The Great Depression and the New Deal

The Great Depression and the New Deal

A Thematic Encyclopedia

Daniel Leab, Kenneth J. Bindas, Alan Harris Stein,

Justin Corfield, and Steven L. Danver, Editors

Volume 2

Santa Barbara, California • Denver, Colorado • Oxford, England

Library of Congress Cataloging-in-Publication Data

The Great Depression and the New Deal : a thematic encyclopedia / Daniel Leab . . . [et al.].
    v. cm.
  Includes bibliographical references and index.
    ISBN 978-1-59884-154-1 (set : alk. paper) — ISBN 978-1-59884-155-8 (set ebook)
1. Depressions—1929—United States—Encyclopedias.   2. New Deal, 1933–1939—
Encyclopedias.   3. United States—Economic conditions—1918–1945—Encyclopedias.
4. United States—Social conditions—1918–1932—Encyclopedias.   5. United States—Social
conditions—1933–1945—Encyclopedias.   6. United States—Politics and government—
1901–1953—Encyclopedias.   I. Leab, Daniel J.
  E801.G74   2009
  973.917—dc22   2009031352

14 13 12 11 10   1 2 3 4 5

This book is also available on the World Wide Web as an eBook.
Visit www.abc-clio.com for details.

ABC-CLIO, LLC
130 Cremona Drive, P.O. Box 1911
Santa Barbara, California 93116-1911

This book is printed on acid-free paper ∞

Manufactured in the United States of America

Contents

About the Editors

Kenneth J. Bindas, professor and chairperson, Department of History, Kent State University (KSU), has written extensively on the intersection of popular music, politics, and race, class and gender and uses this information in his classroom. He has been the recipient of both the Distinguished Teaching Award and the Diversity Leadership Award at KSU. He has also co-produced and directed a television documentary entitled *Invisible Struggles,* which uses oral histories to tell the story of segregation and power in a small northeast Ohio city during the 1950s and 1960s. He is currently writing a monograph on the power and meaning of modernity in 1930s American thought and culture.

Justin Corfield was born in England, and was educated at St. Paul's School, London; and the University of Hull; gaining his doctorate from Monash University in Australia. He has been teaching history and international relations at Geelong Grammar School since 1993. He has written and co-authored a number of books including: *Khmers Stand Up!: A History of the Cambodian Government 1970–1975, The Ned Kelly Encyclopedia,* the *Encyclopedia of Singapore,* and *The History of Vietnam.*

Steven L. Danver is Professor of Social Sciences in the Center for Undergraduate Studies at Walden University. His research has focused on the history of the American West and of American Indian groups in the United States. He has written for, edited, or co-edited numerous reference works including ABC-CLIO's *Seas and Waterways of the World: An Encyclopedia of History, Uses, and Issues,* its *Revolts, Protests, Demonstrations, and Rebellions in American History* encyclopedia, and its *Popular Controversies in World History* series. He has been managing editor of *Journal of the West* since 2004. His current research focuses on the long history of one of the most important issues of relevance to American Indians and non-Indians in the 20th and 21st century west— the use and allocation of the region's scarce water resources.

Daniel J. Leab is Professor of History at Seton Hall University and the founding editor of *American Communist History.* At Seton Hall he was Director of the American Studies Program and established and directed (1990–96) the university's multicultural program. His academic career began in the history department at Columbia University, where he was also associate dean of Columbia College, before joining the university's central administration as an assistant provost. He has twice been a Senior Fulbright Scholar at the University of Cologne and in 2008 was a visiting professor of history there. His books include *A Union of Individuals: The Formation of the American Newspaper Guild, 1933–1936,* and *From Sambo to Superspade: the Black Image in American Film.* His most recent book is *Orwell Subverted: The CIA and the Filming of "Animal Farm."* Forthcoming is a collection of essays about the "long civil rights revolution" co-edited with David Levering Lewis and Michael H. Nash. For two decades Leab was editor of *Labor History,* and in 1997 for his efforts he won the John Commorford Prize of the New York State Labor History Association.

Alan Harris Stein is an archival oral historian and associate director of the Consortium for Oral History Educators, located at the Martha Ross Center for Oral History at the University of Maryland. He has been active in the national Oral History Association since 1995 and is treasurer of the National New Deal Preservation Association. In 2007 he received the Society of American Archivists' Spotlight Award—being the second recipient of the award that recognizes an individual who works for the good of the profession and archival collections, work that would not typically receive public recognition. His uncle worked on the Federal Writers' Project in Chicago.

List of Contributors

Nicole Anslover
Waldorf College, Forest City, Iowa

Randal Beeman
Bakersfield College,
Bakersfield, California

Walter Bell
Aurora University, Aurora, Illinois

Kenneth Bindas
Kent State University, Kent, Ohio

Kevin Brady
Texas Christian University,
Fort Worth, Texas

Ron Briley
Sandia Preparatory School,
Albuquerque, New Mexico

Stephen Burgess-Whiting
University of Guelph,
Guelph, Ontario

Lynn Burlbaw
Texas A&M University, College Station,
Texas

Ron Capshaw
Midlothian, Virginia

David Carletta
Michigan State University,
East Lansing, Michigan

Justin Corfield
Geelong Grammar School,
Corio, Australia

Steven L. Danver
Walden University, Minneapolis,
Minnesota

Peter L. de Rosa
Bridgewater State College,
Bridgewater, Massachusetts

Greg Dehler
Front Range Community College,
Westminster, Colorado

Petra Dewitt
Missouri University of Science
and Technology,
Rolla, Missouri

Kerry Dexter
Tallahassee, Florida

Steven Dimmick
San Francisco, California

Merrill Evans
Michigan State University,
East Lansing, Michigan

Richard M. Filipink
Western Illinois University,
Macomb, Illinois

James Frusetta
College of William and Mary,
Williamsburg, Virginia

Michael Greaney
Center for Economic and Social Justice,
Arlington, Virginia

Theresa Hefner-Babb
Lamar University, Beaumont, Texas

Chuck Howlett
Moloy College,
Rockville Centre, New York

Kevin Kern
University of Akron, Akron, Ohio

Leigh Kimmel
Indianapolis, Indiana

Daniel Leab
Seton Hall University, South Orange,
New Jersey

William Leeman
Coventry, Rhode Island

Robert Leeson
Murdoch University, Perth, Australia

Fred Lindsey
John F. Kennedy University,
Pleasant Hill, California

Tess Mann
San Diego, California

Greg Moore
Notre Dame College,
South Euclid, Ohio

Sarah Munro
Friends of Timberline,
Portland, Oregon

Keith Murphy
Fort Valley State University, Fort Valley,
Georgia

Mitchell Newton-Matza
Olive-Harvey College, Chicago, Illinois

David A. Norris
Wilmington, North Carolina

Lee Oberman
Catonsville, Maryland

Dave Powell
Gettysburg College, Gettysburg,
Pennsylvania

Jessica Richman
Stanford University, Stanford, California

Jason Roberts
George Washington University,
Washington, DC

Charles Rosenberg
Milwaukee, Wisconsin

Mark Schwartz
Alexandria Library, Alexandria, Virginia

Kate Stewart
University of Iowa, Iowa City, Iowa

Lonn Taylor
Fort Davis, Texas

Tanfer Tunc
Hacettepe University, Ankara, Turkey

Heather Vaughan
Albany, California

Ronald Young
Canterbury School,
Fort Myers, Florida

The Artistic Depression

The cultural history of the Depression era is rich, perhaps superseded only in profundity by the 1960s. The historical circumstances that created each of these epochs could hardly be more different; and yet, in many ways, the significance of their cultural production is very similar. The culture of the sixties was borne in an era of comfort and prosperity, begun during the middle part of the decade before, its motivation stemmed from the relative ease and power at which Americans existed. Literature, art, music, television, radio, and film all spoke to this burgeoning of what *Life* magazine had labeled in 1941 as the American century. The magazine's publisher, Henry Luce, who also published *Time,* made this announcement in an effort to convince the American people and their leaders that intervention in World War II was necessary to save the world from the ravages of dictatorship in the guise of Hitler and National Socialism, although he was also suspect of the socialism of the USSR's Josef Stalin. He suggested that the time had come for the United States to step up and accept the responsibility that had been ordained since the country's founding in the early 17th century and to fulfill the ideals set forth by the founding fathers in the Revolutionary era

The subsequent involvement in the war by the United States and the eventual victory by the Allies over the Axis powers brought Luce's belief to fruition, as the country emerged from the conflict as a world power. The war had devastated most of Europe and Asia and the United States, after considerable debate, deviated from its traditional foreign policy of relative isolationism (conforming to the Monroe Doctrine [1824] and the Roosevelt Corollary [1901]) and became actively involved in rebuilding the world and fulfilling the destiny that so many had deemed manifest in the country's creation. With the Truman Doctrine (1947) and the Marshall Plan (1948), the country embarked upon a course of both world leadership and sustained economic growth. The Doctrine announced the American intention to help any country resisting the threat of communist takeover with military aid, while the Plan outlined ways in which the United States would assist economically those countries who would agree to free market economy

363

and, at least tacitly, democracy. These efforts outlined the basic ideologies at work during the era of the sixties that produced the tremendous cultural outpouring—prosperity and tension. The commitment of America to stop the spread of what was perceived as Soviet communism meant that the country became involved more actively in world affairs, either directly with military action such as Korea and Vietnam, or indirectly through economic and military aid. The implements of this containment policy were funneled through the newly created Department of Defense (1946) via its iconic headquarters the Pentagon. The contracts it distributed to American manufacturers helped to stimulate the economy and stabilize the economy. By the time the United States became actively involved in Vietnam in 1964, the American economy was the strongest on the world and its people were among the most prosperous, which of course made many question both the nature of this comfort and the meaning of its power. In the end, the creators of culture questioned the definition of America—from its people, economy, and its institutions.

The Depression era could not have been more different, or the same. The creators of the era's music, film, radio, literature, and art were enmeshed in the worst economic calamity in the nation's history. The aftermath of the stock market and banking collapse that began in the fall of 1929 resulted in not only massive unemployment and suffering, but a questioning of the validity and meaning of democracy itself. The causes of the crisis were hotly debated, but certainly the policies of the New Era, a term coined by President Herbert Hoover (1929–33) which involved raising tariffs on foreign goods to encourage American production and consumption, coupled with immigration restrictions to limit the number of workers in the marketplace and thus reduce both labor union activism and raise wages, as well as limited government regulation of the stock market and banking industries, spurred an economic boom for the country. This was the era of heroes, of those men and women who personified the American individualism that Hoover defined in his 1922 book of the same name. Strong, relentless, and willing to surmount all obstacles, nothing could stop these individual heroes from success. The newspapers were littered with these individuals, whether they be politicians like Hoover himself—he had been orphaned and had risen to become not only president, but also a very wealthy civil engineer—industrialists like Henry Ford, aviators like Charles Lindbergh and Amelia Earhart, athletes like Jack Dempsey, Red Grange, and of course, Babe Ruth. The continued growth and popularity of the movies added other names to the lexicon of American heroes: Charlie Chaplin, Harold Lloyd, Gloria Swanson, Tom Mix, Norma Talmadge, Rudolph Valentino, Douglas Fairbanks Sr., Colleen Moore, Norma Shearer, John Barrymore, Greta Garbo, Lon Chaney, Sr., Clara Bow, and "Little Mary" Pickford. These actors and the powerful studio and theater owners like Adolph Zukor, the Warner Brothers, Louis B. Mayer, Joseph P. Kennedy, and Samuel Goldwyn helped to reinforce President Hoover's general idea that individualism made America great and less government meant more prosperity. It was on this rhetoric that he was elected president in 1928.

The halcyon days of the Hoover's New Era ended rather abruptly, for by the end of his first year in office the country witnessed over 640 bank closures and the worst single day (to that point) on Wall Street, immortalized as Black Tuesday, October 29, 1929. The New Year would offer little respite as the economic situation continued to deteriorate as the gross national product dropped to barely above 12 percent and business failures reached record levels at over 26,000. The banking crisis continued as more than 1,500 more banks closed, losing over one billion dollars of depositor's money. It became increasingly clear that what many had hoped would be a short term crisis was now becoming a much more entrenched economic crisis. Hoover was not reluctant to try to stave off a further slide, proposing a series of bills to help stabilize the banking system and protect home mortgages, but these did little to abate the slide. Unemployment grew to over 16 percent in 1931 and the gross national product continued its downward spiral.

Increasingly, any action Hoover took either did little to slow the economic collapse or was perceived as helping the rich at the expense of the people. The election year 1932 proved pivotal. The nation's economy was nearly at rock bottom—unemployment would go beyond 25 percent across the nation with some cities, like Toledo, Ohio, approaching 60 percent. High school graduates, finding few opportunities in their hometowns, took to the rails, hoboing across the country in the hopes of finding employment. By some estimates, over 250,000 young people rode the rails in 1932, an example of the dire consequences of what was now commonly known as the Depression. The Southern Pacific estimated that it removed over 600,000 illegal riders from its train in 1932 alone. Hoovervilles—minimal housing sometimes constructed by cities but most often simply shanty-towns located near rail depots—began to dot the landscape. These were followed by other Hoover-isms, like the Hooverwagon (a model T being pulled by a mule), Hooverhankerchief (one's sleeve), or Hooverchicken (virtually anything that could be caught and eaten like chicken). While the president proposed legislation such as the Reconstruction Finance Corporation as an attempt to funnel money into the nation's banks in the hopes of reviving the economy and stimulating employment, the people were losing hope in their government's ability to address their needs. This demoralization was augmented by Hoover himself, who regularly proclaimed that people needed to pull themselves up by the bootstraps, or, with the Washington state bumper apple harvest of 1930, sell apples on street corners as an example of finding individual means of creating jobs. Perhaps the most glaring event that tarnished Hoover's reputation among the people in 1932 was the Bonus March calamity. In June and July 1932 veterans from across the country—some estimates putting the number to 20,000—descended on Washington, D.C., to lobby Congress to pass a Bonus Bill. This act would have allowed veterans from World War I, nearly five million men, to receive their $2,500.00 bonus for serving ahead of its slated 1945 date. Some veterans needed the money immediately, the bill's sponsors reasoned, and the Federal government should help them since they had helped to win the Great War. Every day and night beginning in early June until July veterans marched in front of the capital building with placards reading "Pass the Bill," or "You Didn't Leave us in 1917–18, So Don't Leave Us Now." These were massive demonstrations of desperation by any account and while Hoover understood their plight, he did not support the bill and promised a veto should it pass both Houses. After passing the House the Senate rejected the bill and by the end of June many of the veterans left the Capitol. However, about 3,500 remained, taking up residence in some of the abandoned federal buildings lining Pennsylvania Avenue. Hoover and others wanted these squatters out and in late July ordered the Washington, D.C., police, in conjunction with the U.S. Army, to remove these malingerers. The police and nearly 600 Calvary and a few tanks were to escort the remaining veterans out of town, but the situation quickly got out of control and Major General Douglas MacArthur, ignoring Hoover's orders not to cross into Anacostia Flats, Maryland, ordered his troops in to the Hooverville. The tear gas canisters that had been lobbed into the camp started fires in tents and other dwellings and soon the camp was ablaze. Photographs in the nation's newspapers and newsreel images shown in movie houses seemed to reaffirm to many that Hoover had little concern for the people, thus helping to secure the victory for Franklin D. Roosevelt (FDR) in the November election.

FDR came into the White House in perhaps one of the most crucial times in America's history. Jefferson and Lincoln were other presidents who faced dire circumstances right from the start of their administrations. By the time FDR took the oath of office (in March in those days), the Depression was in full force and the country was not only mired in economic calamity, but the people's faith in democracy was increasingly challenged. In the 50 years or so leading up to the Crash and Depression, the country had come to equate the ideals of democracy with the tenets of capitalism, so that in many people's minds, the failure of one signaled the demise of the other. Many questioned whether or not a system so rooted in capitalism could survive and challenged the effectiveness of any reform FDR might propose. As president, he reacted swiftly, promising the American people a vague yet powerful message of a New Deal. His was a pragmatic approach—try something and if it works keep doing it—and one that had to balance the needs of commerce with those of the people. FDR had to offer salvation for the nation's banking system, for example, while also providing relief to the masses of un- and under-employed. He had to maintain the credo of individualism that encouraged innovation and ambition while asking people to work together and work for the commonwealth. The emergency gave FDR power though, and he used it to pass through Congress in his first 100 days some of the most comprehensive and important legislation in history. Not all of the bills were successful—the National Industrial Recovery Act and the Agricultural Adjustment Act were struck down as unconstitutional in 1935 for example—but they displayed to the people that government was at least trying to do something.

Some of the programs were almost immediate successes, like the Civilian Conservation Corps (CCC). In March of 1933 FDR proposed legislation that would tackle the problem of young men without work. It was estimated that over 40 percent of those between the ages of 16 and 24 were neither employed nor in school. FDR sought to take these young men and use their energy and potential to salvage the nation's forests and parks and build a legacy for future generations. Young men between the ages of 17 and 25 could sign onto the CCC for 30 dollars a month, 25 of which they were to send to their families, and work in military-styled camps in the nation's parks and national forests. Over the next nine years more than 3 million men would serve on this tree army and would plant 2 billion trees (saving from erosion over 40 million acres of farmland) and help to develop over 800 new state parks. They would also carve out trails and work to make the National parks more open to the public. But even more importantly, the CCC infused a sense of commitment and faith into the scores of young people who served and those family members it helped.

The goals of the CCC—relief, recovery, and security—became the larger mantra of FDR's New Deal as it entered its second stage in 1935 and would become the foundational ideology for the welfare state programs that would follow. In the spring of 1935 FDR proposed an even more aggressive agenda of legislation aimed at directly giving economic power to the people who needed it the most. Some of the initial 100 days legislation from 1933 continued to achieve results, like the Tennessee Valley Authority (TVA) and the Glass-Steagall Banking Act, while others like the Federal Emergency Relief Act (FERA), while initially constructive, failed to provide the results deemed necessary for continuation. By 1935 FDR and his advisors began to understand that the government's ability to bring about recovery was more complex and so began to focus more on the intangibles of government programs, namely the building of faith and hope in the system. This meant transforming the nature of government in the acceptance of its responsibility for the economic well-being of its citizens. With this in mind, the second New Deal expanded the role of government into social welfare, guaranteeing Americans a stable and decent way of life. The Social Security Act, for example, sought not only to provide retirement pensions, but also to establish aid to widows and orphans, and even more significantly, create an unemployment relief fund to help those thrown out of work by no fault of their own. Along these same lines, the Wagner Act, also known as the National Labor Relations Act, gave tacit federal approval for the right of workers to form and join unions, with the idea in mind to stabilize the workplace and guarantee livable wages for all workers. Over the next six years over six million Americans would join unions and begin to negotiate wages that would propel the country into an era of almost unlimited prosperity after World War II. One of the largest and most comprehensive of the second New Deal efforts was the Works Progress Administration (WPA) led by the president's good friend and confidant Harry Hopkins. Committed to the idea of work relief—whereby the unemployed were given jobs by the government in occupations that mirrored their private sector employment— Hopkins sought to transform the morally degenerative notion of relief into recovery. Those employed on the WPA, and there were projects for nearly everyone, came away not only with the money necessary to sustain life and family, but also with a sense of pride that they had contributed something tangible and meaningful for their wages. During its tenure until 1942, the WPA employed over 8,500,000 Americans and built 651,087 miles of roadway, 95,110 public buildings, 3,238 public recreation facilities, 953 airports, planted 184,843,967 trees and shrubs, preserved over 84,000,000 jars of food which were distributed to schools where they served over 1,200,000,000 billion school lunches. The WPA had projects for nearly every occupation. Federal Project One, for example, created jobs for unemployed writers, artists, musicians, actors, directors, and stage hands. The Federal Music Project (FMP) gave thousands of free or low cost performances to nearly two and half million Americans, while Federal Art Project (FAP) murals decorated hundreds of public buildings and spaces. The WPA left virtually no occupation without an opportunity and the result was a nearly religious dedication to FDR and with him the United States. In the pages that follow, several selections discuss the breath and significance of WPA sponsored projects. Discussions concerning the development and building of the Timberline Lodge or the facilities on Davis Mountain outline the complex government interactions with the private sector and symbolic importance of such comprehensive structures. There are also essays outlining the value and significance of WPA sponsored art projects joined together under the label Federal Project One, including the Writers', Arts, Music, and Theater projects, as well as examinations of the men and women who led these ventures.

Other programs followed the WPA model, like the National Youth Administration (NYA), the Rural Electrification Administration (REA), and the Farm Resettlement Administration (FSA), to name a few. All sought to bring the country together through work and sacrifice; and to stimulate the economy by putting the money directly into the hands of the consumers. FDR and the WPA understood that broadening the delineation of needs would open up new markets. In a needs assessment in 1936, the WPA suggested that tobacco, movies, radio, newspapers, magazines, and music should be joined with traditional needs of food, clothing, and shelter. The government believed that by increasing the standard of living, not only would business be rewarded with increased consumption, but the consumer would benefit with an increase in their way of life. The pursuit of the American Way became attached to the general promotion of the American Dream, a term coined earlier in the era. This shift in ideology as to need helped encourage the emerging entertainment and culture industries, as well as others,

President Franklin D. Roosevelt delivers one of his popular fireside chats, a series of evening radio talks to the American public. Roosevelt used these chats to explain New Deal programs during the Great Depression and war policies during World War II. (Library of Congress)

and stimulated the general movement toward a new economy focused not on the production, but on the consumption of goods. The problem with the economy, FDR and his advisors came to reason, was that the people were not spending enough. First the government had to get more money into the economy and through government programs like the WPA, NYA, CCC, TVA, REA, FSA and many others, the government pumped billions of dollars into the economy.

And to help the people better understand this reformation, FDR talked directly to the people using one of the emerging industries his programs were tangentially encouraging to grow; the radio. The era of the thirties is often called the Golden Age of radio. By 1937 24.5 million people owned a radio and listened for at least five hours a day, meaning over 41 million daily listeners. The three networks—NBC Red, NBC Blue, and CBS—crisscrossed the country, unifying the listeners and projecting information and entertainment to a national audience like no other time in America's history. After World War II it was estimated that 82 out of every 100 listened regularly to the radio. Programming ran the gamut from comedy shows like *Amos and Andy, George Burns and Gracie Allen, Fibber McGee and Molly,* or *The Jack Benny Show* to adventure and soap operas like *The Shadow* and *Captain Midnight,* to *Lux Radio Theater* and many other formats. Working to make the Depression era radio's 'Golden Age' was advertising. Studies showed that people who listened to radio advertisements were 35 percent more inclined to buy the item they heard advertised and that more than 75 percent usually bought items because they heard about them via an advertisement over the radio. It seems curious that in an era of economic decline there was an increase in advertising and a general encouragement of consumption. But, one of the central features of FDR's New Deal was to get money into the hands of the people, as he and his advisors believed one of the main causes for the slow economic recovery was the limited circulation of species. In other words, the people were not buying enough. During the era advertisers used the traditional methods of selling that had been defined in the earlier era—fear and competition—but added to this mix a reliance on brand loyalty and an almost patriotic duty to consume. Increasingly, the emphasis on consumption over production within the American economy meant that the people were now expected to buy and circulate the money the government was providing through its many programs. Advertising did its part by using radio and print ads to sell the new America, introducing to the people the more modern versions of products and announcing how new technology and innovation had made them better and much more modern than their predecessors. Radio programming catered to this idea by seeking corporate sponsorship for their programs and linking the commodity to the program. Thus, product sponsorship sought to cater to the program's audience and increasingly advertiser's companies had more influence over the structure of the broadcast so as to best utilize the time on the air to market their brands. The intersection of advertising and production meant that programs were written to introduce the ads and, for example, musical programming was designed so that no one song would last too long as to divert the attention span, and usually more upbeat songs or music preceded an advertising spot. In the selections that follow, you will read about action adventures featuring *The Lone Ranger, Flash Gordon,* and *Superman,* about the hysteria caused by the radio broadcast of *War Of the Worlds,* about the homespun humor of *Lil' Abner,* and the development of news reporting by Edward R. Murrow. And in this mix, the people listened to FDR's Fireside Chats, experiencing for the first time the same cultural event simultaneously; listening to their president together. The effect was tremendous support for FDR and his programs; for the entertainment industry it meant a revival and boom.

Music was one of the most popular forms of entertainment used by the network programmers. Over 51 percent of all broadcast time, according to a 1938 Federal Communication Commission study, and up to one-third of all radio programming featured music. And, four out of five listeners in who participated in the Robert and Helen Lynd's *Middletown Revisited* study preferred popular music over all other programming. Radio stations like Chicago's WLS, Atlanta's WSB, and New York City's WNBC featured shows like the National Barn Dance, the Grand Ol' Opry, and the countless remote Swing broadcasts from the swank NYC hotels. Radio broadcasts helped to spur a popular music revolution, seeking to exploit an emerging youth market. Nearly 40 percent of the country's population was under 25 and these new consumers, many delaying marriage because of the Depression and many more with limited spending money, represented an under-tapped market. Like the 1960s, companies viewed these young people as potential customers and saw in their youth the potential not only for the immediate sale, but for a life-long affinity and brand-loyalty. Jazz, later rebranded as swing, and hillbilly music were two emerging popular music forms from that era. Both had developed out of the relatively new recorded music industry born in the early 1920s and were made up primarily of what would be best termed working-class listeners. Both were later rebranded, jazz into swing as mentioned above, and hillbilly into western, then country and western, and finally country. Regardless of their name, the majority of performers came from socio-economic backgrounds where their families or they made little money and were often raised in the poorer rural areas or grew up in the many urban ghettos. One study suggests that 85 percent of hillbilly performers came from rural and farming backgrounds while another study reveals that 65 percent of swing musicians came from urban working class backgrounds. The music they played and recorded in the 1920s represented only a small segment of the recording industry, as the price of record players was still a bit high, the technology of recording and playing back not yet very sophisticated, and a general attitude among executives from larger companies and distributors that only good or cultivated music should be promoted. Jazz and hillbilly music were small, segmented markets that often competed with regional and ethnic recordings. The economic collapse in 1929 meant that sales had fallen from over 79 million dollars in that year to less than 11 million in 1932. The industry remained in a slump and only began to emerge after 1935 with several developments: the coin-machine player or jukebox, the swing music explosion, and the profitability of B-grade western movies which featured hillbilly music. The essays that follow document this significant musical explosion, and discuss the most significant of the genre's musicians, like swing's Gene Krupa, Teddy Wilson, Helen Humes, Count Basie, the Dorsey Brothers, Fletcher Henderson, and Mary Lou Williams and hillbilly's Roy Acuff, Bob Wills, Jimmie Rodgers, and Roy Rogers, as well as George Gershwin, Marc Blitzstein, Roger Sessions, Roger Thomson, Woody Guthrie, and even American Federation of Musicians union leader James Petrillo, all designed to provide the reader with an understanding of the diversity of the music of the time and the role music played in the lives of those going through the Depression era.

The music industry boomed as result of radio and advertising. Jukebox profits soared to over 20 million dollars a year. Swing made up 85 percent of all record sales and was generating 100 million dollars a year by 1939. B-Grade westerns were filling theaters. Between 1930 and 1954 over two thousand B-Grade movies, where western music played the central role, were released and Gene Autry, Roy Rogers, and Tex Ritter were among the top 10 film draws during the period. Between 1932 and 1941 record sales increased by 500 percent with 40 to 70 percent going on to the 350,000 jukeboxes scattered throughout the country. Popular music utilized radio and film to gain a greater share of the audience, and their sound and imagery reflected the ambivalence of America during the Depression era. Hillbilly performers came from traditional white Anglo American stock while swing was represented by multiethnic and occasionally racially mixed performers. Hillbilly songs spoke of the days gone by and used nostalgia for a rural and simpler past as a way to deal with the uncertainty of the future. Hillbilly performers dressed in cowboy garb and emphasized their western roots, even if the west was Alabama. Performers like Gene Autry, Roy Rogers, Roy Acuff, Tex Ritter and many more used their individual identity to promote their songs. Meanwhile, swing suggested the energy, vitality, and perhaps chaos of the urban American experience. Its tone and players reflected a more cosmopolitan, modern sound, even if it emanated from Paducah, Illinois. Their band outfits reflected the urban image of a slicker, full-on with coat and tie. From the bandstand these bands, or collectives of musicians working to create a unified sound, were made up of a variety of ethnic groups and played to urban audiences whom they mirrored. Like hillbilly performers, they were also very focused on the individual, not just in the naming of the band but also in the featuring of soloists and the star system. Both were overwhelmingly male and women were used in both as singers, mothers, sisters, lovers, and pals, but were rarely accorded equality within the band.

The vision of women within the bands mirrored to a large degree their place within American society during the era. During the 1920s, women had experienced some employment and status gains—a total increase of nearly 50 percent in the professional trades—but many of the advantages were lost with the onset of the Depression. By the time FDR came into the White House, over two million women were out of work and faced a society that overwhelmingly believed that during this economic crisis a woman's proper place was in the home and not competing with men for jobs. Amazingly, 75 percent of the nation's women agreed. Marriage and childbirth rates dropped as divorces increased. Advertising used the fear of a woman working to sell commodities and by 1939 over 90 percent of men polled believed married women should not be allowed, by law, to work outside the home. But, true to the New Deal's commitment to inclusion, and with the sage advice of his wife Eleanor, FDR and his trusted advisor Harry Hopkins began to first speak out about the plight of women in the Depression, and, as the New Deal programs began to achieve results, focused attention on getting women back to work. The WPA, for example, could claim by 1936 that nearly 16 percent of all of its workers were women and in some categories, like professional-technical, held 33 percent of the positions. While these numbers did not reflect the depth of the need for women workers, it was an indication by the administration that the government recognized and understood their plight.

American culture played a central role in maintaining an ideology of power for women during this era. Led in many ways by the example of Eleanor Roosevelt and other influential public servants like Frances Perkins, women negotiated between the social roles proscribed for them and the ideals they held for themselves. Vivian Leigh's portrayal of Scarlett O'Hara in *Gone with the Wind,* as one of the essays suggests, points to how women were able to carve out places for themselves outside of the male power structure. Other essays explore this concept further, discussing the importance of writers Pearl Buck and Virginia Woolf, and actors Katharine Hepburn, Greta Garbo, and Mae West. So while women continued to struggle to gain employment equality and social acceptance, significant models of power encouraged their resilience, which eventually found definition in the iconic Rosie the Riveter of World War II.

Hollywood played a major role in American culture not only for women, but for all segments of the population. This was truly the Golden Age of film, with stars like Errol Flynn, Charlie Chaplin, Shirley Temple, Ginger Rogers, William Powell, Laurel and Hardy, W. C. Fields, Helen Hayes, the Marx Brothers, Margaret Dumont, Bette Davis, and so many more performing in virtually every type of visual entertainment. One could go to the theater and watch Tom Mix and later Gene Autry and Roy Rogers in B-Grade westerns, which were later made into feature films, most notably with the release of *Stagecoach,* featuring a young John Wayne. In the early part of the era some films offered the audience escapism, like the films by Busby Berkeley, which suggested that the hard times were only temporary and that good times waited just around the corner. Movies like *Bringing up Baby,* or *The Thin Man,* or *My Man Godfrey* relied on stock images of the wealthy and oftentimes portrayed them as weak and flighty. Ordinary people were portrayed as earthy and real, quick to act and with a sense of purpose. Clark Gable's role in *It Happened One Night,* explored later in this book, details the manner in which the ordinary people—workers—were seen to be the salt of the earth and uncorrupted by the ease of wealth. Perhaps the most salient of these images came from Henry Fonda's portrayal of Tom Joad in the film adaptation of John Steinbeck's *The Grapes of Wrath,* where the plight of the people is offset by the greed and maliciousness of the propertied class. In the film, and in the minds of many Americans during the era, the government was clearly on the side of what came to be called "the common man." Other films that portrayed this include Jimmy Stewart in *Mr. Smith Goes to Washington,* Henry Fonda in *Young Abe Lincoln,* or the many films directed by Howard Hawks, including *Dawn Patrol* and *The Road to Glory,* or the many directed by John Ford, including *The Informer, Tobacco Road,* and the earlier mentioned *Stagecoach,* and films with Spencer Tracy and Gary Cooper, to name a few. There were also many "common women" portrayed in film, as the many roles played by Bette Davis, Katharine Hepburn, Joan Crawford and many more testify. One of the clearest examples of this is the portrayal of Dorothy by Judy Garland in *The Wizard of Oz.* In the end it's Dorothy who provides the escape and also serves as an instructor to her fellow travelers to look inside for the answers they seek from authority.

The escapism and common person theme were but two of the themes Hollywood exploited during the era. Others included horror, gangster, comedy, and fantasy through cartoons. Actors Bela Lugosi and Boris Karloff thrilled audiences in films like *The Mummy, Dracula, The Invisible Man, Dr. Jekyll & Mr. Hyde, Frankenstein,* and *The Werewolf.* Each of these revolved around a solitary scientist dedicated to the pursuit of knowledge regardless of the consequences, which, as it turns out, always proves to be their undoing. In the end, the monsters they create either have to conform to the accepted rules of science and society, or be destroyed. The individualistic pursuit of the scientist served as a subtle warning to the viewing audiences, reminding them what becomes of a person so convinced of their own righteousness that they ignore the norms and values of their society. The same ideal held for the era's gangster movies, where the stories focused on the ambition and drive of an individual to dominate and control their empire, only to be brought down by their own greed or selfishness. Paul Muni in *Scarface,* Edward G. Robinson in *Little Caesar,* James Cagney in *Public Enemy,* and Humphrey Bogart in *Dead End* or *The Petrified Forest,* all shared the same fate—death caused by their strict adherence to individualism. The era also saw some of the greatest film comics of all time in W. C. Fields, the Marx Brothers, Abbot and Costello, the Little Rascals, and even a more serious but still funny, Charlie Chaplin. In the cartoon fantasy world created through the talents of Walt Disney and his staff of artists, the dangers and mysteries of nature were made safe and harmless, and through hard work and persistence, any task could be successful. The most obvious example of this was the 1940 surprise movie hit *Fantasia,* where Mickey Mouse's antics as the sorcerer's apprentice mixed classical music with artful and detailed animation. This film, as well as earlier full-length versions of classic fairy tales like *Sleeping Beauty* and *Snow White,* made adorable the patterns of nature and brought young children into the theaters by the droves.

The movies, like the music and the government programs discussed before them, all reinforced the belief that only through the cooperation of ordinary Americans could the problems of the Depression be solved. This encouraged a gentle form of nationalism throughout American culture, where artists, who a decade previously had derided and criticized American civilization, now saw in the heroic struggles of the American people a sense of honor and pride. Roger Sessions, Virgil Thomson, Aaron Copland, Peggy Seeger, William Grant Still, and many other American composers began to mine the rich traditions of American music to create their symphonies. Copland's *Fanfare for the Common Man, Appalachian Spring,* or *Billy the Kid* reminded the listener of the various types of people that made up the country and built within the music a sense of pride in America. Within art, this tendency was labeled the American regionalist style, where artists like John Steuart Curry, Georgia O'Keefe, Edward Hopper, and Thomas Hart Benton used their canvases to display the various regions and people of the country and within their presentation, a sense of togetherness. Perhaps the most famous example of this is Grant Wood's "American Gothic," with its stark presentation of father and daughter standing steadfast against the rush of time and trouble. Theirs is a resolute focus, a knowing look that suggested survival.

This attitude was also displayed through fiction, as writers wrote about ordinary people struggling to define themselves against the tide of change and crisis. Ernest Hemingway's *For Whom the Bell Tolls,* William Faulkner's *Absalom, Absalom,* or *As I Lay Dying,* Howard Fast's *Power* and *Citizen Tom Paine,* John Dos Passos's *The Big*

Money and the *USA* trilogy, Zora Neale Hurston's *Their Eyes Were Watching God,* F. Scott Fitzgerald's *Tender is the Night,* as well as more radical literature from Mike Gold, Jack Conroy, and many others. Margaret Mitchell's *Gone with the Wind* perhaps gave the most popular version of the resilience and radicalism that was the undercurrent of American literature during the era. This runaway best seller's main character, Scarlett O'Hara, vows to survive even as her beloved Tara is destroyed by the invading Federal forces hell-bent on ending the Civil War. Her resolve to rebuild her destroyed life served as a visual cue to many readers who saw similarities in the struggles of the Depression with those of the reluctant heroine. Poetry too applauded the ordinary pursuits of America's people, with Robert Frost's descriptions of the joys of ordinary pursuits, Carl Sandburg's poem *The People, Yes,* and the lyrical imagery of Archibald MacLeish capturing the people's imagination.

During the Depression era sporting events helped to reinforce the culture of inclusion established by FDR and presented in the various cultural expressions listed above. Gone were the selfish players like Ty Cobb and the self-styled one-man slugging machine Babe Ruth. In their stead came Lou Gehrig, Joe DiMaggio, and Lefty Gomez of the Yankees, which was the most dominant team of the era, winning the pennant four years running from 1936 through 1939. Another great team was the St. Louis Cardinals with the stellar brother pitching tandem of Dizzy and Paul Dean, and the hitting of Leo Durocher and Pepper Martin. Baseball had retained its place as America's sport during the era and by the end of the decade saw the establishment of organized Little League baseball for youngsters. America's pastime grew in the Depression era as it provided a cheap form of entertainment and the league worked to build its audience by providing radio broadcasts of games, playing its first games under the lights so that workers could better attend without losing a day's wages, and also by legitimizing its legacy with the opening of the Hall of Fame in Cooperstown, New York in 1939. During this era, African American players were not allowed in the all-white major leagues, and many great players like Satchel Paige and Josh Gibson thrilled crowds in the Negro National League formed in 1933 and the Negro American League formed in 1937. These leagues would continue until baseball began to integrate with Jackie Robinson and Satchel Paige in the late 1940s.

One would hardly recognize the National Football League in the early part of the decade, with teams representing Frankfort, Pennsylvania, and Portsmouth, Ohio. Stalwarts like the Green Bay Packers and Chicago Bears dominated early in the era, but as the Depression wore on the face and nature of the game changed. First, the ball itself was slimmed down to afford better control for passing as the rules changed to allow the quarterback greater mobility to throw from anywhere behind the line of scrimmage. This resulted in higher scoring games and opened the offense up, making the game more exciting to watch for the spectators and forcing the coaches to create newer defensive schemes emphasizing precision and collective action. By 1933 enough teams were solvent to form two divisions—East and West—with the champions of each meeting in a final game to determine the overall champion. The Chicago Bears won the first title, as the great Red Grange and Bronko Nagurski played both offense and defense to defeat the New York Giants. Players at this time were allowed to play with any team that paid them the most, so those teams with the most money tended to dominate the small market teams. In order to make for more balanced competition, in the spring of 1935, team owners agreed to create a college player draft, which called for teams to select players going from the team with the worst record to the champion. Detroit, Chicago, and the Giants dominated until the Washington Redskins drafted Sammy Baugh and he led them to the 1937 championship. Sammy Baugh made the Washington club one of the best for years to come.

Just as Hollywood and radio can point to the Depression era as its Golden Age, so too can another American cultural artifact from the era, the comic book. Beginning in 1933, publishers began reprinting popular newspaper cartoon strips on inexpensive newsprint and selling these collections as books in many of the nation's cities. In 1935, the first comic book of an original cartoon was released and the rush was on. The 1938 publication of *Superman* unleashed a flood of super hero comics published primarily by DC Comics. Heroes like Batman and later his ward Robin, Wonder Woman, Flash Gordon, The Green Lantern, the Atom, Hawkman, and Aquaman spawned rival publisher Marvel Comics to create the Human Torch, the Sub-Mariner, and of course, Captain America. The popularity of these comics led to radio shows oftentimes taken right from the book, and many of these super heroes remain part of the American lexicon. That the Depression era would adopt people who were often ordinary citizens by day but heroes at night and in disguise again points to the profundity of the common person ideology prevalent throughout the era. For various reasons, the Depression era saw

Grade schoolers in San Augustine, Texas, snip comic strips, collecting their favorites into books, 1939. (Library of Congress)

a concerted effort for entertainment and recreation. It was during this time that board games like Monopoly (1935), Scrabble (1938), and Sorry (1934) were popularized.

This ideology of inclusion that transcended FDR's New Deal and seeped into American culture would serve the country well, for as the decade came to a close the issues of the home front were increasingly taking a backseat to growing crises throughout the world. The aftermath of World War I had encouraged the American people and Congress to support non-intervention in European and Asian affairs during the 1920s and the economic calamity of the thirties reinforced this type of isolation. It is important to note however, that while many histories of the era claim that the country was isolationist, the United States was very active in foreign policy activities in Central and South America, supervising protectorates in Puerto Rico, Cuba, and Panama, as well as control over the Dominican Republic and Nicaragua. For most Americans however, the notion of isolationism focused on the tensions caused by first the creation of the Soviet Union in 1918 and then by the sweep of fascist governments in Europe, first in Italy in 1922 with Benito Mussolini and culminating in the rise of Adolf Hitler in Germany in 1933 and Francisco Franco in Spain in 1939. When Hitler began to rearm Germany in repudiation of the Versailles agreement in 1934 and Italy invaded Ethiopia in 1935, the United States responded by passing the first of a series of laws, called Neutrality Acts, designed to prevent the country from being drawn in to a European conflict as had happened between 1914 and 1917. The first act prohibited sales of munitions to combatants and imposed a travel restriction, and would be followed by two other Neutrality laws placing further restrictions on loans, travel, and increasing the ban to include the Spanish Civil War. FDR was uncomfortable with these laws, believing that it restricted his and the country's ability to counter aggressive actions against allies. He enunciated this in a 1937 speech where he warned that such laws prevented the country from helping good countries against bad ones. But the people and Congress were not swayed and in 1939 another law—cash and carry—was passed. The situation in Asia was just as tense, as Japanese military expansion came into conflict with American and western designs in the Far East. Japan saw itself as the protector of the region, much the same way as the United States viewed its relationship to Central and South America. This ran counter to the ideals of the United States, Britain, and other western nations, as well as China. When the Japanese formally seized control of Chinese Manchuria in 1931, which they had occupied since their defeat of the Russians in 1905, and made it in effect their colony, the United States was powerless to oppose them, which led to increased tension between the two countries. When in 1937 Japanese and Chinese troops fired on each other near Beijing, the Japanese used the event as a justification to invade northern China—to protect it—and quickly forced the Chinese in Nanking to submit. Over the next several months the Japanese executed several hundred thousand civilians in order to bring order to the area. The United States was again powerless, and although able to sell arms to the Chinese government, America also continued to supply the Japanese with much needed steel, oil, and other raw materials until the summer of 1941.

By 1939 it was clear to all observers that war in Europe was imminent, even as Hitler had agreed the year before at the Munich conference that his demands for more German living space had been met. This fallacy was exposed when on September 1, 1939, the German army launched an attack on Poland from the west. This *blitzkrieg* forced England and France to declare war on Germany but they did little to prevent the downfall of Poland. By November the Polish army had been vanquished and the country fell to the invaders. The Soviet Union, which sent troops into Poland from the east in order to protect it in accordance with an earlier secret treaty with the Germans, also sought to protect Finland, Estonia, Lithuania, and Latvia by invading these countries in November. In December, Germany signed a treaty with Italy and Japan, creating the Pact of Steel alliance. The next year would find Germany invading the lowland countries of Europe and France as the Japanese moved into Southeast Asia. The American people, while critical of the Germans, Italians, and Japanese, were adamant that the United States not get involved. FDR used his executive powers to freeze German assets, lend the British 50 destroyers for naval leases in Canada, Bermuda, and Greenland, and by the summer of 1941, impose a total trade embargo on the Japanese. All signs pointed to American involvement at this point, but the questions remained—how? On December 7, 1941, the Japanese launched a surprise naval and air attack on American military facilities at Pearl Harbor, Hawai'i and within a week the United States found itself at war with Japan, Germany, and Italy. The American people were quick to support the new war—mainly to seek revenge on the Japanese—by joining the military and advocating unity in this time of struggle. As 1942 dawned, the country found itself involved in a life or death struggle, and over the next several years its resolve would be tested as tens of thousands of American soldiers would die and the home front would be strained over the demands of war. The cultural movements of the Depression era helped prepare the people for this national cause by emphasizing inclusion, acceptance, and Americanism.

The essays in *The Great Depression and New Deal: The Artistic Depression* were written by distinguished members of the history profession and are designed to introduce, not exhaust, any potential topic. This volume is best used as an opening to a more detailed study regarding the Depression era and American culture. The task of the scholars here was more difficult than normal, for they had to condense an entire person, band, career, book, film, or show into fewer than 500 words. This makes the job more difficult, for the writer must focus on just those things that are most significant. There are no words to waste. No ideas to wrestle with. The writers had to be concise and provide the reader with enough of an interesting story so as to invite further inquiry. Each essay reflects how those particular scholars choose to see the past and project to the reader their intended image or idea. So while the career of Abbott and Costello, for example, may not seem all that compelling on the surface, the essay here is littered with ways in which they superseded being simply popular comedians and came to represent American values and ideology during the 1930s and 1940s.

The study of culture and specifically popular culture has had a tumultuous ride within the study of history. And, while the canon now includes cultural history, divisions remain over the import and influence of this new way of viewing the past. What appears in *The Great Depression and New Deal: The Artistic Depression* is a reflection of the growing interest in things popular in the past; and what's more, the essays use this desire to introduce to the readers a more complex discussion of the topic. History is an attempt to derive meaning from the past in order to better understand the present situation. While discussions concerning politics and economics oftentimes create a linear and therefore rational representation of the past, culture and the stories of ordinary people provide a more introspective and nuanced view. From these essays the reader will not only get an understanding of what American culture was like in the 1930s, but also what the people, the consumers of the culture, thought interesting, humorous, challenging, artful, and worthy of their patronage. In an age of inclusion, the consumer of culture replaced the wealthy patron and art came to represent more closely that always-difficult term, the people.

Kenneth J. Bindas

References and Further Reading

Bergman, Andrew. 1971. *We're In the Money: Depression America and It's Films.* New York: New York University Press.

Bindas, Kenneth J. 1995. *All Of This Music Belongs to the Nation: The WPA's Federal Music Project and American Society.* Knoxville: University of Tennessee Press.

Bindas, Kenneth J. 2001. *Swing, That Modern Sound.* Oxford: University of Mississippi Press.

Cohen, Lizabeth. 1990. *Making a New Deal: Industrial Workers in Chicago, 1919–1939.* New York: Cambridge University Press.

Collier, James Lincoln. 1989. *Benny Goodman and the Swing Era.* New York: Oxford University Press.

Cooney, Terry A. 1995. *Balancing Acts: American Thought and Culture in the 1930s.* Woodbridge, CT: Twayne.

Denning, Michael. 1996. *The Cultural Front: The Laboring of American Culture in the Twentieth Century.* Brooklyn, NY: Verso.

Graff, Ellen. 1997. *Stepping Left: Dance and Politics in New York City, 1928–1942.* Durham, NC: Duke University Press.

Kenney, William Howland. 1999. *Recorded Music In American Life: The Phonograph and Popular Memory, 1890–1945.* New York: Oxford University Press.

Leuchtenburg, William E. 1995. *The FDR Years: On Roosevelt and His Legacy.* New York: Columbia University Press.

Lynd, Robert S., and Helen Merrell Lynd. 1937. *Middletown in Transition: A Study in Cultural Conflicts.* New York: Harcourt, Brace & World.

MacDonald, J. Fred. 1979. *Don't Touch That Dial: Radio Programming in American Life from 1920–1960.* Chicago: Nelson-Hall.

Marchand, Roland. 1985. *Advertising the American Dream: Making Way for Modernity, 1920–1940.* Berkeley: University of California Press.

Marquis, Alice G. 1986. *Hopes and Ashes: The Birth of Modern Times, 1929–1939.* New York: Free Press.

McElvaine, Robert S. 1993. *The Great Depression: America, 1929–1941.* New York: Random House, 1984.

Pecknold, Diane. 2007. *The Selling Sound: The Rise of the Country Music Industry.* Durham, NC: Duke University Press.

Pells, Richard H. 1973. *Radical Visions and American Dreams: Culture and Social Thought in the Depression Years.* Middletown, CT: Wesleyan University Press.

Smith, Terry. 1993. *Making the Modern: Industry, Art, and Design in America.* Chicago: University of Chicago Press.

Smulyan, Susan. 1994. *Selling Radio: The Commercialization of American Broadcasting, 1920–1934.* Washington, DC: Smithsonian Institution Press.

Stowe, David W. 1994. *Swing Changes: Big-Band Jazz in New Deal America.* Cambridge, MA: Harvard University Press.

Reference Entries

Abbott and Costello

Abbott and Costello, made up of William "Bud" Abbott and Lou Costello, were a popular comedy duo who made their mark in the show business media of radio, film, and then television. Many of their routines remain famous into contemporary times, including their infamous "Who's On First" skit which was popular in both radio and film. Both their routines and images continue to be used today as symbols of American comedy.

Both members of the team hail from New Jersey. Abbott was born William Alexander Abbot in Asbury Park, on October 2, 1897. Costello was born Louis Francis Cristillo, in Paterson, on March 6, 1906. Both members had a background in burlesque, and while Abbot earned a reputation for being a good straight man, Costello faced a few more obstacles before achieving his success. They teamed up in 1936 and began to make their mark in both burlesque and radio. Their appearance on the Kate Smith Radio Hour opened the doors to fame, performing their infamous "Who's On First" comedy baseball skit, a routine that remained popular for decades.

They next turned to Hollywood. Universal studios signed the duo, featuring them in *One Night in the Tropics* (1940). Although not the stars, they performed "Who's On First" for the first time on film. Their first starring role came in 1941 with *Buck Privates*, which made them instant celebrities. While they made a variety of Hollywood comedies, many of their productions featured them in war propaganda films and they made many personal appearances In the war bonds drive. In *Buck Privates* they joined the army; they also joined the air force (*Keep 'Em Flying*) and navy (*In the Navy*). In *Keep 'Em Flying,* Costello encouraged citizens to enlist in the armed forces; as his character was facing the prospect of being rejected for military service, Costello pleaded with the base commander to at least let him be the a waterboy for the greatest team in the world.

Many of their non-military themed films included *Hold That Ghost, Who*

Done It?, and *Hit the Ice.* After a brief lull in their popularity, with the 1948 release of *Abbott and Costello Meet Frankenstein,* the team again achieved box office success. A variety of similarly themed films followed. In the early 1950s the team began the move into television. While many of their shows were merely reworkings of their old bits, many future comedians would cite Abbott and Costello as an influence on their own work.

Costello died of a heart attack in 1959. Abbott tried to make a comeback in the early 1960s, and began providing voiceovers for a series of short cartoons using the images of the duo. He died of cancer in 1974. Abbott and Costello hold their own place in American popular culture. A film version about their lives aired in 1978, and their "Who's On First" routine has been repeated, and even parodied, by many others.

Mitchell Newton-Matza

References and Further Reading

Costello, Chris. 1981. *Lou's On First.* New York: St. Martin's Press.

Furmanek, Bob, and Ron Palumbo. 1991. *Abbott and Costello in Hollywood.* New York: Perigee.

Acuff, Roy (1903–92)

Called the "King of Country Music," Roy Acuff and the Smokey Mountain Boys became a fixture on Nashville's Grand Ole Opry from the 1930s to 1990s and during the Depression and World War II era, played an instrumental role in commercializing "hillbilly music" into the more respectable "country western" categorization.

Acuff was born September 15, 1903, in Maynardsville, Tennessee, just north of Knoxville. His father was a Baptist minister who moved his family to a Knoxville suburb, Fountain City, in 1919. Rather than focusing upon his father's hobby of playing the fiddle, Acuff was an excellent high school athlete with a passion for baseball. His career was cut short in 1929 when his health was threatened by severe sunstroke.

While regaining his health, Acuff rediscovered his interest in music and began playing the fiddle. In 1932, he joined Doc Hauer's traveling medicine show, a form of vaudeville popular in rural areas during the 1920s and 1930s. Able to develop his fiddling and showmanship, Acuff formed a string band known as the "Crazy Tennesseans" in 1934 and performed on radio station WNOX in Knoxville.

Acuff and his band soon won renown for their rendition of the gospel song "The Great Speckled Bird," drawing the attention of W. R. Calaway, who represented the American Record Company. He invited Acuff and his band to Chicago to record for the label and the October 1936 session produced the hit recordings "Wabash Cannonball" and "Freight Train Blues." The success of these recordings provided Acuff with an opportunity to perform at the Grand Ole Opry in February 1938. The response to Acuff's "The Great Speckled Bird" was enthusiastic, and by 1939, Acuff was a featured performer with the Opry. Finding that the name "Crazy Tennesseans" presented a somewhat negative image of his home state, Acuff changed the name of his band in 1938 to the Smokey Mountain Boys. The group, featuring performers such as "Bashful Brother Oswald" Kirby on the Dobro, toured the world and recorded a string of hits in the 1940s and 1950s; including "Night Train to Memphis," "Will the Circle Be Unbroken," and "Smokey Mountain Melody." Acuff became so well known that it is reported that the Japanese in World War II attempted to anger American soldiers by shouting, "To Hell with Roy Acuff."

In 1948, Acuff made an unsuccessful entry into politics as the Republican nominee for governor of Tennessee. Far more lucrative was the formation of the song publishing company Acuff-Rose with popular songwriter Fred Rose, who signed such stars as Hank Williams. Acuff also founded his own record company, Hickory, which was successfully managed by his wife, Mildred Louise Douglas Acuff.

In 1962, Acuff was the first living member to be inducted into the Country Hall of Fame. His last chart hit was "Precious Jewel" in 1987. With the death of his wife Mildred in 1981, the Opry built a cottage near the facility where Acuff lived in his final years. He continued to record and perform at the Opry until his death on November 23, 1992. Acuff was acclaimed for his influence as a vocal artist, businessman, and contributor to the country music genre.

Ron Briley

References and Further Reading

Acuff, Roy. 1983. *Roy Acuff's Nashville: the Life and Good Times of Country Music.* Nashville, TN: Perigee.

Escott, Colin, and Vince Gill. 2006. *The Grand Ole Opry.* Nashville, TN: Center Street.

Hagen, Chet. 1982. *Country Music Legends.* Nashville, TN: Thomas Nelson.

Malone, Bill C. 1985. *Country Music, U.S.A.* Austin: University of Texas Press.

Schlappi, Elizabeth. 1993. *Roy Acuff: The Smokey Mountain Boy.* New York: Pelican.

Astaire, Fred (1889–1987)

One of America's favorite entertainers, Fred Astaire danced with a winning, effortless style that drew life from ingenious combinations of tap, ballroom, and ballet dancing. The debonair, elegant dancer moved top hat and tails, his signature, from Broadway to Hollywood, where he became a star.

Astaire was born Frederick Austerlitz on May 10, 1899, in Omaha, Nebraska, the son of brewer Frederick E. Austerlitz. Astaire's father had emigrated from Vienna, Austria and found his way to the Midwest. Astaire's older sister Adele showed early promise as a dancer, and their mother, Ann, an enthusiastic supporter, brought the two children to New York in 1904, adopted the stage name Astaire, found dance instruction for the youngsters, and tried to spot a break in the entertainment world for a brother-sister song and dance act. The duo made their vaudeville debut in 1906 and continued their stage apprenticeship for more than a decade. By 1917, Adele and Astaire were appearing in stage musicals, and by the time Adele left the stage to marry in 1932, the popular team had ten musicals to their credit. Adele was the audience favorite. "The perfect dancing team since they were children," notes writer Arthur Jackson, "the Astaires came, were seen, and conquered with their personal dancing style and strangely enough, Adele's winsome personality rather than Fred's retiring demeanor." The Astaires' last show together was *The Band Wagon* in 1931, but they had sparkled and dazzled earlier in two George Gershwin musicals, *Lady, Be Good!* (1924) and *Funny Face* (1927), and Vincent Youmans's *Smiles* (1930).

Astaire was then paired with Claire Luce in Cole Porter's *Gay Divorce* in

1932. The show ran only 32 weeks, but it contained Astaire's choreography for the romantically seductive "Night and Day." Jackson points out that *Gay Divorce* "made Fred Astaire a star...in his first solo performance." The show was made into the film *The Gay Divorcée,* starring Astaire and Ginger Rogers, in 1934. In assessing the show, *New York Times* reviewer Brooks Atkinson wrote, "As a solo dancer Mr. Astaire stamps out his accent with that lean nervous agility that distinguishes his craftsmanship, and he has invented turns that abound in graphic portraiture. But some of us cannot help feeling that the joyousness of the Astaire team is missing now that the team has parted." Others were less kind, and one critic suggested, "Two Astaires are better than one." Fearing that he would not fare well without his sister, Astaire rethought his position. Hollywood beckoned, and films seemed the answer. In 1933, Astaire headed for California. That year, he appeared in *Flying Down to Rio* with Rogers and went on to dance with her in nine more films, including *Top Hat* (1935), *Swing Time* (1936), and *Shall We Dance* (1937), movies considered by many to be among the best musicals ever made.

For Astaire, dancing was not enough. A perfectionist, he involved himself with film staff and choreographers, especially Hermes Pan, his longtime associate. Astaire expressed both story and character through dance sequences, and dances were filmed with long, sweeping shots that avoided close-ups. The result was a heightened sense of the close interplay between dancers. In the 1940s and 1950s, Astaire continued to develop new dance routines, always carefully rehearsed, with stars like Eleanor Powell, Rita Hayworth, Judy Garland, and Bing Crosby.

In 1949, he received a special Academy Award for his contributions to film. His studied, casual singing inspired songs by Irving Berlin, George Gershwin, Vincent Youmans, and Cole Porter, and he made his mark in dramatic roles, on television, and with his own songs.

But it is Astaire's dancing that sticks in the mind. Dance critic Arlene Croce wrote "Astaire was the first dancer to establish himself on the screen, and the greatest. He raised technical standards in every department—camerawork, cutting, synchronization, scoring. He inspired the best efforts of the best song writers, and his personal style set a criterion for masculine elegance that has persisted through two generations." She adds this about his partnership with Rogers: "With Astaire and Rogers, it's a matter of total professional dedication; they do not give us emotions, they give us dances, and the more beautifully they dance, the more powerful the spell that seems to bind them together." Astaire died in Los Angeles on June 22, 1987, of pneumonia.

References and Further Reading

Adler, Bill. 1987. *Fred Astaire: A Wonderful Life: A Biography.* New York: Carroll & Graf.

Astaire, Fred. 2000. *Steps in Time: An Autobiography.* New York: Cooper Square Press.

Billman, Larry. 1997. *Fred Astaire: A Bio-Bibliography,* Westport, CT: Greenwood Press.

Cohan, Steven. 2002. "'Feminizing' the Song-and-Dance Man: Fred Astaire and the Spectacle of Masculinity in the Hollywood Musical." In *Hollywood Musicals, the Film Reader.* ed. Steven Cohan. New York: Columbia University Press.

Genne, Beth. 2004. "'Dancin' in the Street': Street Dancing on Film and Video from Fred Astaire to Michael Jackson." In *Rethinking*

Dance History: A Reader. ed. Alexandra Carter. New York: Routledge.

Giles, Sarah. 1988. *Fred Astaire: His Friends Talk.* New York: Doubleday.

Autry, Gene (1907–81)

Gene Autry was a Hollywood legend who started his career as a popular western singer in the 1930s and 1940s. He went on to perform in dozens of westerns for Republic Studios and became the first of the singing cowboys. Autry was also a songwriter, producer, television performer, and businessman. One of the hardest working men in show business, his prolific and successful career made him the only entertainer to earn five stars on the Hollywood Walk of Fame.

Autry had a modest childhood. He was born on September 29, 1907, to a struggling livestock dealer and his wife near Tioga, Texas. He joined the church choir at the age of 5 and learned to play guitar from his mother at age 12. Employed as a telegraph operator for the Frisco Railroad in 1927, Autry decided to pursue music as a career. Will Rogers heard him singing and recommended that he move to New York and try his luck with radio. Autry followed Rogers's advice, but initially he was not well received in New York. He did better when he moved to Tulsa, took a job at a local radio station, and became known as Oklahoma's yodelin' cowboy. When Autry returned to New York, he recorded some of Rogers's songs as well as his own. His first success, "That Silver-Haired Daddy of Mine," was released in 1931 and sold 1 a million copies. He then began performing regularly on "National Barn Dance," a popular radio show broadcast out of Chicago. With the money he earned from his radio performances, Autry began a publishing company so that he could retain the rights to the songs he had written.

Autry went to Hollywood in 1934 and sang one song in the western movie *In Old Santa Fe.* Studio executives were impressed. The next year Bob Nolan wrote the hit song "Tumbling Tumbleweeds," Hollywood writers scrambled to fashion a movie around the song. Autry got the starring role in this movie, the first of the western musicals. This new movie genre became so popular that between 1934 and 1942, Autry starred in six to eight such movies a year. During World War II, he enlisted in the Army Air Corps and became a pilot. His military service ended in 1946 and after the war, Autry returned to filmmaking and recording but also began a television career. In 1949, he wrote the Christmas song, "Rudolph, the Red-Nosed Reindeer," which quickly became popular. Between 1951 and 1954, he hosted "The Gene Autry Show" and produced many television series, including "Annie Oakley," "The Adventures of Champion," and "Buffalo Bill Jr." In 1966, he hosted the syndicated television series "Gene Autry's Melody Ranch." He received his five stars on the Hollywood Walk of Fame for his work in film, television, radio, music, and theater.

In 1956, Autry stopped performing and focused on managing his business empire. He owned radio and television stations, real estate, and oil wells. He became the original owner of the baseball team the California (now Anaheim) Angels in 1960 during the expansion of the American League. Baseball was one of the only fields in which Autry did not achieve top honors, since the Angels never got to the World Series during his lifetime. He regularly attended most home games, however, even though he sold one-quarter interest in the team to the Walt Disney Company in 1996.

Throughout his years of business dealings, Autry collected Western memorabilia and art. In December 1988, the Gene Autry Western Heritage Museum opened in Los Angeles' Griffith Park. Autry believed that the West had been very good to him and saw his investments in the museum as a way of showing his gratitude. The museum houses a wide range of exhibits from both the historical West and the West of Hollywood legend. Guns once owned by Annie Oakley and Wyatt Earp are displayed along with the costumes of TV's Lone Ranger and Tonto.

Autry married his second wife, Jackie Ellam Autry, in 1981. He died in their home in Studio City, California on October 2, 1998.

References and Further Reading

Autry, Gene. 1978. *Back in the Saddle Again.* Garden City, NY: Doubleday.

Cusic, Don. 2007. *Gene Autry: His Life and Career.* Jefferson, NC: McFarland & Co.

Malone, Bill C. 1985. *Country Music, U.S.A.* Austin: University of Texas Press.

George-Warren, Holly. 2007. *Public Cowboy No. 1: The Life and Times of Gene Autry.* New York: Oxford University Press.

Rothel, David. 1988. *The Gene Autry book.* Madison, NC: Empire Publishing Co.

Basie, William "Count" (1904–84)

William James "Count" Basie was one of the most important jazz band leaders from the 1930s until his death, and along with Duke Ellington is recognized as one of the two greatest jazz musicians.

Born on August 21, 1904, at Red Bank, New Jersey, Basie's father was a coachman for a wealthy family, and then later a groundsman. His mother taught him how to play the piano, and he soon became a drummer. In his teens he played in Harlem with Fats Waller, and by the 1920s was touring many parts of the United States. It was while playing at Kansas City, Missouri, that Basie was dubbed "Count" by a radio broadcaster who was comparing him to Duke Ellington.

In 1934 Basie established his own band, but later returned to the Bennie Moten Band, based in Kansas City, in which he had played earlier in his career. Moten died in 1935, and Basie formed a new band, drawing much talent from the Moten Band. Late in 1936 Basie's band moved from Kansas City to Chicago, and in October of that year a recording was made of the band, but had to be published under the name Jones-Smith Incorporated because Basie had already signed a business deal with Decca although he did not record his first session with them until January 1937. After only a short time in Chicago, Basie's band moved to New York City where they continued to play until the 1950s.

During the second half of the Great Depression, many people were inspired by the upbeat jazz music of Basie, who became a celebrity in the United States and internationally. As well as his musical talent, he was also able to build up a band which included some of the greatest jazz musicians of the period. Even Billie Holiday was a vocalist for Basie in 1937–38. The music that the band played was forceful, and the band collectively composed their music and then memorized it for performances so that they did not have to use sheet music.

Renowned jazz musician, William James "Count" Basie helped to pioneer the swing era in New York clubs during the late 1930s. (AP/Wide World Photos)

Count Basie's band sold countless records during the late 1930s through the 1950s. By that time the band was quite different, included excellent sight readers, continued to draw great talent, and performed with many famous people including Ella Fitzgerald and Frank Sinatra. In 1974 Basie and his band appeared in the Hollywood film *Blazing Saddles*. Basie suffered from diabetes and arthritis, but continued to insist on leading his band right up to a month before his death, on April 26, 1984.

Justin Corfield

See also: Goodman, Benny, Ellington, Duke.

References and Further Reading

Dance, Stanley. 1980. *The World of Count Basie.* New York: C. Scribner's Sons.

Murray, Albert. 1985. *Good Morning Blues: The Autobiography of Count Basie.* New York: Random House.

Schuller, Gunther. 1989. *The Swing Era.* New York: Oxford University Press.

Biddle, George (1885–1973)

George Biddle was a famous American artist who was born on January 24, 1885, to a well-known Philadelphia family. He was educated at Groton School where he was a classmate of Franklin Roosevelt. He went to Harvard University in 1904, graduating in 1908, and then gained a law degree in 1911 and returned to Philadelphia, where he passed his bar examination.

But in 1911 he left the United States to study art, his true vocation.

After studying at the Académie Julien, Paris, he returned to Philadelphia to attend the Pennsylvania Academy of the Fine Arts. In 1914 he returned to Europe and studied art at Munich, and then Madrid, where he, respectively, studied the works of Rubens and Velasquez. When the United States entered World War I, Biddle enlisted in the army. After the war Biddle visited many places around the world, including Tahiti, and then returned to France. Later he went to Mexico where he embarked on a short trip with the famous Mexican artist Diego Rivera, thus becoming involved in the Mexican mural movement.

During the 1930s, Biddle started producing what became known as social art. He urged Franklin Roosevelt to establish the Federal Art Project, which became part of the Works Progress Administration. The project was responsible for the funding of the production of several thousand pieces of artwork. Biddle was involved in producing paintings, lithographs and drawings of actual people or real events. One of the more famous of his works was a mural called *The Tenement,* held at the Justice Building in Washington, D.C. Another was a lithograph image *Catfish Alley,* influenced by a visit to Charleston, South Carolina. In 1939 some of Biddle's works were shown at the New York World Fair.

When World War II broke out, Biddle became chairman of the U.S. Department of War's Art Advisory Committee. He traveled with the 3rd Infantry Division on Operation Torch, and recorded the work of the soldiers at Algeria, Tunisia, Sicily, and then the Italian mainland. Some of his artwork depicting the exploits of the U.S. soldiers in the Mediterranean was published in *Life* magazine. Back in the United States after the war, Biddle was appointed to the U.S. Commission of Fine Arts, and died on November 6, 1973, at Croton-on-Hudson, New York.

Justin Corfield

See also: Diego, Rivera; Federal Art Project; Pollock, Jackson.

References and Further Reading

Biddle, George. 1939. *An American Artists' Story.* Boston: Little, Brown & Co.

Biddle, George. 1957. *The Yes and No of Contemporary Art.* London: Oxford University Press.

Pennigar, Martha. 1979. *The Graphic Work of George Biddle.* Baltimore, MD: Garamond/Pridemark Press.

Blitzstein, Marc (1905–64)

Marc Blitzstein's operas fused traditional and popular musical styles. Committed to leftist politics and art accessible to the people, Blitzstein is perhaps best remembered for his 1937 working-class opera *The Cradle Will Rock.*

Blitzstein was born on March 2, 1905, in Philadelphia, Pennsylvania. His father was a banker and his mother encouraged her son's musical interest. Blitzstein was something of a child prodigy, beginning piano lessons at age three and performing as a soloist with the Philadelphia Orchestra by his 15th birthday. He was a product of the Philadelphia public schools and attended the University of Pennsylvania. In 1922, he left the university to study with Alexander Siloti in New York. Two years later Blitzstein enrolled at the Curtis Institute of Music in Philadelphia.

In 1926, Blitzstein expanded his studies abroad, traveling to Paris and Berlin for compositional work with Nadia Boulanger and Arnold Schoenberg. While in Berlin, Blitzstein was exposed to the work of Bertolt Brecht. He returned to the United States in 1928, supporting himself as a performer and music teacher. Although he was a homosexual, Blitzstein married novelist Eva Goldbeck in 1933, but the marriage ended three years later with Goldbeck's death. Influenced by the ideas of Brecht and Hanns Eisler, Blitzstein was increasingly drawn to the importance of creating art for the masses. He wrote for journals such as *New Masses* and joined the Communist Party during the 1930s Popular Front era. Blitzstein also joined the Group Theatre in New York, working with socially conscious artists such as Elia Kazan and Clifford Odets.

Embracing the idea of music for the people, Blitzstein composed *The Cradle Will Rock,* under the auspices of the Federal Theater Project and Works Progress Administration (WPA). Threatened with Congressional budget cuts for supporting radical and controversial art, the WPA pulled funding from the show on the day it was scheduled to open. Although locked out of the Maxine Elliott Theatre, Blitzstein, director Orson Welles and producer John Houseman were able to procure a venue. Blitzstein played the score from an on-stage piano, while actors performed their parts from the audience. The opera celebrated the triumph of the working class and played for over 100 performances at the Mercury Theatre.

During the Second World War, Blitzstein was stationed in England with the U.S. Eighth Army Air Force, and this experience formed the basis for the symphony *Airborne* (1946), first performed by his friend Leonard Bernstein. During the post war period Blitzstein also came under fire for his political beliefs and in 1951 was subpoenaed to testify before the House Committee on Un-American Activities. In private testimony, he admitted his membership in the Communist Party but refused to name associates. He was blacklisted by the film industry, but he continued a career in the theater. He adapted Lillian Hellman's play *The Little Foxes* as the opera *Regina* (1949), fusing the traditions of European opera with American popular music. He also enjoyed commercial success with his translation of Brecht's *The Threepenny Opera* (1952) and *Juno* (1959) based upon Sean O'Casey's *Juno and the Paycock.*

Blitzstein died on January 22, 1964, in Martinique after being beaten by three Portuguese sailors following a sexual encounter. At the time of his death, Blitzstein was working on an opera based upon the case of Sacco and Vanzetti. Lauded by Bernstein as a major force in American music, renewed interest in Blitzstein's work was stimulated by the 1999 Tim Robbins's film *Cradle Will Rock.*

Ron Briley

See also: Federal Theater Project.

References and Further Reading

Chase, Gilbert. 1987. *America's Music: From the Pilgrims to the Present.* 3rd ed. Urbana, IL: University of Illinois Press.

Gordon, Eric. 1989. *Mark the Music: The Life and Work of Marc Blitzstein.* New York: St. Martin's Press.

Lehrman, Leonard. 2005. *Marc Blitzstein: A Bio-Bibliography.* New York: Praeger.

Bogart, Humphrey (1899–1957)

Widely considered one of the greatest film actors of all time, Humphrey DeForest Bogart created cynical but largely sympathetic characters in classic Hollywood movies like *Casablanca* (1942) and *The African Queen* (1951). Standing 5 foot 10 inches and weighing about 150 pounds, Bogart often created formidable tough guys on screen, his intense presence more a creation of his weary eyes and dark good looks than his physical stature.

Bogart was born on January 23, 1899, in New York City. His parents were Maud Bogart, an artist, and Dr. Belmont DeForest Bogart, a well-established surgeon. Well off, the family lived on Manhattan's Upper West Side, and Bogart attended the elite Trinity School. He then entered Philips Academy in Andover, Massachusetts, but the school expelled him for poor grades. He left school during World War I to join the U.S. Navy, serving from 1918 to 1919. The war ended right after he enlisted however, so most of his military career was spent on the ship *Leviathan,* transporting U.S. soldiers home.

When Bogart returned from his stint in the navy, he was offered a clerical position by William A. Brady, the owner of a stage company who was also a neighbor of the Bogarts. Soon, Bogart was promoted to stage manager. His first foray into acting came in 1920 while on a road tour of a Brady production, and he first stepped foot onto a New York stage in the 1922 production of *Drifting*. He would remain in theater, acting in a slew of both hits and failures, for the next 13 years. During this time, he married twice: to Helen Menken in 1926 (they divorced the following year) and to Mary Philips in 1928 (the couple split in 1938).

Although he had taken several screen tests, Bogart's lucky break didn't come until 1930, when he began appearing in small film roles. It wasn't until 1936, however, with his terrifying performance as Duke Mantee in the film version of *The Petrified Forest* (he had played the role on Broadway the previous year), that Hollywood took notice of him. Although not an instant film star, he never went back to the stage. Bogart's believability as a sinister gangster got him typecast as a "tough"—both bad guy and good (but flawed) guy—in films like *High Sierra* (1941), which established him as a top-ranking movie star, and the plot-twisting *The Maltese Falcon* (1942). Although miscast as a romantic lead and misused in a western or two, Bogart emerged to star in classics like *Casablanca* (1942), *The Big Sleep* (1946), and John Huston's *The Treasure of the Sierra Madre* (1948). These films solidified the persona of "Bogey" as a world-weary, cynical, sometimes snarling thug and sometimes a sardonic, reluctant hero. It was a long way from his prep-school boyhood.

Bogart was in a stormy marriage to his third wife, Mayo Methot, when he met Lauren Bacall on the set of *To Have and Have Not* in 1944. Then 45, he fell in love with the 20-year-old actress. The film made her a star, and he divorced Methot to marry Bacall in 1945. Bogey and Bacall were one of the most celebrated couples in Hollywood. Bogart, who had no children with his first three wives, fathered a son, Stephen, and a daughter, Leslie, with Bacall. Although Bogart was a heavy drinker, he was known as competent and professional on the movie set, and Bacall has indicated that their relationship was a loving one despite his alcoholism. Bogart and Bacall starred in three more crime stories together: *The Big Sleep* (1946), *Dark Passage* (1947), and *Key Largo* (1948), each of them darkly atmospheric and filled with seductive chemistry. Bogart won his only Academy Award for his role as a grizzled man who pilots a riverboat toward a showdown with a World War I German ship in 1951's *The African Queen*. In the powerful *Caine Mutiny* (1954), Bogart proved he could penetrate the soul of paranoia in his portrayal of Captain Queeg.

Bogart was diagnosed with esophageal cancer in 1956, just after he finished work in *The Harder They Fall*, which would be his last film. He died on January 14, 1957, having been on top of his game for 20 years.

Kellie Searle

References and Further Reading

Bogart, Stephen Humphrey. 1995. *Bogart: in Search of my Father*. New York: Dutton.

Duchovnay, Gerald. 1999. *Humphrey Bogart: A Bio-Bibliography*. Westport, CT: Greenwood Press.

McCarty, Clifford. 1995. *The Complete Films of Humphrey Bogart*. New York: Carol Publishing Group.

Perry, George. 2006. *Bogie: A Celebration of the Life and Films of Humphrey Bogart*. New York: Thomas Dunne Books/St. Martin's Press.

Sarris, Andrew. 1998. *You Ain't Heard Nothin' Yet: The American Talking Film: History & Memory, 1927–1949*. New York: Oxford University Press.

Tuska, Jon. 1978. *The Detective in Hollywood*. Garden City, NY: Doubleday.

"Brother Can You Spare a Dime?"

Written by composer Jay Gorney and lyricist E. Y. "Yip" Harburg, "Brother Can You Spare a Dime" became perhaps the defining popular song of the Great Depression. The song is a poignant memoir of an "everyman" expressing his disillusionment with the American dream. In it, the narrator recounts how he willingly served his country during World War I and worked hard to plow the country's fields and build its infrastructure, but despite his service and work, he was now reduced to standing in breadlines and begging for spare change. Much of the song's emotional impact comes from the way it contrasts each of the man's worthy accomplishments with the haunting refrain that became the song's title. This is further enhanced by the way the song casts the listener as the passer-by to which the singer directs his story. When the singer at the end reminds the listener that they are in fact old friends, it turns the otherwise impersonal tragedy of a "forgotten man" into something of immediate personal relevance.

Both of the song's authors had personally experienced hard times. Composer Jay Gorney was born Abraham Jacob Gornetzky to a Russian Jewish family that fled a Russian pogrom when Jay was 10 years old. Lyricist Edgar Yipsel "Yip" Harburg (born Irwin Hochberg) grew up in a poor Jewish neighborhood on New York's Lower East Side. He was Ira Gershwin's classmate at the City College of New York and also wrote lyrics for Harold Arlen (including songs for *The Wizard of Oz*) and Jerome Kern. With a melody based on a Russian Jewish lullaby Gorney remembered from his youth, "Brother Can You Spare a Dime's" melancholy tune and lyrics almost prevented it from being included in the Shubert Brothers' 1932 version of their *Americana* musical revue (sometimes referred to as *New Americana*) on Broadway.

From the time *Americana* premiered on October 5, 1932, the song was a show-stopper, having to be moved to the end of the second act to accommodate the encores. As the first popular song to deal with the Depression in any serious way, it became a national sensation as the economy was reaching its worst point in late 1932 and early 1933. Both Bing Crosby and Rudy Valee—two of the most popular male vocalists of the day—charted number one versions of the song at this time, and many other artists covered it in the following years. The song's potency was so great that when Franklin Roosevelt took office he requested (with its authors' assent) that radio stations stop broadcasting it to help lift the country out of the Depression.

Perhaps no other song has better come to represent the Great Depression in American popular culture. Beyond its emotive power as a musical work, its title has been used in the following decades as a colloquial expression and as a title for countless books, television episodes, and a 1975 documentary on the Depression. Its enduring relevance is reflected in the fact that it remains the only protest song ever to make it to number one on the charts; and in its 2005 induction into the Grammy Hall of Fame.

Kevin Kern

See also: Gershwin, George Jacob; Gershwin, Israel (Ira); Radio.

References and Further Reading

Gorney, Sondra K. 2005. *Brother, Can You Spare A Dime?: The Life of Composer Jay Gorney.* Oxford: The Scarecrow Press.

Wilk, Max. 1997. *They're Playing Our Song: Conversations With America's Classic Songwriters.* New York: Da Capo Press.

Cahill, Holger (1887–1960)

The principles guiding Holger Cahill's work as an advocate of arts education, champion of American folk art, and director of the Works Progress Administration Federal Art Project likely trace their origins to the hard work characterizing his distinctly humble background.

The son of Icelandic farmers who migrated to North Dakota in the 1890s, Cahill (born Sveinn Kristjan Bjarnarson) went to work as a farmhand while still a child after his father deserted the family. Frustrated by forced absences from school and poor treatment by his employer, Cahill ran off at the age of 15, supporting himself through various jobs, chiefly manual labor, and supplementing his education with extensive reading. At 26 he hopped a freight train to New York, where he changed his name and eventually enrolled in writing classes at New York University, intent on a career in journalism.

Cahill became a fixture of the 1910s and 1920s Greenwich Village social milieu, associating with other writers and artists such as playwright Eugene O'Neill, and painters John Sloan and Stuart Davis. During this time, as Cahill learned about art while writing essays for the magazine *Shadowland,* he developed an affinity for aesthetic simplicity and disdain for academic elitism which shaped his later career. Under the mentorship of Newark Library and Museum director John Cotton Dana, Cahill expanded into the roles of curator, arts educator, and advocate of American art, especially folk art created by people with little or no formal training.

In a book authored to supplement the Museum of Modern Art's *Art in America* educational radio series (1934–35), Cahill argued that fine art could only flourish in an America where the general public was familiar with art in general and supportive of American artists in particular. This position became a core principle of the Works Progress Administration Federal Art Project (FAP) when Cahill assumed directorship in 1935. Wary of bureaucracy and bureaucrats, Cahill accepted the appointment reluctantly. Though he remained frustrated throughout his tenure by federal procedures, his understanding of the creative process proved essential to mediating between artists and the protocols of government employment.

Deviating from Washington convention established by Treasury Department programs such as the Section of Painting and Sculpture, the FAP under Cahill placed little emphasis on refining public taste. Instead, Cahill prioritized quickly putting as many artists to work as possible, and promoting public interaction with arts and crafts, especially in communities far removed from traditional cultural centers like New York and San Francisco. The quantity over quality approach earned criticism from the art world that the FAP yielded little quality work. Nor did the relief through employment of thousands of artists (5,000 in 1936 alone) appease critics of federal expenditure on art during a time of economic crisis.

Well into retirement, Cahill continued to argue the merits of what he considered the program's key accomplishments: creating opportunities for artists to support themselves through their work; establishing southern and midwestern community art centers where the public could participate in art activities, including some centers which were racially integrated; and the creating the Index of American Art, an illustrated catalogue of American folk art.

Cahill served as FAP director until the program's termination in 1941, then retired to Stockbridge, Massachusetts to write novels.

Tess Mann

See also: Federal Art Project; Works Progress Administration.

References and Further Reading

Cahill, Holger. 1934. *Art in America in Modern Times.* Edited by Holger Cahill and Alfred H. Barr. New York: Reynal and Hitchcock.

Cahill, Holger. 1984. "Document: Letter from Holger Cahill to Edgar P. Richardson on Federal Patronage of the Arts." *Archives of American Art Journal* vol. 24 (3): 22–23.

Jeffers, Wendy. 1991. "Holger Cahill and American Art." *Archives of American Art Journal* 31 (4): 2–11.

McKinzie, Richard D. 1973. *The New Deal for Artists.* Princeton, NJ: Princeton University Press.

Carter, Bennett "Benny" Lester (1907–2003)

Benny Carter was an African American jazz composer, arranger, band leader, alto saxophonist, and trumpeter. Referred to by many of his peers as "the King," Carter was a major figure in the jazz world from the 1920s into the 1990s. During the Depression era, he brought his jazz talents to Europe with a racially integrated band.

Carter was born August 8, 1907, in New York City. His mother, who taught him piano, introduced him to music. While attracted to the trumpet through the influence of neighbor Bubber Miley, who played with Duke Ellington, he became frustrated that he could not quickly master the instrument and shifted to the saxophone. By his mid-teens he was performing at Harlem night spots. Carter briefly attended Wilberforce University, but left school to play with Horace Henderson's Wilberforce Collegians. In 1928, Carter joined the Charlie Johnson's Orchestra and although he had no formal music training, he arranged the sound for the recordings *Charleston is the Best Dance After All* and *Easy Money.* His growing reputation as a performer and arranger led to his appointment as musical director for the Detroit-based McKinney's Cotton Pickers. By 1932, Carter was back in Harlem, forming his own band with such jazz performers as Teddy Wilson and Dickey Wells.

Although fellow musicians praised Carter's band, commercial success was difficult during the early Depression years. Thus, he welcomed the 1933 opportunity to join the Willie Lewis Band based in Paris. While in Europe, Carter played a season at a Dutch seaside resort with an interracial band, a breakthrough moment for integration in jazz. Carter also worked with the British Broadcasting System as an arranger for jazz programs. Carter, however, missed the burgeoning swing music scene in the United States and returned to Harlem in 1938 and quickly found work arranging the recordings for major jazz figures Lionel Hampton, Count Basie, Duke Ellington, and Tommy Dorsey. In 1941, Carter formed a short-lived sextet which included Dizzy Gillespie and Kenny Clarke. The following year, he moved to California where he began a successful film-scoring career, including film scores for *Stormy Weather* (1943), *An American in Paris* (1951), and *The Gene Krupa Story* (1959). While focusing on his career in film and the emerging television industry, Carter continued to perform as a soloist and toured with such all-star groups as Jazz at the Philharmonic and recorded on the Verve record label.

In the 1970s, Carter expanded rather than contracted his activities, touring in the Middle East under the sponsorship of the State Department. He also developed a large following in Japan, frequently commuting to Tokyo for performances. Carter also educated Americans on the importance of jazz by conducting seminars at Princeton, which awarded him an honorary doctorate in 1974. Carter continued to record with jazz giants such as Miles Davis and Dizzy Gillespie and in the 1980s, Carter produced two of his most notable recordings: *A Gentleman and His Music* (1985) and *I'm in for Swing* (1987).

Carter's contributions to jazz were recognized with a Grammy Lifetime Achievement Award in 1987, and in 1996 he was honored by the Kennedy Center. The King's career spanned seven decades. After retiring from performing in 1997, Carter died on July 12, 2003, from bronchitis.

Ron Briley

References and Further Reading

Berger, Monroe, Edward Berger, and James Berger. 1982. *Ben Carter: A Life in American Music.* Lanham, MD: Scarecrow Press, 198.

Carter, Benny. 1998. *Benny Carter Collection.* Milwaukee, WI: Hal Leonard Corporation.

Lewis, Floyd. 2000. *Classic Jazz: A Personal View of the Music and the Musicians.* Berkeley: University of California Press.

Shipton, Alyn. 2007. *A New History of Jazz.* New York: Continuum.

Citizen Kane

Citizen Kane is generally considered to be one of the greatest movies of all time. It was innovative in its use of angles, lighting, and flashbacks. The American Film Institute ranked *Citizen Kane* as the number one movie of all time.

Directed by Orson Welles, the movie debuted in 1941. At the time, *Citizen Kane* was controversial because many believed the portrayal of the main character John Foster Kane was an attack on powerful newspaper publisher William Randolph Hearst. Many reviewers praised the movie, though sales for the movie were weak. One of the reasons for the movie's weak numbers may have been due to many movie theaters not showing *Citizen Kane* for fear of offending Hearst.

The movie is based on the style of the popular newsreel *The March of Time*. *Citizen Kane* begins with the death of newspaper publisher Charles Foster Kane who utters the word "Rosebud" before he dies. The movie brilliantly uses flashbacks and one scene seems to meld seamlessly into another. A journalist interviews people who knew Kane, including his second wife Susan Alexander and his newspaper colleagues. One newspaper colleague still admires Kane while the other is much more cynical about the man. The movie moves between their recollections and the life of Kane, showing him to be a tragic figure. He starts out as an idealist newspaper publisher only to yield by the end of the movie to the temptations of power. By the end of the movie, he is bitter, cynical, and alone. The journalist never figures out the mystery of Rosebud. However, movie viewers are given the answer at the end when a sled labeled "Rosebud" is burned in a stove inside Kane's mansion.

The powerful newspaper publisher Hearst reacted with fury. His lawyers threatened to sue movie directors that showed *Citizen Kane*. Hearst's newspapers refused to cover the movie. Hearst hinted to movie executives that his newspapers would leak damaging articles about their actors. Hearst's threats prompted the studio head Louis B. Mayer to offer to buy the rights to *Citizen Kane* for $800,00 in order to suppress it. There were a number of reasons for Hearst's reaction. One reason for Hearst's anger was the fact that the character John Foster Kane's life story was very similar to that of Hearst. Like Hearst, Kane was a successful newspaper publisher who had started his career as a reformer intent on confronting political bosses. Like Hearst, Kane's newspapers ran headlines that emphasized sex, scandal, and crimes and helped provoke the Spanish-American War. Like Hearst, Kane displayed extravagant tastes for art, and the character of Susan Alexander was very similar to that of Hearst's mistress Marion Davies.

Hearst's efforts at suppressing *Citizen Kane* were not successful. The movie debuted in 1941 to admiring reviews from critics. Yet Hearst's influence undoubtedly reduced sales for the movie. Many movie studios, such as MGM and Fox, did not show the movie due to threats from Hearst and his supporters. The fact that Hearst's newspapers throughout the country refused to publicize *Citizen Kane* probably diminished sales. Hearst's influence could also be seen at the 1942 Oscars. *Citizen Kane* received nine nominations, including best actor, best screenplay, best director, and best picture. However, the only award that the movie received was for best screenplay.

Perhaps the biggest casualty of *Citizen Kane* was its star actor and producer, the young prodigy Orson Welles. Welles was just 24 when he starred and produced *Citizen Kane,* by which time he was an a veteran within the acting profession. As a teenager he starred in several productions on Broadway. In addition, Welles played popular characters on the radio, such as the Shadow. By the late 1930s, he formed his own company called the Mercury Theater and produced his own plays. Before *Citizen Kane,* Welles was most famous for his radio broadcast of H. G. Wells's classic the *War of the Worlds,* which convinced many panic-stricken Americans that Earth was being invaded by aliens.

When Welles started producing *Citizen Kane,* he appeared to have a promising future ahead of him. He was given full control of *Citizen Kane* by RKO Studios as director, producer, and actor. It was assumed that the movie would be a success and that Welles would subsequently produce many successful movies. However, his career was damaged by the controversy over *Citizen Kane* and he never made another movie as significant as *Citizen Kane* nor did he again have complete control over a movie. He repeatedly traveled to Europe throughout the rest of his career to find acting work because Hearst used his influence to exclude Welles from the studio system.

In the years immediately after the debut of *Citizen Kane,* it receded from memory within the United States. Indeed, it was more popular in Europe, where it was first shown in France, Spain, and Norway in 1946. However, *Citizen Kane* became popular again within the United States in the 1950s. Beginning in the early 1960s, it made lists of top 10 movies of all time. Since then, it has generally been considered the greatest or one of the greatest movies of all time.

Jason Roberts

See also: Hearst, William Randolph.

References and Further Reading

Carringer, Robert L. 1985. *The Making of Citizen Kane.* Berkeley: University of California Press.

Heylin, Clinton. 2005. *Despite the System: Orson Welles Versus the Hollywood Studios.* Chicago: Review Press.

Swanberg, W. A. 1961. *Citizen Hearst: A Biography of William Randolph Hearst.* New York: Charles Scribner's Sons.

Thomson, David. 1996. *Rosebud: The Story of Orson Welles.* New York: Alfred A. Knopf.

Walsh, John Evangelist. 2004. *Walking Shadows: Orson Welles, William Randolph Hearst, and Citizen Kane.* Madison: University of Wisconsin Press.

Crosby, Bob (1913–93)

Although often overshadowed by his older brother Bing, Bob Crosby achieved his own measure of fame as a singer, bandleader, and radio, film, and television personality.

Born in Spokane, Washington in 1913, George Robert Crosby was the youngest of seven children. An average student in high school and at Gonzaga College, he expressed a strong desire to become a performer from an early age. Ten years Bing's junior, Bob Crosby spent his adolescence emulating his increasingly famous brother by singing in public and on local radio whenever he could. His first big break came in 1931 when, at Bing's suggestion, the Anson Weeks Orchestra hired him as a singer. After some initial difficulties, he eventually became a more confident vocalist with a style much like his brother's.

Dissatisfied with what he called Weeks's "Mickey Mouse" style of music, Bob Crosby left the band in 1934 and got a job with the new Dorsey Brothers Band, touring with the group and recording the vocals on several songs, including Tommy Dorsey's future signature tune, "I'm Getting Sentimental Over You." His tenure with the Dorseys was unpleasant, however, with Tommy Dorsey in particular treating him poorly. Thus, when disaffected members of Ben Pollack's band bolted in 1935 to form a new group and were searching for a titular leader, Crosby jumped at the chance.

Crosby would later say, "I'm the only guy in the band business who made it without talent" (Chilton 1983, 273) but this understates his role in his band's success. His famous name and pleasing stage presence attracted audiences; and by playing almost no role in the band's musical direction, he allowed its more talented members to flourish. Both the Bob Crosby Orchestra and its sub-group the Bob Cats had at their core musicians from New Orleans, and their music more than any other major band at the time was committed to the Dixieland style. As a result they cultivated a dedicated following of traditional jazz aficionados. From 1935 to 1951, Crosby's band in its various incarnations charted scores of recordings including such major hits as "In A Little Gypsy Tearoom," "Whispers In The Dark," "Day In Day Out," and "Down Argentina Way." It also became famous for such crowd-pleasers as "March Of The Bob Cats," "South Rampart Street Parade," and "Big Noise From Winnetka."

In the 1940s, Crosby began a Hollywood career in addition to his band responsibilities. Although he made more than 20 low-budget films, perhaps his greatest contribution was providing (with his band) part of the soundtrack to the classic *Holiday Inn*. He joined the Marines in 1944 and served as the leader of a 29-piece entertainment unit that toured throughout the Pacific theater. After his return, he resumed band leading, as well as acting as host on a series of popular radio and television shows, including *Club 15* and *The Bob Crosby Show*. Through the 1950s and 1960s, he divided his time between broadcasting and fronting bands, including prolonged residencies at Lake Tahoe and the Rainbow Grill at Rockefeller Center, New York. He continued to perform with his own ensembles and periodic reunions of the Bob Cats until shortly before his death of cancer in 1993.

Kevin Kern

See also: Basie, William "Count"; Ellington, Edward Kennedy "Duke"; Goodman, Benny; Henderson, Fletcher; Swing Music.

References and Further Reading

Chilton, John. 1983. *Stomp Off, Let's Go!: The Story of Bob Crosby's Bob Cats & Big Band*. London: Jazz Book Service.

Oliphant, Dave. 2002. *The Early Swing Era, 1930–1941*. Westport, CT: The Greenwood Press.

Sudhalter, Richard M. 1999. *Lost Chords: White Musicians and Their Contribution to Jazz, 1915–1945*. New York: Oxford University Press.

Davis Mountain Indian Lodge

Indian Lodge is a 39-room hotel located in the Davis Mountains State Park near Fort Davis, Texas and managed by the Texas Parks and Wildlife Department. The original adobe Pueblo Revival Style building, consisting of 16 guest rooms, a lobby, a game room, a dining room, and a manager's apartment, was built in 1934–35 by the Civilian Conservation Corps (CCC) under the supervision of the National Park Service (NPS) as part of the Emergency Conservation Work program in state parks. In 1965–66 an additional 24 guest rooms, new dining and meeting rooms, and a swimming pool were added to the original structure, and the older building was modernized. In 2004–6 the Texas Parks and Wildlife Department renovated the addition and restored the original structure to its 1935 appearance.

Construction on the building was to have started in June 1933, when CCC Companies 879 and 881 arrived in Davis Mountains State Park and established Camp Washington Seawell, named after the 8th Infantry colonel who had established the military post at Fort Davis in 1854. Company 881 was transferred to Roswell, New Mexico in October 1933 but Company 879 remained in the park until June 1935. The initial work on the Lodge proceeded very slowly, and the foundations were not laid until December 1933. The CCC men also built Skyline Drive and numerous picnic shelters within the park.

The first plans for the Lodge, which was originally designated the Indian Village, were drawn up by NPS architect J. B. Roberts. However, when NPS Inspector George Nason visited the site in May 1934 he found the partially constructed building "distinctly lacking in character and atmosphere," and he instructed NPS architects Arthur Fehr and William Caldwell to redraw the plans. Fehr and Caldwell produced a building that was very much in the southwestern romantic mode favored by architects such as John Gaw Meem and Mary Colter, a building that was essentially Pueblo Revival in style with Arts and Crafts details such as wrought iron lighting fixtures and hardware, wooden window sashes, flat rock chimneys and coping, and flagstone walks between the rooms. Caldwell also designed furniture for the Lodge that was reminiscent of the Spanish Colonial Revival furniture being produced in federally funded craft schools in New Mexico at the time. That furniture is still in place in the older section of the Lodge. In February 1935 Nason, fearful that the building would not be completed by the March 31, 1935, deadline established by the NPS's Washington office, eliminated some of Fehr and Caldwell's details, including the stone coping and flagstone walks.

All of the materials for the building were obtained locally. The CCC enrollees made 120,000 adobe bricks on the building site under the supervision of a skilled adobe maker employed as a Local Experienced Man (LEM). The pine roof beams and support columns were cut on the slopes of nearby Mount Livermore, and the river cane that forms the ceilings of the guest rooms was cut near Boquillas on the Rio Grande, about 130 miles south.

The construction of Indian Village (the name was changed to Indian Lodge in July 1936) was plagued with difficulties and problems. It was among the first CCC projects in the state of Texas, and there were no procedures established for estimating costs or purchasing materials when the work started. The first two construction superintendents were inexperienced political appointees of the notorious Miriam Ferguson administration. The first resigned after three months; the second remained on the job for five months. A local newspaper reported after the second superintendent left in March 1934 that the men "lacked plans and materials to proceed." The third superintendent, A. S. Lewis, was an experienced builder and it was not until he took over in May 1934 that substantial progress was made. However, when the building was deemed complete by the NPS and turned over to the Texas State Parks Board on March 31, 1935, it lacked a hot water system and electricity and the gray plaster exterior and interior walls were unpainted. It was opened to the public with these defects in September 1935. Rooms were lit with kerosene lamps and visitors were told that there was no hot water because Indians did not take hot baths. In fact the architects had omitted the hot water system, and the electric generator had not been purchased due to a misunderstanding over whether it was to be bought with state or federal funds.

Hot water and a gasoline-powered electric generator were installed during the first year of operation, but in March 1937 severe leaks in the Lodge's flat roofs resulting from design and construction defects forced its closure for more than a year. Fifty men from CCC Company 1855's Chisos Basin camp established a side camp at the Lodge and rebuilt the roofs and the roof drainage system, and at the same time painted the buildings and built a power line that connected the Lodge to the electric power grid at Fort Davis. When the Chisos Basin camp was closed in December 1937 the men at the Lodge were transferred to CCC Company 1856, based at Balmorhea State Park. The side camp was closed on June 30, 1938, and the Lodge reopened in August 1938. Except for a brief period during the World War II, when it housed the wives of pilots in training at Marfa Army Air Field as permanent guests, and during the renovation and restoration in 2004–6, the Lodge has been open to the public since then. Its spectacular setting with views down Keesey Canyon, its location in a 1900-acre state park with hiking trails and other recreational opportunities, and the cool temperatures resulting from its 5,000-foot altitude have made it one of Texas's most popular summer resorts

Lonn Taylor

See also: Civilian Conservation Corps.

References and Further Reading

Alpine (Texas). *Avalanche, 1933–1938.* National Archives Regional Center, Denver, CO: RG 79, Records of the National Park Service; National Archives, Washington, DC: RG 35, Records of the Civilian Conservation Corps.

Steely, James Wright. 1999. *Parks for Texas: Enduring Landscapes of the New Deal.* Austin: University of Texas Press.

Taylor, Lonn W. 2006. "A History of Indian Lodge in Davis Mountains State Park, 1933–2000." *Report to the Texas Parks and Wildlife Department.* November 15.

Dillinger, John Herbert (1903–34)

John Herbert Dillinger was the most infamous bank robber of the 1930s. He was named "Public Enemy Number One" by the U.S. Justice Department in 1934 and subsequently became the subject of the country's greatest manhunt. The Dillinger saga is shrouded in myth, and he remains even today a potent symbol of the modern American outlaw.

Dillinger was born on June 22, 1903, in Indianapolis, Indiana to middle-class parents. His mother died when he was three, leaving his older sister Audrey in charge of raising him. He rebelled against his father's strict moralizing and discipline, which included terrible beatings. While in the sixth grade, Dillinger became the leader of a neighborhood gang, known as the Dirty Dozen, that stole coal from the Pennsylvania Railroad. In 1920, his family's move to Mooresville, Indiana, a small farming community, curbed

John Dillinger was the most infamous bank robber of the 1930s. He was named "Public Enemy Number One" by the U.S. justice department in 1934 and subsequently became the subject of the country's greatest manhunt. (Library of Congress)

Dillinger's delinquency for a short time, but he soon dropped out of high school and took a factory job back in Indianapolis. He began to read about Wild West outlaws, reveling in the exploits of Jesse James, and spent much of his free time playing baseball, shooting pool, and chasing girls.

Following a failed courtship, Dillinger decided to join the navy in July 1923. He found military life intolerable, however, and deserted in December of that same year. After a few brief relationships, Dillinger married Beryl Hovius on April 12, 1924. He excelled as an upholsterer in a Mooresville furniture factory but quickly tired of normal, married life. Dillinger committed his first major crime on September 6, 1924, when he and a friend, Ed Singleton, got drunk and tried to rob Frank Morgan, an elderly grocer. The attempt failed, and both men were arrested. Dillinger was sentenced to 10 to 20 years in Pendleton Reformatory, while his partner got only 2 to 14 years, which deeply embittered Dillinger. He was punished for trying to escape in 1924, for gambling in 1926, and for destroying property in 1928, but became a model prisoner soon after. In 1929, his wife divorced him. His family minister and Morgan pleaded for his release in 1929, and their request was eventually granted in 1933.

After being released on May 22, Dillinger launched his own response to the country's Great Depression. He and some friends he had made while in prison robbed a bank in New Carlisle, Ohio on June 10, 1933, taking approximately $10,600. Dillinger and various cohorts hit at least 10 other banks during 1933, including the First National Bank of Montpelier, Indiana, the State Bank in Indianapolis, and the Central National

Bank of Greencastle, Indiana. The Dillinger gang became such a problem that Indiana governor Paul McNutt called out the National Guard. Yet Dillinger somehow found time to visit Chicago's 1933 World's Fair twice, attend baseball games with some girlfriends, and visit his father at the Mooresville farm. He had several run-ins with the law and was jailed in Lima, Ohio for almost a month before being freed by some associates on October 12. Dillinger continued to operate without fear, however, raiding police stations on two occasions for guns and ammunition. The phrase "Dillinger Luck" arose during this time to account for the bank robber's amazing ability to elude arrest. The Dillinger gang reportedly celebrated New Year's Eve on Daytona Beach, firing machine guns into the sand.

The year 1934 began with Dillinger and friends robbing the First National Bank of East Chicago on January 15. He was captured by Arizona police only 10 days later. Apparently wielding a crudely carved wooden gun, Dillinger escaped from the Lake County Jail on March 3. Between March 6 and March 23, Dillinger's new gang robbed banks in Sioux Falls, South Dakota and Mason City, Iowa, stealing more than $100,000. The newly formed Federal Bureau of Investigation (FBI) had become involved with the search for Dillinger by this time, and he barely escaped traps on March 31 and April 23. Just as in 1933, however, Dillinger was able to attend a family reunion at the Mooresville farm in early April, bury a friend who had been shot by the police, and undergo plastic surgery in late May. Many of the myths surrounding Dillinger's life and crime spree were created during this time, some of them by FBI director J. Edgar Hoover, who told reporters that Dillinger liked to disguise himself as a nun. On June 22, 1934, while Dillinger was celebrating his 31st birthday, the federal government named him Public Enemy Number One.

Dillinger knew that he would not be able to run for much longer, reportedly telling friends, "I'm traveling a one-way road, and I'm not fooling myself as to what the end will be." He robbed his last bank in South Bend, Indiana, on June 30. On July 22, 1934, Dillinger was betrayed by his girlfriend Anna Sage ("the woman in red") and was shot and killed by federal agents while leaving Chicago's Biograph Theater. Stories and rumors quickly began circulating that Dillinger was still alive and that the agents had shot the wrong man. Many of the myths surrounding Dillinger's life continue to circulate today.

Mark Edwards

References and Further Reading

Block, Lawrence, ed. 2004. *Gangsters, Swindlers, Killers, and Thieves: The Lives and Crimes of Fifty American Villains*. New York: Oxford University Press.

FBI Documents Regarding John Dillinger. Washington, DC: Federal Bureau of Investigation, 1998.

Fredericks, Dean. 1963. *John Dillinger*. New York: Pyramid.

Matera, Dary. 2004. *John Dillinger: The Life and Death of America's First Celebrity Criminal*. New York: Carroll & Graf.

Potter, Claire Bond. 1998. *War on Crime: Bandits, G Men, and the Politics of Mass Culture*. New Brunswick, NJ: Rutgers University Press.

Wild, Roland. 1935. *Crimes and Cases of 1934*. London: Rich & Cowan.

Disney, Walter Elias (1901–66)

Creator of Mickey Mouse, Walter Elias Disney achieved preeminence in movies and television and revolutionized the leisure industry with his theme park, Disneyland. Founder of the largest studio in the world devoted to animated films, he produced such classics as *Snow White and the Seven Dwarfs* and *Fantasia* and was equally successful with such live-action productions as *Mary Poppins.*

Born on December 5, 1901, in Chicago, Illinois, Walt was the fourth son of Elias and Flora Disney. As a result of several family moves, he attended grammar school in Kansas City and high school in Chicago, as well as art classes at the Kansas City Art Institute and the Chicago Institute of Art. In his leisure time, he was always drawing. In late 1918, he went to France as an ambulance driver in the final days of World War I. Employed at an advertising company in 1920, Disney met Ub Iwerks, who later helped develop the Disney style. At the Kansas City Film Ad Company, Disney learned enough about stop motion photography to set up a studio, where he made animated spoofs and fairy tales known as Laugh-O-Grams. Unfortunately, the firm went bankrupt in 1923.

Moving to Hollywood, Disney, his brother Roy, and Iwerks produced a 56 film series inspired by *Alice's Adventures in Wonderland,* involving interaction between a six-year-old girl and cartoon characters. In 1927, Disney conceived the *Oswald the Lucky Rabbit* series for Universal Studios but lost the rights to the character. He vowed never to work for someone else again. With Mickey Mouse, Disney created a character whose optimism appealed enormously to Depression-era audiences. Mickey was introduced to the public in *Steamboat Willie* (1928), the first cartoon to use synchronized sound. Disney himself provided vocalizations for Mickey, Minnie Mouse, and the ship's parrot. Other characters followed, including Pluto, Goofy, and Donald Duck, the studio's most successful star, who was first seen in *The Wise Little Hen* (1934). Competition inspired Disney to develop another kind of cartoon, in which music was used to tell a story. With *The Skeleton Dance* (1929), a series of more than 70 *Silly Symphonies* was initiated, representing the Disney Studio's most creative work. *Flowers and Trees* (1932) was the first cartoon in color and the first to win an Academy Award in the new "Cartoon Short Subject" category. Oscars also went to *Three Little Pigs* (1933), *The Old Mill* (1937), and *The Ugly Duckling* (1939), the last *Silly Symphony.*

Believing that the future belonged to feature films, in 1934, Disney began his most ambitious project, requiring 750 artists and quadrupling the original budget. Certain that it would bankrupt the studio, the industry labeled it Disney's Folly. When it premiered on December 21, 1937, *Snow White and the Seven Dwarfs,* based on Grimm's fairy tale, made instant film history. Disney received a Special Academy Award for "a significant screen innovation," and the film, universally acknowledged as a movie milestone, earned $8 million on its initial release, four times its cost. Entering its golden age, the Disney Studio achieved a level of success that continued unabated for five decades, producing a stream of animated classics, live-action films, and documentaries, and garnering numerous awards. Among the studio's best animated features are

Pinocchio (1940); *Fantasia* (1940), a collaboration with conductor Leopold Stokowski, featuring the music of Johann Sebastian Bach, Ludwig van Beethoven, Peter Ilyich Tchaikovsky, Modest Moussorgsky, and others; *Dumbo* (1941); *Bambi* (1942); *Cinderella* (1950); *Alice in Wonderland* (1951); and *Peter Pan* (1953). *Sleeping Beauty* (1959), Disney's most ambitious and expensive animated film, was a financial disaster but had dazzling animation effects set to the score of Tchaikovsky's ballet of the same name.

The studio also produced dozens of public service films for the U.S. government, the armed forces, and various institutions. During World War II, it provided brilliant animation for the "Why We Fight" series supervised by Frank Capra. Even its cartoons served the war effort, notably the Oscar-winning *Der Fuehrer's Face* (1942), in which Donald Duck has a nightmare that he is in Nazi Germany.

Treasure Island (1950) was the first all live-action feature film for the studio and the first in a series of swashbuckling adventures produced at Disney's British studio, which also included *The Story of Robin Hood* (1952) and *Kidnapped* (1960)—all with British casts. Among the most successful ventures in live-action were *20,000 Leagues under the Sea* (1954), *Old Yeller* (1957), and *The Parent Trap* (1961). One of Disney Studio's biggest commercial and critical hits was *Mary Poppins* (1964), a lavishly produced musical integrating a live-action story of a British nanny (Julie Andrews) with ingenious animated sequences. The film was nominated for 13 Academy Awards and won 5 (including Best Actress for Andrews).

Disneyland, the studio's first television venture, premiered on ABC in October 1954. Its programming, representing the diversity of the Disney product, included many of its cartoons, live-action, and nature subjects, but new material premiered as well, like the *Davy Crockett* series. Other Disney television programs included *The Mickey Mouse Club,* an instant success at its premiere in 1955; *Zorro,* a weekly adventure series; and *The Wonderful World of Color,* which premiered on NBC in 1961.

The view of America—and life in general—projected through the varied products of the Disney Studio was remarkably consistent. Whether embodied in the contests between good and evil in *Snow White* or *Sleeping Beauty,* or in the celebration of traditional family and patriotic values through heroes like Johnny Tremain and Davy Crockett, Disney's was the personality and vision that marked every work. This was both his genius and the reason that, over the years, so many artists and directors—including loyal collaborators like Ub Iwerks—found him tyrannical and left the Disney Studio. Perhaps the ultimate symbols of Disney's empire are the two amusement parks he created. The first, Disneyland, opened in Anaheim, California in 1955, and the second, Walt Disney World, in Orlando, Florida in 1971. Today, versions of Disneyland exist around the world. The Disney company remains one of the most successful merchandising businesses of the century, producing numerous commodities linked to its films, including books, comics, records, toys, clothes, games, and watches. The income from such sources had reached $130 million annually by 1986.

After Disney's death on December 15, 1966, the studio's fortunes varied but have markedly improved since the late 1970s. Under the banner of Touchstone Pictures, it has produced many live-action successes, including *Splash* (1984) and *The Color of Money* (1987). *Who Framed Roger Rabbit* (1988), co-produced by Steven Spielberg, was an extraordinary integration of live action and animation. An ebullient tribute to the achievements of Disney and his contemporaries, the film's animation won a Special Academy Award. The studio's pure animation impulse was revitalized with *The Little Mermaid* (1989), *Beauty and the Beast* (1991), *Aladdin* (1992), *The Lion King* (1994), *Pocahontas* (1995), *The Hunchback of Notre Dame* (1996), *Hercules* (1997), and *Mulan* (1998), and with Pixar Studios pioneered the art of computer animation in *Toy Story* (1995), *A Bug's Life* (1998), and *Toy Story 2* (1999).

References and Further Reading

Barrier, Michael. 2007. *The Animated Man: A Life of Walt Disney*. Berkeley: University of California Press.

Feinstein, Stephen. 2005. *Read About Walt Disney*. Berkeley Heights, NJ: Enslow Publishers.

Jackson, Kathy Merlock. 1993. *Walt Disney, a Bio-Bibliography*. Westport, CT: Greenwood Press.

Thomas, Bob. 1976. *Walt Disney: An American Original*. New York: Simon and Schuster.

Watts, Steven. 2001. *The Magic Kingdom: Walt Disney and the American Way of Life*. Columbia: University of Missouri Press.

Dorsey, Tommy (1905–56)

Trombonist and orchestra leader Tommy Dorsey led the quintessential big band of the swing era. As a trombonist, Dorsey had no equal. His seemingly effortless breathing control technique helped to create his "singing" trombone style and made him the master of his genre.

Thomas Francis Dorsey was born on November 19, 1905, in Shenandoah, Pennsylvania. The son of an amateur musician and bandleader, he was taking cornet lessons by the time he was a toddler. To make sure that his sons would practice their instruments, Dorsey's father would hide their shoes so they couldn't play outside. Dorsey and his brother Jimmy played in their father's band, and by the time the brothers were teenagers, they started their own band called Dorsey's Wild Canaries. In 1922, the Dorsey brothers joined the Scranton Sirens, and in 1924, they joined Jean Goldkette's big jazz band in Detroit. At about that time, Tommy switched from playing the trumpet to playing the trombone, while Jimmy played the alto saxophone and clarinet.

In 1927, the brothers moved to New York, where they embarked on extremely successful careers as freelance musicians. The success of the Dorsey brothers was even more impressive because their careers in New York started at the same time as the Great Depression. Very few artists were successful at making a living during those hard times. In 1934, after the repeal of Prohibition triggered a resurgence in nightlife and entertainment, the brothers established the Dorsey Brothers Orchestra. Tommy and Jimmy Dorsey had vastly different personalities, and they fought constantly. Tommy was a single-minded perfectionist, and his brother was easygoing but always challenging Tommy. They had a falling out in 1935 that led them to establish separate careers. For nearly two decades, the brothers rarely spoke or played together.

Tommy Dorsey took over leadership of Joe Haymes's big band, known for its Dixieland style, in 1935. He gradually shifted the band's style to a more tightly knit, harmonized, melodic, and danceable kind of swing jazz. By 1940, his orchestra was at the pinnacle of popular dance music. That year, he signed a 24-year-old singer by the name of Frank Sinatra, who began his phenomenal rise to superstardom under Dorsey's influence. The coming of Sinatra was a turning point in the swing era, as the singers became perceived as the stars to the accompaniment of the big bands. Other singers in Dorsey's orchestra included Connie Haines and Jo Stafford. The Dorsey brothers reunited briefly in 1947 to work together on the semibiographical film *The Fabulous Dorseys.*

The big band era largely came to an end after World War II, but Dorsey's band was one of the few big bands that managed to survive. He and his brother reconciled in 1953, and his band became known as Tommy Dorsey and His Orchestra, featuring Jimmy Dorsey. Tommy Dorsey died in Greenwich, Connecticut on November 26, 1956, and his brother died seven months later.

The Tommy Dorsey Orchestra released dozens of singles, including "I'm Getting Sentimental Over You" (1935); "Marie" (1937); "Song of India" (1937); "Boogie Woogie" (1938); "Hawaiian War Chant" (1938); "Music, Maestro, Please" (1938); "I'll Be Seeing You" (1940); "I'll Never Smile Again" (1940); "Yes, Indeed!" (1941); "Well, Git It!" (1941); "On the Sunny Side of the Street" (1944); and "Opus No. 1" (1944). The Dorsey Brothers Orchestra's singles include "My Melancholy Baby" (1928); "Praying the Blues" (1929); "Oodles of Noodles" (1932); "Fidgety" (1933); "Shim Sham Shimmy" (1933); "Stop, Look, and Listen" (1934); "Sandman" (1934); "Tailspin" (1935); "Dippermouth Blues" (1935); "Parade of the Milk Bottle Caps" (1936); "John

Silver" (1938); "Dusk in Upper Sandusky" (1939); "My Prayer" (1939); "Contrasts" (1940); "Amapola" (1941); "Green Eyes" (1941); "Maria Elena" (1941); "Blue Champagne" (1941); "Embraceable You" (1941); "Tangerine" (1941); and "Brazil" (1942).

Lisa McCallum

See also: Goodman, Benny.

References and Further Reading

Dorsey, Tommy. 1944. *The Modern Trombonist: A Complete Method for Trombone.* New York: Embassy Music.

Dicaire, David. 2003. *Jazz Musicians of the Early Years, to 1945.* Jefferson, NC: McFarland.

Levinson, Peter J. 2005. *Tommy Dorsey: Livin' in a Great Big Way: A Biography.* Cambridge, MA: Da Capo Press.

Stockdale, Robert L. 1995. *Tommy Dorsey: On the Side.* New Brunswick: Institute of Jazz Studies, Rutgers, State University of New Jersey; Metuchen, NJ: Scarecrow Press.

Crow, Bill. 2005. *Jazz Anecdotes.* New York: Oxford University Press, 2005

Sanford, Herb. 1972. *Tommy and Jimmy: The Dorsey Years.* New Rochelle, NY: Arlington House.

Dos Passos, John (1896–1970)

Dos Passos was born in Chicago on January 14, 1896. His father was a wealthy and well-known corporate lawyer while his mother was the scion of a well-heeled Virginia family. Because Dos Passos's parents were married—but not to one another—when he was born, Dos Passos spent much of his childhood traveling with his mother in Europe to avoid the possibility that his illegitimate birth might scandalize his father. The sense of alienation and the search for identity Dos Passos experienced in these early years would later shape the poetry and prose he wrote as an adult.

Like many other writers of the "Lost Generation," Dos Passos was deeply affected by the tumultuous events of the early 20th century. Also, like many of his cohorts (including Ernest Hemingway, e.e. cummings, and W. Somerset Maugham), Dos Passos witnessed these events first-hand. During World War I Dos Passos agreed to join the Norton-Harjes Ambulance Corps in Europe. His first novel, *One Man's Initiation: 1917,* was published in 1920, and it was followed by another novel, *Three Soldiers,* which brought Dos Passos his first taste of popular and critical acclaim. Both focused on his experiences in Europe. In 1925, Dos Passos published *Manhattan Transfer,* which cemented his reputation as one of the most prolific and innovative writers working at the time. Unlike his first two novels, which dealt explicitly with the experience of World War I, *Manhattan Transfer* more broadly explored the alienating tendencies of modern life, focusing especially on the perils of unfettered capitalism and the shallow nature of peoples' lives during the "Jazz Age." The novel also represented a crucial turning-point for Dos Passos stylistically; it was inspired, at least in part, by the experimental prose employed by James Joyce in his ground-breaking novel *Ulysses.*

After the success of *Manhattan Transfer,* Dos Passos increasingly turned his attention to political concerns. When the Italian immigrants Sacco and Vanzetti were sentenced to die in 1927, Dos Passos was among a cadre of influential writers and intellectuals who agitated for their release. His major work, known colloquially as the *U.S.A. Trilogy,* was comprised of three separate novels. They were published together in 1938, at the height of the Great Depression. In *U.S.A.,* Dos Passos combined the impressionistic styling of his earlier work with a new sense of realism and explored the themes of the collected novels as stream-of-consciousness musings. Viewed together, the novels also betrayed Dos Passos's increasingly cynical views of the future of American democracy, views which were shared by many Americans who had become disillusioned as a result of the ongoing economic and social malaise.

Later in life, Dos Passos repudiated his own left-leaning views and gradually embraced more conservative, even reactionary, political positions. Though he continued to write until his death in 1970, Dos Passos never again achieved the acclaim that had followed *U.S.A.* From a literary standpoint he was enormously influential; from a political standpoint, his life represents many of the conflicted and conflicting views of the tumultuous 20th century.

Dave Powell

References and Further Reading

Carr, Virginia Spencer. 1984. *Dos Passos: A Life.* New York: Doubleday.

Ludington, Townsend. 1980. *John Dos Passos: A Twentieth Century Odyssey.* New York: Dutton.

Rosen, Robert C. 1981. *John Dos Passos, Politics and the Writer.* Lincoln: University of Nebraska Press.

Sanders, David. 1987. *John Dos Passos: Comprehensive Bibliography.* New York: Garland.

Whittemore, Reed. 1993. *Six Literary Lives: The Shared Impiety of Adams, London, Sinclair, Williams, Dos Passos, and Tate.* Columbia: University of Missouri Press.

Earhart, Amelia Mary
(1897–1937)

A pioneering aviator, Amelia Earhart became a symbol of both women's growing independence and the rising prominence and importance of the airplane in American life.

Born in Atchison, Kansas on July 24, 1897, Amelia Mary Earhart was an independent child and something of a daredevil, even from an early age. Her parents, Edwin Earhart (a lawyer) and Amy Otis Earhart, struggled financially for the first years of Earhart's life, relying greatly on Earhart's maternal grandparents for support. Contributing to these financial problems was Edwin's alcoholism, resulting in a divorce for the couple in 1924. Earhart and her younger sister spent a great deal of their childhoods with their maternal grandparents, who were strict, conservative people and attempted to restrain Earhart's tomboyish ways. Her parents' financial problems compelled Earhart to begin working at young age and encouraged her desire for independence. During World War I, she worked as a Red Cross nurse in Toronto, Canada. After the war ended, Earhart moved to New York, where she attended Columbia University, earning a degree in nursing.

Sometime before 1921, Earhart flew as a passenger in an airplane for the first time, probably at a local air show. In January 1921, she met Neta Snook, a woman pilot, and began taking flying lessons from her. In 1922, Earhart bought her first plane, a yellow Kinner Canary biplane, and quickly set about breaking her first record. She was the first woman to fly higher than 14,000 feet. Although Earhart continued to work as a nurse, she

A pioneering aviator, Amelia Earhart and her navigator, Fred Noonan, disappeared over the Pacific during a planned round-the-world flight on July 2, 1937. Ever since, Earhart has been the subject of speculation and conspiracy theories. (Library of Congress)

was fascinated by flying. After Charles Lindbergh completed the first solo flight across the Atlantic on May 20–21, 1927, she became even more dedicated to aviation. In 1928, Captain H. H. Railey asked her to join a publicity flight across the Atlantic, making her the first woman to make the flight, although she would only be a passenger. She accepted, and the flight on June 17–18, 1928, propelled her to stardom. Although her duties during the flight were limited to keeping the flight log, in the public's mind, she had become the female version of Lindbergh and the most famous woman aviator in the world.

After her Atlantic flight, Earhart devoted herself full time to aviation, leaving her nursing position. She served as the aviation editor for *Cosmopolitan* magazine and published a book about her transatlantic flight, *20 Hrs., 40 Min.,* in 1928. She also found work as a consultant and promoter for several early airline companies. With her publisher husband, George P. Putnam (whom she had married in 1931), Earhart embarked on a series of promotional flights, most notably the Women's Air Derby in 1929 (a race from Santa Monica, California to Cleveland, Ohio). She continued to break records, setting a women's speed record of 181 miles per hour in 1929 and an altitude record of 18,451 feet in 1931. She also served as a founder and president of the Ninety-Nines, a club for woman pilots. In 1932, exactly five years after Lindbergh's historic flight, Earhart became the first woman to fly solo across the Atlantic. In her single-engine Lockheed Vega, she flew from Newfoundland to Ireland in the record-breaking time of 14 hours and 56 minutes. This adventure brought her more fame and honors. Later that same year, she published another book about flying, *The Fun of It.* In 1935, Earhart set her sights on even greater glory. She became the first person to complete solo flights from Hawaii to California (which covered more distance than her Atlantic flight had) and from Los Angeles to Mexico City and to make nonstop flights between Mexico City and Newark, New Jersey. For her pioneering aviation efforts, she received the Distinguished Flying Cross at a joint session of Congress and met President Franklin D. Roosevelt at the White House. She also began serving as a career counselor for women students at Purdue University.

In 1937, Earhart concentrated all of her energy on completing a round-the-world flight. In 1924, a group of army pilots had completed a series of such flights, but they had taken a circuitous route that had allowed them to remain close to land. Earhart planned to follow the much more dangerous equatorial route, which would cover more than 29,000 miles. She hoped to discover the effects of distance flying on humans, particularly looking at levels of fatigue and the impact of diet. She recognized that such a trip would be impossible to complete alone, so hired a navigator, Fred Noonan, to accompany her. Public interest in the trip was tremendous, with Earhart's husband Putnam handling all of the publicity and fundraising. With financial help from Purdue University, Earhart had a twin-engine Lockheed Electra plane specially built for the trip. The Electra was considered extremely advanced for its time. Earhart and Noonan set out from Oakland, California on March 17, heading west for Hawaii, but after completing this first leg of the trip, the plane crashed upon takeoff from Hawaii. The passengers were uninjured, but the plane required extensive repairs, forcing Earhart to postpone the entire trip. On June 1, Earhart and Noonan set out again, this time traveling east from Oakland to Miami, Florida. By June 30, they reached New Guinea, having nearly completed their journey and traveling over the Caribbean, South America, Africa, India, the Dutch East Indies, and Australia (a trip covering 22,000 miles). This next leg of the trip was the most dangerous and would require expert navigation and flying. From New Guinea, the flight was scheduled to go to Howland Island, a tiny island near the equator that was not much more than an airstrip. The trip from New Guinea was more than 2,500 miles over the Pacific Ocean, with no landmarks to guide them. Earhart and Noonan left New Guinea in mid-morning on July 1 and disappeared, never reaching Howland Island. The last radio contact made with Earhart was at 8:44 A.M. on July 2. Earhart stated that overcast weather conditions and strong winds had contributed to them missing Howland Island and they were running out of fuel. The U.S. Navy made an extensive search for Earhart and the plane that ultimately covered more than 25,000 miles in the Pacific, but no trace of the plane or its crew was ever found. Since her disappearance, theories as to her fate have abounded, including speculation that she had secretly been flying a surveillance mission for the U.S. government and was then captured by the Japanese. Most experts agree, however, that the most likely theory is that her plane crashed into the Pacific after running out of fuel, killing both her and Noonan.

References and Further Reading

Blair, Margaret Whitman. 2006. *The Roaring 20: The First Cross-Country Air Race for Women.* Washington, DC: National Geographic.

Butler, Susan. 1997. *East to the Dawn: The Life of Amelia Earhart.* Reading, MA: Addison-Wesley.

Burke, John. 2007. *Amelia Earhart: Flying Solo.* New York: Sterling.

Haugen, Brenda. 2007. *Amelia Earhart: legendary aviator.* Minneapolis, MN.: Compass Point Books.

Holden, Henry M. 2003. *American Women of Flight: Pilots and Pioneers.* Berkeley Heights, NJ: Enslow Publishers.

Micklos, John Jr. 2006. *Unsolved: What Really Happened to Amelia Earhart?* Berkeley Heights, NJ: Enslow.

Ellison, Ralph Waldo (1914–94)

Ralph Waldo Ellison, whose novel *Invisible Man* has become a classic of modern American fiction, wrote compellingly of the experience of African Americans in a society that has tended to ignore their problems.

Ellison was born on March 1, 1914, in Oklahoma City. Among the role models available to him in his youth, he was deeply impressed by the jazz musicians, and when he entered Tuskegee Institute in Alabama in 1933, he expected to study classical music. In 1936, while still an undergraduate, Ellison headed for New York City and intended to work there for a summer. He never returned to Tuskegee. The following year, he met Richard Wright, who asked him to write a review for a magazine called *New Challenge.* Wright influenced Ellison's ideas about social justice and provided a literary role model. A number of Ellison's early stories published in *New Masses,* a left-wing magazine, presented characters and situations that foreshadowed Ellison's novel *Invisible Man.* "Slick Gonna Learn" is an example of a story that also shows Wright's influence. During the years surrounding World War II, Ellison wrote and abandoned a book-length manuscript and composed a series of stories, like "Flying Home," that explored the concept of the antihero, a protagonist notable for the lack of heroic qualities. In 1945, he began to concentrate his efforts on *Invisible Man,* though the novel had been on his mind for some time. He worked for seven years on the manuscript; the book was published in 1952.

Invisible Man concerns an unnamed African American man who travels from the South to the North and from ignorance to understanding. The narrative is framed by a prologue and an epilogue in the protagonist's voice, set in an underground room in which he has taken refuge from the hurt and hardship of life outside. The action of the story begins in the South during the Great Depression as the protagonist graduates from high school and prepares to enter an all-black college. He arrives at college with naive dreams of success, but he grows disillusioned by the corruption he sees in the hollow philanthropy of a white trustee and the naked ambition of the black college president. After a painful encounter in which he tries to show a founder of the school how most southern blacks live, the protagonist is expelled. He heads to New York City in search of a job. When he fails to find white-collar employment, he signs on at a paint factory, again with bad results. After he rouses a crowd witnessing an eviction, he catches the attention of the Brotherhood, a radical group similar to the Communist Party. He hopes to work within the Brotherhood for social change, but he finds himself hampered by tokenism. After a Harlem race riot in which his physical safety is threatened, the protagonist realizes he must deal explicitly with the issue of race and the invisibility of the black man in white America, and he goes underground. *Invisible Man* was published as the American civil rights movement was beginning to emerge. The book quickly became known not just for its literary quality but also for its articulation of many of the values of the movement. The novel earned the National Book Award in 1953, as well as honors from the National Newspaper Publishers Association and the National Academy of Arts and Letters.

In 1964, Ellison published a collection of essays, *Shadow and Act,* which contain his reflections on literature—particularly his own literary career—music, and race. Excerpts have been printed from a long second novel on religion and politics, but the book remains unpublished after three decades. A second collection of essays, *Going to the Territory,* was published in 1986.

Ellison held a number of visiting professorships at such institutions as the University of Chicago, the University of California at Los Angeles, and Yale University. He retired in 1979 after nine years as Albert Schweitzer Professor in the Humanities at New York University. He is a recipient of both the Presidential Medal of Freedom, awarded to him in 1969 by President Lyndon B. Johnson, and the National Medal of Arts. Ellison died at his home in New York City at the age of 80 on April 16, 1994.

References and Further Reading

Busby, Mark. 1991. *Ralph Ellison.* Boston: Twayne Publishers.

Butler, Robert J., ed. 2000. *The Critical Response to Ralph Ellison.* Westport, CT: Greenwood Press.

Hersey, John, ed. 1974. *Ralph Ellison: A Collection of Critical Essays.* Englewood Cliffs, NJ, Prentice-Hall.

Morel, Lucas E., ed. 2004. *Ralph Ellison and the Raft of Hop: A Political Companion to "Invisible Man."* Lexington, KY: University Press of Kentucky.

Tracy, Steven C., ed. 2004. *A Historical Guide to Ralph Ellison.* New York: Oxford University Press.

Warren, Kenneth W. 2003. *So Black and Blue: Ralph Ellison and the Occasion of Criticism.* Chicago: University of Chicago Press.

Evans, Walker (1903–75)

Born in St. Louis, Missouri in 1903 and raised in Chicago, Walker Evans dropped out of Williams College after one year, spent another studying in Paris, then moved to New York where he fruitlessly tried to find work as a writer and took up photography as a sideline. From this unlikely beginning emerged a profoundly influential figure in American photography, art, and journalism. Like Alfred Stieglitz and the pictorialists, Walker Evans strongly believed in photography as an art. However, he rejected the pictorialist painterly style, pursuing an aesthetic informed by the clean economy of modernism and a principle of straightforward truthfulness.

Best known for his work of the 1930s while under contract to the Resettlement Administration (RA), and later the Farm Security Administration, Evans's photographs are often characterized by a sober, direct realism. Though Evans did occasionally use a 35 mm camera, most memorably in a series of photographs taken covertly on the New York subway (published in 1966 as *Many Are Called*), for his RA photographs Evans favored an 8" × 10" view camera. The large format allowed Evans to capture exceptional and nuances of light and texture lending visual intensity to studies of storefronts, windows, and interiors. Given the longer exposures typically required, where Evans included people his subjects often address the camera with frank directness as they pose for him.

Though Evans preferred his work to be considered in artistic terms, he gained notice working as a photojournalist, including assignments for *Fortune* which would be an important source of income through most of his life. In 1935 he began his association with the RA, documenting the administration's relief efforts in rural towns. Though the regular income and freedom to occupy himself entirely with photography was welcome to Evans, he chafed under the direction of administrator Roy E. Stryker. In part this stemmed from conflicting principles. Steadfastly apolitical, Evans had qualms about contributing to what he considered propaganda. When the RA was embroiled in controversy after it became known Arthur Rothstein had moved a steer's skull for compositional variety, Evans took the side of critics who lambasted the Rothstein for subverting the facts of a scene as it had been found. Above all, Evans regretted terms of his employment stipulating the federal government would retain the rights to work he created while a member of the unit (now held by the Library of Congress). The terms did not deter him from pursuing side projects, including a collaboration in the summer of 1936 with author James Agee on a magazine assignment to document the lives of Southern tenant farmers. While the article never materialized, in 1941 the project was published in book form as *Let Us Now Praise Famous Men.* Work from Evans's RA period also appeared in his portfolio *American Photographs,* published by the Museum of Modern Art in 1938.

Evans continued contributing work to *Fortune* until 1965, when he took a teaching position at Yale and resumed his quest for greater artistic independence. Though the work of his later years is often characterized as uneven, it was in his later years that Evans formed important relationships with the succeeding generation of photographers, notably Dianne Arbus, Lee Friedlander, and Robert Frank, whose 1959 work *The Americans* strongly evoked Evans's *American Photographs.*

Tess Mann

References and Further Reading

Curtis, James C., and Sheila Grannen. 1980. "Let us now appraise famous photographs:

phy." *Winterthur Portfolio,* 15 (1): 1–23.

Galassi, Peter. 2000. *Walker Evans and Company.* New York: Museum of Modern Art, distributed by H. N. Abrams.

Mellow, James R. 1999. *Walker Evans.* New York: Basic Books.

Stotts, William. 1973. *Documentary Expression and Thirties America.* New York: Oxford University Press.

Fantasia

A financial disaster when originally released in 1940, *Fantasia* evolved through various edits and releases to become both a critical and financial success for producer Walt Disney. It is now considered one of the top 100 most important films in cinematic history, and along with *Snow White and the Seven Dwarfs* (1937) one of only two Disney cartoon films selected for preservation in the National Film Registry for its cultural and artistic importance. It remains an compelling example of the marriage of animation and music enjoyed by both critics and moviegoers alike.

In the late 1930s, Mickey Mouse, Walt Disney's avatar, no longer held the public's imagination as he once had when he first appeared in the late 1920s. While working on a Mickey Mouse comeback short, which Disney conceived without dialog but set to the music of Goethe's *The Sorcerer's Apprentice,* Disney met world renowned conductor Leopold Stokowski. Fascinated by the project, Stokowski offered his services for free. Once all animation was complete on the most expensive cartoon ever created to that point, Disney knew he could never make a profit. So, with Stokowski's help, decided to produce an entire feature film built around this musical concept. Stokowski also hinted that this feature should be called "Fantasia," denoting a medley of familiar themes with variations and interludes.

Disney, cleverly, placed the more abstract music and visual coupling at the beginning of the short. Among the animated stories, Disney also edited in live-action scenes, which featured Stokowski, the Philadelphia Orchestra that performed seven of the pieces, and the critic Deems Taylor, who acted much like a Greek chorus explaining the action of the intent of the feature. To heighten the audience's sense of being at a live concert, "Fantasound," a precursor to modern surround sound, was developed.

After a very abstract opening piece, Depression era audiences enjoyed shorts of program music, that is, classical music that tells a story with sound and theme, although the intended story to be told by the original composer can not be assumed to match how *Fantasia* weaves a narrative around the notes. Bach's *Toccata and Fugue in D Minor* is set to a pattern of light and superimposed shadows of a live-action concert stage. Tchaikovsky's *Nutcracker Suite* runs through the seasons of the year, with a menagerie of characters including fairies, flowers, and fish. Igor Stravinsky's *The Rite of Spring* flew in the face of tradition, hosting battling dinosaurs in their most realistic portrayal in film to date. Beethoven's *6th symphony* included centaurs and nudity that shocked some of the nation. Ponchielli's *Dance of the Hours* showcases hippos attempting ballet. Mussorgsky's *Night on Bald Mountain* summons nightmares as its lead demon, Chernabog, raises the creatures of the night, only to be chased away by morning church bells. With so much variety, moviegoers were enthralled and alarmed, and the critics split.

Mark Schwartz

References and Further Reading

Eliot, Marc. 1993. *Walt Disney: Hollywood's Dark Prince.* Secaucus, NJ: Carol Publishing Group.

Taylor, Deems. 1940. *Walt Disney's Fantasia.* New York. Simon and Schuster.

Thomas, Frank. 1981. *Disney animation: The Illusion of Life.* New York. Abbeville Press.

Faulkner, William Cuthbert (1897–1962)

William Cuthbert Faulkner crafted a set of intricately woven stories and novels depicting the tragic lives of a people inhabiting a fictional county in rural Mississippi. His extraordinary imaginative power and the depth of his insight into the human condition have led to his reputation as one of America's greatest novelists.

Born on September 25, 1897, in New Albany, Mississippi, Faulkner moved to Oxford, Mississippi at the age of five. His father, Murray Falkner, owned a livery stable and then a hardware store, finally becoming business manager of the University of Mississippi in Oxford. Faulkner dropped out of school in the 11th grade. Anxious to serve in the military during World War I but unable to join the U.S. Army because he was too short, Faulkner signed on with the Canadian Division of the Royal Air Force. The war ended before he could see combat, but he received his commission as a second lieutenant in 1918. It was during this period that Faulkner changed the spelling of his name, adding the *u* from an earlier family spelling.

After the war, Faulkner was admitted to the University of Mississippi as a special student, but he dropped out early in his sophomore year. He did begin to write stories and poems for student publications, however. He held a number of odd jobs—house painter, dishwasher, and store clerk—as he tried to establish himself as a writer. In 1922, he became postmaster for the University of Mississippi, a job at which he was inept and which he resigned in 1924. A fellow townsman, Phil Stone, helped Faulkner by suggesting authors to read and keeping him in touch with literary movements of the day. Faulkner had gone with Stone to New Haven and later moved to New York in order to try to become acquainted with the literati. Stone also helped finance the publication of Faulkner's first book, a collection of poems called *The Marble Faun* (1924).

In 1925, Faulkner moved to New Orleans, where he became acquainted with Sherwood Anderson. Anderson encouraged him to write his first novel, *Soldier's Pay* (1926), and gave it to his own publisher. An experimental novel about World War I, the book did not sell. Late in 1925, Faulkner took a walking tour through Italy, Switzerland, and France; the trip provided material for later stories. Faulkner then returned to Mississippi, where he wrote *Mosquitoes* (1927), a satiric novel about the New Orleans artistic community. With his third novel, *Sartoris* (1929), Faulkner began to mine the territory in northern Mississippi in which he had grown up. He invented Yoknapatawpha County and its county seat of Jefferson, a composite of several Mississippi towns. He drew upon the characters he had known in childhood and upon his own family history. Faulkner's great-grandfather, William Clark Falkner, provided the model for Colonel John Sartoris, while his grandfather, John Wesley Thompson Falkner, seems the likely source for "Old Bayard" Sartoris. The novel focuses on "Young Bayard" and his bitter return from World War I to his small-town home, where his violent anger puts him at odds with the more genteel ways of his kinsfolk and the townspeople. Faulkner's imaginative return to his roots unleashed a torrent of creative energy, and he wrote a series of major novels in quick succession. In 1929, he published *The Sound and the Fury,* his first radical experiment in narrative form and, by some estimates, his finest work. The novel tells the tale of the Compson family from four different perspectives in succession: through the eyes of the idiot son Benjy; his hypersensitive, intellectual brother Quentin; their greedy, petty-minded brother Jason, and finally Dilsey, the black servant who really holds the family together. The Compson family had been Southern aristocracy but had fallen: the mother to whining and imagined illness, the father to drink, and a daughter, Caddy, to sexual debauchery. In *As I Lay Dying* (1930), Faulkner again used multiple streams of consciousness—this time creating 59 separate interior monologues and time shifts—to tell the tale of a disintegrating Southern family, the Bundrens. Written in only six weeks, the novel describes the death of a poor woman who lives in the hills and her family's obstacle-laden journey to Jefferson to bury her. Faulkner claimed to have written *Sanctuary* (1931) in only three weeks, but when it came back from the publisher in galley form, he decided it was so bad he had to tear it down and rewrite it, bearing personally the expense of resetting the

galleys. The novel describes lawyer Horace Benbow's efforts to exonerate Lee Goodwin of rape and murder charges. Benbow's work is thwarted, however, when the rape victim, Temple Drake, lies to protect the real villain, and Goodwin is killed by townspeople. Perhaps owing to the shocking nature of the story, *Sanctuary* became Faulkner's first popular success. In *Light in August* (1932), Faulkner fashioned a plot of enormous complexity, featuring a large cast of characters whose psychologies he probed using multiple flashbacks and shifts in chronology. The story centers on Joe Christmas, who does not know whether he is black or white and who is taunted mercilessly by the children in the orphanage where he has been placed by his white grandfather. In later years, he begins an affair with a wealthy white woman who wishes to exploit him and pushes him to assume a black identity. When Joe murders her, he is hunted down and brutally killed. *Absalom, Absalom!* (1936), considered by some to be Faulkner's masterpiece, reintroduces the character of Quentin Compson and follows his detective work as he tries to uncover the story of Thomas Sutpen, a local plantation owner murdered many years before. Sutpen's dreams of social prominence had been dashed when, returning from meritorious service in the Civil War, he found his son gone and his plantation in ruins. His attempt to produce a new heir with a poor white girl led to his death at the hands of her grandfather. Faulkner turned his attention to shorter fiction, occasionally lengthening a short story into a thin novel; *The Unvanquished* (1938), *The Hamlet* (1940), and *Go Down, Moses* (1942) are examples. The author frequently reintroduced characters from earlier stories. Lucas Beauchamp, the black hero of Faulkner's story "The Fire and the Hearth," is saved from a lynching in his novel *Intruder in the Dust* (1948). Temple Drake, the rape victim of *Sanctuary,* comes to atonement in *Requiem for a Nun* (1951). Not all of Faulkner's fiction, however, arose from Yoknapatawpha County. *A Fable* (1954) retells the story of Christ's passion through the experience of a French corporal on the Western Front during World War I. *The Town* (1957) and *The Mansion* (1959) complete the story of the rise of the poor white Snopes family, begun in *The Hamlet. The Reivers* (1962), Faulkner's final book, is a nostalgic and amusing account of a boy's initiation into manhood.

Faulkner became internationally known after he was awarded the Nobel Prize for Literature in 1949. Whereas previously he had spent most of his time in Oxford, traveling to Hollywood from time to time to work on movie screenplays, afterward he traveled widely for the U.S. Department of State. Meanwhile, the honors continued. He won the National Book Award for *The Collected Stories of William Faulkner* in 1951 and for *A Fable* in 1955, the Pulitzer Prize for *A Fable* in 1955 and for *The Reivers* in 1963, and the Gold Medal for Fiction of the National Institute of Arts and Letters in 1962. Faulkner died of a heart attack on July 6, 1962.

References and Further Reading

Friedman, Alan Warren. 1984. *William Faulkner.* New York: F. Ungar.

Inge, M. Thomas. 1999. *Conversations with William Faulkner.* Jackson: University Press of Mississippi.

Kopley, Richard, ed. 1997. *Prospects for the Study of American literature: A Guide for Scholars and Students.* New York: New York University Press.

Millgate, Michael. 1966. *The Achievement of William Faulkner.* Reprint, New York: Vintage Books, 1971.

Porter, Carolyn. 2007. *William Faulkner.* New York: Oxford University Press.

Swisher, Clarice, ed. 1998. *Readings on William Faulkner.* San Diego, CA: Greenhaven Press.

Federal Art Project (1935–39)

The Federal Art Project (FAP) was founded in August 1935 as a part of the Works Progress Administration's (WPA) Federal Project Number One, also known as Federal One. Federal One handled the WPA's fine arts organizations, employing artists, musicians, actors, and writers. The largest of the New Deal visual arts organizations, the FAP hired artists to create new works of art for public institutions, teach art classes, and research American art. Holger Cahill, former acting director of the Museum of Modern Art, was the National Director of the FAP.

FAP artworks included murals, easel paintings, lithographs, etchings, prints, and sculpture. The project also encouraged traditional American crafts. Another assignment was the creation of posters for federal theatre and music programs. Artists were paid hourly wages that varied according to the cost of living in their region. Top pay, such as in New York City, ran about $100 a month.

Another purpose of the FAP was spreading appreciation of art among a broad spectrum of Americans. Federal Art Centers were established in cities and small towns in every state. The centers offered free art classes, art libraries, and hosted traveling art exhibits as well as dance, music, and theatrical programs.

Depression-era federal art most often falls under the genre of American Scene. While absorbing some modern stylistic influences, American Scene painters celebrated U.S. history, folklore, and local traditions. Their emphasis on American heritage was a source of pride and reassurance during the Depression. Scenes of everyday life exemplified the belief that the lives of ordinary people were worthy of being portrayed in fine art.

Not all government-sponsored Depression-era public art was created by the FAP. The well-known series of post office murals, for instance, were done under the auspices of the Section of Fine Arts, under the Treasury Department. Dorothea Lange, Walker Evans, and other well-known photographers contributed to major photographic projects made by the Farm Security Administration and other federal agencies.

While the number of actual Communists involved with the FAP was very small, artists who dealt with leftist themes such as social justice, poverty, and unionization of workers drew sharp conservative opposition against the program. Conservative attacks in Congress led to the reorganization of the FAP into the WPA Art Program in September 1939. Federal funding was sharply cut and control was turned over to individual state projects. The WPA Art Program was transferred to the Defense Department to become the Graphics Section of the War Service Division in 1942, and officially ended on June 30, 1943.

In its eight years, the FAP sponsored the creation of over 225,000 works of art for the people of the United States. Millions of children and adults were introduced to art through classes, lessons, and local exhibits. Notable artists who received employment through the FAP included Jackson Pollock, Jacob Lawrence, Stuart Davis, and Raphael Soyer.

David A. Norris

See also: Biddle, George; Cahill, Holger; Federal Music Project, Federal Theater Project.

References and Further Reading

Bustard, Bruce I. 1997. *A New Deal For the Arts.* Washington: National Archives and Records Administration.

McKinzie, Richard D. 1973. *The New Deal For Artists.* Princeton: Princeton University Press.

Library of Congress. *By the People, For the People: Posters from the WPA, 1936–1943.* Available at: http://memory.loc.gov/ammem/wpaposters/wpahome.html. Accessed October 1, 2007.

Federal Music Project (1935–39)

The Federal Music Project (FMP) was founded in August 1935 as a part of the Works Progress Administration (WPA)'s Federal Project Number One, also known as Federal One. Federal One handled the WPA's fine arts organizations, with separate agencies to employ artists, musicians, writers, and actors. The FMP hired musicians as instrumental and vocal performers, composers, teachers, and researchers. The director of the FMP was Dr. Nikolai Sokoloff, the former conductor of the Cleveland Orchestra.

While upholding the democratic tendencies of the New Deal, the FMP mainly sought to share highbrow classical music and opera with all Americans, rather than to endorse popular music. Sokoloff's emphasis on classical music avoided conflict

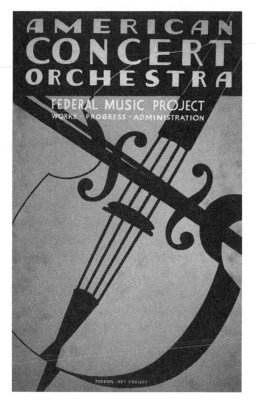

Poster created by the Federal Art Project for a performance of the Federal Music Project, 1936. (Library of Congress)

over the promotion of avant-garde and politicized works, which caused controversy at the Federal Art Project and Federal Theatre Project. A drawback to this emphasis on classical music was the reduction of employment of musicians who played popular, folk, or jazz music.

Employment by the FMP was spread across the nation, but was necessarily concentrated in large cities, where most professional musicians lived. Live and radio concerts by symphony orchestras, chamber ensembles, dance bands, and solo performers were sponsored by the agency. Posters were sometimes provided by the Federal Art Project. Music classes were offered to children and adults.

The FMP showed some interest in American folk music, gathering some 2500 songs by mid-1938. State WPA music projects, notably those of Florida and California, recorded hundreds of folk songs in different genres. Under the heading of novelty bands, the FMP employed some traditional Mexican, Hawaiian, and American cowboy musicians. More extensive documentation of Depression-era folk music was done by the Library of Congress, as part of its Archive of American Folk Song, which began in 1928. Scholars took recording equipment to remote areas in every state of the Union, harvesting a rich legacy of American musical tradition that would have been lost within a few years.

In 1939, the FMP was reorganized into individual state music projects administered as the WPA Music Program. Sokoloff resigned that same year. Federal funding for music was sharply reduced, although it was supplemented by varying degrees of state and local support.

After the United States entered World War II, the dwindling WPA Music Program shifted its emphasis to helping the war effort. Their concerts entertained servicemen waiting for transfer overseas, and boosted the morale of wartime civilians. Federal funding shrank until the program ended with little fanfare in 1943.

By 1939, the FMP had played almost 225,000 performances to audiences totaling over 148 million. In its eight years, the project gave millions of Americans their first taste of classical music, and encouraged new respect for America's musicians and composers.

David A. Norris

See also: Federal Art Project; Hillbilly Music; Swing Music; Works Progress Administration.

References and Further Reading

Bindas, Kenneth J. 1995. *All of This Music Belongs to the Nation: The WPA's Federal Music Project and American Society.* Knoxville, TN: University of Tennessee Press.

Moore, Earl Vincent. 1939. *Final Report of the Federal Music Project, October 10, 1939.* Washington, DC: Government Printing Office.

Federal Theatre Project (1935–39)

The Federal Theatre Project (FTP) was established as a New Deal agency under the auspices of the Works Progress Administration (WPA). The FTP was to provide employment for artists, writers, and directors, as well as introduce theatre to a broad national audience. During its four year existence, the FTP employed approximately 10,000 people per year and provided 1,200 productions to an audience estimated at over 25 million people in 40 states. Many of the productions dealt with topical issues, and the FTP proved controversial, leading Congress to halt funding for the program.

The WPA was headed by Harry Hopkins and established by Congress in 1935 to provide meaningful employment for Americans during the Depression. Included within the WPA were projects for art, music, writers, and theatre. While often criticized for waste and political bias, the arts programs accounted for less than one percent of the WPA budget.

The FTP was established on August 27, 1935, and Hopkins tapped Hallie Flanagan, a theatre professor at Vassar, to administer the project. During her tenure at Vassar and Grinnell College in Iowa, Flanagan was influenced by European and Soviet artists who believed that drama could be employed to encourage social and political change. Flanagan envisioned that the FTP would be more than a temporary work relief project. She hoped to create a national theatre culture geared to a mass audience which would continue after the expiration of federal funding.

To implement her ideas, Flanagan encouraged living newspaper productions, which would use a documentary montage technique to introduce topical issues through the voice of common people. Many of these dramas sparked controversy. The State Department protested *Ethiopia* (1936) for violating the nation's neutrality policies, while *Triple-A Plowed Under* (1936) examined New Deal farm programs. Playwright Elmer Rice, who was the FTP director in New York, resigned after what he termed government censorship with the production of *Ethiopia.*

The FTP also included Negro and children's units. The Negro unit, which was headed by black actress Rose McClendon, employed 851 African American artists and included over 70 plays such as *Swing Mikado, Haiti,* and *Voodoo Macbeth.* While some in Congress criticized the expenditure on black theatre, even the children's unit was subject to controversy. For example, *Revolt of the Beavers* was denounced for fostering socialistic principles.

Perhaps the most controversial FTP production was the staging by Orson Welles and John Houseman of Marc Blitzstein's opera *Cradle Will Rock,* extolling the union movement. Reservations regarding the production led to cancellation of the show's opening on July 14, 1937. Houseman and Welles led the audience to another theatre where Blitzstein played the music from an onstage piano and the performers delivered their lines from off stage. Shortly thereafter, Welles and Houseman left the FTP to form the Mercury Theatre.

Controversial productions such as *Cradle Will Rock* and *It Can't Happen Here* (1936), a dramatization of Sinclair Lewis's novel dealing with the emergence of fascism in America, continued to draw the ire of congressional critics such as Congressman Martin Dies. Flanagan was called before the House Un-American Activities Committee, where the FTP was denounced for waste and fostering leftist politics. On June 30, 1939, the FTP was terminated when Congress ended funding for the program. An experimental and unique effort to provide theatre for the masses and address cultural class divides was over.

Ron Briley

See also: Federal Art Project; Federal Music Project.

References and Further Reading

Craig, E. Quita. 1980. *Black Drama of the Federal Theatre Era: Beyond the Formal Horizons.* Amherst, MA: University of Massachusetts Press

De Hart, Jane Sherron. 1967. *The Federal Theatre, 1935–1939: Plays, Relief and Politics.* Princeton, NJ: Princeton University Press.

Flanagan, Hallie. 1965. *Arena: The History of the Federal Theatre.* New York: B. Blom.

O'Connor, John, and Lorraine Brown, eds. 1978. *Free, Adult, Uncensored: The Living History of the Federal Theatre Project.* Washington DC: New Republic Books.

Federal Writers' Project (1935–39)

The Federal Writers' Project (FWP) is the most widely known of the four major cultural work relief programs—the others being the Federal Theatre Project, the Federal Music Project, and the Federal Arts Project—created under the Works Progress Administration (WPA) to provide work for the American creative community. The best known and most popular of the FWP projects was the *American Guide Book Series* that published guidebooks to each of the states, major cities, and interstate highway routes. Writers' Project investigators also interviewed former slaves and set their memories down in narratives that preserved slavery's human face. Folklorists employed by the FWP recorded the bleak lives of black and white sharecroppers in the South and of Appalachian natives.

Like the other cultural programs, the FWP originated in a number of state projects created under the Federal Emergency Relief Act (FERA) passed by Congress in March 1933. Cultural work relief programs had strong support in the Roosevelt Administration from many of the president's closest advisors and from First Lady Eleanor Roosevelt. With creation of the WPA in early 1935, director Harry Hopkins decided to provide funding for creative programs designed to revive American culture, strengthen public appreciation of arts and literature, and provide thousands of impoverished writers, artists, musicians, and playwrights with work. The WPA created the National Office of the Federal Writers' Project in the summer of 1935. That office provided oversight for the FERA-created state writers' programs and presided over the creation and expansion of more projects.

The FWP posed organizational problems for the WPA because writers worked alone and because of the difficulty in establishing criteria to determine who was eligible for aid. Like most WPA programs, the FWP was organized by state. Each state writer's project answered to state and national WPA officials as well as senior FWP officials. Each program within the FWP had its own national editor who directed subordinate editors at the state level. To give the FWP direction, Harry Hopkins selected Henry Alsberg, a lawyer and journalist who had been involved in liberal or left causes since World War I, as the FWP's National Director. The choice proved to be a good one. Alsberg combined a genuine sympathy for the plight of writers in need of relief with an idealistic concept of writing as an art and as a conduit for the expression of the national character.

Alsberg faced competing views concerning criteria for determining who deserved funding. The Author's Guild, the oldest and most established of the writers' organizations, insisted that a writer had to be a recognized professional with at least two books. The Newspaper Guild supported anybody whose name had appeared in print. The most radical of the organized writer's groups, the Writer's Union, included anybody who had earned a living as a writer and could produce a manuscript acceptable to a review committee.

Because Alsberg and the senior FWP leadership could not agree on universal eligibility requirements, responsibility for determining who should receive aid often fell to FWP officials at the state level. The result was a wide variation in the selection of participants and programs that gave free rein to creative differences and contributed to continuing turbulence within the FWP.

The lack of clear direction in the FWP left it open to growing criticism from Congress that it was wasting money and not providing aid to enough workers to justify funding. By mid 1935, however, the idea put forward by a number of writers' organizations as early as summer 1934 that a series of guides to the United States should be the centerpiece of the FWP gained support from Alsberg, Hopkins, and the senior leadership in the WPA. The idea fit perfectly with the emphasis on regionalism that prevailed in the WPA cultural programs. It also addressed a genuine need since no comprehensive guide to the United States had appeared in more than 30 years.

The main reason that FWP and WPA officials settled on the *American Guide Book* series as the program's centerpiece, however, is that it suited their function as a relief agency. Project employees had to be selected from the relief roles and the guide books best suited the talents of these individuals. The emphasis on the state, city, and highway guides, moreover, meant that the project could employ persons with varied training—typists, teachers, librarians, mapmakers, and lawyers among others—who would have no role in a program dedicated solely to the support of professional novelists, poets, essayists, and other writers.

The *Guidebook* series also directly addressed the goal of all four of the cultural projects—to create a more accessible culture and give the general public a greater appreciation of the nation's culture as a whole. FWP officials viewed the guides as an educational exercise aimed at helping Americans accept, understand, and celebrate their own diversity. Project officials believed this cultural education could overcome the fragmentation involved in modern industrial society—fissures made worse by the Depression—without demanding total conformity.

This romantic nationalist vision of diversity within a greater cultural unity also influenced the other FWP programs for folklore, social-ethnic, and black studies. The FWP's cultural pluralism was not limited to white Americans. Alsberg and his allies believed that the FWP should also study blacks, ethnic groups, regional cultures, and the nation's folklore. He appointed Sterling Brown, an African American poet and literary critic, as Negro Affairs editor for the FWP. In addition, Alsberg pushed for the hiring of black writers and scholars to work on projects, such as the ex-slave narratives, that explored the black experience in the United States.

Likewise, FWP folklorists sought the roots of American folklore in the experiences of previously unstudied groups, such as miners, sharecroppers, loggers, and cowboys. FWP investigators developed folklore and oral history projects that would empower the voiceless to speak for themselves, resulting in publications that created an encounter between reader and narrator that allowed the reader to understand the speaker's perspective. The outcome was the voice of America's blacks, workers, and farmers made real to mainstream middle-class Americans.

The Federal Writers' Project's work reflected the New Deal's goals and ideals. It provided work relief for thousands of writers and support workers. Through its programs it gave the diverse elements of American society an opportunity to understand each other thus furthering the vision of President Roosevelt, Harry Hopkins, Henry Alsberg, and other New Dealers of a cooperative commonwealth.

These efforts, however, met with only mixed success. As the political tide turned against the New Deal in the late 1930s the Federal Writers' Project experienced budget cuts and political attacks from hostile congressional conservatives. By the end of 1939, control of the FWP programs was transferred to the individual states, where they faced an uncertain future. Although the FWP never faced the intense political scrutiny that plagued the Federal Theater Project and the Federal Arts Project, right-wing southern Democrats and midwest Republicans still viewed it suspiciously. However, the FWP weathered these attacks and left a wealth of materials on 1930s America that have proven invaluable to later students of Depression-era American society.

Walter Bell

See also: Federal Art Project; Federal Emergency Relief Administration; Federal Music Project; Federal Theater Project; Hopkins, Harry; Roosevelt, Eleanor; Roosevelt, Franklin; Works Progress Administration.

References and Further Reading

Hirsch, Jerrold. 2003. *Portrait of America: A Cultural History of the Federal Writers Project.* Chapel Hill: University of North Carolina Press.

Kennedy, David M. 1999. *Freedom from Fear: The American People in Depression and War, 1929–1945.* New York: Oxford University Press.

Lawson, Alan. 2006. *A Commonwealth of Hope: The New Deal Response to Crisis.* Baltimore, MD: Johns Hopkins University Press.

McDonald, William F. 1969. *Federal Relief Administration and the Arts: The Origins and Administrative History of the Arts Projects of the Works Progress Administration.* Columbus: Ohio State University Press.

Fields, William Claude (1880–1946)

Among the great comic film stars of the 1930s and 1940s, none was as misanthropic, as drunken, or arguably as funny as W. C. Fields.

William Claude Fields' birthday has been recorded as February 10 or April 9, 1879, in Philadelphia, but he was most likely born on January 29, 1880. His parents named him William Claude Dukenfield. His father was a vegetable peddler who had emigrated from England. It is generally reported, and Fields himself said, that he left home at age 11 and lived on the streets, stealing food and getting into frequent fights that would give him his trademark bulbous nose. However, a recent biographer found that Fields didn't leave home until age 18. Apparently, he learned the art of caustic asides from his mother.

Passionate about performing, Fields practiced juggling, and before long, he had established himself as a performer. By his early twenties, he was an international vaudeville star, headlining with Ziegfeld Follies and George White's Scandals and sharing the stage with Fanny Brice, Sarah Bernhardt, Harry Houdini, Maurice Chevalier, and the Marx Brothers. Fields married briefly and had one son. He and his wife separated—it is not clear whether they ever actually divorced—and he remained estranged from his son for many years.

Perhaps as a result of that disastrous union, Fields made wives the butts of countless jokes. On stage, Fields was becoming as famous for his comedy as for his physical talents. By 1920, he was earning $1,000 a week. He made a silent movie, *The Pool Shark,* which reused one of his stage routines and was the first of many confused and chaotic Fields movies.

Fields soon saw that there was significant money to be made in Hollywood, and with the calculation and determination that guided his entire career, he aimed for the West Coast. He also set about building his own legend, a public persona that would be so memorable, it would for years overshadow his true private character. The public Fields hated women and children, was reckless with money, and at the same time was quite stingy. The real Fields was a devoted grandfather, managed his career and money carefully, was generous with his friends, and greatly enjoyed the company of women. The similarities between the two personas were in Fields's acerbic wit and his heavy drinking, which was truly legendary. In the 1920s, Fields appeared in 11 silent films, all mediocre. In 1930, he made a 20 minute film based on one of his vaudeville acts, *The Golf Specialist.* In 1932 and 1933, he made four short films for Mack Sennett, all of which he wrote himself. Those shorts launched his film stardom. In the mid-1930s, Fields starred in a series of films that featured two of his famous on-screen personas: in *It's a Gift* and *The Man on the Flying Trapeze,* he was a beleaguered husband; in *The Old-Fashioned Way* and *Poppy,* he was a pompous charlatan, a con man trying not to give a sucker an even break. A fan of Charles Dickens, Fields commonly borrowed Dickensian names and caricature. However, it was his famous nasally voice that captured the essence of his hapless characters and made him a legend. During the 1930s, Fields's health crumbled under the weight of his heavy drinking. After a period of convalescence, he worked in radio, then abruptly quit after three years to return to film. The years 1938 to 1942 are considered Fields's finest artistically. He starred in *You Can't Cheat an Honest Man, My Little Chickadee* (with cowriter Mae West), *Never Give a Sucker an Even Break,* and *The Bank Dick.* In those films, Fields was at his comic best, still mining the competing roles of sucker or con man and the false respectability of both. At the same time, Fields's movies skewered American hypocrisy and stinginess.

In 1940, Field ran for president on the platform "a chickadee in every pot." He famously said, "When, on next November 5, I am elected chief executive of this fair land, amidst thunderous cheering and shouting and throwing of babies out the window, I shall, my fellow citizens, offer no such empty panaceas as a New Deal, or an Old Deal, or even a Re-Deal. No, my friends, the reliable False Shuffle was good enough for my father and its good enough for me." Throughout his career, Fields was vocal in his opposition to taxation of any kind and creative in his ways of avoiding it. One year, he reportedly tried to deduct his liquor bill as a legitimate business expense. And in an era when many in Hollywood were firmly leftist, even flirting with communism, Fields was a conservative. In his movie *You Can't Cheat an Honest Man,* he even made a joke at the expense of the Wagner Act that had granted new power to labor unions.

After 1942, work for Fields largely dried up. Legend has it that as he lay on his deathbed in a New York hospital under an oxygen tent, he heard newsboys hawking papers outside. He said to his lawyer, agent, and mistress: "Poor little urchins out there. No doubt improperly nourished, ill-clad. Something's got to be done about them." He closed his eyes and a moment later, weakly said, "On second thought—screw 'em." Legend further holds that he is buried under a tombstone that reads, "I'd rather be in Philadelphia." Actually, Fields died in Pasadena, California on December 25, 1946, a month after he had lapsed into a coma. His grandson says Fields regained consciousness for a moment, put a finger to his lips, winked, and died. His tombstone includes no reference to Philadelphia.

Katherine Gould

References and Further Reading

Anobile, Richard J., ed.1969. *Drat! Being the Encapsulated View of Life by W. C. Fields in his Own Words.* New York: New American Library.

Curtis, James. 2003. *W. C. Fields: A Biography.* New York: Knopf.

Fields, Ronald J. 1984. *W. C. Fields: A Life on Film.* New York: St. Martin's Press.

Gehring, Wes D. 1994. *Groucho and W. C. Fields: Huckster Comedians.* Jackson: University Press of Mississippi.

Louvish, Simon. 1997. *Man on the Flying Trapeze: The Life and Times of W. C. Fields.* New York: W. W. Norton.

Rocks, David T. 1993. *W. C. Fields—An Annotated Guide: Chronology, Bibliographies, Discography, Filmographies, Press Books, Cigarette Cards, Film Clips, and Impersonators.* Jefferson, NC: McFarland.

Flanagan, Hallie (1890–1969)

Hallie Flanagan was born in 1890. She attended Grinnell College and taught theater there after graduation. After writing an award-winning play, *The Curtain,* she attended the Workshop 47 at Harvard University, directed by George Pierce Baker and returned to Grinnell to found the college's experimental theater program. In 1925, she accepted a position as the director of the experimental theater at Vassar College. Flanagan was the first woman to receive the Guggenheim Fellowship, which allowed her to tour and study European theaters in the 1920s. She used this experience to transform theater at Vassar with new modernist techniques. In 1931 she co-wrote and directed a play based on the experiences of Arkansas farmers during the drought, called *Can You Hear Their Voices?*

The Works Progress Administration (WPA) created Federal Project One programs that sought to support out of work artists, writers, actors, historians and musicians. WPA Director Harry Hopkins appointed Flanagan as the director of the Federal Theatre Project (FTP) in 1935. The goals of the FTP were initially unclear and many involved in the project questioned the role of the government in artistic productions. Flanagan began her job by researching the problem of unemployed stage actors and theater workers, who had been shut out of jobs with the advent of radio and movies. She developed a plan that focused mostly on New York City's theater and Broadway scene, with local projects across the country receiving funds to start community theaters. From Washington, D.C. Flanagan coordinated the work of many theater projects across the nation in cities such as Boston, Chicago, Seattle, and Los Angeles. The FTP successfully employed thousands of actors and stagehands across the country, even though many theater unions forbade their members from working for FTP productions. Flanagan was instrumental in the creation of a new theater form called the Living Newspaper, in which current events and social issues were presented to local audiences. The FTP also supported children's theaters, marionette shows, and separate projects for African Americans. In New York, many plays achieved great success, such as *Macbeth* directed by Orson Welles.

Because a large portion of the budget of the FTP was spent on productions in New York City, members of Congress representing areas that had no FTP theaters began to criticize the project. The controversial 1937 musical *The Cradle Will Rock,* which addressed labor issues, was shut down due to censorship in the guise of budget cuts. In protest, the actors sang their parts from the audience because the Actor's Union forbade them to appear on stage. In 1939, members of Congress began to accuse the FTP of spreading communist propaganda through its productions, especially the Living Newspaper. Flanagan testified before the House Committee to Investigate Un-American Activities led by Chairman Martin Dies and was questioned about her trip to Russia to study theaters for the Guggenheim Fellowship. In June of 1939, Congress withdrew funding for the FTP and Flanagan returned to Vassar and continued her theater career there and at Smith College until the 1950s.

Kate Stewart

See also: House Un-American Activities Committee, Federal Theatre Project; Works Progress Administration.

References and Further Reading

Bentley, Joanne. 1988. *Hallie Flanagan: A Life in the American Theatre.* New York: Knopf.

Flanagan, Hallie. 1940. *Arena.* New York: Duell, Sloan and Pearce.

McDonald, William F. 1969. *Federal Relief Administration and the Arts*. Columbus: Ohio State University Press.

Flash Gordon

Flash Gordon first appeared as a comic strip hero in early 1934, created by Alex Raymond, to compete with the popular spaceman Buck Rogers, another misplaced earthling batting evil forces in the far reaches of the universe. Technological advances in telescopes and rocketry fueled the public's interest in outer space and theories of space travel, so there was room for two heroes. Flash Gordon, originally cast as a blonde polo player and alumni of Yale University, was the heroic brand of brawn and brains, which intrigued audiences used to heroes with respectable, but predictable, law-enforcement or military backgrounds.

Thrown into orbit when a brilliant, well-meaning, but mad scientist shanghais a crew, Flash and love interest Dale Arden blast off into space to eventually discover the source of the deadly meteors that had been, until recently, pummeling the Earth. The mad scientist, Dr. Hans Zarkov, takes the three voyagers to the planet Mongo, where they find out that the source of the meteors is the intergalactic despot, Ming the Merciless.

Flash, Dale, and Dr. Zarkov, in their struggle to save the Earth in particular and the universe in general, meet in battle and in friendship, a menagerie of human-like creatures who amazingly speak English: King Kala, ruler of an undersea kingdom of Shark Men; Prince Thun, leader of the Lion Men; and Prince Vultan, steward of the flying city of Hawk Men. While the sinister Ming is pictured as looking like a spin on Dr. Fu Manchu, others from outer space look attractively human, such as Ming's daughter, Princess Aura, and Prince Barin, a morally ambiguous figure dressed like Robin Hood. Other characters, especially females, leave little to the imagination, such as Queen Desira, ruler of her Amazon-like jungle kingdom, Tropica.

The Flash Gordon franchise extended itself into radio and film. In 1935, the radio show, *The Amazing Interplanetary Adventures of Flash Gordon,* aired as a 26 episode weekly radio serial. The script was an audio adaptation of the comic strip for most of its run. Gale Gordon, no relation of course, played Flash Gordon, and later appeared on television shows such as Mr. Wilson on *Dennis the Menace.* The radio series veered off the course of the comic strip by crash-landing on the planet Earth and ended in October 1935 with the marriage of Flash and Dale. *The Further Interplanetary Adventures of Flash Gordon* began after a two-day honeymoon as a daily radio show, five days a week, ending on February 6, 1936. Buster Crabbe appeared as Flash Gordon in several serials between 1936 and 1940, which were more popular than the radio show. Radio was a difficult medium for science fiction: sound effects cannot match the fire and smoke of the big screen, even if the smoke from model rockets erroneously rises up in outer space.

In the 1940s and beyond, Flash Gordon ventured from his comic strip, radio, and movies into comic books, television shows, and then again back into movies. His orbit has yet to disintegrate.

Mark Schwartz

See also: *Radio.*

References and Further Reading

Campbell, Roberts. 1976. *The Golden Years of Broadcast.* New York: Scribner's.

Douglas, George H. 1987. *The Early Days of Radio Broadcasting.* New York: McFarland.

Nachman, Gerald. 1998. *Raised on the Radio.* New York: Random House.

Gable, William Clark (1901–60)

Clark Gable was known as the "King of Hollywood" in the late 1930s. He acted in a vast number of films; his most famous role was that of Rhett Butler in 1939's *Gone with the Wind.*

William Clark Gable was born in Cadiz, Ohio, on February 1, 1901. His mother died when he was very young, and his father, an oil driller, sent Gable to live with other family members. Later, Gable returned to Cadiz, where he spent the rest of his youth. At the age of 16, Gable dropped out of school. He later worked with his father in the oil fields of Oklahoma for several years and then joined a traveling theater company. While he was with the company, he met Josephine Dillon, who became his acting coach. Though she was more than 10 years his senior, he married her on December 13, 1924. Gable and Dillon moved to Hollywood so that he could pursue his acting career, and he found work as an extra in several silent movies, including *Forbidden Paradise* (1924) and *The Merry Widow* (1925). Gable and Dillon divorced in April 1930. Following the breakup, Gable went back to the stage briefly, appearing on Broadway, and then returned to Los Angeles, where he played a killer in the play *The Last Mile.*

Clark Gable and Greta Garbo embrace in the film *Susan Lenox: Her Fall and Rise,* 1931. (Bettmann/Corbis)

His performance attracted the attention of film recruiters, which finally landed him his first real part in a movie, a small role in the 1931 film *The Painted Desert.* That same year Gable married another much older woman, Ria Langham.

The early 1930s were productive years for Gable. He worked for both the Metro-Goldwyn-Mayer (MGM) and Warner Brothers studios in such films as *The Finger Points, Night Nurse, Dance, Fool, Dance,* and *A Free Soul,* all in 1931. Gable often played gangsters. His first starring role was in 1931's *Sporting Blood.* Women loved his seemingly dangerous on-screen persona, and MGM capitalized on that image, placing him opposite all of the studio's best leading ladies, including Greta Garbo, Joan Crawford, Norma Shearer, Myrna Loy, and Jean Harlow, with whom he acted in the popular 1932 film *Red Dust.* In 1934, Gable starred with Claudette Colbert in Frank Capra's film *It Happened One Night* and won an Oscar for his performance. Legend has it that Gable's performance also caused an unintended stir in the men's underwear business. In one scene, he removed his shirt to reveal that he wore nothing underneath it, instead of the then-ubiquitous white undershirt. Sales of men's undershirts reportedly plummeted thereafter. In 1935, Gable starred with Loretta Young in *The Call of the Wild.* He also had an affair with her, which resulted in the birth of a daughter whose true parentage was only acknowledged many years later. That year, Gable also played Fletcher Christian in *Mutiny on the Bounty,* which earned a huge sum of money for MGM and brought him an Oscar nomination. He continued to produce hits through the late 1930s, including *Wife vs. Secretary* (1936), *Saratoga* (1937), *Test Pilot* (1938), *Too Hot to Handle* (1938), and the song-and-dance film *Idiot's Delight* (1939). The year 1939 proved to be a busy one for Gable. He and Langham divorced and he married again, to Carole Lombard, with whom he had starred with in *No Man of Her Own* (1932). Also that year, he starred as Rhett Butler in the film version of *Gone with the Wind,* Margaret Mitchell's blockbuster novel about the Civil War and Reconstruction. Gable was reluctant to take the part and the production was plagued with difficulties; however, the film was an immediate success and remains one of the most successful movies ever produced. Gable was at the peak of his popularity and made several successful films over the next three years, including *Boom Town* (1940), *They Met in Bombay* (1941), and *Somewhere I'll Find You* (1942).

By all accounts, Gable was content with his third wife, Lombard, but the marriage came to an untimely end when she died in a plane crash in January 1942. Devastated by the tragedy, Gable volunteered for the U.S. Army and spent several years serving in Europe during World War II. He earned the rank of major and the Air Medal for his participation in bombing raids over Germany, though he spent much of his time making training films and doing public relations tours.

When Gable returned home after World War II, he resumed his acting career with MGM. Though he continued to work regularly, observers have noted that Gable had appeared to lose some of the spark he had prior to Lombard's death, and he never regained his former matinee-idol status. He starred in *The Hucksters* (1947), *Homecoming* (1948), *Any Number Can Play* (1949), *Key to the City* (1950), *Across the Wide Missouri* (1951), *Lone Star* (1952), *Never Let Me Go* (1953), and *Betrayed* (1954), none of which was a major success. His only notable films of the period were 1948's *Command Decision* and 1953's *Mogambo,* a remake of his 1932 film *Red Dust.* In 1949, he married Sylvia Ashley; however, they divorced a few years later. In 1954, Gable left MGM to work as a freelance actor. A year later, he married Kay Spreckels. He continued to appear in films through the late 1950s, including *Soldier of Fortune* (1955); *The King and Four Queens* (1956); *Band of Angels* (1957); *Run Silent, Run Deep* (1958); *But Not for Me* (1959); and *It Started in Naples* (1960). His last film was John Huston's *The Misfits* (1961) with Marilyn Monroe, in which he performed some of his own stunts. Critics deemed it an excellent film.

On November 16, 1960, shortly after he finished work on *The Misfits,* Gable suffered a fatal heart attack and never saw the completed film. He was buried in Los

Angeles next to his third wife, Lombard. His son by Spreckels, John Clark Gable, was born after his death.

Amy Hackney Blackwell

References and Further Reading

Harris, Warren. 2002. *Clark Gable: A Biography.* New York: Harmony Books.

Harris, Warren G. 1974. *Gable and Lombard.* New York: Simon and Schuster.

Spicer, Chrystopher J. 2002. *Clark Gable: Biography, Filmography, Bibliography.* Jefferson, NC: McFarland.

Tornabene, Lyn. 1976. *Long live The King: A Biography of Clark Gable.* New York: Putnam.

Wayne, Jane Ellen. 1993. *Clark Gable: Portrait of a Misfit.* New York: St. Martin's Press.

Garbo, Greta (1905–90)

One of the most famous Hollywood actresses of all time, Greta Garbo embodied romance and mystery in the silent era and the 1930s, playing such tragic heroines as Anna Karenina and Camille. Although she retired from films in 1941 to live a reclusive existence, she remained a fascinating enigma for the next 50 years.

Garbo was born Greta Lovisa Gustafsson on September 18, 1905, in Stockholm, Sweden. She was the third child of Karl and Anna Gustafsson, and the family lived in poor circumstances. She left school at 13 to care for her ill father. At age 14, when he died, she worked in a department store, where she drew attention and was cast in a publicity short. In 1922, she appeared as a bathing beauty in the slapstick feature *Peter the Tramp.* Interested in theater, Garbo won a two-year scholarship to Stockholm's Royal Dramatic Theater Academy, where Swedish film director Mauritz Stiller noticed her and took her under his wing. He made her lose 20 pounds, taught her how to move and dress, and took her out in public to develop her social graces. He changed her name to Garbo and cast her in *The Saga of Gosta Berling* (1924), based on a celebrated novel by Selma Lagerlöf. Impressing film reviewers in Berlin, Garbo was invited by German director G. W. Pabst to play in *The Joyless Street* (1925). Simultaneously, Stiller signed a contract with Louis B. Mayer, head of Metro-Goldwyn-Mayer studios, on the condition that Garbo go to Hollywood with him. In one of the most nearsighted judgments of film history, Mayer was at first reluctant to take Garbo because "in America men don't like fat women."

Unpredictably, Garbo became MGM's biggest star, making 24 movies there between 1926 and 1941. Even before her first film, *The Torrent,* was released in early 1926, the studio realized that she was a screen sensation. Stiller was assigned to direct her second film, *The Temptress* (1926), but problems with studio executives resulted in his dismissal, and direction was completed by Fred Niblo. Stiller returned to Sweden in 1928 and died a year later, leaving Garbo to grieve over her mentor for many years. In her third film, *Flesh and the Devil* (1927), assigned to Clarence Brown, her favorite director, Garbo was cast opposite John Gilbert, Metro's biggest male star at the time. The film's sizzling love scenes, reflecting Garbo and Gilbert's passionate off-screen affair, made it a huge box-office success. One critic remarked, "Never in our screen career have we seen seduction so perfectly done." Garbo demanded a salary increase commensurate with her drawing power, and MGM, in order to profit from the gossip, acceded, raised her weekly salary from $600 to $5,000. She immediately was cast again with Gilbert in *Love* (1927), a modern-dress version of Tolstoy's *Anna Karenina.* Although their affair continued, they never married. In the remaining two years of the decade, Garbo made six more films, including *The Divine Woman* (1928). Based on the life of the actress Sarah Bernhardt, it was the first time she received top billing above the male lead. *A Woman of Affairs* (1929) was her third film with Gilbert. In reviewing *The Kiss* (1929), her last silent film, critic/playwright Robert Sherwood judged it mediocre but called Garbo "the best actress in the world," warranting comparison with Eleanora Duse, Helen of Troy, and Venus. Garbo shunned Hollywood society, avoiding interviews and appearances at premieres, preferring privacy and simple living. Though she was a plain, unglamorous dresser by nature, her screen image exerted a huge influence on women's fashions, hairstyles, and makeup. Her genius was that she knew intuitively exactly how she projected on the screen. The studio complied with her requests for closed sets because Garbo claimed it was the only way she could make her face express things it would not ordinarily.

Afraid that sound would destroy Garbo's image and career, as it had done many others—including Gilbert—MGM delayed casting her in a talking film until 1930 with *Anna Christie.* With her deep throaty voice, so well suited to the character in this adaptation of Eugene O'Neill's play, directed by Brown, Garbo's mystique was, if anything, intensified. "I can't decide whether it's baritone or bass," said one critic, but "there isn't another like it. Disturbing, incongruous, its individuality is so pronounced that it would belong to no one less strongly individual than Garbo herself." Garbo became an even bigger star, by the early 1930s earning a record $270,000 per movie. She played

opposite Clark Gable in *Susan Lenox: Her Fall and Rise* (1931) and was the German spy in *Mata Hari* (1932), costarring Ramon Novarro. In 1932, she was one of an all-star cast in the Academy Award-winning *Grand Hotel,* in which she played a fading, world-weary dancer, briefly regenerated by an affair with shady aristocrat John Barrymore. This role epitomized the air of romantic disillusionment that pervaded nearly all of Garbo's performances and spilled over into the public's impression of her private life. In 1933, Garbo played opposite Gilbert for the last time in *Queen Christina,* again about a doomed love affair and one of her most memorable films. The last shot of the movie is a dazzling long close-up of Garbo's face, holding every secret longing and unfulfilled wish in a mask of the eternal feminine. She remade *Anna Karenina* in 1935 with Fredric March, and in 1937, George Cukor directed her in *Camille,* which, along with *Ninotchka* (1939), was one of her two best films. In the latter, a brilliant satire directed by Ernst Lubitsch, Garbo revealed a talent for comedy as the sober Soviet envoy seduced by Melvyn Douglas and Parisian society. Advertised with the quip "Garbo Laughs!" the film was a critical and box-office success, leading MGM to conclude, erroneously, that her image should change into that of a "fun-loving American glamour girl," according to biographer John Bainbridge. The result was *Two-Faced Woman* (1941), again costarring Douglas. The critic of *Time* magazine said of her character's loose behavior, "It is almost as shocking as seeing your mother drunk." Garbo is reputed to have said about Metro's decision, "They've dug my grave." It was her last film.

Leaving Hollywood at age 36, Garbo was approached repeatedly to make a comeback but was never able to agree on scripts. She became an American citizen in 1951 and lived in total privacy in a Manhattan apartment. Pursued by fans, photographers, and the press whenever she went out, she was forced to wear nondescript clothes and sunglasses in public. It was not uncommon to hear strangers, store owners, or celebrities remark that they "spotted Garbo" on the street or in an East Side store. Garbo was twice voted Best Actress by the New York Film Critics, for her performances in *Anna Karenina* and *Camille,* and received an honorary Oscar in 1954, which she naturally was not present to accept. Though she had publicized relationships with several noted men, including director Rouben Mamoulian, conductor Leopold Stokowski, and nutrition theorist Gaylord Hauser, she remained unmarried. Garbo died on April 15, 1990.

References and Further Reading

Affron, Charles. 1977. *Star Acting: Gish, Garbo, Davis.* New York: Dutton.

Negra, Diane, and Jennifer M. Bean, eds. 2002. *A Feminist Reader in Early Cinema.* Durham, NC: Duke University Press.

Paris, Barry. 2002. *Garbo.* Minneapolis: University of Minnesota Press.

Swenson, Karen. 1997. *Greta Garbo: A Life Apart.* New York: Scribner.

Vieira, Mark A. 2005. *Greta Garbo: A Cinematic Legacy.* New York: Harry N. Abrams.

Gershwin, George Jacob (1898–1937)

George Gershwin, admired by Maurice Ravel and other European composers, wrote songs for Tin Pan Alley, Broadway, and Hollywood, as well as more ambitious works like *Rhapsody in Blue* and *Porgy and Bess.* Jaunty Gershwin songs, many with clever lyrics by his brother Ira, cheered the 1930s and continue as favorites today.

Jacob George Gershwin was born in New York City on September 26, 1898, the second of four children. His parents, Moishe Gershovitz (Morris Gershvin or Gershwin) and Rose Bruskin, were both Russian immigrants. Their first child, Israel (Ira), was followed by Gershwin two years later, Arthur in 1900, and Frances in 1906. Morris changed jobs often, and the Gershwins moved frequently to be near his place of employment—22 times between 1895 and 1917. His parents were not musical, but in 1910, the family purchased a piano, ostensibly for their eldest son. It quickly became clear that Gershwin was a musical child. In 1912, after two years of instruction from neighborhood teachers, Gershwin was accepted as a student by Charles Hambitizer, who took the youngster under his wing, introduced him to the concert hall, and taught him pieces by Claude Debussy, Franz Liszt, and Frédéric Chopin. In 1914, Gershwin dropped out of the New York High School for Commerce to go to work as a song plugger for Jerome H. Remick & Co., a music publishing firm. Day after day of playing honed his piano technique and turned him into an accomplished accompanist.

Gershwin began to compose songs and dreamed of moving from Tin Pan Alley (the district where many publishers of popular music were located) to Broadway. On Broadway, people like Jerome Kern, another New York songwriter with European-Jewish roots, were writing entire scores for the most sophisticated musical stage. In 1917, Gershwin left his job at Remick to take a position as rehearsal pianist for *Miss 1917,* a show written by Kern and Victor Herbert. One year later, Max Dreyfus, head of Harms, another music publisher, recognized Gershwin's talent and offered him $35 a week for the publishing rights to future songs. Before Gershwin was 21, he was known as a pianist, had written the score for a Broadway show, *La La Lucille* (1919), published songs, and had a publisher committed to issuing more. Gershwin wrote 16 full scores between 1919 and 1925. "Swanee," sung by Al Jolson in 1920, was a hit. He composed music for *George White's Scandals,* provided scores for several shows, contributed songs to others, and wrote twice for the London stage. In 1924, he created the score for *Lady, Be Good!* Songs like "Fascinating Rhythm" and "Oh, Lady, Be Good!", with lyrics by Ira, are still popular.

It was band leader Paul Whiteman, however, who catapulted Gershwin to fame. Whiteman's concert "An Experiment in Modern Music" was held at Aeolian Hall on February 12, 1924. Whiteman had commissioned Gershwin to write and perform a serious jazz composition for the occasion; the result was *Rhapsody in Blue.* The audience loved the jazzy, spirited work. Though reviews were mixed, Gershwin's name was made, not just as a songwriter but as a serious composer. In *Rhapsody in Blue,* Gershwin combined the materials of popular music, like syncopated rhythms and bluesy harmonies, with his Tin Pan Alley experience and classical studies to create a concert work. He had studied harmony, counterpoint, orchestration, and musical form with Edward Kilenyi for four years, and the piece reflects his efforts. Gershwin continued to write for the musical theater, producing 10 scores and 1 collaboration between 1926 and 1935. He also

published *George Gershwin's Song-book* in 1932, in which he pointed out that his "rhythms . . . are more or less brittle; they should be made to snap, and at times to crackle." He was concentrating, too, on concert music and study, working with Rubin Goldmark, Wallingford Riegger, and Henry Cowell in the 1920s. A 1928 trip to Europe with Ira and others allowed Gershwin to complete the score for a tone poem, *An American in Paris.* The next year, he conducted the New York Philharmonic in a performance of the work at Lewisohn Stadium and was the conductor and soloist for *Rhapsody in Blue.* Gershwin wrote most of another concert work, *Second Rhapsody for Piano and Orchestra,* while he and Ira were producing music for a Hollywood film, *Delicious* (1931). The 1930s saw more successful Gershwin brothers musicals, among them *Girl Crazy* (1930) and *Of Thee I Sing* (1931), which won a Pulitzer Prize. Tireless, Gershwin toured, performed, wrote songs, and studied composition with constructivist Joseph Schillinger between 1932 and 1936. While working with Schillinger, Gershwin collaborated with his brother and wrote a full-length opera, *Porgy and Bess* (1935). The ambitious work, based on Dubose Heyward's novel *Porgy,* brought together African American folk music and opera. The work is popular today, though when it opened, it ran for only 124 performances and was a financial failure.

Early in 1937, Gershwin was plagued by bouts of dizziness and depression and fell into a coma on July 9. After an operation for a brain tumor, he died in Hollywood on July 11. Novelist John O'Hara wrote, "George Gershwin died . . . but I don't have to believe it if I don't want to." Critic and composer Virgil Thomson commented, "George Gershwin was an exquisite maker of tunes. There is life in them and grace and a wonderful sweet tenderness.... They are music, our music, everybody's music."

References and Further Reading

Carnovale, Norbert. 2000. *George Gershwin: A Bio-bibliography.* Westport, CT.: Greenwood Press.

Ewen, David. 1956. *A Journey to Greatness: The Life and Music of George Gershwin.* New York: Holt.

Pollack, Howard. 2006. *George Gershwin: His Life and Work.* Berkeley: University of California Press.

Rosenberg, Deena. 1991. *Fascinating Rhythm: The Collaboration of George and Ira Gershwin.* New York: Dutton.

Wyatt, Robert, and John Andrew Johnson, eds. 2004. *The George Gershwin Reader.* New York: Oxford University Press.

Gershwin, Israel (Ira) (1896–1983)

Israel "Ira" Gershwin wrote most of the clever lyrics that graced songs by his brother George. The two wrote songs for Tin Pan Alley, Broadway, and Hollywood, as well as more ambitious works like *Rhapsody in Blue* and *Porgy and Bess.* Jaunty Gershwin songs cheered the 1930s and continue today as favorites.

Ira Gershwin was born on December 6, 1896, in New York City. He was interested in literature and studied at City College of New York for two years. He went on to have odd jobs around town while his brother George became well known as a composer and pianist on Tin Pan Alley. Ira Gershwin had a talent for turning a phrase, and his brother asked him to collaborate with him as a lyricist. Their first shared credit was "The First American Folk Song," which was used in *Ladies First* (1918). During his early days as a lyricist, Gershwin used a pseudonym, Arthur Frances (an amalgamation of his other siblings' names), so his brother would not be accused of nepotism and he wouldn't be deemed a "coat-tailer." The first large-scale production the brothers created as a team was *Lady, Be Good!* The musical went on to become a Broadway smash and included such American standards as "Fascinating Rhythm" and "The Man I Love." The following decade of collaboration established the Gershwin brothers as the preeminent songwriting team of Broadway theater. In 1930, Gershwin became the only lyricist to receive the Pulitzer Prize for the musical political satire *Of Thee I Sing.* While the Gershwins continued to produce musical theater, they also began composing music for Hollywood films. Throughout the Great Depression and World War II, Gershwin wrote some of the most enduring song lyrics of the 20th century, like "I Got Rhythm," "Embraceable You," and "'S Wonderful." Many of these compositions would fill the romantic musical comedies of Fred Astaire and Ginger Rogers, helping to define the glamour of Hollywood iconography. The Gershwin's most ambitious composition would be based on DuBose Heyward's popular novel *Porgy* (1925). Gershwin would collaborate with the author on the lyrics that would become the "folk opera" *Porgy and Bess* (1935). Along with Heyward, Gershwin wrote the brilliantly enduring lyrics of "Summertime," "It Ain't Necessarily So," and "I Got Plenty O' Nuthin'." When *Porgy and Bess* opened, it ran only 124 performances and was a financial failure. However, in later years, it became popular and was made into a

1959 movie musical starring Sidney Poitier and Dorothy Dandridge.

Gershwin continued to write his slangy, sophisticated lyrics after his brother died in 1937; he collaborated with Kurt Weill, Jerome Kern, and Harold Arlen. After spending his last years compiling the Gershwin songbook, Gershwin died in Beverly Hills, California on August 17, 1983.

References and Further Reading

Rosenberg, Deena. *Fascinating Rhythm: The Collaboration of George and Ira Gershwin.* New York: Dutton, 1991.

Gone With the Wind (1936)

Gone With the Wind (1936) (*GWTW*), written by Georgia native and journalist Margaret Mitchell, is considered to be one of the greatest American novels of all time. It focuses on the story of protagonist Katie Scarlett O'Hara, a rebellious southern belle of French-Irish descent, whose bucolic life in the antebellum South is transformed by the death and destruction of the Civil War, and the ensuing Reconstruction Era. The 1000+ page novel traces her personal growth from a spoiled, capricious 16-year-old girl to a mature, weathered southern woman who has survived three husbands (Charles Hamilton, Frank Kennedy, and Rhett Butler), three births (Wade Hampton Hamilton, Ella Lorena Kennedy, and Eugenie Victoria "Bonnie" Butler), the loss of her parents (Ellen and Gerald O'Hara), and the loss of their family fortune.

GWTW, which won the Pulitzer Prize in 1937 and is loosely based on Mitchell's own family history, focuses on Scarlett's two obsessions: her familial plantation, Tara, and her childhood sweetheart Ashley Wilkes. The intricate plot, which is sprinkled with racism, sexism, and a mythic glorification of the "Old South," is driven by her passion to secure both. However, despite Scarlett's machinations, she is unable to win Ashley's love, and in the end realizes that her foolish, selfish behavior has cost her the undying adoration of her third husband (and antagonist), Rhett Butler. In the concluding lines of the novel, she comes to terms with her father's aphorism "land is the only thing that matters," and returns to Tara, resolving to win back Rhett tomorrow, for "tomorrow is another day."

GWTW became an instant classic, selling thousands of copies within weeks of publication (by the time the film was released in 1939, it had sold over 1.5 million copies, and had already begun to be translated into dozens of languages). Within a few months of publication, Hollywood producer David O. Selznick purchased the film rights to the book, and began casting what would become an epic American motion picture. After a costly year-long, global search, British actress Vivien Leigh was selected for the role of Scarlett O'Hara, Clark Gable was cast as Rhett Butler, Leslie Howard was chosen to portray Ashley Wilkes, and Olivia de Havilland was selected to play Melanie Hamilton Wilkes, Ashley's wife and Scarlett's nemesis.

The motion picture, which is over three hours long and was one of the first filmed in three-strip Technicolor, functioned as romantic escapism during a very difficult period of time in U.S. history. Its release on December 15, 1939, in Atlanta, Georgia (Mitchell's home town, and the setting for much of the novel/film) came just a few months after the beginning of World War II, and its themes of survival, passion and determination propelled it, and its actors, into instant stardom. In 1940, it was nominated for 13 Academy Awards, and won 8, including Best Picture, Best Director (Victor Fleming), Best Actress (Vivien Leigh), Best Screenplay (Sidney Howard), Best Color Cinematography, Best Interior Decoration, Best Film Editing, and Best Supporting Actress (Hattie McDaniel), who was the first African American to be nominated and awarded an Oscar. The film also received two plaques for production design and technical production. *GWTW* did not receive Oscars for Best Actor, Best Sound Recording, Best Original Score, and Best Special Effects. It was nominated twice for Best Supporting Actress—Olivia de Havilland lost to co-star Hattie McDaniel.

Even though *GWTW* is one of the largest grossing films and best-selling novels of all time, over the past few decades, it has become the target of scholars who have taken issue with its rose-colored depiction of the Antebellum, Civil War and Reconstruction periods. In both the novel and the film the Ku Klux Klan (although never specifically mentioned by name) is portrayed as a heroic organization that protects southern women and the "southern way of life." After Scarlett is attacked by a group of impoverished ruffians in a local shanty town, her second husband Frank Kennedy, and the perpetually chivalrous "southern gentleman" Ashley Wilkes, suddenly attend a "political meeting." They, along with, presumably, other members of the Klan, go and "clean out" (i.e., burn down and terrorize) the shanty. When cornered by U.S. Calvary officers who were expecting trouble after Scarlett's attack,

the "meeting" disperses, leaving Frank mortally wounded and Ashley with an injury, which Rhett helps to conceal. While Rhett himself is not a member of the Klan, in the novel he implies that he would become a member if it meant restoring order in the South.

GWTW has also been criticized for fueling myths and stereotypes about plantation life, romanticizing the destruction of the Confederacy, and perpetuating racist and sexist language and images. The villains of *GWTW* are Unionists, scalawags and carpetbaggers; members of the planting class are portrayed as heroes: belles and beaux who were able to withstand the onslaught of the terrible "Yankees." Moreover, in both the film and novel, slavery is depicted as a benevolent institution. The evils of slavery are never represented; rather, Mammy is merely Scarlett's surrogate mother, and Pork is characterized not as a forced laborer, but as a loyal servant. Moreover, the hardships slaves do encounter befall them after they are released from the "benevolent" grip of their masters. Racist language abounds (in the novel Scarlet describes African Americans as "stupid," and as "black apes"), as does sexist imagery (Rhett manhandles the women in the novel, and in one scene, even rapes Scarlett).

Despite the obvious flaws of *GWTW*, it has inspired numerous sequels including Alexandra Ripley's *Scarlett* (1991), Donald McCaig's *Rhett Butler's People* (2007) and Alice Randall's controversial parody *The Wind Done Gone* (2001), which is told from the perspective of Scarlett's biracial half-sister Cynara (they share the same father, Gerald O'Hara). Thus, it continues to be an enduring, yet troubling, part of the American cultural canon, and will undoubtedly attract adoration, imitation, and criticism for years to come.

Tanfer Tunc

See also: Gable, William Clark.

References and Further Reading

Bergman, Andrew. 1971. *We're In the Money: Depression America and its Films.* New York: New York University Press.

Bridges, Herb. 1998. *The Filming of Gone With the Wind.* Macon, GA: Mercer University Press.

Bridges, Herb, and Boodman, Terryl C. 1989. *Gone With the Wind.* New York: Fireside.

Mitchell, Margaret. 1936. *Gone With the Wind.* New York: The Macmillan Company.

Pyron, Darden Asbury, ed. 1983. *Recasting: Gone with the Wind in American Culture.* Miami: Florida International University.

Pyron, Darden, and Pyron, Darden Asbury. 2004. *Southern Daughter: The Life of Margaret Mitchell and the Making of Gone With the Wind.* Athens, GA: Hill Street Press.

The Good Earth

Both the novel and the motion picture, *The Good Earth,* were instrumental in introducing the cultural and political issues of China to the average American. The story of a family trying to eke out a living in rural, village, and urban settings translated well for Americans during the Depression era. Dramatic reversals of fortunes and startling epiphanies held audiences and readers, but the characterizations of a persevering farmer and his dutiful wife created a measure of empathy for China and its people.

The novel was an immediate bestseller upon its publication in 1931 and received the Pulitzer Prize in 1932. The 1937 motion picture was based less on the book and more on the subsequent adaption for the stage by Donald and Owen Davis. The book, play, and movie follow the arch of Wang Lung, the farmer and husband, and O-Lan, the former servant and wife, from their wedding day to strained family relations between their two sons. Much of what happens in between—working the land, fighting natural disasters, buying land, moving to the city, taking a second wife—occurs in all three narrative forms. While the movie ends with the death of O-Lan, who Wang Lung sees not only as a hard-working wife but as the land itself, the book ends with the sons humoring their father as he loses his status of patriarch.

Particularities of the characters make both the book and the movie of interest to those struggling during the Depression. The land, as the title suggests, is at the center of all things, offering a stability not found in any other aspect of the story, aside from O-Lan's character. Everything is chaotic in the city, particularly when the poor masses riot. While crops may be under siege from insects, the innovative farmers can save some. However, when the city explodes with looting and murder, only the lucky can survive and even prosper. The book and the film treat the raiding of the city's rich home differently: in the book, Wang Lung is handed a bag of gold by a rich man who thinks Wang plans to kill him; in the movie, O-Lan finds a bag of jewels during the riot.

Whether Pearl Buck was attempting to write two universal characters or representatively good Chinese characters is beside the point. Americans stereotyped the Chinese abroad and U.S. government had in place laws against those inside its own borders. What struck Depression era audiences and readers was the odd custom of not being outwardly too thankful for good fortune for fear that the gods, ancestors, or fate might take it away to make the mortals more humble. The love of the land and growing distance between people and the land further struck a universal cord in the human experience.

Mark Schwartz

See also: The Grapes of Wrath.

References and Further Reading

Lawrence, Jerome. 1982. *Actor: The Life and Times of Paul Muni.* New York, G. P. Putnam's Sons.

Buck, Pearl S. 2005. *The Good Earth.* New York: Pocket Book.

The Grapes of Wrath

John Steinbeck's 1939 Pulitzer Prize winning novel, *The Grapes of Wrath,* and the subsequent film of the same title directed by John Ford and released in 1941, have become important sources in the historical understanding of the Great Depression and the New Deal. Reflecting the anticapitalist and pro-populist sentiments of the period, Steinbeck's best-seller was very controversial at the time of its publication, and many scholars suggest Ford's film version of the book could not have been made during or after World War II due to the strong critique of American society implicit in the story. Other scholars argue that Ford watered down Steinbeck's tone from a socialist-realist polemic into a nostalgic tribute to the enduring spirit of the American people.

Decades after the Great Depression, teachers and academics continue to assign *The Grapes of Wrath* to students seeking to understand the tumultuous 1930s. Steinbeck spent a great deal of time researching for his novel, traveling throughout California and the Southwest to document the plight of the Okies, Arkies, and other Dust Bowl refugees as they landed in the state in the mid-1930s by the hundreds of thousands. He first wrote on the subject in a series of articles in the *San Francisco News,* published as *The Harvest Gypsies* in 1936.

The Dust Bowl became the emblem of the Great Depression even before Steinbeck's novel and Ford's film. Director Pare Lorentz had photographed and interpreted the devastation of the dust storms in his 1936 film *The Plow That Broke the Plains* for the United States Farm Security Administration. The government had also hired photographers such as Dorthea Lange and Walker Evans to capture the plight of the Okies, just as Woody Guthrie and others depicted the same story in songs such as "Dust Bowl Blues" and "Do Re Mi."

The Grapes of Wrath tells the story of the Joad Family from Oklahoma. The book opens with a dramatic (perhaps melodramatic) portrayal of the impact of drought and dust storms, along with a treatment of a merciless system wherein smaller farmers were being "tractored out" of their family farms by larger farmers backed by faceless banks in the East. While this part of the novel is poignant, Steinbeck makes many errors of history and geography in the book. For example, he has the Joad family farmstead located outside of the area of Oklahoma gripped by dust storms, and he fails to note (as did Carey McWilliams, another author on the subject) that the settlement of

Oklahoma was doomed from the beginning due to poor land and high rates of farm tenancy.

The main character of the book is Tom Joad, who returns home from prison in the opening section of the story, only to find out that his family and most of his neighbors have lost their farms and are heading to California, lured by promises of jobs and visions of largesse in the Golden State. After an arduous, impossibly difficult trip across the desert in their worn out jalopy, the Joads and their defrocked preacher companion finally make it to the Central Valley of California, though one of the family members and the elderly Grandmother who had encouraged the migration died in the trip across the wilderness.

Landing in California, the Joads quickly find out that there are far more workers than available jobs. In fact, by the mid-1930s there were three workers for every agricultural job in California, with the average wage at a less than subsistence level of under $300 per year. Living on their paltry savings and occasional work, the Great Depression takes a toll on the Joad family, with pregnant sister Rose-of-Sharon's husband Connie running away and the family suffering from a variety of indignities and oppressions, living out of their car as migrant workers.

Eventually Tom and others try to organize for better treatment and pay, and are forced into a violent confrontation with thugs hired by the large, impersonal agricultural companies that were, in the eyes of Steinbeck, the incarnation of modern agribusiness in the American West. Old Stock farmers from pioneer roots, the Joads find themselves among the millions of displaced people in the Depression, seeking a better life but facing hostile natives who see the arrival of the Okies as an invasion. Indeed, the State of California attempted to shut its borders to the onslaught of people from the Dust Bowl regions. Thus, the film can be interpreted as a symbolic statement on both the decline of American individualism and of the decline of the Jeffersonian, agrarian ideal.

Both the book and the film find a heroic savior in the form of the New Deal of Franklin Roosevelt. The Farm Security Administration (originally the Resettlement Administration) built 12 federal migrant labor camps during the late 1930s and early 1940s. The camps provided clean shelter, hot showers and food, and school and recreational opportunities for the children of the migrants, all in an atmosphere of convivial self-government. In *The Grapes of Wrath* the Joad family's only good fortune is spending time in the government camp, where they could once again live as humans instead existing as hungry vagabonds facing the vagaries on minimal employment, exploitative pay, and the red-bating goons patrolling California's farm regions.

Steinbeck had visited the Arvin Federal Relief Camp (Weedpatch Camp) when researching the novel; and the camp administrator served as a prototype for the benevolent government administrator in the book and film. Indeed, parts of the film were actually shot on sight at the Weedpatch Camp, located about 15 miles south of Bakersfield near Arvin, California.

As the novel and film were highly critical of the people and institutions in California's agricultural towns, there was a backlash against the novel in Central California and elsewhere. The Salinas Public Library refused to buy the book, even though Steinbeck was a local boy, and the Kern County (California) Board of Supervisors banned the book from the classrooms and libraries for several years due to its unflattering portrayal of the area. The attempts to suppress the book engendered a long free speech battle in the cities like Bakersfield.

John Ford, known for his classic Westerns, proffered a film interpretation of Steinbeck's book in 1941. Though the film is true to the story and the spirit of the novel, Ford did change the ending. In the novel's climatic scene Rose-of-Sharon's baby is stillborn, and she uses her milk to suckle a starving man. Ford's film ends with a central character, Ma Joad, making an impassioned statement on the capacity of the common folk to survive in the face of dogged circumstances.

As the United States was preparing for eventual entrance into World War II, films and books critiquing the unjust nature of the Depression were falling out of vogue. Ford's sensitivity to the rising patriotism of the period is perhaps reflected in the changed ending. The film is credited for losing Americans from escapist movies, therefore setting the stage for more realistic films that shed light on the social problems of the day. Ford won the Academy Award for Best Director in 1940.

Randal Beeman

See also: Dust Bowl, Guthrie, Woodrow Wilson; The Good Earth; Migrant Agricultural Labor; Steinbeck, John.

References and Further Reading

Lingo, Marci. 2003. "Forbidden Fruit: The Banning of The Grapes of Wrath in the Kern County Library." *Libraries and Culture* 38 (Fall): 351–77.

McDermott, Robert, ed. 1990. *Working Days: The Journals of The Grapes of Wrath.* New York: Penguin.

McWilliams, Carey. 2001. "The Joads at Home." In *Fool's Paradise: A Carey McWilliams Reader,* eds. Stewart, Dean, and Gendar, Jeannine, 99–106. Berkeley, CA: Heyday Books.

Pauly, Thomas M. 1993. "*Gone With the Wind* and *The Grapes of Wrath* as Hollywood Histories of the Depression." In *Hollywood's America: United States History Through Its Films,* eds. Mintz, Steven, and Roberts, Randy, 103–11. New York: Brandywine Press.

Shindo, Charles J. 1997. *Dust Bowl Migrants and the American Imagination.* Lawrence: University Press of Kansas.

Guthrie, Woodrow Wilson (1912–67)

The legendary Woody Guthrie is best remembered for such songs as "This Land Is Your Land" and "Reuben James." His belief that music could change social conditions influenced a younger generation of singers that included Bob Dylan and Joan Baez. Coming of age in the migrant labor camps of California during the Great Depression, Guthrie's songs honored working people and called attention to the social inequities that they faced.

Woodrow Wilson Guthrie was born on July 14, 1912, in Okemah, Oklahoma, the third of five children. His father, Charley, a real estate speculator with political ambitions, supported the family comfortably until Guthrie was seven. Then, his father's prosperity—undermined by alcoholism and threatened by the oil boom—foundered. Things went from bad to worse for the family. In 1919, his oldest sibling, Clara, died in a fire. In 1927, his father was badly burned in

Woody Guthrie inspired the Beats with his love for America and his readiness to make music a form of social protest. (Library of Congress)

another blaze. Thereafter, Charley left Okemah to join his two younger children, who lived with his sister Maude in Texas, and to recuperate. Meanwhile, Guthrie's mother, Nora, was afflicted with Huntington's disease, a degenerative neurological disease, and was consigned to a mental institution. Now on his own at 15, Guthrie drifted and was sporadically taken in by friends and relatives. A restless loner, Guthrie spent his days reading in the public library and went to school infrequently until he dropped out at 16. He taught himself to play the harmonica and the guitar and performed at barn dances and revival meetings, in pool halls and bars. In 1929, he rejoined his family in Pampa, Texas. Six years later, Guthrie headed for California, one of thousands of Okies who fled the Dust Bowl in the 1930s. That hobo life, punctuated by menial jobs and occasional street singing,

shaped his convictions and heightened his sense of mission.

In 1937, Guthrie's radio program, "Here Come Woody and Lefty Lou," was heard over KFVD in Los Angeles. Guthrie went on to broadcast in New York with "Cavalcade of America" and "Pipe Smoking Time." By 1938, he was on the west coast again singing in migrant camps and on radio shows with Will Geer and Cisco Houston. A mimeographed songbook he put together, *On a Slow Train through California,* found its way to folk singer Pete Seeger. Guthrie and Seeger met at a concert for migrant workers in 1940. That year, ethnomusicologist Alan Lomax, the son and collaborator of folklorist John Lomax, recorded Guthrie's *Dust Bowl Ballads* for the Library of Congress Archive of Folk Song. Following Guthrie's relocation to New York, Lomax introduced Guthrie to the city's liberal café society and helped him search out publishers and sponsors for his works. In 1941, the Almanac Singers formed in New York with Guthrie, Seeger, and others. The group toured the country and settled in Greenwich Village later that year. Guthrie founded and worked briefly with the Headline Singers (Huddie Ledbetter, Sonny Terry, and Brownie McGhee) and wrote an article for the magazine *Common Ground.* The piece led to an autobiography *Bound for Glory* published in 1943. Early writings, spurred by his sympathy for the underdog, were published in *The Daily Worker* and *People's Daily World.* In 1943, Guthrie joined the U.S. Merchant Marine with Houston. In the course of their travels during World War II, they collected musical instruments, sang in North Africa, the United Kingdom, and Sicily, and survived dangerous torpedo attacks. After Guthrie's discharge in

1945, he recorded hundreds of songs for the Folkways label.

The more than 1,000 songs written or adapted by Guthrie (he often put new words to old tunes) were nearly all inspired by his life on the road. He sang of hard times in the Great Depression, the Dust Bowl drought, unions, and the New Deal. He performed frequently at protest meetings, on picket lines, and on marches, and his lyrics urged action as they underlined his beliefs. "This Land Is Your Land" and "Union Maid" are especially well known, as are "So Long, It's Been Good to Know Ya," "Goin' Down the Road," "Roll on Columbia," "Reuben James," and "Pastures of Plenty." Guthrie also wrote songs like "My Car" and "Why Oh Why" for children. Guthrie's column for the communist paper *People's Daily World* made him a target during the Mc-Carthy era. By the mid-1950s, he was seriously ill, struck down by Huntington's disease. By the 1960s, he was bedridden and his son, Arlo, began to perform his songs. It was at this time that the young Dylan began to visit him regularly.

Guthrie died in Brooklyn on October 3, 1967. After his death, *Tribute to Woody Guthrie* concerts were recorded at Carnegie Hall in January 1968 and the Hollywood Bowl in September 1970. A year later, he was inducted into the Songwriters' Hall of Fame. A film, *Bound for Glory,* starring David Carradine as Guthrie, was released in 1976. He was inducted into the Rock and Roll Hall of Fame in 1988. In 1998, Guthrie's daughter Nora asked British folk singer Billy Bragg and American rock band Wilco to put music to the hundreds of unpublished song lyrics discovered after Guthrie's death. The resulting *Mermaid Avenue* and *Mermaid Avenue II* were critically praised and spurred new interest in Guthrie's work.

References and Further Reading

Cray, Ed. 2004. *Ramblin' Man: The Life and Times of Woody Guthrie.* New York: W. W. Norton.

Garman, Bryan K. 2000. *A Race of Singers: Whitman's Working-Class Hero from Guthrie to Springsteen.* Chapel Hill: University of North Carolina Press.

Guthrie, Woody. 1943. *Bound for Glory.* New York: E. P. Dutton.

Jackson, Mark Allan. 2007. *Prophet Singer: The Voice and Vision of Woody Guthrie.* Jackson: University Press of Mississippi.

Klein, Joe. 1980. *Woody Guthrie: A Life.* New York: A. A. Knopf: Distributed by Random House.

Santelli, Robert, and Emily Davidson, eds. 1999. *Hard Travelin': The Life and Legacy of Woody Guthrie.* Hanover, NH: University Press of New England.

Hammett, Samuel Dashiell (1894–1961)

Samuel Dashiell Hammett's detective stories, particularly *The Maltese Falcon* and *The Thin Man,* brought hard-edged characters, seamy action, and the ambiance of the urban underworld to a genre that had been dominated in the previous generation by the elegance and rationality of Sherlock Holmes.

Hammett was born in St. Mary's County, Maryland on May 27, 1894. Educated at the Baltimore Polytechnic Institute until the age of 14, he served in the U.S. Army's Motor Ambulance Corps during World War I. He worked variously as a newsboy, freight clerk, messenger, stevedore, advertising manager, and finally for several years as a private detective for the Pinkerton Agency before turning to writing full time in 1922.

Hammett began publishing detective stories in *Black Mask,* a pulp magazine, in 1923. From the start, he ignored conventions of the genre. Whereas most contemporary stories featured detective heroes who solved crime after crime using flawless procedure and impeccable logic, Hammett's detectives grumbled about the inadequacy of fingerprints as clues and faced files full of unsolved cases. They worked in cities gone to seed and spoke the language of the criminals they hunted. Hammett's story "Fly Paper," published in *Black Mask* in 1929, is often cited as the first true example of so-called hard-boiled fiction. In 1929, Hammett published *Red Harvest* and *The Dain Curse* and in 1930, *The Maltese Falcon,* in which he introduced his sleuth, Sam Spade. In *The Glass Key* (1931), Hammett's own favorite book, detective Ned Beaumont runs down the bootlegger who murdered the son of a public official and takes the girl of the town's political boss away from him. *The Thin Man* (1932) features Nick Charles, a former detective who solves a murder when he discovers that the suspected murderer, the thin man, was himself slain months earlier by the real murderer. In 1934, *The Thin Man* became a successful movie starring William Powell and Myrna Loy. Among Hammett's later detective novels were *The Continental Op* (1945), *Nightmare Town* (1948), *The Creeping Siamese* (1950), and *Woman in the Dark* (1951).

Hammett, who lived in Hollywood from 1930 to 1942, became a successful screenwriter and co-wrote *City Streets* (1931) and *Woman in the Dark,* as well as two sequels to *The Thin Man* released in 1936 and 1939. He also consulted in the screen versions of his novels like *The Maltese Falcon;* directed by John Huston, it was the role of Sam Spade that made Humphrey Bogart a household name. Perhaps most notable among his screenplays was *Watch on the Rhine* (1943), about a refugee from Nazi Germany who murders his blackmailer, which Hammett adapted from the play by Lillian Hellman. Hammett and Hellman had begun a long-term relationship in 1930; they lived and worked together after Hammett's 1937 divorce from Josephine Dolan.

After 1946, Hammett taught creative writing in New York City. He served as president of the Civil Rights Congress of New York during 1946–47. In 1951, he was sentenced to six months in prison for contempt of Congress when he refused to cooperate with the anticommunist investigation led by Senator Joseph McCarthy and the House Un-American Activities Committee. After Hammett's death on January 10, 1961, Hellman edited a collection of his works, *The Big Knockover: Selected Stories and Short Novels,* published in 1966. One of the stories, "Tulip," is the closest Hammett got to writing autobiographically.

References and Further Reading

Dooley, Dennis. 1984. *Dashiell Hammett.* New York: F. Ungar Publishing Co.

Gregory, Sinda. 1985. *Private Investigations: The Novels of Dashiell Hammett.* Carbondale: Southern Illinois University Press.

Hamilton, Cynthia S. 1987. *Western and Hard-Boiled Detective Fiction in America: From High Noon to Midnight.* Iowa City: University of Iowa Press.

Metress, Christopher, ed. 1994. *The Critical Response to Dashiell Hammett.* Westport, CT: Greenwood Press.

Symons, Julian. 1985. *Dashiell Hammett.* San Diego: Harcourt Brace Jovanovich.

Hammond, John (1910–87)

Jazz aficionado John Hammond had a gift for spotting new talent and remarkable tenacity in boosting careers of jazz, blues, and rock-and-roll artists. He was especially influential during the 1930s when he promoted recordings by Count Basie, Fletcher Henderson, Billie Holiday, Benny Goodman, and countless others.

John Henry Hammond Jr. was born on January 15, 1910, to New York City wealth and privilege: his mother was a Vanderbilt, his father a banker and lawyer. He was sent off to Hotchkiss, a prestigious preparatory school. While there, he frequently traveled to Harlem to listen to African American blues singers. Hammond entered Yale University in 1930 but dropped out in his sophomore year to follow his jazz interests.

Hammond began to write for British publications like *The Gramophone* and later, in 1931, *Melody Maker.* At age 21, an inheritance enabled him both to produce the music that had fascinated him since he was a teenager and to bring black and white musicians together— an unheard-of phenomenon at that time. Hammond's goal was to find jazz musicians and record them. He tried unsuccessfully to produce records, and it was not until a 1933 trip to England that, in the words of James L. Collier, the "young, brash, opinionated rich man's son" who had been haunting American Depression-ridden record companies, got a break. He met Sir Louis Sterling, president of the English Columbia Gramophone Company. Hammond returned to New York to produce records for English Columbia: eight sides by the Fletcher Henderson Orchestra, eight by Benny Carter's big band, four by a Benny Goodman group, and another four by a Joe Venuti sextet. In 1934, Hammond helped form Goodman's orchestra and secured bookings for him. The association of the two men was to be a long one and was strengthened by Goodman's marriage to Hammond's sister, Alice, in 1941. In the late 1930s, Hammond was often to be found at Café Society, a Greenwich Village interracial night club where the band was directed by pianist Teddy Wilson. At that time, Hammond was a powerful figure in the jazz world because of his control of jobs and his many press contacts. Concerts in 1938 and 1939 at Carnegie Hall, "Spirituals to Swing," showcased and promoted Hammond's discoveries.

As swing bands lost ground in the late 1940s, Hammond was less influential, but he continued his work in the record industry with Columbia Records, Brunswick-Vocalion, Keynote, and others. He later was responsible for starting Bob Dylan, Bruce Springsteen, and Stevie Ray Vaughan on their recording careers. Through the years, his writings appeared in *Down Beat, The Brooklyn Eagle, The Nation, Tempo, Chicago News, New Masses,* and European magazines, including *Jazz Hot.* His autobiography, written with Irving Townsend, *John Hammond on Record,* appeared in 1977. Hammond died on July 10, 1987.

References and Further Reading

Prial, Dunstan. 2006. *The Producer: John Hammond and the Soul of American Music.* New York: Farrar, Straus and Giroux.

Hammond, John, with Irving Townsend. 1977. *John Hammond on Record: An Autobiography.* New York: Ridge Press.

Hawkins, Coleman (1904–69)

Coleman Randolph Hawkins, always open to new ideas, transformed the tenor saxophone from vaudeville novelty to serious jazz instrument. His constantly evolving style with its tone, technical proficiency, and powerful harmonic improvisation inspired contemporaries, while his musical flexibility and experimentalism continue to influence new generations of admirers.

Hawkins was born on November 21, 1904, into a middle-class family in St. Joseph, Missouri. His mother, a school teacher and organist, started him on the piano at five and the cello at seven. On his ninth birthday, he received a tenor saxophone. Sent to Chicago for high school, Hawkins went on to study harmony and composition at Washburn College in Topeka, Kansas.

In 1921, Hawkins landed his first professional job with the 12th Street Theater Orchestra in Kansas City. Blues singer Mamie Smith performed there that summer with the Jazz Hounds, and she asked Hawkins to tour with the group. By March 1922, he was performing and recording with Smith in New York. Hawkins traveled to California with the Jazz Hounds in 1923 but in June, returned to New York to freelance. He recorded his first solo, "Dicty Blues," with the Fletcher Henderson Orchestra in August. Hawkins stayed with Henderson until 1934 as a featured soloist at Roseland, the New York dance hall, through the 1920s.

The "Dicty Blues" documents Hawkins's early solo style: big-toned, energetic, slap-tongued. Louis Armstrong's brief tenure with the Henderson Band (1924–25) affected Hawkins. Exposure to Armstrong's improvisations led Hawkins to the more melodic and swinging jazz style. He dropped the slap-tongued attack for softer tonguing, especially in ballads. From pianist Art Tatum, Hawkins learned how to anticipate harmonic changes by playing chords before their statement by the rhythm section.

Hawkins's musical reputation led him to leave the Henderson Orchestra in 1934 to accept an invitation from Jack Hylton, a successful British bandleader. Hawkins stayed abroad for five years, but when war threatened in 1939, he returned to New York. Soon thereafter, he recorded "Body and Soul," a landmark performance. Many consider that best-selling jazz performance a masterpiece. Gunther Schuller has written that it "pulled together in one majestic...improvisation the various strands of Hawkins's previous stylistic exploration [with] seamless inner unity." Hawkins recorded "Body and Soul" again in 1959. The later version, from the Playboy Jazz Festival in Chicago, is another example of Hawkins's virtuosity. From the early 1940s, Hawkins played with small groups and was able to embrace the new harmonic challenges of bebop. In the following years, he toured Europe and recorded at home with groups that included musicians like Miles Davis, Fats Navarro, and Milt Jackson. He was heard frequently in the 1960s at New York nightclubs until his health began to fail. His final concert took place at Chicago's North Park Hotel on April 20, 1969. Hawkins died on May 19, 1969, in New York City.

References and Further Reading

Burnett James, selected discography by Tony Middleton. 1984. *Coleman Hawkins.* New York: Hippocrene.

Chilton, John. 1990. *The Song of the Hawk: The Life and Recordings of Coleman Hawkins.* Ann Arbor: University of Michigan Press.

Deveaux, Scott. 1997. *The Birth of BeBop.* Berkeley: University of California Press.

Giddins, Gary. 1998. *Visions of jazz: The First Century.* New York: Oxford University Press.

Kirchner, Bill, ed. 2005. *The Oxford Companion to Jazz.* New York: Oxford University Press.

Hearst, William Randolph (1863–1947)

Through the sensationalism he promoted in his journalistic empire and his own lavish lifestyle, William Randolph Hearst became one of the best-known public figures of his day.

Hearst was born on April 29, 1863, in San Francisco, the son of a millionaire miner and rancher. Enrolling at Harvard in 1882, he was expelled three years later because of a tasteless prank. Undaunted, Hearst persuaded his father to let him take over the family's failing newspaper, the *San Francisco Examiner,* in 1887. He modeled the paper after Joseph Pulitzer's *New York World,* with its mixture of sensationalism and reform, and hired a talented, well-paid staff. After initially going into debt, Hearst finally began to make a profit with the paper.

With his purchase of the *New York Journal* in 1895, Hearst challenged Pulitzer on his own turf. He brought the best of his San Francisco staff to New York, lured other talented people away from the New York papers, and slashed the price of his paper to one cent. When the Cubans revolted against Spanish rule, Hearst tried to outdo Pulitzer in printing exaggerated accounts of Spanish "atrocities." The circulation war between the two papers produced "yellow journalism," or an excessively lurid style of reporting. Also, by firing public sentiment against Spain, Hearst and Pulitzer helped promote the Spanish-American War of 1898. Hearst's enthusiasm for the war was illustrated in the well-circulated story of his dealings with sketch artist Frederic Remington. Hearst had sent Remington to Cuba to make sketches of Spanish atrocities. Remington, however, found nothing outrageous in Cuba and sent Hearst a telegraph telling him so. Hearst wired back, "You furnish the pictures and I will furnish the war." The Spanish-American War not only increased the circulation of Hearst's newspapers, it also increased Hearst's fame across the nation.

In 1903, Hearst married a showgirl, Millicent Willson. Millicent quickly shed her image as a stage performer, however, and assumed the characteristics of a high-society wife. Harboring political as well as journalistic ambitions, Hearst made a successful bid for a seat in Congress in 1903, serving until 1907. Despite an undistinguished record, he made a determined but ultimately losing effort to win his party's presidential nomination in 1904. He then tried for the mayoralty of New York City, taking on the Democratic machine of Tammany Hall and almost winning in 1905. The following year, he struck a bargain with Tammany Hall that he hoped would win him the governorship, but he was defeated. Hearst then launched his own personal third party, the Independence Party, but in the presidential election of 1908, it polled less than 100,000 votes and soon sank into oblivion.

Despite political activity, Hearst did not ignore newspapers. His journalistic empire grew through buying or starting newspapers in Chicago, Los Angeles, Boston, Baltimore, Pittsburgh, Atlanta, Seattle, and other cities. He also acquired such magazines as *Cosmopolitan, Good Housekeeping,* and *Harper's Bazaar* and created both the King Features Syndicate and the International News Service to supply newspapers throughout the country with news and features. In 1913, he branched into motion pictures by producing a weekly newsreel.

Not afraid of taking unpopular stands, Hearst opposed U.S. entry into World War I and was accused of being pro-German as a result. After the war, Hearst took a stand against America's joining the League of Nations and helped to keep the nation from participating in the World Court. Throughout the 1920s, Hearst was riding high. His handpicked candidate, John F. Hylan, was mayor of New York, enabling Hearst to influence city government for eight years. Hearst also started a motion picture company aimed at making a star of a Ziegfield Follies girl, Marion Davies, whom Hearst had met and fallen in love with in 1917 and who became his closest companion despite the fact that he was already a married man with a family. His wife refused to divorce him, despite the openness of his affair with Davies. Indulging his taste for luxury, Hearst began building a mansion at San Simeon on the California coast, where he entertained prime ministers and film stars in a princely manner. Throughout his life, he indulged his passion for art, buying vast amounts of paintings, sculptures, artifacts, furniture, and, jewelry while traveling around Europe. At one point, he bought an entire castle, with all of its furnishings, in England. Many of these treasures he put on display at San Simeon, but the majority remained in warehouses in New York.

In 1932, Hearst wielded political clout by swinging the Democratic presidential nomination in Franklin D. Roosevelt's favor through his control of the California delegation. He soon turned against Roosevelt, however, because of the latter's attempts to regulate business, and by 1935, Hearst papers were calling Roosevelt's New Deal the "Raw Deal." The Great Depression, combined with Hearst's spendthrift ways, almost cost him his empire. He not only lost control of his publishing ventures, but also suffered the humiliation of seeing many of his art treasures sold at auction at Gimbel's department store in New York City. With World War II and the return of prosperity, Hearst succeeded in regaining a measure of control over a publishing conglomerate that, though diminished in size, was still the largest in the nation. He also consolidated his hold over the motion picture industry during the 1930s. When the brilliant young filmmaker Orson Welles produced *Citizen Kane,* a movie based on a thinly veiled account of Hearst's life, Hearst exerted his power in Hollywood to blacklist Welles and nearly ruined the younger man's career.

After suffering a heart seizure in 1947, Hearst spent his last few years as an invalid, who, nevertheless, managed to read the various papers he owned and issue instructions to editors. Hearst died at Marion Davies's Beverly Hills home on August 14, 1951, at the age of eighty-eight.

References and Further Reading

Coblentz, Edmond D., ed. 1952. *William Randolph Hearst, a Portrait in his Own Words.* New York: Simon and Schuster.

Davies, Marion. 1975. *The Times We Had: Life with William Randolph Hearst.* ed. Pamela Pfau, and Kenneth S. Marx. Indianapolis, IN: Bobbs-Merrill.

Littlefield III, Roy Everett. 1980. *William Randolph Hearst, His Role in American Progressivism.* Lanham, MD: University Press of America.

Procter, Ben. 1998. *William Randolph Hearst: The Early Years, 1863–1910.* New York: Oxford University Press.

Procter, Ben. 2007. *William Randolph Hearst: Final Edition, 1911–1951.* Oxford; New York: Oxford University Press.

Walsh, John Evangelist. 2004. *Walking Shadows: Orson Welles, William Randolph Hearst, and Citizen Kane.* Madison: University of Wisconsin Press/Popular Press.

Hemingway, Ernest Miller (1899–1961)

Ernest Miller Hemingway, author of such classics as *The Sun Also Rises, A Farewell to Arms,* and *For Whom the Bell Tolls,* is regarded as the quintessential American novelist and one of the great prose stylists writing in English in the first half of the 20th century.

Hemingway was born in Oak Park, Illinois on July 21, 1899. His father, a physician, instilled in his son a love of hunting, fishing, and sports. His mother, who had once aspired to being an opera singer, taught him an appreciation for art and music. In 1917, the young Hemingway skipped college and found a job at the *Kansas City Star.* He tried unsuccessfully to enlist in the army but instead joined the Red Cross ambulance corps in 1918. Severely wounded in Italy after only a few weeks' service, he was decorated by the Italians as a war hero. After marrying Hadley Richardson in 1921, Hemingway traveled to Europe as a correspondent for the *Toronto Star.* He joined a community of expatriate writers living in Paris and was guided in his early literary efforts by Gertrude Stein and Ezra Pound.

Hemingway's seven years in Paris shaped his style and gave him characters and subjects. He worked as a journalist to pay the rent while he concentrated on learning to write; nevertheless, as he experimented with both poetry and fiction, laboring to strip the language bare of unnecessary adornment, he may have been helped by his newspaper experience, which had taught him an economy of style. Though at first he considered himself a disciple of Sherwood Anderson, Hemingway soon found a voice that struck the other writers of his acquaintance as rare and original. As F. Scott Fitzgerald was moved to advise his editor at Scribner's, Maxwell Perkins, "I'd look him up right away. He's the real thing."

A collection of Hemingway's stories, *In Our Time* (1925), attracted attention for

Ernest Hemingway is regarded as the quintessential American novelist and one of the great prose stylists writing in English in the first half of the 20th century. (Library of Congress)

its narrative technique, featuring his spare prose and objective description. It also introduced Nick Adams, a character who became a type for many later Hemingway protagonists. The book chronicles Nick's exposure to a series of violent experiences that culminate with his sustaining a severe wound during World War I. Hemingway's first major work, *The Sun Also Rises* (1926), established him as a writer of international reputation. Jake Barnes, an American journalist living in Paris, wounded in the war, and sexually impotent as a result, loves the beautiful and promiscuous Lady Brett Ashley. Because Jake is unable to consummate their relationship, Brett turns to other lovers before returning hopelessly to him. The novel's depiction of what Gertrude Stein called the Lost Generation—disillusioned with traditional values and caught in aimless hedonism—caused a sensation. In 1926, Hemingway left Hadley and their three-year-old son, Bumby, for Pauline Pfeiffer, whom he had come to know in Paris. They married and settled in Key West, Florida in 1928 and began a succession of travels that would eventually take them to Cuba, Africa, Spain, and Italy. In 1928, Hemingway's father committed suicide. Earlier that year, Pauline had delivered a son, Patrick, by Cesarean section, a traumatic event Hemingway worked into his next novel, *A Farewell to Arms* (1929). Gregory, Hemingway's third son and last child, was born in 1931. In *A Farewell to Arms,* Frederic Henry, an American lieutenant in the Italian ambulance service during World War I, falls in love with an English nurse, Catherine Barkley. With the Italians in retreat and Catherine pregnant, Frederic eventually deserts his unit. Catherine and the baby die in childbirth, but Frederic nevertheless has found strength in their love. "The world breaks

every one and afterward many are strong at the broken places," he says.

During the 1930s, Hemingway lived in Key West, Florida, hunted in Wyoming and Africa, and fished in the Gulf Stream off Cuba. He wrote *Death in the Afternoon* (1932), an extended essay in which he explored bullfighting in Spain as a ritual, and *Green Hills of Africa* (1935), an account of a big-game expedition. During the years 1933 to 1936, Hemingway published a number of his best-known short stories, including "A Clean, Well-Lighted Place," "The Short Happy Life of Francis Macomber," and "The Snows of Kilimanjaro." *To Have and Have Not* (1937), perhaps Hemingway's most experimental novel, tells the story of Harry Morgan, an ex-police officer who runs a charter boat in Florida and Cuba and who gets mixed up in smuggling during the Great Depression. Harry fits the mold of the Hemingway hero: a rugged individualist, he prides himself on his prowess as a fighter and a lover. The novel uses multiple narrative perspectives, a device that lets the reader see how little any single character's view actually represents the full story. In 1937, Hemingway returned to Spain as a correspondent covering the civil war. Ardently pro-Loyalist, he helped raise money for ambulances and medical supplies. Out of this experience came *For Whom the Bell Tolls* (1940), describing three days in the life of Robert Jordan, an American fighting for the Loyalist forces in Spain. Jordan is assigned to blow up a bridge behind enemy lines to slow the movement of Fascist forces after a Loyalist attack. The guerrillas learn that the Loyalist attack cannot succeed, but Jordan blows the bridge as instructed. He is wounded during the retreat and is left behind to meet certain death at the hands of the Fascists.

In 1950, Hemingway published *Across the River and into the Trees,* an unsuccessful novel about an aging American colonel who spends his last weekend in Venice with a beautiful, young Italian countess. *The Old Man and the Sea* (1952) was much more successful. In 1952, *Life* magazine published the entire text in a single issue, an unprecedented experiment. Hemingway was awarded a Pulitzer Prize in 1953 and a year later, the Nobel Prize for literature. In the story, an old Cuban fisherman fights a giant marlin for three days, finally subduing it, only to have the carcass attacked by sharks. The old man brings home only the skeleton of the great fish, but he has shown his stature through the quality of his elemental struggle. Hemingway continued to write, but he produced no more works of such importance. In 1953, in the midst of an African safari, he suffered serious head and abdominal injuries in a plane crash. A long, painful period of recuperation followed, and for the first time, Hemingway found his prodigious physical strength sapped, his energy gone, and with it his concentration. He grew displeased with the draft of a book about the safari. With the rise of Fidel Castro in Cuba, the Hemingway's moved permanently to Ketchum, Idaho. There, he worked on a collection of sketches based on his life in Paris during the early days of his career, published after his death as *A Moveable Feast* (1964). Suffering the effects of a lifetime of injuries, plus mild diabetes and depression, Hemingway saw his physical powers wane further. He was troubled by a loss of memory that hindered his efforts to write about his Paris years. After enduring months of hospitalization at the Mayo Clinic in Rochester, Minnesota, he grew suicidal. On July 2, 1961, he shot himself in Ketchum.

References and Further Reading

Wagner-Martin, Linda. 2000. *A Historical Guide to Ernest Hemingway.* New York: Oxford University Press.

Meyers, Jeffrey, ed. 1982. *Hemingway: The Critical Heritage.* Boston: Routledge & Kegan Paul.

Berman, Ronald. 2001. *Fitzgerald, Hemingway, and the Twenties.* Tuscaloosa: University of Alabama Press.

Civello, Paul. 1994. *American Literary Naturalism and its Twentieth Century Transformations: Frank Norris, Ernest Hemingway, Don DeLillo.* Athens: University of Georgia Press.

Tyler, Lisa. 2001. *Student Companion to Ernest Hemingway.* Westport, CT: Greenwood Press.

Lee, A. Robert, ed. 1983. *Ernest Hemingway, New Critical Essays.* Totowa, NJ: Barnes & Noble.

Henderson, Fletcher (1898–1952)

The pioneering arrangements by Fletcher Hamilton Henderson and Don Redman allowed sparkling improvisations by such stellar musicians as Louis Armstrong and Coleman Hawkins to emerge from choruses marked by sharply defined rhythms presented by Henderson's whole band. Those innovations helped shape what was to become swing.

Born to a middle-class African American family in Cuthbert, Georgia on December 18, 1898, Henderson studied music with his mother, a classically trained piano teacher. He earned a degree in chemistry and mathematics at Atlanta University, where he played baseball and acquired the nickname Smack, in reference to the sound of the impact of a baseball makes when hit by a bat. In 1920, Henderson went to New York to find a job as a chemist. Youth and race worked against him, and he was unsuccessful in his search. To support himself, he turned to working as a song demonstrator for the Pace-Handy Music Company, an early African American music publisher. In 1921, Harry Pace established Black Swan, the first African American recording company, and Henderson moved over to Black Swan as a musical jack-of-all-trades. While employed there, Henderson put together groups to accompany featured Black Swan singers and thus became a bandleader by default rather than by design. His bands performed at dances and clubs and worked at the Broadway nightclub Club Alabam. In 1924, an offer came from the Roseland Ballroom. A whites-only spot, it grew to be the best-known dance hall in New York City. Henderson stayed at Roseland for 10 years, and his work there brought him recognition and fame.

Henderson's group, one of many that came into being because of the social dancing fad, developed from an unremarkable dance band into a lively jazz orchestra. The change came not only in response to the attractions of the exciting new style but also because of the musical innovations of Armstrong. Armstrong arrived in 1924, and his short stint with Henderson's New York band was critical for the growth of jazz. While Armstrong's melodic improvisations and swinging rhythms were shaping New York City's music and musicians, the Henderson band's music director, Redman, was working out his new arrangement patterns of brass and reed interplay, patterns that became formulas for big bands in the years to come. Instrumental solos were inserted between set arranged sections, and Armstrong was the spectacular early soloist. Redman and Henderson established and brilliantly developed that basic formula.

The creative Armstrong, having made his mark on the Henderson style, returned to the greener pastures of Chicago in the fall of 1925. By 1926, according to Armstrong biographer James L. Collier, the band "was playing excellent jazz, with first-rate soloists and an ability to make the arranged passages swing." The Fletcher Henderson Orchestra successfully blended the steady tempo, syncopation, lilt, and notation of swing into pleasing concoctions and became a model for jazz bands until the mid-1930s. Redman wrote most of the Henderson band arrangements until 1927, when he left to become music director of McKinney's Cotton Pickers. Henderson took over most of that work, though he continued his practice of buying arrangements from freelance musicians. He had found his métier. His arrangements, for example, "King Porter Stomp" and "Wrapping It Up," were playable, clean, and relaxed.

The unassuming Henderson had a knack for spotting new talent and hired most of the major African American jazz players of the era, many of whom, like Armstrong and Lester Young, made their names with him. Management skills, however, were not his strength, and as a result, his group broke apart all too frequently. In 1934, due to financial reverses, he sold some of his work to Benny Goodman for Goodman's new band. Nevertheless, Henderson's popular arrangements ushered in the widespread success of swing bands that continued for a decade, from 1935 to 1945. Henderson directed bands until 1939, when he was hired by Goodman as a full-time staff arranger. In 1941, he returned to band-leading but wrote arrangements for a living, unable to keep pace with the swing band boom he had helped create. In December 1950, he had a stroke that left him partially paralyzed. Henderson died on December 29, 1952, in New York City.

References and Further Reading

Magee, Jeffrey. 2005. *The Uncrowned King of Swing: Fletcher Henderson and Big Band Jazz.* New York: Oxford University Press.

Allen, Walter C. 1973. *Hendersonia, the Music of Fletcher Henderson and his Musicians.* Highland Park, NJ: Walter C. Allen.

Dicaire, David. 2003. *Jazz Musicians of the Early Years, to 1945.* Jefferson, NC: McFarland.

Miller, Paul Eduard, introduction by Fletcher Henderson. 1978, c1939. *Down Beat's Yearbook of Swing.* Westport, CT: Greenwood Press.

Hepburn, Katharine Houghton (1907–2003)

Katharine Hepburn, at the top of her profession for more than 60 years, was arguably one of the most highly regarded and universally respected of all Hollywood actresses. Equally brilliant in comedy and drama, she is the only actress to have won four Academy Awards.

Katharine Houghton Hepburn was born on May 12, 1907, in Hartford, Connecticut. She was the second of six children and the first daughter of Thomas and Katharine Houghton Hepburn. Her father, from a poor and simple family, was a doctor; Hepburn's first ambition was to become a surgeon just like him. Her mother—whose family, the Houghtons, was one of America's foremost dynasties—was active in the woman suffrage movement in the early 1900s, joined Margaret Sanger's crusade for birth control

in the 1920s, and was one of the founders of the organization later known as Planned Parenthood. Hepburn marched for these causes with her parents and supported similar causes—such as the pro-choice movement—in the 1970s and 1980s. To biographer Christopher Andersen she said, "[T]he single most important thing anyone needs to know about me is that I am totally, completely the product of two damn fascinating individuals who happened to be my parents."

As a young girl, Hepburn was an accomplished painter, sculptor, and athlete. A tomboy for much of her childhood, she shaved her head at age nine to keep the boys from pulling her hair. She attended West Middle School in Hartford and later Hartford's Oxford School. Inspired by her grandfather's stories, she became interested in drama at age 10, performing plays on a makeshift stage in a shed at the family's country house in Fenwick. In 1921, the tragedy of Hepburn's older brother Tom's apparent suicide devastated her. She left school, was given private tutors, and spent a great deal of time watching silent movies as an escape, secretly dreaming of becoming an actress. At Bryn Mawr, Hepburn began studying medicine, but as a result of poor academic performance and eccentric behavior (swimming nude in a fountain), she almost flunked out. She switched her major, became active in the college's drama society, and graduated with honors in 1928. Her senior year performance as Pandora in *The Woman in the Moon* won the attention of a friend of theatrical producer Eddie Knopf, who as a result of Hepburn's persistence gave her first professional, non-speaking role as one of Catherine the Great's ladies-in-waiting in *The Czarina*. Hepburn's first speaking role was in Knopf's stock company's production of *The Big Pond,* but when they reduced her to understudy for the Broadway opening, she refused. Her first role on Broadway was in *These Days,* after which she was understudy and then fill-in for Hope Williams in Philip Barry's *Holiday.* Williams was a strong influence on Hepburn's acting and vocal style.

In 1928, Hepburn married Ludlow Ogden Smith, whom she had met during her senior year at Bryn Mawr and, for the next several years, appeared in a number of plays, making her biggest impression as an Amazon in *The Warrior's Husband* in 1932. In that year, she tested for the role of Sydney in the film *A Bill of Divorcement,* which was to star John Barrymore. She won the part and signed a contract with producer David O. Selznick for $1,500 a week. Remarking on Hepburn's initial impact on film audiences, Selznick said that while her look was totally new and unglamorous for Hollywood, she proved instantly to be a unique screen personality. The film was directed by George Cukor, with whom Hepburn formed a lasting friendship and from whom she learned the subtle differences between stage and film acting. In the course of her career, she made nine other features with Cukor, including *Little Women* (1933); three of the nine films she made with Spencer Tracy—*Keeper of the Flame* (1942), *Adam's Rib* (1949), and *Pat and Mike* (1952)—and two television films, "Love Among the Ruins" (1975) and "The Corn Is Green" (1979). Hepburn's second film, also produced by Selznick, was *Christopher Strong* (1933), directed by Dorothy Arzner, one of Hollywood's few women directors. Her initial success peaked when she won her first Oscar for her third film, *Morning Glory* (1933). She continued to develop as an actress with an amazing range— playing the spunky backwoods heroine in *Spitfire* (1934), the homespun girl of

Booth Tarkington's *Alice Adams* (1935), *Mary of Scotland* (1936), an ambitious actress in *Stage Door* (1937), and the flighty Susan in the screwball masterpiece *Bringing Up Baby* (1938). The latter, a brilliant comic performance, was also her most scintillating teamwork with Cary Grant, with whom she also appeared in *Sylvia Scarlett* (1935), *Holiday* (1938), and *The Philadelphia Story* (1940), all directed by Cukor. In the 1940s, Hepburn began a long personal and professional relationship with Tracy. Their first film together was *Woman of the Year* (1942), in which Hepburn is a political commentator and Tracy a sportscaster. Besides the three directed by Cukor, their other notable film was Frank Capra's political satire *State of the Union* (1948). Their last was the preachy *Guess Who's Coming to Dinner* (1967), which was Tracy's last screen appearance and which won Hepburn a second Oscar. While their relationship never led to courtship or marriage, Hepburn said in her autobiography, "We just passed twenty-seven years together in what was to me absolute bliss. It is called love."

In the 1950s, Hepburn gave several memorable performances as spinsters: as the missionary in John Huston's *The African Queen* (1951), she is won over by equally memorable Humphrey Bogart as a drunkard sea captain; in *Summertime* (1955), she has an autumnal love affair with Rossano Brazzi while vacationing in Venice; and in *The Rainmaker* (1956), she is wooed by charming con man Burt Lancaster. She also gave two striking performances as neurotic mothers in screen adaptations of Tennessee Williams's *Suddenly, Last Summer* (1959) and Eugene O'Neill's *Long Day's Journey into Night* (1962). Her third Oscar was for *The Lion in Winter* (1968) and her fourth for *On Golden Pond* (1981), which costarred

Henry Fonda. Her most recent appearances were in the television movies *Laura Lansing Slept Here* (1988), written especially for her, and *One Christmas* (1994). In 1994, she also appeared with Warren Beatty in *Love Affair,* a remake of *An Affair to Remember.*

Divorced from Ludlow Smith in 1934, Hepburn never remarried, believing that she could not be successful at both marriage and a career. Toward the end of her life, Hepburn noted, "I have no fear of death—must be wonderful, like a long sleep—but let's face it: it's how you live that really counts." The legendary actress passed away at her home in Old Saybrook, Connecticut on June 29, 2003, at the age of 96.

References and Further Reading

Britton, Andrew. 2003. *Katharine Hepburn: Star as Feminist.* New York: Columbia University Press.

Edwards, Anne. 2000. *Katharine Hepburn: A Remarkable Woman.* New York: St. Martin's Press Griffin.

Hepburn, Katharine. 1991. *Me: Stories of my Life.* New York: Ballantine Books.

Hepburn, Katharine. 1987. *The Making of The African Queen: or, How I Went to Africa with Bogart, Bacall, and Huston and Almost Lost My Mind.* New York: New American Library.

Higham, Charles. 2004. *Kate: The Life of Katharine Hepburn.* New York: Norton.

Mann, William J. 2006. *Kate: The Woman Who Was Hepburn.* New York: H. Holt.

Hillbilly Music

During the years of the Great Depression, hillbilly music was the name given to what has today evolved into old time, string band, bluegrass, Americana, and country music. Ever since people from England, Ireland, and Scotland interacted with people from Africa along the east coast of America, this music had been evolving, and it would continue to do so through the decades, expanding to take in influences from other immigrant groups, and moved and changed by the mountains and plains and cities in which the musicians found themselves.

Fiddle, guitar, banjo, and mandolin were the instruments most used in hillbilly music: portable, melodic, and in the case of fiddle and banjo especially, able to be heard equally well across a crowed dance floor and a mountain hollow. This sort of music was, up until just before the Great Depression, music made face to face, on the front porch and in the community. As the 1920s unfolded, that began to change.

In the years just before the Great Depression, the newly developing industry of radio and the expanding business of record companies had both begun to see potential in this style of music, which had been identified with the back roads and backwoods of the rural south. Many rural southerners were moving to towns and cities, and wanted to hear the music of home; radio stations might be based in cities, but their signals reached rural areas as well; and for those who had no electricity, the record companies could still offer a chance to hear the music, with hand cranked record players.

In 1927 Ralph Peer, a scout for Victor Talking Machine Company, was looking for the next big star to follow the success of fiddlers Eck Robertson and Vernon Dalhart in the hillbilly market. At a scouting trip in Bristol, Tennessee he recorded The Carter Family and Jimmie Rodgers, who would both come to define hillbilly music during the Great Depression, and influence artists across the decades from that day to this.

Jimmie Rodgers, The Singing Brakeman as he was known from his days working the railroad, mixed up sounds and influences from blues, country, jazz, creating a fresh sound. Rodgers leave a legacy of songs including "T for Texas," "Blue Yodel," "Miss the Mississippi and You," "My Rough and Rowdy Ways," "Waiting for a Train," and "Somewhere Down Below the Dixie Line."

A. P. (Alvin Pleasant) Carter, his wife Sara Dougherty Carter, and his sister-in-law Maybelle Addington Carter, had three part harmony that became the signature sound of country music harmony, and Maybelle's unique approach to guitar, the "Carter Scratch," as well as the ability to create new songs that lived in tradition. During the great Depression, Carter songs including "I'm Thinking Tonight of My Blues Eyes," "Will the Circle Be Unbroken," "Wildwood Flower," "ALittle Darlin' Pal o' Mine," "Storms Are on the Ocean," "No Depression in Heaven," and "Keep on the Sunny Side" spoke to those down and out as well as those fighting their way up from hard times.

Kerry Dexter

See also: Autry, Gene; Radio; Rogers, Roy; Swing Music.

References and Further Reading

The Carter Family: Their Complete Victor Recordings [sound recording]. 1993–98. Cambridge, MA: Rounder Records.

Kingsbury, Paul, and Alanna Nash. 2006. *Will The Circle Be Unbroken?* Nashville, TN: Country Music Hall of Fame Press; New York: Dorling Kindersley.

Oermann, Robert K. 1999. *A Century of Country* New York: TV Books.

Various artists. 1991. *The Bristol Sessions* [sound recording] Nashville: Country Music Hall of Fame Press.

Hines, Earl "Fatha" (1903–83)

One of the most formidable talents in jazz history, "Fatha" Hines was not only a major bandleader of the 1930s but is also considered to be the first modern jazz pianist.

Born to a musical family in Duquesne, Pennsylvania in 1903, Earl Kenneth Hines played cornet before switching to piano at age nine. He later credited his mature, trumpet-style of piano playing (in which his right hand played the melodic line in octaves and mimicked a trumpet's phrasing) to his early horn experience. He was playing professionally before the end of high school, and toured with Lois Deppe's band before moving to Chicago's vibrant jazz scene in 1924, first as a soloist and then as a member of several bands.

In Chicago he also began playing with Louis Armstrong, participating in many of his "Hot Five" and "Hot Seven" sessions as well as the duet *Weather Bird*, all considered defining recordings in jazz history. By 1928 Hines had started a 12-year residency as leader of his own band at the Grand Terrace nightclub. Although a haven for gangsters (Al Capone was once Hines's patron), the Grand Terrace gave Hines nationwide exposure through its nightly, coast-to-coast radio broadcasts on NBC. His modest recording success at this time included such songs as "57 Varieties" and "Boogie Woogie on the St. Louis Blues." After leaving the Grand Terrace over a contract dispute in 1940, he toured with varying degrees of success for the next few years, including a stint heading Duke Ellington's Orchestra in 1944.

With the end of the big band era, Hines engaged in small-ensemble work before starting a four-year run with Louis Armstrong's All-Stars in 1947. Despite a later successful European tour with Jack Teagarden, Hines became increasingly frustrated with the business side of music during the 1950s. He had almost quit entirely by 1964 when he decided to appear in what became a critically acclaimed series of solo engagements in New York that revived his career. This second career was prolific, enhancing his public profile and resulting numerous engagements and new recordings until a few years before his death in 1983.

Although never as big a commercial success as such bandleaders as Benny Goodman or Glen Miller, Hines nevertheless stands as one of the most important figures in jazz history. Not only did he help start the careers of such jazz greats as Charlie Parker, Dizzy Gillespie, Billy Eckstine, and Sarah Vaughn, he also profoundly influenced the direction of piano jazz. Technically, only Art Tatum could rival his dexterity and command of the keyboard, and few could match his trademark, lightning-fast runs or inventive improvisations. Musically, Hines helped change the role of piano in jazz, extending its influence beyond the rhythm section and integrating it more fully into the orchestration of the band. His style and melodic use of the left hand broke with previous conventions and earned him critical acclaim as the first modern jazz pianist. His work inspired generations of piano artists (including Teddy Wilson, Nat King Cole, Erroll Garner, and Claude Bolling), many of whom would agree with Count Basie that Hines was the world's greatest pianist.

Kevin Kern

See also: Basie, William "Count"; Ellington, Edward Kennedy "Duke"; Radio; Swing Music.

References and Further Reading

Dance, Stanley. 1977. *The World of Earl Hines.* New York: Charles Scribner's Sons.

Dicaire, David. 2003. *Jazz Musicians of the Early Years, to 1945.* Jefferson, NC: McFarland and Company.

Oliphant, Dave. 2002. *The Early Swing Era, 1930–1941.* Westport, CT: Greenwood Press.

Schuller, Gunther. 1989. *The Swing Era: The Development of Jazz, 1930–1945.* New York: Oxford University Press.

How to Win Friends and Influence People (1936)

Dale Carnegie's seminal self-help book *How to Win Friends and Influence People* was published in 1936, and it has been a bestseller, off and on, ever since, with nearly 15 million copies sold. Some editions not only sport the smiling elfish visage of Dale Carnegie, but also were imprinted with a copy number appearing on the cover in red. Today, there are many tie-in books and courses to the ideas that Carnegie put forward so plainly so many years ago. Contemporary readers may confuse him with the millionaire Andrew Carnegie, or believe he is related to the Carnegie clan. He actually changed his birth name from "Carnegey" to Carnegie to encourage this association.

Dale Carnegie was born into poverty, later attending Warrensburg State

Teachers College in Missouri. Before becoming a salesman for Armour and Company, he sold correspondence courses to ranchers. His dream of becoming an actor was quickly dashed in New York City, but it was there that he first began to teach his courses in public speaking. His tool to get the most reluctant speakers to speak naturally was to ask them speak about something that made them angry. Much of his teaching and his experience with students helped him write *How to Win Friends and Influence People.*

By today's standard, most of the advice given by Carnegie may be considered by some as old hat: smile, don't criticize, praise, avoid an argument, see the other person's point of view, allow the other to save face, and ask questions about the other person's interest. What makes the book still as readable today as it was during the Depression, is that Carnegie takes his own advice of dramatizing personal ideas. It is the stories, taken from Carnegie's life and the lives of famous individuals that have inspired several generations. Confucius, Abraham Lincoln, and Jesus Christ might appear within pages of each other, illustrating the same point with direct quotes. Carnegie weaves the Golden Rule of "doing to others what you would want them to do to you" throughout the book.

What strategies Carnegie proposes that are still fresh today include the ideas that someone could change another person's behavior by simply reacting to them in a certain way and that someone could create an unknown desire in another person for something. Other ideas seem like shrewd management: leaders should talk about their mistakes before pointing out someone else's mistakes, and leaders should presuppose that those around them have established good reputations which should be praised and continued.

All Carnegie's ideas can be classified in three general categories known to readers of self-help books: the power in positive thinking, walk in someone's shoes, and that honey attracts more flies than vinegar.

References and Further Reading

Carnegie, Dale. 1981. *How to Win Friends and Influence People.* New York: Pocket Books.

Kemp, Giles, and Clafin, Edward. 1989. *Dale Carnegie: The Man Who Influenced Millions.* New York: St Martin's Press.

Schiffrin, Andre. 2001. *The Business of Books: How the International Conglomerates Took Over Publishing and Changed the Way We Read.* New York: Verso.

Stine, Jean Marie. 1997. *Writing Successful Self-Help and How-To Books.* New York: Wiley Books.

Humes, Helen (1913–81)

Helen Humes was a prominent jazz and blues singer. She was born on June 23, 1913, in Louisville, Kentucky, into a musical family, learning to play the trumpet and the piano as a small girl. She sang with the local Sunday School Band, and when she was 13 she recorded several blues songs for Okeh Records.

As a teenager, she decided to move to New York where she found work with Stuff Smith and Al Sears. Soon she started working as a recording vocalist with Harry James's Big Band. The songs she recorded included "Jubilee," "I Can Dream Can't I," "That's the Dreamer in Me" and "Song of the Wanderer." In the late 1930s, Humes initially turned down an invitation to replace Billie Holiday as the lead female vocalist, although she did eventually replace her in Count Basie's band in 1938. In 1941, she left Basie and moved to California to continue her repertoire of singing ballads and popular songs.

Throughout the 1940s and 1950s Helen Humes was a solo performer, although she did work with a number of other singers including Nat King Cole. In 1950, she recorded Benny Carter's "Rock Me to Sleep"; and in the same year she established her own independent record company called Discovery Records. Her major song during this period was "Million Dollar Secret" (1950). Managing to bridge the divide between big band jazz swing and rhythm and blues, she made a number of appearances in southern California throughout 1951, and in the following year she recorded her famous song "Wheel of Fortune."

In September, 1952, Humes extended her stay at the Brown Derby in Honolulu, Hawaii, and in August of the following year she was a featured performer at Gene Norman's 4th Annual Rhythm & Blues Jamboree at the Shrine Auditorium, in Los Angeles, before embarking on a tour of Australia. Remaining popular, she recorded three albums in 1959–61 and toured with Red Norvo. Later she moved permanently to Hawaii and in 1964 she went to live in Australia. She returned to the United States but when her mother died in 1973, sold her piano and records and decided not to sing again. However, later the same year the music critic Stanley Dance convinced her to appear at the Newport Jazz Festival with Count Basie. This led to a come back of sorts and she would later play at the Cookery in New York, and later in Los Angeles. She died on September 9, 1981, at Santa Monica, California.

Justin Corfield

See also: Basie, William "Count"; Radio; Swing Music.

References and Further Reading

Dahl, Linda. 1984. *Stormy Weather: the Music and Lives of a Century of Jazzwomen* New York: Pantheon.

Placksin, Sally. 1982. *American Women in Jazz: 1900 to the Present: Their words, Lives and Music.* New York: Seaview Books.

Eileen M. Hayes and Linda F. Williams, eds. 2007. *Black Women and Music: More than the Blues.* Urbana: University of Illinois Press.

I Am a Fugitive from a Chain Gang (1932)

Both Robert E. Burn's autobiographical book, *I Am a Fugitive from a Georgia Chain Gang* (1932), and the geographically challenged motion picture, *I Am a Fugitive from a Chain Gang,* tell the tale of northerner World War I veteran, shell-shocked and so down on his luck that he ends up on a southern chain gang after disputable involvement in a petty theft. While the sensational book describing the living hell of the chain gang has fallen out of popularity, the movie, starring Paul Muni cast into Burn's circumstances as James Allen, remains a viewable classic and a study in successful social-protest filmmaking.

The film went into production within the same year as the best-selling book's publication. Georgia officials took note of the book and voiced exception to the film: Warner Brothers dropped "Georgia" from the film's title and all other references to the state from the film. While the film uses double-exposures of Muni's character walking over a map background in several transitions, Georgia, much less any southern state, is not clearly visualized as the place where his first crime of petty theft is committed.

The film, which took little money to make, proved a cash cow to Warner Brothers by becoming Warner Brothers' biggest money-maker since the Depression began. American men, identifying with the film's protagonist, so desperate that he tried to pawn his war metals, were particularly drawn to film.

All moviegoers were moved by one of the most famous endings in the history of film. Although the implied message of the film may have been to shed light on the dark existence of those working on a chain gang, another message was taken away by the audience. After Muni's character has been through the wringer of the chain gang, the insecurity of leading a double life as a successful citizen, and the victim of the broken promises of the legal system, he becomes the man he was accused of being at the beginning of the film. Now a fugitive for the second time, the girl of his dream asks him how is he abiding in his nightmare on the streets. He answers that he steals, and he fades back into the shadow. The fugitive's story was an inversion of a Horatio Algiers tale of rags to riches. One exchange early in the film draws this point out. He tells his mother, who wants him to take a paper-pushing job at a local company, that he wants to do something worthwhile with his life, and she asks how he could talk like that.

The film was nominated for three Oscars, including Best Picture, despite its downbeat ending. Since the film was made so close to the date of the book's publication, it did not include the somewhat happy ending of the real Robert E. Burns's life: with Georgia Governor Arnall's help, Burns had his sentence commuted as time served. The chain gangs were shortly thereafter abolished.

References and Further Reading

Bergman, Andrew. 1971. *We're In the Money: Depression America and its Films.* New York: New York University Press.

Burns, Robert Elliott. 1997. *I Am a Fugitive from a Georgia Chain Gang!* Reprint, Athens: University of Georgia Press.

LeRoy, Mervyn. 1974. *Mervyn LeRoy Take One.* New York: Hawthorn Books.

I Am a Fugitive from a Gang. 1932. Hollywood, CA:. Filmstrip.

It Happened One Night

Based on at least one short story by Samuel Hopkins Adams, *It Happened One Night,* a romantic comedy meets road trip movie, went the distance from sleeper to blockbuster to win the top five best Academy Awards of 1934: Picture, Actor (Clark Gable), Actress (Claudette Colbert), Director (Frank Capra), and Adaptation (Robert Riskin). It took over 40 years before another movie, *One Flew Over the Cuckoo's Nest,* achieved the same status.

It may be considered an excellent picture simply for being one of the first screwball comedies: its characters, in a battle of wits from the start, are sometimes employed, often drunk, but always jaded. The film focuses on the edgy relationship between journalist (Gable) and an heiress (Colbert) who recently married a playboy whom her overprotective father despises. The early hint of a rich man hating another rich man, not simply for marrying his daughter, gives the serious examiner of this film the first clue that this film may be concerned with more than romantic love. *It Happened One Night* is also just as concerned about money, if not more so. In the great scheme of the comedy, if Colbert's heiress falls in love with Gable's journalist, not only is she marrying into an occupation that often bottom feeds on gossip of high society, but she would, if she were to marry him, marry beneath her class. She has everything to lose, and he has everything to gain. Whether she ends up with him is not in question for the audience. What is in question is how they end up together by the end of the picture.

Even though he is cynical and broke, Gable's character refuses to profit off of his association with Colbert's character. He not only rejects making a deal with another man who wants to cash in on a reward offered by her father, but refuses money from the father himself. He only wants to set the financial record straight by submitting an itemized billing for travel expenses.

Other situations reinforce the underlining structure of who has money and who does not throughout the picture. In one scene, a poor boy refuses money from the budding pair because his mother, if she were well enough to answer herself, would not want him to take it. But not all the folks populating his picture are so civil: this movie has a gallery of thieves, all of which Gable has to chase after or instruct in the ways of righteousness.

While it paints a picture of the role of class in society, it is more obviously about sex. There are several famous scenes: the blanket barrier set up in a hotel room the couple share before they become involved, pillow talk in haystacks, and Colbert's hitching up her skirt for more than a glimpse of her leg in order to catch a ride with a passing car. Aside from the filmmakers making money off of the sexuality in this movie, the sexuality had monetary ramifications for other industries. After Clark Gable took his shirt off and showed the audience and Colbert his bare chest, the sales of undershirts plummeted. Further, women began to use buses in droves, the mode of travel for the first half of this romantic comedy.

Mark Schwartz

See also: Gable, William Clark.

References and Further Reading

Ina Rae Hark, ed. 2007. *American Cinema of the 1930s: Themes and Variations.* New Brunswick, NJ: Rutgers University Press.

Bret David. 2007. *Clark Gable: Tormented Star.* New York: Carroll & Graf.

Everson, William K. 1976. *Claudette Colbert.* New York: Pyramid Publications.

Jukebox

A jukebox is a piece of phonographic equipment with a mechanism to exchange multiple disks and a coin-operated actuator. The etymology of the term is uncertain, but is often traced to an African American slang term meaning "to dance."

In its first several decades of existence, the jukebox faced harsh competition from coin-operated player pianos. However, those devices were severely limited in the number of songs they could play, and the perforated rolls they used for storing the playing instructions meant songs were not random-access. By the 1930s, the record-changing mechanisms in jukeboxes had become sufficiently sophisticated that it was possible for a user to choose any song at random from the collection of disks in the machine, simply by pressing a button. Furthermore, the purchase of Victor, an important phonograph brand, by the Radio Corporation of America (RCA) brought the technical sophistication of radio to sound reproduction, giving recorded sound a more lifelike quality.

As a result, the years between 1934 and 1940 marked the jukebox's greatest popularity. The Great Depression had limited people's ability to purchase records and phonographs for themselves, while radio had made a wide variety of music popular and in demand. As a result, being able to go into a restaurant or bar and listen to a favorite song by slipping a nickel into the slot was a popular way of hearing music. Furthermore, the end of Prohibition brought bars back out into the open as legal establishments, greatly expanding the market for these mechanical music boxes.

The jukeboxes of the 1930s were handsome artifacts, their lines heavily influenced by the Art Deco movement. Many had wide bands of lights and intricate woodwork, or streamlined chrome lines. As a result, using a jukebox was an experience in its own right.

Leigh Kimmel

See also: Swing Music; Hillbilly Music; Radio.

References and Further Reading

Bunch, William. 1994. *Jukebox America: Down Back Streets and Blue Highways in Search of the Country's Greatest Jukebox.* New York: St. Martin's Press.
Goldstein, Paul. 2003. *Copyright's Highway: From Gutenberg to the Celestial Jukebox.* Stanford, CA: Stanford Law and Politics.
Segrave, Kerry. 2002. *Jukeboxes: An American Social History.* Jefferson, NC: McFarland & Co.
Steffen, David J. 2005. *From Edison to Marconi: The First Thirty Years of Recorded Music.* Jefferson, NC: McFarland.

King Kong

King Kong premiered to Depression era audiences in the spring of 1933, and since then the world of movies and their interpretation has never been the same. This film has inspired heated debates among critics and audiences, has influenced filmmakers through its use of special effects, and has launched a franchise of Kong-related movies, including the sequel Son of Kong, which also came out in 1933 to bad reviews.

The plot is a "Lost World" story, made popular 50 years prior to King Kong by writers like Arthur Conan Doyle and H. Rider Haggard. As Age of Exploration was winding down, stories of lost civilizations became more poignant. King Kong is a huge gorilla on Skull Island, a remote island, where the natives offer human sacrifices to Kong by way of a huge wooden door. It is to this island that successful filmmaker Carl Denham, played by Robert Armstrong, must go. Before he embarks, he needs a female lead, so he takes to the streets of New York, which are filled with woman struggling through the Depression, and finds Ann Darrow, played by Fay Wray, groping at an apple, as if to steal it.

King Kong stands atop New York's Empire State Building as he holds an airplane during an attack by fighter planes in a scene from the 1933 film *King Kong*. (AP/Wide World Photos)

After a meal, Darrow is on the ship, where she falls in love with its captain, Jack Driscoll, played woodenly by Bruce Cabot. Once they arrive on fog-obscured Skull Island, it begins to dawn on Darrow that she's getting more than she bargained for: the not-so-welcoming natives of the island want to hand her over to Kong, their local monster.

Once Kong arrives on the scene, the development of the characters ends, the non-stop action begins, and we see the characters for what they really are. Screaming Darrow wants to be saved from Kong, heroic Driscoll wants to save Darrow, greedy Denham wants to film and capture Kong, and brutish Kong wants to be left alone with the blonde that he carries around like a doll. Unfortunately

for Kong, he is plagued by humans, dinosaurs, and giant snakes. After Driscoll rescues Darrow from Kong and his oversized world, Denham and crew gas Kong. Next, King Kong appears on Broadway, wants his girlfriend back, kidnaps her and takes her to the top of the Empire State Building only to be pestered by bi-planes shooting at him. The "Old Arabian Proverb," which appears after the overture and the opening credits proves true; that a beast looking upon beauty, that he does not kill, will end up dead. King Kong, riddled by bullets, falls to his death. Denham, looking over the remains of Kong, tells a policeman that it was not the airplanes, but beauty that killed the beast.

In order to understand how such a seemingly simple story as King Kong has raised such diverse and contentious interpretations in the Depression era and time periods since, the last lines of the movie, spoken by the filmmaker within the movie, should be heeded: It wasn't such-and-such, "it was beauty that killed the beast." This is the photo negative of a beauty and a beast fable: the beauty does not fall in love with the beast. No one debates this point. Although there have been some highly specific interpretations of the movie, for example, that President Franklin D. Roosevelt is Denham and the New Deal is King Kong, nothing seems more defensible than the interpretation this is a story of something natural, a gorilla, caught up in circumstances such as capitalism (Denham), romantic love (Darrow), civilization (New York City), and technology (bi-planes with machine guns), and not being able to survive it.

For many critics and audiences in the 1930s and onward, King Kong is about race. The natives of Skull Island, though supposedly in the East Indian Ocean, appear to be African and King Kong is black, and something that the "white man has never seen," according to Driscoll and a tagline for the movie itself. The historical content for this interpretation is not debatable: for a decade prior to the film's release, African Americans were moving to the city and desiring equality and a better life. During the Depression, they were often the populations hardest hit: first to be fired and last to be hired. Whether most white audiences saw King Kong's rampage through New York City as a race riot or his longing for the fair Darrow as ambition to succeed in a white society, some audiences during the Depression did. There is no refuting that King Kong, like African slaves, came to American in chains.

Whether critics need to see King Kong as representative of race or not, there is undeniably the strain of Kong being the owner of a lonely heart. At the top of the Empire State Building, the tallest building in New York City in 1933, Kong is riddled with bullets as Saint Sebastian is with arrows. Kong is most interested in the wounds over his heart, while Darrow seems not to care that he is dying. The audience is expected to feel sorry for Kong, who looks hurt and sorry: the music is not victorious but sorrowful. Kong picks up Darrow, and although he could throw her down, he sets her down again with care and a caress. It is climatic, tragic chords that the audience hears as Kong falls to his death. Driscoll gets the girl, whether the audience wants him to or not.

The picture has also been viewed as tract against women: Darrow may have been groping that apple to steal it in the beginning of the film just as, critics point out, Eve was tempted by an apple in the beginning of the Bible. Darrow is not smart, brave, or independent—very unlike Belle from the classic fable or even Greta Garbo's character in another movie from 1933, *Grand Hotel,* who just wants "to be alone."

The technological advances made by the making of King Kong are irrefutable: although some "stop-action" special effects were used on *The Lost World* eight years earlier, King Kong was a triumph of this method to make inanimate things appear to move. The monster of King Kong, which includes some of the people, is a conglomerate of various models which were moved by small increments for each frame exposed, which creates the illusion of continuous motion as the frames are run for viewing.

Although some filmmakers may have been attracted to King Kong remake projects or films that revive him as a character, all, presumably, have returned, as audience have, to the simian King Kong for his richness in character, which is natural and tragic, and to the story line of a beast that might not prove to be as much of a beast as what kills it.

Mark Schwartz

References and Further Reading

Goldner, Orville, and George Turner. 1975. *The Making of King Kong: The Story Behind a Film Classic.* Stamford, CT: Oak Tree Publishers.

Morton, Ray. 2005. *King Kong: The History of a Movie Icon from Fay Wray to Peter Jackson.* New York: Applause Theatre and Cinema Books.

Price, Michael H., George E. Turner, and Susan Svehla. 2006. *The Amazingly True Adventures of Merian C. Cooper and Ernest B. Schoedsack.* Baltimore, MD: Midnight Marquee Press.

Rony, Fatimah Tobing. 1996. *The Third Eye: Race, Cinema, and Ethnographic Spectacle.* Durham, NC: Duke University Press.

Kirk, Andrew Dewey (1898–1992)

A leading American jazz saxophonist, Andy Kirk was an African American bandleader who achieved much fame during the 1930s throughout the United States.

Andrew Dewey Kirk was born on May 28, 1898, in Newport, Kentucky, and grew up in Denver, Colorado. He started to become interested in music from an early age, studying the piano, singing and playing the alto and tenor saxophone under Wilberforce Whiteman, father of the musician Paul Whiteman. He joined the band of the violinist George Morrison in 1918, playing the bass saxophone and the tuba, before moving to Dallas between 1925 and 1927, where he joined the Dark Clouds of Joy band of Terrence Holder. In 1929, when Holder left, the band elected him as their leader and were renamed the Clouds of Joy, or sometimes the Twelve Clouds of Joy. Performing at the Pla-Mor Ballroom in Kansas City, they made their first recording for Brunswick Records at the end of 1929.

Kirk was never a soloist and did not like playing ensemble parts after the 1930s. Most of the band stuck with Kirk for many years, with Buddy Tate as the tenor saxophonist, Pha Terrell as the singer, Claude Williams as the violinist, and John Williams, the first husband of Mary Lou Williams, as the saxophonist. Other players included Dick Wilson, Kenney Kersey, Don Byas, Fats Navarro, Howard McGhee and also, briefly, Charlie Parker. Mary Lou Williams joined the group as a pianist, although Marion Jackson, the pianist who was replaced, was angered by this. The death of the tenor saxophonist Wilson in 1941, only 30 years old, hurt the band badly. In the same year, Mary Lou Williams left to perform with her own group, but the band continued until 1948. Andy Kirk continued to play jazz occasionally, but moved into real estate and hotel management. He did perform again briefly during the 1960s, and in the 1980s he started working with the New York American Federation of Musicians, performing until just before his death. He died on December 11, 1992, in New York City.

Justin Corfield

See also: Basie, William "Count"; Ellington, Edward Kennedy "Duke"; Goodman, Benny; Swing Music.

References and Further Reading

Claghorn, Charles Eugene. 1973. *Biographical Dictionary of American Music.* West Nyack, NY: Parker Publishing Co.

Claghorn, Charles Eugene. 1982. *Biographical Dictionary of Jazz.* Englewood Cliffs, NJ: Prentice Hall.

Handy, D. Antoinette. 1995. *Black Conductors.* Metuchen, NJ: Scarecrow Press.

Holmes, L. D., and Thomson, J. W. 1986. *Jazz Greats: Getting Better With Age.* New York: Holmes & Meier Publishers.

Kirk, Andy. 1989. *Twenty Years on Wheels, as Told to Amy Lee.* Ann Arbor: University of Michigan Press.

McCarthy, Albert. *Big Band Jazz.* New York: Putnam, 1974.

Krupa, Gene (1909–73)

One of the most famous and flamboyant drummers of the swing era, Gene Krupa was also an influential percussion icon who popularized the drum solo and inspired generations of drummers.

Eugene Krupa was born on the south side of Chicago, the ninth child in a Polish-Catholic family. He gravitated toward music early, starting on the saxophone and then switching to drums. An indifferent student, he left school at 16 to pursue a career in music. Chicago at this time was a jazz hotbed, and Krupa immersed himself in this subculture, particularly emulating the work of drummer Baby Dodds. With other young local artists he helped pioneer what came to be known as Chicago-style jazz, and this group's influential 1927 recordings were among the first to include an entire drum kit.

Krupa's move to New York in 1928 greatly influenced his career. Musically, his introduction to the drumming of Chick Webb profoundly affected his own style. Professionally, he not only played with well-known bandleaders (including Red Nichols, Mal Hallet, and Horace Heidt), but also became George Gershwin's favorite drummer while appearing in the pit orchestras of *Strike Up the Band* and *Girl Crazy*. These successes led to national acclaim after he joined Benny Goodman's band in December 1934. His flashy, gum-chewing demeanor combined with his matinee-idol looks distinguished him from other drummers of his day. These qualities, along with his powerful style (exemplified by his driving beat and drum breaks in the swing anthem "Sing, Sing, Sing" made him a celebrity with the jitterbug set.

Krupa left Goodman in 1938 and formed the first of several bands. In its various incarnations, these bands charted dozens of recordings, including "Drum Boogie" (which, along with "Apurksody," served as one of his themes), "It All Comes Back To Me Now," and "Let Me Off Uptown." Perhaps as significantly, his bands also helped launch the careers of Anita O'Day, Roy Eldridge, Gerry Mulligan, and a number of other jazz artists.

In 1943, an arrest and imprisonment on marijuana possession charges (the most serious of which was later overturned) threatened Krupa's career. Although his band folded as a result, an invitation to join Tommy Dorsey in 1944 helped rehabilitate his public image. After World War II, he toured extensively with his own groups and with stars such as Benny Goodman until ill health (back problems and a heart attack) forced him to slow down in the 1960s. During this period, he and Cab Calloway drummer Cozy Cole also founded a drum school in New York.

Although not the greatest drummer of the swing era—most experts (including Krupa himself) considered Chick Webb to be better—Krupa was nevertheless a seminal figure in jazz and percussion history. Music historians credit him with popularizing the drum solo and influencing the standard drum kit. His showmanship and abilities as a drummer continued to leave their mark long after his death from leukemia in 1973. The long list of drummers who have named him as a major influence extends beyond the jazz community to such rock artists as Keith Moon (The Who), John Bonham (Led Zeppelin), and his own student Peter Criss (Kiss).

Kevin Kern

See also: Goodman, Benny; Swing Music.

References and Further Reading

Blesh, Rudi. 1971. *Combo: USA. Eight Lives in Jazz.* Philadelphia: Chilton Book Company.

Crowther, Bruce. 1987. *Gene Krupa: His Life and Times.* New York: Universe Books.

Dicaire, David. 2003. *Jazz Musicians of the Early Years, to 1945.* Jefferson, NC: McFarland and Company.

Korall, Burt. 1990. *Drummin' Men: The Heartbeat of Jazz.* New York: Oxford University Press.

Kyser, James Kern "Kay" (1905–85)

Titular leader of one of the most prolific and popular big bands, Kay Kyser was also one of the swing era's most famous radio and movie personalities.

Kyser was born in Rocky Mount, North Carolina to an extended family of academics and pharmacists with close ties to the University of North Carolina. Following family tradition, he attended UNC and soon became one of the most popular people on campus and head cheerleader for the Tar Heels. Although he did not play an instrument, his popularity and outgoing personality inspired graduating fellow student Hal Kemp to put his college band under Kyser's leadership. Wishing to adopt a less formal stage name, Kyser began using his middle initial for alliterative effect at this time.

Upon graduation, Kyser toured with his band for a number of years, adopting crowd-pleasing costumes, banter, and novelty numbers as part of his act. The band's big break came in 1934, when Hal Kemp got Kyser to take over for him at the Blackhawk Restaurant in Chicago. Broadcasting over local radio, Kyser and his band devised their trademark singing song title introductions, as well as an audience-participation quiz that eventually became known as *Kay Kyser's Kollege of Musical Knowledge.* Donning academic robes and a mortar board, Kyser would ask audience members questions, responding to incorrect answers with the catchphrase, "That's right, you're wrong!" When NBC picked up the show in 1938, it became a nationwide hit, bringing in millions of listeners each week and rating as a top 10 program each of the 13 years it aired.

Kyser's radio success soon made his band one of the most commercially popular groups of the 1930s and 1940s. Recording over 400 singles, Kyser's band charted scores of top-twenty, dozens of top-ten, 11 number-one, and sold six million records from 1938–48. Among the band's biggest hits were "Praise The Lord and Pass The Ammunition,"

"(I've Got Spurs That) Jingle, Jangle, Jingle," "(There'll Be Bluebirds Over) The White Cliffs of Dover," and such novelty songs as "Three Little Fishies," and "The Woody Woodpecker Song." Kyser also made celebrities out of such band members as trumpeter/singer Merwyn "Ish Kabibble" Bogue and singer Mike Douglas. On top of his tremendous broadcast and recording success, Kyser also had the greatest cinematic presence of any major bandleader, with starring roles in seven films and cameos in several others. His films included *That's Right—You're Wrong* with Lucille Ball and Adolphe Menjou and *You'll Find Out* with Peter Lorre, Boris Karloff, and Bela Lugosi.

Although health reasons kept him out of uniform during World War II, Kyser resolved to perform only for military audiences for the duration, logging hundreds of visits to camps and hospitals in addition to his weekly Saturday shows at the Hollywood Canteen. After the war was over he gradually withdrew from show business, one of his last jobs being a televised version of his *Kollege*. He retired from performing entirely in 1951, becoming a major figure in the Christian Science Church until his death of heart failure in 1985. He was inducted into the Radio Hall of Fame in 1990.

Kevin Kern

See also: Jukebox; Radio.

References and Further Reading

Stowe, David W. 1994. *Swing Changes: Big-Band Jazz in New Deal America.* Cambridge, MA: Harvard University Press.

Whitburn, Joel. 1986. *Pop memories, 1890–1954: The History of American Popular Music.* Menominee Falls, WI: Record Research.

Yanow, Scott. 2004. *Jazz on Film: The Complete Story of Musicians and Music Onscreen.* San Francisco: Backbeat Books.

Let Us Now Praise Famous Men

Let Us Now Praise Famous Men began as a *Fortune* magazine assignment about Southern tenant farming offered to author James Agee in 1936. That summer, Agee and photographer Walker Evans spent two months in Alabama with three sharecropper families, experiencing first-hand the primitive living conditions and encountering people Agee would describe as helpless and ignorant, but painfully aware that they did not live so much as survive.

Though Agee and Evans had both worked for *Fortune* before, neither was strictly a journalist. Agee had published poetry and short stories and later wrote screenplays and novels. Evans was a photographer for the Federal Resettlement Administration, documenting the work of the administration in rural areas. However he considered himself an artist first, and favored the exceptional detail possible with an 8"x10" view camera over the agility of a small 35 mm more typically used by photojournalists.

The photographs Evans produced in Alabama are widely regarded a highpoint of his career. His portrait of Allie May Burroughs, in which the visibly uneasy sharecropper's wife stares directly at the camera, especially typifies the frank honesty Evans strove for, while his interior studies of the farmers' homes are as artistic as they are soberly straightforward.

Agee found writing the text immensely difficult, which determined the ultimate

Portrait of sharecropper's wife Allie May Burroughs, by Walker Evans. (Library of Congress)

fate of the project. The article Agee turned in was pronounced overlong and inappropriate in tone for *Fortune*. Agee revised and expanded the text for five years, finally publishing it as a book in 1941. Agee's prefatory note offers some insight into his struggle with the material, and the tone *Fortune* rejected. Agee noted the "curious" nature of the original assignment, sharply criticizing the magazine, and to some extent himself, for proposing to exploit the unimaginable hardship to sell magazines and justify the publication at a time of economic crisis.

The greater part of the book is in many respects the written equivalent of Evans's photography. By turns intensely literary, even poetic in style, Agee describes the families and their surroundings in vivid detail. Periodically Agee self-consciously reflects on his intrusion as an outsider, and recognizes when his reactionary views of modern life are confronted by the brutally unromantic reality of living without basic conveniences.

The complexities of Agee's text and his conflicted relationship to it became enduring topics of literary criticism assessed in terms ranging from "bourgeois liberalism" to "postmodernist realism." However, when first published, few copies of *Let Us Now Praise Famous Men* were sold and it went out of print until 1960, when proponents of the civil rights movement, who read in it a call to class solidarity, brought it to wider public notice.

Tess Mann

References and Further Reading

Agee, James with Walker Evans. 1960. *Let Us Now Praise Famous Men.* Boston: Houghton Mifflin.

Ward, J. A. 1985. *American Silences: The Realism of James Agee, Walker Evans, and Edward Hopper.* Baton Rouge: Louisiana State University Press.

Mellow, James R. 1999. *Walker Evans.* New York: Basic Books.

Quinn, Jeanne Follansbee. 2001. "The Work of Art: Irony and identification in *Let Us Now Praise Famous Men.*" *Novel: A Forum on Fiction,* 34 (3): 338–68.

Li'l Abner

In 1934, cartoonist Al Capp connected with the hearts and minds of Depression-era Americans with a comic strip about hillbillies which Capp used as a grand satiric platform from which he combined the slapstick humor of the funny-pages with razor-sharp political satire, targeting everything from corrupt politicians and bureaucrats to his fellow cartoonists. Capp's daily strip became such an important part of American popular culture that it transcended its role as political gadfly and left an enduring mark on American language and literature.

Al Capp, born Alfred Gerald Caplin in 1909, said that he inherited his talent as an artist from his father. After a trolley car accident at age nine cost Capp a leg, his father introduced drawing as a form of therapy. This therapy culminated with formal study at several art schools, perhaps most notably at the Designer's Art School in Boston. The training allowed the 19-year-old Capp to become the youngest syndicated cartoonist in the country with the daily one-panel comic *Col. Gilfeather* which was picked up the Associated Press. By 1932, Capp was engaged in "ghosting" the more prestigious boxing comic strip *Joe Palooka* for Ham Fisher.

It was in the *Joe Palooka* strips that Capp first introduced a hillbilly character named Big Leviticus. Capp, anecdotally, claimed to have based his hillbilly characters on people he witnessed while traveling in West Virginia as a youth. In 1934, Capp took the hillbilly idea to United Features Syndicate and the result was *Li'l Abner*.

Set in Dogpatch, U.S.A., *Li'l Abner,* followed the adventures of the titular character and a cast of sidekicks as varied as Joe BTFSPLK, a human jinx who was constantly followed by his own personal rain cloud and Mammy Yokum, the sweet, small matriarch of Dogpatch who could easily "lick" any two men. The strip's plot revolved around Li'l Abner's continuing attempts to escape the marital schemes of his girlfriend Daisy Mae.

The strip's theme reflected Capp's personal politics. Capp, and the denizens of Dogpatch, were clear and vocal supporters of Franklin Delano Roosevelt's liberal New Deal policies. Capp used the strip, and his ability to utilize brilliant and scathing satire of political, as well as cultural issues, to attack those with whom he did not agree. A prime example is Capp's creation of the character "Senator Jack S. Phogbound" who served as a parody of Southern Democrats who did not support the New Deal. Capp's political views changed over the years, so much so that by the 1970s, he was seen as an arch-conservative and was a friend of President Richard Nixon.

Li'l Abner was an immediate success with Depression-era readers. The strip, which was at first carried in only eight newspapers, soon reached a circulation of over 60 million readers. Li'l Abner's adventures were not merely read, they became a part of the culture; adding such terms to the language as: "druthers," "irregardless," and "Kickapoo Joy Juice," as well as such traditions as the "Sadie Hawkins Dance."

Li'l Abner, because of Capp's masterful use of political satire, is considered to be one of the most important American comic strips ever and it is for this reason that author John Steinbeck referred to Capp as the greatest writer in the world.

Keith Murphy

References and Further Reading

Berger, Arthur Asa. 2006. *Li'l Abner: A Study in American Satire.* Oxford: University of Mississippi Press.

Capp, Al. 1956. *The World of Li'l Abner.* New York: Farrar, Strauss, and Young.

Capp, Al. 1989, *Li'l Abner Dailies, 1937: The First Sadie Hawkins Day.* North Amherst, MA: Kitchen Sink Press.

Lippmann, Walter
(1889–1974)

Walter Lippmann was one of the foremost political journalists and political philosophers of the 20th century. From the Progressive era through the early decades of the Cold War, Lippmann's writings on multiple topics influenced the American public and policymakers.

Born in New York in 1889, Walter Lippmann began his prolific career almost immediately after graduating from Harvard. He began publishing discourses on a myriad of topics, starting with *Preface to Politics,* published in 1913. The book asserted that one of the hallmarks of a successful politician was the ability to tap into the needs and wants of his constituency. Lippmann cited Theodore Roosevelt as an excellent example of a policymaker who knew how to capitalize on emotions and gather public support for a cause. Shortly after the book's publication, Lippmann was influential in founding the liberal magazine *The New Republic.*

World War I had considerable impact in shaping Lippmann's thinking. Observing events, he became convinced that domestic and international policies were inextricably linked. His writings on current events and their historical connotations drew the attention of major politicians. Because of his astute political observations, Lippmann was recruited to help President Woodrow Wilson craft the cornerstone of his foreign policy, the Fourteen Points. After helping formulate the plans for making the world safe for democracy, Lippmann was invited to attend the treaty making process in Paris.

During the 1920s, Lippmann continued to develop as a theorist and a journalist. One of his next works was the widely read and respected *Public Opinion,* which examined the role of citizens in a democracy and the media's part in shaping the thoughts and ideas of the public. Lippmann's other major works include *An Inquiry Into the Principles of the Good Society* and *Essays in the Public Philosophy.* Late in the decade, as the Great Depression struck, Lippmann's writings became even more relevant to the American public. He eventually would vocally criticize the collectivism of Franklin Roosevelt's New Deal although he had been an early supporter of the programs. Early on, he voiced the fear that Roosevelt did not have the ability to effectively lead. Also during the 1930s Lippmann began his most famous work, *Today and Tomorrow.* Appearing in 1931, this column appeared in over 200 newspapers for over four decades. It won him a devoted audience, who greatly respected Lippmann's views on the state of America, foreign affairs, fashions, and trends.

Lippmann's writings differed from other journalists in that he engaged heavily in political philosophy, discussing the ethical and moral ramifications of government. Lippmann attempted to combine journalism with the history of ideas and the problem of dealing with current events, thus, he not only reported current events, he analyzed them. To Lippmann, the role of columnists became important because as domestic and foreign affairs became more complex, local papers simply did not have the staffs to keep up with the scope of affairs. Lippmann continued his career, earning two Pulitzer prizes, and influencing political thought and theory for several decades. He was particularly noted for his outspoken views on Lyndon Johnson's handling of the Vietnam War and Great Society during the 1960s.

Nicole Anslover

See also: Roosevelt, Franklin.

References and Further Reading

Blum, Steven D. 1984. *Walter Lippmann, Cosmopolitanism in the Century of Total War.* Ithaca, NY: Cornell University Press.

Kennedy, David M. 1999. *Freedom from Fear: The American People in Depression and War, 1929–1945.* New York: Oxford University Press.

Steel, Ronald. 1980. *Walter Lippmann and the American Century.* Boston: Little, Brown and Co.

Little Caesar (1930)

Little Caesar was released in 1930 by Warner Brothers and, along with *Public Enemy* (1931) and *Scarface* (1932), defined the gangster film genre. All were perceived as glorifying criminal behavior during an era where prohibition and the Depression seemed to spawn such criminal figures as John Dillinger and Bonnie and Clyde. In response to films such as *Little Caesar,* which were accused of promoting disrespect for law and authority, the Catholic Legion of Decency and the Motion Picture Production Code were employed to combat the depiction of the gangster as a folk hero.

The script for *Little Caesar* was based upon a novel by W. R. Burnett, who also received screenwriting credit, and public fascination with the life and career of Chicago crime boss Al Capone. The film was directed by veteran filmmaker Mervyn LeRoy and starred Edward G. Robinson in the title role of Caesar Enrico "Rico" Bandello. Rico and his best friend Joe Massara (Douglas Fairbanks, Jr.) move to Chicago seeking fame and fortune during the Depression era. While Rico begins to advance within the life of organized crime, Joe pursues his dream of becoming a dancer and falls in love with his dance partner, Olga Strassoff (Glenda Farrell). Rico insists that Joe join his gang, but Joe refuses, and at the insistence of Olga, turns Rico over to the authorities. Rico attempts to kill Joe for this betrayal, but his feeling for his friend proves too strong. Rico is gunned down by the police in a shootout, muttering his famous final line, "Mother of mercy, is this the end of Rico?"

Ostensibly, the film promoted the concept that crime does not pay as Rico died in the film's conclusion. *Little Caesar* included a disclaimer to this effect, as did *Public Enemy* and *Scarface.* Nevertheless, the forces of public order feared that unlike the crime pictures of the 1920s, which focused primarily upon detectives and victims of crime, *Little Caesar* would foster a national crime wave. The film's popularity certainly encouraged a number of imitations as over 50 gangster films were made in 1932. Afraid of government censorship, the industry began to enforce the production code values which asserted crime must not be explicitly presented and that criminal activity must never be depicted in a sympathetic fashion. By the mid-1930s gangster heroes such as Robinson and James Cagney of *Public Enemy* were back on the screen, but this time working on the side of the law.

Although unsympathetic to censorship, many film scholars acknowledge the appeal of the gangster hero such as Rico. In the final analysis, Rico dies in a hail of bullets, but for much of the film he is surrounded by beautiful women, wears nice clothes, drives powerful cars, and eats in fancy restaurants; activities denied to most Americans during the early years of the Depression. In his classic essay on the gangster film, Robert Warshow argues that the gangster is a "tragic hero" because of his drive to become a self-made man. With traditional means of advancement blocked because of the Depression or, in the case of Rico, because of discrimination against the new immigration from southern and eastern Europe, the gangster must resort to illegal activities such as providing alcohol during prohibition. In this inversion of the American dream, capitalism is subverted by the individualistic gangster who eventually pays with his life. Rico becomes a somewhat sympathetic character who maintains his allegiance to his best friend and seemingly had no other way to advance in a corrupt society.

This sense of ambiguity continues to resonate with audiences, and efforts at censorship have been unable to muzzle the appeal of the gangster genre and hero defined in 1930 by Edward G. Robinson in Mervyn LeRoy's *Little Caesar*.

Ron Briley

References and Further Reading

Mundy, Jonathan. 1999. *Public Enemies, Public Heroes: Screening the Gangster from Little Caesar to Touch of Evil*. Chicago: University of Chicago Press.

Schatz, Thomas. 1981. *Hollywood Genres*. Philadelphia: Temple University Press.

Shadoian, Jack. 1977. *Dreams and Dead Ends: The American Gangster/Crime Film*. New York: Oxford University Press.

Warshow, Robert. 1979. *The Immediate Experience: Movies, Comics, Theatre & Other Aspects of Popular Culture*. New York: Antheneum.

The Lone Ranger

The Lone Ranger was a popular radio show, which, beginning in 1933, aired nearly 3,000 episodes. George W. Trendle, a lawyer and the person responsible for much of the writing for the radio show, originally pitched his Wild West hero as part Zorro and part Robin Hood. Fran Striker also helped develop the concept and its spin-off, The Green Hornet, featuring the Lone Ranger's nephew. The show attracted an audience of at least 50,000 listeners within six months of first airing.

Its eponymous hero was a Texas Ranger, identified only by the last name Reid, who alone survived an ambush by Butch Cavendish and his "Hole in the Wall Gang." With Tonto, identified as a Potawatomi Native American, at his side, the Lone Ranger apprehended outlaws much like other superheroes, with cunning and, of course, his secret weapon; a gun which shot a silver bullet. He'd always leave the scene, allowing the local law enforcement to sort the bad guys out. Other conventions of the show were catch-phrased as only radio, a verbal medium, could accomplish. The Lone Ranger made his horse, "a fiery horse the speed of light," moved not by a jab with a spur, but a "Hi-yo, Silver, away!" Imaginary onlookers of the final scene would ask, "Who was that masked man?" only to be answered by someone "that was the Lone Ranger." Tonto's handle for the Lone Ranger also fixed itself in the American idiom, addressing his friend as "Kemo Sabe," which means "Faithful Friend" or "Trusted Scout." Although many actors played the Lone Ranger, only John Todd played Tonto; and, whether Tonto was originally a childhood friend of Reid before he became the Lone Ranger, or happened upon him at the massacre, or was saved by the Reid after he became the Lone Ranger is up to some dispute. What may have been most attractive feature about the Lone Ranger was his unwavering character. Frank Striker wrote the character's code down and shared it with all the actors who played the hero, with both Clayton Moore and Jay Silverheels taking it to heart as young radio listeners looked up to them. The creed included that all men are created equal and that at some point all must be accountable for what they have taken from the world.

The Lone Ranger was also a comic strip, distributed by King Features Syndicate for nearly 30 years, and generated two movie serials produced by Republic Pictures during the Depression era. Later, in the 1950s, the Lone Ranger regained popularity as a television program.

Mark Schwartz

See also: Flash Gordon; Mix, Tom; Radio

References and Further Reading

Bisco, Jim. 2005. "Buffalo's Lone Ranger: The Prolific Fran Striker Wrote the Book on Early Radio." *Western New York Heritage* 7 (4).

Campbell, Roberts. 1976. *The Golden Years of Broadcast.* New York: Scribner's.

Douglas, George H. 1987. *The Early Days of Radio Broadcasting.* New York: McFarland.

Dunning, John. 1998. *On the Air: The Encyclopedia of Old-Time Radio.* New York: Oxford University Press.

Nachman, Gerald. 1998. *Raised on the Radio.* New York: Pantheon Books.

Luce, Henry Robinson (1898–1967)

Henry Robinson Luce was probably the most influential magazine publisher in the United States during the first half of the 20th century. He introduced and perfected the first weekly newsmagazine, *Time,* and the first magazine devoted to photojournalism, *Life.*

Luce was born on April 3, 1898, in Dengzhou (present-day Penglai), on the coast of the Shandong promontory in northeast China. He was the eldest of four children of a Presbyterian missionary, Henry Winters Luce, and a Young Women's Christian Association worker, Elizabeth Middleton Root. Aside from 15 months in the United States when the Reverend Luce had a furlough in 1906 and 1907, the boy grew up in China. As a student at a British school, however, he had little familiarity with the Chinese people. In 1912, young Luce traveled alone to England for a year at an English school, where he was treated for his stammer. He then entered the Hotchkiss School in Lakeville, Connecticut, helped by a wealthy family friend, Mrs. Cyrus H. McCormick, of Chicago. At Hotchkiss, he felt an outsider among boys from families of means but found a friend in Briton Hadden, and they both entered Yale University in 1916 and worked on the *Yale Daily News.* After a summer in an army training camp, Luce finished his degree at Yale in 1920 and, thanks to McCormick, spent a year at Oxford.

While reporters on the *Baltimore News,* Luce and Hadden began to plan a new kind of weekly magazine, to be called *Time,* which would give the most important news in a concise and interesting style, covering both sides analytically while telling the reader which side *Time* considered had the better case. The venture's stock was bought by a number of wealthy friends, though Luce and Hadden retained financial control. The first issue, with Hadden as editor and Luce as business manager, was dated March 3, 1923. By 1930, *Time* had a circulation of 300,000. It favored a progressive sort of Republicanism, and early on it had adopted the style that came to be called "Timese;" using distinctive language, sometimes reversing sentence order, and introducing novel words and unusual items of information. Objective reporting was not required of *Time's* writers, who originally were anonymous. The publishers, incorporated as Time Inc., bought the *Saturday Review of Literature* and started an advertising trade journal, *Tide,* both of which were later sold. After Hadden died of septicemia in February 1929, Luce assumed control of the editorial and business sides of the firm. He brought in as managing editor Hadden's cousin John S. Martin, who carried on Hadden's policies and stylistic color. Luce founded still another magazine in 1930, *Fortune,* a monthly focusing on business, notable for its staff of well-known writers, its comprehensive articles, and its high price. During the 1930s, Luce entered the newsreel and radio world with *The March of Time,* presenting the salient events of the week in *Time* style. That events were sometimes dramatized by actors, drawing criticism from some journalistic purists. In any event, neither the radio program nor the newsreel survived beyond the late 1940s. In November 1935, having divorced his first wife, Luce married Clare Boothe, an editor and later a well-known playwright. While Clare Boothe Luce had no appointive position, she undoubtedly influenced her husband's publications and is said to have inspired his creation of *Life* magazine a year later. Certainly it was Luce's interest in the image and his awareness of the technical advances in photography and printing that led him to plan another pioneer periodical, whose title he bought from a long-lived humor magazine. In November 1936, the first issue of *Life* appeared. Its editorial method, using pictures as *Time* used words, was an instantaneous success. In a month, circulation passed ½ million and a year later, approached 2 million. *Life* became the principal vehicle for Luce's editorial statements as he began to concern himself with public issues.

Though Luce had been impressed by "strong men" like Benito Mussolini and Francisco Franco—though not Franklin D. Roosevelt, whose hostility to big business made him uneasy—he saw Adolf Hitler as a serious danger to the United States and Europe and supported aid to Great Britain and intervention in World War II. In China, which he and his wife visited in 1941, he saw Gen. Chiang Kai-shek as a paragon of leaders, despite the military gains of the Chinese communist forces. After the success of the revolution, he opposed recognition of the government of Mao Zedong and, through his editorial pronouncements and connections, may have influenced American policy for decades. In the 1940 presidential election, Luce favored Wendell Willkie's candidacy as the most reliably interventionist possibility among Republican hopefuls. He and Clare had a hand in Willkie's campaign speeches, and the Time Inc. publications were at the service of the campaign. Willkie's defeat, it is said, ended Luce's hope of becoming secretary of state. Once the United States entered World War II, Luce fell in with Roosevelt's leadership. In early 1941, Luce published an editorial essay in *Life* entitled "The American Century," claiming that the United States would now take Great Britain's place as the leader among nations. It provoked much controversy. Socialist leader Norman Thomas attacked Luce's "nakedness of imperial ambition," though Dorothy Thompson found merit in it. Even during the war, Luce began to see the Soviet Union as an eventual impediment to America's leadership. He was pleased with President Harry Truman's postwar challenges to Moscow, though his hope of encouraging military aid to Chiang Kai-shek came to nothing. *Life* and *Time* supported Dwight D. Eisenhower's campaign with enthusiastic coverage, though Luce found his foreign policy as president too moderate. Luce was obsessed with the competition to best the Soviet Union in space exploration. When Eisenhower appointed Clare ambassador to Italy, Henry spent most of the years 1953 to 1957 with her in Rome, commuting as necessary to New York. He pressed President John F. Kennedy to take a more forceful stand toward Communist Cuba, and he urged aggressive involvement in Vietnam. While the international views Luce voiced in his publications encountered ongoing criticism from liberals, they were probably approved by most of his upper-middle-class readers.

After Luce became editorial chairman of Time Inc. in 1964, he and his wife lived mostly at a winter home in Phoenix, Arizona. During the remaining three years of his life, they continued to travel, and Luce took up the study of religion and supported a movement to achieve world peace through law. He died on February 28, 1967.

References and Further Reading

Baughman, James L. 1987. *Henry R. Luce and the Rise of the American News Media.* Boston: Twayne Publishers.

Herzstein, Robert E. 2005. *Henry R. Luce, Time, and the American Crusade in Asia.* New York: Cambridge University Press.

Herzstein, Robert E. 1994. *Henry R. Luce: A Political Portrait of the Man Who Created the American Century.* New York: C. Scribner's Sons.

Kobler, John. 1968. *Luce: His Time, Life, and Fortune.* Garden City, NY: Doubleday.

Jespersen, Christopher. 1996. *American Images of China, 1931–1949.* Stanford, CA: Stanford University Press, 1996.

Martin, Ralph G. 1991. *Henry and Clare: An Intimate Portrait of the Luces.* New York: Putnam's Sons.

Mix, Tom (1880–1940)

Tom Mix's film career as a Western hero spanned from 1910 to 1935, during which he made over 300 pictures. In the 1920s, Mix was making over $17,000 per week in Hollywood, establishing the image of the honest and noble cowboy hero upon which Roy Rogers and Gene Autry would build in the 1930s and 1940s. Mix made fewer films during the Depression era, as he returned to his love of performing riding tricks before live audiences. The Western image fashioned by Mix continued to influence filmmakers well after his death in a 1940 automobile accident.

Mix was born Thomas Hezikiah Mix on January 6, 1880, in Mix Run, Pennsylvania. When he was eight years old, his father moved the family to DuBois, Pennsylvania, where he served as a stableman. Mix followed in the footsteps of his father, working with horses after dropping out of school following the fourth grade.

When he was 18, Mix enlisted in the army. Although the horseman claimed to have served with Theodore Roosevelt at the Battle of San Juan Hill during the Spanish-American War, Mix never saw combat or left the United States during the conflict. Mix's stories regarding exploits in the Boxer Rebellion and Boer War proved equally apocryphal, but he did form a friendship with legendary lawman Wyatt Earp. After reenlisting in 1901, Mix got into difficulty with the military the following year when he failed to return from a furlough during which he married school teacher Grace Allin. The marriage was annulled, and Mix received an honorable discharge.

Pursuing his passion for horses and the West, Mix moved to Guthrie, Oklahoma, where he worked in a variety of jobs. In 1905, Mix was employed at the Miller Brothers 101 Real Wild West Ranch near Bliss, Oklahoma. The 101 Ranch served as both a working ranch and Western entertainment experience. Mix performed in a Wild West show for the 101, gaining the attention of William Selig. In 1909, he began appearing in pictures made by the Chicago-based Selig Polyscope Company. After learning the business in features such as *Chip of the Flying U* (1914) and *The Days of the Thundering Herd* (1914), Mix was given his own series with *The Real Things in Cowboys* (1914). Mix parted with Selig over financial issues, and in 1917 he signed with William S. Fox.

Working with Fox throughout the 1920s, Mix replaced the taciturn and realistic William S. Hart as the film industry's leading Western star. In films such as *Riders of the Purple Sage* (1925) and *The Last Trail* (1927), Mix developed the image of the clean-cut and straight-shooting cowboy who always fought on the side of justice. Mix's films also included roping and riding tricks featuring his show horse, Tony. Mix took great pride in doing all of his own stunts, although he was often injured. Off the screen, Mix was better known for a flamboyant lifestyle, which included five marriages.

Apparently concerned about the transition to talking features, Mix retired from film in 1932. He was lured out of retirement in 1935, however, to appear in *The Miracle Rider* (1935), a serial for Mascot Pictures. During the 1930s, Mix was well compensated for his performances on the circus circuit. From 1929 to 1931, his appearances with the Sells-Floto Circus reportedly earned $20,000 per week. In 1934, Mix purchased an interest in the Samuel B. Gill Circus, and the cowboy star toured in his own show. He also sold his name to the popular 1930s Tom Mix radio show. On October 12, 1940, Mix was killed when the automobile he was driving overturned near Florence, Arizona.

Ron Briley

See also: Autry, Gene; Hillbilly Music; Rogers, Roy.

References and Further Reading

Jensen, Richard D. 2005. *The Amazing Tom Mix: The Most Famous Cowboy of the Movies*. Lincoln, NE: iUniverse.

Mix, Olive Stokes, and Eric Heath. 1957. *The Fabulous Tom Mix*. Englewood Cliffs, NJ: Prentice-Hall.

Mix, Paul E. 1972. *The Life and Legend of Tom Mix.* New York: A. S. Barnes.

Mr. Smith Goes to Washington

Mr. Smith Goes to Washington is one of the most celebrated movies of all times: the film was nominated for 11 Academy Awards in 1939, a year critics still call "the greatest year in film history," when it competed with other historically important and wildly popular films such as *The Wizard of Oz, The Hunchback of Notre Dame,* and *Gone with the Wind.* It is estimated to be director Frank Capra's most watched film after *It's A Wonderful Life.*

The plot is rather simple, yet the film never drags as the suspense climbs over a runtime of more than two hours. A stooge governor needs to appoint a replacement for one of his unnamed state's positions in the U.S. Senate. The state's media mogul and robber baron named Jim Taylor, played by character actor Edward Arnold, instructors the governor, deep in his pocket, to pick another "yes" man. The governor, influenced by his children and a chance encounter with a newspaper article, selects Jefferson Smith, played brilliantly and bumbling by James Stewart, the head of the Boy Rangers and editor of their magazine. Smith's folksy reputation, idealistic outlook, and willingness to please should make him easy to control, or so thinks the governor, Mr. Taylor, and the senior senator of the state, Joseph Paine, played by seasoned actor Claude Rains, who happens to be a long ago friend of Smith's father, an idealistic and murdered journalist.

Though under the wing of Senator Paine, Smith becomes the laughing stock of Washington, D.C., after he press covering the Senate paint him as a bumpkin, having no business in Washington, which Smith admits is true when he confronts the members of the press, including Diz Moore, played by veteran actor Thomas Mitchell. To keep Smith out of trouble and to make him feel like he does have a reason to be in Washington, Paine suggests Smith propose a bill for a national camp for boys.

Smith seeks the help of his jaded secretary Clarissa Saunders, played by Jean Arthur, to write his boys camp bill. Saunders soon realizes that Smith's proposed camp is on the very site that "political boss" Taylor and his "machine" want to build a dam. Saunders knows that this dam is "graft" in a bill that Paine has been trying to pass.

The corruption of Washington hits Smith hard, and Smith refuses to sell out to Taylor, even after Paine lectures Smith that this is the way things work in Washington. Smith's rejection of Taylor prompts Taylor to create false evidence, forging papers that Smith owns the land in question for his camp. Smith, so upset by Taylor's power and Paine's complicity, makes ready to leave Washington, but Saunders steps in and inspires him to stay and fight, using his own idealistic words back at him. She launches him in a filibuster, allowing him to dominate the floor of the Senate. While Smith talks until he is hoarse, many rally around him, including the press, the page boys, and the president of the Senate. Taylor, however, controls the media in their home state and goons destroy the papers Smith's boy rangers try to deliver that cover that "Smith tells the truth."

What would seem to be a crushing blow to Smith is the bins of letters written by the people of his state telling him to give up the floor of the Senate. Seeing that the filibuster is killing Smith, Saunders wants him to stop. Nevertheless, Smith stands tall, after seeing a smile from the president of the Senate. After he slumps over on the letters, as his father once did over his desk, Paine flees the floor. He attempts to shoot himself, and after he fails at that, he bursts back onto the floor, confessing to all that Smith is innocent and that it is he that should be expelled.

Mr. Smith Goes to Washington was uniformly criticized by both the press and politicians, from the moment it premiered in Washington, D.C., in October 1939. The movie-going public, however, loved it, despite it being called anti-American and unpatriotic. Americans were drawn to Frank Capra's movie and critics now cite the movie as the first "whistle blower" movie made. Out of the 11 nominations for Oscars, it won only one; Best Screenplay. Today, it appears on lists of the most pro-American movies made, perhaps due to the fact that neither the home state nor even political parties are ever named.

Mark Schwartz

References and Further Reading

Capra, Frank. 1971. *Frank Capra, The Name Above the Title: An Autobiography.* New York: Macmillan Company.

Jones, Ken D., McClure, Arthur F. and Twomey, Alfred E. 1970. *The Films of James Stewart.* New York: Castle Books.

Sennett, Ted. 1989. *Hollywood's Golden Year, 1939: A Fiftieth Anniversary Celebration.* New York: St. Martin's Press.

Edward R. Murrow (1908–65)

Born Egbert Roscoe Murrow in Guilford County, North Carolina, near Greensboro, on April 25, 1908, Murrow's career as a journalist coincided with the advent of new ways of delivering the news and he parlayed this into becoming the most respected journalist of his generation. Murrow began his career in broadcast journalism in 1930 when he helped create a program for the Columbia Broadcasting System (CBS) called *University of the Air;* he would go on to become one of the most recognizable people in television.

Though Murrow was born in North Carolina, he spent most of his early years in the state of Washington. His parents moved there in 1913, when Murrow was only five. Back in North Carolina the family had lived in spare quarters with no running water, no electricity, and no telephone, but they lived in reasonable comfort. Murrow's parents moved the family west to take advantage of the opportunity to claim land being granted to homesteaders by the federal government. As a high school student, Murrow distinguished himself as an excellent debater as well as a fine athlete; he also served as president of the student body during his senior year and even drove the school bus.

After graduating from high school in 1926, Murrow spent a year working as a logger where he was able to witness the violence that often erupted between laborers and their bosses. Murrow saw union organizers intimidated, beaten, and even lynched. Union members were also accused of being communist sympathizers; later in life, Murrow fought similar accusations leveled by Senator Joseph McCarthy against various Americans,

Edward Roscoe Murrow was an independent-minded newsman who emphasized plain speaking and straightforward reporting on a high level of integrity. In the words of the *New York Times,* "No other figure in broadcast news left such a strong stamp on both radio and television." (Library of Congress)

including Murrow himself. Murrow's campaign to rebuke and discredit McCarthy was profiled in the 2005 motion picture *Good Night, and Good Luck.*

Before exposing the demagoguery of McCarthy, Murrow had established himself as an honest and courageous war correspondent. He was sent to London by CBS in 1937, where he provided stirring reports from the front lines of the conflict that would become World War II. Many regarded Murrow's heroic reporting as a crucial part of the effort to help mobilize Americans for the long war they would eventually join. After the war Murrow returned home to host the innovative programs *See it Now* and *Person to Person* on CBS, establishing himself as a true

pioneer of the nascent television news industry.

Murrow's upbringing seemed to prepare him for his life as a journalist. His steadfast faith in the wisdom of the American people, which was hewn partly during the hard years of the Great Depression, manifested itself throughout Murrow's career. By the time of his death from lung cancer in 1965, Murrow was widely seen as the conscience of journalism and as a champion of the underdog. His unwavering allegiance to the values of the society in which he was raised— where, as he saw it, hard work and fairness should be elevated above nearly all other values—helped cement Murrow's reputation as one of the most influential Americans of the 20th century.

Dave Powell

References and Further Reading

The Museum of Broadcast Communications. *Edward R. Murrow.* Available at: http://www.museum.tv/archives/etv/M/htmlM/murrowedwar/murrowedwar.htm.

Edwards, Bob. 2004. *Edward R. Murrow and the Birth of Broadcast Journalism.* Hoboken, NJ: John W. Wiley and Sons.

Halberstam, David. 1994. *The Powers That Be.* New York: Knopf.

Murrow, Edward R. 1941. *This is London.* New York: Simon and Schuster.

O'Neill, Eugene Gladstone (1888–1953)

If Eugene Gladstone was not America's first great modern playwright, as many have claimed, certainly he was the first to achieve international stature and to claim an important influence on a later generation of writers like Tennessee Williams, Arthur Miller, and Edward Albee. Much of his work was autobiographical, drawing on the troubled and complicated relationships of his family as well as his experiences at sea.

O'Neill was born on October 16, 1888, in New York City to a theatrical family. His father, James O'Neill Sr., had worked with James A. Herne and David Belasco and spent most of the latter part of his career touring in the lead role of one of the most popular melodramas of the 19th century, *The Count of Monte Cristo*. For the first seven years of his life, O'Neill accompanied his father on the road and as a result, developed an ambivalent attitude (at times extending to outright detestation) toward the commercial theater. Rebellious and dissipated, he left Princeton University in his first year, married Kathleen Jenkins in 1909 (the union was dissolved three years later), contracted malaria while prospecting for gold in Honduras, worked as a seaman on several occasions (including a three-month stint on a Norwegian square-rigger, a hitch on a cattle boat, and service as an able seaman on freighters and luxury liners), and wrote for several newspapers. During a stay in a sanatorium in 1912 for the treatment of tuberculosis, he began writing his first plays (many of which were derivative of the styles of melodrama popularized by his father).

At Harvard University in the fall of 1914, O'Neill enrolled in the legendary "47 Workshop" playwriting course taught by Professor George Pierce Baker. A year later, with a trunk full of short plays, he went to Provincetown, Massachusetts, where with the assistance of other young playwrights like George Cram Cook and Susan Glaspell, he had his play *Bound East for Cardiff* produced in 1916 at the Wharf Theater. In the fall of that year, the Provincetown Players relocated to New York and pledged to present a program of new, experimental plays. Among the O'Neill plays produced between 1916 and 1918 were the four short plays later collected as *S. S. Glencairn (Bound East for Cardiff, In the Zone, The Long Voyage Home, The Moon of the Caribees)*. With the Pulitzer Prize-winning play *Beyond the Horizon* (1920), O'Neill, now married to Agnes Boulton, moved from the little theaters of Greenwich Village to the more commercial houses of Broadway. A remarkably fertile period ensued throughout the decade of the 1920s. *Anna Christie* (1921) won him a second Pulitzer Prize and was filmed in Hollywood in 1930 with Greta Garbo in the title role. He experimented with the techniques of European expressionism in *The Emperor Jones* (1920) and *The Hairy Ape* (1922); with the devices of the Greek theater (masks and choruses) in *The Great God Brown* (1926) and *Lazarus Laughed* (1928); and with the trappings of melodrama (like the aside, or spoken thoughts) in *Strange Interlude* (1928). The last play was produced under the auspices of the Theatre Guild, whose large subscription audience and prestige ensured it a fair measure of commercial success. *Strange Interlude* brought him to the crest of his popularity, earning him more than $250,000 and a third Pulitzer Prize. The association with the Guild lasted the rest of O'Neill's life.

In 1929, O'Neill divorced Boulton, left his two children, and married Carlotta Monterey, who ultimately survived him. Thus began a period of artistic consolidation and maturation but also of family turbulence. His subsequent plays subsumed frankly experimental techniques and traditional forms into a wholly unique and unified vision. The trilogy *Mourning Becomes Electra (Homecoming, The Hunted, The Haunted,* 1931), the nostalgic comedy of *Ah, Wilderness!* (1933), and the epic lengths of *The Iceman Cometh* (1946) and *Long Day's Journey into Night* (1956), for which he won a posthumous Pulitzer Prize, all displayed characters and themes of displaced persons, dysfunctional families, dreams as coping mechanisms for otherwise sordid lives, and an overall sense of alienation from history. O'Neill claimed to detest the "photographic" plays of his contemporaries and referred to his own method as supernaturalism, by which he meant using symbolism in a realistic way. For example, the character of Yank in *The Hairy Ape* is both a specific character and a representation of humanity in general; and the site of Harry Hope's saloon in *The Iceman Cometh* becomes, in Act Two, an evocation of the Last Supper.

Although never wholly free of the commercial lures of the theater, O'Neill nonetheless remained a stubborn individualist to the end. He always tried to cleave to the proclamation he made in 1923: "I intend...to write about anything under the sun in any manner that fits the subject. And I shall never be influenced by any consideration but one: Is it the truth as I know it—or, better still, feel it? If so, shoot, and let the splinters fly wherever they may." His perseverance won him a Nobel Prize for literature in 1936.

After a failed production by the Theatre Guild in 1947 of *A Moon for the Misbegotten* (1942–43), O'Neill wrote no new plays. He died on November 27, 1953, of Parkinson's disease after many years of seclusion and personal unhappiness. His widow, as the heir in control of the estate, sanctioned world premiers in Stockholm of two more plays, *A Touch of the Poet* (1958) and *More Stately Mansions* (1962). It was the Broadway premiere of *A Long Day's Journey into Night* (1956), however, that sparked the O'Neill revival that continues unabated around the world.

References and Further Reading

Berlin, Normand. 1982. *Eugene O'Neill.* New York: St. Martin's Press.

Bloom, Harold, ed. 2007. *Eugene O'Neill.* New York: Bloom's Literary Criticism.

Bogard, Travis. 1988. *Contour in Time: The Plays of Eugene O'Neill.* New York: Oxford University Press.

Diggins, John Patrick. 2007. *Eugene O'Neill's America: Desire Under Democracy.* Chicago: University of Chicago Press.

Houchin, John H., ed. 1993. *The Critical Response to Eugene O'Neill.* Westport, CT: Greenwood Press.

Manheim, Michael. 1998. *The Cambridge Companion to Eugene O'Neill.* New York: Cambridge University Press.

Petrillo, James C. (1892–1984)

A prominent U.S. trade unionist, James Caesar Petrillo was born on March 16, 1892, in Chicago, Illinois, the oldest son of Joseph and Evelina Petrillo, both migrants from Italy. As a boy he became interested in playing the trumpet, decided to become a full-time musician, and in 1919 started working as an organizer for the American Federation of Musicians (AFM), part of the American Federation of Labor.

Beginning in 1922, when Petrillo became the president of the local branch of the Musicians' Union, he worked to maintain employment for his members.

Many felt their jobs threatened by the better quality recording equipment being developed in the later 1920s and 1930s. Elected president of the American Federation of Musicians in 1940, he remained a major force in the union through the 1960s.

Perhaps most famously, Petrillo organized a strike that lasted from 1942 until 1944 when no union members were allowed to take part in commercial recordings. These were known as the "Petrillo Bans" and the aim was to force record companies to promise to pay royalties for records sold. Up to that point most musicians were paid for recording sessions at an hourly rate regardless if the recording became popular. Furthermore, the use of recorded music on the radios made it even more difficult for many musicians to earn money performing live. Petrillo exempted those musicians who played for radio broadcasts sponsored by the U.S. or state governments, and also anything connected with the war effort. In 1948, when Petrillo saw that television could provide companies with a legal loophole, he called another strike. The recording companies had stockpiled material to use, however, and the strike failed. Ten years later, following complaints over Petrillo's use of union funds, many musicians left the AFM and formed the Musicians Guild of America, getting the right to negotiate with the main Hollywood film studios.

Petrillo died on October 23, 1984. The Petrillo Bandshell in Grant Park, Chicago, was named after him.

Justin Corfield

See also: Federal Music Project; Swing Music.

References and Further Reading

Leiter, Robert D. 1953. *The Musicians and Petrillo* New York: Bookman Associates.

Seltzer, George. 1989. *Music Matters: The Performer and the American Federation of Musicians.* Metuchen, NJ: Scarecrow Press.

Sengstock, Charles A. 2004. *That Toddlin' Town: Chicago's White Dance Bands and Orchestras, 1900–1950.* Urbana: University of Illinois Press.

Pollock, Jackson (1912–56)

Jackson Pollock was one of the leading abstract expressionists of the post-World War II era. Though his paintings were derided by much of mainstream America, his work inspired a generation of young artists.

Pollock was born on January 28, 1912, in Cody, Wyoming. His parents, Leroy and Stella Pollock, were farmers who had moved to Wyoming from Iowa. Pollock's father worked a variety of odd jobs, and the Pollock family moved frequently while his father looked for work. Pollock spent most of his childhood in southern California and Arizona. As a teenager, Pollock attended Manual Arts High School in Los Angeles. In school, he frequently found himself in trouble. He was eventually expelled for fighting and left school without graduating. However, he had developed an enthusiasm for art in high school. After leaving Manual Arts, he moved to New York City, where two of his brothers lived. There, he took art classes with a number of important artists of the day, most significantly Thomas Hart Benton, who was to become the young man's mentor. Pollock's art of this period reflects the popular social realism of the era. His paintings from the late 1930s, such as *Threshers* and *Going West,* are highly stylized representations of working life, with a political dimension.

Living in New York, Pollock found work with a federal government arts project, part of the Depression-era Works Project Administration. He produced art for the federal government until 1943 at a salary of $95 per month, but most of the dozens of paintings he produced during this time are lost. While working as a government artist, Pollock attempted to confront his growing problem with alcoholism. Though he underwent treatment several times, he never successfully overcame his problem. His career was marred by arrests for public drunkenness. When the United States entered World War II in late 1941, Pollock was rejected by the draft board as unfit for service. He remained in New York during the war, where his painting finally began to be noticed by the art world. He found a patron in Peggy Guggenheim, an art collector and the owner of a gallery called "Art of this Century." Guggenheim organized a series of showings of Pollock's works and began paying him a salary in exchange for the rights to sell his paintings. With Guggenheim's financial assistance, Pollock was able to stop working for the first time in his life and devote himself entirely to his painting. He then enjoyed his most creative period, producing works that were presented in a series of major shows throughout the country between 1944 and 1946. During the war, Pollock married Lee Krasner, a fellow artist he had met in an art gallery in 1935.

As Pollock's work became more popular, it also became more abstract. Living in New York, he was influenced by the works of Picasso, Kandinsky, and other abstract painters. In 1945, Pollock and Krasner left New York to live and paint on a farm on Long Island. In late 1946, Pollock began experimenting with what he called the "action" style of painting, an abstract approach in which he dripped paint onto the canvas. This would become his signature style. Pollock had developed an interest in Eastern philosophy and Jungian psychology and was convinced that the drips made on the canvas were the result of a psychic energy that was unconscious, but premeditated. Some of his most important works from this era include *Lucifer, Number 5,* and *Lavender Mist.* New York critics hailed Pollock's new approach as an important step in freeing modern art from the limitations and barriers of convention, but mainstream America derided his works as childish, and Pollock became a figure of ridicule. Public criticism of his art made it difficult for Pollock to earn a living selling paintings in the early 1950s. He experimented briefly with more conventional genres of art, though he returned to his "action" paintings from time to time. The final years of his life saw him produce few new works and return to drinking and problems with the law.

He was killed in an automobile crash on August 11, 1956.

James Burns

References and Further Reading

Karmel, Pepe, ed. 1999. *Jackson Pollock: Interviews, Articles, and Reviews.* New York: Museum of Modern Art: Distributed by H. N. Abrams.

Leja, Michael. 1993. *Reframing Abstract Expressionism: Subjectivity and Painting in the 1940s.* New Haven, CT: Yale University Press.

Lewison, Jeremy. 1999. *Interpreting Pollock.* London: Tate Gallery Publishers.

Ratcliff, Carter. 1996. *The Fate of a Gesture: Jackson Pollock and Post-War American Art.* New York: Farrar, Straus, Giroux.

Solomon, Deborah. 1987. *Jackson Pollock: A Biography*. New York: Simon and Schuster.

Porgy and Bess

Based on the 1926 novel and 1927 play *Porgy* by DuBose Heyward, the 1935 opera *Porgy and Bess* was conceived by composer George Gershwin as an American folk opera. DuBose Heyward's wife, Dorothy, who also co-wrote the stage drama, and George Gershwin's brother, Ira, wrote its lyrics; DuBose also completed the opera's libretto. George Gershwin considered it to be his best work.

The story takes place in the fictitious neighborhood of Catfish Row in Charleston, South Carolina, and concerns the African American community struggling with poverty, drug use, and strained romantic relationships. Porgy is a physically disabled beggar, and Bess is under the thumb of her ignoble boyfriend, Crown. During the first act, Crown kills another man while drinking and gambling. Crown flees the scene, leaving Bess to be taken care of by Porgy. When Crown returns for Bess, Porgy kills him. Porgy flees and returns for Bess as a richer man, but Bess has run off with a drug dealer named Sportin' Life. Porgy sets off to find Bess, singing, "Oh Lawd, I'm on my way."

Every aspect of the opera was controversial from its onset. Most critics and audiences did not even consider it to be an opera, and many thought the opera was racist, depicting African Americans as violent and prone to vice. Very few criticized the music, which skillfully synthesized European classical opera with American jazz and folk music. The opera's most well known song, "Summertime," an American musical standard, has been interpreted by musicians and singers worldwide.

The world premiere occurred at the Colonial Theatre in Boston on September 30, 1935. It ran on Broadway for 124 performances. The tour began on January 27, 1936, in Philadelphia and ended in Washington, D.C., on March 21, 1936. The cast, mostly African Americans and not Caucasians in blackface, demanded that the audiences in Washington, D.C., be integrated. The integrated audience was the first in the National Theatre's history. Other casts and audiences, after becoming familiar with the opera, have forced the opera to close early or even before it opens, believing the opera reinforces negative stereotypes of African Americans. In Europe, it was well received as mostly white casts performed it in blackface. The Nazis, however, did not like the opera and closed its production in occupied Copenhagen after 22 sold-out performances.

Since the Depression, the opera has experienced several revivals in several different mediums. In 1959, a film version debuted with Sidney Poitier as Porgy after Harry Belafonte refused the part. The filmmakers dubbed over actual actors that were also singers, such as Sammy Davis, Jr. and Dorothy Dandridge, for voices that sounded more operatic. The Gershwin estate was not happy with the end product, and it has only aired on television once in 1967. It is currently unavailable to the public. In 1993, a stage production was telecast in America and Britain, and in 2006, it was rewritten as a musical (with spoken dialog) for the London stage.

Mark Schwartz

See also: Federal Music Project; Federal Theatre Project; Gershwin, George Jacob; Gershwin Israel (Ira).

References and Further Reading

Alpert, Hollis. 1990. *The Life and Times of Porgy and Bess: The Story of an American Classic.* New York: Knopf.

Capote, Truman. 1956. *The Muses Are Heard.* New York: Random House.

Fisher, Burton. 200. *D. Porgy and Bess.* Coral Gables, FL: Open Journeys Publishing.

The Public Enemy

Based on the novel *Beer and Blood* by Kubec Glasmon and John Bright, *The Public Enemy,* a blockbuster in 1931, is considered to be Hollywood's first attempt to show the societal cause of criminal behavior. To offset any criticism of the film as merely exploitive of Chicago gangland criminality, Warner Brothers ran a polemic disclaimer before the show began, explaining that the film is attempting to show "an environment that exists today," rather than "glorify" criminal behavior. James Cagney plays Tom Powers and Edward Woods plays Matt Doyle, though the two rising stars were initially cast in the opposite roles.

Both the book and the movie follow two young men as their urban environment turns even more challenging and troublesome with the onset World War I in 1917 and then Prohibition in 1919. The film emphasizes these two years by printing them in screen-high numerals before two scenes, reinforcing that both the country and the lives of our characters will be changed by the two events. With the United States entering World War I, Tom Power's older brother, Mike, enlists, which brings their mother to tears and shows the Cain and Abel alignment of the two bothers. A larger, more dramatic scene soon follows with the advent of Prohibition, perhaps not as surprising to the Depression era audience as it is to a modern audience. In the last days when buying alcohol is still legal, a consumption chaos takes over the city streets: the film pans a flower truck hauling away crates of drink and a baby displaced out of a carriage to make way for bottles of booze.

The trajectory of the two men's lives in crime set a standard for gangster movies to follow for a century: an early mentor in crime is later killed by his students, an early robbery goes terribly wrong, and an early love relationship is not ended on the best of terms. The killing of the first mentor takes place off the screen, a pan from him playing the piano as if begging for his life, his song punctuated only by the sound gunshot. The first bungling at grand theft is absurd as Cagney, acting out of character as nervous, shoots at a stuffed bear (which should have been replaced by a mannequin) at a fur warehouse. Finally, Cagney's first love gets it in the kisser with a grapefruit as his way of ending a lovers' spat: this shocking scene, by that era's standard, is said to be responsible for violence towards women in movies for years to come.

As most gangster films and morality plays end, so does *The Public Enemy.* While Warner Brothers claimed this film's characters were fictional, much has been made of its storyline being taken from the lives of actual criminals of its day. Real life gangster Earl Weiss shoved an omelet into his girlfriend's face, Louis Alterie killed a horse out of revenge for what the horse did (rather than its rider), while several famous gangsters, as lone gunmen, have taken on a room full of rivals with expectations of leaving unharmed. Even to a modern audience, this film, launching Cagney into stardom, has stood the test of time, though the character Cagney played, like most celluloid criminals, did not survive.

Mark Schwartz

See also: Bogart, Humphrey; Scarface: The Shame of the Nation.

References and Further Reading

Dickens, Homer. 1989. *The Complete Films of James Cagney.* New York: Citadel Press.

Rafter, Nicole. 2000. *Shots in the Mirror.* New York: Oxford University Press.

Sklar, Robert. 1994. *City Boys.* Princeton, NJ: Princeton University Press.

Radio

The 1930s began the second half of the Golden Age of Radio. Although the heady days of the late 1920s, with its rampant speculation on the stock of the Radio Corporation of America (RCA), often referred to simply as "radio," were over, radio became an even more important element of people's lives. After the stock market crash of 1929, people going on relief would often beg and plead to be permitted to retain their radios. To many, a radio was thus no longer a luxury, but a necessity.

By 1929, most of the key inventions that made broadcast radio possible were in place. Although a few hobbyists were still using crystal detectors (a primitive transistor using a point-contact on a germanium crystal, tricky in the absence of understanding of semiconductor theory), most consumer radios were based upon vacuum tubes. The superheterodyne circuit made tuning easier

and more stable, and regenerative amplification made possible loudspeakers that would allow an entire roomful of listeners to enjoy a radio at once. Transmitters were moving increasingly away from Alexanderson alternators to giant triode vacuum tubes.

In fact, the only major technological breakthrough in the 1930s was the development of frequency modulation, or FM, by Edwin Howard Armstrong. RCA head David Sarnoff had asked Armstrong to develop a static-free radio, expecting some kind of an add-on filter, not an entirely new form of transmission. Although virtually free of static, FM would have instantly made obsolete the entire installed user base of radios. As a result, Sarnoff did not implement FM, leading to a tragic and bitter fight that ended only with Armstrong's death.

For most people, the technical aspects of radio development were of little interest. Far more important was its role as an entertainment medium. In the 1930s, radio offerings were not limited to news, sports, and music, nor were playlists organized around morning and evening drive times. Radio had not yet become primarily a background medium, to be enjoyed as one was doing something else.

One of the most popular radio shows was *Amos n' Andy.* The eponymous protagonists were two African American men who had joined the Great Migration from the rural South and settled in Chicago. Their struggles to come to grips with urban culture served as the basis of the show's humor. Because the actual actors were white men, and because the show played upon stereotypes of African Americans, many people found it offensive, and some even petitioned to have it removed from the airwaves. However, *Amos n' Andy* was so popular

Men break the windows of an automobile to produce a crashing sound for a radio broadcast at the NBC sound effects studio, Chicago, December 1930. (Library of Congress)

that it continued to air throughout the radio era, and even briefly translated into television.

However, not all radio shows were comedies. There were adventure shows such as *The Lone Ranger* and *The Shadow,* as well as radio adaptations of various theatrical plays. As a result of the development of radio networks, which transmitted radio feeds via telephone wires and rebroadcast them on stations across the nation, the radio created a national culture. One could go anywhere across the country and have a reference to such programming understood.

Radio also became one of the principal channels for the dissemination of political ideas. One of the first people to see the potential of radio for transmitting a partisan political message was a Catholic

priest, Father Charles Coughlin. When he arrived as pastor of the Church of the Little Flower in the Detroit suburb of Royal Oak, Michigan in 1926, he met with the hostility of the local Ku Klux Klan klavern. Not to be swayed by bullies, he composed a series of fiery sermons about religious freedom. However, he also knew that if he merely delivered them as homilies in his Masses, they would not reach the ears of those who needed them most. As a result, he approached a local radio station and was given an airtime slot, allowing him to reach the entire community.

His style was so successful that his radio program soon became a regular feature. He expanded his horizons beyond mere anti-Catholicism to tackling all the problems he saw besetting the ordinary people of his parish. He condemned rapacious corporations, particularly after the Depression brought poverty to many working people, and at first was friendly to President Franklin D. Roosevelt's New Deal. However, as the years went by, his rhetoric took on a darker cast, incorporating anti-Semitic themes and catchphrases and even attacking President Roosevelt. Only after the United States entered World War II did the local bishop finally order him to cease speaking publicly on political subjects, effectively silencing him.

President Roosevelt also was quick to grasp the power of radio. In his series of Fireside Chats he created a sense of intimacy with his listeners that would have been impossible with traditional political rhetoric. Instead of being the remote politician shouting from a podium, he made listeners feel as though he were sitting right there with them, having a conversation. In the dark days of the Depression, that ability was critical in rebuilding the confidence of ordinary Americans in their government and its ability to cope with the economic crisis.

Leigh Kimmel

See also: Roosevelt, Franklin; War of the Worlds.

References and Further Reading

De Forest, Lee. 1950. *Father of Radio: The Autobiography of Lee De Forest.* Chicago: Wilcox and Follett Co.

Leinwoll, Stanley.1979. *From Spark to Satellite: A History of Radio Communication.* New York: Charles Scribner's Sons.

Lewis, Tom. 1991. *Empire of the Air: The Men Who Made Radio.* New York: Edward Burlingame.

Lyons, Eugene. 1966. *David Sarnoff.* New York: Harper and Row.

Royal, Brian. 2005. "Radio: The Life Story of a Technology." *Greenwood Technographies.* Westport, CT: Greenwood Press.

Sobel, Robert. 1986. *RCA.* New York: Stein and Day.

Rivera, Diego (1886–1957)

Diego Rivera was one of the most influential artists of the 20th century, incorporating trends such as symbolism, cubism, social realism, and surrealism with the pre-Columbian and indigenous heritage of his native Mexico.

Born in Guanajuato to a family with liberal traditions, Rivera began formal art studies at age 11 at the Academy of Bellas Artes. When he was 21, Rivera traveled to Europe, where he spent the next 14 years studying the masters in Spain, France, Belgium, Italy, and England, and painting with many renowned artists. During this rich time immersed in European art history, Rivera was influenced by classical, impressionist and cubist movements. Symmetry, proportion, use of the human figure, and the practice of drawing before painting were all features Rivera used from his classical background.

Homesick, Rivera returned to Mexico in 1921, where he was commissioned to paint murals, giving him the opportunity to paint on a much wider scope, conveying complex historical themes. Rivera was a populist who took a deep interest in working people, joined the Mexican Communist Party, and visited Russia. Throughout his life, Rivera described himself as a Marxist, but he had conflicts with the Mexican Communist Party, which expelled him in 1929. Critics refer to Rivera's work as expressing a conversation between art and revolution.

Rivera's work began to be recognized in the United States. In 1929, the American Institute of Architects awarded a medal to Rivera, in recognition of his role in reviving the fresco, a mural painted directly onto wet plaster, which united art and architecture. Rivera's first one-man exhibition in the United States was held in San Francisco in 1930. Following this, Rivera painted frescoes at the San Francisco Stock Exchange and at the California School of Fine Arts in 1931. In December of 1931, the recently opened Museum of Modern Art in New York honored Rivera with a retrospective of paintings in many different media. When he traveled to New York to prepare for the show, Rivera spent a little over a month rapidly painting seven new movable frescoes to add to the exhibit. In 1932, the Detroit Institute of Arts awarded Rivera a commission to paint frescoes in a garden court on the general theme of Detroit industry. Edsel Ford, of the automotive family, funded this project. In preparation, Rivera visited many factories in Detroit, observing the manufacturing processes for automobiles, weapons, pharmaceuticals, and chemicals. In the 27 frescoes, Rivera expressed many of his favorite themes: the nobility and diversity of the working class, a fascination with the internal workings of machines, a synthesis of realism and symbolism, and the role of technology and scientific research in bettering mankind. The recognizable faces in the frescoes included Louis Pasteur, Henry Ford, and Thomas Edison.

Some observed an irony in the contrast between Rivera's wealthy patrons and his left-wing sympathies. Unemployed and underemployed Mexican workers came to the Detroit Institute of Arts to watch Rivera. Mexican workers were often the first to be laid off during the Great Depression, and the United States government pressured them to return to Mexico. In Detroit, Rivera formed the League of Peasants and Workers to protect the rights of Mexican nationals, whether they wished to stay in the United States or return to Mexico. The Detroit frescoes quickly drew complaints from some political and religious leaders who felt the content was revolutionary. Museum authorities worked with labor leaders and religious groups to launch a vigorous public relations campaign in favor of Rivera's work. Record crowds visited the Detroit Institute of Arts and popular support grew. Edsel Ford helped to turn the tide in favor of the frescoes by publicly defending them.

In March of 1933, Rivera traveled to New York, where he had been commissioned to compose murals in the lobby of the RCA building at Rockefeller Center. The overall theme was new frontiers. Work proceeded smoothly until Rivera painted Lenin's face into the mural. Rockefeller requested that an anonymous face be painted over Lenin's, to avoid the potential of offending the many visitors to Rockefeller Center. Rivera refused, and he was removed from the project, although he was paid in full. The murals were covered, and a year later they were destroyed. After Rivera was removed from the Rockefeller project, a previously agreed commission in Chicago was canceled. Rivera recreated the destroyed murals at the New Workers' School in New York City, using movable walls. He painted another version of the Rockefeller murals at the Palace of Fine Arts in Mexico. Rivera continued as a left-wing sympathizer and he convinced the Mexican government to offer political asylum to Leon Trotsky. When Trotsky and his wife arrived in Mexico in 1937, they stayed with Rivera and his wife, painter Frida Kahlo.

From 1935 to 1943, Rivera received no commissions from the Mexican government. However, he had ample commissions for sketches, oils and water colors from other patrons. Admirers gave many examples of Rivera's work to the San Francisco Museum of Art. In 1939, the museum hosted a Rivera exhibition. The same year, Rivera was invited to paint movable frescoes in honor of the Golden Gate International Exposition, on the theme of the cultural union of North and South America. This was Rivera's last work in the United States. He spent most of his remaining years painting in Mexico, for both government and private commissions. In 1955, he traveled to Poland and Russia to paint, and in Moscow he was treated for cancer. In 1957, he died of heart failure at his studio in Mexico.

In connection with the Great Depression and the New Deal, Diego Rivera was best known for his left-wing political views, for his exalted depiction of working people, and for his murals, which influenced public art in the United States, through the Works Progress Administration Federal Art Project.

Merrill Evans

See also: Federal Art Project.

References and Further Reading

Anonymous. 1999. "The Arts: Diego Rivera, Art and Revolution; Cleveland Museum of Art Premieres Retrospective." *Hispanic Outlook in Higher Education* 9 (20): 6.

Craft, Catherine. 1999. "Review: Diego Rivera, Houston and Mexico City." *Burlington Magazine* 141: 776–77.

McMeekin, Dorothy. 1985. *Diego Rivera: Science and Creativity in the Detroit Murals.* East Lansing: Michigan State University Press.

Valdés, Dennis Nodín. 1988. "Mexican Revolutionary Nationalism and Repatriation during the Great Depression." *Mexican Studies* 4: 1–23.

Wolfe, Bertram D. 1963. *The Fabulous Life of Diego Rivera.* New York: Stein and Day.

Rockwell, Norman (1894–1978)

The work of illustrator and commercial artist Norman Rockwell is as notable for its enduring popular success as for the critical hostility it has traditionally drawn from the fine art world. From the 1920s through 1950s Rockwell's gently humorous depictions of everyday Americans reached an audience of millions via *The Saturday Evening Post.* Though his magazine covers and illustrations occasionally offered somber reflections on serious issues, Rockwell is broadly, and often dismissively associated with sentimental, middle-class Americana. However, want of critical respect in no way inhibited his illustrations from becoming deeply ingrained in the visual vocabulary of the United States.

Inspired by illustrators like A. C. Wyeth, Howard Pyle, and Arthur Rackham, Rockwell began drawing at a young age. He studied at New York's Chase School of Art, the National Academy of Art, and the Art Student's League, and became a regular contributing illustrator for *Boy's Life,* the magazine of the Boy Scouts of America, in late 1912. By 1916 Rockwell had assumed the role of art director for the magazine, illustrated books for its editor Edward Cane, and begun a lucrative sideline in commercial and free-lance illustration.

As a non-athletic young man who had grown up in urban and suburban New York, Rockwell relied heavily on research and live models to illustrate outdoors activities with a precision of detail that became a hallmark of his style. His use throughout his career of family, friends, and neighbors as models gave the characters in his illustrations an endearing, non-idealized individuality American readers found especially appealing.

In 1916, Rockwell received his first commission for a cover from the magazine with which his career would become indelibly linked, *The Saturday Evening Post.* For covers like *Boy with Baby Carriage* (May 20, 1916), *Redhead Loves Hatty Perkins* (September 16, 1916), *Schoolitis* (October 5, 1916), and many to follow, Rockwell drew from familiar territory; the trials and antics of youth.

As he tried his hand at other subjects, including occasional period subjects reminiscent of Pyle, Rockwell's signature themes began to emerge: the quirks and foibles of everyday Americans; the nobility of home and community; awkward coming of age experiences; and humorous vignettes of cultural change such as the emergence of automobile culture. Small town America would also assume an increasingly prominent role after 1939, when Rockwell moved to Arlington, Vermont. In addition to his work for the *Post,* he continued accepting commercial work for companies ranging from Massachusetts Mutual Life Insurance to Coca-Cola, and provided illustrations for Heritage Press editions of *Tom Sawyer* and *Huckleberry Finn* in 1935, and *Little Women* in 1938.

Despite his early and escalating success, Rockwell experienced a period of profound artistic frustration in the 1920s he would never entirely shake. He traveled to Europe in hopes of learning a modern style the fine arts world might better respect, only to have his efforts rejected by *Post* editor George Horace Lorimer. Though Rockwell came to accept and cultivate his natural strengths as a representational artist, and though he never failed to appreciate the mass audience available to him through the *Post,* the sometimes vicious critical rejection continued to depress him.

While Rockwell enjoyed a degree of creative latitude, as an artist on commission he chiefly produced material that would sell, which during the Depression was predominantly light-hearted. In a 1971 interview for the *New York Times Magazine* (Reeves 1971, 42), Rockwell acknowledged that Lorimer also instructed him to not portray black people except in roles of servitude. Well into the following decades, Rockwell's subjects remained almost exclusively white and middle class. However, the dominant social concern of the 1930s, economic crisis, did crop up in the details of otherwise innocuous images, such as *Ticket Agent* (April 24, 1937), depicting a comically bored ticket clerk surrounded by advertisements for holiday destinations Americans could no longer afford to visit.

During World War II, Rockwell produced several of his most familiar and emblematic works, including the unabashedly patriotic *Rosie the Riveter.* With the American flag behind her, the muscular, red-headed Rosie—modeled after a figure by Michelangelo—eats a sandwich, her rivet hammer and lunch box on her lap and a halo behind her head, while one foot crushes a copy of

Adolf Hitler's *Mein Kampf.* In 1943, inspired by President Roosevelt's address to Congress, Rockwell painted a series of covers known as *The Four Freedoms: Freedom of Speech, Freedom to Worship, Freedom from Fear,* and *Freedom from Want,* the last an often-referenced and parodied image of Thanksgiving dinner. The images proved so popular, the *Saturday Evening Post* and the U.S. Treasury Department toured the original paintings for a savings bond drive. Other Rockwell images of the war era evoked warm but quiet somberness, such as *Homecoming GI* (May 26, 1945), depicting in de-saturated tones a soldier dwarfed by a modest home, standing subtly but significantly apart from his family.

As photographic covers came into favor, the *Post* offered Rockwell fewer assignments, mostly portraits. After 47 years and more than 300 covers, he and the magazine finally parted company in 1963. The most significant works of Rockwell's later career would be produced for *Look* magazine, notably *The Problem We All Live With* (1964), commenting on violence directed at children during the integration of schools, and *Southern Justice: Murder in Mississippi* (1965), memorializing the deaths of three civil rights workers. On the whole, however, Rockwell struggled to produce images in step with the era of Vietnam and Nixon. Though he remained active into the 1970s, the peak of his career was firmly behind him. He died at his home in Stockbridge, Massachusetts in 1978.

While retrospective exhibitions in the late 20th century drew large audiences, attempts to integrate Rockwell into the canon of American masters proved less successful. However, the late 20th and early 21st centuries saw the emergence of scholarship examining the nature of prejudice against Rockwell, and discussing his broader cultural relevance.

Tess Mann

See also: Cahill, Holger; Federal Art Project; Rivera, Diego.

References and Further Reading

Finch, Christopher. 1975. *Norman Rockwell's America.* New York: Abrams.

The Saturday Evening Post Norman Rockwell Book. 1986. New York: Bonanza Books. Distributed by Crown Publishers.

Reeves, Richard. 1971. "Norman Rockwell is Exactly Like a Norman Rockwell," *New York Times Magazine.* February 28.

Hennessey, Maureen Hart, and Anne Knutson, eds. 1999. *Norman Rockwell: Pictures for the American People.* New York: Henry N. Abrams.

Johnston, Patricia, ed. 2006. *Seeing High and Low: Representing Social Conflict in American Visual Culture.* Berkeley: University of California Press

Rodgers, Jimmie (1897–1933)

Acknowledged as the Father of Country Music, Jimmie Rodgers was inducted into the Country Music Hall of Fame in 1961. His ability to incorporate hillbilly and blues elements into his songs also made Rodgers an important influence upon the formation of rock music, and in January 1986, he was among the first musicians selected for membership in the Rock and Roll Hall of Fame. Born into humble circumstances in rural Mississippi, Rodgers enjoyed his greatest success between 1927 and his premature death in 1933. His ballads, spirituals, and blues songs gave voice to the concerns of common people during a difficult time.

Rodgers was born September 8, 1897, in Meridian, Mississippi. His mother died when Rodgers was only four years of age, and he was raised by his father, a foreman on the Gulf, Mobile & Ohio Railroad. Struggling economically, Rodgers dropped out of school at age 14 and worked as a water boy in the rail yard. While working for the railroad and studying the singing style of black railroaders, Rodgers learned to play the guitar and banjo.

His 1917 marriage to Stella Kelly resulted in a divorce two years later. The following year, Rodgers wed Carrie Williamson and the couple had two children, one of whom died at six months of age. Rodgers supported his family by railroading; often suffering through long separations from his family. The work also took its toll upon his health, and in 1924 Rodgers was diagnosed with tuberculosis. The following year, Rodgers was performing in black face with a traveling medicine show in Tennessee and Kentucky. During this time, Rodgers began to develop his talent for yodeling, which appeared to be a way for the white entertainer to reflect the wails of blues singers. Rodgers earned enough money to invest in a tent carnival. The show, however, was destroyed, and in 1926, Rodgers was back railroading in Asheville, North Carolina.

But Rodgers had not given up on music, and in 1927, he formed the Jimmie Rodgers Entertainers, featuring the singer's flair for yodeling. The big break for Rodgers came in August 1927, when Ralph Peer, representing the Victor Talking Machine Company, was conducting recording sessions in Bristol, Tennessee. Peer recorded Rodgers and the Carter Family; artists who brought respectability to the hillbilly genre. Separate recording sessions for Rodgers and his band were arranged as the band believed that Rodgers was planning to audition alone. Rodgers performed "Sleep, Baby, Sleep" and "Soldier's Sweetheart," accompanied by the Carter Family. Peer was impressed and signed Rodgers to a contract.

Although the Bristol sessions did not result in major record sales, Peer arranged another recording session in November 1927 at the RCA Victor Camden, New Jersey studio. Rodgers recorded the songs "T for Texas," "Away Out on the Mountain," and "Rock All Our Babies to Sleep," all of which became hits for the singer.

By the fall of 1929, Rodgers was a major music star, appearing in the Columbia-Victor film, *The Singing Brakeman*. As the country was beset be depression, Rodgers was earning $2,000 a month and living a life of luxury. Many of his hits, including "Hobo Bill's Last Ride," "Waitin' for the Train," and "Lullaby Yodel," were written by his sister-in-law Elsie McWilliams. Rodgers also recorded for RCA with jazz greats Earl Hines and Louis Armstrong. His songs regarding hobos, cowboys, railroads, traveling, and relationships gone sour resonated with the public, and his recordings sold over six million copies.

Commercial success, however, did not improve his health, and Rodgers continued to suffer from tuberculosis. In May 1933, Rodgers journeyed to New York City to record a session with the Carter Family. While his voice remained strong enough to sing "I'm Free from the Chain Gang Now" and "Yodeling My Way Back Home," he began to hemorrhage and died on May 26, 1933. Weeping fans greeted the train bearing his body back to Mississippi. His music captured the lives and dreams of common Americans during the depression era.

Ron Briley

See also: Autry, Gene; Hillbilly Music; Wills, Bob.

References and Further Reading

Porterfield, Nolan. 1979. *Jimmie Rodgers: The Life and Times of America's Blue Yodeler.* Urbana: University of Illinois Press.

Rodgers, Carrie. 1975. *My Husband, Jimmie Rodgers.* Reprint, Kila, MT: Kessinger Publishing, 2007.

Rodgers, Jimmie. 1989. *The Jimmie Rodgers Collection.* Milwaukee, WI: Hal Leonard Corporation.

Rogers, Roy (1912–98)

Born into a poor working-class family, Roy Rogers journeyed to California in the early 1930s, fashioning a career as a singer and cowboy film star. Between 1943 and 1951, Rogers starred in 48 Western films for Republic Pictures. When his film career faltered in the post war period, Rogers turned his attention to television and a successful business career. In 1989, he was inducted into the Country Music Hall of Fame.

Rogers was born Leonard Frank Sly on November 5, 1911, in Cincinnati, Ohio. His mother, Mattie Womack Sly, was disabled from a bout with polio, and his father, Andrew Sly, was a factory worker. The family lived on a houseboat on the Ohio River for eight years, and Rogers worked on a family farm. Rogers played guitar with his father and learned yodeling from his mother. He abandoned his ambition to become a dentist when he dropped out of high school following his sophomore year, accepting a job with a Cincinnati shoe factory.

In 1930, Rogers moved with his family to California, where he worked as a truck driver and migrant worker picking peaches. After finding little success with local bands, Roger joined with Bob Nolan and Tim Spencer to form Sons of the Pioneers. Displaying strong harmonies, the group was signed by Decca Records and achieved hits with "Tumbling Tumbleweeds" (1934) and "Blue Prairie" (1936). Rogers married Lucile Ascolese in 1933, and the couple divorced in 1936. That same year he married Grace Arline Wilkins, who died from an embolism in 1946.

Billed as Dick Weston, Rogers played a villain in the Gene Autry picture, *The Old Corral* (1936). Rogers got his big break in the film industry in 1937, when Republic, following a financial dispute with Autry, tapped Rogers to replace the singing cowboy in *Under Western Skies.* The picture proved a hit, and the studio assigned the stage name of Roy Rogers to the young performer. After Autry's return in Republic in 1938, Rogers played in smaller budget films, but he did receive good reviews for his work in director Raoul Walsh's *Dark Command* (1940) with John Wayne.

When Autry left the studio in 1942 for the military, Rogers assumed his role as the "King of the Cowboys." In films such as *Heart of the Golden West* (1942), *Silver Spurs* (1943), and *The Man from Music Mountain* (1943), Rogers developed the singing cowboy formula, featuring his horse Trigger, sidekick George "Gabby" Hayes, the Sons of the Pioneers, and co-star Dale Evans. Rogers was also a popular rodeo performer, and at the peak of his fame in the mid-1940s, he was receiving an estimated 75,000 fan letters per month.

Following World War II, Hollywood turned to more adult themes in its Western films, and Rogers moved into television. *The Roy Rogers Show* ran on NBC from 1951 to 1957. The program featured Trigger, as well as co-star Dale Evans, whom Rogers married in 1947. The couple recorded the show's trademark theme song, "Happy Trails." The popularity of *The Roy Rogers Show* with children offered the star considerable merchandising opportunities, and the Rogers name and image appeared on over 400 products.

During the 1960s, Rogers and Evans also toured with evangelist Billy Graham's crusades, testifying to their Christian beliefs. Rogers also teamed with the Marriott Corporation to develop a fast food restaurant chain under his name. The chain included over 800 restaurants and was sold to Hardee's in 1990. The poor Ohio boy who moved to California during the Depression certainly found fame and fortune in Hollywood. Rogers died on July 6, 1998, at his ranch near Victorville, California.

Ron Briley

See also: Autry, Gene; Hillbilly Music; Rodgers, Jimmie Rodgers.

References and Further Reading

Morris, Georgia, and Mark Pollard, eds. 1994. *Roy Rogers: King of the Cowboys.* San Francisco: Collins.

Phillips, Robert W. 1995. *Roy Rogers: A Biography, Radio History, Television Career Chronicle, Discography; Filmography, Comicography, Merchandising and Advertising History.* Jefferson, NC: McFarland & Company.

Rogers, Roy, and Dale Evans, with Jane Stern and Michael Stern. 1994. *Happy Trails: Our Life Story.* New York: Simon & Schuster.

Rosie the Riveter

Rosie the Riveter is a World War II icon that emerged during the early years of U.S. participation in the war, 1942–45. Symbolizing the approximately 6 million American women who worked in the U.S. service sector (mostly in the defense industries producing ammunition, weapons, artillery, airplanes and tanks), Rosie inspired a whole generation of daughters, mothers, sisters, and wives to enter the U.S. workforce and replace the American men fighting on behalf of the Allies.

As soon as the U.S. entered WWII in 1941, it became clear that in order to secure victory, hundreds of thousands, if not millions, of new employees would be

"We Can Do It," a poster by J. Howard Miller, is the quintessential image of the female defense worker during World War II. The image of the factory woman, depicted in many ways and popularized as "Rosie the Riveter," became a national symbol of American unity and patriotism. (National Archives)

needed to fill the positions that soldiers had vacated. Middle class women over the age of 18 suddenly emerged as a potential pool of employees, however, up until this point in history, only a minority of women from this age group had ever worked in the public sector, and very few had worked in "blue collar" factory jobs. Persuading this segment of the population would be a difficult task, especially given the nature of the positions that needed filling (working in factories, especially those producing military wares, was considered both masculine and "lower class"). In 1942, the U.S. government, through the War Manpower Commission and the Office of War Information, began advertising campaigns in newspapers, ladies' magazines and on billboards, linking female participation in the defense industry to patriotism, empowerment, and military victory. The breakthrough came when the War Advertising Council's Women in War Jobs Campaign asked 20-year-old Midwesterner Rose Will Monroe, who was a fighter plane riveter building bombers for the U.S. Air Force, to appear in a film about the war effort on the homefront. Dubbed "Rosie the Riveter" in the ensuing poster campaign, Monroe became an instant cultural icon. Although J. Howard Miller's famous "Rosie the Riveter" poster *We Can Do It!* was actually modeled on Michigan factory worker Geraldine Doyle, it was Monroe's public persona, combined with Norman Rockwell's May 29, 1943, *Saturday Evening Post* cover and Redd Evans and John Jacob Loeb's song "Rosie the Riveter," that popularized the icon.

The Rosie propaganda campaign succeeded in attracting millions of women into the U.S. workforce. Although some voluntarily returned to their positions as homemakers after the war, others were forced to leave their positions when the soldiers returned and began seeking employment, Rosie continues to be a potent cultural symbol of the Great Depression/ WWII era. The women who remained in the workforce owe their success, in part, to the wide-spread acceptance of the U.S. government's women in the workforce campaign, which helped dismantle stereotypes about working women. Second and Third Wave feminists have claimed Rosie as a symbol of female empowerment, and renewed interest in Rosie iconography is booming, especially since Rose Monroe's death in 1997. In 2002, Rockwell's original painting of Rosie—transposed over an American flag, and stepping on a copy of Adolph Hitler's autobiography *Mein Kampf*—sold for almost $5 million (US).

Tanfer Tunc

See also: Roosevelt, Eleanor.

References and Further Reading

Gluck, Sherna Berger. 1988. *Rosie the Riveter Revisited: Women, the War, and Social Change.* New York: Plume.

Frank, Miriam. 1982. *Life and Times of Rosie the Riveter: The Story of Three Million Working Women During World War II.* New York: Clarity Education Production.

Honey, Maureen. 1985. *Creating Rosie the Riveter: Class, Gender, and Propaganda During World War II.* Amherst: University of Massachusetts Press.

Kessler-Harris, Alice. 1982. *Out to Work: A History of Wage-Earning Women in the United States.* New York: Oxford University Press.

May, Elaine Tyler. 1988. *Homeward Bound: American Families in the Cold War Era.* New York: Basic Books.

Rogers, Donald. 1973. *Since You Went Away: From Rosie the Riveter to Bond Drives, World War II at Home.* New Rochelle, NY: Arlington House.

Scarface: The Shame of the Nation (1932)

Despite the release of *Scarface: The Shame of the Nation* being postponed two years as its director Howard Hawks fought against censors, the film is considered to be among Hollywood's first gangster films. To offset any criticism that the film glamorizes gangsters, a subtitle was added, a statement prefaced the show, and several characters editorialize on the blood-shed, even if the audience never saw any blood. The biggest change was the ending; a judge offers a first-person point-of-view tongue-lashing before the crime boss dangles in the shadows of the gallows.

Under the resourceful direction of Hawks, Paul Muni swaggers as well as any other actor playing a gangster loosely based on Al "Scarface" Capone. Ben Hecht, a friend and colleague of Hawks, used his real life experience as a Chicago reporter in revising a script based on a novel by Armitage Trail. The movie follows actual events such as the St. Valentine's Day Massacre of a rival gang, a hit in a hospital room, and another murder in a flower shop.

The gangsters are apish, which is not to say that the actors ape gangsters. They seem authentic, but they are childishly amoral, not understanding the causes or even the effects of their atrocious behavior. Muni's character even seems sexually attracted to his own sister, though the incestuous relationship is made less obvious due to a preemptive cut by Hawks. Their relationship is a tangle that the average moviegoer, even of today, may not understand, and one wonders if the omitted scene might have shed light on this subplot. The relationship was not at the center of the controversy that preceded the release of the film, however. Its violent plot and its failure to praise the police led to it never being shown in many states and its postponed release in Al Capone's own city of Chicago.

As with many of Howard Hawk's films, the Academy of Motion Picture Arts and Sciences paid little attention to the artfully crafted movie—action-packed with over 30 murders, yet artistically shot to hide the blood while heightening the drama. Fifty years later, Brian De Palma dedicates his own *Scarface* film to Ben Hecht, yet his eponymous character is from Cuba, a runner of cocaine instead of alcohol, and ends in a shoot out, more in line with Hawks's first cut of his gangster genre masterpiece. In 1994, the United States National Film Preservation Board inducted the once controversial Hawk movie into the National Film Registry, preserved as a national treasure by the United States Library of Congress.

Mark Schwartz

See also: Little Caesar; Public Enemy.

References and Further Reading

Lawrence, Jerome. 1982. *Actor: The Life and Times of Paul Muni.* New York: G. P. Putnam's Sons.

Rafter, Nicole. 2000. *Shots in the Mirror.* New York: Oxford University Press.

Sklar, Robert. 1994. *City Boys.* Princeton, NJ: Princeton University Press.

Sergeant York (1941)

The most popular film of 1941, *Sergeant York* was directed by Hollywood legend Howard Hawks, (with screen writing assistance from John Huston), produced by Jesse Lasky, and starred Gary Cooper as Medal of Honor winner Alvin York, the most venerated World War I soldier produced by the United States during World War I. (Cooper won the Academy Award for Best Actor for his interpretation of York.) By tracing York's evolution from pacifist to war hero, the film also served to help guide the United States away from its isolationist position in the years leading up to American involvement in World War II.

Audience members connected with Hawks's film version of Alvin York, and Gary Cooper, one of the biggest stars of his time, was York's personal choice to play him on the silver screen. Though nostalgic by today's standards, and shot entirely on studio sets rather than on location, the film is still accessible to Americans, as judged by its ubiquitous appearance on cable television to this day.

The story begins with York's conversion from a carousing hardscrabble farmer into a hard-working Christian. Nearly killed in a thunderstorm, York accepted Christianity and began to work to save money for a better piece of land and to win the affection of a local girl while facing off against her more prosperous suitor. Things appear to be working out well for York when he receives his draft notice, as did millions of American farm boys, in the summer of 1917. York seeks status as a conscientious objector while undergoing training with a variety of recruits taken from across the United States.

Recognizing York's skills as a soldier and natural leader, his commanding officers employ the heroes of American history to convince York that his Christianity would not be diminished by devotion to freedom and country. York makes the decision to fight, confident that an American victory will end the destructive war. Launched into battle in France, York heroically fights his way to the rear of an enemy position, killing numerous German soldiers and capturing 132 of the enemy. Like most Hollywood versions of history, for dramatic purposes the film included many composite characters, made-up scenes, and other inaccuracies.

York remained a pacifist after World War I, and was an outspoken opponent of American entry into World War II before Pearl Harbor. He was hesitant to allow the film to be made due in part to the fear that it would serve as pro-war propaganda. Apparently, York's distaste for Hitler and the Nazis convinced him to cooperate with the production and appear at the film's premiere on July 2, 1941.

Prior to the outbreak of World War II, the mostly Jewish moguls of Hollywood had been reluctant to make films that openly advocated American intervention in World War II. Public sentiment remained strong against intervention until 1941, and groups like the American First Committee attempted to maintain the isolationist policies of the United States in the 1930s. Fearing an anti-Semitic backlash of blame if America was brought into the war due to Hollywood propaganda, the studios began to follow the lead of President Roosevelt in preparing Americans for the great crusade with a series of commitment films such as *Sergeant York* and *Casablanca*.

Randal Beeman

References and Further Reading

Beck, Ken. 2007. "York Was Reluctant to Make Film." *Tennessean*, September 15.

Gabler, Neal. 1988. *An Empire of Their Own: How the Jews Invented Hollywood.* New York: Anchor Books.

Graebner, William. 1998. *The Age of Doubt: American Thought and Culture in the 1940s.* New York: Waveland Press.

Sessions, Roger Huntington (1896–1985)

Roger Huntington Sessions is remembered for his dense, demanding music and for 50 years of teaching. He reached beyond American interest in a strictly national style to lead an international approach to composition. He encouraged students, among them Milton Babbitt, to master their craft and to pursue the highest ideals.

Sessions was born in Brooklyn, New York on December 28, 1896. At age 11, he intended to become a composer. At age 14, he entered Harvard University and earned a bachelor's degree in 1914. Sessions next studied with Charles Ives's teacher at Yale University, Horatio Parker, and in 1917, he earned a bachelor's degree in music and the Steinert Prize for his *Symphonic Prelude.*

While teaching theory at Smith College (1917–21), Sessions studied with composer Ernest Bloch in New York and in 1921, became Bloch's assistant at the Cleveland (Ohio) Institute of Music. In 1923, Sessions composed incidental music for *The Black Maskers,* a symbolist play of Leonid Andreyev that was to be performed at Smith College. The score, dedicated to Bloch, is thought by most to be Sessions's first real masterpiece.

Sessions resigned his Cleveland position in 1925 after Ernest Bloch was dismissed from the institute. Sessions traveled abroad and spent several years in Florence, Rome, and Berlin. He produced his First Symphony (1926–27) while abroad, a piece that reflects Sessions's neoclassicism and the influence of Igor Stravinsky. That early symphony, the first of nine, is Stravinskian in that it is less dense and less chromatic than Sessions's later symphonies. In the *Piano Sonata no. 1* of 1930, Sessions began to move away from the neoclassic idiom to create a work that composer Aaron Copland called "a cornerstone upon which to build an American music." By 1935, when Sessions joined the faculty at Princeton University, he had completed a violin concerto. The work reveals his individualism, and Copland notes "an almost tactile sensibility" in the music. Yet, Sessions was expending most of his energy on teaching. To remedy the dearth of new works, he forced himself to write at least one short piece every day or so. Under pressure from his publisher to provide something for publication, he agreed to submit four of those pieces, which together were published as *Pages from a Diary* (1940). The work shows Sessions's music becoming more chromatic.

The Second Symphony (1944–46) is dedicated to the memory of Franklin D. Roosevelt and exhibits a new emotional strength and drama. Some sense of key remains in that and other works of the period, including the *Piano Sonata no. 2* and the one-act opera *The Trial of Lucullus* (1947). In 1947, Sessions began to work on his opera *Montezuma;* he finished in 1963 and within a few years, had incorporated the 12-tone system into his work. He noted later that he "came to [the system] by degrees and used it for [his] own purposes. [He] never tried to force [himself] into a style…because [he] wanted to find [his] own style." *Montezuma,* an ambitious work, was scored to a libretto by Antonio Borgese. The libretto was based on Bernal Díaz del Castillo's chronicle of the Spanish conquest of the Aztecs in the 16th century. Peter Maxwell Davies said in his *New York Times* review, April 21, 1964, "There is little doubt that this is Sessions' masterpiece; it is also his most problematic and difficult work...[and] marks...a huge step in the history of American music."

After Sessions retired from Princeton University in 1965, he became Bloch Professor at Berkeley (1966–67), Norton Professor at Harvard (1968–69), and a faculty member of the Juilliard School. He completed four more symphonies; the very successful cantata *When Lilacs Last in the Dooryard Bloomed* (1970), after Walt Whitman; and in 1981, at 84, composed the *Concerto for Orchestra* to mark the Boston Symphony Orchestra's 100th anniversary. Sessions died in Princeton, New Jersey on March 16, 1985.

References and Further Reading

Bindas, Kenneth J. 1995. *All of this Music Belongs to the Nation: The WPA's Federal Music Project and American Society, 1935–1939.* Knoxville: University of Tennessee Press.

Sessions, Roger. 1987. *Conversations with Roger Sessions.* Boston: Northeastern University Press.

Prausnitz, Frederik. 2002. *Roger Sessions: How a "Difficult" Composer Got That Way.* New York: Oxford University Press.

Kirkpatrick, John. 1988, c.1987. *The New Grove Twentieth-Century American Masters: Ives, Thomson, Sessions, Cowell, Gershwin, Copland.* New York: Norton.

Shaw, Artie (1910–2004)

Artie Shaw was a prominent U.S. jazz musician, clarinet player and popular band leader during the 1930s and 1940s. A keen jazz player, he has been noted as being one of the few outstanding jazz players whose commitment to jazz remains uncertain. He was born Arthur Jacob Arshawsky on May 23, 1910, in New York City, and grew up in New Haven, Connecticut, where, as a boy he was subjected to anti-Semitic taunts. He began playing music when young, appearing in his high school band and becoming a professional by the time he was 15 years old. Shaw soon became a close associate of Willie "the Lion" Smith at jam sessions and by the age of 21, he was a studio musician.

In 1935, Shaw surprised his audience by performing one of his original compositions with the accompaniment of a string quartet and a rhythm section. Not pleased with the reception, he retired from music for a year. When he returned, his *Begin the Beguine,* recorded in 1938 was a great success in which Shaw playing the clarinet suddenly became famous.

In 1938 Shaw signed Billie Holiday as a vocalist and became the first white bandleader to hire a full-time black female singer. Holliday, however, did not remain with Shaw for long on account of hostile audiences in the southern states, and also music company executives who wanted a more conservative style. Over the next few years Shaw was immensely successful and his name became equated with that of Benny Goodman, with Shaw being dubbed the "King of the Clarinet." Shaw continued to experiment with different musical instruments and a large number of hits resulted in his selling of more than 100 million records. At his height, he was said to be making $60,000 per week.

Shaw moved to Mexico in 1939 and lived there and in the United States, enlisting in the U.S. Navy in World War II. He formed his own band which served in the Pacific, playing to naval service personnel for 18 months. The performances took him to places such as Guadalcanal. Shaw became exhausted from travelling and returned to the United States where he received a medical discharge.

Returning to the music scene in the late 1940s, Shaw started performing classical music in New York at Carnegie Hall, and also with the New York Philharmonic Orchestra. However, Shaw remained unsettled and took more time out from his music. His taking of sabbaticals became a major part of his career and while Count Basie and Duke Ellington led one orchestra during their period of fame, and Benny Goodman, owing to an illness, led two, Shaw led five different orchestras. Part of this has been put down to his troubled private life—he married eight times. It has also been suggested by some writers that he may never have liked jazz music. He was also, in 1953, brought before the House Un-American Activities Committee after he stated his support for the Constitution of the Soviet Union. He died on December 30, 2004.

Justin Corfield

References and Further Reading

Shaw, Artie. 1952. *The Trouble with Cinderella: An Outline of Identity.* New York: Farrar, Straus & Young.

Simosko, Vladimir. 2000. *Artie Shaw: a Musical Biography and Discography.* Lanham, MD: Scarecrow Press.

———

Sokoloff, Nikolai (1886–1965)

The important Russian American conductor and violinist, Nikolai Sokoloff, was born on May 28, 1886, at Kiev, Russia, the son of Gregory and Marie Sokoloff. His father taught him the violin, and the boy won a scholarship to study the violin at the Yale University School of Music at the age of 14. He spent three years studying under Charles Martin Loeffler, and in 1911 toured France and England. Becoming a prominent violinist, he was appointed as the musical director of the San Francisco People's Philharmonic Orchestra from 1916 until 1917. During this brief tenure, he included women in his orchestra and insisted on paying them at the same rates as the male musicians.

In 1917 Sokoloff became the first violin at the Boston Symphony Orchestra, and in the following year was appointed as the founding conductor and music director of the Cleveland Orchestra in Ohio, and remained in that position until 1932. He had been president of the Fairfield County Music Association in Connecticut, and also later Musical Director and Conductor of the New York Orchestra, the Cincinnati Symphony Orchestra, the Detroit Symphony Orchestra and, briefly, the London Symphony Orchestra. In 1923 he performed at the National Welsh Festival an Annanford, Wales, and in 1924, performed in London. He was a guest conductor at the New York Philharmonic Stadium Concerts in 1925, the Philadelphia Orchestra in 1926, and again in 1929, and guest conductor for the San Francisco Symphony Orchestra in 1927, and also for the San Mateo Philharmonic Society.

From 1935 until 1939 he was the Director of the Federal Music Project (FMP), a program established under the New Deal to get musicians to perform, and also educate members of the public about music. It aimed to help musicians who were particularly hard hit by the Depression, and led to the creation of 34 new orchestras, and the formation of a Composers' Forum Laboratory which hosted many musical festivals. There were also many music classes, and the FMP sponsored research into ethnomusicology, especially cowboy music, Creole music and African American music and traditions.

Sokoloff directed the Seattle Symphony Orchestra from 1938 until 1940, and the San Diego Symphony Orchestra in 1939–41. Moving to La Jolla, California, in 1941 he founded and was musical director of the La Jolla Musical Arts Society, a position he held until 1961. He died on September 25, 1965.

Justin Corfield

See also: Federal Music Project; Sessions, Roger.

References and Further Reading

Bindas, Kenneth J. 1995. *All of This Music Belongs to the Nation: The WPA's Federal Music Project and American Society.* Knoxville: The University of Tennessee Press,.

Sokoloff, Nikolai. 1936. *The Federal Music Project.* Washington, DC: Government Printing Office.

Who Was Who in America Vol. 4: 1961–1968. 1994. New Providence, NJ: Marquis Who's Who.

Stagecoach (1939)

Based on Ernest Haycox's short story "The Stage to Lordsburg" for *Collier's Magazine, Stagecoach,* less obviously than the title of the tale of the American West on which it was based, smacks of Chaucer's *Canterbury Tales.* Unlike Chaucer, the life stories of the characters are not so much told but brought out through dialogue among the characters inside the coach and at rest stops along the way. The characterizations, too, tip their hats to Chaucer: the goodhearted woman of pleasure; the seeming upright banker; the rascal as a Confederate veteran; the family-centered merchant of whiskey; the Yankee doctor rife with both wisdom and whiskey; the simple yet true horse driver; the pregnant wife of a high ranking soldier; the marshal literally riding shotgun; and the role that made John Wayne famous, the falsely accused man who escaped from jail to kill the brothers who framed him. If the conflicts within each character and the conflicts between each character were not enough, Geronimo, the infamous Apache, is on the warpath in locality.

John Ford, who was beginning to glean critical success as a director of better than "B" pictures, did much with the story adapted for film by his regular partner, Dudley Nichols. The film had all the trappings of a Western but rose above the confined genre by breaking social prototypes through the positioning of characters against each other as the exterior pressure of the Apaches increases. Although the drunk doctor, played by Thomas Mitchell, who won an Oscar for his role, and the Southern gentlemen rascal, played skillfully by John Carradine, exchange barbs concerning the proper way to refer to the American Civil War, of which both are veterans, they aid and comfort the pregnant woman and fight attacking Apaches as brothers-in-arms. Each character has an exchange with all other characters that shows their true character. Much is made of John Wayne as the outlaw Ringo Kid, taking a liking to Claire Trevor as the prostitute, who has been run out of town and now wants to show her heart of gold. By the end of the film, Ringo forgives all and the prostitute begins to forgive herself. Less clichéd is the whiskey salesman who becomes, for the first and last time in the film, indignant, over the group's forgetting to circle the wagons around the baby which is born at a rest stop with the help of the sobered doctor. Further, as an indicator that this film came out during the Great Depression, the corrupt banker goes on a tirade on how the government has no right to inquire how men in his business go about their work. It is the banker, and not the outlaw, who meets with the long arm of the law by the end of the film.

Although the film has some traditional trappings, such as a chase scene involving Apaches, and a cavalry-to-the-rescue scene, *Stagecoach* was a breakthrough for its director, John Ford, and its leading man, John Wayne. It elevated the Western out of Saturday matinee entertainment to serious motion picture art. *Stagecoach* was nominated for seven Academy Awards, winning two.

Mark Schwartz

See also: John Ford; John Wayne.

References and Further Reading

Bergman, Andrew. 1971. *We're In the Money: Depression America and its Films.* New York: New York University Press.

Lusted, David. 2003 *The Western.* Harlow, England; New York: Pearson/Longman.

Tag, Gallagher.1986. *John Ford: the man and his films.* Berkeley: University of California.

Stagecoach. 1939. Hollywood, CA:. Filmstrip.

Steinbeck, John (1902–68)

Novelist, playwright, short-story writer, and essayist John Steinbeck was born in Salinas, California, on February 27, 1902. By the time of his death in 1968, Steinbeck was recognized around the world not only as one of the quintessential American writers but also as an extraordinarily articulate and passionate defender of the "common man."

Steinbeck, along with the characters he created, came to personify the spirit of those who were hit hardest by the Great Depression: migrant families desperate to find food and work, immigrants searching for the same, and any kind of working-class person fighting against his boss for better pay and better working conditions. Steinbeck's work was also grounded in the physical landscape that surrounded him as a boy and for most of his adult life. He wrote extensively and eloquently about the way people are connected to land and in his many short stories, novels, essays, and plays, Steinbeck returned often to the theme of people adapting to the environment that surrounds them. He is best known for writing *The Grapes of Wrath,* which was published in 1939, and he received the Nobel Prize for Literature in 1962.

Steinbeck was born in a house located on Central Avenue in Salinas, the son of the county treasurer and a school teacher. He developed a love of the written word early in his life as his mother exposed Steinbeck to various classic literary works, including Dostoevsky's *Crime and Punishment* and the work of the great poet Milton. After graduating from high school, Steinbeck attended Stanford University from 1920 to 1926. At Stanford, Steinbeck studied biology but he did not complete his degree; he decided long before he left school that his professional goal was to become a writer. After leaving Stanford, he moved to New York City to try his hand at writing professionally.

In 1929, Steinbeck published his first book, entitled *Cup of Gold.* It was followed by short story collections entitled *Pastures of Heaven* (1932) and *The Long Valley* (1938). In each of these collections, Steinbeck's home in California's Salinas Valley played a prominent role. He also wrote a book with his friend Ed Ricketts, a marine biologist, titled *The Sea of Cortez* in 1941. That book emerged from an expedition Steinbeck and Ricketts undertook together in the Gulf of California and firmly established two themes that would be constantly reiterated in Steinbeck's work: the interdependence of all living things and the prominent role that the physical environment plays in the lives of humans.

But it was Steinbeck's novels that would earn him lasting fame. He published his first, *Tortilla Flat,* in 1935. The following year, Steinbeck published *In Dubious Battle,* which described a strike led by migrant workers in California's apple country. His novel *The Red Pony,* which was originally published in serial form, appeared in 1937 and was made into a movie in 1949, one of several film scripts Steinbeck would ultimately write.

Also in 1937, Steinbeck published *Of Mice and Men,* which helped to introduce him to the American reader. *Of Mice and Men* tells the story of two ranch workers named Lennie and George who move from place to place in search of work, driven by the dream of one day owning their own farm. The descriptions of life among itinerant farm workers and the tragic end to the story foreshadowed what was to come in Steinbeck's masterwork, *The Grapes of Wrath,* which appeared in 1938.

Besides being Steinbeck's unquestioned masterpiece, *The Grapes of Wrath* is also one of the great masterpieces of American literature, and arguably one of the greatest novels ever written in the English language. The novel, which chronicles the experiences of the Joad family as they travel from Oklahoma to the promised land of California, not only brought Steinbeck's many influences together—including his affinity for exploring human relationships and the connection between humans and their environment—but did so at precisely a moment in history in which the story of migrant families like the Joads needed to be told. The story of the Joads also paralleled the larger issues facing Americans as a whole during the Great Depression. Steinbeck was awarded the Pulitzer Prize in 1940 for *The Grapes of Wrath,* and the novel was made into a film that same year by director John Ford. Though the ending was changed to emphasize the New Deal programs of President Franklin Roosevelt, probably to inspire beleaguered Americans affected by the Depression, but also to avoid censorship because of a controversial final scene in the novel, Steinbeck agreed that the film version was an accurate and commendable representation of the novel itself.

After the success of *The Grapes of Wrath,* Steinbeck eventually moved to New York. Though the novel was well received by many critics and much of the public, it also received its share of criticism, much of which came from large landowners and banking interests and even from some members of Congress. The story of the Joads struck a chord with many Americans that continues to resonate even today.

After the start of World War II, Steinbeck served as a war correspondent for the New York Herald-Tribune. During and after the war, he wrote several pieces that described his experiences, including *The Moon is Down* (1942),

Lifeboat (which was made into a film directed by Alfred Hitchcock in 1944), and *A Medal for Benny* (1945). After the war Steinbeck continued to write prolifically, publishing such notable works as *Cannery Row* (1945), *East of Eden* (1952), *The Winter of Our Discontent* (1961), and *Travels With Charley* (1962), which described his experiences as he took a cross-country trip in a pickup truck with his dog, Charley. He was recognized for his artistry when he awarded the Nobel Prize for Literature in 1962. John Steinbeck died in New York of a heart attack on December 20, 1968, at the age of 66.

Dave Powell

See also: Hemingway, Ernest Miller; Gone With the Wind.

References and Further Reading

Benson, Jackson J. 1984. *True Adventures of John Steinbeck, Writer: A Biography.* New York: Viking Press.

George, Stephen K. 2002. *John Steinbeck: A Centennial Tribute.* Westport, CT: Praeger.

George, Stephen K. 2005. *The Moral Philosophy of John Steinbeck.* Lanham, MD: Scarecrow Press.

Steinbeck, John. 1975. *Steinbeck: A Life in Letters.* New York: Viking Press.

Steinbeck, John. 1989. *Working Days: The Journals of The Grapes of Wrath.* New York: Viking.

Superman

Perhaps the most famous comic book character of all time, Superman made his debut in Action Comics #1 in 1938. Created in Cleveland, Ohio in the early 1930s by Joel Siegel and Jerry Schuster, Superman was originally conceived as a bald-headed villain with telepathic powers. The concept failed to sell, however, and the character was redone as a heroic figure. Later revisions led to the introduction of the character's unique powers and abilities, along with his now-famous costume. The super powers were explained by making Superman an alien sent to Earth by his biological parents, Jor-El and Lara, as the only survivor from the doomed planet Krypton. Still, it was not until 1938 that Siegel and Schuster were able to sell their creation to DC Comics. They received $130 for the rights to Superman, agreed to supply DC with material for stories and were placed on salary.

The character quickly became popular, and the Man of Steel had his own comic book launched in 1939. He continued to appear in Action Comics and also appeared from time to time in other DC titles. Siegel and Schuster originally drew and wrote the stories, but as Superman's popularity increased and Schuster's eyesight began to fail, the two established a studio to handle the increasing workload. Writing and drawing teams were organized and eventually took over the production of stories and artwork.

Siegel and Schuster freely admitted that their creation was a reflection of popular culture at that time. Both were avid readers of pulp and science fiction magazines, and movie actors provided a source of names for the characters that populated Superman's universe. Edgar Rice Burroughs's John Carter tales were a source of inspiration, and Schuster, who drew Superman, noted that his work was influenced by popular artists such as Alex Raymond and Burne Hogarth. Movies were equally influential, particularly the swashbuckling adventure films of Douglas Fairbanks, Sr.

Created as a rather hard-boiled and aggressive character, Superman originally battled typical villains of the day such as gangsters and petty criminals, and often tossed them around like rag dolls, unconcerned with the physical injuries that his great strength could cause. Some of these injuries were clearly fatal, although these were rarely shown. Ultimately this side of Superman was softened, and editorial policy established in 1940 forbade Superman from taking a life.

From the beginning Superman was "more powerful than a locomotive, faster than a speeding bullet and able to leap tall buildings at a single bound," as he was described on the popular radio program and in the Max Fleischer cartoons in the 1940s, as well as the 1950s television program. At first, Superman could perform amazing feats of strength, had skin that could only be penetrated by an exploding artillery shell and could jump about an eighth of a mile in a single leap. In time, his leaping prowess evolved into the ability to fly. Ultimately Superman was able to fly through outer space, and could even travel to other stars and planetary systems, apparently as a result of limitless speed combined with his powers of flight.

His other powers increased as well until he acquired the abilities that are familiar today. Besides super strength, super speed and flight, Superman has a range of extraordinary visual powers, most notably X-ray and heat vision. He has super hearing, is invulnerable to everything except Kryptonite and magic, and he can use his breath to freeze objects or blow them over with the force of a tornado or hurricane. Eventually Superman became so powerful that writers were hard pressed to think up believable story lines for him.

An entire universe sprang up around Superman as well. Youthful super-adventures were chronicled in *Superboy* magazine that appeared in 1945. A host of recurring characters populated Superman's world: his adoptive parents, Ma and Pa Kent, his love interest, *Daily Planet* reporter Lois Lane, his pal, cub reporter Jimmy Olsen, and the *Planet's* editor, Perry White, being the most recognizable. Even his Kryptonian parents appeared on occasion. And, of course, there is Superman's secret identity: mild-mannered reporter Clark Kent. Among the most notable villains were Superman's arch-enemy, Lex Luthor, the magical imp from the Eighth Dimension, Mr. Mxyzptlk, the alien Brainiac, and the monstrous Bizarro. The Man of Steel has also joined forces with other superheroes, such as Batman, Wonder Woman and a superhero team called the Justice League of America. An interesting note is that many of the characters have names that begin with the initials LL, such as Lois Lane, Lex Luthor, and Superboy's girlfriend, Lana Lang, among others.

Superman quickly made the leap from comic books to other media. He was the star of a popular radio serial in the 1940s as well as the Fleischer cartoons, he appeared in a movie serial, *Superman,* in 1948, followed by *Atom Man vs. Superman* in 1950. A television series was launched in 1952 and ran for more than 100 episodes, coming to an end in 1958. A Broadway musical in 1966 was a flop, but the character appeared in a number of television cartoon shows in the late 1960s and 1970s. In 1978, *Superman, the Movie,* the first of four theatrical releases starring Christopher Reeve, revived the character's film career. A number of television programs and cartoon shows appeared afterwards, with *Lois and*

Clark: The New Adventures of Super-man (1993–97) and the most successful, *Smallville* (2001–present), a reworking of the Superboy theme.

Superman's saga was revised in the 1980s by John Byrne in order to simplify what had become a complex series of storylines and characters. Superman's powers were reduced somewhat and characters such as Superboy and Supergirl were eliminated entirely. In an early 1990s storyline Superman was killed by a creature called Doomsday and subsequently resurrected. The long romance between Lois Lane and Superman reached its climax with their marriage in 1996.

Superman was the first super hero to appear in comic books and as such he has become a literary icon. A wide variety of other comic book heroes with remarkable powers or abilities followed, but none have achieved the iconic status enjoyed by the Man of Steel. Superman's significance as a cultural symbol, both within the United States and globally, has generated much commentary by scholars, critics and others over the years. While the character of Superman has undergone numerous and occasionally dramatic changes throughout nearly 70 years, he seems to remain as relevant to Americans today as he was when he first appeared in 1938.

Greg Moore

See also: Radio.

References and Further Reading

Daniels, Les. 1998. *Superman: The Complete History: The Life and Times of the Man of Steel.* San Francisco: Chronicle Books.

Daniels, Les. 2004. *DC Comics: A Celebration of the World's Favorite Comic Book Heroes.* 2nd ed. New York. Virgin Books.

Eury, Michael, Adams, Neal, Swan, Curt, and Anderson, Murphy. 2006. *The Krypton Companion.* Raleigh, NC: Two Morrows Publishing.

Yeffeth, Glenn, ed. 2006. *The Man From Krypton: A Closer Look at Superman.* Dallas, TX: Benbella Books.

Swing Music

Swing music developed from the incorporation of elements of western classical art music with the jazz music of the 1920s, a combination which generally smoothed the rhythms and introduced a wider variety of instrumentation. While jazz music was dominated by African Americans, many white musicians made a name for themselves in swing music. The period of swing music is sometimes also known as the Big Band Era, although some historians of music would distinguish the swing music of the 1930s from that of the 1940s and early 1950s, which remained popular into the beginning of the rock era.

Swing music was also distinguished from the jazz of the 1920s by a more elegant, well-designed image of the bands. The jazz bands of the Roaring Twenties were professional in their appearance and on-stage demeanor, while the big bands of the 1930s would arrange themselves in neat rows behind handsome music stands, generally ornamented with the monogrammed initials of the band's leader. Conductors such as Benny Goodman, Tommy Dorsey and Glenn Miller often outfitted their bandsmen in handsome uniforms, and Duke Ellington's band even had multiple outfits for various occasions.

Swing music also reduced the degree of improvisation in performances. Whereas in jazz a score was at most a jumping-off point for wild improvisations in which

A swing band plays at a community center dance in Brooklyn, New York, 1941. (Rothstein, Arthur. *The Depression Years As Photographed by Arthur Rothstein.* Dover Publications, 1978)

performers sought to outdo one another, swing music was heavily based upon written scores. When the Glenn Miller Band played "In the Mood" at a club in Los Angeles, it would sound almost exactly like their rendition of the song in Chicago. The individual players were no longer independent actors negotiating an *ad hoc* performance, but had become subordinated to the score and the conductor.

The venues in which they played also differed. Jazz musicians of the 1920s often found employment in less acceptable establishments, such as brothels or speakeasies. Listening to jazz had a certain flavor of the forbidden, which made it exciting. By contrast, many big

swing bands, particularly white bands, played in more upscale venues such as hotels and dance halls, giving them a respectable image.

However, swing music was not without its critics. In particular, its energetic rhythms came under fire because of the physical responses it tended to inspire in its listeners: toe-tapping, finger-snapping, swaying bodies, etc. To the dedicated concert-goer accustomed to the staid decorum of the symphony, such behaviors were gauche, excusable only in young children. As a result, many highbrow critics condemned swing as being uncultured and representative of a lower order of society, fearing that its proliferation would result in the deterioration of standards of music appreciation throughout society. Many of these critics simply ignored the fact that swing was first and foremost a genre of dance music, and as such it was somewhat irrational to expect people to sit still and listen passively to melodies intended to inspire movement.

Even on the dance floor, swing was not immune from attacks. Particularly in dance halls that had been heavily dominated by aficionados of the waltz and other classical dance steps, the movements followed by swing dancers were often met with hostility. The derogatory term "jitterbugging" was often applied to the rapid movements that characterized swing dancing. By the end of the 1930s some midwestern dance halls began actively prohibiting the characteristic moves of the "bug." Generally their rationale was that jitterbugging took up too much space, and on a crowded dance floor it was disruptive to other dancers. One Indianapolis ballroom went so far as to ban a list of specific behaviors after jiggerbuggers and waltzers came to blows.

However, the opprobrium that fell upon swing music was not confined to dance hall owners. Commentators spoke of swing as having a jungle beat that inflamed the animal passions, and sought to connect it with delinquency and crime. There were even experiments that purported to show deleterious effects of swing music. Some of them appear to have been hoaxes with racially tinged humor, such as the ones that supposedly exposed various species of monkeys and great apes to recordings of a number of swing bands. One held at Oberlin College had a little more claim to scientific respectability, involving having 10 musicians tap out straight and syncopated rhythms while having various physiometric measuring devices attached to their bodies, and comparing their physical reactions to the two kinds of rhythm.

Hollywood got into the act with *Strike Up the Band,* a 1940 musical about a young man who forms a swing dance band with the high goal of showing that American musical genres are as good as classical genres imported from Europe. In the end, swing became a mainstream genre, and by the middle of the 1950s, its listeners were leveling the same accusations against "that new rock and roll music" as had been leveled against swing by their elders. The term "big band music" for swing actually rose in the beginning of the rock era, comparing the large swing bands to the smaller ensembles typical of rock.

Leigh Kimmel

See also: Basie, William "Count"; Ellington, Edward Kennedy "Duke"; Goodman, Benny; Hillbilly Music; Kirk, Andrew Dewey.

References and Further Reading

Belaire, David. 1996. *A Guide to the Big Band Era: A Comprehensive Review of All the Recorded Hits and All the Hitmakers.* Santa Ana, CA: Winged Note Press.

Bindas, Kenneth J. 2001. *Swing, That Modern Sound: The Cultural Context of Swing Music in America, 1935–1947.* Jackson: University Press of Mississippi

Ehrenberg, Lewis A. 1998. *Swingin' the Dream: Big Band Jazz and the Rebirth of American Culture.* Chicago: University of Chicago Press.

Oliphant, Dave. 2002. *The Early Swing Era: 1930 to 1941.* Westport, CT: Greenwood Press.

Stowe, David W. 1994. *Swing Changes: Big Band Jazz in New Deal America.* Cambridge, MA: Harvard University Press.

Yanow, Scott. 2002. *Swing: Great Musicians, Influential Groups.* San Francisco: Miller Freeman.

Tatum, Art (1910–56)

The remarkable Arthur Tatum Jr. was one of the greatest pianists jazz has produced. His reputation rests on an amazing technique and outstanding powers of invention. A major influence on alto sax great Charlie Parker, Tatum's free improvisational style and technical acrobatics were forerunners of modern jazz.

Tatum was born on October 10, 1910, in Toledo, Ohio. Nearly blind from birth, he had no sight in one eye and only partial vision in the other. His parents were supportive of his musical inclination. From the age of three, he played by ear. Later he studied piano and managed to master Braille so that he could read music. Tatum did not pursue a career as a classical pianist despite being encouraged to do so by his teacher, Overton G. Rainey. Extraordinary talent notwithstanding, career opportunities in classical music were, for African American musicians, nonexistent at the time. Tatum turned instead to what he heard on piano rolls, recordings, radio broadcasts, and from musicians who played in the area. Stride pianist Fats Waller was an early, important influence.

By 1926, Tatum was playing locally in Ohio. In 1929 and 1930, his performances were broadcast over WSPD in Toledo, once as a partner of Teddy Wilson. He went to New York in 1932 as accompanist for jazz singer Adelaide Hall, and in 1933, he recorded his first solo. New York City was the scene of Tatum's first "cutting" contest, a performance competition among musicians. He won with a formidable rendering of *Tiger Rag,* having faced down James P. Johnson, Willie ("The Lion") Smith, and Fats Waller.

After-hours solos at New York's Onyx Club did not bring in enough money, and Tatum returned to the Midwest. He was in Cleveland from 1934 to 1935 and in Chicago the following year. By 1937, thanks to New York club dates and radio jobs, his reputation was established. He toured England in 1938, conquered London, and appeared in New York and Los Angeles in the late 1930s and early 1940s. In 1943, he founded his own trio with Tiny Grimes on electric guitar and Slam Stewart on double bass.

A complex person, Tatum was a favorite of jazz fans but never became generally popular. Recordings produced by Norman Granz in the 1950s brought together some fine small ensembles and yielded an extraordinary series of solo performances. Tatum, however, was a subject of controversy, especially during the years preceding and following his death. According to critic-scholar Gunther Schuller, conflicting opinions about the pianist's importance stem from "the uniqueness and solitary nature of his art." Not of the mainstream, Tatum was essentially a loner: most often he performed alone and did not follow musical fashion. The disagreements spring from differing assessments of his creativity and of his influence on the course of jazz. As *New Yorker* writer Whitney Balliett says, "No one ever knew exactly what he was or what to do with him."

All critics concede that his technical mastery was matchless. Tatum's astonishing style was distinguished by "its speed and accuracy, and its harmonic and rhythmic imagination." Tatum continued to grow musically until the end of his life. By abandoning the restrictions imposed by the stride style, he was able to play with greater rhythmic freedom. Until his death in Los Angeles, California on November 5, 1956, he played solo or in ensemble, in clubs or in concert.

References and Further Reading

Bindas, Kenneth J. 2001. *Swing, That Modern Sound.* Jackson: University of Mississippi Press.

Laubich, Arnold. 1982. *Art Tatum, a Guide to his Recorded Music.* New Brunswick, NJ: Institute of Jazz Studies, Rutgers University; Metuchen, NJ: Scarecrow Press.

Lester, James. 1994. *Too Marvelous for Words: The Life and Genius of Art Tatum.* New York: Oxford University Press.

Giddins, Gary. 1998. *Visions of Jazz: The First Century.* New York: Oxford University Press.

Fell, John L. 1999. *Stride!: Fats, Jimmy, Lion, Lamb, and all the Other Ticklers.* New Brunswick, NJ: Institute of Jazz Studies Rutgers, State University of New Jersey, Scarecrow Press.

Williams, Martin T. 1993. *The Jazz Tradition.* New York: Oxford University Press.

Temple, Shirley (1928–)

During the Great Depression, child actress Shirley Temple provided American film audiences with what President Franklin D. Roosevelt termed a much needed "infectious optimism." Although she was the number one box office attraction in the United States from 1935 to 1938, she was unable to expand her career into more adult roles in the 1940s.

Shirley Temple was born April 23, 1928, in Santa Monica, California. Her father, George Francis Temple, was a banker, while her mother Gertrude Amelia Krieger, was an ambitious stage mother, who enrolled her three-year old daughter in dancing classes. In the early 1930s, Temple appeared in the *Baby Burlesque* films in which children in diapers mimicked adult roles. The film production code halted these questionable films in 1933. The following year Temple was signed to a Fox Studios contract to appear in *Stand Up and Cheer,* gaining acclaim for the song "Baby Take a Bow." Meanwhile, the film *Little Miss Marker,* which she had previously made with Paramount, was released several weeks after *Stand Up and Cheer.* Based upon a story by Damon Runyon, *Little Miss Marker* teamed Temple with veteran actor Adolphe Menjou. The film proved a major box office hit for the six-year old who tamed the hearts of audiences and a cynical bookie portrayed by Menjou. Temple followed this success with *Baby Take a Bow* (1934) and *Bright Eyes* (1934) in which an orphaned Temple sang "On the Good Ship Lollipop," a tune which would always be identified with the mop-haired child star.

The following year Daryl F. Zanuck featured Temple in four Fox pictures and pioneered a merchandising bonanza with Temple products such as dolls and dresses. In *The Little Colonel* and *The Littlest Rebel,* Temple danced with Bill "Bojangles" Robinson. Temple's status as a child deflected criticism of an interracial dancing couple, but the films certainly reflected stereotypes of blacks comfortable with the institution of slavery. In *Our Little Girl,* Temple used her charms to reunite estranged parents, while *Curly Top* featured the hit song "Animal Crackers in My Soup." In 1935, Temple was the recipient of a special Juvenile Performer Academy Award for recognition of her outstanding contributions to film entertainment.

Temple continued to churn out hits throughout the 1930s, featuring musical numbers and the ability of the diminutive child, often orphaned or abandoned, to win over the hearts of crusty authority figures. She impersonated Ginger Rogers and danced with a Fred Astaire doll in *Stowaway* (1936). More international settings were provided for Temple in *Heidi* (1937) and John Ford's *Wee Willie Winkie* (1937), in which Temple became the mascot for a British regiment in India. The following year Temple was cast in one of her most beloved roles, *Rebecca of Sunnybrook Farm.*

The 1940 production *The Blue Bird,* however, was the first Temple vehicle to lose money, and Fox released her from her contract at age 12. Although Temple continued to make films throughout the 1940s, such as *Since You Went Away* (1944), *The Bachelor and the Bobby-Soxer* (1947), and *Fort Apache* (1948) with her husband John Agar whom she wed in 1945, audiences failed to accept the child star as a mature adult.

She divorced Agar in 1950 and married television producer Charles Black, whom she met in Hawaii. Two brief television comebacks in 1958 and 1959 failed, and Temple retired from acting. But she did not remain out of the public eye. After unsuccessfully running for Congress as a Republican, Temple was appointed as the U.S. Representative to the United Nations by President Richard Nixon in 1969. She also served as the American Ambassador to Ghana (1976) and Czechoslovakia (1989). She survived a bout with breast cancer in 1999, and in 2005, Temple was awarded the Screen Actors Guild Life Achievement Award. Temple's spunky character was, indeed,

an inspiration for many Americans during the Depression years.

Ron Briley

See also: West, Mae.

References and Further Reading
Black, Shirley Temple. 1989. *Child Star, USA.* New York: Warner Books.

Hammontree, Patsy Guy. 1998. *Shirley Temple Black: A Bio-Bibliography.* Westport, CT: Greenwood Press.

Windeler, Robert. 1995. *The Films of Shirley Temple.* New York: Citadel Press.

Thomson, Virgil Garnett (1896–1989)

Virgil Garnett Thomson was a composer of uniquely American music whose rhythms were modeled on American speech patterns and the harmonies of Protestant hymnbooks. His work was also strongly influenced by the rebellious French composer Erik Satie and French impressionist composer Claude Debussy. One of Thomson's best-known compositions is *Four Saints in Three Acts,* a comedy opera whose libretto Gertrude Stein wrote.

Born in Kansas City, Missouri on November 25, 1896, Thomson went to the city's public schools. He had learned to play piano by age 5, and by age 12 was taking lessons with the best teachers in the area. Thomson concentrated on studying the organ from 1909 until 1917, during which time he also served as organist in his family's Baptist Church and in other Kansas City churches. After serving in a field artillery unit with the army during World War I, Thomson returned to the United States and entered Harvard University in 1919. At the university, he studied both music theory and practiced extensively and began to compose there in 1920. He toured Europe with the Harvard Glee Club in 1921, occasionally conducting the group, and then stayed in Paris for a year on a traveling fellowship.

While in Paris, Thomson composed more music and published his first critical work, music reviews for the *Boston Evening Transcript.* When he returned to the United States, he continued his education at Harvard but took a job as organist and choirmaster at King's Chapel in Boston. Thomson graduated from Harvard in 1923 and having received a Juilliard Fellowship, traveled to New York for a year of study. In 1924, he went back to Harvard to teach as an assistant instructor and supplemented his meager income by writing music reviews for *Vanity Fair.* His writing attracted so much attention that many friends and colleagues suggested he take up music criticism professionally. Thomson declined, however, determined to pursue his career as a composer and musician.

In the fall of 1925, Thomson returned to Paris, where he would stay until 1940 and where he would come to accept his homosexuality. His first composition of that period was the *Sonata da Chiesa,* a neoclassical chamber work for five instruments that Thomson later called his "graduation piece." In late 1926, Thomson met Gertrude Stein, then a young writer living in Paris, and immediately found himself part of the fashionable crowd that surrounded Stein and her companion, Alice B. Toklas. He made a great deal of valuable connections among Parisian society among Stein's associates, but most important to his future was his collaboration with Stein herself on a comedy opera, which they named *Four Saints in Three Acts.* Meanwhile, Thomson's career as a composer was beginning to take off, and in 1928, he put together the first show devoted entirely to his music. It featured four pieces for organ derived from Protestant hymns called *Variations on Sunday School Tunes,* his first symphony, the *Symphony on a Hymn Tune, Five Phrases from the Song of Solomon,* and *Capital, Capitals,* another Stein collaboration. The concert was successful, but the music was considered somewhat controversial because of its austerity and dissonance. It was also at that point that Thomson began developing the style of the musical "portrait." He wrote more than 100 of those portrait-like pieces during his long career. By 1929, Thomson's music was so much in vogue that the fashionable thing at private parties was to present all-Thomson programs.

From 1931 to 1934, Thomson worked mostly on getting the staging done for *Four Saints.* He employed lighting experts, choreographers, costume designers, and a conductor, but not until later did he have the idea that would make the show such a hit: casting the opera entirely with African Americans. The show premiered on Broadway on February 20, 1934, and was such a hit that Thomson became nationally famous overnight. He returned to Paris, and living off his royalties from the show, composed incidental music for several productions. In 1936 and 1937, respectively, he wrote musical scores for the films *The Plough That Broke the Plains* and *The River,* both of which were praised by music critics. Those scores were filled with references to cowboy songs, old popular tunes, and Southern spirituals. His compositions for the ballet *The Filling Station* in 1938 also received rave reviews.

Thomson wrote his first book, *The State of Music,* in 1939. The following year, when France fell to the Nazis, the composer fled to New York and got a job as chief music critic for the *New York Herald Tribune,* where until his retirement in 1954 he would develop and perfect the writing style that he came to be known for. By the end of his tenure at the paper, Thomson had become known as the country's premier music critic. In the meantime, in 1947, he wrote his second opera, the comedic *The Mother of Us All,* whose libretto Stein also wrote. Thomson won a Pulitzer Prize in 1948 for his score for the film *Louisiana Story.*

Thomson spent the majority of the 1950s and 1960s traveling the world, lecturing at universities, going to music conferences, writing critical articles, and conducting. He was appointed to the American Academy of Arts and Letters in 1959. Thomson had written the bulk of his music by the 1950s, but some notable exceptions are *Missa Pro Defunctis* (1960); his third and last opera, *Lord Byron,* in 1968; and *Fanfare for Peace* (1979). He also wrote a number of books on music, including *The Musical Scene* (1945), *The Art of Judging Music* (1948), *American Music since 1910* (1971), and *Music with Words* (1989). Thomson received a National Book Critics Circle Award for his *Virgil Thomson Reader* in 1983, the same year he earned the coveted Kennedy Center Honor. He continued working into his eighties and died at the famous Chelsea Hotel in New York City on September 30, 1989.

Amanda de la Garza

References and Further Reading

Bindas, Kenneth J. 1995. *All of this Music Belongs to the Nation: The WPA's Federal Music Project and American Society, 1935–1939.* Knoxville: University of Tennessee Press.

Kostelanetz, Richard, ed. 2002. *The Virgil Thomson Reader: Selected Writings, 1924–1984.* New York: Routledge.

Levy, Alan Howard. 1983. *Musical Nationalism: American Composers' Search for Identity.* Westport, CT: Greenwood Press.

Meckna, Michael. 1986. *Virgil Thomson, a Bio-Bibliography.* Westport, CT: Greenwood Press.

Tommasini, Anthony. 1997. *Virgil Thomson: Composer on the Aisle.* New York: W. W. Norton.

Thomson, Virgil. 1988. *Correspondence/Selections.* New York: Summit Books.

Thomson, Virgil. 1977, c.1966. *Virgil Thomson.* New York: Da Capo Press.

Watson, Steven. 1998. *Prepare for Saints: Gertrude Stein, Virgil Thomson, and the Mainstreaming of American Modernism.* New York: Random House.

Timberline Lodge

Timberline Lodge is probably the largest resort structure constructed and furnished by hand under the Works Progress Administration (WPA). It is a ski resort at 6000 feet on the southern slope of Mount Hood, 60 miles from Portland, Oregon. In 22 months, from December 1935 (when the WPA administrators in Washington, D.C., approved the first application) until February 1938 (when the lodge was opened to the public), local administrators rushed to construct and furnish this "Playground for Everyone." The project was completed in record time.

Local administrators of the U.S. Forest Service were searching for ways to develop recreational opportunities in the national forest on Mount Hood at the same time that local businessmen, sports enthusiasts and Emerson J. Griffith, Oregon's WPA administrator, were striving to build a ski resort. In September 1935, Griffith submitted the application to construct a ski lodge, and in December 1935, the project was approved, without any drawings or assessment. The Forest Service rushed to find an architect, and local businessmen organized the Mount Hood Development Association to raise $20,000 for the "sponsor" contribution by selling bonds. Gilbert Stanley Underwood, an architect experienced in designing such national park lodges as The Ahwahnee in Yosemite National Park and Grand Canyon Lodge (since rebuilt), was retained as consulting architect. Forest Service architects—Tim Turner, Linn Forrest, Howard Gifford, and Dean Wright—executed final drawings for the building and designed wrought-iron decoration and hardware and some heavy furniture for the lodge. The building was conceived in three parts—a hexagonal "headhouse," and two asymmetrical wings. Working with pioneer, Indian, and wildlife themes, interior designer, Margery Hoffman Smith, metalwork supervisor Orion B. Dawson, and woodwork supervisor Ray Neufer furnished the lodge with hand-wrought ironwork, hand-made wood furniture and hand-woven, hooked, and sewn fabrics. Blacksmiths made a pair of dining room gates, spiral and animal-shaped andirons, hardware for the doors, light fixtures, and straps on high ceiling beams in the lobby. Frequently working without designs, workers in the WPA woodshop constructed handmade furniture, including hexagonal oak coffee tables, angled three-sided couches, wood and iron bed frames, chairs, tables, chests, and coat racks. A special chair with arms was made for President Franklin Roosevelt to use when he came to dedicate the lodge. Hand-carved newel posts illustrating animals native to the Mount Hood area and a carved Indian head door carried out the decorative schemes. Textiles included hand-woven upholstery and draperies, hand-hooked rugs, and hand appliquéd curtains in the guestrooms, created in designs based on local wildflowers. Hand-painted lithographs and watercolors of local wildflowers were hung on the walls of all the guestrooms.

Several of Oregon's most highly regarded artists were commissioned to paint murals and paintings for the lodge, including C. S. Price, Darrel Austin, Howard Sewall, and Charles Heaney. The murals and paintings created for the lodge by Price and Heaney are the largest and among the most significant of their careers. Wildlife themes were illustrated in carved wood panels by Erich Lamade and Florence Thomas, and in wood marquetry murals by Aimee Gorham. Virginia Darcé depicted the lumberjack Paul Bunyan in opus sectile glass mosaics, and Douglas Lynch illustrated mountain activities in painted and carved linoleum panels.

The WPA initially approved $275,000 for the lodge project, but actual construction and furnishing costs exceeded one million dollars. Multiple applications were approved by WPA administrators in Washington, D.C. Because New Deal projects were intended to create work, the WPA required that labor costs account for 90 percent of the project and materials the remaining 10 percent. The materials for construction of Timberline Lodge were far higher even in the initial application.

Local administrators attempted to use the furnishing projects to generate a local craft industry. The designs for the furniture were compiled into books so that the pieces could be replicated. An effort was also made to use local materials, such as flax for woven upholstery and draperies, in order to revive the lagging flax industry in Oregon. Due to the economy and other factors, these attempts were unsuccessful at that time.

When President Roosevelt came to the northwest to dedicate Bonneville Dam on September 28, 1937, he and Eleanor Roosevelt motored around Mount Hood with Oregon's Governor Charles Martin and visited Timberline Lodge. Despite personal concerns over costs, he dedicated the lodge "as a monument to the skill and faithful performance of workers on the rolls of the Works Progress Administration." The lodge was opened to the public on the weekend of February 4, 1938. It was operated by Timberline Lodge, Inc., a private group of Portland businessmen many of whom had been active in the Mount Hood Development Association. The Forest Service administered the lodge through a special use permit.

In 1939, WPA funds were used to construct the Magic Mile—the second chairlift in the world (after the one at Sun Valley, Idaho). A ski hut that served as the terminus of the lift was also built and named Silcox Hut after Chief Ferdinand Silcox, the head of the Forest Service who supported the ski lift construction and who died unexpectedly prior to its completion.

The lodge was operated for four years prior to World War II and was then closed for the duration of the war. It re-opened in December 1945, and was run by a series of managers until 1955. Richard L. Kohnstamm organized R.L.K. and Company, which has successfully operated the lodge and surrounding facilities for over 50 years. Although the textiles have worn out, most of the original art and wood and metal furnishings remain. With the assistance of the local, non-profit Friends of Timberline, new textiles based on original designs have been created. Local blacksmiths have made hand-wrought handrails, door latches, lamps and other iron work to replace broken or missing originals or to provide needed safety improvements in the style of original furnishings. Woodworkers have similarly replaced broken or missing pieces and adapted designs to satisfy current preferences (for queen-size beds rather than twin-size, for example). This National Landmark embodies some of the finest examples of New Deal art and craftsmanship.

Sarah Munro

See also: Davis Mountain Indian Lodge; Hopkins, Harry; Works Progress Administration. Harry Hopkins.

References and Further Reading

Gohs, Carl. 1972. *Timberline: A Common Ground Between Man and the Spirit of the Mountain.* Portland, OR: Metropolitan Printing.

Griffin, Rachael, and Sarah Munro, eds. 1978. *Timberline Lodge.* Portland, OR: Friends of Timberline.

Rose, Judith, ed. 1986. *Timberline Lodge: a Love Story.* Portland, OR: Friends of Timberline and Graphic Arts Center Publishing Company.

Tobacco Road (1932)

Tobacco Road, the novel (1932), the Broadway play (1933), and the film (1941), were all met with widespread controversy, much financial gain, and some critical success. The conflict of the characters, trapped between a growing industrialization of farming and the gravity of the Depression, would normally be sympathetic characters like those of John Steinbeck; however, *Tobacco Road's* poor, white southern farmers are unsympathetic and, some say, despicable. Their ignorance, lascivious behavior, and tendency towards violence make *Tobacco Road* a problematic plot to pigeonhole. Some critics and audiences have labeled the story as an American tragedy, while other have marked it the most extreme example of a southern grotesque. The naturalistic style of the novel's author, Erskine Caldwell, in dialect, dialog and demagogy, elevate it above genre.

Although the film by director John Ford does not follow Caldwell's novel as closely as the Broadway play adapted by Jack Kirkland, the plot spins around the Lesters, a destitute family of sharecroppers, and other desperate characters: Jeeter Lester, who loves the land and lusts after Sister Bessie; Jeeter's son Dude, who wants a new Ford; Sister Bessie, who seeks God's approval to marry Dude and purchase him a new Ford; and Jeeter's two daughters Ellie Mae and Pearl who spend much of the beginning of the book trying to steal turnips from Pearl's husband, Lov Bensey. Several of the women have facial deformities and, by legal standards, marry men too old or young for them.

A car lover may feel more depressed over what happens to the Ford than the population of *Tobacco Road.* The car is driven over Grandma Lester and an unfortunate black man, run without enough oil, and used to haul wood. When Jeeter and his wife die in a fire, after spending much time worrying about their own deaths which seem inevitable and imminent, the rubberneckers to this story who enjoyed the antics might be sad, while others who did not care for these characters, who care only for themselves, might be relieved.

As far as *Tobacco Road* being a testament to how hard life was during the Depression, Jeeter does note how many of his daughters have run off to live a better life in the city. The Lesters are without credit or money to buy seeds to, in turn, grow food to make money. The story describes a downward spiral, caused by both the conditions of the country and the reactions of the characters. The worst criticism of Caldwell's work is that his story, if seen as grotesque, portrays life during the Depression in a black comedy that onlookers can dismiss while laughing. The most generous observation of the work, especially during the time it was popular, is that it allowed the destitute to be entertained, even if they were unaware that more sophisticated readers might see them as a butt of their own joke.

Mark Schwartz

See also: Faulkner, William Cuthbert.

References and Further Reading

Caldwell, Erskine. 1947. *Tobacco Road.* New York: Modern Library.

Cook, Sylvia. 1991. *Erskine Caldwell and the Fiction of Poverty.* Baton Rouge, LA. Louisiana State University Press.

Tag, Gallagher. 1986. *John Ford: The Man and his Films.* Berkeley, CA: University of California.

Ward, Helen (1916–98)

A singer who rose to national fame with the Benny Goodman Band, Helen Ward helped redefine the role of popular female vocalist during the swing era.

Born in New York City, Helen Ward began playing piano at the age of three and took up singing as a teenager. Despite her lack of formal training, her duo act with family friend and songwriter Burton Lane got her noticed by several New York bandleaders. Nye Mayhew, Eddy Duchin, and Enrique Madriguera all had her sing with their bands after she finished high school, and by the age of 18 she was singing regularly with Roxanne's Orchestra on New York's WOR radio station. Thus, she was actually was a bigger name than Benny Goodman in 1934, when she agreed as a personal favor to sing with his new band on its first audition. That audition ultimately led to the Goodman band's first job and its formative stint on NBC's national *Let's Dance* radio show.

Ward accompanied the band on the cross-country tour in 1935 that established Goodman's reputation and traditionally marks the beginning of the swing era. Her swinging vocals and enthusiastic, alluring stage presence distinguished her from other vocalists and quickly made her a favorite of the college-age men who were a large part of Goodman's core audience. Ward recorded frequently with Goodman's band, charting a number of songs including such number one hits as "It's Been So Long," "The Glory of Love," "You Turned the Tables on Me," "Goody Goody," and "These Foolish Things." Despite this success, the stresses of touring and her turbulent personal relationship with Goodman (which included an informal marriage proposal that he later broke) made her increasingly unhappy, and at the age of 20 she retired to marry childhood sweetheart Albert Marx.

Her retirement was brief, and from 1937 to the early 1940s, she recorded with several artists, including Teddy Wilson, Joe Sullivan, and Gene Krupa. Her biggest hit of this period 1939's number one hit *Day In, Day Out* with Bob Crosby's band. Through the forties and fifties she worked in radio production and toured periodically, including stints with Hal McIntyre, Harry James, Peanuts Hucko, and an ill-fated reunion tour with Goodman in 1953. After a long period out of the spotlight, she resumed singing in New York clubs in 1979, and released her last recording, *The Helen Ward Song Book, Vol. 1* in 1981.

Although Ward's professional career was much more sporadic than that of many of her contemporaries, her significance to popular music was immense. Apart from the important part she played in making Goodman's band a success, Ward also played a fundamental role in changing the nature of female pop vocals. Before she joined Goodman in 1934, few major bands had a "girl singer" (as all female band vocalists were called at the time), and those that did tended to favor sweet, trained voices, primarily on ballads. Ward's confident, bouncy, and relatively unembellished singing of jazzy tunes helped define the standard swing-era vocal style and became a model for most of the female big band vocalists who followed her.

Kevin Kern

See also: Crosby, Bob; Goodman, Benny; Humes, Helen.

References and Further Reading

Collier, James Lincoln. 1989. *Benny Goodman and the Swing Era.* New York: Oxford University Press.

Firestone, Ross. 1993. *Swing, Swing, Swing: The Life and Times of Benny Goodman.* New York: W. W. Norton & Company.

Friedwald, Will. 1996. *Jazz Singing: America's Great Voices from Bessie Smith to Bebop and Beyond.* New York: Da Capo Press.

War of the Worlds

The radio adaptation of H. G. Wells's science fiction novel *War of the Worlds* aired on October 30, 1938, as a Halloween night special, live from CBS in New York City. Orson Welles, in his early twenties, directed and performed the play written by Howard Koch with considerable input from Welles and other members of CBS's *Mercury Theatre On the Air.* The hour long show competed with the much more popular show, *Chase and Sanborn Hour,* which featured Don Ameche and two other popular radio stars.

The adaptation is most famous for its format and its ensuing panic, whether widespread or isolated. The format of the show was that of a news broadcast, not a typical format for fiction, but not unheard of as a storytelling technique. Welles's show was the first to use this format on record in the United States. The fact that most of the voices could have been recognizable from other stories told by CBS's *Mercury Theatre On the Air* did tip off some listeners that these were fake news flashes interrupting entertainment not usual for the normally broadcasted show.

What made this adaptation different were the infrequency of the announcement reminding the listener that this was indeed not really happening, and the length of the fake broadcast, which lasted an hour. Those listeners who just tuned in from the more popular Don Ameche bit of the *Chase and Sanborn Hour* would miss the first disclaimer that this was a radio play and not a real news broadcast. In fact, if listeners switched after the Don Ameche bit, they would have heard a news report that Martians had been seen stepping out of their space ships.

The Martians, in the fake news broadcast and in the novel, were less than friendly. They had ray guns and traveled in monstrous machines to cross rivers and fields, passing easily over wooded areas. They sprayed poison gas and seemed attracted to New York City in a very pre-Christmas shopping rush. While H. G. Wells's novel had the Martians landing in England, Orson Welles's Martians landed on the East Coast of the United States.

While the broadcast aired, listeners began to flock to Grover's Mill, in New Jersey, to catch a glimpse of the focal point of the alien invasion. By the time the broadcast was over, the local police had to quell crowds, informing people, some of whom were armed with weapons, that it had only been a science fiction radio show. Anecdotal and documented incidents include a panicked person shooting a farmer's water tower, fleeing citizens refusing to pay for gas because the end of the world was nigh, and churches opening for congregations to pray. According to reports, all educational levels were susceptible to the story: several professors from nearby Princeton University made a road trip to the site where the unidentified flying objects were first seen.

The next day, *The New York Times* ran the headline: "Radio Listeners in Panic, Taking War Time Drama as Fact." Although the headline is slightly misleading, the use of the word "War" is intriguing to social scientists. Some listeners did not believe it was Martians invading, but that an actual invasion was taking place by

William Dock, a resident of Grovers Mill, New Jersey, carries a shotgun ready to ward off strange creatures from Mars, October 31, 1938. Residents of the area fled after fictitious news bulletins broadcast over the Mercury Theater of the Air by actor Orson Welles (during a dramatization of H. G. Wells's book *The War of the Worlds*) said that the first space ship carrying invading martians had landed here. (Bettmann/Corbis)

Germans with a new technology, perhaps dressed as Martians. Other social scientists, in retrospect, believed that the panic over the broadcast had been exaggerated by the contemporary media. Thus, the media was creating panic over how easily Americans panic. Whether this is indeed the case, over 12,000 newspapers worldwide ran stories about the panic within a month of that Halloween night. Adolph Hitler stated that the panic proved that democracy was deteriorating in America.

The public, nevertheless, wanted CBS and Orson Welles to be punished for what many people considered a prank rather than a mistake. CBS and Welles apologized and this seemed to be enough for most of America. CBS promised to never use this fake broadcast format again. Welles was less apologetic. In fact, two years later, Orson Welles and H. G. Wells were interviewed together and both made jokes about the event.

The airing and the controversy around its presentation made Orson Welles a household name and afforded him the opportunity for tremendous creative control when he directed his first film, *Citizen Kane,* three years later. A multitude of books, films, and television shows reference, in scholarly seriousness or in parody, the show and the incidents around it. Undoubtedly, it is the most famous and notorious radio show in history.

Since the Depression, there have been countless books, films, radio and television shows that attempt to document or fictionalize the ensuing panic, some scholarly, some realistically, some comically. Whether the aftermath of this radio show is a textbook example of mass hysteria or how the media loves to report on itself is still up for debate. One thing is certain—other programs that use this type of broadcast format in latter years have yielded similar results. In Ecuador, a radio show using a fake news broadcast panicked and then outraged listeners to such a degree that they burned the radio station down to the ground.

Mark Schwartz

See also: Citizen Kane; Federal Theatre Project.

References and Further Reading

Campbell, Roberts. 1976. *The Golden Years of Broadcast.* New York: Scribner's.

Douglas, George H. 1987. *The Early Days of Radio Broadcasting.* New York: McFarland.

Nachman, Gerald. 1998. *Raised on the Radio.* New York: Random House.

Welles, Orson, and Peter Bogdanovich, 1992. *This is Orson Welles.* New York: Harper Collins.

West, Mae (1893–1980)

Mae West began her acting career as a child performer in Vaudeville shows in Brooklyn. In the 1920s, West began to write and star in her own Broadway shows. She was arrested for public obscenity in 1927 for writing and starring in the play titled *Sex* about a wandering prostitute. Her next effort was *Diamond Lil*, a smash hit based on the 1890s saloon culture of New York's Bowery district. This was the role in which West would develop into an icon—the sultry saloon-keeper who spouted memorable sexual innuendos and one-liners with unmatched wit.

In 1932 West headed to Hollywood to start her contract with Paramount Studios. From the beginning, West felt like an outsider in the movie business. Although her public persona would indicate otherwise, she usually spent every night at home working on scripts rather than out socializing with Hollywood stars. Her first movie, *Night After Night,* was lukewarm, but in 1933 she starred in two movies that revitalized the flagging Paramount Studios: *She Done Him Wrong* and *I'm No Angel,* both with Cary Grant. The former was a doctored version *of Diamond Lil,* which was supposed to have been too risqué to ever reach the big screen. While conservatives were outraged with West's blatant sexual come-ons, both movies ran successfully for weeks across the nation. Other movies West starred in during the Depression include *Belle of the Nineties* (1934), *Goin' to Town* (1935), *Klondike Annie* (1935), *Go West, Young Man* (1936), and *My Little Chickadee* (1940).

West came to symbolize a new era of Hollywood during the Great Depression. While stars like Marlene Dietrich and Greta Garbo had popularized the masculine, svelte look, West's voluptuous curves represented health and bounty in an era of depravity. She also created bold female characters that openly enjoyed sex with no apologies or victimhood. The coming repeal of prohibition also made West's barroom scenes with a drink in hand appealing to audiences.

On the other hand, West's movies provoked outrage among censors. The Production Code (also known as the Hays

Code) was created in 1930 with the aim of regulating offensive material in the motion picture business. The code was not enforced until Mae West created such a stir with both *She Done Him Wrong* and *I'm No Angel.* Her next movie, *Belle of the Nineties,* was targeted by the Hays Office to prove that they could enforce the Production Code. Even though the movie was drastically edited in order to be approved by the Hays Office and appeared on banned list anyway, it still was very successful. After a dispute with Paramount, West worked at Universal for one film, but left the movie business in the early 1940s. In the 1960s and 1970s she recorded several albums and wrote an autobiography. She made a brief comeback in the 1970s by appearing on television shows and a few movies, capitalizing on her well-known diva personality.

Kate Stewart

References and Further Reading

Erens, Patricia, ed. 1979. *Sexual stratagems: The World of Women in Film.* New York: Horizon Press.
Leider, Emily Wortis. 1997. *Becoming Mae West.* New York: Farrar, Straus and Giroux.
Louvish, Simon. 2005. *Mae West: "It Ain't No Sin."* New York: Thomas Dunne Books.
Watts, Jill. 2001. *Mae West: An Icon in Black and White.* Oxford: Oxford University Press.

Williams, Mary Lou (1914–81)

A prominent American jazz stride pianist, composer and music arranger, Mary Lou Williams was born Mary Elfrieda Scruggs on May 8, 1914, in Atlanta, Georgia, the daughter of Mose and Virginia Winn. A child prodigy, she grew up in Pittsburgh, Pennsylvania, attending Western House High School. She taught herself how to play the piano, giving her first public performance when she was six, and becoming a professional musician as a teenager. She soon took her stepfather's surname, performing as Mary Lou Burley.

Marrying saxophone player John Williams at the age of 16, she joined his band Andy Kirk's Twelve Clouds of Joy, in 1930, and soon became the band's leading soloist, composer and arranger. She also wrote for other bands including that of Benny Goodman, for which she wrote "Roll 'Em." Her husband later left the band to join Terrence Holder, and Mary Lou Williams took over leadership of it, and then she herself left to join Holder.

Working for Duke Ellington for six months in 1941 as his staff arranger, in 1942 she and her second husband, Harold "Shorty" Baker formed their own group, after which she performed solo for much of her life until the 1970s. She was also involved in encouraging the bebop movement of Thelonious Monk. Mary Lou Williams was also involved in arranging music for Glenn Gray, Earl Hines, Bob Crosby, and Louie Armstrong. She was a member of the American Society of Composers and Publishers, and was the composer of the Zodiac Suite, which included 12 compositions based on astrology. In 1946 she played with the New York Symphony Orchestra.

Closely involved with the Abyssinian Baptists, she met a Roman Catholic priest called John Crowley who was a keen jazz enthusiast, and throughout the 1940s and 1950s played at clubs throughout the United States and Europe. In 1957 she became a Roman Catholic, and recorded some cantatas and masses, devoting some years to religious works. Donating 10 percent of her profits to the poor, she wanted to encourage people throughout the United States to appreciate jazz. In the 1970s she conducted the first Roman Catholic mass for which all the music was jazz. In 1976 she received a D.F.A. from Bates College, Lewiston, Maine, and then taught at Duke University as Artist-in-Residence from 1977 until her death, on May 28, 1981, from cancer. She had received a number of honorary doctorates, and Duke University established the Mary Lou Williams Center for Black Culture in 1983.

Justin Corfield

See also: Basie, William "Count"; Goodman, Benny; Kirk, Andrew Dewey; Swing Music.

References and Further Reading

Dahl, Linda. 1999. *Morning Glory: A Biography of Mary Lou Williams.* New York: Pantheon.

Holmes, L. D., and Thomson, J. W. 1986. *Jazz Greats: Getting Better with Age.* New York: Holmes & Meier Publishers.

Kernodle, Tammy L. 2004. *Soul on Soul: The Life and Music of Mary Lou Williams.* Boston, MA: Northeastern University Press.

Lyons, L. 1983. *The Great Jazz Pianists: Speaking of their Lives and Music.* New York: W. Morrow.

Wills, Bob (1905–75)

During the Great Depression, fiddle player and band leader Bob Wills forged a blend of country and jazz music which became known as Western swing. By the late 1930s, Bob Wills and His Texas Playboys were the most popular dance band in the Southwest. In the post World War II period, Wills and his band performed on the national level until he was slowed by health issues in the early 1960s. The contribution of Wills to America's musical heritage was recognized with induction into the Country Music Hall of Fame (1968) and the Rock and Roll Hall of Fame (1999).

Wills was born James Robert Wills in Kosse, Texas on March 6, 1905. When he was eight years of age, the Wills family moved to Hall County in the Texas Panhandle. Dropping out of school following the seventh grade, Wills worked in the cotton fields with his family. He learned to play the fiddle from his father, John Tompkins Wills, and he became familiar with the blues, hearing the music of African Americans with whom he picked cotton.

In the early 1920s, he traveled around Texas and Oklahoma, working the fields as a day laborer and playing the fiddle for dances. He also developed a drinking problem which would plague him for the rest of his life. After trying his hand at barbering, Wills moved to Fort Worth, Texas in 1929, playing for dances and appearing on radio station WBAP. Two years later, he formed The Light Crust Doughboys (named after their sponsor), working for future Texas governor and senator W. Lee "Pappy" O'Daniel.

Willis had a falling out with O'Daniel, and in 1933 he moved to Tulsa, Oklahoma, where he formed Bob Wills and His Texas Playboys. The band was a popular fixture on Tulsa radio station KVOO, adding drums, strings, horns, and steel guitar to the infusion of hillbilly, jazz, and blues labeled Western swing. By the late 1930s, the band was playing for large dance audiences throughout the Southwest. His recording "San Antonio Rose" (1940) became the band's only gold record. While establishing a national musical reputation, Wills struggled with bouts of alcoholism which contributed to a troubled personal life. Between 1935 and 1941 he was divorced four times. His 1942 marriage to Betty Anderson lasted until his death and produced four children.

During the early 1940s, Wills appeared in *Take Me Back to Oklahoma* with Tex Ritter, and he would eventually perform in 19 films. In 1942, his musical and film career was interrupted when he enlisted in the Army. Military service, however, failed to stall the popularity of Wills and his band. In the late 1940s and early 1950s, Bob Wills and His Texas Playboys were touring nationally. In 1947, Columbia Records released over 70 recordings by the band.

By the late 1950s and the arrival of rock and roll, Western swing proved far less popular and commercial. After suffering serious heart attacks in 1962 and 1964, Wills curtailed his performing. In 1969, Wills's musical contributions were recognized by the Texas state legislature, and the day after the ceremony he suffered the first of several debilitating strokes. Wills recovered to join some of his former band mates to record *For the Last Time: Bob Wills and His Texas Playboys* (1973), which garnered a Grammy award. Later that year, he suffered another stroke and slipped into a coma. Wills eventually died on May 13, 1975, in Fort Worth. By the time of his death, the Western swing music which Wills pioneered during the 1930s was making a comeback with younger audiences, and Wills continues to be popular with country dancers.

Ron Briley

See also: Hillbilly Music; Rodgers, Jimmie; Swing Music.

References and Further Reading

Knowles, Ruth Sheldon. 1995. *Bob Wills: Hubbin' It.* Nashville, TN: Country Music Federation.

McLean, Duncan. 1998. *Lone Star Swing: On the Trail of Bob Wills and His Texas Playboys.* New York: Norton.

Townshend, Charles R. 1976. *San Antonio Rose: The Life and Music of Bob Wills.* Urbana: University of Illinois Press.

Wilson, Teddy (1912–86)

A prominent U.S. jazz pianist, Theodore Shaw "Teddy" Wilson was one of the most important pianists of the swing period, with his solo recordings being extremely popular during the 1930s. Influenced by Earl "Fatha" Hines, he remained a distinctive player in his own right, and he, in turn, was an influence for Nat King Cole.

He was born on November 24, 1912, at Austin, Texas. He grew up in Tuskegee, Alabama and studied the piano at Tuskegee Institute where his parents taught, and also attended Talladega College. He then moved to Detroit where he found work as a professional musician, before moving to Chicago, Illinois, where he played with Jimmie Noone, and then worked in the bands of Speed Webb and Louis Armstrong, joining Benny Carter's *Chocolate Dandies* in 1933. Two years later he joined with Benny Goodman to form the trio with Goodman and Gene Krupa, the drummer. This was later expanded to include Lionel Hampton as the Benny Goodman Quartet. In these performances Wilson became the first African

American to perform in public in a jazz group that had previously been all-white.

In 1935, with the support of jazz writer and producer John Hammond, Teddy Wilson managed to get a contract with Brunswick Records to record hot swing arrangements. These proved popular for juke boxes, and Wilson was also involved in recordings with Buck Clayton, Roy Eldridge, Red Norvo, Ben Webster, and Lester Young. He left Goodman in 1939.

Although he led in his own band in 1939 and the first part of 1940, Wilson performed more easily with others and in 1940 until 1944 led a sextet which performed at Café Society. Far more comfortable as a leader of small ensembles, and as a soloist, in 1950 he took up a position as an instructor at the Juilliard School in New York in 1950, and went on important tours of the Soviet Union in 1962 and Japan in 1971. One of his early albums was *The Didactic Mr. Wilson* (1953). He also played himself in *The Benny Goodman Story,* (1955), played at the Newport Festival in 1973, and at a concert at Carnegie Hall in 1982. Retiring to Hillsdale, New Jersey, Wilson performed occasionally as a soloist until the 1980s. He died on July 31, 1986, at New Britain, Connecticut.

Justin Corfield

See also: Basie, William "Count"; Goodman, Benny; Krupa, Gene; Swing Music.

References and Further Reading

Lyons, L. 1983. *The Great Jazz Pianists: Speaking of their Lives and Music.* New York: W. Morrow.

Wilson, Teddy. 2001. *The Teddy Wilson Collection.* Milwaukee, WI: Hal Leonard Corporation.

Wilson, Teddy, Humphrey Van Loo, and Arie Ligthart. 1996. *Teddy Wilson Talks Jazz: The Autobiography of Teddy Wilson.* Herndon, VA: Cassell.

The Wizard of Oz (1939)

The Wizard of Oz is Metro Goldwyn and Mayer's (MGM) 1939 blockbuster film, based on L. Frank Baum's beloved American fairy tale: *The Wonderful Wizard of Oz* (1900). The film, featuring the breakthrough performance of Judy Garland, has become one of the best known and most popular American movies of all time. *The Wizard of Oz* has created a set of iconic characters, such as the Wicked Witch of the West and the Tin Man. In addition, the film has also given generations of Americans such memorable catchphrases as "Lions, and tigers, and bears, oh my!" and "Somewhere over the rainbow."

The film is the simple story of a young girl named Dorothy who hits her head during a Kansas twister and winds up in the Land of Oz. Dorothy promptly kills an evil witch, by landing her home atop the witch, an event which launches Dorothy on an odyssey in which she acquires a Scarecrow, Tin-man, and Cowardly Lion as companions (along with her dog Toto) *en route* to seeking out the Wizard of Oz. On the way she ends up killing another wicked witch, and then returning to obtain her and her companions' hearts' desire. Then Dorothy awakens to find out that this magical Technicolor world was just a dream and she has returned to sepia-toned Kansas. Despite the Depression and the growing military aggression in Europe, 1939 was a banner year for

The Scarecrow, played by Ray Bolger, and Dorothy, played by Judy Garland, encounter some hazards on the way to Oz in the 1939 film *The Wizard of Oz*. Along with *Gone with the Wind, The Wizard of Oz* was one of the most famous movies of the 1930s. (AP/Wide World Photos)

American filmmakers. Silent films had recently given way to "talkies" and now full color films were replacing black and white standards. During 1939, 22 other films, which are now considered classics, were also released including: *Gone With the Wind, Dark Victory,* and *Of Mice and Men.* Out of that crowded field of now classic films, *The Wizard of Oz* stood alone, with over three million dollars in box office receipts in 1939.

This success took a long time to reach the silver screen. What began as Baum's popular children's tale had already been adapted for stage and screen numerous times including Baum's 1902 stage adaptation (with illustrator W. W. Denslow)

and Baum's 1908 film adaptation. The now iconic adaptation of *The Wonderful Wizard of Oz* began in 1934 when MGM mogul Samuel Goldwyn bought the rights to Baum's novel. He intended the film as a vehicle for Shirley Temple whom he wanted to star as Dorothy. By the time filming began, Temple's popularity was down, so Goldwyn had a hot property and no ingénue. Arthur Freed, who was a songwriter for MGM, and a fan of the Oz books, was looking for the right property to feature actress Judy Garland. Freed, who wanted to be a producer, convinced MGM to buy the rights to *The Wonderful Wizard of Oz* from Goldwyn. MGM paid Goldwyn $75,000 for the rights for the film (compared to the $50,000 paid for *Gone With The Wind*) named Mervyn Leroy producer (Freed settled for assistant) and signed Victor Fleming (who would later leave in 1939 to work on *Gone With the Wind*) to direct MGM Production number 1060: *The Wizard of Oz*. The film's production was budgeted at 2.7 million dollars and filming was set to commence in October of 1938.

This was where the production threatened to unravel. The difficulties began with the writers who were hired to adapt Baum's well-known book into a musical film. Although three writers are given credit for the script: Noel Langley, Florence Ryerson, and E. A. Woolf, by the time the film was completed, a mob of writers and lyricists had worked to produce the final version of the script, including such notable writers as Sid Silvers, Herman J. Mankewicz (*Citizen Kane*) and Ogden Nash. The Director's chair was equally unsettled—four directors helmed the film at some point. Richard Thorpe was initially hired and lasted 2 weeks, his replacement, George Cukor, lasted just days, Victor Fleming, the director of record, directed for 4 months, and King Vidor filmed the final 10 days of production of which most consisted of the austere sepia-toned opening and closing sequences of dreary Kansas farmlands. It was also highly unlikely that, in 1939, *The Wizard of Oz* would have been made as a big budget, "prestige," film by a major studio. When the "talkie" became the staple of the industry, studio executives frowned on high-concept fantasy films for fears that the movie-going public of the day just wouldn't accept nor understand them. Then, in 1937, Disney Studios crushed that stereotype with *Snow White and the Seven Dwarfs,* which broke all box-office sales records;

the race was on to get fantasy projects into theatres.

The Wizard of Oz officially premiered on August 15, 1939, at Grauman's Chinese Theatre in Hollywood (following the first publicized showing August 12 in the Strand Theatre in Oconomowoc, Wisconsin). The film was received with strong reviews which praised the performances of Garland as Dorothy and Bert Lahr as the Cowardly Lion. Unfortunately, thanks to a high turnover rate at theatres due to the sheer number of high-quality films made that year, films were not staying in theatres for very long. This, coupled with the onslaught of World War II in Europe, which decimated foreign earnings, limited the film's total box office take to 3 million which meant that *The Wizard of Oz,* when the cost of production, distribution, and publicity were all figured in, lost money in its initial release.

Much has been made about both the book and the film's allegorical meanings. Baum, as a journalist, wrote editorials calling for the extermination of local Native American tribes, was exposed to the Great Depression of 1893, the formation and rhetoric of the Populist party. Some, most notably Henry M. Littlefield in his 1963 essay *The Wizard of Oz: Parable on Populism,* claim that the book is an allegory for the failed Populist movement. The problem with this argument is that despite the editorials he wrote, Baum was never a political activist. Others have seen allegories hidden within the film; the most prominent claim is that the film was a call for American isolationism despite the looming war in Europe. Another theory is that the film is an allegory of President Franklin D. Roosevelt's New Deal. Neither of these theories is likely as Mayer, MGM's head was a devout member of the Republican Party.

The Wizard of Oz is ranked in nearly all top-10 best films of all time lists and was one of the first 25 films to be put on the National Film Registry which is reserved for culturally or historically significant films.

Keith Murphy

References and Further Reading

Baum. L. Frank. 2003. *The Wonderful Wizard of Oz*. Philadelphia, PA: Running Press.

Cox, Stephen. 2002. *The Munchkins of Oz*. Nashville, TN: Cumberland House.

Harmetz, Alijean. 1977. *The Making of the Wizard of Oz: Movie Magic and Studio Power in the Prime of MGM*. New York: Alfred A. Knopf.

Scarfone, Jay, and William Stillman. 1999. *The Wizardry of Oz: The Artistry and Magic of the 1939 Classic*. New York: Random House.

Swartz, Mark Evan. 2000. *Oz Before the Rainbow: L. Frank Baum's the Wonderful World of Oz on Stage and Screen to 1939*. Baltimore, MD: John Hopkins University Press.

Woolf, Samuel J. (1880–1948)

In 1927, Samuel Johnson Woolf told George Bernard Shaw that if the playwright hoped for immortality in the United States, he would need the help of a Woolf likeness. He was only half joking. For more than 20 years famous men and women became more familiar to the public through Woolf's loose, informal charcoal studies and anecdotal articles written for the *New York Times*.

Born in New York, Samuel Johnson Woolf first learned drawing from an uncle who illustrated humor magazines. Later studying at City College and the Art Students' League, Woolf could support himself by the age of 23 through portrait commissions. He showed his work in competitions, winning several awards, including the Hallgarten prize for best picture from the National Academy of Design, and in 1903 rented space in the Holbein Studio on West Fifty-fifth Street which counted among its tenants at various times George Inness, John Singer Sargent, and Childe Hassam.

When Woolf found himself financially struggling after the Panic of 1907, he began to supplement his income through illustration, which ultimately led to a long career in newspapers. At the outbreak of World War I, Woolf was appointed a special correspondent to the American Expeditionary Forces. In 1923, *New York Times* Sunday Editor Lester Markel invited Woolf to illustrate features and articles for the *Times* magazine. Woolf also supplied the *Times* with several portraits of President Roosevelt, all drawn from life, the first following Roosevelt's election as Governor of New York in 1928.

In July of 1927, while Woolf was on assignment in London, he was granted his hard-won sitting with George Bernard Shaw. Encouraged by *Times* London bureau representative Fitzhugh Minnigerode to write an account of the visit, Woolf's career was refigured again to include writing. Between 1927 and 1948 Wolf wrote profiles of notable figures. A charcoal portrait accompanied each profile, drawn while Woolf engaged the subject in conversation. While some of Woolf's sitters took up specific issues they wished to address, the artist's easy manner, and the periods of quiet which ensued while he sketched often relaxed sitters and resulted in conversations as informal as Woolf's drawing style. Woolf's subjects included composer Irving Berlin; physicist Albert Einstein; New York Governor, Al Smith; New Deal critic Colonel Frank

Knox; First Lady Eleanor Roosevelt; and the occasional ordinary person, such as peanut vendor Steve Vasilakos who plied his trade outside the Whitehouse through six administrations.

In addition to his profile series, in the 1920s through mid-1930s Woolf also contributed about 200 portraits to *Time* magazine, including *Time's* first full color cover featuring Walter P. Chrysler (January 1929) and the 1928 "Man of the Year" portrait of Charles Lindbergh. During World War II, Woolf worked again as a correspondent, for the Newspaper Enterprise Association. His career at the *New York Times* extended up to his death in 1948. Despite suffering immobilization from amyotrophic lateral sclerosis (ALS), or Lou Gehrig's disease, Woolf's last story, a profile of Roosevelt's first vice president, John Nance Garner, ran two days after Woolf died.

Tess Mann

References and Further Reading

Markel, Lester. 1948. "From the Woolf Album: Portraits from the artist's work-and a tribute to the reporter." *New York Times,* December 12, SM12.

Meschutt, David. 1986. "Portraits of Franklin Delano Roosevelt," *The American Art Journal* 18 (4): 2–49.

New York Times. 1948. S. J. Woolf (obituary), December 4: 13.

Voss, Fred. 1998. "Being on Time." In *Faces of Time: 75 Years of Time Magazine Cover Portraits.* Boston: Little Brown and Company

Woolf, Samuel Johnson. 1941. *Here Am I.* New York: Random House.

The Ethnic Depression

The Great Depression destroyed the fabric of American society. Yet, it did relatively little damage to the upper echelons of that society many of whom, thanks to their economic underpinnings, escaped its impact. And nor did the situation change much for those at the other end of the social spectrum, since for the latter—especially the ethnics—conditions remained dire. For the offspring of the "new immigrants" (e.g., Italians, South Slavs, Spanish speakers mostly from Mexico, and Jews from the Russian Pale), notwithstanding all their aspirations, their lives had not improved notably during the uneven prosperity of the New Era of the 1920s.

Nor had the situation of the Native Americans or the African Americans (neither those who had remained in the Southern United States and in 1930 represented about 75 percent of the black population; only during the latter 1930s did it begin in large numbers to move North and to a lesser extent West). Their opportunities were severely limited by a U.S. Supreme Court 1896 decision (*Plessy v. Ferguson*) which called for blacks to be treated as "separate but equal" which in reality meant for decades judicial support for Jim Crow segregation.

Louis Adamic, a Yugoslav immigrant, had, during the 1930s (and even more so in the 1940s) become a perspicacious and noted social commentator because of his discussions of the American way of life and the changes it was undergoing. He was not alone in his comments, but certainly was among the most successful of the pioneers and well known because of his Balkan background. It had long been established social policy to transform newcomers to the United States, and certain classes of citizens such as the blacks, into clones celebrating a particular kind of white Protestant Anglo Saxon America.

Typical had been the policy at some of the factories where Henry Ford produced automobiles *and* Americans of a particular kind. On a given day various ethnics in their native costumes would walk onto a stage on which there was a great *paper mache* cauldron representing the much touted "Melting Pot" which represented the influence of America on these inhabitants, with their peculiarities of dress, language, and custom. They would walk into that contraption and come out the other side dressed in the clothes of an American, having symbolically shed their foreign ties.

As Adamic pointed out, people may have changed their dress but not their way of life, which was bound up, for example, with their language, their eating habits, and their socialization patterns. In many an immigrant family not everyone spoke English, and often the language of choice in the home was a native tongue. People banded together in fraternal bodies based on their geographic background, often maintaining prejudices from the old country. Thus the mafia was Sicilian and not generally Italian; the welcome was for the paisan from Palermo, not the one from Naples. So too, blacks distinguished between people of color from the West Indies and the American South.

Employers, for all their lip service to the melting pot, used the cultural and other differences among their workers to forestall unionization. Ford was notorious for his use of African American workers. Unlike many employers, he did offer them employment at relatively decent wages but the company knew that with their employment there was a labor pool that could, because of the racism of their white co-workers, be used as scabs.

The steel companies were notorious for putting men from different ethnic backgrounds together in the gangs which worked in the mills. Often their language differences resulted in serious accidents, but it kept them from being successfully organized. These situations changed during the 1930s because the need to improve their dreadful conditions helped to make it necessary for the union organizers to overcome ethnic differences.

Various writers from the different ethnic groups published works of fiction during the Great Depression that were grounded in their own experiences and highlight the many difficulties they and their fellow men and women faced. Much of this writing is now dated, both socially and politically, and often is not very good prose, but does describe, perhaps too emotionally but very usefully, the social problems caused by the Depression, its impact on living conditions, on the shortage of employment, and on the problems faced by minorities living in a prejudiced and distressed United States.

As can be graphically seen from works of literature, discrimination was a pervasive and immutable fact of American life not only during the Great Depression. What happened during those years built on the multitude of barriers erected during the previous decades. The authors detailed not only their own contemporary experiences but also the various ways that previous generations had been kept in their place.

It is worthwhile noting that Catholics also suffered at the hands of their fellow Christians. While the widespread use of slogans such as "No Irish Need Apply" had fallen into disuse, just prior to the Great Crash of the stock market in 1929, Al Smith, the Democratic candidate in the presidential election of 1928, lost votes because of his Catholic religion (the "Solid South" had in part because of his religious beliefs deserted the Democratic Party, which it would not do again until after World War II when the issue of civil rights for African Americans reared its head, and in the 1948 election split the Party).

Some indication of the difficulties of life for the average Irish Catholic can be gleamed from the writing of novelist James Farrell who produced perhaps the most notable work dealing with this subject. A prolific writer, he produced a series of novels as well as several short stories dealing with Irish lower middle class life in Chicago. His trilogy *Studs Lonigan* (published between 1932 and 1935) is a forceful portrait of a Catholic youth unable to cope with his society; the author's view of it is stark, but he later sought to emphasize the "spiritual poverty" of that life.

Pietro di Donato's 1939 *Christ in Concrete* treats the Church less kindly in one of the best novels treating Italian American life, although much of it is set before the Depression. Still, graphic and muscular in its details about life in the New York City slums and the dangers of working class life (bricklayers and others in the building trades suffer fatal accidents), the novel—based on the author's own experiences—depicts a family's economic helplessness when there is no breadwinner, and thus the importance of a job.

Italians also were the subject of other writers using fiction as a means of dealing with difficulties faced. The novelist John Fante, in a series of angry novels including *Wait Until Spring* (1938), *Bandini* (1938) and *Ask The Dust* (1939), concentrated on the problems faced by Italians in Los Angeles (a far cry from the ghettos on the East Coast), as did Jo Pagano in a series of moving short stories.

During the 1930s Native Americans continued to suffer from all kinds of discrimination but received relatively little attention in the literature of the day. Thanks to the efforts of various New Dealers, the depressing situation of Native Americans received official attention and some improvement, but little was written about them in contemporary literature. Previously novels had presented Native Americans as implausibly noble (the models which had an impact well beyond their publication date or the Great Depression were the treacly, preachy 1884 Helen Hunt Jackson effort *Ramona* or Zane Grey's more robust and much less sentimental *The Vanishing American* published in 1925) or treacherously villainous (the pulp adventure magazines of the 1930s).

The "reservation Indian" had become, after Franklin D. Roosevelt's (FDR) ascendancy to the presidency in 1933, a subject of concern and of interest; melodrama and sentimentality gave way to a more realistic view of how Native Americans could or would adjust to the dominant white civilization which surrounded them. 1930s novels and short stories by writers like Edward Corle and Oliver La Farge, authors since their time unhappily much neglected, dealt with attempts of the Native American to adjust to a modern world. Some New Deal projects apotheosized the Native Americans; a 1939 competition to select the best mural design for a post office in the 48 states concentrated on depicting the natural life of Native Americans.

The bitter discriminatory treatment suffered by Mexicans in the United States continued in the 1930s to be a subtext in novels such as Dane Coolidge's *Gringo Gold* (1939) dealing with the mid-19th century California bandit Joaquin Murietta, who, legend has it, took to outlawry as a result of the mistreatment of him and his family by American miners. The contemporary problems faced by Mexicans and their progeny in the United States are the subject of somewhat obscure 1930s authors like Marta Roberts, who in her 1940 novel *Tumbleweeds* movingly depicts what they faced "on relief," and better known authors like John Steinbeck in the less serious *Tortilla Flat* (1935) who treated the characters in this novel much less graphically than he had the Okies and other migrant workers in his masterful *The Grapes of Wrath* (1939).

Contemporary literature by Orientals about the rampant discrimination during the 1930s against them in the Western United States, especially California, is sparse. The Japanese, whether American citizens or not, faced a fierce racial intolerance fueled by their success in the service industries, the maritime trades, and agriculture. State laws in various western states forbade marriage between them and a Caucasian, a situation accepted by Herbert Hoover—president between 1929 and 1933, who asserted there were "biological and cultural grounds why there should be no mixture of Oriental and Caucasian blood." The legal restrictions on immigration of Orientals antedated the 1930s, and were deeply rooted in decades-old attitudes that had occasionally exploded in violence, and in 1942 would result in deportation of West Coast Japanese Americans to concentration camps.

While the availability of 1930s writing in English by Orientals about their American experiences is limited, subsequent memoirs of individuals such as the Japanese American communist Karl G. Yoneda (*Ganbatte: 60 Year Struggle of a Kibei Worker*), and the writings of the Filipino radical Carlos Bulosan, record the racial injustice that made the lives of them and their fellows so difficult during the decade.

During the latter part of the 19th century Chinese in the United States were the main target of the campaign against Orientals undertaken by militant American racists. For various reasons (e.g., the sentimental public attachment to the activities, adventures, and putative achievements of U.S. missionaries in China, fear of the growing political and military power of Japan—recognized by their inclusion in various disarmament conferences as well as a changing American diplomatic attitude towards that country), and the venom spewed by the contemporary media—notably the newspapers controlled by the influential press lord William Randolph Hearst who propagandized against Japan ceaselessly as "the Yellow Peril," the Japanese in the Western United States, especially California, came to bear the brunt of attacks on Orientals.

In that state, as elsewhere in the American West, there were during the 1930s a variety of organizations—who somewhat mistakenly described themselves as "civic minded"—agitated against the Issei (the Japanese who had migrated to the United States, and were denied American citizenship) and the Nisei (the children of the Issei who by virtue of their birth in the United States were American citizens). Among these organizations were posts of the American Legion, various union locals, and branches of the Native Sons and Daughters of the Golden West.

Their actions without any doubt affected the mindset of the Issei and Nisei, who on the one hand were not accepted as Americans because of the theories and actions of these racists and who on the other hand had become too assimilated to be at ease with the increasingly aggressive teachings and actions of Imperial Japan, which, during the 1930s, reached out to dominate Asia by any means possible. The Japanese Americans, in facing their racist detractors, faced a conundrum: if as a result of adopting American manners and mores to their way of life they moved into the market place and competed successfully their critics charged them with being too aggressive or of "not knowing their place"; if the Issei and Nisei lived among themselves the charge was that they rejected American values and were "too clannish."

Where, in contrast to the Chinese who had preceded them to the United States, the Japanese initially had been welcomed, the very success of the Japanese in California and the Pacific Northwest stimulated racist feelings against them. They had been initially accepted as convenient, cheap labor but by dint of hard work and seizing upon whatever opportunities became available they had become frightening competitors, and continued to be so demonized because despite the economic impact of the Depression they suffered fewer setbacks than many of their contemporaries.

At one point the average production per acre for all California farmers was estimated at less than $42.00 while the per acre productivity of the Japanese farmer was estimated to be about $141.00. At the end of the 1930s, notwithstanding the economic drawbacks of the hard times and the discriminatory treatment the Issei and Nisei faced as targets of blatant and sometimes violent prejudice, the Japanese produced about 40 percent of California's truck crops even though they owned only one about 1 percent of the state's cultivated land.

The sharecroppers and tenant farmers found all over the South, both black and white, also faced oppression and violence, but for African Americans the situation was more dire since they did not have the illusion of white superiority to which the political demagogues of the region often appealed. Attempts by the exploited tillers of the soil were often met with harsh reprisals. The Southern Tenant Farmers Union (STFU), organized in 1934, and active chiefly in the Arkansas delta region, attempted to bring

Japanese American farmer harvests cauliflower on a ranch near Centerville, California. Photograph by Dorothea Lange. (Library of Congress)

together both blacks and whites to improve the lot of both. The banding together of tenants would certainly have aroused the landowners but the implication of the possibility of racial equality led to a fierce response.

Socialists attempted to aid the members of the STFU to gain their rights, but proved to be too weak to counter the ruthless brutality of the local authorities and the indifference of the Roosevelt administration. Some officials of the Agricultural Adjustment Administration, the New Deal's tool for assisting the recovery of American agriculture, attempted to aid the exploited, but they were purged from the agency in 1935. Socialist Party leader Norman Thomas and his associates went to Arkansas to help the STFU, but were soon not allowed to speak publicly; at one meeting from which Thomas was driven a landlord roared at him "we don't need any Gawd-damn Yankee bastard to tell us what to do with our niggers"; ultimately, after being manhandled, he and his colleagues left for Memphis and safety.

Terror was common but it was felt most keenly by the union's African American supporters. The cabin of a black preacher who had served as a chaplain for a union local was riddled with bullets; a black church which had served as a union meeting place was burned to the ground; a black minister who had worked as a union organizer was shot dead and there was no organization. Thomas met with President Roosevelt asking for Federal intervention but got nowhere. The Secretary of Agriculture refused to respond to any pleas.

The union hung on despite the terror and in October 1934 did manage to win a strike that brought about some gains. In 1937 the union, barely alive, became part of the newly established CIO. Subsequently it became a lobby in Washington, D.C., fighting for legislation to aid the exploited. Their problems were never fully solved, but they were at least ameliorated by changing conditions. With mechanization there was less need for tenants and sharecroppers. With the coming of the war many whites moved to the new industries and left agriculture behind. So too did many of the blacks as they moved north and became urban dwellers facing different problems. Both black and white authors dealt with the racial problems faced by African Americans during the 1930s. Often politically committed, these authors dealt with both the urban blacks of the North and their Southern rural counterparts, and such issues as lynching, segregation, perversion of the law, and economic discrimination. Overall the situation of African Americans in the 1930s was treated realistically by authors of both races. However, the traditional stereotypes did not wholly disappear; they still could be found in romantic Civil War epics like *So Red The Rose* (1934) and *Gone With The Wind* (1936) as well as in the Hollywood versions of these novels and in numerous other movies. Yet, in much of the literature of the day the "contented darky" gave way to the exploited individual, and more sensational aspects such as the inequitable treatment of African Americans replaced the traditional folksy, sentimental treatment. In works that concentrated on contemporary black men and women, a much more accurate picture could be found.

Writers like the white author Erskine Caldwell, in his treatment of race relations in the South in a 1935 short story collection *Kneel to the Rising Son,* presented a grim but more realistic view of the relationship in the South between the average white and African Americans, in which the latter were often fatally demeaned as part of an exploitative economic, politically unjust system. Numerous white authors had written about black life in pre-Depression New York City. The eccentric white poet Maxwell Bodenheim in his 1931 novel *Naked on Roller Skates* presented an interesting contemporary view of "slumming" in Harlem, in which the black population also faced exploitation.

There had been no absence of black authors dealing with the African American communities in the North and South as well as the difficult relationship between races. Typical of such writers who published in the 1930s was Countee Cullen, whose 1932 novel *One Way To Heaven* dealt with Harlem's assumed sophisticates and their hardworking everyday counterparts. Langston Hughes, whose most well-known efforts came after the 1930s, drawing on his experiences published a 1930 novel about black life in a Kansas town (*Not Without Laughter*) and four years later drew together various published class-conscious short stories about the divisive relationships between the races, written from an angry black point of view (*The Ways of White Folks*). Richard Wright wrote with even more bite. His 1938 collection of long short stories (*Uncle Tom's Children*) deals in tough-minded fashion with racial conflict in the contemporary South, and the ruthless suppression of blacks.

For Wright the progeny of Uncle Tom have to fight just as hard for their very existence as their forebears did in his time. *Native Son* (1940) is an angry novel, later turned into a movie, dealing with a young black man (Bigger Thomas) who finds himself hemmed in by the social restrictions of a white-dominated Chicago, commits as a result, somewhat inadvertently, a murder which he brutally tries to cover up, and becomes a symbol. Wright very effectively describes Bigger Thomas's feelings and in dealing with the psychology of relations between the races argues forcefully for giving blacks the rights due a native son.

Hughes and Wright, like so many African Americans (and Jews) and other minorities, were for a while attracted to the Communist Party, which during much of the 1930s seemed to be the most outspoken champion of those dispossessed by the ravages of the Depression. The Party's politics and those of its fronts and the groups it dominated with which minorities interacted are an important part of their story during the Depression.

The Communist Party of the United States of America (CPUSA) was part of the Communist International. Also known as the Comintern and the Third International, it had been organized in 1919, and followed in the footsteps of the First and Second Internationals, 19th century groupings of Marxist parties and labor organizations. The political critic Theodore Draper, and the many historians and political scientists who have echoed his views, cogently argued that the ultimate direction of the CPUSA was determined by the Comintern's Soviet controlled leadership and that the American Communist Party served as an "instrument of the Russian Communist Party."

Subscribers to this view consider very important the significant changes in the Party line during the Great Depression. Beginning in 1928, Communist leaders argued the post-World War I world was entering a "Third Period" of capitalism's collapse, an argument that seemed remarkably prescient with the onset of the Great Depression. In dealing with that collapse the CPUSA, like other communist parties elsewhere in the world, was committed to a militancy which rejected working with other leftist groups or middle class reformers.

In 1935 the Seventh World Congress of the Comintern decreed, given the dangers of fascism and its threat to the Soviet Union, that communists should seek cross-class alliances with progressive forces, confirming actions which had already taken place in countries like France where the Party had joined in with other Left groups to form a Popular Front to combat reaction. The Party line changed again after the 1939 pact between Nazi Germany and the Soviet Union, and blamed the coming of World War II on the failed policies of the capitalist democracies. The Communist Party, however a local chapter implemented the official line, had to that point been an outspoken critic and determined foe of fascism. The pact which revived the sectarianism of the Third Period reversed that policy.

Many in various academic disciplines accept that during the Third Period the CPUSA echoed the sectarian line imposed by the Comintern but forcefully argue that whatever the leadership may have done, many American Communists dedicated to improving the lot of the working class and to ending *de facto* intolerance and *de jure* discrimination suffered by minorities, aided them in gaining their rights. In furtherance of such goals, goes the argument, while on the one hand adhering to Party doctrine, members undertook to do what was necessary to aid the victims of a broken economy and of institutional discrimination.

Once the line changed to the Popular Front, the various national Parties such as the CPUSA operated in the mainstream of reformist politics, which in the United States meant that the Party undertook successful coalition-building in such New Deal era ventures as industrial unionism and civil rights activism, and cooperated formally with groups on the left who, during the Third Period, had been attacked (the Socialists, for example, had been excoriated as "Social Fascists").

The Party never escaped its ethnic heritage. When the CPUSA left its underground status in the 1920s the bulk of the membership lay in the foreign language federations, especially that of the Finns, deserters from the Socialist Party. By the onset of the Depression Jews had become more prominent in the Party, in part because of Communist strength in New York City, a center of Jewish life in America. The Party grew very slowly during the Third Period, hampered by its sectarianism. During the Popular Front, the Party's membership did grow.

All during the 1930s Party members were very active in its reaching out to African Americans. And the Party and its front organizations, such as the International Labor Defense (ILD), in many situations were the only ones who minority groups could count on for legal assistance or for publicity when their tenuous civil rights were violated, a common occurrence.

It has been argued that for much of the Depression years the CPUSA was less enthusiastic about dealing with Mexican Americans than with African Americans; one reason may be the confusion aroused by a change in the census; during the first two decades of the 20th century Spanish speakers in the United States, mostly living in the Southwest, were counted as Caucasians, but for the 1930 census they were identified as a separate racial category (an action hotly and strongly protested by Latino activists).

During the 1930s only Mexico City had more Mexicans than Los Angeles. There, as in the Southwest in general, there were no Jim Crow statutes as in the South legislating relations between the races, but custom—often enforced illegally—held back the progress of Mexican Americans, who faced residential restrictions and segregation at work and social establishments. Various groups and individuals, such as the American Civil Liberties Union, the Socialist Party, and unaffiliated liberals tried to aid Mexican Americans in obtaining their rights, improving their lot., and stopping the mass deportation of Mexicans at the growing season's end when their services were no longer needed, but probably the most vociferous, if not the most effective, were the Communists.

Starting in the early 1930s Communists and their close allies in auxiliary organizations attempted to unionize the exploited Mexicans working in the canneries and as stoop labor in the fields, initially with little success. In part because of determined opposition by management and local government, but also, according to some sources, because the Communists involved, both during the Third Period and the time of the Popular Front, failed to understand the national, ethnic, and class dimensions of Mexican Americans.

The Communist Party, dominated United Cannery. Agricultural, Packing, & Allied Workers of America, building on earlier abortive Party efforts, did have in the later 1930s some effect before failing after World War II. The union was remarkably diverse in membership, organizing not only Mexicans but other minorities as well as poor whites in areas as disparate as the Southwest and New Jersey, but never became a mass organization.

Although overall the CPUSA certainly was not shy in its importuning on behalf of Mexican Americans, the Party and its allies pulled out all the stops in their strenuous efforts to win over African Americans. In part this campaign resulted from an initial failure to enlist blacks in the Party's ranks. For much of the 1920s the Communists stressed class and not race. Blacks felt excluded. In 1928 Party organizer James W. Ford, who would be its vice-presidential candidate in 1932 (the first African American in the 20th century to be on a national ballot) announced at the Comintern's Sixth World Congress in Moscow that the CPUSA had only about 50 black dues-paying members. It would seem that most African Americans felt that being black was enough of a burden without adding a further drawback by being identified as a "Red." As the conservative black weekly *The Pittsburgh Courier* later commented: "the position of the American Negro is precarious enough with out making it more so by joining a crew espousing the overthrow of the government..."

During the 1930s the CPUSA paid more attention to blacks than to any other ethnic group in an endeavor to win them over to the Communist cause and away from other African American organizations such as the National Association for the Advancement of Colored People (NAACP), and the National Urban League. The Party vociferously campaigned for antidiscrimination legislation on the Federal and local level, propagandized against what at one point the Party termed "white chauvinism," spoke out diligently for improvements in the lives of blacks, directed Party members to work with people of color for political, economic, and social ends, vigorously publicized legal and social inequities, and argued for an end to peonage. The CPUSA, in recognition of the Depression's greater impact on the already poverty stricken African Americans community, urged substantially more government relief for them.

In the early 1930s the Party did so against the backdrop of one answer by the Comintern to what it dubbed "the Negro Question." That answer determined that "the Negro people" in the United States were an exploited "peasantry;" they were an "oppressed nation." who needed to be freed. Communists subsequently agitated for "black liberation." As the CPUSA defined that term for African Americans in the early 1930s; it meant that in "the Black Belt" (i.e., those Southern U.S. counties in which the preponderance of the population was engaged in agrarian work) the "Negro people" as a "subject nation" were entitled to "the right of self-determination."

The ultimate objective was adding to the Union a 49th State, sometimes referred to in Party propaganda as a "Negro Soviet Republic." As the CPUSA defined this belt of counties, it stretched from eastern Virginia and parts of the Carolinas through Georgia, Alabama, the delta area of Mississippi and Louisiana, and the coastal part of East Texas. The obvious impracticality and impossibility of black separation, even as another State, did not blunt the Party's appeal to African Americans. A 1932 Communist Party presidential election poster underscores the CPUSA's determination to woo African Americans; while the poster does argue for "Self Determination for the Black Belt, in much larger letters it calls for "EQUAL RIGHTS FOR NEGROES EVERYWHERE!!" It is clear that "self determination," even during the Third Period, had a limited appeal, but the cry for "equal rights" could not help but have a real impact. The number of Party members of all races during the early 1930s grew slowly, as did the number of African American members, but by the time of the inception of the Popular Front, the number of blacks attracted by CPUSA activity was rising, especially among younger intellectuals.

Party work, South and North, was not easy, and the "self-determination" line certainly did not help matters, but what did were Communist efforts through local organizations to aid the unemployed by fighting evictions, utility turnoffs, and the inadequacies of relief. Chicago had its "Black Birds" who held "Pot and Pan Demonstrations" (i.e., African American workers who under Communist leadership protested against the effects of the Great Depression on life in the city, and would, for example, aid families to return their furniture to apartments from which they had been evicted). In various parts of the South, Communists often at great personal risk helped organize inter-racial groups, admittedly small in number but vociferous and often fearless, who fought for voting rights for all, racial equality, adequate relief, and the ability to organize unions.

Perhaps most important for the Communist cause among African Americans before the Popular Front brought it more public favor was the Communist stance against the racial injustice represented by the Scottsboro case, in which nine young blacks were fraudulently convicted. In March 1931 the nine "riding the rods" while looking for work got into a brawl with some whites and threw them off a freight train heading for Alabama from Chattanooga. When shortly thereafter authorities boarded the train in Alabama they found two teen-aged white girls with the black youths. Victoria Price and Ruby Bates were prostitutes, but knowing the dire consequences of having voluntary relations with African Americans they quickly charged rape. The black youths—one was 12, two were 14, the oldest was 21; several were crippled and probably incapable of sexual activity—were immediately charged. They had incompetent legal representation, and within three weeks were tried, convicted, and all but one sentenced to death.

The railroading of the youths came to the attention of the Communists who turned these victims of blatant racial injustice into an international *cause celebre*. Communists in different parts of the world organized massive protest demonstrations denouncing the verdicts on behalf of the "Scottsboro Boys," as the defendants became known, demanding "They Shall Not Die." B. D. Amis, then a prominent black communist, coined the phrase.

Black communists showcased by the CPUSA in the United States during its campaign on behalf of the defendants included Ford and William Patterson, an attorney later Executive Secretary of the International Labor Defense (ILD), the CPUSA's legal auxiliary. The international demonstrations in support of the Scottsboro Boys (in places like Latvia and Germany); tours around the United States and to parts of Europe by some of the mothers of the defendants; organized national protests including mass marches in Harlem, Chicago, and Chattanooga—all had an effect (they enhanced the Communist Party's reputation in the black community and may have benefited the Party's coffers, although that charge by its political opponents is the subject of contradictory arguments). The execution was stayed while ILD lawyers appealed the Alabama verdict to the U.S. Supreme Court, which in November 1932 (*Powell v. Alabama*) by a vote of 7–2 ordered a new trial, on the grounds that in a state trial involving a capital offense an indigent defendant was entitled to a competent defense but in this case the defendants had been denied "adequate counsel."

Over the next years the ILD arranged for proper representation, not only using its own talented lawyers, but also by bringing into the Scottsboro trials a noted New York defense attorney, Samuel Liebowitz, who argued for the defendants during a succession of trials. Liebowitz, who served without compensation, was subject to the vilest kind of anti-Semitism while in the South arguing the cases. Despite his best efforts and the rest of the defendants' legal team the verdicts went against the defendants. In the trial of one youth, notwithstanding the recantation of Ruby Bates and the state's flimsy evidence, the "boy" was found guilty. The trial judge courageously set aside the jury's verdict as unwarranted, as being contrary to the weight of the evidence. Tried again, this youth and another were again found guilty. An appeal to the U.S. Supreme Court resulted in an 8–0 decision (*Norris v. Alabama*) in 1935 and the ordering of a new trial, this time on the grounds that although Alabama counties "had qualified Negroes for jury service...there was *prima facie* evidence that Negroes were denied jury duty because of their race."

The ILD attorneys and Liebowitz could stop the imposition of the death sentence but ultimately could not prevent the incarceration of the Scottsboro Boys. The state, over a period of years, refused to relent and continued to prosecute (one defendant was tried four times). The trials all ended with guilty verdicts. Yet by 1936 it was clear that the state was tiring of the controversy. In 1937 trials resulted in five of the defendants being sentenced to lengthy prison terms, but not to death, and four were freed. Although the incarcerated Scottsboro Boys were not forgotten, especially by the black community, interest in them waned as other causes came to the fore.

The Popular Front policies of the CPUSA resulted in a muting of the call for a separate black state in the United States and a willingness for the ILD to join a Scottsboro

These nine African American youths, known as the Scottsboro Boys, were imprisoned in Scottsboro, Alabama, after being falsely accused of raping two white women in a freight car. Here, the young men are pictured conferring with civil rights activist Juanita Jackson Mitchell in 1937. The boys' convictions were overturned in *Powell v. Alabama* (1932), when the U.S. Supreme Court declared that the defendants, who had not been given adequate time to prepare a defense, were denied due process. (Library of Congress)

Defense Committee with organizations such as the NAACP that the communists had previously scorned. The end of Third Period sectarianism meant that communism now sold itself as "Twentieth Century Americanism" and that in the area of race relations the CPUSA now formally worked with other groups advancing the cause of African Americans, campaigning for an end to segregation, disenfranchisement, and lynching, as well as other violent acts directed against blacks.

In the early 1940s as the nation went to war, interest in the remaining incarcerated Scottsboro Boys nearly ceased. The Scottsboro Defense Committee grew inactive and retained little contact with the ILD, which did send a small sum each month to the imprisoned defendants. In 1944 three of them were paroled, although two later were returned to prison as parole violators before finally achieving freedom. The last Scottsboro Boy escaped to Michigan in 1948, and subsequently, upon being discovered there, that state's governor refused extradition.

The hopes of the CPUSA leadership and comintern officials for a massive influx of blacks into the Party as a result of Third Period activity such as the campaign on behalf of the Scottsboro Boys remained illusory. "Self-determination," reckless militancy, a cry to defend the Soviet Union, and Marxist theory could not be offset by the Party's outspoken and vigorous attacks on racial injustice and economic inequity in the United States.

Without any doubt many African Americans appreciated the actions of the ILD and the sincere efforts of individual Party members who marched and demonstrated in support of the Scottsboro defendants or who participated in protests against relief cuts, but this appreciation, even if it resulted in some black support of communist causes, did not translate into formally joining the CPUSA, Moreover, the outspoken hostile response of various parts of white America to Communist Third Period racial activity raised the issue for many in the United States of who speak for the black community.

The NAACP had clashed with the communists about how to proceed with the Scottsboro case. The confrontation resulted in a clear victory for the ILD which, having won the support of the defendants' parents, controlled the case until with the implementation of the Popular Front the Communists agreed to work with other groups. It was not just that the ILD outmaneuvered the NAACP. That organization which had been founded by both African Americans and whites approached the issue of winning black rights very differently than the communists. The NAACP was not a disciplined monolithic organization. Moreover, although not averse to mass actions such as picketing and the use of the boycott, the organization's leaders preferred to engage in political lobbying and to work through the courts. Such tactics did not engage mass support in the black community.

The NAACP did manage in 1932 to obtain a 5–4 U.S. Supreme Court decision (*Nixon v. Condon*) outlawing the white primary in Texas (important because in the then one party South, victory in the Democratic primary was tantamount to election) The Southern states responded by enacting legislation that allowed a political party as a private body to make its own rules about who could participate in a primary, an evasion that despite the NAACP's vigorous legal counter-arguments in a series of legal actions, the Supreme Court accepted, once more effectively disenfranchising African Americans (and not until 1944 would that be rectified in another case involving Texas).

The NAACP's use of civil suits over the years chipped away at the 1896 U.S. Supreme Court "separate but equal" ruling (*Plessy v. Ferguson*) which legally sheltered segregation. An important victory for the NAACP and its then chief counsel Charles Hamilton Houston came in 1938 when the Court ruled 6–2 (*Missouri ex rel Gaines v. Canada*) in what was probably the most important case dealing with segregated schools since the 1890s that a tax-supported state university law school such as that operated by Missouri must provide education for all its citizens, white or black; it was just not enough to be willing to pay for a legal education outside the state because that denied the state's citizens the equal protection and due process under due under the 14th Amendment. Missouri agreed to establish a separate law school for African Americans. Alas, this case was a Pyrrhic victory for the NAACP as the black student Lloyd Gaines chose not to attend a separate law school, and in 1939 disappeared after telling friends in Chicago he was going out to buy stamps; he was never seen again.

In the 1930s the NAACP's litigation path suffered by comparison with the sturm and drang practiced by the communists throughout the decade. Understandably, both during and after the Third Period various black militants were attracted to the communists. Moreover there was an elitist quality to the NAACP. In 1934 W.E.B. Du Bois, one of its founders, editor of its magazine *Crisis,* and a mover and shaker in the organization since its creation in 1909, broke with the NAACP in part because he believed that it was out of step with the bulk of the black community. This was a dramatic switch in his thinking for, thanks to him, one of the NAACP's founding principles was its emphasis on what Du Bois called "the Talented Tenth," the "gifted Negro" who could benefit the race. For him then and for some years, the educated, middle class "Advance Guard of the Race" was the hope of the organization to achieve improvements for blacks. Unfortunately, as he recognized, they numbered hundreds among the millions who made up the black community.

In the early 1930s, as a result of the impact of the Depression and of changing circumstances in the world and the United States, his position changed. He advocated economic self-sufficiency through racial separatism (an attitude which found expression in a mid-1930s campaign in Harlem and other African American ghettos by black radicals against white merchants who refused to hire African Americans, symbolized by the slogan "Don't Buy Where You Can't Work"). Du Bois's revised ideas expressed in issues of *Crisis* clashed with the policies of NAACP leaders, especially Walter White, its executive secretary, a firm and forceful proponent of integration of the races. In 1934 Du Bois resigned his positions with the NAACP. He did not then accept the agenda set out by the communists (although over time he accepted many of their goals and ideas, and a quarter century later joined the CPUSA).

White had joined the NAACP staff right after the end of World War I at the behest of James Weldon Johnson, who set the policies under which the NAACP operated for years. A true Renaissance man, Johnson was a successful novelist, an accomplished poet, a respected critic, an enterprising journalist, a well-received professor, an intelligent diplomat, and an acclaimed song writer. He and his brother were an in-demand Broadway song-writing team, producing a variety of hits. In the early 1900s they collaborated on *Lift Every Voice and Sing* (originally a poem composed in 1900 for a celebration of Abraham Lincoln's birthday at a segregated Jacksonville, FL school; music was added in 1905). Very inspirational, it was adopted in 1919 by the NAACP as a "Negro National Hymn," and became very popular in the black community. It found renewed popularity during the 1960s civil rights movement, and words from it were recited by the black minister offering the benediction at Barack Obama's presidential inauguration in 2009.

Johnson joined the NAACP staff in 1917, became its first African American secretary (i.e., chief operating officer) in 1920, and over the next decade was responsible for its expansion, especially in the South. Johnson worked hard to expose the injustices faced by blacks, both North and South, and to correct them, lobbied diligently but unsuccessfully for passage of federal antilynching legislation (a bill passed the House of Representatives in 1921 but southern Democratic senators filibustered it to death and the threat of such action hindered attempts at further legislation during the rest of the Twenties), and collaborated with liberal white attorneys such as Clarence Darrow, Louis Marshall, and Arthur Garfield Hays to ensure proper legal redress for blacks in high profile cases. The NAACP during his tenure became "a clearing house for civil rights cases."

White, in his early twenties, was involved in African American protest movements in his native Atlanta and helped to set up a NAACP branch there in 1916. His efforts attracted the attention of Johnson. The blond, blue eyed, fair-skinned White, could "pass" for white; he was only 1/64th African American, accepted as he later put it "an invisible pigmentation which marked me...as a Negro." And during the 1920s he used his ability to be taken as white to investigate (sometimes at considerable personal risk) dozens of lynchings and racial incidents, in order to expose the brutality and injustice of what happened to black victims. In 1929 when an ill Johnson took a leave of absence White became the NAACP's acting secretary. And in 1931 he was promoted to executive secretary. For the next decades he became the public face of the NAACP.

That year the NAACP under his leadership enjoyed one of its few 1930s public triumphs as it joined with the American Federation of Labor to defeat President Herbert Hoover's nomination of John J. Parker, a Federal appellate judge, to the U.S. Supreme Court—the first rejection of a presidential appointment since 1894. Organized labor opposed Parker because he had upheld "yellow dog" employment contracts whereby workers agreed not to join unions; the NAACP opposed him because in 1920 as a losing Republican candidate for governor of North Carolina he asserted that "the Negro as a class does not desire to enter politics. The Republican Party of North Carolina does not desire him to do so"; ten years later, while being considered for the Court, he did not disown the statement. The Senate rejected Parker, an able but right of center jurist and one of the youngest men ever to be nominated for the Supreme Court, by a two vote margin (41–39).

White continued the organization's policy of gradualism, of working to break down Jim Crow barriers which kept qualified blacks from enrolling in tax-supported state university graduate and professional schools, of attempting to end legal restrictions based on color, of defending the rights of African Americans, of using publicity and the courts to improve their situation in the United States, of putting together an extraordinary black legal team that began in the 1930s in a series of court cases to chip away at the "separate but equal" doctrine; the legal battle was not finally won until in 1954 the U.S. Supreme Court overturned *Plessy v. Ferguson* in a landmark decision (*Brown v. Board of Education of Topeka, Kansas*) that ruled unanimously that segregated public education was unconstitutional and inherently could not be equal.

One of the stars of that team was Thurgood Marshall, later a much respected Supreme Court justice. The NAACP lawyer won his first civil rights case in 1936 with a decision by a state court that a black man must be admitted to the all-white University of Maryland law school, which earlier, because of his race, had turned away Marshall (who then got his legal training at the all-black Howard University law school). White, an outspoken believer in racial equality and a zealous crusader for integration, staunchly resisted attempts at self-segregation (an important reason for the clash with Du Bois, although their strong egos also played a role). With White at the helm of the NAACP, it eschewed the policies of noisy confrontation advocated by the communists and other radicals. The organization's predominantly black middle class membership had been decimated by the economics of the Depression, and after 1930 he slowly reestablished branches, created some new ones, and built up the NAACP's membership which had fallen to below 30,000, while downplaying the leadership role of whites although they continued to be active (a white man remained president well into the era of the Second Reconstruction). It is a comment on the times that NAACP's policies were seen as militant and to be feared, and not only by those who denied African Americans their rights.

Thanks to White, the NAACP kept its distance from the CPUSA, but it did work in a limited manner with the ILD, as in the case of Angelo Herndon, a black communist organizer for whom it filed an Amicus Curiae brief. The 19-year-old Herndon, convicted in Georgia for inciting "insurrection" (under a Reconstruction-era law) for leading a protest by Atlanta unemployed against cuts in relief, was sentenced in 1932 to the chain gang for 18–20 years; those judging Herndon considered the sentence an "act of mercy" since a death verdict could have been imposed. He became a shirt tail to the Scottsboro case, as the CPUSA agitated "Free Angelo Herndon and the Scottsboro Boys." Herndon, after serving some time, was able to obtain bail and to wait out his lawyers' various appeals until the U.S. Supreme Court, by a 5–4 decision (*Herndon v. Lowry*), disallowed the Georgia law because setting "no ascertainable standard of guilt" was so "vague and indeterminate" it violated the 14th Amendment due process clause; he was set free. During the early 1940s Herndon broke with the CPUSA and ultimately veered away from politics.

For the Communists and the ILD who were involved with other cases involving racial injustice, these cases, while well-fought, paled into less importance during the 1930s than Herndon and Scottsboro, which were the CPUSA's rallying cry in the black community during both the Third Period and the Popular Front. While the Scottsboro and Herndon cases attracted a great deal of attention, White and the NAACP continued to work in their fashion. During the 1930s once again there were attempts to get federal antilynching legislation passed. Gallup polls showed that public opinion, even among some Southerners, favored such legislation. Between 1933 and 1938 over 80 blacks suffered unspeakable brutality as they were viciously and violently lynched. Typical was a 1937 double lynching in Mississippi where two handcuffed African Americans were chained to a tree, mutilated by a blow torch, doused with gasoline, and set afire.

In the four years after FDR took office in 1933, despite a generally favorable response among Federal legislators, even from some Southern white supremacists aghast at the brutal violence unleashed by mob action, antilynching bills introduced into both Houses of Congress were stalled by Southern representatives and senators. Whatever their unspoken fears about an end to white supremacy, their announced concerns were for "states rights." and opposition to another Reconstruction with dictates again from the North. But if nothing else, they were determined, as one historian puts it, "not...to be 'outniggered' in a Democratic primary."

The NAACP's input on the antilynching legislation drive was helped immensely by White's access to President and Mrs. Roosevelt, with whom he could and would informally chat from time to time. She was especially interested in the bettering of the situation of African Americans economically and socially and was a unstinting advocate of equal rights. She had the President's ear, and even though he did not always listen to his wife, her influence was felt.

A woman of great social conscience (the economist and New Dealer John Kenneth Galbraith subsequently dubbed her "Eleanor The Good"), she reached out to the black community; she invited to the White House delegations it had sent to Washington, D.C., had her picture taken with them and African Americans elsewhere, and participated in fund-raisers for black schools and organizations. In 1938, confronted at an interracial meeting with a local Alabama segregation ordinance that required her to sit in the white section of the audience, she moved her chair into the aisle between the two sections. Much of what she did could be considered symbolic, but nonetheless was extremely important in advancing the cause of ending racial oppression and certainly impressed African Americans, who had been denied even such symbolic acts over the years.

She became for many Southern whites a hated woman because of her advocacy of racial equality. In early 1936, Georgia Governor Eugene Talmadge held a convention of individuals opposed to New Deal policies in Macon; each of the 3000 attendees found on their seat a copy of a magazine which, with pictures and bold type, disclosed that the president's wife "entertained Negroes at White House dinners." Thanks to her the complaints of African American leaders could receive a hearing at the White House.

Being able to talk to the president, however, was not always rewarding. White later recalled, whatever FDR's personal sympathies, the president told him "I did not chose the tools with which I must work. Had I been permitted to chose them I would have selected quite different ones. But I've got to get legislation passed...The Southerners by reasons of the seniority rule ...occupy strategic places in most of the Senate and House committees...." As a then key FDR aide Thomas Corcoran later put it: "He does his best with it, but he ain't gonna lose his votes for it." Important members of the White House staff (e.g., Steve Early, FDR's press spokesman; Marvin McIntyre, his appointment secretary; Colonel and later General Edwin "Pa" Watson, his military aide and boon companion) stemmed from the South, shared the prejudices of their section, and tried to bury even limited attempts at racial amelioration which would, in their opinion, offend Dixie voters.

Despite such political reckoning and the necessity for close dealing with Southern legislative oligarchs, FDR, the leader of the Democratic Party, during his first term in office won the African American vote away from the Republicans, the party of Lincoln—deified among blacks by that president's early 20th century political successors as "Emancipator of the Slaves" in a quest for the votes of blacks outside the South. The popular historian William Manchester noted that given the African Americans' traditional ties to the Republicans Party, FDR's ties to the Southern wing of the Democratic Party, and the fact that blacks initially were subject to various kinds of discrimination in the programs established by the New Deal., that at first Roosevelt's appeal seems "baffling." However, whatever the shortcomings of the New Deal with regard to African Americans, and there were more than a few, FDR was helped by the actions of his predecessor. As later playwright and Roosevelt speech writer Robert Sherwood put it: "Herbert Hoover, in the parlance of vaudeville, a good act to follow."

In the 1928 presidential election—thanks in large part to the bigotry which hampered the Catholic Al Smith—the Democratic candidate, the Republican Herbert Hoover had cracked "the solid South." The president and his party's strategists, taking heart from that outcome, in an attempt to energize that region's skeleton Republican Party and continue to gain white votes, acted in a manner that led White to call him "the man in the lily-White House." Hoover closed down the Negro Division of the Republican National Committee, excluded African American workers from jobs in construction at the federally sponsored Boulder Dam project, and his Commission on Law Enforcement refused requests to consider subjects such as lynching and disenfranchisement.

When the administration sent the Gold Star mothers, women who had lost sons in World War I, to France to visit their graves, African Americans were sent on separate ships with inferior accommodations. When a racially mixed delegation met with the vice president, he refused to shake hands with the black member. Fifty-seven lynchings took place during Hoover's term in office; whatever his personal feelings he did not publicly disapprove of them. And it was Hoover who had nominated Judge Parker for a position on the U.S. Supreme Court.

At first, for many African Americans and liberals concerned with the race issue much of the record of the New Deal was damning. The Agricultural Adjustment Administration had failed black tenant farmers (and white ones as well) in the South as payments for crop reduction (undertaken to raise the price of farm products) designed to offset diminished income went not to them but to the white landowners. In 1934 the Federal Housing Administration included restrictive covenants in its contracts and a "whites only" policy was practiced in most of the new housing created by New Deal agencies. The Civilian Conservation Corps (CCC), which employed young men on various nation-wide environmental projects based at camps across the country (with most of their pay going to their families), after a stab at integration established separate facilities for whites and African Americans. At various New Deal project sites such as the Tennessee Valley Authority (TVA), there were separate toilets and water fountains for "coloreds." The National Recovery Administration (NRA)—the centerpiece of the administration's first attempts to combat the effects of the Depression—because of its hiring practices and pay policies, in a play on its name become known to many blacks as the "Negro Run Around" and "Negroes Rarely Allowed".

Yet, a harbinger of the future came in the 1934 elections with the defeat of Chicago Republican Oscar De Priest (the first black congressman elected to the House of Representatives since Reconstruction) by a black Democrat (Arthur Mitchell). African Americans began to benefit from the New Deal, especially after 1935 when it moved into high gear. An analysis of the black vote in 15 wards in 9 Northern cities showed that FDR captured 4 in 1932, 9 in 1936. In 1938 a *Fortune* survey found that over 80 percent of African Americans polled were unhesitatingly for Roosevelt. The alphabet agencies of the New Deal may not have been free of discrimination, but the black community recognized that despite the Dixiecrats, the New Deal offered African Americans relief and jobs, and hope.

The CCC camps may not have been integrated, but enrolled thousands of young blacks. TVA, despite the strong opposition of local employers, annoyed at losing a low wage black labor force to better paid federal jobs, hired hundreds of African Americans. Homes constructed by various New Deal agencies, like much of American housing, may have been limited to "native white American stock," but the Division of Subsistence Homesteads, Federal Emergency Relief Administration and Resettlement Administration built Aberdeen Gardens, a 159-unit "garden city for Negroes" in Newport News, VA.

The Work Progress Administration (WPA), a giant work relief program established in 1935, whose efforts ranged from make-work of little value to the construction of schools, parks, hospitals, playgrounds, and highways, among other projects, employed millions, including thousands of African Americans, a fact that angered those critics who complained about its "mixing of the races" in the agency's various endeavors. Under the WPA's aegis (and subsequent acclaim by both African American and white scholars) an all-black unit of writers interviewed ex-slaves, and put together a very useful and valuable collection of "Slave Narratives," material which might otherwise have been lost to history and has since been mined by historians and others interested in the subject.

Such WPA Arts Projects gave talented blacks a chance to work at their trade. Employment on the Federal Writers Project in Chicago allowed Richard Wright to write *Native Son;* Other writers for whom the WPA became patron included such diverse types as Ralph Ellison, Margaret Walker, and Frank Yerby. Various black performers were utilized extensively by the Federal Theatre Project unit in New York City, headed by Orson Welles and John Houseman, and it was but one of 23 Negro Units scattered across the country in cities like Seattle, Los Angeles, and Chicago (where a director was Shirley Graham, the wife of W.E.B. Du Bois). The WPA funded the Harlem Art Workshop, and in 1937 established the Harlem Community Arts Center, both of which benefited artists as well known as Romare Breardon, Jacob Lawrence, and Charles White, as well as other less notable African Americans.

The Public Works Administration (PWA) built or financed four-fifths of the public works constructed in the U.S. between 1933 and 1937, but never fulfilled the goal of those who established it in the weeks after FDR became president. Secretary of the Interior Harold Ickes, its head, was less interested than Harry Hopkins, the WPA head, in stimulating the U.S. economy by providing jobs than in getting a dollar's worth for every government dollar spent. PWA, before it ceased to exist in 1939, did, without wasting a penny, build a great many post offices, schools, bridges, courthouses, and the like, and did so with significant black labor. Ickes made use of a quota system requiring PWA contractors to hire African American in proportion to their number in a local labor force. Ickes, to the consternation of many in Washington, D.C., desegregated the Department of Interior cafeteria (it took a long time before other Executive Departments followed his example).

Ickes made the Lincoln Memorial over which the PWA held sway available in 1939 for an outdoor concert by the gifted black contralto Marian Anderson. She had been denied the use of Constitution Hall, then the only real concert venue in Washington, D.C., by its proprietor, the Daughters of the American Revolution (DAR), because as its head said, "no Negro would be permitted to appear there." Mrs. Roosevelt loudly resigned from the DAR. White and Marian Anderson's concert manager Sol Hurok suggested as an alternative an open-air concert at a park in Washington, D.C. Ickes, when approached, went to check with FDR for his approval, which was given.

The interior secretary presided over the concert, which took place Easter Sunday afternoon. He estimated that over 75,000 attended, the majority of them African Americans. Marian Anderson began her recital with *America* and ended it with *Nobody Knows The Trouble I've Seen.* By all accounts her concert was an enormous success, majestic in its setting and impressive as a concert. Earlier in the year she had sung at the White House; later in 1939 she would sing there again when the King and Queen of England were guests of the Roosevelts. In the segregated Washington, D.C., of that era, there was no first-class hotel that would accept her. At the time of the Easter Sunday concert, she and her mother were guests in a private home, the town house of a white socialite friend of Mrs. Roosevelt.

The Roosevelt administration employed a significant number of capable African Americans and by 1936 over 40 of them had become mid-range officials in various

New Deal agencies and Departments of the Executive Branch. They belonged to an *ad hoc* caucus known as "the Black Cabinet." These New Dealers included men whose careers in government service began an "Advisor on Negro Problems" in the Interior Department such as Robert Weaver—the first black to obtain a Ph.D. from Harvard— who after successful careers as an academic and in public service became in 1966 the first secretary of housing and urban development, and William Hastie—a brilliant lawyer who scored a number of firsts for blacks with his selection for the Federal Bench, appointment as Governor of the Virgin Islands, and becoming a Federal Appeals Court judge.

The successful well-known black activist Mary McLeod Bethune, who began work with the NYA, in 1936 organized as an informal body the Federal Council on Negro Affairs, which was the basis for "the Black Cabinet." Participants in the network included the best and brightest African Americans serving the New Deal such as Hastie and Weaver as well as some others prominent in the black community such as White and Eugene K. Jones, the then executive secretary of the National Urban League. Bethune had good ties with Eleanor Roosevelt (they had known each other for years), which assured this group access to the White House, if not always a favorable response.

The Black Cabinet had less input and importance than its members hoped and wished for, and got more play in the African American press than its influence warranted. Its members, despite their personal success, often were frustrated by the lack of positive response that they obtained. The racism that permeated much of American society and government blunted their often perceptive comments and intelligent suggestions, which not only would have furthered the cause of African Americans but in general would have improved race relations. Through Eleanor Roosevelt they could reach the president, but a highly pragmatic politician, he would and could only respond up to a point. And Mrs. Roosevelt, for all her deeply felt commitment, understood that fact, although to her credit she was willing to be a nag.

Even FDR, in a convoluted fashion, furthered the possibility of achieving racial justice by reining in some of the power of the South within the Democratic Party. In 1936 at its presidential nominating convention, the Party abolished the rule that a nominee for president had to obtain two-thirds of the convention delegates vote; its abolition ended Southern veto power over presidential candidates. That year for the first time black delegates were seated as more than alternates, and the president arranged for Congressman Arthur Mitchell to give one of the 55 seconding speeches; it highlighted FDR's program for African Americans. FDR, a few years later, encouraged his attorney general to create a Civil Rights Division in the Department of Justice which was done in 1939.

Until the 1930s African Americans had all too often been on the receiving end of violence in what were tagged as race riots, as in the "Red Summer" of 1919. During those months violent disturbances took place all over the United States, which really meant that whites rioted against blacks, at least some of whom were injured fatally, and in the main white casualties, if there were any, were the result of blacks defending themselves. In 1935 a different kind of race riot took place in Harlem, which was a preview of what happened in the 1960s with attacks on property and an absence of clashes between racial groups; the violence was the response of the forces of law and order against the black rioters, who were those in the African American community with the least to lose.

Harlem in 1935 could be said to have been ripe for a riot. About 50 percent of Harlem's families were unemployed. In the fifth year of the Great Depression, despite relief activity by city, state, and federal authorities, the majority of the population suffered. In that part of New York City, the tuberculosis rate for its inhabitants was five times greater than for whites; the rates for pneumonia and typhoid were twice those of whites. It was estimated that two black mothers and two black babies died for every white mother and child. The only hospital in the area had 273 beds and inadequate facilities to service about a quarter of a million blacks. Housing was poor and the average rent in Harlem was about twice as much as a similar white family paid. And while unemployment was very high, stores and businesses which serviced Harlem—often owned or operated by Jews—generally did not hire African Americans except in the most menial positions.

The riot began on the afternoon of March 19, 1935, when a 16-year-old black Puerto Rican youth was apprehended by chain store employees while trying to steal a pocket knife. He bit the hand of one of them. After police arrived the store's manager declined to press charges, and the boy was taken out the back entrance. Shortly thereafter an ambulance arrived to treat the manager and his assistant who, in addition to the bite, had suffered scratches and bruises while apprehending the youth. A crowd gathered and assumed the youth had been taken out the back in order for the police to beat him. When an ambulance left the scene empty, many in the growing crowd assumed that the youth had been killed. A hearse happened to be across the street and members of the crowd, which had continued to grow, assumed that it was calling for the body of the youth.

More police arrived and assured the growing crowd the youth was okay. The crowd demanded to see him. The police tried to disperse them. Word spread through Harlem that the youth had been beaten by the police and killed. At the end of the day Mayor LaGuardia issued a statement urging Harlem to remain calm. But to no avail. Handbills, one headed "Child Brutally Beaten," were distributed. Various militant white and African American speakers attempted to address the thousands who had gathered outside the store; the police arrested them for "unlawful assemblage." Someone threw a brick through the store's window; looting began. It quickly spread as all through Harlem's main shopping area, store windows were smashed. Police tried to stop the crowds by circulating photos of the youth alive but were hooted down by those who argued that the pictures were phony.

Looting and disorder continued through the night, as white-owned businesses were targeted. Some shops posted signs that read "COLORED STORE" or "COLORED EMPLOYED HERE." Some times it helped, sometimes it did not. By the end of the next day order had been restored, but the cost was high. The rumored murder of a young black shoplifter by white police had resulted in the death of three African Americans, serious injuries to nearly 60 more, and an estimated $200,000,000 in property damage. A Mayor' Commission on Conditions in Harlem attributed the riot to "the aggressions of the police," "racial segregation," and "injustices of discrimination in employment."

Quick thinking by the proprietor of this store, who hastily plastered his display window with signs proclaiming it a "colored store," saved this shop from destruction when rioters swept through Harlem shattering store windows on March 19, 1935. (AP/Wide World Photos)

Many black militants ignored the other causes and blamed the Jews who operated most of the stores which were looted, which, in keeping with the contemporary practices of American society, failed to hire people from the community. The militants' approach fit in with the anti-Semitism flourishing in the mid-1930s. American Jews had been castigated as "Christ killers" and ritual murderers by much of Western society for centuries. The United States had been relatively free of such buncombe, however. The first Jewish immigrants, mostly Sephardic Jews, had come to the United States during colonial days. The later Jewish immigrants to the United States came from Central Europe and had lived in America relatively free from the restrictions suffered in the old country. Some had assimilated very well. The socially prominent Belmonts, for example, could trace their lineage back to the German Jewish Schoenbergs (both names mean beautiful mountains).

Anti-Semitism, although it existed, had been a relatively negligible factor in American life until the latter part of the 19th century when it emerged as a social force. During the 1890s many Populists had condemned the Jew as responsible for the hard times occasioned by the Panic of 1893 and its aftermath. The argument was that the international connections and unrestrained greediness of Jewish financiers and bankers had enabled Lombard Street (the home of English banking) to wreck the American economy. These Jews were responsible for the hard times faced by American farmers and small businessmen. The issue of whether the Populists were anti-Semitic or class conscious has been argued by scholars ever since. However, anti-Semitism in the United States had grown as the number of Jewish immigrants from Eastern Europe—strange in their ways and makeup and alien to how American viewed themselves—increased dramatically during the 1880s and 1890s.

In any event, unlike the Europe from which the Jews had emigrated, there was little overt or coordinated violence directed against them. There was nothing like the state organized pogroms in early 20th century Russia. A notable exception was the 1915 lynching in Georgia of Leo Frank, the Jewish manager of an Atlanta pencil factory accused of the rape and murder of a teenage employee. Frank, the only Jew ever lynched on American soil, although born in Texas and married to the daughter of a prominent Southern Jewish family, had been brought up and educated in the North. His murder resulted as much from resentment against the cultural judgments of Northerners about the South as from the anti-Semitism successfully stirred up by local rabble rousers. However, as one writer succinctly put it: "Wrongly Accused, Falsely Convicted, Wantonly Murdered."

During the 1920s anti-Semitism became more overt with such activity as industrialist Henry Ford's subvention of *The Dearborn Independent;* advertising itself as "Chronicler of the Neglected Truth," it published hate material about "The International Jew: The World's Problem" including the anti-Semitic hate literature like *The Protocols of the Elders of Zion.* A forgery produced by Russian Tsarist police in the late 19th century, the *Protocols* purport to be transcripts of secret meetings by international Jewish conspirators to take over the world. The *Protocols,* like compilations of anti-Semitic material from the *Independent,* became central texts of 1930s anti-Jewish Nazi propaganda, had wide circulation among U.S. anti-Semites, and still do overseas, especially in the Middle East. Law suits and threats of a boycott forced Ford to end his support of the weekly in 1927.

During the late 1930s Detroit was again a center of anti-Semitic publishing activity, however. Father Charles Coughlin, a Roman Catholic parish priest in Royal Oak, a suburb of "the Auto City" had gained a national following through weekly radio broadcasts (*Fortune* dubbed him "just about the biggest thing that ever happened to radio"). At first the priest outspokenly supported FDR and the New Deal; "Roosevelt or Ruin," "the New Deal is Christ's Deal," were Coughlin's themes. His impact on the country is a telling indication of the changing American response to Catholics, since before Father Coughlin parted company with FDR he had many non-Catholic followers. He broke with the president over various issues and in 1936 joined a coalition of fringe groups that put up a candidate for the presidency who got swamped in FDR's overwhelming victory that year.

Father Coughlin's influence began to wane; as it did he became avowedly antiSemitic in virulent attacks on "Franklin D. Rosenfeld" and the "Jew Deal." There had always been a tinge of Populist bigotry in the priest's attacks on international bankers. Now, weekly in nationwide radio broadcasts and in his magazine *Social Justice,* Coughlin attacked the Jewish cabal advising FDR, justified the Nazi persecutions, attacked the international Zionist conspiracy: at one point in a New York City rally he shouted at an approving audience "When we get through with the Jews in America, they'll think the treatment...received in Germany was nothing." There are some indications that in the late 1930s Nazi Germany provided Coughlin's operation with some funds.

In 1938–39 admirers of Coughlin enrolled in organizations like his Christian Front that included the Christian Mobilizers (self-defined as "anticommunist" but actually pro-Nazi) and would assault Jews on the streets. desecrate synagogues, vandalize Jewish businesses, and threateningly picket Jewish shops shouting "Don't Buy Here." Most of this activity took place in New York City and Boston (known at the end of the 1930s by Jewish defense groups as "a poisonous city," it was probably among the most important sources of Coughlin funds). Their predominantly Irish American police, at whose communion breakfasts journalists found Coughlin propaganda widely available, seem to have observed but not responded to anti-Semitic violence and vandalism. Nor did these cities' police interfere with aggressive selling at busy street corners by groups of Coughlin supporters of his virulent *Social Justice* (in 1938 it began serializing the *Protocols*) to people assumed to be Jewish in the hope of finding targets to beat up. The Coughlinite police often responded to critics that the salesmen, in making their pitch, were only practicing their right to freedom of speech; the victims were responsible for any violence.

The frequency and intensity of such disturbance increased substantially during World War II with the general American national upturn in anti-Semitism. The violence directed against Jews in the 1930s raises questions about the "whiteness school" of history which argues the U.S. population at this time was divided along racial lines, with public perception of the differences between the various European immigrant groups fading into insignificance after the 1920s, with anti-Semitism subsumed into the broader pattern of prejudice against Southern and Eastern European immigrants which began to disappear as others came to regard them as "white." Anti-Semitism was, it was argued, no different than the antagonism shown to other immigrant groups before they assimilated. As the immigration of Italians was restricted, and their numbers began to stabilize, no longer would they be dubbed "niggers." The proponents of "whiteness" have argued rather tellingly that the United States is "a country that has known no pogroms," and that "no American Jew has been seriously impeded in the practice of his faith."

While organized instances of violence against Jews in the United States are rare, it should not be overlooked that there are individual instances of violence against them. However, even in the late 1930s as anti-Semitism in the United States increased, Jews continued as a group to escape the blatant oppression directed against African Americans and Orientals, the other minorities against whom American bigots focused. As the classics scholar Mary Lefkowitz has summed up the situation of American Jews at that time "anti-Semitism tended to be undercover, passive, and only exclusionary."

Jews in the 1930s did not experience the *de jure* bias legally suffered by African Americans in the Southern United States or that which tormented Orientals in the American West (the legal restrictions against both groups often illegally backed up by an almost barbarous violence). But if anti-Semitism was less visible than the overt racism practiced against people of color in the 1930s, it did exist. The critic Alfred Kazin recalled even in the literary world of New York City "anti-Semitism was obvious";

while freelancing as a book reviewer at that time for the *New York Herald-Tribune* his "very friendly" boss asked "if I thought Jews walked differently from other people." That very liberal man, remarked Kazin, was not overtly anti-Semitic but did view Jews "as *low.*"

The Jews did face a *de facto* discrimination whose impact was hurtful and cruel since, with very rare exceptions, it barred them from many hotels, various resorts, a variety of clubs, some housing, diverse university fraternities, and a wide range of employment opportunities. And in various areas of American life that *de facto* policy did not cease until long after the 1930s were over. (Hotels, for example, continued to be "restricted" even after the wording was dropped by the end of the decade from advertisements and replaced by "select clientele.")

Moreover, what was dubbed "parlor anti-Semitism" obviously did have an effect. In 1940 New York State's medical schools enrolled only 108 Jewish students. During the 1930s various Yale Law School eating clubs were closed to Jews and pressure was put on non-Jews rooming with Jews to change their accommodations. A law school professor would write in his recommendations for outstanding students that this candidate "has no trace of those characteristics one associates with Hebrews."

Supposedly the respected, well known Harvard Law professor Felix Frankfurter could not join an exclusive Boston club, but as a committeeman remarked with a member, he "generally was welcome at lunch." Jews did not study engineering because they knew that even with a first rate academic degree it was unlikely they could find a job in the industry. A common response from a Wall Street firm to which a university's better graduates would be recommended was "We have no prejudices but have found from experience that Jews are so unlikely to click with our clients that we employ them only in very extraordinary circumstances." Faculty liberals at one university considered hire of a librarian with one Jewish parent a real triumph. Jewish graduates did find jobs: student lawyers could usually connect with Jewish law firms, but competition for the limited number of these positions was fierce, whereas non-Jews usually had a choice of offers.

While anti-Semitism did become a more powerful force in American life during the 1930s, it never did win over more than a particular limited slice of the population. By the end of the decade 46 percent of those responding to a *Fortune* magazine poll did not feel that "hostility to the Jewish people" was growing even though a third of the respondents did. The head of the New School for Social Research maintained that "Anti Semitism is on the increase in America" but argued he had found that those promoting it were "far from a majority."

The journalist W. L. White believed in 1938 that by and large Americans did not approve of the anti-Semitic policies instituted by the Nazis in Germany and Austria (after annexed in 1938). And White, while admitting that unfortunately anti-Semitism did exist in the United States, argued that "the hag ridden intellectuals of the eastern seaboard" were wrong in their assessment about a positive future for American anti-Semitism, pointing out that when, in the late 1930s, the venomous anti-Semitic Reverend Gerald Winrod ran in Kansas for the Republican senatorial nomination, he got only 52,000 votes out of over 220,000 cast.

It is doubtful that most Americans understood the distinctions between the various branches of American Judaism. In the main Americans were ignorant of the different interpretations of the religion undertaken by American Jews of Orthodox, Conservative, and Reform bent. Nor would most Americans have been aware of the Reconstructionist view of Judaism as divined and preached by Rabbi Mordecai M. Kaplan, who in 1935 formally founded a movement that did not accept a divine basis for the religion but argued that its basis was as a "religious civilization"—Kaplan "reconstructed" Judaism as a "civilization" and "revalued" the commandments God gave Moses as "folkways"; he wanted to provide a rationale for those who wished to keep on living as Jews but could not, or would not accept "the Biblical God of Abraham, Isaac, and Jacob."

It is also doubtful that most Americans understood the class and often economic distinctions between the main Jewish defense groups which spoke out for Jews during the 1930s with varying degrees of success. Although very different in makeup, at the beginning of the 1930s they mainly emphasized mobilization of that gentile American element who had indicated good will toward the Jews, avoided overt or militant advocacy based on Jewish self-interest, and stressed behind-the-scenes negotiations where influence could be utilized. The defense groups' operations changed during the decade as their goals changed. The defense groups' overriding concern at the beginning of the decade was American society's treatment of Jews, but after the Nazis took power in 1933 it became the fate of Germany's Jews. These organizations also had some other interests, stemming to some extent from their substantial support of the NAACP and other African American groups, but did not really encompass larger issues such as the whole field of civil rights, as would in later years be the case.

The Anti-Defamation League had been founded in 1913 by the B'nai B'rith, a fraternal organization organized by Jews of German descent in 1845. By the beginning of the 20th century it had become the major middle class men's service organization in the Jewish community. And its affiliate, the Anti-Defamation League, centered in Chicago during the 1930s, had as its main mission as the combating of negative portrayals of the American Jew in the mass media, including advertising. It supported the effective imposition in 1934 of self-censorship by the American film industry, which resulted in the effective disappearance of Jews from Hollywood film until well after the end of World War II.

The American Jewish Committee (AJC), a much more patrician group, had been founded in 1906 in order to fight the pogroms in Russia. Organized by well-off Jews who were of German descent, it had chapters in various parts of the United States, with the largest and most effective located in New York City. During the 1930s the leaders of the AJC considered themselves the representatives of those who thought of themselves as Americans who happened to be Jewish. It lobbied extensively on behalf of those persecuted by the Nazis, especially to get immigration quotas enlarged and the legal restrictions on entry to the United States modified, although it eschewed boycotts and large scale public protests. The AJC was a patriarchal elite organization which limited its membership. Because its leadership felt Americans who happened to be Jews did not need a homeland, and that establishment of a Jewish state would raise the issue of dual allegiance, it did not support Zionism, and only became a supporter of such a state after the establishment of Israel in 1948.

One of AJC's founders and head for years was Louis Marshall, a very effective lawyer who had defended Leo Frank. Marshall had argued cases for the NAACP (he was one of several Jewish lawyers who had been active on behalf of that organization in civil rights cases before the creation of it own legal team), and written, at the behest of the litigants bringing the case against Ford, the apology the industrialist made when ceasing support for the *Dearborn Independent*. Marshall, who died in 1929, was typical of the older generation of American Jewry which by the time of the Great Depression had been assimilated although it suffered from the exclusionary practices of U.S. society.

The AJC, given the conservative outlook of its leaders and members, feuded with the more left-oriented, democratically operated American Jewish Congress about the role of Jews in the United States, who should represent them, and what their goals should be. The Congress, differing from the AJC, viewed Jews as able to support a Jewish homeland although living in America. The Congress and its initial supporters, such as U.S. Supreme Court Justice Louis D. Brandeis and Harvard Law School Professor Felix Frankfurter, who championed Zionism as being an integral part of being an American Jew, supported the establishment of a Jewish state in Palestine.

Initially organized in 1917 to secure Jewish civil, political, and religious rights in Eastern Europe and Palestine, the American Jewish Congress sent a mission to the Versailles Peace Conference in order to give Jewish people a voice in the discussions about the shape of the post-World War 1 world. Among those who went was the articulate dynamic Rabbi Stephen S. Wise, who two years after the Congress was reorganized on a permanent basis in 1923, was elected its head, a position he held until his death in 1949.

Wise energetically presided over an organization which brought together a wide range of Jews, mostly of Eastern European descent, and in many ways considerably less elite and more diverse than the AJC membership. Wise was a tireless Zionist and an indefatigable supporter of liberal causes; he had helped establish the NAACP and the American Civil Liberties Union, spoken out on behalf of Sacco and Vanzetti, and participated actively in the fight against municipal corruption in New York City. Under his hard-driving leadership the Congress unstintingly supported Zionism and conducted vigorous campaigns for human rights and civic virtue.

After 1933 while the Congress strongly continued its support of such social causes, thanks to Wise it took an active public anti-Nazi stance. Just weeks after the Nazis took control of Germany and began to implement their outrageous anti-Jewish policies, the Congress held a mass protest rally in New York City's Madison Square Garden despite the strong opposition of the German government, the U.S. State Department, and organizations like the AJC and B'Nai B'Brith.

Under Wise's aggressive leadership the Congress held protest demonstrations, staged mock trials of Hitler, and attempted to organize boycotts of German goods, all to mobilize American opposition to the Nazi regime. He and the organization also focused attention on the refugee problem caused by Nazi persecution and in pursuit of rescue and relief of the Jewish victims, and pressed for amelioration of the restrictive American immigration laws and the limits placed by the British government on Jewish immigration to Palestine, which was under that country's control. His campaign unfortunately achieved little as both countries by the end of the decade had tightened their immigration procedures, despite the increasingly desperate situation of German Jewry.

Within weeks of coming to power the Nazis instituted a temporary but effective national boycott of Jewish shops. As Hitler and his minions reorganized German life, Jews were increasingly marginalized, until finally in 1935 the Nuremberg laws barred Jews from much of Germany's economic life and severely limited their civil rights. The November 7, 1938, murder in Paris of a minor German diplomat by a half-crazed, teenaged Jewish refugee resulted in a massive officially sanctioned national pogrom in Germany on the night of November 10–11; all across the country organized mobs destroyed Jewish homes, looted Jewish shops, and burned synagogues; dozens of Jews were murdered, and 20,000 were arrested. The destruction became known as Kristallnacht (Night of Broken Glass) because of the shards of broken glass littering German streets the morning after as a result of Nazi ferocity.

Hitler wanted the Jews, after he had pauperized them, to emigrate; the German Jews were willing to pay to leave Germany and most of world opinion thought emigration would resolve the situation, the problem that remained the subject of much debate domestically in the United States and internationally was where they could go. The American Jewish defense groups tried ineffectually to have the administration pressure the British not to restrict immigration to Palestine. The American Jewish community also hoped that the United States could be a land of refuge. But an isolationist-oriented Congress and a xenophobic public stood in the way of any U.S. action on the international scene even in a modest and mostly symbolic way: in 1935 FDR, much to his surprise and disappointment, failed because of an aroused popular sentiment to get the necessary two-thirds approval from a heavily Democratic Senate for a treaty affiliating the United States with the World Court.

These forces stood squarely in the way of modifying the stern restrictions put in place by the immigration laws of the 1920s, with their emphasis on quotas. Legislative attempts by concerned congressmen to transfer quotas (e.g., the unfilled British quota to Germany) failed, as did efforts to "mortgage" them (i.e., to accelerate immigration by refugees in 1938 and 1939 by adding to the total for those years the quotas for 1940 and 1941). The laws which made no provision for asylum because of religious or political persecution also called for banning "people likely to become a public charge" which allowed the American opponents of Jewish immigration to wrap themselves in the concern that the refugees admitted might become public charges. Certainly, Jews from Germany (and after March 1938 and Hitler's annexation of Austria those from there as well), were invariably stripped of their assets by the Nazis, and in order to come to America had to have someone in the country vouch for their support; no easy task in a Depression-ridden United States.

Bills proposed in Congress during the 1930s to mitigate the restrictions faced as stern opposition as had the proposed antilynching legislation, often from the same sources. And as time would prove, the career foreign service officers administering these laws often were not-so- genteel anti-Semites, who, through rigid interpretation of the laws, placed unnecessary complex procedural barriers in the way of rescue. A Jewish congressman characterized the State Department's consular service as having "a heart best muffled by protocol." Controversy swirled around FDR's response to Jewish immigration to the United States during the 1930s (and later to Hitler's extermination policies).

Both President and Mrs. Roosevelt were sympathetic to the plight of the Jews. Both had long ago overcome the traditional social anti-Semitism of their class. FDR had close Jewish friends and advisers, courted successfully the Jewish vote, and was genuinely outraged by the brutal tactics of the Nazis. He spoke out against Nazi Jewish policies; early on he urged his ambassador to Germany to do what could be done "to moderate the general persecution." Roosevelt called in 1938 for an international conference to deal with the refugee problem (delegates from 33 countries met at the French resort of Evian-Les Bains on the shores of Lake Geneva and accomplished almost nothing).

Roosevelt asserted after Kritallnacht that he "could scarcely believe that such things could occur in a twentieth century civilization" and recalled the American ambassador for "consultation." (And though the United States did not sever diplomatic relations with Germany he never returned to Berlin). The bulk of the U.S. press and prominent gentile Americans as disparate as Herbert Hoover, Harold Ickes, Alf Landon (the 1936 Republican candidate for president), and Al Smith condemned the Nazis and the brutality underlying Kristallnacht.

All through the 1930s public opinion polls showed that the majority of Americans were ill at east with Nazi policies towards the Jews, but sympathy for them did not translate into a willingness to support changes in the immigration laws. While in November 1938 the pollster George Gallup found that 94 percent of those polled disapproved of Nazi treatment of the Jews, a *Fortune* survey recorded that less then 5 percent of those queried favored raising immigration quotas in order to accommodate more refugees.

The president, ever mindful of the expenditure of political capital in support of unpopular causes and after 1937 faced with a deteriorating economy as a recession within the Depression hit home, did not wish to directly confront those hostile to aiding Jewish refugees while attempting to move the United States to action on the international scene. He recognized the tenuousness of his power over an economically wounded country that in response to popular and legislative sentiment had isolated itself diplomatically.

The unhappy fate of the German Jews on the Hamburg-America liner *St. Louis* vividly illustrates the dichotomy found in various public opinion polls and the precarious equilibrium in which FDR's sentiments and official policy were suspended. Nearly 1000 German Jewish refugees sailed to Cuba on the liner but, unhappily, the landing rights bought by a philanthropic Jewish American committee were renounced by the government that had sold them. The passengers were denied admittance and faced with returning to Germany. American Jewish groups were willing to bond the ultimate transit of the passengers from Cuba but to no avail even though many already had quota numbers for immigration to the United States and had sailed to Havana to wait there for their number to come up.

Negotiators begged an unyielding American State Department to allow the refugees to disembark at a U.S. port. A telegram from the passengers to FDR went unanswered, as did petitions from many American groups (both Jewish and Gentile). For days the ship steamed up the Florida coast within sight of various American cities, followed by a Coast Guard cutter assigned to pick up any passenger who might jump overboard to swim ashore. Ultimately attempts to gain entry for the passengers to the United States failed and the ship returned to Europe. Its doomed cargo dispersed to England, France, Belgium, and the Netherlands. Only the 200 or so who went to England escaped the Holocaust.

As in this instance FDR's measured caution and his overall failure to recognize or understand the anti-Semitism of many in the State Department can and should be faulted. So too can his initial response in the early 1940s upon learning of the systematic Nazi extermination of the European Jews. But as many of his biographers and chroniclers of the era point out, the president did as much as his authority allowed to ameliorate the situation of the German and later the Austrian Jews.

After the passage of the Nuremberg Laws at FDR's behest, the State Department instructed consular officials to provide "the most generous and favorable treatment possible" under American law and there was an upturn in the very modest numbers of German Jews admitted to the United States—the number rising from 6,000 in 1936 to 11,000 in 1937 (altogether between 1933 and 1937 about 30,000 German Jews had

Refugees from Europe arrive in New York City, 1940. (Rothstein, Arthur. *The Depression Years As Photographed by Arthur Rothstein*. Dover Publications, 1978)

emigrated to the United States, about 5 percent of that country' Jewish population). Hitler's annexation of Austria led the president to order the merging of the German and Austrian quotas (thus not losing any immigrant spaces) as well as the expediting of Jewish visa applications, actions estimated to have helped 50,000 Jews to escape the Nazis in 1938 and 1939, even though American counsels remained stingy about issuing visas.

Even though over 60 percent of Americans polled in 1939 opposed the proposed admittance of 10,000 refugee children to the United States (their religion in the poll was unspecified but those queried undoubtedly thought they were Jewish), the president tried to have the immigration restrictions on the admittance of the children lifted but failed. Between November 1940 (Roosevelt's re-election) and December 1941 (when the Japanese attack on Pearl Harbor brought the United States into World War II) about 50,000 German Jews were admitted to the United States as FDR overrode the quota system.

Unfortunately the president' fears about the infiltration of Nazi agents among the refugees and concerns about national security were played on by Breckinridge Long, the State Department official whose bailiwick oversaw the visa section. An elegant Southerner, successful international lawyer, and bigot (his diary was full of invective against Jews and Catholics) he successfully played the national security card well into World War II in order to stem immigration by people he deemed undesirable. A 1944 Treasury Department report prepared by non-Jewish officials discussing some of his policies concluded that the State Department was "guilty of obstructionism" that resulted not only in "gross procrastination and willful failure to act, but even of willful attempts to prevent action from being taken to rescue Jews from Hitler."

FDR's wife clashed with Long repeatedly about the admission of refugees, and called him a "fascist." Her attempts to circumvent his authority were only partially successful, as with her intervention (various Jewish groups had aroused her interest) on behalf of 83 German refugees stuck in Norfolk, VA on a Portuguese freighter in August 1940; thanks to her FDR sent an government official there and the refugees were cleared to disembark.

Under U.S. law at the time, the president had only so much power with which to act. He could by force of his personality influence events, however, and he prioritized that capacity during the 1930s when greater Issues than the rescue of the German Jews were perforce on his agenda. Domestic recovery was the overriding concern of the American people, who had little or no interest in foreign affairs. In the 1930s FDR swam with the isolationist tide. He had to accept the political, social, and economic realities which limited his power, and operate within a difficult framework. As Alan Dershowitz has concluded: "Reasonable people can debate specific decisions, indecisions, actions and inactions...But no one should question Roosevelt's motives or good will toward the Jewish victims...." Whatever his shortcomings in the 1930s with regard to the rescue of the German Jews, because of his leadership in the fight against Hitler the president became a folk hero for the majority of American Jews.

For much of the 1930s the Soviet Union also attracted the favorable attention of many American Jews. The Soviets seemed to have reversed the anti-Semitic policies of Czarist Russia. A Jewish CPUSA member later recalled "everything that came out of the Soviet Union sounded wonderful." Not every Jew was a communist, as anti-Semites in the United States and Europe vigorously claimed at the time, but many American communists were Jews. The outspoken anti-Nazi policy of the Soviet Union attracted Jews, as did the politics of the CPUSA, which echoed the Soviets' attack on Hitler and the Nazis and after the Third Period bombastically supported FDR.

Religion played a different kind of role in the various novels dealing with Jewish life in the big city ghetto. Communists and communism did play a role, indicated by the fact that many of the books of the time touch on radical politics, although these works center on the struggle for adjustment by a family or individual who find their religious traditions in conflict with customs, habits, and politics that are perceived to be "American." An important sub-text often deals with the politics of a given situation involving some kind of anti-Semitism, and the fight against it. Because of the temper of the times in the 1930s, novels written during those years often have as a common theme the relationship with various branches of the left (assumed to be fighters against discrimination) and deal with the revolt of Jews, both young and old, against the attitudes of the day.

Among the novels penned both by the politically committed (who felt that in the story of their experiences during the Depression communism had overcome anti-Semitism) and those more interested in literary pursuits there are a number of authors who deserve to be remembered. A sample of the literature includes the following: Henry Roth's moving, insightful novel about a young Jewish boy on New York's Lower East Side, *Call It Sleep,* was rediscovered decades after its initial publication and remains a seminal work; *Jews Without Money* (1930) by Michael Gold (who placed his talents at the service of the Communist Party) had an enormous impact given its images of crime, prostitution, and crowded tenements; Daniel Fuchs, later an award-winning screenwriter, in 1934 published *Summer In Williamsburg,* a kaleidoscopic view of the disparate inhabitants of a Jewish section of Brooklyn; Meyer Levin, a prolific and popular novelist did the same for Chicago in *The Old Bunch* (1937), dealing with a group of Jewish high school graduates from 1921 to 1934 and various themes including racketeering, politics, and education.

Just before the Great Depression set in it seemed that Native Americans might fare better than Orientals, African Americans, or Jews, specifically that the Native Americans would benefit from more enlightened federal policies stemming from the actions of the newly elected Herbert Hoover. In 1929 he appointed as Indian commissioner Charles J. Rhoads, a former head of the Indian Rights Association and active supporter of Native American rights. Rhoads abolished segregated Indian schools and obtained greater appropriations for the Bureau of Indian Affairs, which allowed for a doubling of the funds available for the clothing of Native American pupils and the tripling of their food subsidy. Rhoads also built hospitals and hired better-trained doctors (during his tenure trachoma among the Indians was cut by 50%). However, the Hoover administration continued a policy of assimilating the Native American, ignoring the damage done to Indians by the efforts to abrogate their native culture. The secretary of the interior who oversaw the Bureau of Indian Affairs at one point asserted "the redman's civilization must be replaced by the white man's."

Serious attempts at improving the situation of the often impoverished, alienated, and demoralized Native Americans came with the appointment by President Roosevelt of John Collier as head of the Bureau of Indian Affairs and the passage in 1934 of the Wheeler-Howard Act (the "Indian Re-Organization Act" termed the "New Deal for Indians"). This act reversed a decades long policy of forced assimilation and sought to stop the alienation of Indian lands and to conserve tribal domains, provide for and encourage a larger measure of Indian self-government, safe-guard the rights of individual Native Americans, establish a revolving credit fund to help improve economic life on the reservations, and preserve ancestral traditions. The act also brought a level of gender equality to the reservations, thanks to Collier's intense efforts, which overcame strong resistance, and women were given the right to vote in tribal elections and to hold office.

Collier was a fierce proponent of Native American rights and pushed hard for his policies both in Washington, D.C., and among the tribes. Ultimately 192 of the 263 tribes voted to accept what the federal legislation proposed. But even among those who did there were Native Americans who thought that his vision a more active role for the Bureau of Indian Affairs in the management of tribal lands, of the placing of greater reliance on planning by expert social scientists and the like, and in some instances the imposition of policies on the basis of cold and perhaps more effective planners was just as disturbing as the previous long term neglect. These Native Americans were just as unhappy with imposed advice. Collier's actions in support of his policies, such as his emphasis in favor of tribally held rather than individually held land and the promotion of ancestral traditions as well as arts and crafts enterprises, led to denunciations against him by various Native American groups towards the end of the 1930s. Later he was accused of fostering "back-to-the-blanket" measures, which left men, women, and children ill-equipped to deal with modern American life.

That friction was typical of ethnic groups during the Great Depression. During the 1930s most of their constituents suffered more than did most of their non-ethnic peers. Yet already in the early 1930s some advances had been made. Anton Cermak (fatally wounded in February 1933 by a man who attempted to assassinate president-elect Roosevelt) was the first foreign-born American to be elected a mayor of Chicago. For all their suffering, the members of minority groups ultimately had improved their lot by the end of the 1930s, or at least had created a foundation for that improvement during and after World War II.

Much of the credit belongs to President Roosevelt and the New Deal. The improvements initiated do not at first seem obvious: at the end of the decade African Americans and Orientals still faced legal barriers; according to most sources anti-Semitism increased; many Catholics remained working class. But FDR opened the government to people of merit whatever their background and members of minority groups benefited: The president and the New Deal had by the end of the decade given legitimacy, status, improved conditions, and power to groups that had for generations suffered discrimination socially, economically, and professionally. Not all the minority groups fared equally well, but as Conrad Black convincingly argues "Jews and Catholic, especially the Irish, would wait a long time for a president better disposed to them than Roosevelt." At the beginning of the Great Depression a monopoly on American government at the federal level was held by white, male, Anglo Saxon Protestants. By the end of the 1930s a coalition of economic, ethnic, and cultural minorities held sway. Many of the outsiders had become insiders, and, building on what had been done in the 1930s, that condition would continue apace in the following decades.

Daniel Leab

References and Further Reading

Adamic, Louis. 1938. *My America 1928–1938.* New York: Harper & Brothers.

Bayor, Ronald. 1978. *Neighbors in Conflict: the Irish, Germans, Jews in New York City, 1929–1941.* Baltimore, MD: Johns Hopkins University Press.

Bodner, John, Roger Simon, and Michael P. Weber. 1983. *Lives of Their Own: Blacks, Italians, and Poles in Pittsburgh, 1900–1960.* Urbana: University of Illinois Press.

Carter, Dan T. 1976. *Scottsboro: a Tragedy of the American South.* Baton Rouge: Louisiana State University Press.

Dyja, Thomas. 2008. *Walter White: the Dilemma of Black Identity in America.* Chicago: Ivan R. Dee.

Edgerton, John. 1994. *Speak Now Against the Day: the Generation Before the Civil Rights Movement in the South.* New York: Knopf.

Feingold, Henry. 1995. *A Time for Searching: Entering the Mainstream, 1920–1945.* Baltimore, MD: Johns Hopkins University Press.

Goings, Kenneth W. 1990. *The NAACP Comes of Age: the Defeat of Judge John J. Parker.* Bloomington: Indiana University Press.

Guerin-Gonzales, Camille. 1991. *Mexican Workers and American Dreams: Immigration, Repatriation, and California Farm Labor, 1900–1939.* New Brunswick, NJ: Rutgers University Press.

Kelley, Robin D. G. 1990. *Hammer and Hoe: Alabama Communists During the Great Depression.* Chapel Hill: University of North Carolina Press.

Modell, John. 1977. *The Economics and Politics of Racial Accommodation: the Japanese of Los Angeles, 1900–1942.* Urbana: University of Illinois Press.

Murray, David. 1982. *Modern Indians: Native Americans in the 20th Century.* Durham, UK: British Association for American Studies.

Myrdal, Gunnar. 1944. *An American Dilemma: The Negro Problem and American Democracy.* New York: Harper & Brothers.

Prucha, Francis Paul. 1984. *The Great Father: The United States Government and the American Indians,* 2 vols. Lincoln: University of Nebraska Press

Harvey Sitkoff. 1978. *A New Deal for Blacks: The Emergence of Civil Rights as a National Issue.* New York: Oxford University Press.

Tull, Charles J. 1968. *Father Coughlin and the New Deal.* Syracuse, NY: Syracuse University Press.

Weber, Devra. 1994. *Dark Sweat, White Gold: California Farm Workers, Cotton, and the New Deal.* Berkeley: University of California Press.

Winger, Beth. 1991. *New York Jews and the Great Depression: Uncertain Promise.* New Haven, CT: Yale University Press.

Wyman, David. 1976. *Paper Walls: America and the Refugee Crisis 1938–1941.* Amherst: University of Massachusetts Press.

Reference Entries

Adamic, Louis (1899–1951)

Louis Adamic was a key figure in the history of American ethnicity. Born March 23, 1899, in Blato, Carinola, now Slovenia, to Anton and Ana Adamic, Catholic land-holding peasants, he had a limited education in various local schools before activity in a nationalist student organization necessitated emigration (December 1913) to the United States. Ambitious and hard-working, he found employment at a New York City Slovenian daily, *Narodni Glas* (The People's Voice), first on its loading docks, then in the mail room, and finally as an editorial assistant. After its failure (1916) he held manual labor jobs before enlisting (1917) in the army, serving on the western front during World War I. Naturalized (1918) during service, he was mustered out (1920) in California, ultimately settling there in a San Pedro Croatian fishing community. After various work experiences he determined to become a writer.

Adamic's first publications were translations of Slavic writers. After producing material for the radical pamphlet publisher Haldeman-Julius in the mid-1920s, he became a contributor to the *American Mercury* (his first article in 1928 dealt with "Yugoslav speech in America."). Moving back to New York City (1929) he published *Dynamite* (1931) which dealt pessimistically with "class violence" in the United States; a revised edition (1934) was more temperate. In 1931 he married Stella Sanders, a college-educated Jewish student of modern dance. They had no children.

Laughing in the Jungle, a readable but dark view of his experiences as youngster in his homeland and the United States published in 1932, helped him win a Guggenheim Fellowship, which he used for a year's stay in Yugoslavia, that resulted in *The Native's Return: An American Immigrant Visits Yugoslavia and Discovers His Old Country* (1934). A critical and commercial success (a Book-of-the-Month Club selection and a best seller), it was not without controversy because of negative views of the country's royal government and king,

As in most of his books, he touched on the strengths of American cultural diversity, highlighting not the story of immigration but the contributions of immigrants, especially the more recent groups who differed from the creators of Anglo Saxon America. Acculturation for him did not mean achieving homogeneity, but recognition of diversity's strengths.

Many of his subsequent books and activities highlighted this theme. *Grandsons: A Story of American Lives* (1935) and *Cradle of Life: The Story of One Man's Beginnings* (1936) were novels dealing with Slovene family life. *My America:1928–38* (1938), a fascinating if somewhat disjointed mélange of biographical sketches, opinion pieces, and reportage, was informed by the relationship between his immigrant past and contemporary America. He joined the Foreign Language Information Service Board in 1934 and helped reorganize it in 1940 as the Common Council for American Unity and establish its quarterly, *Common Ground,* serving as co-editor (1940–42). *Common Ground* was one of the first journals to use the word "ethnicity". Adamic got the Carnegie Corporation to underwrite a four volume *Nation of Nations* series and sent thousands of questionnaires to foreign language newspapers; from the responses and his own experiences and investigations he produced works dealing with America's racial and cultural complexity, including *From Many Lands* (1941), *What's Your Name* (1942), and *A Nation of Nations* (1945),

A man of eclectic tastes, Adamic penned a pamphlet study of Robinson Jeffers for the *Washington Chapbook* series (1929), and wrote *The House in Antiqua (1937)* using the restoration of a 300-year-old house to relate a history of the place,

of the Conquistadors, and of the American couple who restored it. In *Two-Way Passage* (1941) he proposed that after the end of World War II, immigrants be sent back to their homelands to educate Europeans in American-style democracy, a suggestion that impressed President and Mrs. Roosevelt, who invited the Adamics to a meal at the White House to meet with Winston Churchill. *Dinner at the White House* (published some time later in 1946) is engaging gossip about what happened but is also a scathing critique of U.S. foreign policy: Churchill is presented as seducing Roosevelt into "counter-revolutionary" foreign policies by arguing the threat of Russia, who Adamic viewed favorably. A footnote maintained that Churchill's Greek policy had been influenced by personal obligations to a bank with Greek interests; Churchill sued and won a substantial out-of court settlement.

During the war Adamic had become an outspoken supporter of Tito's Communist Partisans and disparaged the Yugoslav government in exile. In his influential *My Native Land* (1943) he passionately presented in black and white political developments in his homeland, fervently urging American support for Tito. Such attitudes resulted in severe criticism of Adamic from sections of the American Yugoslav community; even more so when Tito awarded him the Yugoslavian Order of National Unity in 1944. Adamic's attitude toward the USSR changed after Stalin broke with Tito. Adamic's last book *The Eagle and the Roots,* published posthumously (1952), eulogized Tito, maintaining that Yugoslavia was a "democratic force" resisting Stalin and Soviet totalitarianism.

Adamic's reputation was damaged by the Churchill judgment, by his association with communist front groups

(California's Un-American Committee in its reports referred to him as "pro-communist" and "pro-Soviet."), and by his support of Henry Wallace for president in 1948. He was plagued by ill health, diminished finances, and accusations that he was a Soviet agent (after his death a clipping was found in his wallet headlined "Adamic Red Spy, Woman Charges"). He was found dead on September 4, 1951, at his Hunterdon County farm in western New Jersey under mysterious circumstances. Neighbors had smelled smoke and seen flames on his property. After volunteer firemen extinguished the flames, they found him in a second floor study with a gun shot wound to the head and a rifle resting on his lap. Because of the circumstances, and threats that had been made against him, there was speculation that his death was an assassination by some Yugoslav faction or the Soviets, but the coroner eventually ruled the death a suicide and his widow accepted the verdict. Yet questions remained, such as how Adamic could shoot himself in the head and then return the gun to his lap.

Daniel J. Leab

References and Further Reading

Louis Adamic Papers, 1848–1951. Princeton University Library, Manuscripts Division.

Louis Adamic Papers. Slovene American Collection. FBI Files, Immigration History Research Center. University of Minnesota.

Berger, Meyer. 1951. "Adamic Dies of Shot, Home Aflame; Suicide Verdict Studied in Jersey." *The New York Times* (September 5): 1, 13.

Christian, Henry A. 1968. *Louis Adamic: Immigrant and American Liberal*. PhD diss., Brown University.

McWilliams, Carey. 1978. "Louis Adamic, American." *The Nation* (September 22): 230–32.

Velcoli, Rudolph. 1978. "Louis Adamic and the Contemporary Search for Roots." *Ethnic Studies* 2(3); 29–35.

Anderson, Marian
(1897–1993)

Marian Anderson, the first African American to perform at the Metropolitan Opera, was applauded in Europe long before U.S. audiences came to admire and accept her talent. Fine musicianship guided this magnificent contralto voice of remarkable range in a repertoire that included difficult art songs along with deeply felt Negro spirituals.

Born in Philadelphia on February 17, 1897, to working class parents, she had

An African American, Marian Anderson was amazingly popular despite racial discrimination in the United States. Her performance at the Lincoln Memorial in 1939 remains a symbolic event in the civil rights movement. (Library of Congress)

two younger sisters. Her father—an iceman, barber, and laborer in the Reading Terminal Market—died in 1910. Her mother sustained the family as a laundress and employee in Wanamaker's Department Store.

Anderson grew up singing in the Union Baptist Church choirs (starting in the junior choir at age 6, graduating to the senior one seven years later), and by age 10 she already had become known in her South Philadelphia neighborhood as the "baby contralto." Her formal education was limited: she graduated from Stanton Grammar School in 1912, and after a three year hiatus during which her singing helped support the family, she attended the business-oriented William Penn High School and in 1918, anxious for a more academically oriented curriculum, moved to the South Philadelphia High School for Girls, graduating in 1921.

She began vocal training in 1916 and over the next years had various teachers and coaches, including Giuseppe Boghetti, who probably had the most influence on her. Her limited finances as well as racial discrimination prevented her from attending a conservatory, although she earned a scholarship in the summer of 1919 to a course in opera performance at the Chicago Conservatory of Music.

In the next years Anderson achieved increasing public exposure and gained recognition as an important talent. In 1921 she won the National Association of Negro Musicians competition. In 1924 she made her New York City debut at Town Hall (although she disappointed by the poor attendance). In 1925 she beat out several hundred competitors to win the right to appear with the New York Philharmonic at Lewisohn Stadium in New York. *The New York Times* reported,

"Miss Anderson made an excellent impression. She is endowed by nature with a voice of unusual compass, color and dramatic capacity."

Assisted by the Julius Rosenwald Fund, Anderson went to Europe to study in 1926. After returning to the United States in 1930 she gave her first Carnegie Hall concert. Anderson's success in New York led to a contract with the powerful concert manager Arthur Judson. She was the first black artist under his management. More concerts and higher fees followed. On Judson's recommendation, she began study with Frank La Forge, a well-known vocal coach. In 1930 she also gave her first European concerts and subsequently enjoyed successful tours of Germany and Scandinavia. The famed conductor Arturo Toscanini heard Anderson sing in Salzburg, Austria and remarked "Yours is voice such as one hears once in a hundred years."

For all her European success Anderson's American career had not flourished, and she accepted a contract offered by the flamboyant impresario Sold Hurok. He arranged for a second Town Hall concert in December 1935. Anderson returned to America a more mature artist and received critical acclaim for that recital. In his *New York Times* review, Howard Taubman stated, "Let it be said at the outset: Marian Anderson has returned to her native land one of the great singers of our time."

Under Hurok's intelligent and inventive management Anderson became one of the most popular concert artists in the United States, and in the Depression year 1938 she earned over $200,000, an imposing record in any era but even more so in such economic hard times.

In February 1939, Anderson—who had performed at churches and schools in Washington, D.C.—was denied access to the capitol's premier concert venue, Constitution Hall. The Daughters of the American Revolution (DAR), the managers of the hall who followed a "whites only" policy, refused Anderson permission to sing there. The issue gained national attention. The president's wife, Eleanor Roosevelt, resigned from the DAR and with the aid of Secretary of the Interior Harold Ickes, helped reschedule the concert at the Lincoln Memorial. There, on Easter Sunday, April 9, 1939, Anderson, with her habitual dignity, sang to an audience of some 75,000. Her program included "America," Franz Schubert's "Ave Maria," three spirituals, and "Nobody Knows the Trouble I've Seen," and was a rousing success.

Anderson married the architect Orpheus H. Fisher in 1943. The childless couple lived on a farm in Danbury, CT of over 100 acres. She made her television debut on *The Ed Sullivan Show* in 1952, and she continued to perform concerts. Finally, disgracefully late in her career, she was invited to sing at the Metropolitan Opera in New York by Rudolph Bing, the general manager. There, on January 7, 1955, she made her debut as Ulrica in Verdi's *Un ballo in maschera* (*The Masked Ball*). She has spurned attempts to cast her as the slave girl Aida in Verdi's opera of the same name ("I was a contralto, not a soprano. Why Aida?"). In her fifties, no longer in her vocal prime, she was nonetheless the first black singer to appear at the Metropolitan in its 71-year history, and led the way for other singers of color.

Anderson continued to give concerts into her 60s, including a 1957 State Department-sponsored goodwill tour of Southeast Asia. A farewell tour of the United States took her to over 50 cities and concluded with a recital at Carnegie Hall on April 19, 1965; a tribute there in 1977 celebrated her 75th birthday and the artistry that marked her career. Among her many awards are the Spingarn Medal (1939), the Presidential Medal of Freedom (1963), a Congressional Gold Medal (1978), and the first Eleanor Roosevelt Human Rights Award of the City of New York (1984). In 1978 she was among the first five performers to receive Kennedy Center Honors. Anderson, who had gone to live with her nephew (her husband had died in 1986), Oregon Symphony music director James De Priest, having suffered a series of strokes, died of heart failure in Portland, Oregon on April 8, 1993.

References and Further Reading

Anderson, Marian. 1955. *My Lord, What a Morning: An Autobiography*. New York: Viking Press.

Keiler, Allan. 2002. *Marian Anderson: A Singer's Journey*. Urbana: University of Illinois Press.

Kimbrough, Eily. 1960. "My Life in a White World," *Ladies' Home Journal*, September.

Shawcross, Nancy M. 2008. "Marian Anderson: A Life In Song," Available at http://www.library.upenn.edu/special/gallery/anderson/index.html (accessed, September 23, 2009).

The Marian Anderson Papers. Rare Book and Manuscript Library. University of Pennsylvania.

Armstrong, Louis (1901–71)

A towering figure in jazz history, Armstrong—a virtuoso performer, a master of melodic improvisations, daring experiments in tone and pitch, and rhythmic ideas—inspired generations of musicians.

Louis Armstrong was born in New Orleans on August 4, 1901, to Mary Albert (known as "May Ann"), a domestic and sometime prostitute, and Willie Armstrong, a laborer who soon abandoned them. The boy, raised by a grandmother, grew up poor in New Orleans' red-light district; a few blocks filled with dance halls, brothels, honky-tonks, and the constant swirl of blues and ragtime on the verge of becoming jazz.

At a Home for Colored Waifs (to which he was sent repeatedly for delinquency) Armstrong learned to play the cornet. Released in his early teens, he borrowed instruments, sat in at local establishments, and learned his way around the rags, marches, and songs of the day; Joe "King" Oliver, a jazz cornetist and important musical figure, befriended Armstrong, taught him technique, gave him opportunities to play, and presented him with an instrument.

Oliver went to Chicago in 1918; Armstrong replaced him in what was considered New Orleans's leading jazz band, led by trombonist Kid Roy. Armstrong honed his musical skills working in dance halls and on riverboats. In 1922 Oliver invited Armstrong to Chicago to play in his popular Creole Jazz Band. Recordings in Oliver's 1923–24 series reveal the strength and musicianship of Armstrong's improvised second cornet parts, notably in "Dippermouth Blues."

Musicians began to recognize Armstrong as a leader in "hot" music as jazz emerged, a relaxed style less stiff than ragtime. Jazz depended on extensive use of syncopated rhythms and surprising patterns of off-beat, staggered accents filled within a constant tempo. It also depended on a musician's ability to accent the notes a certain way. Armstrong, more than any other player, demonstrated his brilliance as an architect of spontaneous but disciplined improvisations and as an instrumental virtuoso who transcended the traditional ensemble New Orleans improvisation.

In 1924 Armstrong wed Lillian Hardin, the band's pianist. She was the second of Armstrong's four wives (he had married Daisy Parker in 1918, and would marry Alpha Smith in 1938 and Lucille Watson in 1942). There were no children from these marriages. Hardin encouraged Armstrong to go to New York City to join Fletcher Henderson's big band. Armstrong chafed under the strict Henderson rhythms, but found an outlet and opportunity in solos where his free-flowing improvisation enchanted listeners and strengthened his musical reputation.

Over the next years Armstrong moved from cornet to trumpet, and worked with various groups in Chicago and elsewhere—most notably with the "Hot Five" and the "Hot Seven" who he organized and included his wife on piano and Kid Ory on clarinet. Armstrong's recordings of "Big Butter and Egg Man," "Potato Head Blues," and "Struttin" with Some Barbecue" confirmed his international reputation as the most creative jazz musician of his time.

It was during these years Armstrong made his first scat recording. A manner of singing using nonsense syllables, scat presents the voice as a solo instrument. He continued to make effective use of the trumpet, but also made increasing use of his voice. This vocalizing, not limited to scat singing, became an integral part of his performance. In successive recordings Armstrong's solos became more frequent after the success of his scat singing of "Heebie Jeebies."

Armstrong soon adopted the format he used until 1947—a big band as background for his vocal and instrumental solos. He made recordings of then popular songs (e.g., "I Can't Give You Anything But Love," Some of These Days," "When You're Smiling"), often making them standards of the future among younger jazz players and fans. For B. H. Hagin, a 1930s music critic writing in the *New Republic,* Armstrong "offered the…exciting experience of moment-to-moment working of a creative mind with an inventive exuberance controlled by a sense for coherent developing form."

During the 1930s Armstrong began to appear in movies, including Betty Boop cartoons and features with Bing Crosby, such as "Pennies From Heaven" (1936). In 1937 Armstrong became the first African American featured in a network radio series (years later he would appear extensively on TV).

By the mid-1930s the music known as swing largely fostered by Armstrong's work, had become the popular idiom—there were swing bands in dance and concert halls, on screen and radio. Ideas from Armstrong's classics, such as "Mahogany Hall Stomp" or "Gut Bucket Blues" echoed through other bands. Armstrong himself did not make many quest appearances, and his career now depended as much on his humorous vocals such as "I'll Be Glad When You're Dead You Rascal You," as on his more ambitious instrumental efforts such as "Swing That Music" or "Jubilee."

By 1947 the big band ear was drawing to a close, and that year Armstrong appeared in a specially arranged concert at New York's Town Hall, with a small ensemble, including trombonist Jack Teagarden, drummer Sidney Catlett, and Hines. The evening's success led Armstrong to cut back permanently to a small group he called his "All-Stars." Using a repertory that went back to his early years, including a selection of vocal-instrumental successes, Armstrong (now "the grand old man of jazz") pursued a grueling tour schedule.

His appearances included songs like "Blueberry Hill" and "Cold, Cold Heart" that would become standards for younger performers, and songs he made standard such as *Mack the Knife* from *Three Penny Opera* and the title song from the Broadway show *Hello Dolly,* probably the most successful single of his career.

The All Stars toured the world—Armstrong's international travels, some under the auspices of the U.S. State Department, earned him a new nickname, "Ambassador Satch," in addition to many others including "Dippermouth," "Satchelmouth," and "Satchmo." A heart attack in 1959 and other health problems curtailed his performing. He died from a heart attack at home in the Corona section of Queens, New York, on July 6, 1971.

References and Further Reading

Louis Armstrong Archives. CUNY. Queens College. New York.

Armstrong, Louis. 1954. *Satchmo: My Life In New Orleans.* With a new introduction by Dan Morganstern. Reprint, New York: Da Capo Press. 1986.

Bergreen, Laurence.1997. *Louis Armstrong: An Extravagant Life.* New York: Broadway Books.

Berrett, Joshua. 1999. *The Louis Armstrong Companion: Eight Decades of Commentary.* New York: Schirmer Books.

Brothers, Thomas. 2006. *Louis Armstrong's New Orleans.* New York: W. W. Norton.

Collier, James Lincoln. 1983. *Louis Armstrong: An American Genius.* New York: Oxford University Press.

Giddins, Garry. 1988. *Satchmo.* Reprint, New York: Da Capo Press. 2001.

Nollen, Scott Allen. 2004. *Louis Armstrong: The Life, Music, and Screen Career.* Jefferson, NC: McFarland.

Willems, Jos. 2006. *All of Me: the Complete Discography of Louis Armstrong.* Lanham. MD: The Scarecrow Press.

Berlin, Irving (1888–1989)

Perhaps the most prolific songwriter ever, Irving Berlin published some 1,500 songs—from "Alexander's Ragtime Band" to "White Christmas." Beloved from Broadway to Hollywood, he responded to changing times and tastes with main-street language and down-home images as he set Americans singing with his always-irresistible melodies.

Berlin, the youngest of eight children, was born in Mohilev, Russia on May 11, 1888. He was named Israel by his parents, Moses and Lena Baline. Driven from Russia by Jewish persecution, the Balines reached New York in 1892 and settled on the Lower East Side. Berlin's father, a cantor, died three years later.

The young Berlin had two years of schooling before hard times forced him to work selling newspapers and singing on the streets. After he landed a job as a singing waiter at Pelham's Café in Chinatown, he wrote "Marie from Sunny Italy" with the restaurant's pianist, M. Nicholson. Berlin's name appears on the sheet music as I. Berlin. The song, published in 1907, earned him 37.5 cents in royalties. By 1909, he was working as a lyricist and song plugger, and a year later, he was performing his own songs in *Up and Down Broadway,* a revue.

In 1911, Berlin changed his name legally from Israel Baline to Irving Berlin. That same year, he had his first major success with the jaunty "Alexander's Ragtime Band." It was played again and again for dance-crazy Americans. Though not strictly ragtime, "Alexander's Ragtime Band" became one of Tin Pan Alley's greatest ragtime hits. The nickname "Tin Pan Alley," referring to New York's West 28th Street music publishing district, referred to the area's constant musical din.

The next year, a ballad, "When I Lost You," reflected Berlin's mood after his bride's death of typhoid six months after the wedding. He buried himself in work and wrote his first complete score and lyrics in 1914—*Watch Your Step,* a show designed for dancers Vernon and Irene Castle. Berlin, constantly creating, usually at night, contributed to New York revues and operettas—from *Ziegfeld Follies* in 1911 to *The Century Girl* in 1916—and even performed in London as the "King of Ragtime" in 1917.

Drafted into the U.S. Army, Berlin cajoled his World War I superiors into mounting an all-soldier revue, *Yip, Yip, Yaphank,* in 1918. It included the song "Oh, How I Hate to Get Up in the Morning," but "God Bless America" was discarded as unsuitable. After he was discharged, Berlin formed his own music publishing firm—Irving Berlin Music, Inc.—in 1919, and two years later, with producer Sam H. Harris, he built the Music Box Theatre.

The Music Box, still on West 45th Street, opened in September 1921 and was to stage Berlin's revues and showcase his popular songs. Berlin, a good businessman, maintained control of his works. Along with staging his own productions, the hard-working Berlin was writing music for the Flo Ziegfeld Follies, including in 1919, the hit "A Pretty Girl Is Like a Melody," and for Broadway musicals like *The Cocoanuts* (1925), which starred the Marx Brothers.

In 1926, Berlin married socialite Ellin Mackay, the daughter of a Catholic millionaire. Furious, Clarence Mackay disinherited the bride. Berlin's wedding gift to his bride, the rights to the song "Always," more than compensated for her financial loss. In 1946, 20 years later, Ellin received $60,000 in royalties from the song. Ironically, her father's fortune was wiped out by the Great Depression.

Berlin began to pull out of a long dry period with the 1932 success of *Face the Music* ("Let's Have Another Cup o' Coffee") and 1933's *As Thousands Cheer,* both of which were written with Moss Hart. The latter, a clever revue, was based on pages from a daily newspaper. It included a revised "Easter Parade" (from the failed *Smile and Show Your Dimple*), representing the rotogravure section; "Heat Wave," representing the weather report; and the moving "Supper Time," representing the news, with Ethel Waters singing about the lynching of a black man.

Berlin, taken up by Hollywood, produced successful songs for successful movies, including "Cheek to Cheek" and "Top Hat, White Tie, and Tails" for *Top Hat* (1935), with Fred Astaire and Ginger Rogers; "Let's Face the Music and Dance" for *Follow the Fleet* (1936); and "I've Got My Love to Keep Me Warm" for *On the Avenue* (1937).

However, it was *Holiday Inn* (1942), starring Bing Crosby and Astaire, that launched "White Christmas." Berlin had doubts about the song and recalled, "I didn't think it would be a hit. But Crosby saw something there.... When he read the song he just took his pipe out of his mouth and said to me, 'You don't have to worry about this one, Irving.'" Crosby was right.

World War II brought Berlin back to familiar territory with another all-soldier revue, *This Is the Army* (1942, film 1943). "This Is the Army, Mr. Jones" and "I Left My Heart at the Stage Door Canteen" became hits. Berlin toured with the show for three and a half years, earned $10 million for army relief, and once again portrayed the sleepy soldier singing "Oh, How I Hate to Get Up in the Morning." Yet "God Bless America," originally intended for the World War I revue, turned out to be the showstopper.

The postwar *Annie Get Your Gun* (film version 1950) opened in 1946 and became Berlin's longest-running musical. Starring Ethel Merman, the show included the hit song "There's No Business Like Show Business." *Call Me Madam* followed in 1950 (film 1953). Twelve years later, in 1962, the final Berlin show, *Mr. President,* opened. It ran for eight months, received lukewarm reviews, and was to be Berlin's Broadway farewell. He died in Manhattan on September 22, 1989, at the age of 101.

References and Further Reading

Bergreen, Laurence. 1990. *As Thousands Cheer: The Life of Irving Berlin.* New York: Viking Press.

Wilder, Alec. 1972. *American Popular Song.* New York: Oxford University Press.

Bethune, Mary McLeod (1875–1955)

One of the most important African American leaders of the early 20th century, Bethune vigorously promoted education for Blacks, led numerous African American organizations that campaigned for civil rights, and was an important member of President Franklin D. Roosevelt's "Black Cabinet."

Born near Mayesville, South Carolina, July 10, 1875, to Samuel and Patsy McIntosh McLeod, former slaves, she was the 15th of 17 children. Mary McLeod distinguished herself at a young age in Presbyterian-sponsored segregated schools, first attending a local one room school- house run by a black educator, and in 1887 winning a scholarship to Scotia Seminary for Negro Girls in Concord, North Carolina. After graduating in 1894, Dwight Moody's Institute for Home and Foreign Missions in Chicago awarded her a scholarship. After a year there, she attempted to find missionary work but failing that began teaching in various Presbyterian schools for blacks in Maysville, Augusta, Georgia, and Sumpter, South Carolina.

Mary McLeod Bethune fought fiercely to achieve social, economic, and educational opportunities for African Americans, and particularly for African American women. (Library of Congress)

In May 1898, she married Albertus Bethune, a handsome young teacher turned clothing salesman. Their son Albertus McLeod Bethune, Jr., was born February 3, 1899, in Savannah. The family moved to Florida shortly thereafter. In 1907, Albertus left for reasons never disclosed (the marriage apparently was not a happy one), and went back to South Carolina. They never divorced; the husband died October 22, 1918.

Due to her early experiences Bethune would go on to play a prominent role in black education. She started schools first in Palatka, FL, and in October 1904 in Daytona Beach, FL. The Daytona Literary and Industrial School for Training Negro Girls began in a rented house, according to tradition, "with five little girls, a dollar and a half, and faith in God" (Smith) . She believed education was the key to the advancement of African Americans. Like Booker T. Washington at the Tuskegee Institute, Bethune initially promoted vocationalism. Her school's founding curriculum emphasized Christianity, job training for farming and domestic and personal service.

She struggled to keep the school afloat, becoming a self-proclaimed "good beggar." Her efforts included selling homemade pies and ice cream, but also gaining support from white sources such as Rockefeller-sponsored foundations and affluent northerners wintering in the area. Thanks to her zeal and talents the school, despite financial precariousness, gradually developed from a small elementary school emphasizing vocational training, and in 1923 was merged with a more established boys' school, the Cookman Institute of Jacksonville, Florida, to become the Daytona-Cookman Collegiate Institute, which in 1929 became Bethune-Cookman College (receiving state accreditation as a junior college in 1932). In 1936 the school's non-college parts were closed, and seven years later the first four-year graduates received degrees (and since then it has become Bethune-Cookman University with a very diversified academic program).

She was president of Bethune-Cookman from 1923 until 1942 (and in 1946–47), but her service was only partial in the 1930s as she began to play a central role in African American women's political activities, focused on improving the lives of black women. She served as head of the Florida Federation of Colored Women's Clubs from 1917 to 1925. In this capacity, she founded a home for delinquent black girls in Ocala, FL. Bethune served as president of the Southeastern Federation of Colored Women's Clubs from 1920 to 1925, headed up the National Association of Teachers in Colored Schools from 1923 to 1924, and that year was elected president of the National Association of Colored Women, serving two terms until 1928.

Bethune achieved recognition nationally for her work promoting education of African Americans. In 1930, President Herbert Hoover invited her to a conference at the White House to reward her active work within the Republican Party. When Franklin Roosevelt was elected president in 1932, however, Bethune aligned herself with the Democrats, having achieved a splendid personal rapport with Eleanor Roosevelt. In 1935, Bethune—promoting a more radical political agenda—formed the National Council of Negro Women, a coalition of disparate groups (that grew over the years) dedicated to promoting the interests of all black women.

Bethune moved to Washington, D.C., in 1936, joining (as an administrative assistant) the National Youth Administration (NYA), part of the newly established (1935) Works Progress Administration. The NYA, founded to aid Americans aged 16–24 struggling with the Depression's ramifications, provided work-study jobs for youths in school, work-relief and vocational training for youths out of school, and placement services for unemployed youths. Initially one of two black members of the NYA's 35-person National Advisory Committee, her aggressive efforts on behalf of African Americans earned Bethune the full-time staff position. In 1939, when Bethune's NYA unit was moved to the Federal Security Agency, she became director of its Division of Negro Affairs, making her the highest-ranking African American woman in the federal government. Serving until the agency's termination in 1944, she endeavored to gain blacks' equal participation in NYA programs and promoted college education for black students as well as training in necessary skills.

In 1936, Bethune helped organize an *ad hoc* caucus (Federal Council on Negro Affairs), whose members would include black professionals active in New Deal agencies. Also known as the "Black Cabinet," it lobbied for increased benefits for blacks and promoted civil rights for all African Americans. Thanks to her special friendship with Mrs. Roosevelt, Bethune had access to the White House, and attention was paid to her comments. In 1937 and 1939 Bethune helped to organize national conferences on the "Problems of the Negro." Attendees included Eleanor Roosevelt and other important political figures. The conferences promoted integration and publicized the struggles of African Americans.

During World War II Bethune encouraged African Americans to support the war effort, which she viewed as an opportunity to fight for civil rights. She promoted war bonds, agitated for equal treatment of black soldiers, and protested against unfair treatment of black women in the Women's Army Corps. In 1945, as an associate consultant to the U.S. delegation to draft the UN Charter in San Francisco, she was the delegation's only black woman. Bethune returned to Florida in 1949 but despite declining health continued to play a prominent role in American politics, lobbying for equal rights. She suffered a heart attack on May 18, 1955, and died at her home in Daytona Beach.

Jane Dabel

References and Further Reading

Mary McLeod Bethune Papers: the Bethune-Cookman College Collection, 1922–1955. University Publications of America. Amistad Research Center. Tulane University, New Orleans.

Hanson, Joyce A. 2003. *Mary McLeod Bethune and Black Women's Political Activism.* Columbia: University of Missouri Press.

Holt, Rackham. 1964. *Mary McLeod Bethune: A Biography.* Garden City, NY: Doubleday.

McClusky, Audrey Thomas, and Elaine M. Smith, eds. 1999. *Mary MacLeod Bethune: Building a Better World—Essays and Selected Documents.* Bloomington, IN: Indiana University Press.

Black Cabinet

Franklin Roosevelt was the first president to nominate black appointees in an official capacity. Forty-five black advisers served in what was called the Black Cabinet or Black Brain Trust.

The Black Cabinet was larger than any previous black advisory group. Some members participated for only a few months while others stayed for many years. Most Black Cabinet members were intellectuals, not politicians.

The Black Cabinet explained the needs of African Americans to government agencies. In this capacity, it tried to expand employment opportunities for black citizens in government and industry, based on capability and training, not color. During this period, the number of black employees on the federal payroll quadrupled. Segregation was abolished in many government agencies (Franklin 1956, 522).

However, the Roosevelt administration lacked any written policies to help black constituents. At its worst, this hands-off approach meant that policy decisions for African Americans depended upon the dominant personalities in each agency. Roosevelt was so fearful of estranging the southern voting bloc in Congress—which he needed to pass New Deal legislation—that he did not speak out on racial issues (Buni 1974, 211–12). Roosevelt improved this situation by creating the Fair Employment Practices Act through an executive order (Anonymous 2002–3, 46). He also hoped the example of his Black Cabinet would help bring more black voters into the Democratic Party.

The most prominent members of the Black Cabinet were Mary McLeod Bethune, Dr. Robert C. Weaver, and William H. Hastie. Bethune, a college president, had already served on the National Child Welfare Commission, advising Presidents Coolidge and Hoover. During the New Deal, Behune, a friend of Eleanor Roosevelt, directed the Division of Negro Affairs of the National Youth Administration from 1936 to 1944. Weaver, an economist who served in five departments during his government service, publicly predicted that blacks would become a drain on relief services unless they received proportionate access to skilled jobs. When Weaver set up the first affirmative action program for skilled black workers, he was widely criticized as returning to a form of segregation (Wilson 1997, 66). The Black Cabinet was watchful about honoring economic and political equality for black citizens while guarding against separatist initiatives (Franklin 1956, 521–22). Hastie, dean of Howard University Law School, served in the Department of the Interior and in the judiciary before assisting the Secretary of War. In 1942, he resigned to protest what he saw as racial discrimination in the military. The next year, the NAACP honored Hastie with the Springarn Medal, awarded annually to recognize the highest achieving African American.

The Black Cabinet's sphere of influence spread with appointments to numerous other departments, including the Department of Commerce, the Office of Emergency Management, the Office of War Information, the Office of Price Administration, the War Manpower Commission, the United States Housing Authority, the Division of Negro Labor, the Civilian Conservation Corps, the Federal Works Agency, the National Selective Service, and the Social Security Board. The country's entry into World War II and pressure from Eleanor Roosevelt also expanded Black Cabinet (Anonymous 2002–3, 46).

Merrill Evans

References and Further Reading

Anonymous. 2002–3. "Getting to Know the Racial Views of Our Past Presidents: What About FDR?" *The Journal of Blacks in Higher Education* 38: 44–46.

Buni, Andrew. 1974. *Robert L. Vann of the Pittsburgh Courier: Politics and Black Journalism.* Pittsburgh, PA: University of Pittsburgh Press.

Franklin, John Hope. 1956. *From Slavery to Freedom: A History of American Negroes.* New York: Alfred A. Knopf.

Wilson, Francille R. 1997. "'Going, Going, Gone': Social Research, Public Policy and Black Industrial Workers." *Black Renaissance* 1: 66.

Black Legion

The Black Legion was a group within the Ku Klux Klan that was founded by William Shepard in east-central Ohio, and became powerful in the Midwest in the 1930s. At its height it boasted between 20,000 and 30,000 members, and operated from Detroit (where up to a third of its members were based), Michigan, and also from Lima, Ohio, where one of its leaders, Virgil "Bert" Effinger, lived.

Essentially the Black Legion was a vigilante group that served to strike terror into the lives of African Americans and any others who supported Civil Rights. The Black Legion, like the Ku Klux Klan from where it drew its membership, were against African Americans, Roman Catholics, Jews, supporters of, and recipients of, social welfare, communists, trade unionists and labor organizers. It gained its name through the uniforms the members wore, because rather than using the white robes of the Ku Klux Klan, the Black Legion wore black—including hoods, often decorated with the skull and crossbones. They served initially as a "security force" for the "mainstream" Ku Klux Klan in Ohio, often using the guise of a rifle club or a social organization.

Members of the group were alleged to be involved in the murders of numbers of African Americans and Civil Rights activists, including that in 1931 of Earl Little, a prominent Baptist lay speaker and the father of Malcolm X. One group of the Black Legion operated in Michigan under the "command" of Arthur Lupp of Highland Park.

After many years of striking terror through the African American communities, 11 members of this group were convicted of the kidnapping and murder in May 1936 of Charles Poole, an organizer for the Works Progress Administration, who lived in southwest Detroit. They had believed that Poole had been beating his wife, although this was merely the pretext for their attack. The prosecution of these men, and their conviction in September 1936—9 in a jury trial, 2 in a bench trial—showed that the law could act against them, with all 11 sent to jail for life for the killing of Poole. During the course of the trial evidence emerged about many other crimes that these men, and others in the Black Legion, had committed, including some unsolved murders.

The publicity given to the trial showed the men as thugs removing from the "chivalrous" image in which they had tried to portray themselves. This broke their influence and they ceased to have any real importance. In 1937 the Warner Brothers film *The Black Legion,* based on a story by Robert Lord, was screened. This melodrama starred Humphrey Bogart in the pivotal role as Frank Taylor, a poor factory mechanic who is expecting to get a promotion but is disappointed when the foreman's position is given to a foreign-born migrant. The character played by Bogart then joins the Black Legion, but soon recognizes them for what they are, and works against them.

Justin Corfield

References and Further Reading

Detroit News. 1997. "The murder that brought down the Black Legion." Available at: http://apps.detnews.com/apps/history/index.php?id=151. Accessed September 23, 2009.

Brotherhood of Sleeping Car Porters

The Brotherhood of Sleeping Car Porters (BSCP) was the first successful union of predominantly African American workers, and against the most difficult odds won its members better pay and improved working conditions. From the 1930s onward the BSCP leadership and members played significant roles in the campaign to gain blacks' civil rights.

African Americans had worked as porters and maids for the Pullman Company since the latter part of the 19th century when the concern began operating the cars it manufactured for long distance travel by better-off passengers. The blacks employed by Pullman fared better than many African American sharecroppers in the South and black domestics everywhere in the United States. The porters, thanks to their regular steady employment and other material advantages, were a nascent middle class compared to most black workers and were considered an elite in the African American community. But they were exploited and underpaid. The porters depended heavily on tips from white passengers, who as was customary called the porters "George" (Pullman's first name) whatever their name, and routinely subjected them to verbal, often racist, abuse. The porters spent about 10 percent of their time in unpaid set-up and clean-up work, had to pay for their food and lodging when away from home between trips, and were charged if a passenger took a towel or pitcher.

Dissatisfied porters had tried to unionize in the first years of the 20th century but failed. The Pullman Company was a ruthless employer whose network of spies enabled the company to fire and blacklist any employees who discussed union organizing. Moreover, Pullman—for years the largest employer of African Americans—enhanced its reputation in the black community with contributions to ghetto churches, advertisements in the minority press, and support of local organizations. Nor could the porters count on help from a racist organized labor. The Order of Sleeping Car Conductors—the porters' first union—made little headway, and those interested in organization realized they would have to turn to an outsider for help.

In 1925 porters in New York City turned to the socialist intellectual A. Philip Randolph, who, as he was not a porter, could not be fired. In the mid-1920s, despite the company's attempts at intimidation, including assaults on organizers and creation of a company union, Randolph—an attractive competent leader—successfully organized the Brotherhood of Sleeping Car Porters, the first African-American-controlled union in the country. By 1928 the BSCP had garnered the bulk of the porters as members and they authorized a strike. While Milton P. Webster, a union leader in Chicago, the home of most porters, wanted to confront the company, Randolph, who feared that the company could withstand

a walkout, wanted to use the strike vote to broaden support for the union and hoped to gain government intervention, through existing legislation at a time when the nation depended on rail travel. Failing to obtain this, the strike was "postponed." Internal dissension followed, and the gruff Webster became co-leader with the suave Randolph.

Although different types, the two men, once rivals, became good friends and worked well together, providing the union with sound leadership even as the Depression hit home. During this time, much of the membership, happy to have employment, deserted the BSCP. The union's decline was arrested as the result of New Deal labor legislation whose strictures against company unions and for the rights of labor to organize breathed new life into the organization. In 1935 at the BSCP's behest, the National Board of Mediation (which dealt with railroad labor) held an election: Pullman's company union (the Pullman Porters and Maids Protective Association) lost; the BSCP was certified as the official bargaining agent, and the company was compelled to negotiate with the union, finally signing a contract in August 1937. The American Federation of Labor (AFL), the nation's largest labor organization, initially refused to recognize the BSCP, accepting its locals only as individual "federal locals." However, in 1936 the AFL finally accepted the BSCP as a legitimate full-fledged union. It was the AFL's first African American union.

The BSCP combined the fights for unionization and civil rights—its leadership argued that they were the same struggle. Randolph attracted porters to the union by appealing to African Americans' desire for full citizenship rights; unionization—he claimed—meant that

African Americans could enjoy equality of opportunity. E. D. Dixon, a one-time porter and a leader of the 1955 Montgomery bus boycott, credited the BSCP with awakening in him and others the fighting spirit necessary for the civil rights movement. Randolph used his power within organized labor to press for civil rights gains, to improve racial policies in the AFL. He urged African American workers to join the AFL's chief rival, the Congress of Industrial Organizations (CIO), and after the organizations merged in 1955 continued to fight racism in the AFL-CIO and the nation. Through such efforts, Randolph achieved some success in removing obstacles to African American membership and leadership in the union movement. The BSCP had a much larger impact than its numbers (a peak of 20,000) warranted.

Randolph and the union in 1941 threatened an all-black march on Washington, D.C., to protest discrimination in the military services and in defense production, which had grown substantially as the United States prepared to enter World War II. The march was called off after President Franklin D. Roosevelt, although unwilling to deal with armed forces segregation, issued Executive Order 8022 creating the Fair Employment Practices Committee (reconstituted with more power by a 1943 Executive Order) to curb racial discrimination in defense industries and government employment. Webster was a militant successful member. Randolph and the BSCP continued to play a significant role in the civil rights movement, being very active in the 1963 March on Washington for Jobs and Freedom. By the 1970s, the Pullman Company stopped manufacturing sleeping cars as rail passenger travel had dramatically declined in the 1950s and 1960s; the

BSCP had over 15,000 members in 1940 but only about 3000 porters had regular runs by the end of the 1960s. In 1978, the BSCP merged with the much larger Brotherhood of Railway, Airline, Steamship Clerks, Freight Handlers, Express and Station Employees.

References and Further Reading

Records of the Brotherhood of Sleeping Car Porters 1925–1969. Chicago Historical Society and Newberry Library. University Publications of America. *Brotherhood of Sleeping Car Porters: Chicago Division—Records, 1925–1938.* Collection # 5462mf. Kheel Center for Labor-Management Documentation and Archives. Cornell University.

Brazeal, Brailsford R. 1946. *The Brotherhood of Sleeping Car Porters.* New York: Harper and Brothers.

Harris, William H. 1977. *Keeping the Faith: A. Philip Randolph, Milton P. Webster, and the Brotherhood of Sleeping Car Porters, 1925–1937.* With a new Preface. Reprint, Urbana: University of Illinois Press. 1991.

Santino, Jack. 1991. *Miles of Smiles, Years of Struggle: Stories of Black Pullman Porters.* Urbana: University of Illinois Press.

Wilson, Joseph F., ed. 1989. *Tearing Down the Color Bar: A Documentary History and Analysis of the Brotherhood of Sleeping Car Porters.* New York: Columbia University Press.

Buchalter, Louis "Lepke" (1898–1944)

Louis "Lepke" Buchalter was the head of Murder Incorporated and dominated the garments industry in New York before his arrest in the late 1930s. Lepke was one of the most feared gangsters of the 1930s. His crimes led federal authorities, including FBI Director J. Edgar Hoover to consider Lepke "Public Enemy Number One." Lepke ultimately turned himself in to authorities, only to be found guilty and later executed for the murder of a storeowner in the 1930s.

Louis "Lepke" Buchalter was born on February 6, 1898, on Manhattan's Lower East Side to Solomon and Rose Buchalter, who were both Russian immigrants. Lepke attended school until he graduated elementary school in 1912. Afterwards, he spent much of his time in the streets. By 1915, authorities arrested him for burglary.

By the late 1920s, Lepke began infiltrating the garments industry of New York. Lepke used threats of violence to infiltrate unions within the garment industry. By 1929, he supervised a force of over 50 men that included enforcers and bookkeepers. By the early 1930s, Lepke controlled most of the unions within the garment industry.

By 1931, Lepke headed Murder Inc., the enforcement arm of organized crime. It has been estimated that Murder Inc. was responsible for approximately 1,000 murders nationally and 200 in New York between 1931 and 1940. The organization carried out the decisions of organized crime bosses such as Charles "Lucky" Luciano. Lepke oversaw an organization that thoroughly planned and carried out its executions.

By 1936, Special Prosecutor Thomas E. Dewey focused his attention on Lepke. That year, a jury found Lepke and other associates guilty of violating the Sherman Anti-Trust Act through his control of the fur industry. However, Lepke went into hiding and became a fugitive.

While in hiding, Lepke ordered the execution of many witnesses who could have testified against him; many potential witnesses disappeared between 1937 and 1939. However, Lepke's strategy backfired as other former associates targeted by Lepke, such as hit man Abe Reles, eventually testified against him.

However, organized crime figures who faced increased scrutiny from law enforcement in their hunt for Lepke soon convinced Lepke to turn himself in. On 1939, Lepke surrendered to J. Edgar Hoover, believing that his friends in organized crime had negotiated a deal for him. However, there was no deal. Lepke was found guilty of a number of charges including drug smuggling in 1939. Two years later, Lepke was found guilty of first-degree murder and sentenced to death for ordering the execution of storeowner Joseph Rosen in 1936. After years of appeals, Lepke was executed in 1944.

Jason Roberts

References and Further Reading

Burrough, Bryan. 2004. *America's Greatest Crime Wave and the Birth of the FBI, 1933–1934.* New York: Penguin Press.

Gosch, Martin A., and Richard Hammer. 1975. *The Last Testament of Lucky Luciano.* Boston: Little, Brown and Company.

Kavieff, Paul R. 2006. *The Life and Times of Lepke Buchalter: America's Most Ruthless Labor Racketeer.* Fort Lee, NJ: Barricade Books.

Bunche, Ralph (1904–71)

As a high official of the United Nations for 25 years, Ralph Bunche led peacekeeping efforts in troubled areas of the world. He was awarded the Nobel Peace Prize in 1950, the first person of African descent to win that honor.

Ralph Johnson Bunche was born in the Detroit, Michigan ghetto on August 7, 1904. He was orphaned in 1915 and brought up in Los Angeles by his grandfather, a former slave. He was valedictorian of his high school class and a sports champion. Bunche won an athletic scholarship to the University of California at Los Angeles and supplemented it with income from menial jobs. He graduated summa cum laude in 1927, having been a star three-sports athlete and a debater during his college career.

After receiving a master's degree in political science at Harvard University in 1928, Bunche began teaching at Howard University in Washington, D.C., and by 1937, was a full professor. He took a leave of absence for graduate study at Harvard and earned a Ph.D. in 1934

As a high official of the United Nations for 25 years, Ralph Bunche led peacekeeping efforts in troubled areas of the world. (Carl Van Vechten Collection/Library of Congress)

for a dissertation on French colonial administration in West Africa, where he did fieldwork. Postdoctoral studies in anthropology followed, at Northwestern University, the London School of Economics, and the University of Cape Town, South Africa. In 1936, Bunche was codirector of the Institute of Race Relations at Swarthmore College, and from 1938 to 1940, he collaborated on field studies with Swedish sociologist Gunnar Myrdal for the latter's path-breaking study of race relations, *An American Dilemma* (1944).

Bunche left Howard University in 1941 to join the War Department as an analyst for Africa and the Far East for the Office of the Coordinator of Information, later the Office of Strategic Services (the forerunner of the Central Intelligence Agency). For the Joint Chiefs of Staff, he wrote reports of strategic military importance on colonial areas. In 1944, he moved to the Department of State as a specialist in the Division of Territorial Studies, where he was in a position to correct ingrained misconceptions about the peoples of the Third World. He was the first African American to hold the rank of chief in the Department of State.

By 1944, Bunche was in the mainstream of planning for what would become the United Nations (UN). He was a member of the U.S. delegation at both the Dumbarton Oaks Conference, held at Washington in 1944 to plan the organization, and the San Francisco Conference (held in 1945), where the UN and its charter came into being. Bunche was mainly responsible for that document's sections on trusteeship, and in 1946, Trygve Lie, the first secretary general of the UN, asked for Bunche's services. Bunche became the director of the Department of Trusteeship and Information From Non-Self-Governing Territories.

When Israel declared its statehood in May 1948, after the UN had approved a plan to partition the British mandate of Palestine into an Arab state and a Jewish state, the surrounding Arab nations invaded. Bunche, who had been appointed secretary of the UN Palestine Commission, was in the midst of unfolding events. At his request, the UN Security Council ordered an armed force to oversee the partition, under the command of Count Folke Bernadotte of Sweden. When Bernadotte was assassinated, Bunche succeeded him as acting mediator; in 1949, using objectivity, energy, patience, and wisdom, Bunche brought about a cease-fire and armistice. He received the 1950 Nobel Peace Prize, and as a Nobel spokesman said, "The outcome was a victory for the ideas of the United Nations, but...it was one individual's efforts that made victory possible."

During the rest of his career, Bunche worked to make the UN an effective peacekeeping body. In 1955, he became undersecretary for special political affairs, and from 1967 until his retirement in 1971, he was an undersecretary general. In 1956, during a crisis over the Suez Canal arising after a conflict between Israel and Egypt, Bunche directed a neutral peacekeeping force and enabled the canal to reopen. In 1960, he was sent to the newly independent nation of Congo Republic, preventing the government's collapse. He established a peacekeeping force in Cyprus in 1964 and the next year, was in charge of monitoring a cease-fire between India and Pakistan.

Bunche joined Martin Luther King Jr. in the Selma to Montgomery March and agreed with King that the tremendous funds expended on the Vietnam War should instead be spent to fight racism and poverty. In his last years, he was an adviser to the UN secretary general, U Thant. Bunche died on December 9, 1971, at the age of 67 of diabetes and heart disease, leaving his wife, whom he had met and married in college, and three children.

References and Further Reading

Bunche, Ralph. 1973. *The Political Status of the Negro in the Age of FDR.* Chicago: University of Chicago Press.

Cornell, Jean G. 1976. *Ralph Bunche: Champion of Peace.* Champaign, IL: Garrard Publishing Company.

Johnson, A. D. 1978. *The Value of Responsibility: The Story of Ralph Bunche.* La Jolla, CA: Value Communications.

Calloway, Cab (1907–94)

Caben Calloway III was a bandleader, singer, dancer, songwriter, and author. He was best known for his innovative style of scat singing and his signature song "Minnie The Moocher," memorable for its "hi-de-ho" lyrics. Calloway's career spanned more than 60 years, and he was one of the first African American artists to break racial barriers and perform for mostly white audiences.

Calloway was born in Rochester, New York on December 25, 1907, and was raised in Baltimore, Maryland. Influenced by a family of musicians, he joined the Baltimore Melody Boys during high school and studied voice under the tutelage of a local jazz artist, William "Chick" Webb. After he graduated from high school, Calloway briefly pursued a law degree at Crane College in Chicago, Illinois. He realized quickly that he couldn't resist the lure of a career as a musician, and he dropped out of school to follow his dream. He stayed in Chicago and tried playing the drums and saxophone before achieving success as a scat singer. After he appeared in the 1927 musical theater show *Plantation Days,* he was hired for his first solo performance.

Calloway formed his first band, The Alabamians, in 1928. The group disbanded in 1929, when Calloway formed The Missourians. The Missourians began touring in 1929, and they quickly experienced great success. The band's popularity escalated and led to Calloway's first big musical theater gig as a cast member of the New York production of Fats Waller's *Hot Chocolates.*

In 1931, Calloway renamed his band after himself and replaced Duke Ellington as orchestra leader at Harlem's famed Cotton Club. That same year, he made his first recordings. One of those recordings, "Minnie the Moocher," was a worldwide hit and became his signature song for its nonsensical "hi-de-ho" lyrics. Calloway's early music contained heavy allusions to drug use and sex, but he toned down his performances and the content of his songs in the mid-1930s. Over the years, Calloway ensemble members included jazz notables Dizzy Gillespie, Milt Hinton, and Cozy Cole. In the early 1930s, he was immortalized as an animated character in a series of *Betty Boop* cartoons.

Calloway's popularity continued throughout the 1930s, and he had dozens more hit singles, including "St. James Infirmary," "The Jumpin' Jive," "Lady with the Fan," "Zaz Zuh Zaz," "Kickin' the Gong Around," "The Scat Song," "Reefer Man," "Are You Hep to the Jive," and "Are You All Reet." He went on his first of many European tours in 1934. He also appeared in several feature films, including *The Big Broadcast* (1932),

International House (1933), *The Singing Kid* (1936), *Manhattan Merry-Go-Round* (1937), *Stormy Weather* (1943), *Sensations of 1945* (1944), *St. Louis Blues* (1958), *The Cincinnati Kid* (1965), and *The Blues Brothers* (1980).

George and Ira Gershwin used Calloway as the model for the character of Sportin' Life in their 1935 folk opera *Porgy and Bess.* Although he turned down the lead role in 1935, he performed in a road version of the musical in 1952 and made the soundtrack recording of the 1959 film version. After disbanding his orchestra in 1958, Calloway went solo for several years. He returned to the stage in 1974 to play the part of Horace Vandergelder in an all-black performance of *Hello Dolly.*

In 1976, Calloway wrote his autobiography, *Of Minnie the Moocher and Me.* His ebullient performance in the 1980 film *The Blues Brothers* renewed his popularity and exposed him to younger audiences. He continued to play engagements throughout the 1980s and was awarded the National Medal of Arts in 1992. Calloway died on November 18, 1994, at the age of 86.

References and Further Reading

Gale Research. 1997. *Contemporary Black Biography.* Detroit: Gale Research.

Calloway, Cab. 1976. *Of Minnie the Moocher and Me.* New York: Crowell.

Cantor, Eddie (1892–1964)

Eddie Cantor was an American entertainer who was successful on stage, in the movies, and over the airwaves (both radio and television). He was born Israel Iskowitz on January 31, 1892 in New York City. His poor Russian emigrant Jewish parents Meta and Mechel Iskowitz died before he was three. Raised by his maternal grandmother, he took her surname Kantrowitz, later anglicizing it to Cantor—and used the name Eddie for the first time in 1903, supposedly because his childhood sweetheart Ida Tobias, who he married in 1914, wanted a beau named Eddie. Despite rumors of continued infidelity on his part, their marriage, regarded as one of "the most harmonious in the world of show business," lasted until her death (1962); they had five daughters.

He never finished elementary school. His career began in 1907 when he and a friend formed a song and dance team, and included stints in vaudeville and burlesque in the United States and United Kingdom. He often appeared in blackface throughout his career. Ultimately he did star turns—most notably in a Florenz Zicgfield midnight revue and the *Follies* of 1917, 1918, and 1919. Cantor's active stand against management in the 1919 actors' strike ruptured relations with Ziegfield. Thereafter, Cantor starred successfully on Broadway for other producers.

In 1923 he returned to the Ziegfield fold, starring in *Kid Boots* as a country club caddie who bootlegged liquor. Among Broadway's longest running musicals, it proved Cantor could carry a show. Successful in the 1927 *Follies* (the only performer ever to receive featured billing in those revues) he starred to great acclaim in Ziegfield's 1928 musical comedy *Whoopee* as a chronic hypochondriac visiting a dude ranch. During the peak of his career in the1920s, Cantor earned $5,000 weekly, making him the highest-paid comedian in history up to that point. The stock market crash in 1929 severely

hurt him financially. Later that year he published a joke book *Caught Short!—a saga of wailing Wall Street.*

Cantor made some silent films during the 1920s (shorts, a feature version of *Kid Boots*), however, sound enhanced his film career. In 1930 he filmed *Whoopee* for producer Samuel Goldwyn, who oversaw five more Cantor films, notably *The Kid from Spain* (1932) and *Roman Scandals* (1933). Cantor intermittently made films into the 1940s, but his career boomed in radio beginning in 1931 with the *Chase and Sanborn Hour*. His variety shows for various sponsors were rated among the top 10 for a decade. In 1950 he successfully moved into television as a *Colgate Comedy Hour* rotating host. A series of heart attacks forced his retirement.

Cantor was active in charity work, especially the March of Dimes, which battled polio. A strong Zionist, he attacked Hitler from the early 1930s. During World War II he took part in Bond drives, and performed extensively for wounded GIs as part of the "Purple Heart Circuit." Socially conscious, he headed various performers' unions, including the Screen Actors Guild. Cantor received an Honorary Oscar (1956) and was inducted into the Radio Hall of Fame in 2000. Warner Brothers filmed a weak "bio-pic" *The Eddie Cantor Story* (1953), for which he recorded the sound track. He died on October 10, 1964, in Los Angeles.

Justin Corfield

References and Further Reading

Cantor, Eddie. Private scrapbooks. 1930–. University of Southern California.

Cantor, Eddie. 1963. *As I Remember Them.*, New York: Duell, Sloan, & Pearce

Cantor, Eddie. 1930. *Between the Acts*, New York: Simon and Schuster.

Cantor, Eddie, as told to David Freedman. 1928. *My Life is in Your Hands.* New York: Harper and Brothers.

Cantor, Eddie, with Jane Kesner Ardmore. 1957. *Take My Life.* Garden City, NY: Doubleday.

Cantor, Eddie. 1959. *The Way I See It.* ed. Phyllis Rosenteur. Englewood Cliffs, NJ: Prentice-Hall.

Cantor, Eddie. 1934. *Ziegfield, the Great Glorifier.* New York: A. H. King.

Fisher, James. 1997. *Eddie Cantor: A Bio-Bibliography,* Westport, CT: Greenwood Press.

Goldman, Herbert G. 1997. *Banjo Eyes: Eddie Cantor and the Birth of Modern Stardom.* New York: Oxford University Press.

Koseluk, Gregory. 1995. *Eddie Cantor: A Life in Show Business,* Jefferson, NC: McFarland.

Collier, John (1884–1968)

John Collier, an idealistic reformer, became commissioner of Indian affairs in 1933 during the Franklin Delano Roosevelt Democratic administration. The Indian Reorganization Act (IRA), passed by Congress in 1934, was his creation and the centerpiece of the "Indian New Deal." The IRA ended the disastrous allotment policy that had dispossessed Native tribes of tens of millions of acres of reservation lands. Yet, the Indian New Deal left a mixed heritage with respect to the aspirations of many American Indians. Never completely successful, it was criticized and under-funded by its detractors in Congress, and even opposed by many Indian nations and tribes. The legacy of Collier's Indian reform program poses some interesting questions: How did Collier become a passionate admirer of Indian culture and an advocate of cultural pluralism, and how successful was his program of Indian reform? His biography may provide answers to these questions.

John Collier was born in Atlanta, Georgia, in 1884. His father was a lawyer and banker who went on to become mayor of Atlanta. His mother, a New Englander, instilled in her son a love of literature and nature. The family eventually fell on hard times, and both parents died when Collier was a teenager. As a youth he began regular restorative trips to the southern Appalachian Mountains, and a love of the outdoors continued throughout his life. His later interest in folk cultures began during these outings. Collier entered Columbia University in 1902 and later studied at Woods Hole Marine Laboratory in Massachusetts. He soon turned from the study of biology to an interest in social issues. According to Collier's biographer, Kenneth R. Philp, a book by the Russian anarchist, Prince Peter Kropotkin, *Mutual Aid,* caught the young man's imagination and began his interest in the community life of precapitalist societies. It was a harbinger of his later interest in American Indians.

Upon leaving college, he at first took a job as a newspaper reporter. By 1907, however, he had become a reform social worker who for the next 12 years devoted himself to the welfare of European immigrants on Manhattan Island. In this endeavor he shared the interests of early American sociologists in the problems of immigration and urbanization. They, like Collier, believed that the machine age had undermined the old sense of community found in preindustrial societies and left the individual isolated. Crime and social problems were the result.

Collier became civic secretary for the People's Institute, an immigrant betterment organization, and editor of the

Institute's bulletin. The Institute sponsored regular forums on relevant social issues for Jewish and Italian immigrants. The establishment of school community centers was a project of the People's Institute. Collier was a vigorous opponent of Americanization policy that pressured immigrants to give up their native language and culture.

By 1912, Collier had become a frequenter of Mabel Dodge's weekly salons in New York City, where leading intellectuals of the day gathered to share radical ideas. Dodge was to play a pivotal role in Collier's entry into American Indian advocacy a few years later. As a writer, poet, lecturer, and social reformer, Collier continued his social activism, establishing a training school for community workers, and becoming editor of the publication of the National Community Center Conference. In 1916, when funding for the New York operations dried up and political difficulties arose, he moved with his family to Los Angeles, California, to become the director of the state's adult education program. After taking up the new work, he lectured extensively and established public forums similar to those of the People's Institute. His two main themes were the cooperative movement and the "Bolshevik experiment" of the Russian Revolution, both of which he admired. Collier's radical social work roots were to cause him problems later as Commissioner of Indian Affairs when he lobbied Congress for an Indian "New Deal."

By the beginning of the 20th century, Anglo America had been persuaded that Indians were a vanishing race; therefore, the assimilation of the survivors through Americanization and Christianization was made to seem a task of philanthropy. In reality, American Indians had passed the nadir of their population decline and were no longer "vanishing," either physically or culturally. It was at this juncture that the missionary-oriented Indian Rights Association called upon the Indian Office to place a ban on Indian ceremonial dancing. In the early 1920s, Indian commissioner Charles H. Burke banned Indian religious dances, and Secretary of the Interior Albert Fall sponsored legislation that would legitimize the seizure of 60,000 acres of Pueblo lands and the individualization of tribal economic assets.

In 1920, Collier interrupted a wilderness trip to Mexico to visit Taos Pueblo in New Mexico at the urging of his old friend Mabel Dodge. For two years he resided at the pueblo, where he and others from the art community gathered around the fireplace in Mabel Dodge's home to discuss the meaning of Indian life. He came away determined that Pueblo culture, and Indian life in general, must be preserved. After his stay at Taos, Collier returned to California to accept a lecturer position at San Francisco State College.

A strong believer in cultural pluralism, Collier took up the protest from the Pueblos against persecution by the Office of Indian Affairs and its Christian "reformers." The controversy over the Pueblo land grants, part of the larger struggle aimed at stopping reservation land dispossession and pauperization stemming from the 1887 Allotment Act, led to the founding of the American Indian Defense Association (AIDA) by Collier in May, 1923. The political agitation by the AIDA, along with the two-million member General Federation of Women's Clubs and the Indian Rights Association, led to the resignation of Secretary of the Interior Albert Fall from the Harding administration.

The year 1928 saw the issuance of the government's *The Problem of Indian Administration,* better known as the Meriam Report. For Collier it confirmed the horrible legacy of allotment policy and the fact that major reform was needed in Indian administration. When Franklin D. Roosevelt was elected in 1932, the new president chose Harold Ickes as his secretary of the interior. Ickes was a Chicago progressive and former director of the American Indian Defense Association. Collier was then tapped to become the new commissioner of Indian affairs.

By 1934 the new commissioner had drafted a bill that became the framework for the Indian Reorganization Act. It was rough sailing for Collier, however, and Congress ended up dropping key provisions from the bill and amending others. The section of Title II having to do with promoting Indian arts, crafts, skills and traditions was deleted by Congress, as was also the section in Title III having to do with land alienation and the Indian heirship problem. Title IV, dealing with law and order, was dropped entirely. Not to be outdone, Collier launched his Indian New Deal anyway through a series of administrative reforms and edicts to the Office of Indian Affairs. A singular feature of the Indian New Deal was the exclusion of Christian missionaries from the Collier administration and the inclusion of anthropologists in their place. This represented a policy shift from cultural assimilation to cultural pluralism.

The new commissioner's critics, including a number of Indian tribes and reservation superintendents, viewed self-government under the IRA with suspicion, as socialistic and un-American. Collier, on the other hand, proposed that Indian tribes become chartered corporations with the powers of a community or county, a form of limited self-government. The new tribal councils would act as advisory bodies to the secretary of the interior. The IRA self-government provisions were seen by Collier as a form of indirect rule by the federal government and a progressive advance in U.S. Indian policy. By the 1920s and 1930s the European powers had come to favor this form of colonial administration since direct rule, especially by the French, had been such an abysmal failure. From today's perspective, Collier's reform may be criticized as a form of neocolonialism, but taken in the context of the times, his ideas resulted in a progressive shift in federal Indian policy.

Despite the accomplishments of the IRA, World War II drained funds from the reform program and turned Congress and the country to other priorities. Discouraged, Collier resigned on January 10, 1945, after 12 years as the head of Indian affairs. For the next 23 years he continued an active public life. During his tenure as commissioner, Collier helped found the first Pan-American conference on Indian life held at Patzcuaro, Mexico, in the spring of 1940. He headed up a National Indian Institute in 1943 that undertook an important Indian personality research study, founded the Institute of Ethnic Affairs in 1945, and took an active interest in America's newly acquired trusteeships in the Pacific after the war. He published a major work in 1947, *Indians of the Americas,* which was used in anthropology courses for many years. In the same year he became professor of sociology and anthropology at the City College of New York, a position he retained until 1955. His memoir, *From Every Zenith,* came out in 1960, and he died at his Taos residence in 1968 at the age of 84.

How should one evaluate the Collier legacy? In the first place, the IRA resulted in only a partial and imperfect restoration of Indian sovereignty. Furthermore, for all his democratic idealism, Collier's administrative style as commissioner has been criticized as authoritarian and paternalistic. In some cases he manipulated tribal elections to favor IRA acceptance. He also imposed Anglo American model constitutions and charters on traditionally oriented tribes that undercut the political leadership of chiefs and the old band and treaty councils. The Navajo Nation never forgave him for the ruthlessness of his pursuit of the livestock reduction program on their reservation. The Lakota and some other tribes with allotted lands split into factions as a result of the IRA, the bitter legacy of which manifested itself in the occupation of Wounded Knee on the Pine Ridge Reservation in 1973.

It may be that religious freedom was his most lasting accomplishment. In his memoirs, Collier depicts ceremonial tribal dances as the core of Indian religion. "Through the dances are united body and soul, and self with the community, and self and tribe with nature and with God." Upon taking office as commissioner he immediately reversed the old Bureau policy of religious persecution by issuing Circular No. 2970, *Indian Religious Freedom and Indian Culture.* He also issued an order curtailing missionary activity on the reservations. Yet, the issue of Indian religious freedom was excluded from the Indian Reorganization Act. Religious persecution continued in less obvious ways and was not specifically addressed by Congress until passage of the American Indian Religious Freedom Act in 1978, and the Native American Graves Protection and Repatriation Act in 1990. The repatriation of human remains is still not resolved, and the question of sacred lands has scarcely been addressed in terms of public policy.

Steve Talbot

References and Further Reading

Collier, John. 1963 *From Every Zenith.* Denver, CO: Sage Books.

Kelly, Laurence C. 1996 "Indian New Deal," In *Native America in the Twentieth Century: An Encyclopedia:* 218–20, ed. Mary B. Davis. New York: Garland Publishing.

Philp, Kenneth R. 1977. *John Collier's Crusade for Indian Reform: 1920–1954.* Tucson: University of Arizona Press.

Stefon, Frederick J. Fall, 1983, and Winter, 1984. "The Indians' Zarathustra: An Investigation Into the Philosophical Roots of John Collier's New Deal Educational and Administrative Policies," *The Journal of Ethnic Studies* Part I, 11 (5): 1–28; Part II, 11 (4): 29–45.

Deportation

Deportation is the legal means to remove a foreign national who has, in most cases, entered or remains in the host country illegally, or has conducted themselves in manner which deems them a threat to the safety of the host county. However, justification for deportation varies from country to county. The United States has an extensive deportation system designed both as an arm of the country's immigration policy as well as a tool for social control. During the Great Depression America's deportation policy reflected this dual-purpose. As a nation of immigrants, America's immigration policy is also intimately tied to the economic well-being of the country. As a result, during the Great Depression the deportation system also figured into President Franklin Delano Roosevelt's (FDR) New Deal policy. Because these policies were shaped in an atmosphere of uncertainty and anxiety, a political vacuum was created for which American nativist attitudes came to dominate the policy-making process.

The shift in immigration during the preceding two decades prior to the Great Depression saw an influx of eastern Europeans arriving at Ellis Island; and populating America's industrial inner cities. These immigrants, who were at first targeted by American industrialists and political leaders as a vital source for tackling America's shrinking labor force problem, were during the 1930s victimized as aliens responsible for decreasing wages and taking what little jobs that were available away from "real" Americans. The largest number of cases of undocumented immigration, and noncitizens (which includes contract laborers and permanent-resident "green card holders", has always, and continues to be, Mexicans). These legal and illegal immigrants were recruited and exploited by large farm owners across southwestern states.

During the Great Depression Mexican immigrants, including Mexican Americans, became favorite targets of American nativism. FDR's New Deal policies exacerbated the problem. After decades of increased commercial wheat production, especially during the First World War, soil erosion and winds on American Great Plains produced a massive Dust Bowl. From 1935 to 1940 the 50 acres of the once productive southern Plains were diminished to little more than 4 acres of fertile lands. To combat soil erosion and declining food prices FDR's administration instituted the Soil Conservation Service and the Agricultural Adjustment Administration. Neither policy achieved much success, forcing some 300,000 tenant farmers and sharecroppers from the former Cotton Kingdom to migrate west in search of jobs. These American-born refugees, or "Okies" as they were disparagingly called, often found work in the low paying agricultural positions occupied by Mexicans.

The fact the millions of Mexicans had been living in America illegally for years, even decades, suggests the cause for the mass deportation of Mexicans during the 1930s was less about their legal status and more about the fact they were an ethnic minority group taking jobs away from white Americans. Furthermore, tens of thousands of illegal Mexicans were also seeking employment relief from the Depression, thus taxing the limited resources the government was willing, or able, to distribute in relief payments. Mass arrests and raids rounding-up Mexican immigrants were widely publicized, not to ensure Americans of their security, but as a means of intimidation. In 1932 the United States government adopted a voluntary repatriation scheme, which applied to criminals as well, and involuntary (or forced) deportation that resulted in the tens of thousands of Mexicans removed from the American southwest. The results were dramatic, with the Mexican population in the United States dropping nearly 40 percent during the 1930s. It is estimated that approximately 2 million Mexicans, including 1.2 million American-born Mexicans, were deported from the country during this time. Today, in California, the Senate has passed an "Apology Act for the 1930s Mexican Repatriation Program" apologizing "for the fundamental violations of their basic civil liberties and constitutional rights during

A family of Mexican migrant workers stands outside their shack at a California rehabilitation camp in 1935. Photo by Dorothea Lange. Mexican workers were a prime target for those espousing American nativist views during the Great Depression because of the fear that they were taking jobs away from white Americans. (Library of Congress)

the period of illegal deportation and coerced emigration."

Stephen Burgess Whiting

References and Further Reading

Balderrama, Francisco E., and Raymond Rodriquez. 1995. *Decade of Betrayal: Mexican Repatriation in the 1930s.* Albuquerque: University of New Mexico Press.

California State Senate, Judiciary Committee. 2007–8. Available at: http://www.legislature.ca.gov/cgi-bin/port-postquery?bill_number=sb_552&sess=CUR&house=B&author=cedillo. Accessed September 24, 2009.

Daniels, Roger. 2002. *Coming To America: A History of Immigration and Ethnicity in American Life.* 2nd ed. New York: Perennial.

Guerin-Gonzales, Camille. 1994. *Mexican Workers and the American Dream: Immigration, Repatriation, and California Farm Labor, 1900–1939.* New Brunswick, NJ: Rutgers University Press.

Kanstroom, Daniel. 2007. *Deportation Nation: Outsiders in American History.* Cambridge, MA.: Harvard University Press.

De Priest, Oscar (1871–1951)

Oscar Stanton De Priest was the first African American from the North elected to serve in the U.S. House of Representatives.

De Priest was born on March 9, 1871, in Florence, Alabama, to parents who were former slaves. He graduated from

Salina (Kansas) Normal School in 1888 and later settled in Chicago, where he accumulated a fortune managing real estate on the city's South Side. A Republican in a predominantly Democratic political environment, De Priest managed to hold a number of city offices because of his ability to deliver the African American vote and play factions of the Republican and Democratic parties against each other. In 1915, he became the first African American elected to the city council. In 1923, in return for help he provided to the successful Republican candidate for mayor, De Priest was appointed assistant Illinois commerce commissioner, a position that included patronage appointment powers.

In 1928, De Priest supported the white Republican candidate for Congress over a black candidate in the primary election. The white candidate died shortly after winning the nomination. De Priest took his place and went on to win the general election that fall for the House of Representatives.

In Congress, De Priest filed a number of bills designed to protect the civil rights of African Americans. He also traveled extensively in the South at considerable personal peril to encourage African Americans to organize politically. Although attacked by Southern newspapers for stirring up racial hostility by advocating social equality, De Priest refused to be intimidated.

Reelected in 1930, De Priest even managed to hold onto his seat in the 1932 Democratic landslide of Franklin D. Roosevelt, despite his initial opposition to New Deal federal relief. Although his personal popularity remained high, he lost his bid to win a fourth term in Congress to an African American Democratic Party candidate in 1934. Still active in local politics, he was again elected alderman from Chicago's Third Ward from 1943 to 1947. Before his death, De Priest returned to a lucrative real estate business. He died in Chicago on May 12, 1951.

References and Further Reading

Biographical Directory of the United States Congress. Available at: http://bioguide.congress.gov/scripts/biodisplay.pl?index=D000263. Accessed on September 24, 2009.

Gosnell, Harold F. 1967. *Negro Politicians: The Rise of Negro Politics in Chicago.* Chicago: University of Chicago Press.

Divine, Father (c. 1877–1965)

Father Divine was an influential African American religious figure whose integrated (albeit predominantly black) cult-like International Peace Mission Movement achieved its zenith in the 1930s, although continuing in dwindling form after his death.

Controversy beclouds his birth and early life. Apparently he was born George Baker, the son of former slaves. Contradictory sources list various birth places including Georgia and Maryland, but agree that he grew up in poverty with a limited education. He seems to have been an itinerant preacher.

In 1907, Baker joined a Baptist storefront church in Baltimore, whose leader, Samuel Morris, referred to himself as Father Jehovia. Shortly, Baker became known as "the Messenger." By 1912, Baker had formed his own ministry, leaving Baltimore for Georgia, where clashes with local ministers led to vagrancy and "lunacy" charges; convicted, he was promised leniency if he left the state.

After traveling around the country, Baker settled in 1917 in Sayville in Suffolk County, Long Island, New York, calling himself the Reverend Major Jealous Devine. His followers, who believed him to be God, called him "Father" and soon he became "Father Divine." His teachings, which were considered sacred, prohibited tobacco, alcohol, and profanity, established dress codes, and called for celibacy. Divine had a diverse following that by 1926 included both African Americans and whites.

On November 15, 1931, officers arrested members attending Divine's regular service. Fifty-five members, pleading guilty, paid a $5.00 fine. Father Divine and others pleaded not guilty and stood trial. Most found guilty were fined. Justice Lewis J. Smith sentenced Divine to a year in jail and a $500.00 fine. Two days later Smith died of cardiac arrest. For many of Divine's followers, that confirmed his Divinity. A new trial, although ordered, never took place.

Divine's Peace Mission Movement operated hotels, restaurants, and stores while providing jobs, housing, and free meals during the Depression. Divine became famous for his elaborate "Love Feasts," communion banquets, and services. In the mid-1930s, Divine moved his headquarters to Harlem. In January 1936, Divine issued his "Righteous Government Platform" calling for elimination of racial segregation, lynching, and capital punishment and advocating for additional government funds to end unemployment and poverty. In 1940, the movement petitioned for federal prosecution of lynching.

Father Divine's movement grew steadily during the 1930s and gained tens of thousands of followers organized in communities across the country. Over the years he faced a range of accusations, including charges of racketeering. In the early 1940s he moved his headquarters to Philadelphia, and subsequently to "Woodmount," an estate in Gladwynee, a suburb of the city, willed to him by a follower.

Plagued by ill health, he became increasingly reclusive, and as economic conditions in the United States improved, his following, many of whom had been lower class, dwindled. After the death of his first wife, Divine had married a 21-year-old Canadian white woman, Edna Rose Ritchings, on April 29, 1946: "Sweet Angel" assumed the title of Mother Divine and oversaw operations. Father Divine, suffering from diabetes, died on September 10, 1965.

Julius H. Bailey

References and Further Reading

Burnham, Kenneth. 1979. *God Comes to America: Father Divine and the Peace Mission Movement.* Boston: Lambeth Press.

Watts, Jill. 1992. *God, Harlem, U.S.A.: The Father Divine Story.* Berkeley: University of California Press.

Weisbrot, Robert. 1983. *Father Divine and the Struggle for Racial Equality.* Urbana: University of Illinois Press.

Du Bois, William Edward Burghardt (1868–1963)

Writer, scholar, crusader for black rights, W.E.B. Du Bois was one of the most influential African American intellectuals of the 20th century. He studied and promoted the African American heritage and called for immediate equality in civil and economic rights. In all his activities over the decades he stood in sharp contrast to more accomodationist black leaders.

He was born on February 23, 1868, in Great Barrington, MA to parents of mixed racial ancestry (Alfred Du Bois, a laborer, and Mary Silvana Burghardt, a domestic). Less than two years after his son's birth, Alfred Du Bois deserted the family. Mary Silvana Burghardt died (1884) some months before the son graduated from high school—the only black graduate in his class. One of a handful of blacks in the western Massachusetts town of 4,000, Du Bois—an excellent student and encouraged by the high school principal—earned a scholarship to Fisk University, a black institution in Nashville, TN, and attended there from 1885 to 1888. His time in the South exposed Du Bois to the region's cruel, pervasive racism and influenced his later career.

In 1888 Du Bois, aided financially by a prize he won, enrolled at Harvard as a junior, graduating cum laude in 1890. The next year Harvard granted him an M.A., and he undertook further graduate study, followed by a stint (1892–94) at the University of Berlin. His fellowship funds exhausted, he returned to Harvard, completing the requirements for the Ph.D., which Harvard awarded him in 1895 (he was the first African American to be awarded a Harvard Ph.D.). He taught (1895–96) at Wilberforce University in Ohio, an institution supported by a black church. While there his Ph.D. thesis, "The Suppression of the African Slave Trade to the United States of America," was published (1896) and became the standard history of the subject. Scrupulously documented and well-argued, the thesis asserted economic dictates prolonged the trade notwithstanding moral arguments against it, and that economics not moral suasion ended the trade.

At Wilberforce, he met and married (1896) Nina Gomer, a student there. They had a son, who died young (Du Bois maintained his death was due to the inadequate medical facilities available to blacks), and a daughter. Du Bois's wife died in 1950 and he married Shirley Graham, a long-time friend and militant leftist activist, in February 1951. They did not have children.

At the end of 1897 Du Bois began teaching sociology at Atlanta University, a black institution. A year earlier he had undertaken a groundbreaking study of poor urban blacks in Philadelphia. Applying the scientific method to social research, Du Bois produced *The Philadelphia Negro,* published in 1899. Still considered a model study of an African American community, Du Bois's work described in social and economic detail what he termed the "Negro Problem." He initially believed ignorance was at the heart of the problem, but became convinced that the increasing racism of the day and the cultural politics supporting it were also important factors. He undertook a more limited study of some southern black communities, published in 1898 as U.S. Bureau of Labor Bulletin *The Negroes of Farmville, Virginia: A Social Study.* Like the Philadelphia study, it recorded the debilitating social and economic conditions of African Americans and emphasized the need for forceful action to combat discrimination. In 1903 Du Bois produced *The Souls of Black Folks,* a collection of essays on African American culture denouncing the racism of American society.

As Du Bois moved toward a more radical stand, he came into conflict with Booker T. Washington, then the most influential African American in the United States. Washington called for blacks to refrain from demanding social and political equality, in favor of developing their economic standing. He stood for accommodation, education, and racial solidarity. Du Bois argued Washington's program would not end white oppression, and called for political action, a strong civil rights agenda, and leadership by the small elite of "exceptional black men" he called "the Talented Tenth."

He joined with other black radicals in 1904 to form the Niagara Movement, an organization militantly advocating full civil and political rights for African Americans. It soon collapsed from internal tensions. In 1909, Du Bois joined with other blacks and white liberals to form the National Association for the Advancement of Colored People (NAACP). It undertook an active program of lawsuits and lobbying to improve the conditions of African-Americans. In 1910 Du Bois, the organization's only black board member, left Atlanta University to become an active officer of the NAACP and editor of its journal, *Crisis*.

During the next quarter century Du Bois made *Crisis* a vital force in the black community. His editorials, the articles he wrote and solicited, the publication of talented new black writers, all contributed to his vision of the role and place of African Americans in the United States and the world. The monthly issues were uncommonly attractive, intelligent, and inspiring. He urged African Americans to stand up for their rights. After the end of World War I in 1918 he urged returning veterans to fight for democracy in their own country, as they had in France. Du Bois called for an end to lynching and Jim Crow laws in the United States. He commented freely and widely on current events. *Crisis* was in the forefront of the NAACP campaigns to improve the social, economic, legal, and political situation of African Americans.

In 1919, Du Bois sailed to France as the NAACP's observer to the Paris Peace Conference. While there, he attended a Pan-African Congress, the first of a number (1921, 1923, 1927, 1945) with which he was involved, the last of which he helped organize. They were designed to bring world attention to the problems of Africans. The last one he attended, stressing the Africans' need and desire for independence, presaged the end of colonial rule in Africa.

Increased violence and discrimination against blacks during the 1920s, as well as the problems caused by the onset of the Great Depression, caused Du Bois to become more direct action-oriented. His views diverged from the NAACP's traditional legalistic and propagandistic campaigns for integration. His belief in Marxism as a solution to racism and colonialism did not sit well with the organization's officers, especially Walter White, the chief executive, nor did Du Bois's beliefs in voluntary segregation as a means of dealing with the economic harshness of the times. In 1934 Du Bois was forced out after he published in *Crisis* essays averring that separatism could be a useful economic strategy for African Americans.

Du Bois returned to Atlanta University where he taught until pushed out in 1944. The NAACP then took him on as a director of special research (a newly created post). In 1945 he served the NAACP as a consultant to the U.S. delegation at the founding conference of the United Nations Organization in San Francisco. In 1947 he prepared and presented to the UN Commission on Human Rights a 94-page petition he had prepared, protesting the violations incurred by American racism. During these years his influence began to decline, notwithstanding such activity and his prolific publication of newspaper columns, articles, and books, including critiques of colonialism and capitalism as well as his most important historical work *Black Reconstruction in America* (1935). This book systematically re-evaluated the traditional view of African Americans in the South after the Civil War, arguing that the black leadership overall was honest, farsighted, and democratic, a view now generally held by contemporary historians.

Already during the 1930s but subsequently at the end of the 1940s and later, his politics hampered him. He was used by Japan in 1936 as part of its "Negro Propaganda Operations." In the later 1940s, a time when anticommunism was dramatically on the rise in the United States, he increasingly became involved with groups seen as communist fronts, and his increasingly pro-communist opinions lost him his NAACP post. He was an active supporter of the Progressive Party in 1948, helped organize the controversial 1949 New York City conference for World Peace, chaired the advisory council of a group which promoted the supposedly Soviet-inspired Stockholm Peace Appeal calling for a ban on nuclear weapons (which resulted in his being indicted in 1951 for failing to register as a foreign agent, although he was subsequently acquitted).

From 1952 to 1958 Du Bois and his wife were denied passports to travel abroad. After finally attaining them, one of their visits was to the Soviet Union where on May Day 1959 he received a Lenin Peace Prize. In 1961 Du Bois was invited to Ghana (which in 1957 was the first of the newly independent African nations) by its head of state Kwame

Nkrumah in order to work on an "Encyclopedia Africana"—a long-standing pet project of Du Bois. Before leaving for Ghana in October 1961 the 93-year-old Du Bois joined the Communist Party. In February 1963 Du Bois became a citizen of Ghana, dying there on August 27, 1963, just a day before the March on Washington took place and Martin Luther King gave his "I Have A Dream" speech.

Daniel J. Leab

References and Further Reading

W.E.B Du Bois papers. Manuscript and Special Collections Archive, W.E.B. Du Bois Library. University of Massachusetts, Amherst.

Blum, Edward. 2007. *W.E.B. Du Bois: American Prophet.* Philadelphia: University of Pennsylvania Press.

Lewis, David Levering. 2000. *W.E.B. Du Bois, 1868–1919: Biography of a Race.* New York: Henry Holt and Company.

Lewis, David Levering. 2000. *W.E.B. Du Bois, 1919–1963: The Fight for Equality and the American Century.* New York: Henry Holt and Company.

Lewis, David Levering, ed. 1995. *W.E.B. Du Bois: A Reader.* New York: Owl Books.

Rampersad, Arnold. 1976. *The Art and Imagination of W.E.B. Du Bois.* New York: Schocken Books.

Ellington, Edward Kennedy "Duke" (1899–1974)

Composer, pianist, and band leader, Ellington is among the most influential figures in American jazz history. He used vocal and instrumental timbres ingeniously to produce striking new musical textures.

Born in Washington, D.C. (April 24, 1899), he was the son of James Edward

Ellington, a blueprint maker for the Navy Department who moonlighted as a butler, and Daisy Kennedy, a domestic, to whom he was particularly attached. He and his 16-years-younger sister Ruth grew up in a stable, affectionate, middle-class environment. His style of dress and demeanor earned him the nickname "Duke" while still in his teens. At Armstrong High School, a D.C. manual training school for African Americans (he attended from 1914 to 1917 but never graduated), Ellington won an NAACP poster contest. Offered a scholarship to the Pratt Institute of Fine Arts in Brooklyn, NY, Ellington declined, already drawn by opportunities to play piano at dances and parties. By 1918, he was making a good living painting commercial signs and performing in public. On July 2, 1918, he married high school sweetheart Edna Thompson; on March 11, 1919, their son Mercer was born. He and his wife never divorced but had separated by 1930. Ellington's long-time companion Beatrice "Evie" Ellis died in 1976 and is buried alongside him.

Ellington had formed an ensemble that thrived in the Washington, D.C., area and went to New York in 1922 to try his musical wings. He and his Washington sidemen, Otto "Toby" Hardwicke (bass and sax) and Sonny Greer (drums), after a few discouraging months, returned to D.C. In 1923, a group including Ellington, Elmer Snowden (banjo), and Arthur Whetsol (trumpet), found work in Harlem under Snowden's direction. Known as The Washingtonians, they were hired by a new club in the Broadway theatre district (the Hollywood, later Club Kentucky). Ellington became leader because of dissatisfaction with Snowden; Fred Guy replaced him on banjo. The group played this venue periodically until 1927

as well as at other nightclubs in the city and elsewhere. Additions included two trumpet players—one of them James "Bubber" Miley (a jazz specialist who during his stay with the band set its hot driving style)—Joe "Tricky Sam" Nanton (trombone), Harry Carney (baritone sax), Rudy Jackson (clarinet and tenor sax), and Wellman Braud (bass). Ellington, Guy, Greer, and Braud—the rhythm section—stayed together for a decade.

In 1926 Ellington made a deal with Irving Mills, a formidable music publisher with gangland connections. This arrangement (lasting through 1937) brought Ellington publicity and engagements, and assured him control of the orchestra. In 1927 it moved to Harlem's noted Cotton Club. The orchestra expanded again, adding clarinetist Barney Bigard, saxophonist Johnny Hodges, and trumpeters Freddie Jenkins and Cootie Williams. Continuing at the club until 1932, the band often broadcast, appeared in half a dozen movies during the 1930s, and performed around the country. These years consolidated Ellington's reputation for high standards in improvisation and orchestral jazz.

Recordings of Ellington's music including "East St. Louis Toodle oo" (1926) which featured Miley, "Birmingham Breakdown" (1927), and the much admired "Black and Tan Fantasy (1927) enhanced his reputation. The recordings of this period included many "jungle style" numbers. The sound, original to Ellington and Miley, depends on special effects (plunger mutes, mutes on all the brasses, tom-toms, and unusual combinations of instruments). "Mood Indigo," a 1930 hit, made Ellington famous around the world. While his growing success depended in part on his individual players, Ellington blended the special qualities of tone color and timbre each brought to the ensemble into a distinctive sound that defied replication.

Ellington's successes were accompanied by heightened creativity. In 1931, he experimented with longer compositions. *Creole Rhapsody* was followed by *Reminiscin' in Tempo* and *Diminuendo and Crescendo in Blue.* Popular hits included "Sophisticated Lady," recorded in 1933, "Solitude" (1934), and "In a Sentimental Mood" (1935). In other works, his orchestrations matched melody in importance, as in *Daybreak Express* and *Blue Harlem.* Between 1932 and 1942, Ellington's most productive decade, the band (containing six brasses, four reeds, and four rhythm instruments) toured Europe (1933, 1939) and the United States. In 1939, there were three major additions: Billy Strayhorn, arranger, composer, and second pianist, who ultimately became Ellington's closest collaborator; Jimmy Blanton, double bass; and Ben Webster, tenor sax. Strayhorn's "Take the A Train" became the band's theme. Between 1939 and 1942 Ellington's work was, according to many, his most superb. During these years, he composed "Concerto for Cootie," "Ko-Ko," and "Cotton Tail."

By 1946, there were 18 in the band, including Ray Nance, who played trumpet and violin. Unfortunately, as musicians came and went, the musical stability of the preceding years evaporated. Ellington's compositions and performance reflected the uncertainty. A series of ambitious annual Carnegie Hall Concerts began in January 1943 and showcased Ellington works, such as *Black, Brown and Beige,* his first long composition, important because it created a major concert work from jazz elements. Other longer Ellington compositions were introduced in the next years, among them *Liberian Suite* and *Night Creature.* They received mixed reviews.

Ellington continued to tour during the late 1940s and 1950s, but as the big band era faded, royalties from his earlier popular hits subsidized the orchestra. He continued to compose—often more serious works. He created scores for various films including *Anatomy of a Murder* (1959) and *Paris Blues* (1961), and in his final years turned to composing sacred music. He also recorded with John Coltrane, Charles Mingus, and others. In 1965 the Pulitzer Prize music jury recommended a special citation for his long-term achievements. Although the advisory board denied the award because it was not for a specific work, in 1999 on the centennial of Ellington's birth the Pulitzer Board awarded him posthumously a special award citation for that work. Among his many other awards were honorary degrees from Howard University (1963) and Yale University (1967), the Presidential Medal of Freedom (1969), and the French Legion of Honor (1973). Ellington continued to direct the band until his death from lung cancer in New York on May 24, 1974.

References and Further Reading

Duke Ellington Collection. National Museum of American History, Smithsonian Institution, Washington, D.C.

Ellington, Edward Kennedy. 1973. *Music is my Mistress,* Garden City, NY: Doubleday.

Massagli, Luciano, and Giovanni M. Voloonte. 1999. *The New Desor: an updated edition of Duke Ellington's story on records, 1924–1974.* 2 vols. Milan, Italy: privately published.

Collier, James Lincoln. 1987. *Duke Ellington.* New York: Oxford University Press.

Ellington, Mercer, with Stanley Dance. 1978. *Duke Ellington in Person: An Intimate Memoir.* Boston: Houghton, Mifflin.

Blackwell, Earl, ed. 1973. "Ellington, Duke." In *Celebrity Register,* 155–56. New York: Simon & Schuster.

Hasse, John Edward. 1993. *Beyond Category: The Life and Genius of Duke Ellington.* New York: Simon & Schuster.

Lawrence, A. H. 1999. *Duke Ellington and His World.* New York: Schirmer.

Tucker, Mark. 1991. *Ellington: The Early Years.* Urbana: University of Illinois Press.

Ford, Henry (1863–1947)

Henry Ford revolutionized the automobile industry, life in the United States, and possibly western culture with the Model T. His assembly-line production method enabled cars to be made in quantity at a cost that brought them within reach of the average person. His career was stained, however, by his bigotry and antilabor bias.

Ford was born on July 30, 1863, on a farm in Greenfield Township, Michigan, now in the city of Dearborn, adjoining Detroit. He was one of eight children of William Ford, of Protestant Irish ancestry, and Mary Litogot, of a Dutch or Flemish family, who died in childbirth when Ford was 12. Ford went to country schools and early on showed a remarkable mechanical aptitude. At age 15, he was an expert watchmaker. The next year, he left school and worked days as an apprentice in a Detroit machine shop and nights repairing watches to make ends meet. He went on to other mechanical work, becoming familiar with steam engines and early power plants. Young Ford helped occasionally on his father's farm but was determined to leave farming and work with machines.

Henry Ford, founder of the Ford Motor Company, revolutionized the automobile industry, life in the United States, and possibly Western culture with the Model T automobile and assembly-line production method. (Ford Motor Company)

In 1896, drawing on inventions by automotive engineers in Europe and America, Ford constructed his first "horseless carriage," powered by a gasoline motor, in his own workshop. Meanwhile, a job as an engineer for the Edison Illuminating Company supported him as he continued experimenting. In 1899, Ford left the Edison Company and became chief engineer of the Detroit Automobile Company, backed by a group of businessmen. The company did not survive. In 1901 he helped create the Henry Ford Company, but when he did not agree with others in the company as to its goals, Ford left and the firm became the Cadillac Motor Car Company. His chief interest at the time was in producing a fast racing car; although in the long run he was determined to make a car that could be sold to the general public at a low price.

The Ford Motor Company was founded in 1903 with the mission to produce a car that would compete with the Oldsmobile. Ford was vice president in charge of design and production. As the company prospered, Ford bought out most of the other shareholders, and by 1906, he was president and the major shareholder. Two years later, when the company was capitalized at $2 million, Ford introduced his Model T, which was light, durable, cheap, and efficient to run; it sold for $800 to $1,000. By 1916, when 730,000 cars were being turned out, assembly-line production had brought the price down to as low as $345. During the first years, the Model Ts came in a variety of colors, but after 1914, all were black. The ideal car for rough country roads, farms, and small towns, the Model T took the automobile out of the luxury class and made it an affordable necessity for the ordinary family. It also speeded up the urbanization of the United States and stimulated a transportation revolution the world over.

The assembly-line method meant tedious monotony for the worker, who typically repeated a certain movement many times as the belt went past. Labor discontent and turnover were an inevitable consequence. The year 1914 saw Ford's introduction of a remedy: a minimum wage of $5 for the eight-hour shift, contrasted with an average daily wage of around $2 at other Detroit auto factories. This seemingly revolutionary policy made Ford world famous as a humanitarian, though less attention was paid to the reality that numerous Ford workers did not qualify for the $5 rate. Ford quipped that he wanted his employees to be able to afford the price of a Model T.

With the outbreak of World War I, Ford displayed another aspect of his humanitarianism—his conviction that the war was started by a ring of international financiers. In 1915, he sponsored a "peace ship" that carried him and pacifist delegates to Europe. The American public, increasingly pro-Allied, was hostile to Ford's expedition, and nothing came of it. When the United States entered the war in 1917, Ford's factories filled numerous government contracts for trucks, tanks, airplane motors, submarine chasers, and armaments, and he declared he would operate without profit. In fact, no profits were turned over to the government.

Though nominally a rather unpolitical Republican, Ford (after the fiasco of the peace ship) had supported President Woodrow Wilson's reelection in 1916 and his internationalist policies. Wilson persuaded him to run for the U.S. Senate on the Democratic ticket. He lost by a thin margin and blamed it on the international financiers and the Jews. When the *Chicago Tribune* called him an "ignorant idealist," he sued the newspaper. At the trial, cross-examination exposed his ignorance of general knowledge. The jury found the newspaper guilty of libel and awarded Ford damages of six cents. Embittered, Ford became more and more preoccupied with anti-Semitism and printed attacks on Jews in the newspaper *Dearborn Independent,* which he had acquired as a propaganda medium. Later, he apologized publicly for his tirades against the Jewish people.

By 1920, Ford (with his wife Clara and his son Edsel, who had become president) was the sole owner of one of the world's largest manufacturing enterprises, by then worth $100 million. Two years later, he began making a luxury car, the Lincoln. In 1927, the outmoded Model T was discontinued (after 15 million had been made) in favor of the Model A, designed to compete with General Motors' Chevrolet and the Chrysler Corporation's Plymouth. Not a success, the Model A was replaced in 1932 by the V-8. By 1936, the Ford company had sunk to third place in the car industry.

Ford controlled his company despotically, discouraged the introduction of modern methods of management, and fiercely resisted unionization. In 1934, he refused to sign the New Deal's industry-wide code. After General Motors and Chrysler recognized the United Automobile Workers of America (UAW) in 1937, Ford held out and allowed his security boss to use intimidation, brutality, and terror against union organizers until 1941, when he accepted the UAW contract. Split by factions and losses, the company had seriously declined.

When World War II broke out in Europe in 1939, Ford supported the isolationist stand of the America First Committee through his friend Charles Lindbergh. He had been accused of Nazi sympathies after he accepted a decoration from Adolf Hitler's government in 1938. The company, however, became heavily involved in American defense production by 1941, notably at its huge Willow Run plant, where thousands of B-24 Liberator bombers were built.

In his retirement, Ford gave his attention to the historical restorations, reproductions, and museums that he had endowed, including Greenfield Village in Dearborn, Michigan, a shrine to his close friend Edison. After his death on April 7, 1947, his grandson Henry Ford II took over the company and began to rebuild it. The preponderant share of the stock passed to a small family trust, which became the richest private foundation in the world—the Ford Foundation.

References and Further Reading

Collier, Peter, and David Horowitz. 1987. *The Fords: An American Epic.* New York: Summit Books.

Nevins, Allan, and Frank E. Hill. 1954–63. *Ford.* 3 vols. New York: Scribner.

Frazier, E. Franklin (1894–1962)

Dr. Edward Franklin Frazier (1894–1962), a black sociologist and educator, became one of the principal voices in the Africanisms debate which included such notable scholars as Melville Herskovits, Lorenzo Dow Turner, and W.E.B. Du Bois. Born in Maryland at the height of the Black Nadir, Frazier graduated from Baltimore's Colored High School in 1912 and attended Howard University to study Latin, Greek, German and mathematics. After graduating from Howard, he taught throughout the South until 1919 when he enrolled in graduate school at Clark University in Worcester, Massachusetts. Frazier earned a Master's degree in sociology and became a research fellow at the New York School of Social Work in 1920. In 1922, he began a two year teaching stint at Morehouse College before serving as the director of the Atlanta School of Social Work until 1927. After earning a Ph.D. in sociology at the University of Chicago in 1931, Frazier taught at Fisk University for three years. In 1934 he became chair of Howard University's sociology department, a position he held until his retirement in 1959.

Author of more than 10 books and dozens of journal articles, Frazier contributed to a number of scholarly debates and was widely recognized as the

E. Franklin Frazier (1894–1962), a professor at Howard University for many years, is one of the leading American social scientists of the 20th century, and one of the closest students of African American life during the Great Depression. He is best known for his monograph, *The Negro Family in the United States* (1939), which became controversial in the 1960s and 1970s when its findings were interpreted by some as arguing that the structure of the African American family was significantly responsible for persistent inequality. (Photographs and Prints Division, Schomburg Center for Research in Black Culture, The New York Public Library, Astor, Lenox and Tilden Foundations)

leading authority on the black family in America. His distinguished career led to a number of achievements. Frazier earned a Guggenheim Fellowship in 1940; he became the first black president of the American Sociological Association (ASA) in 1948; and, for his life-time contributions to the field of sociology, Frazier was a recipient of the ASA's MacIver Award. Despite the universal acclaim for his contributions, Frazier was not averse to controversy and took a number of unpopular stances throughout his long career. While an instructor at Morehouse College, Frazier published an article entitled *The Pathology of Race Prejudice* which associated racism with mental illness. While this conclusion has become accepted by many social scientists, in 1927 it cost Frazier his teaching position at Morehouse and was one of the factors which prompted his move to Chicago.

Perhaps the most significant controversy Frazier was involved in was the so-called Africanisms debate and his long-standing rivalry with anthropologist Melville Herskovits. The opening salvo in the debate was launched in 1939 with the publication of Frazier's *The Negro Family in the United States.* Championing what became known as the "catastrophist school," Frazier argues that slavery had effectively destroyed the black family and this reality facilitated the "Americanization" of slaves and the complete annihilation of African culture in the United States. Even after the publication of Herskovits's monumental *The Myth of the Negro Past* two years later, Frazier refused to waiver in his contention that African culture had largely disappeared in North America.

In a 1949 work entitled *The Negro in the United States,* Frazier dedicated the first chapter to attacking Herskovits's thesis that the African contributions to African American culture were substantial. While Frazier, for the first time, acknowledged the presence of certain Africanisms, he also contended that "conditions of life destroyed the significance of the African heritage" (3). It is important to note that Frazier was likely responding to the social environment around him more than to the particulars of his ongoing debate with Herskovits. He was born in the midst of the Black Nadir when African Americans had to face the brutal combination of legally sanctioned segregation, political disfranchisement, unprecedented levels of racial violence, and an anti-black propaganda campaign in the media. In this hostile climate, any claims that African Americans were somehow different from whites would further justify their debased treatment. Even as late as the 1960s, in *The Negro Church in America* published posthumously in 1963, Frazier would continue the Africanisms debate. Although he made important contributions in a number of areas, it is now clear that Frazier was wrong when he claimed that enslaved Africans in North America were completely stripped of their cultural heritage.

Walter Rucker

References and Further Reading

Edwards, G. Franklin, ed. 1968. *E. Franklin Frazier on Race Relations: Selected Papers.* Chicago: University of Chicago Press.

Frazier, E. Franklin. 1939. *The Negro Family in the United States.* Chicago: University of Chicago Press.

Frazier, E. Franklin. 1949. *The Negro in the United States.* New York: Macmillan & Co.

Frazier, F. Franklin. 1963. *The Negro Church in America.* New York: Schocken Books.

Herskovits, Melville. 1958, c.1942. *The Myth of the Negro Past.* Boston: Beacon Press.

Goodman, Benny (1909–86)

Benny Goodman, the "King of Swing," ushered in the big band era and delighted a generation of fans. Known for lilting tempos and high ensemble standards, he improvised seamlessly, constantly exploring harmonic and instrumental possibilities. By hiring both black and white musicians for public performances, Goodman also broke existing color barriers.

Goodman was born one of 12 children in Chicago, Illinois on May 30, 1909. His parents, Dora and David Goodman, came from eastern Europe, and his father supported the family by working in the stockyards or at a tailoring shop. At the arrangement of his father, Goodman and two of his brothers received musical training at a local synagogue. Goodman moved on to Jane Addams's Hull House, where he studied clarinet with band director James Sylvester. Franz Schoepp, a classically trained clarinetist, taught Goodman for two years. A superior teacher, Schoepp gave Goodman an excellent technical foundation and a serious attitude toward musicianship.

In 1921, Goodman's imitation of Ted Lewis, a vaudeville clarinetist, at the Central Park Theater in Chicago launched his career. The next year, while a student at Harrison High School, he played with the Austin High School Gang, a group including Jimmy McPartland, Bud Freeman, Frank Teschemacher, and Dave Tough, who had attended the same Chicago high school and were inspired by older New Orleans jazz musicians. Meanwhile, Goodman listened to King Oliver, Louis Armstrong, and clarinetists like Jimmie Noone.

In 1923, Goodman joined the musicians' union; the same year, he met cornetist Bix Beiderbecke. Beiderbecke's lyricism and quiet understatement helped shape Goodman's style. In 1925, Goodman joined Ben Pollack's band in Los Angeles and returned with the group to Chicago in 1926, the year he recorded his first solo, "He's the Last Word." In 1928, the band went to Manhattan. Goodman remained with Pollack until 1929, when he decided to settle in New York City. He established himself as a session musician, working for radio and recording studios and on Broadway. He played in orchestras for *Strike Up the Band* and *Girl Crazy,* two George Gershwin shows, and he met John Hammond and pianist Teddy Wilson, both central to his later success. In 1941, Goodman married Hammond's sister, Alice.

In 1934, with Hammond's encouragement, Goodman formed his first big band. He was booked at Billy Rose's new Music Hall and later that year was featured on the NBC radio series "Let's Dance." Drummer Gene Krupa joined the band, and at the urging of Hammond, Goodman hired Fletcher Henderson as arranger. High performance standards, unusual for the time, were evident in the broadcasts.

A 1935 jam session led Goodman to invite Wilson to record with Krupa and himself. As the Benny Goodman Trio, they recorded four songs. Goodman's solo on "After You've Gone" displays both his dazzling technique and his always disciplined presentation. After a discouraging tour sponsored by MCA, Goodman played in what he thought would be his final band performance on August 21, 1935, at the Palomar Ballroom in Los Angeles. The huge crowd, however, electrified by the music, roared its approval. The performance excited the public and the critics and ushered in the swing era. Goodman was toasted as the "King of Swing," and from 1936 until the early 1940s, the popular Goodman band dominated the market.

At the time of Goodman's big band triumphs, he experimented with smaller ensembles. A trio or quartet was featured in big band performances and pioneered the public appearance of racially mixed band members. The quartet—Goodman, Krupa, Wilson, and Lionel Hampton (who played vibraphone)—made musical history.

In the late 1930s, Goodman explored classical music, initially at Hammond's instigation. Hammond, who played viola, put together a string group and with Goodman played Wolfgang Amadeus Mozart's *Clarinet Quintet.* Goodman's interest grew, and he began study with Reginald Kell, the reigning classical clarinetist. Goodman went on to appear with major American orchestras and to record works by Leonard Bernstein, Claude Debussy, and Igor Stravinsky. He contributed to the repertory by commissioning pieces for clarinet from Bela Bartok in 1938, Aaron Copland in 1947, and Paul Hindemith also in 1947.

Goodman's illness in the early 1940s forced the band to dissolve. Later the same year, however, he re-formed it and began to play more modern arrangements. Eventually, Goodman hired bebop musicians like Fats Navarro and Charlie Christian, but he never really embraced the new style.

For 30 years, Goodman toured the world, appeared in films like *A Song Is Born* (1948), recorded, and even held a repeat Carnegie Hall concert in 1978 to mark the 30th anniversary of his first concert there in 1948. A film biography, *The Benny Goodman Story,* appeared in 1955, and Goodman received a Kennedy Center Honors award in 1982. Goodman died in New York City on June 13, 1986.

References and Further Reading

Collier, James L. 1989. *Benny Goodman and the Swing Era.* New York: Oxford University Press.

Kappler, F., and G. Simon. 1979. *Giants of Jazz: Benny Goodman.* New York: Time-Life.

Schuller, Gunther. 1989. *The Swing Era: The Development of Jazz, 1930–1945.* New York: Oxford University Press.

Harlem Riot (1935)

On March 19, 1935, an African American teenager named Lino Rivera attempted to steal a knife from the Kress store on 125th Street. Store employees confronted Rivera, who bit one of them in a scuffle. The employees took him to the basement and a woman in the store believed they were going to kill him. Because one of the employees called an ambulance for his injured hand and a hearse was parked near the store, other shoppers and bystanders assumed Rivera had been killed, even though the manager told the crowd that he had been released. The local police arrested the woman who had originally spread the rumor of Rivera's death.

Later that day, a crowd gathered at the store to protest the treatment of Rivera. They picketed the store and a few men attempted to make speeches as the police tried to disperse the crowd, which had begun to smash the windows at the Kress store. Around this time, a group called the Young Liberators and the Young Communist League both circulated leaflets stating that a 12-year-old boy had been brutally beaten and urged sympathizers to organize and protest the treatment of African Americans. As the night progressed, thousands of people destroyed commercial property and looted stores around Harlem's 125th Street neighborhood. Seventy-five people were arrested for rioting and 64 were injured, including 7 policemen.

A 16-year-old boy named Lloyd Hobbs was shot to death by the police.

The local press initially reported that the riot was caused by communist agitators and instigated by criminals and hoodlums. Mayor Fiorello LaGuardia established a committee to study the riot. It was composed of 14 white and African American community leaders, including E. Franklin Frazier, Countee Cullen, and A. Philip Randolph. Committee members read police reports and interviewed hundreds of people who had witnessed or participated in the riot. In March of 1936, the committee submitted its 35,000-word report to Mayor LaGuardia, who did not release it to the public. On July 18, 1936, the *Amsterdam News* published the report in its entirety for the public.

The committee came to different conclusions about the riot than had been initially reported by the press and the police. The report covered many local problems, such as New Deal relief, jobs, housing, education, recreation, health, crime, police brutality, and racism. Many who witnessed the scene at the Kress store reported that the police had ignored requests for information. Because the Great Depression had been especially hard on African Americans in Harlem, this small incident sparked rage among citizens frustrated with discrimination, job losses, and police brutality. Although communists did circulate leaflets, the committee concluded that they could not be blamed for instigating the riot. The report made a final recommendation that in order to prevent future riots, the city of New York needed to respond to the specific needs of Harlem residents: more jobs, better education and housing, and respect from the police and other authorities.

Kathryn Stewart

References and Further Reading

The Complete Report of Mayor LaGuardia's Commission on the Harlem Riot of March 19, 1935. New York: Arno Press. 1969.

Greenberg, Cheryl. 1992. "The Politics of Disorder: Reexamining Harlem's Riots of 1935 and 1943." *Journal of Urban History* 18: 395–441.

Greenberg, Cheryl Lynn. 1991. *"Or Does it Explode?" Black Harlem in the Great Depression.* New York: Oxford University Press.

Hastie, William Henry (1904–76)

A brilliant lawyer, Hastie—for years in the forefront of the fight for Black Civil Rights—had a remarkable career marked by a series of "firsts" for African Americans (as governor of a U.S. territory—Virgin Islands, and as a judge on a U.S. District Court and a Federal Appeals Court).

Born in Knoxville, TN on November 17, 1904, the only child of William H. Hastie, the first African American clerk at the U.S. Pension Bureau, Washington, D.C. (who died while his son was a teenager) and Roberta Childs, a teacher. He was valedictorian (1921) at the segregated, academically oriented DC Dunbar High School.

He graduated Phi Beta Kappa from Amherst in 1925. After teaching at the New Jersey Manual Training and Industrial School for Colored Youth, he attended Harvard Law School on a partial scholarship, became the second black to serve on the law review, earning an LL.B. (1930). Admitted in 1931 to the D.C. bar, he joined the prestigious black law firm Houston and Houston. In addition

to private practice, Hastie taught law at Howard University, and continued his education, earning an S.J.D. from Harvard in 1933.

In the early 1930s Hastie, along with Charles Houston and Howard law student Thurgood Marshall, later both vital figures in the fight for civil rights, became involved in the NAACP's systematic challenges to education segregation (Hastie's cases included attempting to enroll a black student at the University of North Carolina and challenging racial pay discrimination for North Carolina African American teachers). He continued working with the NAACP in litigation even after becoming an Assistant Solicitor in the Interior Department (1933), advising on racial issues, and was a member of the "Black Cabinet."

Hastie married (1933) Alma Syphax, daughter of a black, socially prominent Washington, D.C. family; they ultimately divorced. In 1943 he married Beryl Lockhart, daughter of a wealthy Virgin Islands black family; they had two children (William and Karen).

From 1937 to 1939 Hastie served as a U.S. District Court judge in the Virgin Islands, the first African American appointed to the Federal Bench. In 1939 he became Dean of the Howard University Law School, serving until 1946, taking a leave (1941–43) to serve as a civilian aide to the secretary of war to advise on army dealings with African Americans in the military. Hastie, frustrated by its discriminatory practices and segregationist policies, resigned in protest.

During the 1940s he assisted in the NAACP's fight for legal redress, often with politically left allies. In 1946 he became Virgin Islands governor (the first African American appointed to such a position) and in 1949 was nominated for a judgeship on the U.S. Court of Appeals for the Third Circuit (DE, NJ, PA, Virgin Islands). Confirmed in 1950 after Senate hearings marred by Red-baiting, he became the first African American appointed to a Federal Appeals Count. Hastie served with distinction, and was considered for the Supreme Court appointment. Appointed chief judge in 1968, he retired in 1971 becoming, a senior judge. He suffered a heart attack while playing golf and died at a suburban Philadelphia hospital on April 14, 1976.

Daniel J. Leab

References and Further Reading

Chadbourn, Erika, S, Lynne Hollyer, and Richard McNally, eds. 1984. *William Henry Hastie: An Inventory of His Papers in the Harvard Law School Library.* Cambridge, MA: Manuscript Division, Harvard Law School Library.

Lester, Robert, ed. 2006. *African Americans in the Military: Subject Files of Judge William Hastie, Civilian Aide to the Secretary of War.* Bethesda, MD: microform, compiled by Eric H. Doss. UPA collection from Lexis/Nexis.

McGuire, Phillip. 1988. *He, Too, Spoke for Democracy: Judge Hastie, World War II, and the Black Soldier.* Westport, CT: Greenwood Press.

Ness, Jerry N. 1972. *Oral History Interview with Judge William H. Hastie.* Truman Library and Museum. Available at: http://www.trumanlibrary.org/oralhist/hastie.htm. Accessed September 24, 2009.

Ware, Gilbert. 1984. *William Hastie: Grace Under Pressure.* New York: Oxford University Press.

Holiday, Billie (1915–59)

A jazz original who died too young, Billie Holiday, often called Lady Day, was a

Billie Holiday, often called "Lady Day," was a model for countless singers. Her smoky voice, wonderful melodic lines, emotional quality, and remarkable way with lyrics reflect her admiration for Louis Armstrong, an inspiration she always acknowledged. (Library of Congress)

model for countless singers. Her smoky voice, wonderful melodic lines, emotional quality, and remarkable way with lyrics reflect her admiration for Louis Armstrong, an inspiration she always acknowledged.

Holiday was born Eleanora Fagan in Philadelphia on April 7, 1915, to unmarried teenage parents. Her father, Clarence Holiday, left the family early and in the 1930s played banjo and guitar with the Fletcher Henderson Orchestra in New York. Holiday's harsh, uncertain, tumultuous childhood included suspected rape at the age of 10, time in a Catholic home for girls, four months in a New York Welfare Island state institution, prostitution to support her ailing mother, and little formal schooling. Holiday chose the name "Billie Holiday," taking the name of the silent film star Billie Dove and her father's last name.

In the early 1930s, Holiday began to perform—at a small club in Brooklyn, then at Pod and Jerry's in Harlem. By 1933, she was singing at Monette's, another Harlem club, where producer/critic John Hammond heard her and was struck by "her dignity and sensitive phrasing." Hammond arranged recording sessions for Holiday with Benny Goodman and helped her with bookings at New York clubs. Early recordings like "Your Mother's Son-in-Law" and "Riffin' the Scotch" hint at the unique phrasing and timing that set her apart from many of the singers of the day.

By 1935, Hammond was recording Holiday frequently, often with pianist Teddy Wilson and other expert jazz musicians. Wilson commented, "I had never heard a girl with a sound like Billie's. She could just say 'Hello' or 'Good Morning' and it was a musical experience. And her singing, in a very integral way, was a reflection of her whole psychology, her experience. What you heard when she sang was the very essence of her character."

The next seven years were extraordinarily productive and were to be the peak of Holiday's career. Many recordings, among them "Body and Soul" and "Love Me or Leave Me," included the accompaniments of tenor saxophonist Lester Young, Holiday's friend and musical alter ego, the man who first called her Lady Day. Young's sensitive playing and the accompaniments of Buck Clayton, along with an experienced rhythm section, highlighted and enhanced Holiday's expressiveness and way with words.

Holiday also appeared with Henderson and Jimmie Lunceford and, on occasion, sang with her own bands in New York clubs. In 1937, she joined the Count Basie Orchestra, left after a few months with some ill-feeling, and in 1938, moved on to Artie Shaw's band where she became one of the first black singers to be featured by a white orchestra.

By 1939, Holiday was headliner at Café Society, a racially integrated Greenwich Village club that was fast becoming fashionable. That year, she recorded what was to be a great artistic and commercial success, "Strange Fruit." Words from his own poem were set to a haunting melody by Lewis Allen and performed beautifully and from the heart by Holiday. The early protest song, controversial because of its explosive political content, concerned lynching. Holiday wrote her own still-heartbreaking song of childhood and poverty, "God Bless the Child."

Popular in New York clubs from 1939 to 1943, Holiday appeared in a movie, *New Orleans,* in 1946 with Armstrong and Kid Ory, but her performing career was sabotaged by destructive personal habits. Arrested several times on narcotics charges, her cabaret card was revoked. Cabaret cards, New York police licenses, were required of artists performing where liquor was sold. For 12 years after her 10-month term for drug possession at the Federal Women's Reformatory at Alderson, West Virginia, she was not able to work in New York nightclubs.

From 1944 to 1950, Holiday recorded for Decca, but alcohol and narcotics were destroying her voice and her body. Soon after her last performance in May 1959, she was hospitalized with a kidney ailment. She died on July 17, 1959, not long after being arrested in her hospital bed, perhaps unjustly, on a narcotics charge. She was 44.

According to critic Nat Hentoff, "This was a woman who was as deeply pervasive an influence on jazz singing as Armstrong and Charlie Parker were on jazz instrumental playing."

References and Further Reading

Chilton, John. 1975. *Billie's Blues: The Billie Holiday Story, 1933–1959*. New York: Da Capo Press.

Holiday, Billie, and William Dufty. 1956. *Lady Sings the Blues*. New York: Doubleday.

James, Burnett. 1984. *Billie Holiday*. New York: Hippocrene.

Hughes, (James) Langston (1902–67)

For over five decades, James Langston Hughes, who early on dropped his first name, was a versatile, prolific, innovative, critically acclaimed writer whose poetry, fiction, essays, and plays captured the essence of the black experience in America. Hughes wrote for, and about, men and women struggling for survival and equality from the 1920s through the 1960s, and especially in the 1930s in support of the ideas he set forth was also politically active.

Born February 1, 1902, in Joplin, Missouri, to James Nathaniel Hughes, a bookkeeper, and Carrie Mercer Langston, a teacher, he had a peripatetic childhood living in Colorado and various parts of the Midwest, with diverse surrogate parents while his father and mother searched for employment. By 1915 the son was living in Lincoln, Illinois with his mother who had remarried. He finished grammar school there, and after the family moved to Cleveland, graduated (1920) from Central High School.

After graduation he spent time in Mexico teaching, began his literary career with the publication of well-received free-verse poems (including the now classic "The Negro Speaks of Rivers") in *Opportunity* and *Crisis,* and entered Columbia University in 1921, though he withdrew the following year. For four years, Hughes worked at odd jobs on board ship and abroad, while his verse began to appear in magazines. In 1926, he enrolled at (predominantly black) Lincoln University. By graduation (1929), he had published two volumes of verse: *The Weary Blues* (1926) and *Fine Clothes to the Jew* (1927) evidence Hughes's interest in music as these books took the blues and blues musicians as subjects and incorporated blues lyrics into the structure of the title poem of *The Weary Blues.* Throughout his career, Hughes experimented with verse forms drawn from the lyric structures of blues, bebop, progressive jazz, and gospel, using them in his writing. He regarded music as the most representative element of black culture.

Hughes's poetry earned him notice among the African American cultural movement of the later 1920s known as the Harlem Renaissance, and a patron—the elderly Charlotte Mason, a white woman known as "Godmother," who aided some of the movement's writers and artists. Her support enabled Hughes to finish his first novel, *Not Without Laughter* (about a black boyhood in the Midwest), published in 1930, but they had a traumatic break as his writing became more political in character. As the Great Depression hit, the suffering he witnessed radicalized him. Furthermore, visits to Haiti and Cuba convinced him that the United States had acted as an imperialistic power in the Caribbean. In 1932, he left for the USSR as part of a failed film project about American race relations, and wrote some of his most radical poetry. Hughes's short stories collected in *The Ways of White Folks* (1934) reflect his growing anger and general pessimism about black life in the United States.

Communism attracted him as it did many of his peers because it promised an alternative to a racist America. He was involved with various communist activities, including the agitational John Reed Clubs of the early 1930s, signed a statement (1938) supporting Stalin's purges, and prior to Germany's 1941 invasion of Russia worked with the Party-lining American Peace Mobilization, which, during the Nazi-Soviet Pact, agitated to keep the United States out of World War II. He apparently never officially joined the Party, however. After being called (1953) to testify before Senator Joseph McCarthy's committee, Hughes distanced himself from his radical past; his 1959 collection *Selected Works* ignores his more controversial poetry.

In 1942, he began writing a column for the *Chicago Defender,* an African American weekly (years later shifted to the *New York Post).* He introduced the character of Jesse B. Semple (nicknamed "Simple"), a black, urban workingman whose shrewd, assertive, and lively humor filled the column for 20 years. Hughes eventually published five books based on these columns, beginning with *Simple Speaks His Mind* (1950). Simple was an important voice of racial protest, as well as black affirmation.

Hughes's politics evolved as times changed, but he held fast to a belief in the black popular imagination, and he wrote for the broadest audience possible. The late 1930s saw production of a host of Hughes's plays, including most prominently *Mulatto,* a tragedy about interbreeding among races, which ran on Broadway in 1935 (and was produced as a musical version—*The Barrier*—in 1950). Other Hughes plays produced in those years were *Little Ham* (1935), *Joy to My Soul* (1937), and *The Organizer* (1939). His play *Don't You Want to Be Free?* was the first production of the Harlem Suitcase Theatre, founded by Hughes in 1938. *Street Scene,* originally a play by Elmer Rice (1929), was turned into a musical with lyrics by Hughes and music by Kurt Weill. Opening on Broadway in 1947, it became a great success, ending years of financial insecurity for Hughes and enabling his purchase of a house in Harlem (where he lived until his death). He wrote the books for various of musicals, including *Simply Heavenly* (1957), *Esther* (1957), and *Port Town* (1960). His plays *Black Nativity* (1961) and *Jerico-Jim Crow* (1963) incorporated gospel music.

Ever productive, Hughes wrote volumes of verse, including *Fields of Wonder* (1947) and *One-Way Ticket* (1949). His *Montage of a Dream Deferred* (1951) and *Ask Your Mama* (1961) took their forms from jazz; the latter written for musical accompaniment. *The Panther and the Lash* (1967) reflects Hughes's growing support for the black militants active in the United States during the late 1960s. His other publications included two more collections of short stories, *Laughing to Keep from Crying* (1952) and *Something in Common* (1963); another novel, *Tambourines to Glory* (1958); a history of the NAACP, *Fight for Freedom* (1962); a second volume of autobiography (1956, the first appeared in 1940); and several books of fiction and nonfiction for children.

Hughes never married. His biographers concluded that he was a very closeted homosexual. Hughes's many honors included election (1961) to the National Institute of Arts and Letters as well as honorary doctorates from Lincoln (1943) and Howard (1963) universities. He died May 22, 1967, from complications after abdominal surgery related to prostrate cancer, at the Polyclinic Hospital, New York City.

References and Further Reading

Langston Hughes Papers. James Weldon Johnson Memorial Collection, Beinecke Rare Book & Manuscript Library, Yale University, New Haven, CT.

Hughes, Langson. 1940. *The Big Sea.* New York: Alfred A. Knopf.

Hughes, Langston. 1956. *I Wonder as I Wander.* New York: Rinehart.

Ostrom, Hans. 2002. *A Langston Hughes Encyclopedia.* Westport, CT: Greenwood Press.

Rampersad, Arnold. 1986–88. *The Life of Langston Hughes.* 2nd ed. 2 vols. New York: Oxford University Press.

Rampersad, Arnold, 2002. *The Collected Works of Langston Hughes.* 16 vols. Columbia: University of Missouri Press.

Indian Reorganization Act (1934)

The more than 70 years since the passage of the Indian Reorganization Act (IRA) in 1934 have provided many opportunities for examination of the conventional wisdom is that it was a signal example of federal administrative reforms favorable to American Indians, reversing decades of land alienation and cultural abuses caused by the 1887 Indian Allotment Act. John Collier was Indian commissioner from 1933 to 1945 during President Franklin D. Roosevelt's Democratic administration, and the IRA was Collier's brainchild and the centerpiece of the reforms. Collier, a radical social worker who became an anthropologist, was both a prolific writer and a skilled propagandist. His books, *Indians of the Americas* (1947) and *From Every Zenith* (1962), have been widely read and put the best possible interpretation on the Indian New Deal. Until recently, conventional wisdom has followed Collier's interpretation. The question remains, however, was the IRA truly an Indian agenda, and was it fairly and intelligently applied? In short, how should one evaluate the IRA legacy?

A 20-year appraisal of the IRA took place in conjunction with the annual meeting of the American Anthropological Association in 1953. It included John Collier himself, along with several prominent Indians and anthropologists. When the 50th anniversary of the IRA occurred in 1984, scholars, Indian leaders, and political activists began another reevaluation. The Institute of the American West, for example, held a conference at Sun Valley entitled "Fifty Years Under the Indian Reorganization Act—Indian Self-Rule," in which many notables participated in a series of panels. Both appraisals during these past reevaluations were uniformly positive.

In the past few decades, however, scholars have taken yet another look at the IRA and Collier's administrative reforms. Kenneth Philp's biographical study, *John Collier's Crusade for Indian Reform, 1920–1954,* came out in 1977, and Lawrence Kelly's *The Assault on Assimilation: John Collier and the Origins of Indian Policy Reform* appeared in 1983. Philp generally follows Collier's favorable view of the IRA. Kelly, on the other hand, emphasizes the failure of the IRA legislation as passed by Congress to attain Collier's idealistic reform goals. He also faults the Collier administration for its failure to extend the act's limited benefits to the majority of Indians. Two other scholars who have written major re-evaluations are Graham Taylor and Lawrence Hauptman. They, too, are critical of the Indian New Deal as not being all that it was purported to be. We should also mention Deloria and Lytle who present an insightful analysis of the IRA in *The Nations Within: The Past and Future of American Indian Sovereignty.*

In 1977 the American Indian Policy Review Commission reported its findings to Congress on the economic, social and political conditions of the Indian tribes and nations. Its findings, as Graham Taylor observes, seem to indicate that the twin goals of the IRA (Indian economic development and the restoration of Indian self-determination through a council system of government) have been notable failures of existing Indian policy. As a result, as the Meriam Report found in 1928, American Indians continued to rank at the bottom of virtually every social indicator fifty years later.

New criticism of the IRA incorporates the views of traditional Indians, many of whom opposed the IRA and the Indian New Deal from its very beginnings. The traditional Indian movement has historically struggled to achieve three goals: (1) a viable land base for economic self-sufficiency and nationhood, (2) political self-determination through sovereignty under the treaties, and (3) cultural rights—language, religion, and heritage. John Collier's two aims under the Indian New Deal, on the other hand, were (1) to preserve the Indian people as a "race" and as distinct cultures—which Collier termed "grouphood," and (2) to preserve and develop resources, including land. The means to achieve these goals for Collier were "tribal" organization

and economic incorporation under the IRA. For traditional Indians, however, the means to their goals is for the United States to return to the treaty relationship (treaty federalism), and to recognize the Indian peoples as sovereign with the right to self-determination.

The 1920s: Protest from the Pueblos

The first two decades of the 20th century were particularly onerous for American Indians within the borders of the United States. Not only had the 1887 Indian Allotment Act resulted in reservation land loss and impoverishment, but the government's policy of Americanization and cultural assimilation ushered in a virulent period of ethnocide. One of the worst manifestations was the federal crackdown on Indian religious ceremonies. The pro-assimilationist Indian Rights Association led an attack on "indecent" ceremonies among the Indian Pueblos of the Southwest, and the Board of Indian Commissioners deplored the fact that tribal rituals were still being conducted on many Indian reservations. In its 1918 report, the Board described the Indian dances as evil and a reversion to paganism. On April 26, 1921, Indian Commissioner Charles H. Burke issued Circular 1665 that outlawed the Plains Sun Dance and other traditional religious ceremonies, to be punished by fines or imprisonment. The Native American (peyote) Church also came under attack. This period of Indian policy also saw many other instances of religious abuse.

About the same time that the assault on Indian culture and religion was occurring, Secretary of the Interior Albert B. Fall led an attack on Indian rights through his sponsorship of the Bursum and Indian Omnibus bills in Congress. The former bill would have confirmed white encroachment on 60,000 acres of Pueblo Indian land, while the Omnibus bill sought to individualize remaining tribal assets, including timber, coal and other minerals, thereby ending federal trusteeship responsibility. Fall also attempted to create a national park out of part of the Mescalero Apache Reservation that bordered his Three Rivers ranch that would enhance the value of his own property. When oil was discovered on the Navajo Reservation in 1922, he issued a ruling that opened all executive order reservations to exploration by oil companies under the 1920 General Leasing Act. These were the federal Indian policies that struck at Indian sovereignty, especially in New Mexico, and which led to the protest from the Pueblos and the entry of John Collier as an advocate for Indian rights.

Instead of destroying Native societies and cultures through forced assimilation, John Collier believed in a policy of cultural pluralism and Indian administration through indirect rather than direct U.S. rule. The controversy over the Pueblo land grants (part of a larger struggle against landlessness stemming from allotment) and religious dancing led to the formation of the American Indian Defense Association in May, 1923. Facing criticism from Collier and the Pueblo Indians, New Mexico Democrats and the two-million member General Federation of Women's Clubs, Fall was forced to resign from the Harding administration. He was replaced in 1923 by Dr. Hubert Work, who was described as the last of the frontier commissioners. Secretary Work was under the influence of Christian missionaries and opposed Indian dancing, but he had to back off from former Commissioner Burke's order prohibiting the theocratic Taos and Zuni Pueblos from withdrawing selected Indian youth from Bureau of Indian Affairs schools for traditional religious training.

Despite Collier's advocacy work, the Bureau continued its policy of suppressing Indian religious ceremonies. The issue came to a head during the summer of 1925 at Taos when the Pueblo's officials disciplined two members of the Native American Church for invading traditional religious ceremonies. The Indian Bureau thereupon arrested virtually the entire governing body of Taos Pueblo. Collier's Defense Association provided bail and lawyers, and the All-Pueblo Council swung into action, denouncing the Bureau's effort to destroy Indian self-government. Collier took Pueblo representatives on a tour of Utah and California in the cause of Indian religious freedom and to raise money for its defense. Secretary Work denounced these activities, saying that "propagandists are touring part of the country with a company of dancing and singing Pueblos in full Indian regalia in order to awaken people to the 'crime' in New Mexico. There is no crime in New Mexico." Congressman Scott Leavitt of Montana sponsored a bill drafted by the Bureau that would give Indian superintendents the power to throw any reservation Indian in jail for six months and levy a $100 fine without trial. Because of the work by the Defense Committee the Leavitt bill did not get out of committee.

In 1928, on the eve of the Indian New Deal, a government commission issued a landmark report to Congress, "The Problem of Indian Administration." Collier declared that the Mciram Report, as it was popularly called, had "blasted apart the walls of the dungeon called the Indian affairs system" and constituted a major indictment of the Indian Bureau. The report made it clear that allotment policy had not produced assimilation and was, in fact, an unmitigated disaster judging by any social or economic indicator one could apply. The Indian population had actually decreased since the passage of the 1887 Indian Allotment Act. There were more landless Indians than before; Indian trust lands had decreased in value; family income was as low as $48 per year on some reservations; the annual death rate had increased; and the Indian land base had shrunk from 137 million acres to a mere 47 million. Collier saw horrible material and spiritual decline as a result of the allotment policy.

As the Depression deepened, the Bureau began a retreat from instituting reform, and Congress was less inclined to vote for Indian appropriations. In March, 1932, representatives of 49 Indian tribes petitioned the U.S. Senate, alleging that the Hoover administration had reneged on its promises for Indian reform as recommended in the Meriam Report. After his election in 1932, President Roosevelt received a document signed by more than 600 educators, social workers and other concerned citizens, drawing attention to the extreme situation of the American Indians. The signers asserted that "your administration represents almost a last chance for the Indians."

The Indian New Deal (1933–37)

Harold Ickes, who became FDR's new secretary of the interior, was a Chicago Progressive reformer and former director of the American Indian Defense Association. Collier became commissioner of Indian affairs on April 2, 1933. A cultural pluralist, Collier sought to reverse the policy of forced assimilation and its

detrimental economic exploitation and land dispossession. He still believed in eventual assimilation, but at a slower and more equitable pace and without the loss of community solidarity and Indian values. He proposed that government follow a colonial policy known as indirect administration.

Upon taking office, Collier immediately instituted recovery measures legislated under the "New Deal" FDR administration. He successfully established a separate Civilian Conservation Corps (CCC) for Indians known as Emergency Conservation Work (ECW). The conservation of reservation lands and the training of Indians to utilize their own lands and resources distinguished it from the regular CCC, a jobs program for the unemployed. Before its demise in 1943, the ECW had employed 85,349 enrollees from 71 different reservations with a total of $72 million in appropriations. This Indian CCC was perhaps the most successful of Collier's Indian New Deal reforms, and it was very popular at the grassroots level on the reservations.

Collier initiated many other reform measures as well, all of which became known as the "Indian New Deal." The assimilationist-minded Board of Indian Commissioners was abolished in May, 1933, and by the following August Collier persuaded Ickes to declare a temporary cessation of further Indian land allotments, sale of allotted lands, the issuance of certificates of competency, and similar measures. Of equal importance was the cancellation of debts owed by Indian tribes to the federal government. Because of the debt cancellation and the appropriation of more than $100 million in relief programs, American Indians were able to survive the worst years of the Great Depression and even enjoy a higher standard of living than they had a decade earlier. In some respects, the impact of the Depression in the wider society was already reversing the process of assimilation by driving Indians back to their reservation homelands for economic survival.

Other Indian New Deal reforms included the creation of an Indian Arts and Crafts Board, a reservation court system, and a directive ordering the Indian Service to observe "the fullest constitutional liberty in all matters affecting religion, conscience and culture." The ban against religious dances was lifted, and government repression of Indian languages in Bureau schools was ended. The major accomplishment of the Collier administration, however, was the passage of the Indian Reorganization Act.

Indian Reorganization Act (1934)

In a meeting held at the Cosmos Club in Washington, D.C., in January, 1934, Collier laid out his ideas for a basic piece of legislation to correct the evils of 47 years of allotment policy. To this meeting he had invited representatives from organizations that formed the nucleus of Indian reform: the American Indian Defense Association, Indian Rights Association, National Association on Indian Affairs, American Civil Liberties Union, National Council on American Indians, and the General Federation of Women's Clubs. Later the same month, he tested the waters for his ideas in a circular to reservation superintendents, tribal council members, and individual Indians in a document entitled "Indian Self-Government." Despite the mostly negative replies, Collier nevertheless advanced plans to draft a bill for major Indian reorganization. The primary thrust of Collier's draft legislation was self-government,

a policy that ran directly counter to the previous policy of assimilation. The completed Collier Bill contained 48 pages and 4 major titles, each divided into a number of substantive sections. The final Indian Reorganization Act (IRA) as passed by Congress, on the other hand, omitted important parts of two of Collier's original titles and one title altogether, the one dealing with a proposed Court of Indian Offenses. Although the three remaining titles—self-government, education, and Indian lands—were all substantively reduced in content, they at least made it into the new law.

The bill was signed into law June 18, 1934, as the Wheeler-Howard, or Indian Reorganization Act, but it bore little resemblance to Collier's original bill. Opposition to the Collier Bill came from Indians who favored assimilation, western Congressmen (many of whom were reflecting special interests in their home states containing Indian reservations), missionaries, and Bureau personnel. The powerful Indian Rights Association still favored the melting-pot concept, but hoped that the legislation with its provision for educational training would promote assimilation. Only the section of Title II in the original bill that dealt with education came through relatively unscathed. The act in its final form eliminated four key features of Collier's draft bill: (1) the tribes were denied the right to take over heirship lands; (2) the section setting up a reservation court system was eliminated; (3) social units smaller than the tribe, e.g., local or community level groups, were not empowered, although Alaska Native villages were later included when the IRA was amended in 1936; (4) the section on promoting Indian culture and traditions was deleted.

Self-Government

Title I of the IRA gave Indian tribes the right to organize for the purposes of local self-government and economic enterprise. Collier's bill would have conferred limited self-government on reservation Indian groups or communities, treating them as municipalities, but the final version of the IRA limited this provision to tribal units only. The first step in the process was for a tribal committee to draft a constitution. Then an election would be held to ratify the constitution, with a majority vote of reservation members necessary for adoption. Approval by the secretary of the interior was also required. Congress modified this section of Collier's bill by cutting the annual appropriation for the organization of tribal governments from $500,000 to $250,000.

Deloria and Lytle in *The Nations Within* point out that the self-government provision of the IRA helped to define important powers of Native American political entities. With the support of Collier, after the IRA was passed, a ruling by the Solicitor of the Interior Department found that the powers conferred under the act's self-government provision were inherent in the tribes' and nations' status as domestic, dependent nations. These powers are a tribe's right to adopt its own form of self-government, to determine tribal membership, to regulate the disposition of tribal property, and to proscribe the rules of inheritance on real and personal property.

Tribal Business Corporations

An emphasis on economic development was an important feature of the IRA. Upon receiving a petition from at least one-third of the adult reservation Indians, the Secretary of the Interior could issue a charter of incorporation. When ratified by a majority of reservation members, a Native tribe or nation could then engage in business enterprises. The IRA also established a revolving loan fund of $10 million for economic development. This was twice the amount that Collier had suggested in his original bill.

Education and Employment

The education provisions of Title II were not controversial, and Congress raised the appropriation from Collier's $50,000 to $250,000. Congress, on the other hand, limited the amount to loans rather than outright grants and training was primarily for vocational education. An important clause in Title I waved a civil service requirement for employment in the Indian Service, thus establishing the principle of "Indian preference" in hiring. Omitted from Title II was Collier's draft section declaring that it would be the policy of Congress "to promote the study of Indian civilization, including Indian arts, crafts, skills and traditions," This entire section was struck out. Congress, it would seem, was not interested in promoting the Indian heritage.

Indian Lands

A key part of Title III was the section abolishing the 1887 Indian Allotment (Dawes) Act. Title III also declared it the policy of the United States to undertake a constructive program of Indian land use and economic development, with a pledge to consolidate Indian land holdings into suitable economic units. Two million dollars was set aside annually for land acquisition.

The new law also extended indefinitely the trust period of allotted lands as a protection against loss of Indian lands to non-Natives. Under the previous system, allotted lands were held in trust for 25 years, after which they were vested into the ownership of the Indian allottee. At the same time, however, they became subject to state taxes. As a result, the Indian landowner almost always lost his land because of non-payment of taxes, or else was forced to sell to a non-Indian.

The lands provisions of the Collier Bill were so controversial in the Congressional debate that its original 21 sections were reduced to 8, thus negating many of Collier's plans for significant land reform. The Collier Bill had addressed the land alienation and heirship problems with language ensuring that previously allotted lands would be returned to tribal ownership. In the Collier draft, the secretary of the interior was empowered to compel the sale or transfer of trust allotments to tribal governments, and trust allotments not immediately returned would revert to tribal status upon the death of the landowner. Congress modified this section by making it voluntary rather than compulsory. In addition, the land title would now pass to the heirs and not to the tribe upon the death of the Indian landowner. This dealt a deadly blow to Collier's efforts to consolidate fragmented Indian parcels and return them to the tribal estate.

Under the IRA as passed by Congress, the Bureau of Indian Affairs became a real-estate entity for thousands of Indian heirs possessing an interest in ever smaller pieces of inherited land from an original allotment. Today, the number of heirs to an original 160-acre allotment distributed under the 1887 Allotment Act in many cases exceeds one hundred. Tens of millions of dollars are lost every year to Indian tribes through the Bureau's practice of renting or leasing these un-economical interests in allotted or heirship lands to non-Indian farmers and ranchers at low rates, who then combine the parcels into viable economic units. The heirship problem has continued to become more unmanageable with each passing generation. Because of allotment, which the IRA stopped but did not reverse, 25 reservations have greater non-Indian than Indian populations and 38 have lost at least half of their original reservation land base to non-Indians.

Indian Law and Order

Title IV of the Collier Bill that would have created a Court of Indian Affairs was eliminated entirely from the Indian Reorganization Act. It also would have removed IRA tribes from state jurisdiction in Indian cases, heirship cases, and appeals from tribal courts. Title IV also stipulated that law and order must be consonant with Indian customs and traditions. Although the then existing tribal court system needed significant improvement and stability, and the federal attempt to deal with Indian legal problems was woefully inadequate, Collier realized that it was politic to give up Title IV more or less as a sacrificial lamb to a not-too-friendly Congress.

Voting

Part of the Congressional debate concerned the voting or ratification by the tribes and nations for self-government under the IRA provisions. An early version of the bill merely specified "three-fifths of the Indians on the reservation or territory covered by the charter." The House bill changed this to a simple majority vote. Finally, a supplementary act passed in 1935 resolved the question to "the vote of a majority of those voting."

Collier lost out to Senator Burton Wheeler, a sponsor of the legislation, with respect to the blood quantum legal definition of an American Indian under the IRA legislation. Collier wanted one-fourth "blood," but Wheeler insisted on one-half "blood."

Within a year from the date of passage of the IRA the secretary of the interior was to call for a referendum election on the reservations. Each tribe was to discuss the provisions of the act and then vote on whether to accept or reject it. Senator Wheeler favored a simple majority vote, but Collier managed to insert language that would make the IRA operative on a reservation *unless a majority of the tribal members voted to exclude themselves from the act.* In other words, those adult Indians not voting could be counted as voting for the IRA. In this way, Collier's stratagem resulted in more tribes and nations coming under the IRA than would otherwise have been the case. No matter how small the number of eligible Indians voting in favor of the IRA, by counting the non-votes as "yes," IRA acceptance was virtually assured. A case in point is the Santa Ysabel tribe in California that came under the IRA because 62 eligible tribal members who did not vote were counted as being in favor of adoption. Another example is the vote manipulation that took place on the bitterly divided Hopi Reservation. A plurality of Hopi "progressives" voted for the referenda while a larger number of traditional Hopi "voted" by not voting. The Collier administration nonetheless ruled that the Hopi had voted to accept the IRA. As Kenneth Philp points out in his biography of Collier, at least 17 Native American polities

that voted to reject the IRA were considered as being in favor of it. Collier knew that on many of the reservations the more traditional, full-blood Indians would refuse to participate in the IRA elections, preferring instead to assert their tribal sovereignty under the treaties.

A related feature of the IRA was the provision that allowed a tribe only one chance to either accept or reject it. Any benefits of the new law would be lost forever if a tribe wanted to take a "wait and see" approach.

When administrative manipulation of the voting was exposed, Collier was forced to agree that Congress should amend the IRA. In June, 1935, an amendment was passed that extended the deadline for referenda for another year. It also clarified the voting requirements by stipulating that a majority of those voting would determine whether a tribe accepted the IRA or not. At the same time, a distressing feature of the majority rule amendment was that it also contained a provision that 30 percent of the eligible adult Indian population had to participate in the referendum in order for a majority of "no" votes to reject the act. If the number of voters did not amount to 30 percent, then even an overwhelming number of "no" votes could not result in the IRA being rejected. On the other hand, the same rule did not apply for a tribe voting to accept the IRA. Theoretically, even a one percent voter participation could effect acceptance of the IRA.

Extending and Applying the IRA

Because a number of nations and tribes did not want to participate in certain provisions of the new law, and because of political pressure brought by special-interest groups, a section of the IRA provided for exclusions and modifications.

Congress passed the Alaska Reorganization Act on June 1, 1936, that included Alaska Natives at the village level under the IRA provisions. The original IRA, on the other hand, had limited its provisions to tribes only. Ultimately, 66 Alaskan Native groups adopted constitutions and corporate charters under this law. The Oklahoma Indian Welfare Act was passed in the same month, which included the Indian tribes of that state.

According to the reorganization plan, after a tribe or nation voted to accept the IRA, then it would draw up a constitution and by-laws, submit them to a referendum, have the secretary of the interior certify the results, and then start operating as a corporate tribal council. Of the 181 tribes accepting the Indian Reorganization Act between 1934 and 1945, only 96 adopted a tribal constitution, and only 73 tribes ever received corporate business charters. Seventy-seven tribes with a population of 86,365 members rejected the IRA outright. Several of these were large reservation groups, such as the Klamath Indians of Oregon and the Crow of Montana. An especially bitter blow to Collier was the rejection of the IRA by the Navajo Nation. With 98 percent of the eligible Navajo voting, the tribe rejected the Act by 419 votes. The Navajo had not forgiven the Collier administration for its drastic livestock reduction program on the reservation that had reduced many of the small herding families to destitution.

Councils vs. Communities

Graham Taylor stood alone as the only contemporary critic to raise the question of Native political organization and the nature of Indian communities at the time the IRA went into effect. He believed that the Indian responses to the act differed because each Indian group was at a different point on the assimilation-traditional continuum. There were great differences among the reservations in terms of intermarriage, English literacy, Anglo American education, and acceptance of Christianity. These differences provoked factional strife on most reservations at the time. Many of the mono-lingual, full-blooded, traditional Indians were unfamiliar with parliamentary procedures, their aboriginal political systems having been a council of elders and chiefs acting on the unanimity principle. Consequently, many of the traditionals boycotted the IRA proceedings altogether. For most reservation Indians, the "tribal governments" established under the IRA constitutions were a totally new and unfamiliar form of political organization. At Hopi it was primarily the more acculturated villages on the First Mesa that strongly supported the IRA and drew up the tribal constitution, while the villages on the other mesas, being more traditional, either vacillated or withheld their support.

The misreading by Congress and Collier on the question of Indian social organization defies explanation because many of Collier's closest advisers were anthropologists. Yet Collier and his Applied Anthropology Unit, in pressuring Native American peoples to accept the IRA, neglected the existing social organization of Indian communities, the nature of which varied tremendously from reservation to reservation. Many of the Six Nations Iroquois were still committed to a confederacy based on the clan system; the Choctaw, Cherokee, Chickasaw and Creeks had a history of secular Indian republics; the Shoshones and Paiutes of Nevada, Utah and Wyoming were organized only at the level of the extended family band; the Rio Grande Pueblo societies were settled, agricultural villages run as theocracies; and the full-bloods among the Plains Indians were organized into a complex of band councils under traditional chiefs. If the goals of the Indian reform were cultural preservation and economic self-sufficiency, then it would have made sense for reorganization to be tailored to each specific situation. Instead, the "tribal" governments established under the IRA constitutions were a totally new and unfamiliar level of socio-political organization for many Indian populations.

Evaluation

John Collier continually defended the IRA and the Indian New Deal programs during his tenure as commissioner of Indian affairs. He was forced to appear before Congress several times to justify the reforms, and there were two attempts by Congress to repeal the Act, although both were ultimately unsuccessful. The House Appropriations Committee under-funded IRA programs, and by 1944, the Senate Committee on Indian Affairs had also come to oppose the commissioner and his program of Indian reform. Among the most active Indian opponents of the IRA was the American Indian Federation, which joined forces with American pro-Nazi groups in labeling Collier a communist.

In hindsight one can conclude that the self-government provisions of the IRA, although important, were problematic in their impact on Indian communities, but Collier's most lasting achievement was economic development. Much of the Indian New Deal involved bringing needed resources to economically depressed reservation communities. Collier's economic policies also helped Indians rebuild their badly depleted land base, if only modestly; Indian land holdings increased from 48 to 52 million acres, and almost 1 million acres of surplus land was returned to Native tribes and nations.

Following Collier's resignation in 1945, federal Indian policy became stridently regressive for the next two decades during the termination and relocation policy periods in which the limitations of Indian "self-government"—the relative powerlessness of the tribes under the IRA—became apparent. Federal policy did not improve until the federal War on Poverty in the early 1960s and the resurgence of American Indian activism.

Steve Talbot

References and Further Reading

Deloria, Jr., Vine, and Clifford Lytle M. 1984. *The Nations Within: The Past and Future of American Indian Sovereignty.* New York: Pantheon Books.

Hauptman, Lawrence M. 1984 "The Indian Reorganization Act.," In *The Aggressions of Civilization: Federal Indian Policy Since the 1980s,* ed. Sandra L. Cadwalader, and Vine Deloria, Jr., 131–48. Philadelphia, PA: Temple University Press.

Jorgensen, Joseph G, and Richard O. Clemmer. 1980. "On Washburn's 'On the Trail of the Activist Anthropologist': A Rejoinder to a Reply," *The Journal of Ethnic Studies* 8 (2): 85–94.

Kelly, Lawrence C. 1983. *The Assault on Assimilation: John Collier and the Origins of Indian Policy Reform.* Albuquerque: University of New Mexico Press.

Philp, Kenneth R. 1977. *John Collier's Crusade for Indian Reform, 1920–1954.* Tucson: University of Arizona Press.

Taylor, Graham D. 1980. *The New Deal and American Indian Tribalism: The Administration of the Indian Reorganization Act, 1934–45.* Lincoln: University of Nebraska Press.

Jeffries, Herb (1911–   )

The band vocalist and actor Herb Jeffries became popular during the 1930s starring as Herbert Jeffrey in low budget Westerns advertised as "all colored pictures" made by white producers and directors for African-American audiences, and shown primarily in segregated theatres.

Herbert Jeffries was born Umberto Alejandro Ballentino on September 24, 1911 (some sources say 1913) in Detroit to an Irish mother and a father (who he never knew) of mixed ancestry. He chose "to be black" in order to get a job with an African-American music group at a time when segregation was the order of the day in the music world. He became well known as a vocalist with various big bands and was a popular singer when he was tapped to play a "singing cowboy" named Bob Blake in a series of all-black Western films.

The westerns were made during a period when there was racial segregation at most movie theatres in the U.S. As a result some independent companies had made cheaply-produced all-black films for African-American audiences. Among those produced during the 1930s were the Jeffries westerns. The first in which Jeffries appeared was HARLEM ON THE PRAIRIE (1937), also known as BAD-MAN OF HARLEM. He played a black cowboy who aids a former outlaw turned traveling medicine show proprietor whose daughter is threatened by one time partners who want stolen gold believed to be still in his possession. Playing one of the hero's sidekicks in the film was the comedian Mantan Moreland, who later achieved some fame in the Charlie Chan films.

Jeffries playing under the name Herbert Jeffrey followed up this film with three more all-black Westerns: TWO GUN MAN FROM HARLEM (1938), THE BRONZE BUCKAROO (1939), and HARLEM RIDES THE RANGE (1939). As before in each of these they followed a standard formula for such films: he plays a singing cowboy who aids a damsel in distress in various situations, aided by comic relief sidekicks, who help him to overcome a stock villain. Although these films were popular with African Americans, some commentators felt that the white creators were exploiting their black performers and felt that the roles played by Jeffries and other blacks helped to reinforce the racial stereotypes found so often in mainstream American films.

In 1942 his recording of "Flamingo" with the Duke Ellington Orchestra was a hit. After serving in World War II Jeffries lived in France for some years (where for a time he owned a night club in which he performed) before returning to the U.S. in the 1950s. During the 1960s and 1970s he acted in various TV shows. In 1995 he recorded an album THE BRONZE BUCK-AROO RIDES AGAIN on the Warner Western label. The following year he was a recipient of a Golden Boot award for his contribution to the Western genre, and in 2004 he was inducted into the Western Performers Hall of Fame at the National Cowboy and Western Heritage Museum in Oklahoma City. His 1930s westerns are often screened on the Turner Classic Movies channel series celebrating black film performers.

Among his five wives was Tempest Storm, the fabled burlesque dancer. AMS Pictures has produced (2008) a 45 minute documentary A COLORED LIFE: THE HERB JEFFRIES STORY

Daniel J. Leab

References and Further Reading

HARLEM ON THE PRAIRIE, THE BRONZE BUCKEROO, HARLEM RIDES THE RANGE, TWO GUN MAN FROM HARLEM in Patricia King Hanson, et xl, eds, *The American Film Institute Catalog of Motion Pictures Produced in the United States: Feature Films, 1931–1940*, Berkeley, et al: University of California Press, 1993.

Gary Brumbrough, "Herb Jeffries," IMDb (International Motion Picture Data Base).

Noah Arceneaux, "The Western Films of Herb Jeffries: the Man who brought Color to the Western," *Filmfax,* April-May, 2003, 70–78.

Kaplan, Mordecai (1881–1983)

A prominent New York rabbi and educator, Kaplan founded the Reconstructionist Judaism movement which he wanted to be a separate religious denomination. From the 1930s he was a major influence on thought in New York, and his ideas have been condemned or praised by many critics.

Mordecai Menahem Kaplan was born on June 11, 1881, at Swenziany in Lithuania, then a part of the Russian Empire. When he was eight his parents Israel and Anna Kaplan migrated to the United States with their family, and Kaplan grew up in New York, attending the College of the City of New York and Columbia University, and then becoming a rabbi at the Jewish Theological Seminary in New York in 1902. Soon he was one of the major forces in the creation of the Young Israel movement of Modern Orthodox Judaism, and was also a co-founder of the Society for the Advancement of Judaism.

Influenced by the philosophy of John Dewey, Kaplan was drawn to Dewey's ideas of using religious terminology along with atheistic beliefs which allowed those who had lost faith in mainstream religious teachings to follow philosophical beliefs. Essentially Kaplan felt that God was the sum of natural processes rather than a personal being. This rapidly led to criticism of him by mainstream Jewish thinkers in Young Israel and other bodies who condemned him as a heretic, and eventually started ostracizing him.

From 1909 until 1932, Kaplan was principal of the Teachers Institute of the Jewish Theological Seminary of America, and was then dean from 1931 until 1946. He was also professor of homiletics at the Rabbinical School of the Jewish Theological Seminary of America from 1910 until 1947, and professor of philosophies of religion from 1947 until his retirement in 1963. Five years later, with his son-in-law and closest "disciple" Ira Eisenstein, he founded the Reconstructionist Rabbinical College where Reconstructionist Judaism was formerly presented as a different religious denomination.

Kaplan was also the editor of the *Jewish Reconstructionist Papers* in 1936, and author of a number of books including *The Future of the American Jew* (1948), *A New Zionism* (1955), *Questions Jews Ask* (1956); *Judaism as a Civilization: Toward a Reconstruction of American Jewish Life* (1957); *Judaism without Supernaturalism* (1958); *The Greater Judaism in the Making* (1960), and *The Meaning of God in Modern Jewish Religion* (1962). Rabbi Kaplan married his first wife Lena Rubin in 1908, and they had four children. She died in 1958 and he married Rivkah Rieger. He died on November 8, 1983.

Justin Corfield

References and Further Reading

Alpert, Rebecca T., and Jacob J. Staub. 1985. *Exploring Judaism: A Reconstructionist*

Approach. Wyncote, PA: Reconstructionist Press.

Kaplan, Mordecai M. 1957. *Judaism as a Civilization: Toward a Reconstruction of American Jewish Life.* Philadelphia, PA: Jewish Publication Society.

Kaplan, Mordecai M. 1962. *The Meaning of God in Modern Jewish Religion.* Detroit, MI: Wayne State University Press.

Ledbetter, Huddie
(1885–1949)

The great bluesman Huddie William Ledbetter, better known as "Leadbelly", wandered the South and honed his solo style doing time in prison. His moving songs employed echoes of African music in improvised laments that sang of the hard times he knew all too well.

Born near the Texas border in Mooringsport, Louisiana on January 21, 1885, Leadbelly grew up on a backwoods farm in the Lake Caddo district. His father, Wes, was a hardbitten, hardworking sharecropper who with great effort had bought his own land. His mother, Sally, half Cherokee, worked with her husband to clear the land and work the soil and to grow and harvest cotton.

Leadbelly was, by his own account, a formidable farmhand, but he liked good times and had an ear for music. As a teenager he went to the local country dances, called sooky jumps, and began to perform on Saturday nights. His uncle taught him to play the accordion, and on his own he picked up guitar, mandolin, harmonica, and piano. He was big, strong, short-tempered, and lethal in a fight. After his second child was born out of wedlock, he was forced out of the area.

Fanin Street, the red-light district of Shreveport, attracted the rebel, and it

The great bluesman Huddie William Ledbetter, better known as "Lead Belly," honed his solo style doing time in prison. His moving songs employed echoes of African music in improvised laments that sang of the hard times he knew all too well. (Library of Congress/American Memory; The Charles L. Todd and Robert Sonkin Migrant Worker Collection, 1940–41)

was there he first heard the barrelhouse blues that inspired his rhythmic, strumming guitar style. He moved on to the black section of Dallas, where he met rural blues singer Blind Lemon Jefferson and adopted some of Jefferson's songs, including "Match Box Blues" and "C. C. Rider." During the Texas years Leadbelly took up the 12-string guitar.

Leadbelly courted trouble. He gambled, womanized, drank, and brawled. In 1917, he killed a man and in 1918, under the name of Walter Boyd, was sentenced to 30 years in the Huntsville, Alabama prison. His release in 1925 is said to have come about after he asked for a pardon in a song he improvised when Texas governor Pat Neff visited the prison.

In 1930, he ran afoul of the law again. Convicted of assault, he was sentenced to 10 years in the state prison at Angola, Louisiana. Folklorists John Lomax and Alan Lomax discovered him there in 1934 and recorded him. According to legend, another plea for pardon, recorded by Lomax, was delivered to O. K. Allen, the governor of Louisiana, who released him. But, according to jazz writer Leonard Feather, the discharge was routine.

Leadbelly recorded additional folk songs and blues for Lomax and, with Lomax as his manager, toured the Northeast. Leadbelly married, settled in New York City, and continued to record blues, ballads, spirituals, prison work songs, country dance tunes, and cowboy songs for John and Alan Lomax for the Library of Congress.

Though he served a year for assault starting in 1939 in a New York prison, New York City and Leadbelly were compatible. Jazz, its roots in the blues, was in the air, and jazz lovers admired Leadbelly as a blues singer. The folk revival movement of the late 1930s and early 1940s embraced his music, too, especially protest songs like "Scottsboro Boys." He performed in nightclubs, singing and playing his guitar, often sliding a knife on the strings to produce voicelike sounds. Among his best-known songs recorded commercially in the 1940s are "Goodnight Irene," "Rock Island Line," and "Good Morning Blues." Gradually, however, he fell out of favor with audiences. In 1949, shortly before his death, he sang in Paris. At the end of the year, poor and all but forgotten, Leadbelly died in New York's Bellevue Hospital on December 6, 1949.

References and Further Reading

Barlow, William. 1989. *"Looking Up at Down": The Emergence of Blues Culture.* Philadelphia, PA: Temple University Press.

Lomax, John, and Alan Lomax. 1936. *Negro Folk Songs as Sung by Lead Belly: "King of the Twelve-String Guitar Players of the World," Long-time Convict in the Penitentiaries of Texas and Louisiana.* New York: Macmillan.

Louis, Joe (1914–81)

Considered one of the best heavyweight boxing champions, the African American Louis held the title longer than anyone else who fought in this division; his career during the 1930s promoted the American Dream of racial unity, national strength, and unlimited opportunity.

Joseph Louis Barrow was born on May 13, 1914, near Lafayette, Alabama, to a tenant family that lived in a one-room shanty. In 1916 his father, Munroe Barrow, was committed to a mental institution. After his death some years later, his wife married Pat Brooks and their family, which now included eight children, moved in 1926 to Detroit, where Louis received a minimal education. Slow of speech, he was placed in a vocational school (leaving at 17), worked at odd jobs, and served as a sparring partner in a local gym from the age of 16. There he learned the rudiments of boxing while working on Ford's assembly line. Although he lost his first fight Louis proved to be a very successful amateur fighter (winning 50 of his 54 amateur fights, 43 by knockouts). He lost the name Barrow by accident, by incorrectly filling out an application, and thereafter was always known as Joe Louis. In April 1934, he won the Amateur Athletic Union light-heavyweight title in St. Louis, and turned professional three months later.

His prowess in the ring brought Louis to the attention of John Roxborough, a black Detroit ghetto numbers king, who joined with Julian Black, a Chicago African American saloon and numbers operator, to sponsor the boxer's professional career. They put Louis in the care of Jack Blackburn, a successful African American lightweight who had gained a reputation as a trainer and, until his 1942 death, would intelligently handle Louis. Recognizing the impact of the color line in 1930s American life, which in boxing had been exacerbated by the attitude and antics of the black champion Jack Johnson that had resulted in outstanding fighters of color being denied title fights, Black and Roxborough set up rules for Louis so he would not seem "uppity," arrogant, or flamboyant: Louis was never to be photographed or filmed alone with a white woman, never to attend a nightclub alone, and never to gloat over a fallen opponent of any color. In public, until his death, Louis almost always acted according to these rules.

With Blackburn guiding him, Louis won a series of fights, earning him the nickname the "Brown Bomber." As a fighter, he was known for his forceful punches, careful footwork, and calm demeanor. Louis's choice of opponents also had great significance in both the boxing world and larger world events. In 1935, he beat former heavyweight champion Primo Carnera, an Italian who for many antifascists was regarded as a symbol of dictator Benito Mussolini. After defeating Carnera, Louis took on several other former heavyweight champions and won all fights but one against German Max Schmeling in June 1936. On June 22, 1937, Louis challenged the world heavyweight championship titleholder James J. Braddock, and knocked him out in the eighth round. Over the next 12 years, he successfully defended his title 25 times; more defenses than any previous champion.

One of Louis's most important fights came on June 22, 1938, when rematched against Schmeling. Louis knocked him out in 124 seconds of the first round, a record unequaled in championship bouts. Schmeling, because of Hitler's boastfulness about the boxer as a model of "racial superiority," had become identified with Nazi racial theories. As world war loomed in the late 1930s, Louis's victories over Carnera and Schmeling buoyed American patriotism. Louis, notwithstanding his public deference to white society, inspired African Americans (as *Ebony* put it "Joe's victory was their victory, a means of striking back at an oppressive…hateful environment"); his success as a boxer was applauded but he also appeared to be prospering in a white-dominated world. With the second Schmeling bout, in an ironic twist, all of America lavished praise on Louis and his boxing ability, which had become a symbol of opposition to Hitler and Nazi policies.

The proceeds of his title defense before his induction in the army in 1942 went to armed forces relief funds, as did the proceeds from his last title defense until after the war. His army career consisted of morale-boosting visits to military bases and hospitals as well as exhibition bouts whose proceeds went to armed forces relief funds. Between 1942 and 1945 he traveled over 21,000 miles and staged nearly 100 boxing exhibitions before approximately 2,000,000 soldiers. After the war he defended his title four times, retired in 1949, fought and lost in 1950 to Ezzard Charles who had succeeded him as champion, and after a string of unimpressive bouts was knocked out by Rocky Marciano in October 1951. Louis's attempted comeback stemmed from his tax woes (he owed the IRS a million dollars), a tax burden he would be plagued by for much of the rest of his life.

In 1935, he married Marva Trotter, a stenographer from Chicago. She divorced him in 1945, mainly because of Louis's predilection for adultery, which included a torrid affair with Lena Horne. He remarried Marva in 1946; they divorced again in 1949. They had a daughter (Jacqueline, born 1943) and a son (Joe Jr., born 1947), but Louis had little to do with raising them. Louis's 1955 marriage to Rose Morgan, a Harlem beauty shop operator, was annulled in 1958. The next year he married Martha Jefferson, an attorney, who survived him.

His earnings from boxing had been considerable but quickly disappeared through high living, gifts to family and friends, love of gambling, and payment of back taxes. After leaving the ring he tried various careers including wrestling and sports promotion, but suffered from ill health. Toward the end of his life, Louis—who had developed a drug problem—spent much of his time working as a greeter for Caesar's Palace in Las Vegas. He died April 12 1981 of cardiac arrest in Las Vegas, and was buried in Arlington National Cemetery.

Daniel Leab

References and Further Reading

Astor, Gerald. 1974. *"And a Credit to his Race": the Hard Life and Times of Joseph Louis Barrow, a.k.a. Joe Louis.* New York: Saturday Review Press.

Bak, Richard. 1996. *Joe Louis: The Great Black Hope.* Dallas, TX: Taylor Publishing.

Barrow, Joe Louis Jr., and Barbara Munder. 1988. *Joe Louis: 50 Years An American Hero.* New York: McGraw-Hill.

Davis, Lenwood G., compiler, with Marsha L. Moore. 1983. *Joe Louis: A Bibliography of Articles, Books, Pamphlets, Records, and Archival Materials.* Westport, CT: Greenwood Press.

Harding, Robert S. ed. 1987. *Guide to the Julian Black scrapbooks of Joe Louis, 1935–1944,* Washington, DC: Archives Center, National Museum of American History, Smithsonian Institution.

Hietala, Thomas R. 2002. *The Fight of the Century: Jack Johnson, Joe Louis, and the Struggle for Racial Equality.* Armonk, NY: M. E. Sharpe.

Joe Louis, with Edna and Art Rust, Jr. 1978. *Joe Louis, My Life.* New York: Harcourt, Brace, Jovanovich.

Joe Louis. 1953. *The Joe Louis Story.* New York: Grosset & Dunlap.

Joe Louis. *My Life Story.* London: Eldon Press, 1947.

Joe Louis Scrapbooks, 1935–1944. 1986. 304 microfiches, Alexandria, VA: Chadwyck-Healey.

John Roxborough scrapbook of Joe Louis, Michigan Historical Collections, University of Michigan, Ann Arbor, MI.

Margolick, David. 2005. *Beyond Glory: Joe Louis vs. Max Schmeling and a World on the Brink.* New York: Alfred Knopf.

Mead, Chris. 1985. *Champion—Joe Louis, Black Hero in White America.* New York: Scribner.

Nagler, Barney. 1972. *Brown Bomber.* New York: World Publishing Co.

McGowen, Dean. 1981. "Joe Louis, 66, Heavyweight King Who Reigned 12 Years Is Dead," Obituary, *The New York Times* April 13.

March on Washington Movement

In 1941, A. Philip Randolph pushed for an all-black march on Washington to demand equal rights in government positions, in the defense industry and the military. The organizers canceled the march when President Franklin D. Roosevelt issued Executive Order 8802.

The onset of World War II in Europe and the subsequent enforced war preparation created millions of new jobs, especially in the defense industry. This seemed to offer new opportunities for African Americans to improve their status and finally reach full citizenship. Hoping to take part in the economic upswing, African Americans migrated from the South to the new jobs centers. However, blacks met with racism, exclusion and often violence. The situation was not much different in the U.S. Armed Forces where African Americans served in segregated units and were mostly assigned to service units. The federal government tended to ignore the issue or even support racial discrimination.

In contrast to World War I, African Americans were no longer willing to tolerate their underprivileged and oppressed status based on the separate-but-equal premise. They demanded federal and state officials as well as the president intercede and force companies to hire on an equal basis. The NAACP and the National Urban League joined a number of groups that focused on equal rights in employment. They demanded the creation of a committee to scrutinize and investigate racial discrimination. Government officials, however, did not consider it necessary to establish a separate committee to cover race issues.

A Philip Randolph, the president of the Brotherhood of Sleeping Car Porters, believed a mass demonstration in Washington would be the most effective way to address the employment inequities faced by African Americans. His idea for the march was strongly influenced by Ghandian concepts of nonviolent civil disobedience and his labor experience in protest marches and in rallying. Putting massive pressure on the government to demand jobs and equal participation in national defense was the only promising strategy for change. Having petitioned relentlessly, he got frustrated with the reluctance of companies, the government and the American president to make changes.

In January 1941, Randolph founded the March on Washington Movement (MOWM) and called for 10,000 African Americans to join this protest march in Washington, D.C., scheduled for July 1st 1941. Its specific aim was the issuance of an executive order by the president to abolish racial discrimination in the government, military and national defense industry.

The African American community hailed and supported Randolph's call for an African American mass march on Washington. The MOWM made extensive use of the African American press that acted as an important information link between the organizers and the participants in the march. Randolph used his methods of communication and the following he had established during his fight for the Brotherhood of Sleeping Car Porters in the same way. The leading civil rights organizations, the NAACP and the National Urban League, among others, embraced Randolph's plan and joined forces with him, as their appeals to President Roosevelt demanding a reformation of the defense program, had not been crowned with success.

Randolph planned to exclude white supporters from the march, an idea initially met with protest. In an effort to build black self-esteem and community, he wanted the march to be all-black—organized, financed, and carried out solely by blacks. Furthermore, he feared that white communists would infiltrate and co-opt the march, thereby discrediting the event.

The March on Washington Committee, responsible for rallying and organizing, was made up of people from various civil rights movements, churches, and black organizations and acted nationally and locally. They planned the marchers to walk silently behind muffled drums through the city to the Lincoln Memorial. The numbers of people wanting to participate rose rapidly above 10,000. By June, 1941, the organizers expected 100,000 African Americans to participate.

The initial reaction of the government was a demand to call off the march, arguing that it would only stir racial hatred. The unwillingness of the organizers to comply with the president's request and the rising numbers of African American willing to participate started to concern government officials, and President Roosevelt sent his wife Eleanor, along with Fiorello LaGuardia, the mayor of New York, to talk with and appease Randolph and White on June 13th. They were unsuccessful in convincing the organizers to call off their march.

On June 19, 1941, the president finally met personally with Randolph and White. They informed Roosevelt that 100,000 people were planning to march and that only the issuance of an executive order to ban all racial discrimination in the war industries and armed forces could prevent the march and satisfy the African American community. Despite serious reservations within the government, Roosevelt acquiesced at least partially to the demands of the MOWM. On June 25, 1941, Roosevelt issued Executive Order 8802 that prohibited employment discrimination on the basis of race, creed, color, or national origin in federal agencies and war-related industries. The order established the Federal Employment Practices Committee (FEPC) to monitor employment in defense industries and government agencies. Roosevelt, however, was not willing to end segregation in the military. To the dismay of many of his followers, Randolph called off the march on Washington.

Cancellation of the march notwithstanding, Randolph continued his March on Washington Movement, organizing local rallies and marches to protest race discrimination. However, most established civil rights movements no longer supported Randolph, but criticized him for his methods. Despite this fall from grace, his MOWM and Randolph's methods were the paragon for the March on Washington in 1963.

Christine Knauer

References and Further Reading

Barber, Lucy G. 2002. *Marching on Washington: The Forging of an American Political Tradition.* Berkeley: University of California Press.

Bracey, John H. Jr., and August Meier. 1991. "Allies or Adversaries? The NAACP, A. Philip Randolph and the 1941 March on Washington," *Georgia Historical Quarterly* 75: 1–17.

Garfinkel, Herbert. 1959. *When Negroes March: The March on Washington Movement in the Organizational Politics for FEPC.* Glencoe, IL: Free Press.

Pfeffer, Paula F. 1990. *A Philip Randolph, Pioneer of the Civil Rights Movement.* Baton Rouge: Louisiana State University Press.

Sitkoff, Harvard. 1971. "Racial Militancy and Interracial Violence in the Second World War," *The Journal of American History* 58: 661–81.

Wynn, Neil A. 1976. *The Afro-American and the Second World War.* New York: Holmes & Meier Publishers.

Migrant Agricultural Labor

Migrant agricultural labor seized unprecedented public concern during the Depression, when close to half a million land-owning or tenant farm families were dispossessed, roaming the highways in search of work. Those from Oklahoma and Arkansas were epitomized in John Steinbeck's novels *The Grapes of Wrath* and *In Dubious Battle*. But many sectors of American agriculture relied on transient labor from the late 19th century. In 1910, of 10,250,000 unskilled workers in the United States, at least 3,500,000 were migratory, including field hands, lumberjacks, oil field workers, and miners.

America's western wheat fields relied on migrant labor from the 1870s. The Agricultural Workers Organization 400 of the Industrial Workers of the World, from 1915 through 1919, represented a workforce decades old. Wheat farmers with as little as 100 acres might need five to seven extra hands to bring in the crop; migrants rolled from Texas north to the Canadian Prairie Provinces with the advancing harvest. Then there was corn husking in Iowa or Nebraska and potato picking in Minnesota. Tractors and mechanical harvesters, introduced as early as 1909, phased out the need for migrant harvest hands in these crops after 1920.

Mechanization turned cotton farm families in the south out on the road in the 1930s. In the eight states producing most of the country's cotton in 1935, a majority of the 2.1 million farmers were share-croppers (537,000) or other tenants (800,000). A cotton farm of 2,500 acres, which had 24 tenants, could be worked by 1937 with only 6 tenants due to mechanization. Anywhere from three to nine families were displaced by one tractor. Reduction of cotton acreage under the Agricultural Adjustment Act (AAA) created further incentives to eliminate sharecroppers, while payments to reduce acreage provided funds for mechanization. Expanding industry might have absorbed displaced agricultural workers, but during the Depression thousands of industrial workers were already unemployed. Tenant farmers became migrants seeking temporary work of the kind familiar to them. Fewer than 16,000 westbound migrants came from the dryland wheat farms of the Dust Bowl, extending from the Kansas-Colorado border to the Texas panhandle.

... To the California Line

California agriculture, with 45,000 orange and lemon trees bearing fruit by 1870, employed several ethnically defined migrant work forces long before the Depression. When the transcontinental railroad was completed, Chinese laborers found work during harvest season, settling the rest of the year in urban centers such as San Francisco. Japanese laborers were imported in the 1890s to work in sugar beets. Both became less available due to the Chinese Exclusion Act of 1882, California's Alien Land Act of 1913, and 1924 restrictions on Japanese immigration. Need for seasonal labor grew by at least 80 percent from 1909 to 1936, as acreage was shifted to more labor-intensive crops; planting of grapes, apples, and peaches doubled, while orange production rose from 14.4 million boxes to 35 million. By 1920, over 50 percent of farm laborers in California migrated from Mexico, some returning home, others settling in the barrios of Los Angeles and San Diego. Most remaining jobs were held by Filipinos. As Mexican and Filipino workers demanded higher wages, state authorities sought to repatriate as many as possible, and California growers were receptive to a new, less established, work force.

From July 1935 through December 1939, 350,000 heads of families seeking manual employment were counted at border check stations entering California by auto. Others arriving by bus, passenger trains, and freight trains were not counted; most of these were single transients. Checks in 1936–37 on the race of 202,000 families migrating into the state showed 187,000 classified as "white," 8,000 "Mexican," 3,000 "Negro," 2,800 "Filipino" and 1,300 "other." The net migration of 1.2 million into California 1930–40, over two thirds after 1935, was smaller, but more destitute, than 1920–30.

Between 1932 and 1937, cotton production in California and Arizona rose from 236,000 bales to 919,000, drawing people experienced in growing and harvesting cotton. However, cotton acreage was reduced by the AAA in the late 1930s in California to one half the 1937 total. Population increases of 40 to 50 percent

was observed in the cotton-growing counties of California. A California State Chamber of Commerce committee on "the Migrant Problem" observed in 1940 "the group as a whole does not possess unsatisfactory work habits," but "they are probably accustomed to a slightly slower tempo of work than is expected in California," having been "tenant farmers who were masters of their own time." Some migrants found their way north to Oregon and Washington, where up until the 1920s most farm families picked and packed their own fruit, or hired migratory Native American pickers.

Uneven distribution of Farm Security Administration subsistence grants may have sustained migration into the late 1930s. In 1938, only two percent of total grant money went to the states of Oklahoma, Texas, Arkansas, and Missouri, although these states contained

Sharecropper family from Oklahoma arrives in California, 1935. Photo by Dorothea Lange. (Library of Congress)

18 percent of the farm population. North Dakota and South Dakota, with 2.3 percent of the farm population, received as much as 55 percent of the FSA money. In 1939, the four states contributing most of California's incoming migrants received 12 percent, and the Dakotas' share went down to 34 percent.

While advocates for migrant workers, such as Paul S. Taylor, his wife, photographer Dorothea Lange, and Carey McWilliams, sought to solve problems of California agriculture by forging a class-conscious work force, many of the migrants simply wanted 60 acres of land to work for themselves, "and so do away with a lot of relief." A study of social attitudes among migrants turned up the suggestion to "set a man up back East on a little piece of land and say to him, 'Now work or starve'." It was the landowning system in California, with its foundation in the Spanish period and continued under American rule, that displaced family farmers found alien. Those called "farmers" in California seemed "just holders of the farm and the other man does the labor."

Deep in the Heart of Texas . . .

Migratory labor appeared in Texas in new cotton growing regions between the 1870s and 1920s; large farms in the high plains, lower Rio Grande valley, the area around Corpus Christi, and El Paso, did not rely on tenants as east Texas cotton growers did. Mechanization reduced the need for labor prior to the harvest, which remained a labor-intensive job done by hand; more workers were needed than could be employed locally year-round. After 1920, thousands of acres were also planted in citrus fruits and vegetables for shipment north and east. These crops required large amounts of labor during peak seasons, provided by migrating families, primarily Mexican, moving across the state.

Of 103,393 Mexican-born people living in the United States in 1900, 68 percent lived in Texas. By 1930, the national total was 639,017, of which 41 percent lived in Texas. In the 1920s, a Mexican family was estimated to need 287 pesos a month to live, but a bread-winner for a family of five often made 35–36 pesos a month, less than $17 in U.S. currency. By comparison, $1.75 a day picking cotton in Texas looked very good. As late as 1929, migration statistics suggested that 90 percent of Mexican laborers went back and forth across the border from homes in Mexico to seasonal jobs in Texas. By the 1930s, the migrant workers referred to as "Mexican" included citizens of both the United States and Mexico.

Growers preferred Mexican workers; the hard physical labor in a hot climate, dry or humid, was not attractive even during the Depression, while newly arrived Mexicans would work for low wages. Racial prejudice added a peculiar twist: Ruth Allen wrote in the University of Texas Bulletin No. 3134, The Labor of Women in the Production of Cotton, "one of the factors that is making the Mexican a welcome laborer in some sections of the State is that the American landowner and his wife dislike to see 'white people living that way' ". Cross-border migration came to a near-halt during the Depression, but a large pool of migrants remained in Texas for the work still available.

The Works Progress Administration sponsored a study of Mexican workers living in the Crystal City area in 1938. It found that local employment was available in the spinach fields from late November until the end of March. Most then left to work in sugar beet fields in other states, while some migrated to Texas onion fields for April and May work, or chopped cotton around Corpus Christi, then during summer and fall picked cotton in various parts of the state. From 1925 into the 1930s, Mexicans experienced in cotton picking were sent by train to Mississippi. From the early 1920s, and continuing through the 1930s, sugar beet growers and processors in the Rocky Mountain and midwestern states began recruiting migrant labor from Texas. As horses were replaced with tractors between 1915 and 1935, larger acreage could be planted by a small permanent work force, but a large number of temporary laborers were required for hoeing and harvest. Until the immigration quotas of the early 1920s, this industry had relied on "unassimilated immigrants," Spanish Americans, German Russians, middle-Europeans, Orientals, some coming seasonally from nearby cities.

As early as 1923, the Texas Bureau of Labor Statistics began opening free employment offices to regulate the flow of migrant labor, and eliminate exploitive private employment agencies. In 1928, these offices were closed, in favor of the Farm Placement Service of the federal Department of Labor. In 1930, FPS placed 369,000 cotton pickers, 12,000 cotton choppers, and 26,800 fruit and vegetable workers. After the Wagner-Payser Act delegated this responsibility to states in 1933, with matching federal funds, Texas established the State Employment Service in 1935. Farm wages in Texas dropped sharply during the Depression, often by 40 to 50 percent. Farm prices fell by 50 percent, and demand for labor dropped, as farmers tried to limit expenses, or simply reduced planting, while unemployed industrial workers came out to agricultural regions looking for work. In a miniature of the migration to California, tenant farmers from eastern Texas displaced by AAA looked for jobs in western Texas.

... Them Guv'ment Camps ...

The most significant government program to assist migrants was a series of camps providing temporary housing. Camps provided by growers were characteristically crowded and unsanitary, having perhaps one hose for water, lacking hot water, and providing few if any bathing facilities. Where available, government camps provided a respite from being driven down the road by the enforcement of vagrancy laws, as rural communities dependent on migrant labor were unable to provide for workers during periods of unemployment. They also made migrants less dependent on grower good will for a place to stay—if an employer paid too little, a family breadwinner could turn down the job and go someplace else. "At the gov'ment camp, I is a free citizen." This very fact led many growers to propose that camps be located on their property, under their control, with low-interest government loans paying for construction. Lee A. Stone, county health officer for Madera County, presented this position to a California Conference on Housing of Migrant Agricultural Laborers in November 1935.

The first camp in Marysville, California, was constructed in 1935 with funds from the Federal Emergency Relief Administration. The same year, responsibility was transferred to the Resettlement Administration. Camps were opened at Arvin in Kern County (Weed Patch), Indio, Calipatria, Firebaugh, Schafter, Tulare, Thornton, Visalia, and Woodville. Efforts were made to develop a democratic self-governing community, with written constitutions, under the benign direction of a camp manager, who in fact had ultimate decision-making power. Participation in elected camp councils varied; Conrad C. Reibold wrote that the Firebaugh Camp, which he managed, could not fill council vacancies. Tom Collins, the first manager of both the Marysville and Weed Patch camps, proclaimed that the camps "will make available for the farmers of the State of California, contented, clean and willing workers." In 1938, the Farm Security Administration began plans for camps in Texas. Facilities offering "the barest minimum of decent living facilities" were established by 1941 at Raymondville, Robstown, Sinton, Weslaco, Harlingen, McAllen, Crystal City, Princeton, and Lamesa, housing 1,119 families, a tiny fraction of the migrant work force.

Migrant workers formed unions in many places, but these seldom lasted more than a few years. The CIO's United Cannery, Agricultural, Packing and Allied Workers of America was active in both California and Texas, while the independent Asociacion de Jornaleros in Laredo, TX, became the Agricultural (Federal) Labor Union 20212 (AFL), followed by Fruit and Vegetable Workers Union Local 20363 in the lower Rio Grande valley. The last major piece of New Deal legislation, the Fair Labor Standards Act of 1938, excluded agricultural workers from its protection. World War II absorbed large numbers of migrant laborers (particularly native-born white Americans) into industry, but some extended families from Oklahoma stayed on the road picking crops into the 1980s. Selective Service took many men temporarily out of the labor market. In 1942, the government initiated the first in a series of programs contracting for labor from Mexico to work in agriculture, while growers in Texas and California encouraged a growing stream of illegal immigrants, commonly known as "wetbacks"—by 1950 the number crossing the border may have been one million a year.

Charles Rosenberg

References and Further Reading

Coalson, George O. 1977. *The Development of the Migratory Farm Labor System in Texas: 1900–1954.* San Francisco: R and E Research Associates.

Conrad, David E. 1965. *The Forgotten Farmer: The Story of Sharecroppers in the New Deal.* Urbana: University of Illinois Press.

Daniel, Cletus. 1981. *Bitter Harvest: A History of California Farmworkers 1870–1941.* Ithaca, NY: Cornell University Press.

Dubofsky, Melvyn, and Stephen Burwood, eds. 1990. *Agriculture during the Great Depression.* New York: Garland.

Foley, Neil. 1997. *The White Scourge: Mexicans, Blacks, and Poor Whites in Texas Cotton Culture.* Berkeley: University of California Press.

Renshaw, Patrick. 1999. *The Wobblies: The Story of the IWW and Syndicalism in the United States.* Chicago: Ivan R. Dee.

Robinson, Harold S. 1940. *Report of the California State Chamber of Commerce Statewide Committee on the Migrant Problem.* California State Chamber of Commerce.

Shindo, Charles J. 1997. *Dust Bowl Migrants in the American Imagination.* Lawrence: University Press of Kansas.

Mitchell, Arthur W. (1883–1968)

The first African American to be elected to the U.S. Congress as a Democrat, Arthur Wergs Mitchell was born on December 22, 1883, near Lafayette, Chambers

County, Alabama, the son of ex-slaves, both of whom were born in Alabama. When he was 14 he left home to go to Tuskegee Institute, Alabama, and while he was there he worked on a nearby farm, and then also as an office boy for Booker T. Washington. After leaving the Tuskegee Institute, he went to Columbia University for a short period before continuing his studies at Harvard University, and at Wilberforce University, Ohio.

Mitchell started teaching at a number of schools in rural Alabama, and then founded and became president of the Armstrong Agricultural School in West Butler, Choctaw County, Alabama. He was listed as president of the school when he was registered for the draft in World War I. Admitted to the bar in Washington D.C., he practiced law for 10 years, and he became involved in real estate. Moving to Chicago, Illinois, Mitchell practiced law there, and initially started working for the Republican Party, being in the state from where Abraham Lincoln, the first Republican president, came. However, he gradually found his views more and more closely aligned to the Democratic Party of Franklin D. Roosevelt.

In 1934 Mitchell defeated African American Republican congressman Oscar de Priest and was elected to the U.S. House of Representatives for the 1st congressional district of Illinois. In Congress he introduced civil rights bills against lynching and to remove discrimination. He also filed lawsuits against the Illinois Central and Rock Island Railroads after he was forced to sit in a segregated train carriage as it was about to pass through Arkansas. The court reached the U.S. Supreme Court which ruled that the railroad company had violated the Interstate Commerce Act.

Although he was reelected in 1936, 1938, and 1940, in 1942 Mitchell decided not to stand for reelection, and resumed his law practice. He also spent much of the rest of his life campaigning for civil rights, giving many public lectures. He retired to Petersburg, Dinwiddie County, Virginia and farmed twelve acres there, known as the "Land of a Thousand Roses." He had married Annie Harris, also from Alabama, and they had one son, Arthur, born in about 1916 in Georgia. Arthur Mitchell died on May 9, 1968, and was buried on his property.

Justin Corfield

References and Further Reading

Biographical Directory of the United States Congress 1774–2005. 2005. Washington, DC: U.S. Government Printing Office.

Garraty, John A., and Carnes, Mark C., eds. 1999. *American National Biography*. New York: Oxford University Press.

National Association for the Advancement of Colored People (NAACP)

There are many social historians who suggested that the concept for the National Association for the Advancement of Colored People (NAACP) was envisioned soon after Booker T. Washington completed his 1895 Atlanta Exposition Speech, where he called on African Americans to accommodate themselves to the racially divided circumstances in the United States. Washington and his Tuskegee Machine, a political network, was the dominant voice and the interpreter of African American people at the turn of the century. He suggested that African Americans lived segregated lives and developed themselves socially and economically through self-help programs while waiting for white America's political system to gradually accept them.

However, in general, most experts agree that the NAACP owes its existence to the political movements of the Niagara Movement, a group of black intellectuals led by W.E.B. Du Bois, William Monroe Trotter, and a small body of white "neo-abolitionists," many of whom were descendants of those who led the antebellum fight against slavery and were distressed by the lost of legal rights and the social status of African Americans.

The Niagara Movement, organized in 1905, was the first significant alliance for black protest in the 20th century and represented the attempt of a small, but articulate group of "radicals" to challenge the accommodation theories of Booker T. Washington. It developed after several failed attempts at reconciling the two factions of benevolence and hostility into American political life. The Niagara Movement was the actual precursor to the NAACP. The organization was adamant in its opposition to Washington's accommodation theories, as well as its commitment to civil equality; however, the organization survived only a few years of existence.

It was the race riot in Springfield, Illinois, in August 1908 that caught the attention of William English Walling (1877–1936), a white socialist, who called for citizens to come to the assistance of African Americans and to fight for racial equality. The St. Louis Riot also caught the attention of Mary White Ovington (1865–1952), a white journalist and social worker from a well-to-do abolitionist family. Ovington contacted Dr. Henry

Moskowitz (1879–1936), a New York labor reformer and social worker. These three professionals are considered the principal founders of the NAACP. Others who joined them were Oswald Garrison Villard (1852–1949), grandson of the abolitionist William Lloyd Garrison and newspaper publisher, and Charles Edward Russell (1860–1941), a socialist, whose father was an abolitionist editor of a newspaper in Iowa.

Ovington also invited two prominent African American clergymen, Bishop Alexander Walters of the African Methodist Zion Church and Minister William Henry Brooks, of the St. Mark's Methodist Episcopal Church, both of New York. Together, the group issued a call for a conference in New York on February 12, 1909 (Abraham Lincoln's one hundredth birthday). Sixty people, seven of whom were African Americans, heeded the call, including W.E.B. Du Bois, Rev. Francis Grimke (1852–1937), Mary Church Terrell (1863–1954), and Ida B. Wells (1862–1931). As a result of the solicitation, the National Negro Conference met at the Charity Organization Hall in New York City on May 31 and June 1, 1909. The Conference created the National Committee for the Advancement of the Negro, or the Committee of Forty, a permanent organization to develop plans for an effective confederation to address "the needs of the Negro." The Committee's plans were implemented, as well as the organization's permanent name, the National Association for the Advancement of Colored People. The NAACP was organized as a small, elite confederation, which would rely on agitation and legal action against racial discrimination. The organization chose to include the phrase "colored people" in its title to emphasize the broad and anti-imperialist concerns of it founders.

In its first year, the new NAACP launched programs to increase the industrial opportunities for African Americans and to obtain a greater protection for them in the South, by crusading against lynching and other forms of violence. Throughout the early years, the NAACP devoted most of it resources to seeking an end to lynching and other forms of mob violence through press publicity, campaigns, as well as with pamphlets, in-depth studies, and other educational activities. The NAACP received its first substantial publicity with a protest campaign in Coatsville, Pennsylvania in 1911, held after a lynching.

When the NAACP hired W.E.B. Du Bois as director of publications and research, it was considered one of its most important acts. It was his visionary ideas and "militant" programs that were regarded as major contributions to the association. In 1910, Du Bois initiated the Crisis Magazine, which mixed political articles with works by African Americans writers, poets and artists, which soon became an instrument of the "black" freedom struggle. By 1912, the NAACP had created branches in Boston, Massachusetts, Baltimore, Maryland, Detroit, Michigan, Indianapolis, Indiana, St. Louis, Missouri, and Quincy, Illinois. The following year, other branches were created in Chicago, Illinois, Kansas City, Missouri, Tacoma, Washington, and Washington, D.C. Membership in the organization was contingent upon acceptance of its philosophy and programs.

During the early days, the national staff of the NAACP was largely white, while the local branches were heavily African American. Whites had the financial resources to devote themselves to the NAACP. Whites had the education, the administrative experience, and the access to money that was required to build the organization. Despite the early contribution of white activists, African Americans became increasing uneasy about their control of an organization that was meant for African Americans. The problem of white control caused considerable conflict between white and black members. At the base of the difficulty was that the organization gave the appearances of inferiority or subservience and the fear that whites would refuse to aid an African American affiliation and would compromise the NAACP's integrationist program.

Recognizing the problem, the whites acknowledged the difficulties of having white leadership, but felt it was a necessary evil until African Americans had sufficient resources to run the organization without assistance. It wasn't until 1916 when the NAACP brought another black person to the board—that was James Weldon Johnson, a writer for the New York Age, noted for his tenacity as a field operative.

There were a number of significant events during the NAACP's early years that helped define the organization. The first was the NAACP's 10-year protest campaign for the withdrawal of D. W. Griffith's bigoted film *The Birth of a Nation,* in 1915. The NAACP charged that the film assassinated the character of African Americans and undermined the very basis of the struggle for racial equality. The death of Booker T. Washington and the end of the effective opposition by advocates of accommodation with the South's Jim Crow policies, as well as, World War I, which set the NAACP on its primary mission—to fight the legal and political course against racial violence.

The strengthening of the branch structure highlighted the influence of the

NAACP. Initially, the progress was slow, but by the end of 1919, the association had 310 branches, including 31 branches in the South. The NAACP's total membership jumped from 9,000 in 1917 to 91,000 in 1919. With the development of the NAACP, it signaled the rising influence of paid African American staffers within the organization.

During the next decade—the "the New Negro Era,"—the NAACP made it clear that its reliance on agitation and education was found to be ineffective against racial violence. Walter White gave a report on the 30 years of lynching in the United States, which eventually led to laws to combat the crime, but both Presidents Coolidge and Harding blocked legislation during their administrations. There was criticism that the organization was too involved in legalism and there was not enough support for self-defensive efforts against racial violence. Additionally, there was a strong rivalry with Marcus Garvey's Universal Negro Improvement Association. Garvey belittled the interracial and integrationist philosophy, of the Association and its white/light-skinned, middle-class leadership, while the NAACP viewed Garvey's Back to Africa Movement as chauvinistic and overly visionary.

In the 1930s, James Weldon Johnson retired from the NAACP and Walter White replaced him. White hired Roy Wilkins, manager of the Kansas City Call newspaper, as his assistant. It started during the 1920s and 1930s with 325 branches, located in every state except Maine, New Hampshire, Vermont, Idaho and North Dakota. The branches served as information centers for the national office and stimulated the cultural life of African Americans. In the early part of the century, the NAACP had significant success winning court cases, particularly in housing segregation, and the reversal of death penalty cases. The acquittal of Dr. Ossian Sweet of Detroit, battles over the "White Primaries," and the "Scottsboro Boys," became a part of its legacy. The core of the NAACP's struggle for the passage of antiviolence and civil rights laws waged through much of the 1940s.

As a continuation to block passage of civil rights laws, the NAACP in the 1950s continued to concentrate its efforts in the courts. It took decisive efforts to end the "separate by equal doctrine" particularly, in the cases of *Sweatt vs. Painter* and *McLaurin vs. Oklahoma,* but its landmark case occurred on May 17, 1954, with the *Brown vs. Board of Education.* This school desegregation case was its "crowning glory."

The NAACP was challenged in the 1960s by a new generation of more militant activists, who took the position of "direct action," as opposed to legal and political agitation. The new challengers used "sit downs/ins," most notably, the North Carolina Agricultural and Technical College (NCA&T) lunch counter protest. It was this protest that propelled sit-ins across the country in the 1960s.

Following the NAACP's forced desegregation of the University of Florida, in 1958, it filed similar lawsuits again the University of Georgia, in 1961 and the University of Mississippi, in 1962. It also lobbied for a meaningful civil rights law, in 1963, as well as a national fair employment practice law. The network was also instrumental in organizing the March on Washington and the Civil Rights Act of 1964, which was followed by the 1965 Voting Rights Act and its extension in 1970.

By the early 1970s, the NAACP faced new and more difficult problems than in the past. The problem centered on "systemic discrimination," which was more difficult to identify than state-imposed segregation and required new strategies. Its initial challenge came with the designing and implementing a conviction for affirmative action.

The election of Ronald Regan as president in 1980 came at a time when the NAACP was groping for new programs for new challenges. The Reagan administration was blamed for destroying the effectiveness of the United States Civil Rights Commission, the Civil Rights Division of the Justice Department, and the Equal Employment Commission. In 1984, clergyman and president of the NAACP Benjamin Hooks led a massive march on Washington to protest the "legal lynching" of civil rights by the Regan Administration.

The nineties saw the retirement of Benjamin Hooks as the NAACP's Executive Director. The NAACP's Board of Directors selected Reverend Benjamin F. Chavis, an official of the United Church of Christ to replace Hooks. Because he was much younger than his predecessor, Chavis was chosen to revitalize the NAACP by finding new funding sources and to reach out to young African Americans; however, Chavis was criticized by the NAACP's "old guard" for reaching out to black radicals, such as Minister Louis Farrakhan. As a consequence, the membership of the NAACP fell dramatically. Chavis also angered board members with his unauthorized policy implementation and as a consequence he was supplanted by Kweisi Mfume, in 1996, who remained president and CEO of the NAACP until his recent retirement in January, 2006.

The NAACP began the 21st century by taking another long stride toward fulfilling its mission of fighting for the rights of minorities. It worked to be recognized by the United Nations as a nongovernmental organization (NGO). NGO status would allow the NAACP to be a consultant to the United Nation, proposing items for the agenda of the world organization and making presentations to its members. This expanded status and role was an example of the expanding focus the NAACP acquired under the leadership of former U.S. Congressman. In 2002, the NAACP monitored elections in the African nation of Zimbabwe, and Africa became an increased focus of the organization's activity. Also, in 2002, Mfume met with Fidel Castro, Cuban officials, and Cuban dissidents in an effort to promote human rights in Cuba and expand trade between that nation and the United States. In 2003, the NAACP began working on issues concerning the Caribbean and Latin America.

Mfume received credit for fixing the NAACP's mid-1990s substantial deficit, and expanding the organization's global efforts, but Mfume also received criticism for the failure to bring "new life" to the organization, as well as maintaining the tradition of boycotts, marches, and fund-raising reminiscent of the 1960s, but out-of-date in today's political atmosphere. By today's standards, there is a strong feeling that NAACP has "lost its way," and has contributed little in the way of "fresh thinking" in its continued battle for civil rights and economic programs. In recent years, despite its past brilliancy, criticism of the NAACP has generally increased. Critics have said that the biggest need for this proud organization is for it to bring a new and more motivated membership to the affiliation, not just to expand its stagnant numbers and inadequate budget, but also to reach out to black youth, who are largely ignored. Expositors also suggest that the NAACP should help close the distance between the black middle class and the black poor, as well as black conservatives and traditional liberals. The NAACP has the challenge of representing a more pluralistic African American community.

As evidence of the need to increase its membership, the NAACP's 500,000 constituency is no larger today than it was in the 1940s, when the modern civil rights movement was just getting under way. Yet, the African American population in the United States has more than doubled since then to approximately 36 million. According to its records, the NAACP has an average spending year in the amount of $27 million, which is said to be grossly inadequate, particularly in wake of the following social indicators—African Americans are still twice as likely as whites to be unemployed, and three times as likely to be poor. The incomes of African Americans still trail the national average and they graduated from college at only half the rate of whites.

Analysts continue to suggest that the key to growth and change for the NAACP is the youth. Only 14 percent of the NAACP members are under 25, whereas most members are over 40. The NAACP's ties to its cultural leaders is said to be weaker than in the past. Years ago celebrities appeared at NAACP events to help boost the cause. While this is still true to a large degree, there are plenty of high-profile sports and entertainment figures who could help mobilize young people, if the organization made the effort to reach out to them. With more influence, the NAACP could tackle more issues, perhaps to slow the tide of the black high school drop-out rate or find a way to stop the joblessness in the African American community or help to boost home ownership, the chief source of wealth in America. Only 48 percent of African Americans own their homes, while the rate of home ownership for whites is over 75 percent. Several factors explain this difference, including the poor credit scores and below average wages and discrimination of African Americans, all factors that have or will eventually affect young people.

Today, there are 2,200 local offices with branches in Germany, Japan and South Korea and the suggestion is that there is a need for more innovative thinking to help solve some of the problems in the African American community and to help restore the luster of the NAACP to keep it in forefront of civil rights organizations. No one expects the NAACP or like organizations to solve all of African Americans' problems, but fresh leadership and creative thinking could go a long way toward invigorating black achievement, improving the nation along the way.

Fred Lindsey

References and Further Reading

Guterl, Matthew Pratt. 2001. *The Color of Race in America, 1900–1940.* Cambridge, MA: Harvard University Press.

Kellogg, Charles. 1967. *NAACP: A History of the National Association for the Advancement of Colored People.* Baltimore, MD: John Hopkins University Press.

Rhym, Darren. 2002. *The NAACP.* White Plains, NY: Chelsea House.

"How the NAACP Could Get Its Clout Back. 2005." *Business Week* February 21.

Weldon, Carolyn. 1998. *Inheritors of the Spirit: Mary White Ovington and the Founding of the NAACP.* New York: John Wiley Press.

National Council of Negro Women (NCNW)

The National Council of Negro Women (NCNW), founded on December 5, 1935, became the first umbrella organization to consolidate the power of all black women's groups to more effectively gain action from national government. NCNW founder, Mary McLeod Bethune, as past president of the National Association of Colored Women (NACW), saw women's potential for organizing and fundraising. In 1929, she invited organizations to meet and form a national council dedicated to African American women's issues, as white women had earlier done through the National Council of Women. Twenty-nine women representing 14 organizations attended the founding meeting at the 137th Street Branch of the YWCA in Harlem. Debate ensued, leaving the NACW leadership split on the value of the new organization. Supporters, including Mary Church Terrell, Dr. Dorothy Ferebee, and Charlotte Hawkins Brown, selected Bethune as the first president.

Bethune used her friendship with Eleanor Roosevelt to gain assistance from the federal government on race issues. Bethune, as the head of the Division of Negro Affairs at the National Youth Administration (1936–43), viewed racial inclusion as a means to influence policy. Bethune helped organize the Federal Council on Negro Affairs (informally called the Black Cabinet), which brought more managers and administrators into Washington, D.C. She used this power base to advance the rights of black women. By 1937, the NCNW gained public attention from the National Conference on the Problems of the Negro and Negro Youth held at the Labor Department. In 1938,

more recognition came with the Conference on Governmental Cooperation in the Approach to the Problems of Negro Women and Children, held at the Department of the Interior. These conferences created public recognition of the NCNW and brought its leaders into direct discussions with government officials.

Under Bethune, the NCNW grew in members, structure, and recognition, developed a full-time paid staff, and purchased a national headquarters building in 1943. The NCNW became the clearinghouse for information related to black women and race issues and disseminated this information through its publication, *Aframerican Woman's Journal.* During World War II, the NCNW campaigned for integration of the military and for admission of black women into the Women's Army Corps (WACS). NCNW sponsorship resulted in the *S.S. Harriet Tubman,* the first ship to honor a black woman. Bethune represented the NCNW as an advisor to the United States delegation at the founding conference of the United Nations in 1945. By 1949, the NCNW represented 22 national organizations including sororities, professional associations, occupational societies, women's auxiliaries, denominational groups, and clubs.

Well-qualified and dedicated women followed Bethune. Dorothy Boulding Ferebee (1949–53) and Vivian Carter Mason (1953–57) continued the direction of the NCNW. Dorothy Irene Height (1957–98) created a professional staff capable of program delivery and won tax-exempt status in 1966 enabling the NCNW to gain grants and contributions for its programs addressing youth, health, employment, hunger, civil rights, international relations, and family life. Growth in membership through affiliation progressed through the years from 500,000 in the 1930s to four million by the 1980s. Government agencies recognized the NCNW as the predominant national organization, hence, reinforcing the organization's representative power.

Collaboration and coalition building remain. Dorothy Height continues as president emerita and chair following her retirement in 1998. The NCNW belief in commitment, unity and self-reliance appears in their current promotion of financial security, health issues, achievement, and recognition of African American women leaders.

Dorothy Salem

References and Further Reading

Collier-Thomas, Bettye. 1981. *N.C.N.W., 1935–1980*. Washington, DC: National Council of Negro Women.

Height, Dorothy I. 2003. *Open Wide the Freedom Gates: A Memoir*. New York: Public Affairs.

Jesse Owens at the start of his record-breaking 200 meter race at the 1936 Olympic Games in Berlin. The grandson of a slave, Owens won four gold medals in track and field at the summer games. (Library of Congress)

Owens, Jesse (1913–80)

Jesse Owens was among the finest athletes ever born in the United States. A track and field star at an early age, Owens smashed record after record at the 1936 Olympic Games in Berlin, where Nazi leader Adolf Hitler's claims of Aryan superiority were shown to be laughable. Owens was a hero to many Americans, but particularly to African Americans.

James Cleveland Owens was born on September 12, 1913, on a tenant farm in Danville, Alabama, one of seven children. Before the family moved to Cleveland, when Owens was still a boy, they all worked in the cotton fields. In Cleveland,

Owens attended a local grade school and then entered Fairview Junior High, where he tried out for the track team. The coach was amazed when Owens set a new national junior high school record by running the 100-yard dash in 10 seconds flat.

After Fairview, Owens attended Cleveland's East Technical High School, during which he competed in the 1933 National Interscholastic Championships at the University of Chicago. He stunned everyone at the meet by winning the 100-yard dash with a time of 9.4 seconds, the 220-yard dash in 20.7 seconds, and the long jump with a record-setting leap of 24 feet, 9-5/8 inches.

As a college freshman at Ohio State University, Owens paid for school with jobs as a gas station attendant and as a page in the state House of Representatives. As a student, he was particularly interested in ceramics and wanted someday to teach at a black college. He started practicing track again in 1934 under Coach Larry Snyder and achieved even better times and distances, earning the nicknames "Brown Bombshell" and "Buckeye Bullet."

At the National Collegiate Athletic Association track and field championships hosted by the University of Michigan in 1935, Owens brought the crowd to its feet. Within 45 minutes, he broke three world records and tied a fourth by running the 100-yard dash again in 9.4 seconds, running the 220-yard in 20.3 seconds, running the 220-yard low hurdles in 22.6 seconds, and long jumping 26 feet, 8-1/4 inches.

In 1936, Owens competed in the Berlin Olympics as a member of the U.S. team. As Hitler and his cronies extolled the virtues of Aryan blood, Owens won his first two Olympic gold medals and established new world records in the 100- and 200-meter sprints (10.3 seconds and 20.7 seconds, respectively). After German long jump champion Lutz Long set an Olympic record with his jump of 25 feet, 5-27/32 inches, Owen set a world record with his leap of 26 feet, 5-5/16 inches.

Following the event, Long strolled around with his arm around Owens's shoulders while Hitler waited to congratulate his Aryan champion. The image became a lasting one for the 1936 Games as the world prepared for war. Owens also set a new world record at the Olympics as a member of the U.S. 400-meter relay team, which ran the event in 39.8 seconds, but his long jump record would stand untouched for the next 25 years.

Exhausted by his efforts at the Olympics, Owens received a hero's welcome when he returned to the United States. However, the Amateur Athletic Union suspended him when, with his coach's consent, he passed up a scheduled exhibition tour of Sweden. Later in 1936, Owens announced that he was going to begin a new career as a professional entertainer and soon was appearing in a tap-dancing act with Bill Robinson. He gave political speeches to support the presidential campaign of Alf Landon, and with the income he made from other such jobs, he had enough by the end of the year to buy a big house for his parents in Cleveland. In 1937, Owens earned his bachelor's degree from Ohio State and continued his eclectic career in show business.

From 1936 to 1939, Owens led a swing orchestra, won a sprint against a race horse in Cuba, and played a detective in a Hollywood movie. Toward the end of that period, he began to turn his attention to establishing himself in the business world. To that end, he started his own dry-cleaning shop, worked for the Cleveland Parks Department, and was a salesperson for a distilling corporation. In the summer of 1939, however, Owens ran into financial trouble when the dry-cleaning business went under and he lost $40,000 in investments on the stock market.

Bankrupt, Owens was forced to get a regular job. From 1940 to 1942, he worked in the Office of Civil Defense in Philadelphia as national director of physical education for African Americans. Until 1946, with a short break for military service, he worked at the Ford Motor Company as director of African American personnel and then became director of sales and sports for Detroit's Leo Rose sporting goods company. That year, he also became co-owner of a black baseball club in Portland, Oregon and the leader of an African American touring basketball team. The latter job gave Owens another chance to be in the public eye, which he loved.

In 1949, Owens gained some renewed public interest when *Ebony* magazine's sportswriters dubbed him one of the 10 "greatest Negro athletes of all time," and in January 1950, the Associated Press sportswriters named him the world's "top track performer since 1900." While he appreciated the honors, he still had to pay the bills. Owens moved from Detroit to Chicago, where he continued his career as a sales executive and did a great deal of work for organizations supporting young athletes. He went to Berlin in 1951 at the invitation of the U.S. Army and the U.S. high commissioner; he appeared with the Harlem Globetrotters in the Olympic Stadium and urged an audience of 70,000 Germans to "stand fast with us for freedom and democracy."

After returning to the United States, Owens accepted a post as secretary of the Illinois Athletic Commission in 1952 but resigned in 1955 to do a goodwill tour of India for the Department of State. He donated the modest proceeds he earned from the tour to Indian programs for young athletes. Back in Illinois, he spent the rest of his life organizing sporting events for children and young people. His business exploits included operating a public relations and marketing firm in Chicago and later in Phoenix. He was also somewhat famous as a speaker at business conventions around the country. Starting in 1970, he supported his family with the proceeds from several books he wrote on his experiences as an African American athlete. In 1976, President Gerald Ford awarded Owens the Medal of Freedom. Owens died of lung cancer on March 31, 1980, in Tucson, Arizona.

A decade later, President George Bush posthumously awarded him the Congressional Medal of Honor.

References and Further Reading

Adler, David. 1992. *A Picture Book of Jesse Owens*. New York: Holiday House.

Kaufmann, Mervyn D. 1973. *Jesse Owens*. New York: Crowell.

Owens, Jesse. 1972. *I Have Changed*. New York: Morrow.

Owens, Jesse. 1970. *The Jesse Owens Story*. New York: Putnam.

Owens, Jesse. 1976. *Track and Field*. New York: Atheneum.

Sabin, Francene. 1986. *Jesse Owens: Olympic Hero*. Mahwah, NJ: Troll Associates.

Polier, Justine Wise (1903–87)

Justine Wise Polier was the first woman Justice in the State of New York. Sitting on the bench of the Family Court, she worked to fight for the rights of the poor and disenfranchised. She was born Justine Wise on April 12, 1903, at Portland, Oregon, her father being Rabbi Stephen Wise and her mother being Louise Waterman Wise. Her father, a rabbi, had been a founder of the American Jewish Congress and also the National Association for the Advancement of Colored People, while her mother, an artist and social worker, had been a founder of the Free Synagogue Adoption Committee in 1916.

Growing up in New York, she attended Bryn Mawr, Radcliffe, and Barnard, and in 1925 went to New Haven to attend the Yale Law School where she became the editor of the *Yale Law Review*. She married Leon Arthur Tulin, a professor of criminal law at Yale, in 1926 and they had a son, Stephen. Leon died in 1932 from leukemia. Four years later she married Shad Polier, and they had a daughter and a son.

Although she managed to become an effective lawyer, Justine Tulin became more concerned with social legislation—she had worked at the Elizabeth Peabody Settlement House while attending Radcliffe. Tulin worked as the first woman referee and then the Assistant Corporate Council for the Workmen's Compensation Division. In 1935 she was offered the position as a judge on the Domestic Relations Court, by Fiorello H. LaGuardia. She accepted and became the first woman judge in the State of New York.

An opponent of segregation, Polier, making judgments about the New York school system, did what she could to try to remove a system which she saw as institutionalizing racism. She became active with groups involved in helping the poor, and worked hard with African American community leaders. From 1941 until 1942 she took a leave of absence to serve as Special Council to Eleanor Roosevelt, Office of Civilian Defense. In 1942 she helped with the establishment of Wiltwyck School for Boys. A committed Zionist, she was vice president of the American Jewish Congress and was the president of its women's division. Although she only planned to spend a few years as a judge, Justine Polier saw that she was able to make a real difference to the lives of so many people that she remained as a judge for nearly 40 years, retiring in 1973 and becoming Director of the Juvenile Justice Project of the Children's Defense Fund. She died on July 31, 1987, in New York City. Her book, *Juvenile Justice in Double Jeopardy* was published posthumously in 1988.

Justin Corfield

References and Further Reading

Nadell, Pamela Susan, and Jonathan D. Sarna, eds. 2001. *Women and American Judaism.* Hanover, NH: Brandeis University Press, University Press of New England.

Polier, Justine Wise, and James Waterman Wise, eds. 1956. *The Personal Letters of Stephen Wise.* Boston: Beacon Press.

Poston, Ted (1906–74)

Ted Poston was a journalist and short fiction writer; among the first African American reporters employed by a white daily newspaper. Born Theodore Roosevelt Augustus Major, July 4, 1906, at Hopkinsville, Kentucky, he was one of eight children of Ephraim and Mollie (Cox) Poston, both schoolteachers also involved in publishing a black weekly. The mother died when Ted, as he became known, was 10. He began his journalistic career in his early teens on the family's *Hopkinsville Contender* which, when deemed too controversial in 1921, moved out of state. His older brothers Ulysses and Robert published it occasionally in Detroit before establishing *The New York Contender.* Robert, a militant Garveyite, died in 1924; Ulysses ultimately left journalism to become a real estate broker. Ted Poston studied journalism at Tennessee Agricultural and Industrial College (now Tennessee State University) graduating with a B.A. in 1928.

He moved to New York City to work with Ulysses on the *New York Contender,* but found work as a writer with the Al Smith presidential campaign. Subsequently, while attempting to jump-start his journalism career, he supported himself as a waiter at Harlem's Cotton

Club, a Pullman porter, and a dining car waiter. His freelance efforts included a *Pittsburgh Courier* column "Harlem Shadows" and reporting for the *New York Amsterdam News*. In 1932 he was one of 22 blacks sent to Russia by the Comintern to make a propaganda film about American race relations. The project failed, ending acrimoniously with participants feuding among themselves.

Back in the United States he worked for the *Amsterdam News,* becoming city editor in 1935. Poston became active in the fledgling Newspaper Guild but was fired in 1936 for supporting a strike by its unit against the *News.* After a stint with the Federal Writers' Project he began providing articles on a space-rate basis to the *New York Post* and soon was employed full-time, making him one of the first African American journalists working for a major U.S. newspaper.

In 1940 he took a leave of absence to serve in various government wartime positions—including head of the Office of War Information's Negro Desk. He was also a member of the informal network of African Americans (known as the "Black Cabinet") advising the Roosevelt Administration. Poston, who at the war's end returned to the *Post,* later stressed that his reporting was not limited to racial events (for a time he covered New York's City Hall), but his most dramatic writing dealt with race relations. His coverage of Southern racial unrest won him in 1950 a George Polk Award, the American Newspaper Guild's Heywood Broun Memorial Award, and an award from the Irving Geist Foundation. And over the years, often literally at risk to life and limb, he reported on important events in the civil rights struggle.

Ill health forced his retirement in 1972. Married three times (1935, 1941, 1957), he kept several women on the side. A contributor of short fiction and serious articles to various periodicals, Poston had planned to write more short stories about his Kentucky childhood, some of which had been anthologized. He died on January 11, 1974, in Brooklyn, New York.

Justin Corfield

References and Further Reading

Hauke, Kathleen A. 1999. *Ted Poston: Pioneer American Journalist.* Athens: University of Georgia Press.

Carson, Clayborne, et al, eds. 2003. *American Journalism, 1941–1963,* Part One of *Reporting Civil Rights.* New York: Library of America.

Poston, Ted. 2000. *A First Draft of History,* ed. Kathleen A. Hauke. Athens: University of Georgia Press.

Poston, Ted. 1991. *The Dark Side of Hopkinsville.* ed., ann. Kathleen A. Hauke, Athens: University of Georgia Press.

Randolph, A. Philip (1889–1979)

A. Philip Randolph, in a long life committed to racial justice, won respect for his quiet dignity and his firmness. A union organizer and socialist early in life, he became the country's best-known black trade unionist and a nationally prominent leader in the struggle for civil rights.

Born in the small town of Crescent City in central Florida, on April 15, 1889, Asa Philip Randolph was the second son of a self-educated minister of the African Methodist Episcopal Church, James William Randolph. His mother, Elizabeth Robinson, a strongly religious woman, had married at 13. Both parents were the children of slaves. Two years after Asa Randolph's birth, the family moved to Jacksonville. He attended Methodist-supported schools, including the Cookman Institute from which he graduated in 1907. He worked at odd jobs, acted in amateur dramatics, and gave public readings in the precise diction his father had taught him. The family atmosphere was relatively intellectual. Young Randolph became acquainted not only with Shakespeare and Dickens, but with the writings of Frederick Douglass, Booker T. Washington, and W.E.B. Du Bois.

In 1911, Randolph headed for New York City, washing dishes on a passenger ship to pay his way. He worked at various menial jobs while attending night classes at the City College of New York, where he began reading Marx and became interested in union organizing. In 1914 he married Lucille Campbell Green, a graduate of Howard University, who owned a beauty parlor and shared Randolph's political views. Randolph and his friend Chandler Owen joined the Socialist Party in 1916 and the next year, with Lucille Randolph's backing, founded a socialist journal, The Messenger, which supported the Industrial Workers of the World and opposed the United States entering World War I. Randolph became celebrated for his eloquent speech-making at street-corner rallies, in which he urged blacks not to fight in the war. He was arrested by federal agents on charges of treason, which were dropped.

In the 1920s, Pullman porters—all black Americans, employed on the railway sleeping cars—had to work 400 hours a month for a salary of $67.50 and had no assured rest periods between runs. In 1925, impressed by Randolph's speaking and activism, a group of porters asked him to organize an independent labor union. The Pullman Company had forced them to join a company-controlled union. As he was not a Pullman employee, he could not be fired or harassed by the company. With help from a liberal foundation, the Garland Fund, Randolph organized the Brotherhood of Sleeping Car Porters, which attracted more than 50 percent of the porters as members. In 1928, the Brotherhood joined the American Federation of Labor (AFL). Yet the union had been unable to win recognition from the Pullman Company or the Federal Railway Mediation Board. With the aid of William Green, president of the AFL, Randolph got the Railroad Transportation Act amended to cover the Pullman porters. On August 15, 1937 (the union's 12th anniversary), the Brotherhood and the Pullman Company signed the first contract between an American corporation and a black union. The contract cut the work month by almost half and provided for a significant increase in wages.

Randolph was now an important figure in the emerging civil rights movement. He was named the first president of the National Negro Congress (NNC), which he led until 1940 when he resigned because of supposed communist influence in the organization. In the same year Randolph—with executive secretary of the National Association for the Advancement of Colored People (NAACP), Walter White, and other leaders—met with President Franklin D. Roosevelt to press for integration of the armed forces and the employment of black workers in the defense plants. The president promised that blacks would be eligible for combat duty; segregation, however, would continue. To force an executive order to end discriminatory hiring practices in defense plants, Randolph called for a show of strength:

a massive march on Washington in July 1941. The president vainly attempted to dissuade Randolph and the other black leaders. On July 1, six days before the march was to occur, Roosevelt signed an executive order barring discrimination in defense plants and in government service and creating a temporary Fair Employment Practices Committee. Though integration of the armed forces was not achieved, Randolph called off the march. Some activists accused Randolph of backing down on integration, but thousands of jobs in defense industries were opened up for blacks.

After the war ended, Randolph led in organizing the League for Nonviolent Civil Disobedience Against Military Segregation and again called for a march on Washington. Furthermore, he advised young African Americans to resist the draft. President Harry Truman, who was also concerned about losing the black vote in the next election, issued an executive order in July 1948 banning racial discrimination in the armed forces. Again Randolph called off his campaign, having won his major battle.

Though Randolph's influence waned in the 1950s as younger black leaders came to the fore, he continued his fight against racial discrimination in the labor unions and, in 1957, was elected a vice president of the AFL-CIO. His last confrontation with an American president occurred in 1963, when John F. Kennedy attempted to dissuade black leaders from staging a demonstration for civil rights legislation. Randolph was honorary director of the March on Washington for Jobs and Freedom, on August 28, 1963, when 200,000 people congregated at the Lincoln Memorial, to be addressed by Randolph, Martin Luther King Jr., and other leaders.

The Civil Rights Act of 1964 was passed with the active encouragement of President Lyndon B. Johnson, who that year awarded Randolph the highest civilian honor, the Medal of Freedom. Also in 1964 Randolph established the A. Philip Randolph Institute, under the direction of Bayard Rustin, which pledged among other goals to foster cooperation between organized labor and the black community.

In his last years, Randolph counseled young African Americans to follow his principles of nonviolence and pacifism, not always with success. He died in his apartment in the Chelsea district of New York on May 16, 1979, at the age of 90.

References and Further Reading

Anderson, Jervis. 1973. *A. Philip Randolph: A Biographical Portrait.* New York: Harcourt Brace Jovanovich.

Harris, William H. 1977. *Keeping the Faith: A. Philip Randolph.* Urbana: University of Illinois Press.

Reid, Ira de Augustine (1901–68)

Ira de A. Reid served in the vanguard of black sociologists. As professor, researcher, government consultant and author, he attempted to improve the condition of African Americans, using data that had never before been collected.

Reid received his B.A. in 1922 from Morehouse College, a part of Atlanta University Center. He earned his M.A. from the University of Pittsburgh in 1925, and his Ph.D. from Columbia University in 1939. Reid also held an honorary law degree from Morehouse.

Reid's interests ran parallel to trends at the Chicago School of Sociology, where sociologist Robert Park, who had once assisted Booker T. Washington, was a powerful force. The goal was to collect and analyze data using quantitative methods. This system would develop rich ethnographies which would shed new light on problems in African American culture, leading to creative solutions (Watts 1983, 281–83). This ethic was prominent throughout Reid's career.

Reid served the New York Urban League as industrial secretary from 1924 to 1928; he then became research director of the National Urban League from 1928 to 1934. As national research director, Reid made headlines with statistics showing that 22 trade unions barred black workers from membership, resulting in the exclusion of 225,000 black workers from representation and benefits (Anonymous 1930, 11).

Reid was professor of sociology at Atlanta University from 1934 to 1946. During his academic career, he served the Roosevelt administration as consultant on minorities for the Social Security Board and the War Manpower Commission. At Atlanta University, Reid and W. E. B. Du Bois were colleagues and frequent collaborators in furthering African American scholarship, including the founding of *Phylon: The Clark Atlanta University Review of Race and Culture* (Aptheker 1997, 187–88). As an undergraduate, Martin Luther King Jr. studied sociology with Reid.

Reid published his scholarly books during the 1930s and early 1940s, covering black immigration, labor issues, and urban workers with exhaustive research methods. His best known books include *Negro Membership in American Labor Unions, Adult Education Among Negroes, The Urban Negro Worker in the United States, 1925–1935* (coauthor), *The Negro Immigrant, In a Minor Key: Negro Youth in Story and Fact,* and *Sharecroppers All* (coauthor).

In *Sharecroppers All,* a representative work, Reid and coauthor Arthur Raper documented the economic disparities between the North and the South which led to social problems such as badly underfunded schools. The South's rich national resources, in the authors' view, did not benefit its people proportionately, with the sharecropper the worst off. Reid and Raper saw this as colonialism (Duffus 1941, BR 9).

Reid was appointed visiting professor of Negro culture and education at New York University for 1946–47, the first time an African American had received a full-time faculty appointment there. In 1947, Reid was named professor and chairman of the department of sociology and anthropology at Haverford College, a post he held until 1966. During Reid's academic career, he also taught at Columbia, Pennsylvania State, and Harvard universities. Overseas, he taught in the Virgin Islands, Nigeria, and Tokyo. Reid died in 1967.

Merrill Evans

References and Further Reading

Anonymous. 1930. "Says 22 Unions Bar Negro." *New York Times,* February 20: p. 11.

Aptheker, Herbert, ed. 1997. *The Correspondence of W. E. B. Du Bois: Selections 1934–1944,* Vol. II. Amherst: University of Massachusetts Press.

Duffus, R. L. 1941. "A Grim but Able Study of the American South: Far Too Many People, Say These Southern Authors, Are on a Sharecropper Basis." *New York Times,* Sunday, 2 February: p. BR 9.

Watts, Jerry G. 1983. "On Reconsidering Park, Johnson, DuBois, Frazier and Reid: Reply to Benjamin Bowser's 'The Contribution of Blacks to Sociological Knowledge.'" *Phylon* 44: 273–91.

Robeson, Paul (1898–1976)

Paul Leroy Bustill Robeson, son of a former slave, became an American icon as an athlete, singer, and actor—a beloved figure until the McCarthy era, when he was attacked and ostracized for his outspoken criticism of racial injustice and his close ties with radicalism and the Soviet Union.

Robeson was born on April 9, 1898, in Princeton, New Jersey. He was the youngest of eight children born to the Reverend William Robeson, former pastor of the Witherspoon Street Presbyterian Church, and Anna Bustill. The Reverend Robeson was born a slave on a North Carolina plantation in 1845, escaped at 15, and eventually studied for the ministry. He was forced to resign from the Princeton church in 1901 because of some irregularity in the church's business records, and had to work as a coachman. His wife, a teacher, who belonged to a free Philadelphia family of considerable distinction, died of burns in a household accident when Robeson was six.

Robeson's father moved the family to Somerville and took over a Methodist church. Robeson went to the town's integrated high school, where his baritone voice began to be noticed. An athlete and top student, he won a four-year scholarship to Rutgers University (the state institution), the first of his family to attend a white college. At Rutgers, he was the only African American student. He was popular, an admired orator, Phi Beta Kappa in his junior year, and the leading athlete—he earned 12 varsity letters in four sports and was an All-American football end in 1917 and 1918. In 1919, he received his bachelor's degree with honors and the next year, entered Columbia University Law School.

In 1920, Robeson was persuaded by another student, Eslanda Goode, to take the lead in a play, *Simon the Cyrenian,* at the Harlem YMCA and later at a downtown theater. He and Goode were married in 1921 and went to England, where he performed in another play at a provincial house and had the experience of traveling without worry of Jim Crow laws. Robeson took his law degree at Columbia in 1923 and joined a New York law firm, where he encountered some bias. When the Provincetown Players approached him, he was glad to take leading parts in two plays by Eugene O'Neill at their playhouse in Greenwich Village: *The Emperor Jones* and *All God's Chillun Got Wings.* His performances were widely praised, and in 1925, he repeated the role of Brutus Jones, a black dictator, in London, where his debut was described as triumphal.

In the 1925–26 season, Robeson embarked on his first concert tour in America and abroad, singing spirituals and folk songs. His baritone voice became world famous in concerts and hundreds of recordings. He was able to perform songs in 20 languages. In 1934, he performed concerts in the Soviet Union on his first visit there. Robeson alternated recitals with roles on stage; one of the most famous was as Joe in the musical *Show Boat,* singing "Ol' Man River." His renditions of "Ballad for Americans" and "Joe Hill" were equally famous. Robeson won the greatest honors for his performance in William Shakespeare's *Othello,* which

Scene from *Othello* with Paul Robeson and Uta Hagen as Desdemona, Theatre Guild production, Broadway, 1943–44. (Library of Congress)

he first played in London in 1930, then on the stage in New York during the winter of 1943 and 1944, and then on tour. He played in a number of films and was said to be the first African American actor not to play cinema parts that were racist stereotypes. Robeson said that he did not succeed to his satisfaction in that respect because of the movie industry's attitude toward African Americans, and he gave up working in films.

Robeson became more and more, as he said, a spokesman "against anti-Semitism and against injustices to all minority groups." In the late 1940s, as the cold war gathered force, he became identified with radicalism and was called a communist or a communist sympathizer, though in fact he was never a Communist Party member. A large segment of the public as well as the government turned against him, but he only stated his opinion of the Soviet Union more forcefully. When in 1949 he was to sing at a left-wing music festival in Peekskill, New York, right-wing extremists stopped it by storming the gathering and injuring many people, while the police looked on. The next year, the State Department revoked Robeson's passport and refused to return it unless he signed an oath that he was not a communist. In 1952, the Soviet government's award to him of the Stalin Peace Prize appeared only to confirm what his adversaries claimed. A legal battle over the passport issue went on for eight years, until the U.S. Supreme Court found the government's action in such cases unconstitutional.

In 1958, Robeson gave a farewell concert at Carnegie Hall, made a brief concert tour, recorded one more album, and left the country. While he and his wife moved about in the Soviet Union, Eastern Europe, and London, his health went into decline, and he was often in hospitals. In 1963, after the Robesons returned to the United States, he announced his retirement from the stage and refused press interviews concerning a rumor that he had turned against Marxism. Robeson's wife died in 1965, and he moved to Philadelphia to live with a sister.

On April 15, 1973, shortly after Robeson's 75th birthday, entertainment stars and civil rights leaders organized a birthday salute at Carnegie Hall. Those on the platform included former U.S. attorney general Ramsey Clark; Pete Seeger; and Coretta Scott King, who said that before Martin Luther King Jr., Robeson had "tapped the same wells of latent militancy" among African Americans. The tide of feeling against Robeson was turning. Rutgers University held a symposium on his life, and in 1975, the FBI declared that "no further investigation is warranted." When Robeson died in a Philadelphia hospital on January 23, 1976, after a stroke, the white press praised him as "a great American," but Coretta Scott King deplored "America's inexcusable treatment" of a man who had had "the courage to point out her injustices."

References and Further Reading

Duberman, Martin Bauml. 1988. *Paul Robeson.* New York: Knopf.
Robeson, Paul. 1958. *Here I Stand.* New York: Othello Associates.

Robinson, Bill (Bojangles) (1878–1949)

Both major guilds of tap dancers, The Hoofers and The Copasetics, called Bill "Bojangles" Robinson the greatest tap dancer of all time. He delighted fans as he brilliantly tapped his way from vaudeville to Broadway to Hollywood over a 50-year career that earned new respect for African American dancers.

Robinson was born in Richmond, Virginia on May 25, 1878, and was orphaned before he was eight. He danced in the street for pennies as a child and never had formal dance training. At the age of 12, he began to tour with the show *The South Before the War.*

According to a childhood friend, Robinson came to New York in 1898. He got a job at Minors Theater in the Bowery and later danced at various restaurants; played vaudeville with his partner, George Cooper; and toured abroad. Robinson found his niche in vaudeville and fought his way to the top, becoming one of the few black dancers who performed solo on the Keith Theater circuit. At his peak, he was earning $6,500 a week.

With the help of his agent, Robinson created variety and cabaret acts that played at clubs and on the black theater circuit from the Apollo Theater in New York to the Alcazar in San Francisco. Occasionally, he left vaudeville for Broadway shows.

Blackbirds of 1928, which opened May 9, 1927, made Robinson's name known. It was in that show that "Bojangles, whose Stair Dance was now acclaimed, became the first Negro dancing star on Broadway," according to Marshall Stearns, a writer on music and dance. (According to one source, the nickname means "happy-go-lucky"; another says it suggests "powerful squabbler.")

The musical *Brown Buddies* opened October 7, 1930. Stearns noted how "critic after critic was delighted by the manner in which Bojangles watched his feet: 'He croons with his feet and laughs with them and watches them in wide-eyed amazement,' wrote Richard Lockridge in the *Sun,* 'as they do things which apparently surprise him as much as they do the rest of us.' " Robinson appeared in other Broadway shows, including two based on Gilbert and Sullivan works: *The Hot Mikado* (1939) and *Memphis Bound* (1945).

Not known as a choreographer, Robinson may have interpolated his old acts into new shows and probably introduced earlier routines into films like *From Harlem to Heaven* (1929) and *Stormy Weather* (1943). The latter is known for its fine display of his dance style. In the 1930s, Robinson appeared in four Shirley Temple films, where his dazzling flight-of-stairs routine was recorded.

"Robinson," said Stearns, "invented no new steps; rather, he perfected and presented them....His Stair Dance, up and down a set of steps, with each step reverberating at a different pitch, was the most famous, but he had other favorites." His "contribution to tap dancing is exact and specific: He brought it up on the toes, dancing upright and swinging.... The flat-footed wizardry of [others]... seemed earthbound compared to the tasty steps of Bojangles, who danced with a hitherto-unknown lightness and presence." Robinson died in New York on November 25, 1949.

References and Further Reading

Stearns, M., and J. Stearns. 1979. *The Jazz Dance: The Story of American Vernacular Dance.* New York: Macmillan.

Haskins, James. 1988. *Mr. Bojangles: The Biography of Bill Robinson.* New York: William Morrow.

Scottsboro Case

The Scottsboro case grew out of rape charges filed in March 1931 against nine African Americans (Roy Wright, 12 or 13, Andy Wright 19, Haywood Patterson, 17, Eugene Williams, 13, Clarence Norris, 19, Olen Montgomery, 17, Willie Roberson, 17, Ozzie Powell, 16, and Charles Weems, 19). Hoboing, and in search of employment, they hopped a freight train, got into a fight with some whites, and tossed these youths off the train, one whom complained to a local sheriff. At Paint Rock, in northern Alabama, the authorities boarded the train, found the young African Americans and two white girls of dubious repute (Victoria Price, 19, and Ruby Bates, 17) who claimed that the nine had raped them. The nine, despite their denials, were jailed at Scottsboro, the county seat, where doctors found no evidence of rape after examining the girls. But given the place and its culture, the nine were speedily tried (without proper representation), found

guilty, and sentenced to death, except for Roy Wright—later sentenced to life imprisonment because of his young age.

With the execution date set for July 10, 1931, the case took on amazing dimensions: the National Association for the Advancement of Colored People (NAACP) became involved, as did the International Labor Defense (ILD), a Communist organization. The NAACP and the Communists, who would use the case to their advantage in world-wide propaganda, battled for control of the defendants; the ILD won. Lawyers associated with the ILD appealed the convictions; the Alabama Supreme Court upheld them in a 7–1 decision, although they sent Eugene Williams to Juvenile Court. In November 1932, the U.S. Supreme Court reversed the convictions, ruling in *Powell v. Alabama* that the defendants who had become known as "the Scottsboro Boys" had lacked adequate counsel.

The ILD hired as lead attorney, Samuel Leibowitz—a flamboyant, extremely successful New York criminal lawyer, to represent Patterson, who was re-tried alone. Despite their best efforts, which included a recantation by Ruby Bates, in April 1933 Patterson was sentenced to death. In June 1933 the conviction was set aside as not justified by the evidence by the presiding judge, James E. Horton, a decision that ruined his career and life. Later that year Patterson was re-tried and the jury again imposed the death penalty, as was also done after a quick trial for Clarence Norris. The trials of the remaining defendants were postponed until all appeals had been exhausted.

Alabama's highest court upheld the convictions. In April 1935 the U.S. Supreme Court in *Norris v. Alabama* unanimously reversed the convictions because of the absence of African Americans from the rolls of the juries which indicted and tried the defendants. In November 1935 new indictments were returned against all nine, including the two whose cases had been transferred to Juvenile Court. Meanwhile a Scottsboro Defense Committee (SDC) had been organized which included not only the ILD (two of whose attorneys had been arrested and charged—much to the outraged dismay of Leibowitz—of trying to bribe Victoria Price to change her testimony) but also the NAACP and other organizations including the American Civil Liberties Union, the Urban League, and the League for Industrial Democracy. The SDC attempted to deal with local prejudice by enlisting Alabama lawyers to assist Leibowitz.

Patterson tried for the fourth time in January 1936, was again found guilty, but this time sentenced to 75 years in prison. Subsequently during June/July 1937 there were more trials of the Scottsboro Boys: Clarence Norris received a death sentence (this was later commuted to life in prison), Andy Wright and Charles Weems received sentences of 99 years and 75 years respectively. Ozzie Powell (shot during an altercation with a sheriff and permanently brain injured) was sentenced to 20 years for assault. But state officials, anxious to end the controversial case (prior to the May 1937 death of the main state prosecutor there had been some talk of a deal), dropped the rape charges against Powell and Roy Wright, Olen Montgomery, Eugene Williams, and Willie Roberson.

The remaining defendants eventually found their way to freedom. Andy Wright was paroled in 1944, but was re-arrested because of parole violations, and in 1950 was the last Scottsboro Boy to be set free. Powell and Norris were paroled in 1946. Patterson escaped to Michigan in 1948,

published his autobiography *Scottsboro Boy* in 1950; Alabama claimed him but Michigan's governor refused extradition. In 1989 Norris, who with NAACP aid received a pardon (1976) from Alabama's governor died—the last of the Scottsboro Boys. The case was an unfortunate manifestation of the racial prejudice which dominated the legal system and culture of the South at that time, of which the treatment of the Scottsboro Boys and their ultimate fates (which for many included poverty, alcoholism, failed marriages, and continued disillusionment) is a shameful example.

Daniel Leab

References and Further Reading

Carter, Dan T. 1979. *Scottsboro: a Tragedy of the American South.* rev. ed., Baton Rouge: Louisiana State University Press.

Goodman, James E. 1994. *Stories of Scottsboro.* New York: Pantheon Books.

Linder, Douglas O. 1999. *Famous American Trials: "The Scottsboro Boys" Trials, 1931-1937.* Available at: http://www.law.umkc.edu/faculty/projects/Ftrials/scottsboro/scottsb.htm. Accessed September 24, 2009.

Lindner, Douglas. 2000. *The Trial of the "Scottsboro Boys."* Available at: http://jurist.law.pitt.edu/trials4.htm. Accessed September 24, 2009.

Reynolds, Quentin. 1950. *Courtroom: In the Criminal Courtroom with Samuel S. Leibowitz, Lawyer and Judge.* New York: Farrar, Straus & Company.

Smith, Ferdinand (1893–1961)

The secretary and treasurer of the National Maritime Union (NMU), Ferdinand Smith was one of the major figures in leading radical maritime groups during the late 1930s, and one of the most powerful trade unionists of African ancestry in the 1930s and 1940s.

Born in 1893 in Jamaica, Ferdinand Smith was the chief steward with the Luchenbach Steamship Company, which was involved in intercoastal trade. The company often hired seamen who then worked for no wages until someone on the company payroll resigned and they were given a salaried position. Although working on a limited budget, Smith was always able to feed his crew well, and became popular with many people. As a result, after the S.S. *California* strike in March 1936, the existing labor system was overhauled, and the seaman established the NMU, Smith was elected as the secretary in spite of the fact that the ship owners did not sign contracts ending racial discrimination until July 15, 1944, partly after pressure from Smith and others.

The creation of the NMU helped the seamen bargain for better wages and conditions, but also brought Ferdinand Smith to the attention of the authorities. His radicalism, aggressive trade unionism and his questionable immigration status led to his surveillance by the private detectives hired by the shipping companies and also the police and FBI.

On the cultural side, it was said that it was Ferdinand Smith who inspired Langston Hughes, the African American poet and novelist, to make his first voyage to Africa. Hughes mentions an enigmatic "F.S." in his work, and it seems likely that this was Smith. Certainly Smith and Hughes corresponded actively until Smith's death.

With the start of the "Red Scare" from 1949, the authorities moved in on Smith who was working in Harlem for the NMU. He was an active member of the American Communist Party, and in 1951 he was arrested and deported as an illegal alien, and also for alleged communist sympathies. Back in Jamaica, Hughes married and continued his radical labor campaigns. He remained active in politics, although he chose to exclude himself from the local telephone directory. He died in 1961 in Jamaica.

Justin Corfield

References and Further Reading

Horne, Gerald. 2005. *Red Seas: Ferdinand Smith and Radical Black Sailors in the United States and Jamaica.* New York: New York University Press.

Southern Tenant Farmers Union

The Southern Tenant Farmers Union (STFU) arose from the same sharecropping economy that gave rise to the Farmers' Alliances and People's Party in the 1890s, plus the impact of Agricultural Adjustment Act (AAA) policies on landowner to sharecropper relations. Socialist Party presidential candidate Norman Thomas suggested a sharecroppers union to two party members in Tyronza, Arkansas: Clay East, the respected owner of a local filling station, and H. L. Mitchell, originally from Halls, Tennessee, who owned a dry cleaning business. National party leadership was unenthusiastic; East and Mitchell's personal familiarity with local sharecroppers brought the STFU into being. East also served for a time as town constable, giving the infant union a few months of protection from harassment.

In July 1934, a meeting of 11 white and 7 black sharecroppers in the Sunnyside Schoolhouse formed STFU. At its height, the organization may have had 25,000 members, mostly in Arkansas and Oklahoma, with some in southern Missouri and smaller numbers in Mississippi, Louisiana and Tennessee. J. R. Butler served as president, E. B. McKinney as vice-president, and Mitchell as executive secretary. A young organizer named John Handcox gave the labor movement some of its best-known anthems, including "Roll the Union On" and "We Shall Not Be Moved."

As with many crops, AAA sought to remove a surplus from commodity markets, paying for acreage to be plowed up or not planted. Powerless, often illiterate tenants, who were entitled to half the payments, were often presented with forms waiving this share, or authorizing their landlord to cash a check made out to both tenant and landlord. When federal bale tags were issued under the Bankhead Act to control the amount of cotton that could be marketed, landlords summarily required tenants to turn over their tags. Many tenants found their rent raised by the amount of their AAA share. Others found that their entire acreage was taken out of production, while the landlord allocated the permitted production to other acres of his property.

Many plantations shifted from sharecropping to day labor. AAA rulings prohibited shifting production from tenants to wage employment, but few tenants knew that, and local county agents were quite cooperative. Day laborers were not entitled to a share of AAA payments. Landlords had more money (from the AAA) to pay cash wages with. And with sharecroppers denied acreage to grow a crop, the number of people seeking to be hired grew. Within AAA, there was tension between the Extension Service conservatives and the Cotton Section, headed by Cully Cobb, against the more liberal Office of General Counsel, headed by reformist lawyer Jerome Frank. Chester Davis, in charge of the AAA, wanted no controversy; Agriculture Secretary Henry Wallace didn't want to embarrass an important New Deal program. Writing in glowing terms of "a democratically administered machine for dealing with agricultural problems" which he did not want "subordinated to a local machinery operated from Washington," Wallace was unaware that the majority of southern farmers were tenants, who were not represented on local county committees.

The first locals in Tyronza were interracial, partly because both white and black members worked side by side and knew each other personally. In the Marked Tree area, separate Negro and white locals persuaded a number of poor whites who might have had doubts to join. The tactic of dual locals was repeated in many areas, as was deployment of white organizers to win over tenants of their own color, and black organizers to gain the confidence of theirs. Most important decisions were taken at mass meetings of all members in an area.

Efforts to suppress the STFU began in January 1935, when Justice of the Peace J. C. McCroy convened a jury of planters, businessmen, and one sharecropper in Marked Tree to convict the union's most skilled white organizer, Ward Rodgers, a Methodist minister from western Arkansas, on a vague accusation as "an organizer for the Communist Party and advocating racial equality right here in Arkansas." Rodgers was sentenced to six months in jail, a $500 fine, plus costs. He also lost his federal relief job as an adult educator. Soon after, meetings in Gilmore, Birdsong, and other locations were invaded by deputies, often drunk, who beat men, women and children and arrested organizers for "disturbing the peace." As the homes of STFU secretaries, organizers, and even attorney C. T. Carpenter were riddled with bullets by night riders, many fled to Memphis, inspiring a headline in the *Marked Tree Tribune:* "Citizens Ask Reds to Leave."

Although the Cross County prosecuting attorney alleged that the STFU "collected $35,000 in dues last year from ignorant Negroes and white people," dues in 1935 were less than $500. Financial support was the most essential form of outside aid, with three fourths of STFU expenditures provided by Strikers Emergency Relief Committee and the American Fund for Public Service. Other support came from the American Civil Liberties Union, the Socialist Party, and the Church Emergency Relief Fund of the Federal Council of Churches of Christ in America. Heading into 1936, special support committees were formed in northern cities, with contributors including columnist Drew Pearson and Supreme Court Justice Louis Brandeis.

In August 1935, the STFU took its first strike vote, calling for an increase in tenants' share, then 40 to 60 cents per hundred pounds of cotton, to a dollar. Faced with a new wave of terrorism by local officials, but noting that pay scales had actually risen to 75 cents, the STFU ended the strike in October. The following year, tenants drummed up support for another strike with "the marches"— a long single file line with eight feet between each picket, calling on workers to leave the fields. STFU members were evicted from many plantations, and organized tent colonies, which drew

further violent reaction, including a stick of dynamite thrown into one settlement by night riders. Breaking up a meeting of 450 tenants with STFU attorney Herman Goldberger and two organizers in the Providence Methodist Church near Earle, deputy Everett Hood remarked "There's going to be another Elaine Massacre, only the next time we'll kill whites as well as niggers."

Accounts of these events brought to Washington by the STFU were a major impetus for the LaFollette Committee investigation into terrorism by management against union organizing. The STFU's own evidence was downplayed in committee proceedings, so that southern senators would not derail the investigation. The 1936 marches coincided with President Roosevelt's visit to Arkansas to praise Senate Majority Leader Joseph T. Robinson—a close ally of the planters, although he had intervened to dampen violence by local sheriffs in 1935. The STFU had some influence on the Farm Security Administration's creation of cooperative farms at Dyess, Twist Plantation in Poinsett County, Lake View in Phillips County, and Plum Bayou and Lake Dick in Jefferson County. But under pressure from the American Farm Bureau Federation, FSA appropriations were reduced to almost nothing after 1942, under cover of war-time necessity to reduce "nonessential" government expenditures.

When the STFU's third annual convention assembled in January 1937, most leaders wanted to join the Congress of Industrial Organizations—at its peak of inspiration to workers across the country, leading epic battles in the auto and steel industries. Real life conditions for rural farm laborers, with or without tenancies, clashed with both the financial requirements of trade union organization, and the rigid ideological categories applied by communist leadership in the CIO's newly formed United Cannery, Agricultural Packing and Allied Workers of America, known by the unwieldy acronym UCAPAWA. The CIO union, led by Don Henderson, had a good strategy for west coast agriculture: cannery workers employed year-round would be a base for hiring halls, which could enlist seasonal field workers. Henderson's plans that the union be "centralized and coordinated so that we can build a union that will have the prestige and power that it ought to have" required reliable per capita dues payments.

Southern tenant farmers seldom had cash except once a year, at "settling time" after the crop was sold—if then. STFU leaders had asked for a dime a month, gotten it sometimes from about one sixth of the enrolled members, and kept all the rest in good standing. UCAPAWA wanted 50 cents a month, without fail. In addition, Henderson and his party comrades insisted that landless hired laborers and tenant farmers were distinct classes of people, who should be in separate organizations. This had no basis in the reality of southern agriculture. The STFU reluctantly joined UCAPAWA in September 1937, and disaffiliated in March 1939. The accompanying personality clashes, factional disputes, and general confusion among membership reduced the STFU to a hollow shell. The New Deal gave way to the priorities of World War II, without a breakthrough for farm labor either in legal protection or successful organization.

Charles Rosenberg

References and Further Reading

Fannin, Mark. 2003. *Labor's Promised Land: Radical Visions of Gender, Race, and Religion in the South.* Knoxville: University of Tennessee Press.

Grubbs, Donald H. 1971. *Cry From the Cotton: The Southern Tenant Farmers' Union and the New Deal.* Chapel Hill: University of North Carolina Press.

Hawkins, Van. 2007. *Plowing new ground: the Southern Tenant Farmers' Union and its Place in Delta history.* Virginia Beach, VA: Donning Co. Publishers.

Mitchell, H. L. 1979. *Mean Things Happening in This Land.* Montclair, NJ: Allanhead, Osmun & Co.

Standing Bear, Luther (1868–1939)

Luther Standing Bear was the most significant Native American writer of the early 20th century. His four books about his experiences growing up on a Sioux reservation are important historical documents that preserve much of the cultural heritage of his people.

Standing Bear was born Ota Kte on the Pinewood Indian Reservation in South Dakota in December 1868. His Sioux name means "plenty kill," and he was the son of the Sioux chief Standing Bear and his wife Wastewin. The year he was born, the Sioux signed a treaty with the U.S. government that removed them from their ancestral lands on the plains and placed them on a reservation.

Standing Bear spent his childhood on the reservation in South Dakota. When he became a teenager, he went to study at the newly founded Carlisle Indian School in Pennsylvania, where he was a member of the school's first graduating class. When he arrived at the school, he told the teachers that his name was Ota Kte, son of

Luther Standing Bear was one of the most widely known Lakota advocates for Indians in the early 20th century. (Library of Congress)

Standing Bear. The teachers ignored his Sioux name, and he was known thereafter as Standing Bear. At Carlisle, the Native American students received a vocational education.

After graduation, Standing Bear returned to his reservation and found that his education had little value there. He worked in the reservation post office and on a small ranch and succeeded his father as leader of his clan. He also married shortly after returning to South Dakota, though little is known about his family life.

Standing Bear bristled under the control of the government officials responsible for life on the reservation. He eventually left the reservation and worked in a variety of jobs. He was a preacher, a schoolteacher, and a clerk in a dry-goods store. In 1902, he auditioned for Buffalo Bill Cody's Wild West Show. The show took him all over the country and even to Europe for a year. His career with the show ended in 1905, after he was injured in a train accident while on tour. In 1912, he moved to California, where he found work playing a Native American in the movies. He went on to have a long career in Hollywood.

Standing Bear published his autobiography, *My People the Sioux,* in 1928. The book was an attempt to preserve the way of life that he had known as a child on the plains. It contains detailed descriptions of Oglala Sioux traditions and folklore. It also describes the changes that transformed his community in the late 19th and early 20th centuries. The book was well received by critics, who found it a simple, honest, and compelling account of a vanishing lifestyle.

Standing Bear followed his autobiography with another memoir, *My Indian Boyhood,* which was published in 1931. This was a children's book that explained the lifestyle of Sioux children. Like his earlier book, *My Indian Boyhood* contains much valuable ethnographic information about the 19th-century Sioux. Standing Bear published the book in the hope of disabusing American children of many of the stereotypes they had about Native Americans.

Standing Bear's next book was *Land of the Spotted Eagle,* another nonfiction account of Sioux life. In this book, he attempted to explain some of the important religious, social, and philosophical traditions of his community. Like his earlier works, the book was filled with details and observations about Sioux life that would otherwise have been lost to history. Standing Bear published his final book, *Stories of the Sioux,* in 1934; it was a collection of Oglala Sioux folklore.

This book, like his other three, drew on traditions he had learned from tribal elders when he was a child.

Standing Bear's books also revealed to the American public many of the injustices carried out against the Oglala Sioux by the U.S. government. In his later life, he became an activist for Native American rights and worked to improve conditions for the people living on the reservations. He was a member of the National League for Justice to the American Indian. He also remained active in Oglala Sioux politics throughout his life.

While pursuing a career as a writer, Standing Bear continued to act in Hollywood westerns. He lived in California for the final years of his life and died in Huntington Park on February 20, 1939.

James Burns

References and Further Reading

Ellis, Richard N. 1985. "Luther Standing Bear: 'I Would Raise Him to Be an Indian'." In *Indian Lives: Essays on Nineteenth-and Twentieth-Century Native Americans,* L. G. Moses, and Raymond Wilson, eds., 138–57. Albuquerque: University of New Mexico Press.

Dockstader, Frederick J. 1977. *Great North American Indians: Profiles in Life and Leadership.* New York: Van Nostrand Reinhold.

Jordan, H. Glenn, and Thomas M. Holm. 1979. *Indian Leaders: Oklahoma's First Statesmen.* Oklahoma City: Oklahoma Historical Society.

Thorpe, Jim (1888–1953)

Hailed as the greatest athlete of the first half of the 20th century, Jim Thorpe excelled in football, baseball, and track.

Born James Francis Thorpe on May 28, 1888, in Indian Territory (now Oklahoma), Thorpe and his twin brother Charles were the second and third children of six. His father, Hiram Thorpe, was of Irish and Sac-Fox Indian descent. His mother was one-quarter French and three-quarters Chippewa Indian, being the granddaughter of the famous Sac-Fox leader, Black Hawk. Thorpe's Indian name was Wa-tho-huck, meaning Bright Path.

One year after Jim and Charles were born, the Thorpe family acquired a 160-acre farm in Oklahoma during the Oklahoma land rush of 1889. Thorpe was an extremely active child and learned how to ride, swim, and hunt at a young age. He was educated at the Sac-Fox reservation school, the Haskell Institute in Lawrence, Kansas, and finally the Carlisle Indian School in Pennsylvania beginning in 1904.

Thorpe hoped to study to become an electrician at Carlisle, but ended up learning to be a tailor. While at the Carlisle School, he became active in organized sports, particularly football. His athletic ability brought him to the attention of Carlisle's athletic coach, "Pop" Warner, who decided to groom Thorpe for track as well as football. Warner elevated Thorpe from the junior varsity to the varsity football team, where he spent most of the 1908 season on the bench, but led the team to an upset victory over the school's rival Pennsylvania late in the season.

During the summer of 1909, Thorpe traveled southward to work on a farm as part of his work commitment to the Carlisle School. He joined the Carolina League and played professional baseball for Winston-Salem, Fayetteville, and Rocky Mount, remaining for the 1910 season as well. In 1911, he returned to Carlisle for two years to complete his education and, at Warner's urging, set his sights on competing in the 1912 Olympics in track and field.

The Olympic Games of 1912 at Stockholm, Sweden represented the pinnacle of Thorpe's athletic career. He competed in both the five-event pentathlon (running broad jump, javelin throw, 200-meter race, discus, and 1500-meter race) and the 10-event decathlon (100-meter dash, running broad jump, shotput, running high jump, 400-meter race, discus throw, 110-meter high hurdles, pole vault, javelin throw, and 1500-meter race). In the pentathlon, Thorpe placed first in four out of the five events. In the decathlon, he set a record which would not be broken for another 15 years. His achievements earned him the gold medal in both events. King Gustav V of Sweden proclaimed him to be "the greatest athlete in the world," to which Thorpe famously replied, "Thanks, King."

In January 1913, however, a scandal erupted when Olympic officials realized that Thorpe had played professional baseball, thus making him ineligible for the Olympics because he had compromised his amateur standing. The Amateur Athletic Union stripped him of his Olympic medals and removed his accomplishments from the Olympic record.

When Thorpe returned to the United States, in 1913, he married Iva Miller in the first of his three marriages. The couple had four children; three daughters and a son. Thorpe continued to play college football and was named to the All-American team. Upon his graduation from Carlisle in 1913, Thorpe returned to professional baseball and joined the New York Giants as a right fielder. Thorpe continued with baseball until 1919, playing at various times for the Giants, the Cincinnati Reds, and the Boston Braves.

In 1920, Thorpe helped organize the American Professional Football Association (which became the National Football League in 1922) and served as the organization's first president. He also played for teams in Canton (Ohio), New York, and St. Petersburg (Florida). In 1926, Thorpe remarried to Freeda Kirkpatrick. The couple had four sons. He retired from football in 1929 and moved to Hollywood, where he tried to sell his life story. Although Metro-Goldwyn-Mayer (MGM) bought the rights, the picture was never made, and Thorpe turned instead to writing, publishing a book for the 1932 Olympics held in Los Angeles entitled *Jim Thorpe's History of the Olympics*. Ultimately, he ended up working construction and appearing in bit parts in films. His one significant role was as a supporting character in the 1937 Errol Flynn film, *The Green Light*.

He returned to Oklahoma in 1937 and became active in Native American affairs. In 1940, he embarked on a public lecture tour across the United States, speaking on current sports, his own career, the importance of sports in American life, and Native American culture. Too old for active military service during World War II, Thorpe briefly joined the merchant marines in June 1945. Also in June of the same year, he married for the third time, to Patricia Gladys Askew. After the war ended, he returned to California, where in late 1949 Warner Brothers acquired the rights to his life story and began production on *Jim Thorpe, All-American* (1951), with Burt Lancaster playing the title role. Thorpe was given a generous payment for his story and was retained as a technical advisor.

In 1950, a poll among nearly 400 Associated Press sports writers selected Thorpe as the greatest athlete and greatest football player of the first half of the 20th century, choosing him over Babe Ruth, Ty Cobb, Red Grange, and Jack Dempsey, among others. At the same time, he was inducted into the college and pro-football halls of fame. He died in 1953.

Efforts to have Thorpe's Olympic medals and records reinstated had begun in the late 1930s. Finally, in 1982, these efforts by his supporters paid off when the International Olympic Committee returned Thorpe's name to their record books and restored his medals to his family.

References and Further Reading

Foner, Eric, and John A. Garraty, eds. 1991. *The Reader's Companion to American History,* Boston: Houghton Mifflin.

Wheeler, Robert W. 1981. *Jim Thorpe: The World's Greatest Athlete.* Norman: University of Oklahoma Press, 1981.

Vann, Robert L. (1879–1940)

Robert Lee Vann, a black editor, publisher, politician, and lawyer, built the *Pittsburgh Courier* into one of the country's foremost black weekly newspapers. Under his leadership, the powerful newspaper was read by a quarter of a million people. In its heyday, Vann's paper distributed 14 editions throughout the country and influenced many important political contests. The *Pittsburgh Courier* rose to national prominence in its campaign for racial equality in the armed forces during the 1930s (Buni 1974, xi).

Born in a rural area of North Carolina, Vann attended Richmond's Virginia Union University, then graduated from Western University of Pennsylvania Law School in Pittsburgh, a rags-to-riches story.

After law school, Vann served as legal counsel to *Pittsburgh Courier* and soon became its editor and publisher, positions he held for the rest of his life. Having a forum to communicate enhanced Vann's career on all fronts. He also served as assistant city solicitor for Pittsburgh, at that time the highest city government position filled by an African American.

Vann turned a calculating eye to the Republican and Democratic parties, believing black people should use the power of the vote to advocate for advantageous legislation (Jackson 1975, 175).

From the time of the Civil War, the Republican Party that fought against slavery was seen as the obvious choice for black people. In particular, black middle class citizens viewed voting Republican as a badge of respectability. However, the Depression changed people's thinking, as many members of the black middle class lost ground (Banner-Haley 1998, 191–98).

Although Franklin Roosevelt's promise to look after the "forgotten man" was as yet unproven, the *Pittsburgh Courier* felt the Republican response to the Depression had damaged the economy across the board. The *Courier* and seven other black newspapers urged readers to join forces with white citizens to defeat Hoover (Martin, 91). This marked a seismic shift in the political landscape.

Despite the extensive campaign to persuade black people to vote for the Democratic Party, FDR did not receive a majority of black votes in 1932 (Martin 1971, 92–93). Even so, Vann's endorsement marked the beginning of an exodus of black supporters from the Republican Party. Roosevelt appointed Vann as assistant United States attorney general, a prestigious title, although it did not carry very much power or responsibility.

Ironically, once the New Deal gained popularity and the Democrats started to win by landslides, the influence of black voters was diluted in the large majorities (Jackson 1975, 175–76). However, the *Pittsburgh Courier* continued as a powerful opinion leader in local and state politics, and in the black community across the country.

Critics paint a complex picture of Vann, a highly accomplished individual who built an influential black power base (Jackson 1975, 174). However, some look at Vann's record and wonder whether at times he was driven by self-interest rather than by conviction, perhaps blunting some of his potential (Buni 1974, xiii). He was seen as a chameleon who switched political parties yet another time, to Wendell Willkie and the Republican Party in 1940, just before Vann died.

Merrill Evans

References and Further Reading

Banner-Haley, Charles Pete. 1998. "*The Philadelphia Tribune* and the Persistence of Black Republicanism during the Great Depression." *Pennsylvania History* 65: 190–202.

Buni, Andrew. 1974. *Robert L. Vann of the Pittsburgh Courier: Politics and Black Journalism.* Pittsburgh, PA: University of Pittsburgh Press.

Jackson Jr., Luther P. 1975. "Review of *Robert L. Vann of the Pittsburgh Courier: Politics and Black Journalism,* by Andrew Buni." *Political Science Quarterly* 90: 174–76.

Martin, Charles H. 1971. "Negro Leaders, the Republican Party, and the Election of 1932." *Phylon* 32: 85–93.

Weaver, Robert (1907–97)

Robert Clifton Weaver became the first African American appointed to the Cabinet when President Lyndon B. Johnson asked him to head the Department of Housing and Urban Development in 1966.

Weaver was born on December 29, 1907, in Washington, D.C. He earned a bachelor's degree in economics in 1929 and a master's degree two years later at Harvard. After spending a year as a professor of economics at the Agricultural and Technical College of North Carolina in Greensboro, Weaver returned to Harvard and earned a Ph.D. in economics in 1934.

In 1933, Weaver began a long career in the federal government. He held a number of different staff positions in the New Deal government of Democratic president Franklin D. Roosevelt, serving as an expert on manpower, housing, and urban and black affairs. He founded the so-called Black Cabinet, a group of knowledgeable New Deal government officials who worked behind the scenes to integrate the federal government and to ensure that black Americans obtained a share in the New Deal-sponsored relief projects, subsidized housing, and federally funded jobs.

After World War II, Weaver briefly served with the United Nations Relief and Rehabilitation Administration mission in the Soviet Union and held a wide variety of teaching and private foundation positions. Two books he published at this time—*Negro Labor, a National Problem* (1946) and *The Negro Ghetto* (1948)—reinforced his reputation as a leading national expert on economic and racial housing pattern issues.

From 1955 to 1961, Weaver held various New York state and city housing posts and was appointed by President John F. Kennedy to the federal Housing and Home Finance Agency in 1961. He also published two more books: *The*

Urban Complex (1964) and *Dilemmas of Urban America* (1965).

President Johnson appointed Weaver as the secretary of Housing and Urban Development (HUD) in 1966. While at HUD, Weaver attempted to encourage housing integration. He viewed the *de facto* segregation patterns of whites in the suburbs and blacks in the inner cities as the root cause of segregated schools and many other racial problems in America.

Upon leaving federal government service in January 1969, Weaver became president of Baruch College (1969–70), professor of urban affairs at Hunter College (1970–78), and director of urban programs for Hunter College's Brookdale Center on Aging.

Weaver died in July 1997 at age 90 in New York City.

References and Further Reading

Current Biography Yearbook, 1961. New York: H.W. Wilson Co.

Who's Who Among Black Americans, 1990–1991. Detroit: Gale Research.

White, Walter F.
(1893–1955)

Walter White served the cause of African Americans as assistant and executive secretary of the National Association for the Advancement of Colored People (NAACP) for nearly 40 years. He came to be the most devoted fighter in the effort to stamp out lynching in the United States after World War I.

Walter Francis Walter was born on July 1, 1893, in Atlanta, Georgia to George W. White, a mail carrier, and Madeline Harrison, a school teacher. Five thirty-seconds of his ancestry was African American. Walter was blond, blue-eyed, and of light complexion and could have passed for white. He chose, with the rest of his family, to identify with his black ancestry. He attended the preparatory school of Atlanta University, which had been founded in 1867 for the education of blacks, and went on to graduate from the university in 1916. He worked as a clerk, then as a cashier, for the Standard Life Insurance Company. His first activist involvement was in a protest move against the Atlanta Board of Education, which had planned to eliminate the seventh grade from black schools in order to free funds for a new white high school. The protest succeeded.

In December 1916, White was a leader in the founding of a local branch of the young NAACP and was elected its secretary. When the writer James Weldon Johnson, the national secretary of the NAACP, visited and learned of White's activities, he hired him as his assistant secretary in the New York office. Upon Johnson's retirement in 1931, White was promoted to national executive secretary, a post he held until the end of his life.

During the 1920s, White focused his attention on lynching and personally investigated 41 lynchings and 8 race riots. In Southern towns, pretending to be a white reporter for a Northern newspaper, he circulated freely, interviewing white people about racial tensions. After a violent lynching and riot in an Arkansas town, White, in his reporter pose, interviewed imprisoned black men, lynchers, and even the state governor; he managed to escape on a train just ahead of a white crowd who had discovered his identity. He wrote a novel about lynching, *The Fire in the Flint* (1924), and another about passing as white, *Flight* (1926).

In 1929, he published a study of lynching, *Rope and Faggot: A Biography of Judge Lynch,* written on a Guggenheim Fellowship.

White led the NAACP's campaign to get antilynching legislation through the Congress. Two bills passed the House of Representatives in 1934 and 1937, but both failed in the Senate. For his work lobbying Congress and bringing racial violence to public notice, White was awarded the Spingarn Medal in 1937.

The NAACP legal department, under White's direction, began a long campaign in the courts to have state-enforced segregation declared illegal. (The legal strategy, plotted by Thurgood Marshall—later a justice of the U.S. Supreme Court—led to the Supreme Court's decision in 1954 that overturned the "separate but equal" doctrine.) In 1941, White joined A. Philip Randolph in persuading President Franklin D. Roosevelt to issue an executive order banning discrimination in defense plants and setting up the Fair Employment Practices Commission. During World War II, White toured every war theater as a *New York Post* correspondent, investigating discrimination against African American service men and women. His book *A Rising Wind* (1945) reported his findings and strengthened the case for President Harry Truman's executive order desegregating the armed forces in 1948.

When the Daughters of the American Revolution refused the singer Marian Anderson permission to sing in Constitution Hall in 1939, White joined Eleanor Roosevelt in arranging for the concert to take place at the Lincoln Memorial before 75,000 people. He rendered a different kind of service in August 1943, at the height of a violent race riot in Harlem, when he toured the streets all night with Mayor Fiorello La Guardia, calming the excited crowds.

White was an adviser to the U.S. delegation at the San Francisco conference to found the United Nations in 1945. Later, he traveled worldwide, lecturing on race relations, and developed a special interest in India and the West Indies. He wrote two weekly newspaper columns, one for the black *Chicago Defender* and another for a syndicate of white papers.

White's activities outside the NAACP and his autocratic manner of administering his staff caused him difficulties. He was criticized by W.E.B. Du Bois, one-time editor of the NAACP journal *Crisis,* who charged that White's involvements compromised NAACP policy. When Du Bois was abruptly discharged from his professorship at Atlanta University in 1944, however, White used his influence to have him reinstated. In the postwar years, the NAACP came under criticism from more radical African American activists for being too conservative, averse to direct action, even timid. Such criticism reflected on White's leadership.

White married Leah Powell, an NAACP employee, in 1922, and they had two children. After a divorce, in 1949, White married the writer Poppy Cannon, who was white. White died suddenly of a heart attack on March 21, 1955, having served as NAACP secretary until his death.

References and Further Reading

Cannon, Poppy. 1956. *A Gentle Knight: My Husband, Walter White.* New York: Rinehart.

White, Walter. 1948. *A Man Called White: The Autobiography of Walter White.* New York: Viking Press.

Wise, Stephen (1874–1949)

Born in Erlau, Hungary, near Budapest, Wise moved to New York at the age of one. The son of a rabbi, Wise was a precocious student. He graduated from Columbia University in 1892 and received his Ph.D. there in 1901. Before beginning his doctoral studies he became an ordained rabbi in Vienna in 1893. A free thinker, social reformer, critic of Tammany Hall, and supporter of liberal theological views, Wise established the Free Synagogue in New York in 1907. For close to 40 years he conducted his services at Carnegie Hall. Wise also founded New York's Jewish Institute of Religion in 1922. During his long and distinguished career Wise held many offices, including editor of the journal *Opinion* and president of the American Jewish Congress (1925–49).

Prior to United States entry into World War I Wise, along with Protestant theologian and Unitarian minister John Haynes Holmes, helped found the American Union Against Militarism. Initially, Wise opposed the war but once the U.S. intervened he strongly supported Wilson's Fourteen Points. In 1919, after visiting Europe and witnessing the destruction, he renewed his ties with peace groups. Even Hitler and the Nazis' initial persecution of the Jews did not cause the ardent Zionist to call for American intervention in European affairs. Only after Germany attacked Poland in September 1939 did Wise actively urge American aid to the

Dr. Stephen S. Wise, President of the American Jewish Congress, speaks before a crowd at Madison Square Park on July 31, 1945, regarding the horrors faced by Jews in Europe. (Bettmann/Corbis)

Allies. He continued to caution against military intervention until the Japanese attack on Pearl Harbor.

First and foremost, Wise was a Zionist. He supported the establishment of a permanent homeland for the Jewish people. In 1939, he criticized the British *White Paper* imposing severe limitations on Jewish immigration into the British-mandate Palestine. In the fall of 1942, after Wise heard from Vienna about Hitler's "final solution"—the massive liquidation of Jews in Europe—he immediately informed the American government. On November 24, 1942, he went public with the news when he did not hear back from the White House. From 1943 to 1946, he co-chaired the Zionist Emergency Council. Throughout the war years Wise also became embroiled in controversy with Cleveland rabbi Abba Hillel Silver. Wise was a Democrat and strong supporter of Franklin D. Roosevelt. Silver, a Republican, opposed Wise's continued support for cooperation with Great Britain after the contents of the *White Paper* were made public. Wise was also a close ally of Chaim Weizman, a powerful figure in the World Zionist Organization; Silver backed the more militant David Ben-Gurion, chair of the Jewish Agency. Neither leader was willing to compromise.

The controversy came to a head in March 1944 when the White House authorized Wise to say that FDR never approved of the British *White Paper* and that the president favored the creation of a Jewish state in Palestine. Bristling at these comments, Silver quickly wrestled control of the American Zionist movement away from Wise. At a December 1946 meeting of the World Zionist Organization in Switzerland, Silver effectively downplayed Wise's influence and managed to cast him aside. Wise, angry at this turn of events, soon left the World Zionist Organization. In March 1948, Wise criticized the Truman administration for failing to insist upon implementing the United Nation's plan to partition Palestine between Arabs and Jews. A few months later his criticisms were muted when the state of Israel was created. The following year, after his autobiography was completed, Wise died in New York City. He lived long enough to witness his dream of the creation of a Jewish state in Palestine become reality.

Charles F. Howlett

References and Further Reading

Kennedy, David M. 1999. *Freedom from Fear: the American People in Depression and War, 1929–1945.* New York: Oxford University Press.

Lipstadt, Deborah E. 1986. *Beyond Belief: the American Press and the Coming of the Holocaust, 1933–1945.* New York: Free Press.

Urofsky, Melvin I. 1981. *A Voice that Spoke for Justice: The Life and Times of Stephen S. Wise.* Albany: State University of New York Press.

Voss, Carl Hermann. 1964. *Rabbi and Minister: The Friendship of Stephen S. Wise and John Haynes Holmes.* Cleveland, OH: World Publishing Company.

Wise, Stephen S. 1949. *Challenging Years.* New York: G. P. Putnam's Sons.

Wright, Richard (1908–1960)

Richard Nathaniel Wright, best known for his first published novel, *Native Son,* introduced a new realism to literary treatments of America's racial problems, rendering sympathetically the always fearful, sometimes violent psychology of the oppressed.

Wright was born on a plantation near Natchez, Mississippi on September 4, 1908, the son of a sharecropper and a teacher. Abandoned by their father in 1911, Wright and his younger brother lived with their mother in the homes of relatives in Tennessee, Arkansas, and Mississippi. The children were often hungry and had little opportunity for formal schooling. After his mother suffered a stroke in 1919, Wright lived with an aunt and uncle, then with his grandmother. He attended a public junior high school in Jackson, Mississippi and graduated first in his ninth grade class in 1925.

At 15, Wright left home, moved to Memphis, and took a succession of menial jobs in order to support himself. Four years later, he moved to Chicago and found a job as a postal clerk, which he held until it was eliminated during the Great Depression in 1931. He joined the Communist Party in 1933.

Wright moved to New York City in 1937 to become Harlem editor of the *Daily Worker.* In the same year, he completed a manuscript for a first novel, "Cesspool," but was unable to find a publisher. This heavily autobiographical work remained unpublished until three years after Wright's death, when it was printed as *Lawd Today* (1963).

Wright's first published volume was a collection of short stories, *Uncle Tom's Children* (1938). Included is "Big Boy Leaves Home," a tale of truant African American youths caught swimming in a whites-only stream. Their discovery leads to violence and the killing of a white man; Big Boy escapes, but his friend Bobo is lynched. *Uncle Tom's Children* caused a sensation for its honest rendering of the victimization of African Americans in a society marked by Jim Crow laws and mob justice. The novel won first prize in a contest sponsored by *Story* magazine for writers supported by the Federal Writers Project.

The novel *Native Son* (1940) proved even more shocking to prevailing literary sensibilities, and it became a best-seller. Acting out of fear, the protagonist, Bigger Thomas, accidentally smothers a wealthy young white woman when he holds a pillow over her head to avoid having his innocent presence in her bedroom detected by her mother. His act is discovered, and he flees with his mistress, Bessie. Desperate for his own survival, he murders Bessie and goes into hiding. He is finally caught and executed, but he comes to see his own violence as a necessary rebellion against his fate as an African American man. Until *Native Son,* most American fiction had treated men like Bigger stereotypically as either subhuman thugs or helpless victims; the novel lent a new complexity to literary discourse on the subject of race and opened a new channel for African American fiction.

Wright became a national spokesman on issues relating to African American experience, a role he pursued in his next two books, *Twelve Million Black Voices* (1941) and *Black Boy* (1945). The first, a social history, recounts African Americans' struggles from slavery, their oppression in the contemporary South, the migration of many African Americans to the North, and their sufferings in urban, industrial society. *Black Boy* is an autobiographical account of Wright's life from ages 4 to 19. It compellingly places Wright's own experience of extreme poverty and racism into a broad social context. Portions of the original manuscript that dealt with his life after his move to Chicago were published separately as *American Hunger* in 1977.

Alienated by the continuing experience of racism in America, Wright moved permanently with his wife and daughter to Paris in 1947. There, he wrote *The Outsider* (1953), a novel about a man who escapes the pressures of marriage and family by taking advantage of a mistaken report of his death to create a new identity for himself. *Savage Holiday* (1954), remarkable because it features white characters and ignores the subject of race, concerns a white man's suppressed love for his own mother and the violent rage that leads him to murder the woman he marries as a substitute for her. *The Long Dream* (1958) recounts a young African American man's coming of age in Mississippi and his coming to terms with the white man's political and economic power.

During the Paris years, Wright began to use the American experience of slavery as a framework for the interpretation of world events. *Black Power* (1954) offers his impressions as an African American of a trip to the Gold Coast shortly before it became the independent nation of Ghana. *The Color Curtain* (1956), a report on the Bandung Conference of nonaligned nations of the Third World, argues that race is the key factor determining the development of emerging nations in Asia and Africa. *Pagan Spain* (1956) indicts the mores of Catholic Spain during the regime of Francisco Franco, comparing religious intolerance to racism. *White Man, Listen!* (1957) collects lectures made throughout Europe warning Western society of the perils of continuing to deny freedom to large portions of the world's population.

At the time of his sudden death of a heart attack in Paris on November 28, 1960, Wright was at work on a new collection of short stories. *Eight Men* was published in 1960.

References and Further Reading

Fabre, Michel. 1973. *The Unfinished Quest of Richard Wright.* New York: Morrow.

Gayle, Addison. 1980. *Richard Wright: Ordeal of a Native Son.* Garden City, NY: Anchor Press/Doubleday.

Walker, Margaret. 1988. *Richard Wright, Daemonic Genius: A Portrait of the Man, A Critical Look at His Work.* New York: Warner Books.

Primary Sources

Robert M. La Follette, Jr., February 2, 1932—Relief

Source: Congressional Record, 72nd Congress, 1st Session (1931–32), 3068–70, 3080–82, 3092, 3095.

Mr. President, we are in the third winter of the most serious economic crisis which has ever confronted this country.

Mr. President, the wage earner is not primarily concerned with the fall in prices of securities; he is not forced merely to postpone the purchase of a new automobile; he cannot reduce his living standard by abandoning his country house in Florida during the winter season; he loses his economic all in a period of protracted depression.

During the period since this depression began, this is the first time that Congress has turned seriously to the consideration of the rank and file of the people of the United States.

We met in regular session on the first Monday of last December. Immediately there was ready for the consideration of Congress the major portion of the President's so-called reconstruction program, namely, the bill creating the Reconstruction Finance Corporation. After hearings which lasted four days, the Banking and Currency Committee hurriedly reported the bill to the floor of the Senate. It was taken up and jammed through under whip and spur.

Two billion one hundred and sixty million dollars has already been provided by the Congress and the administration during this depression for the relief of those who own property and securities in the United States. Now, when it is proposed that the Congress shall give consideration to a measure providing for the relief of those in the United States who, through no fault of their own, find themselves destitute, cold, hungry, and homeless, the contention is raised that there is not sufficient evidence to demonstrate the necessity for Federal action on this crisis.

It is contended by the opponents of this measure that the responsibility rests upon the local government, that it rests upon the cities, counties, and States, and that the Federal Government has no obligation to relieve the suffering which is now prevalent in this country. It is said that there is no evidence to support the necessity for Federal action to assist the cities, counties, and States in meeting unemployment relief.

Practically every witness testified to the Herculean efforts that have been made on the part of private agencies and the efforts which have been made on the part of local governments to meet the problem. I think that not one witness would want his testimony to be construed as a criticism of the great efforts which have been made by private charity and by the local governments in trying to meet the situation.

But [we] ... must realize ... that the burden which has fallen upon these communities is so tremendous and is increasing at such a rate that they are all becoming embarrassed in their efforts to keep financially sound.

The attempt has been made on the part of opponents of Federal relief to brand it as a dole and to carry conviction to the country that the inauguration of this policy would undermine our institutions. There is not only the factor of local pride but there is also the factor of the position which the present Republican administration has taken concerning Federal aid for relief, which of course would make it a matter of embarrassment for Republican governors generally to take a position in direct opposition to the policy of the administration.

I think the evidence shows that both public and private agencies within these communities have manfully endeavored to meet the problem which has been thrown upon them. I think, furthermore, it shows that the burden has become so great that they can not adequately meet it.

The municipalities have reached the end of their rope. The suggestion is made that the Federal Government should not do anything because the local communities should do it. Those who make such a contention are making a football of relief .... The municipalities are now being forced to curtail their normal public-works programs because of two things: First, the increasing tax delinquencies, and the resultant diminishing revenues; and, second, they are unable to float perfectly sound securities because of the attitude of the bankers and the condition of the money market.

Mr. President, I do not know what will be required to convince the Members of this august body that there is need for action by the Federal Government. Evidence has been presented here to show the absolute breakdown of family life, the overcrowded conditions. I have demonstrated that those in distress are upstanding, independent, industrious citizens of the country. They have been driven only by sheer force of necessity to seek relief. Six families are crowded into a 6-room house in hundreds and hundreds of instances in [for example,] the city of Philadelphia.

Mr. President, no one can examine this evidence without being convinced that the need for action by the Federal Government in assisting the cities, counties, and States in meeting the problem of unemployment relief is one of the greatest emergencies that has ever confronted this Government ....Failure to step in and to provide more adequate relief will result in breaking up hundreds of thousands of families. It will break down health standards. We shall be paying the toll in malnutrition and its effect upon adults and children for 50 years to come if action is not taken to meet this emergency and to raise the standards of relief. The non-epidemic type of diseases will become prevalent. The public-health director of the State of Pennsylvania has already publicly stated that an increase in tuberculosis, due to malnutrition, was evident in that State. The social progress which we have made in this country during the last 50 years will be wiped out, so far as millions of our population are concerned, if the relief burden is not adequately met. Our institutions themselves may be endangered by a prolongation of this depression, and a failure of Congress to meet its responsibility and to come to the assistance of citizens who are suffering as a result of economic disaster over which they had no control.

I ask Senators also to consider the situation which will confront this Government if no action is taken. True, there have been enormous losses on the part of individuals owning property and securities; but for the most part they have had their standards of living reduced—not wiped out. So far as the wage earners are concerned, they have been catapulted by the effects of this prolonged depression into a bottomless pit of poverty and despair.

Proceed, if you will; make the record that you will extend relief to organized wealth in this situation to the tune of $2,160,000,000, and that you will turn your backs upon the millions of upstanding American citizens who are suffering want, privation, and misery. But I say that if you fail to meet this issue now, you will meet it later. You cannot duck it; you cannot dodge it; you cannot meet it by offering substitutes that fail to meet the emergency character of the situation.

Senators say that this is a problem for local government; that it is no concern of the Federal Government.

Mr. President, the Federal Government is just as much concerned in the future citizenship of this Republic as the local communities, if not more so. If we permit this situation to go on, millions of children will be maimed in body, if not warped in mind, by the effects of malnutrition. They will form the citizenship upon which the future of this country must depend. They are the hope of America.

Franklin D. Roosevelt, the Forgotten Man, April 7, 1932

President's Personal File, National Archives and Records Administration, Franklin D. Roosevelt Presidential Library, Hyde Park, NY.

ALTHOUGH I understand that I am talking under the auspices of the Democratic National Committee, I do not want to limit myself to politics. I do not want to feel that I am addressing an audience of Democrats or that I speak merely as a Democrat myself. The present condition of our national affairs is too serious to be viewed through partisan eyes for partisan purposes.

Fifteen years ago my public duty called me to an active part in a great national emergency, the World War. Success then was due to a leadership whose vision carried beyond the timorous and futile gesture of sending a tiny army of 150,000 trained soldiers and the regular navy to the aid of our allies. The generalship of that moment conceived of a whole Nation mobilized for war, economic, industrial, social and military resources gathered into a vast unit capable of and actually in the process of throwing into the scales ten million men equipped with physical needs and sustained by the realization that behind them were the united efforts of 110,000,000 human beings. It was a great plan because it was built from bottom to top and not from top to bottom.

In my calm judgment, the Nation faces today a more grave emergency than in 1917.

It is said that Napoleon lost the battle of Waterloo because he forgot his infantry— he staked too much upon the more spectacular but less substantial cavalry. The present administration in Washington provides a close parallel. It has either forgotten or it does not want to remember the infantry of our economic army.

These unhappy times call for the building of plans that rest upon the forgotten, the unorganized but the indispensable units of economic power, for plans like those of 1917 that build from the bottom up and not from the top down, that put their faith once more in the forgotten man at the bottom of the economic pyramid.

Obviously, these few minutes tonight permit no opportunity to lay down the ten or a dozen closely related objectives of a plan to meet our present emergency, but I can draw a few essentials, a beginning in fact, of a planned program.

It is the habit of the unthinking to turn in times like this to the illusions of economic magic. People suggest that a huge expenditure of public funds by the Federal Government and by State and local governments will completely solve the unemployment problem. But it is clear that even if we could raise many billions of dollars and find definitely useful public works to spend these billions on, even all that money would not give employment to the seven million or ten million people who are out of work. Let us admit frankly that it would be only a stopgap. A real economic cure must go to the killing of the bacteria in the system rather than to the treatment of external symptoms.

How much do the shallow thinkers realize, for example, that approximately one-half of our whole population, fifty or sixty million people, earn their living by farming or in small towns whose existence immediately depends on farms. They have today lost their purchasing power. Why? They are receiving for farm products less than the cost to them of growing these farm products. The result of this loss of purchasing power is that many other millions of people engaged in industry in the cities cannot sell industrial products to the farming half of the Nation. This brings home to every city worker that his own employment is directly tied up with the farmer's dollar. No Nation can long endure half bankrupt. Main Street, Broadway, the mills, the mines will close if half the buyers are broke.

I cannot escape the conclusion that one of the essential parts of a national program of restoration must be to restore purchasing power to the farming half of the country. Without this the wheels of railroads and of factories will not turn.

Closely associated with this first objective is the problem of keeping the home-owner and the farm-owner where he is, without being dispossessed through the foreclosure of his mortgage. His relationship to the great banks of Chicago and New York is pretty remote. The two billion dollar fund which President Hoover and the Congress have put at the disposal of the big banks, the railroads and the corporations of the Nation is not for him.

His is a relationship to his little local bank or local loan company. It is a sad fact that even though the local lender in many cases does not want to evict the farmer or home-owner by foreclosure proceedings, he is forced to do so in order to keep his bank or company solvent. Here should be an objective of Government itself, to provide at least as much assistance to the little fellow as it is now giving to the large banks and corporations. That is another example of building from the bottom up.

One other objective closely related to the problem of selling American products is to provide a tariff policy based upon economic common sense rather than upon politics, hot-air, and pull. This country during the past few years, culminating with the Hawley-Smoot Tariff in 1929, has compelled the world to build tariff fences so high that world trade is decreasing to the vanishing point. The value of goods internationally exchanged is today less than half of what it was three or four years ago.

Every man and woman who gives any thought to the subject knows that if our factories run even 80 percent of capacity, they will turn out more products than we as a Nation can possibly use ourselves. The answer is that if they run on 80 percent of capacity, we must sell some goods abroad. How can we do that if the outside Nations cannot pay us in cash? And we know by sad experience that they cannot do that. The only way they can pay us is in their own goods or raw materials, but this foolish tariff of ours makes that impossible.

What we must do is this: revise our tariff on the basis of a reciprocal exchange of goods, allowing other Nations to buy and to pay for our goods by sending us such of their goods as will not seriously throw any of our industries out of balance, and incidentally making impossible in this country the continuance of pure monopolies which cause us to pay excessive prices for many of the necessities of life.

Such objectives as these three, restoring farmers' buying power, relief to the small banks and home-owners and a reconstructed tariff policy, are only a part of ten or a dozen vital factors. But they seem to be beyond the concern of a national administration which can think in terms only of the top of the social and economic structure. It has sought temporary relief from the top down rather than permanent relief from the bottom up. It has totally failed to plan ahead in a comprehensive way. It has waited until something has cracked and then at the last moment has sought to prevent total collapse.

It is high time to get back to fundamentals. It is high time to admit with courage that we are in the midst of an emergency at least equal to that of war. Let us mobilize to meet it.

Franklin D. Roosevelt on Hawley-Smoot Tariff, September 29, 1932

President's Personal File, National Archives and Records Administration, Franklin D. Roosevelt Presidential Library, Hyde Park, NY.

During the election of 1932, in a speech in Sioux City, Iowa, Democratic presidential candidate Franklin D. Roosevelt blamed President Herbert Hoover for the Great Depression because he had signed the Hawley-Smoot Tariff into law. Roosevelt claimed that the tariff had caused the Great Depression, although Hoover argued that other events around the world had precipitated the crisis.

Mr. Chairman, my friends in Sioux City, my friends in this great State, and, indeed, all of you through the country who are listening on the radio tonight, let me tell you first of all that I appreciate this remarkable welcome that you have given me, and I appreciate, too, the performance put on by the mounted patrol of my fellow Shriners.

Two weeks ago, when I was heading toward the Coast, I presented before an audience in the City of Topeka, what I conceived to be the problem of agriculture in these United States, with particular reference to the Middle West and West, and what the Government of the Nation can do to meet that problem of ours.

I have been highly gratified to receive from all parts of the country and particularly from farm leaders themselves, assurances of their hearty support and promises of cooperation, in the efforts that I proposed to improve the deplorable condition into which agriculture has fallen. The meeting of this farm problem of ours is going to be successful only if two factors are present.

The first is a sympathetic Administration in Washington, and the second is the hearty support and patient cooperation of agriculture itself and its leaders.

I cannot avoid a word concerning this plight of agriculture—what it means to all. It means that the product of your labor brings just half of what it brought before the war. It means that no matter how hard you work and how long and how carefully you save, and how much efficiency you apply to your business, you face a steadily diminishing return. As a farm leader said to me, you have been caught like a man in a deep pit, helpless in the grip of forces that are beyond your control. Still, my friends, it has meant that in spite of the maxims that we have learned when we were in school, that we ought to work and save, to be prudent and be temperate, in spite of all of the rest of the homely virtues, the return on these virtues has belied the hopes and the promises on which you and I were raised.

That is one of the tragic consequences of this depression. The things that we were taught have not come true. We were taught to work and we have been denied the opportunity to work. We were taught to increase the products of our labor and we have found that while the products increase the return has decreased. We were taught to bring forth the fruits of the earth, and we have found that the fruits of the earth have found no market.

The results of our labor, my friends, have been lost in the smash of an economic system that was unable to fulfill its purposes.

It is a moral as well as an economic question that we face—moral because we want to reestablish the standards that in times past were our goal. We want the opportunity to live in comfort, reasonable comfort, out of which we may build our spiritual values. The consequences of poverty bring a loss of spiritual and moral values. And even more important is the loss of the opportunity that we hope to give to the younger generation. We want our children to have a chance for an education, for the sound development of American standards to be applied in their daily lives at play and work. Those opportunities can come only if the condition of agriculture is made more prosperous.

Now, the farmer—and when I speak of the farmer I mean not only you who live in the corn belt, but also those in the East and the Northwest who are in the dairy business, those in the South who are raising cotton, and those on the plains who are raising cattle and sheep, and those in the many sections of the country who are raising cattle, all kinds of things, small fruits and big fruits—in other words, the farmer in the broad sense, has been attacked during this past decade simultaneously from two sides. On the one side the farmer's expenses, chiefly in the [Page 606] form of increased taxes, have been going up rather steadily during the past generation, and on the other side, he has been attacked by a constantly depreciating farm dollar during the past twelve years, and it seems to be nothing less than old-fashioned horse sense to seek means to circumvent both of these attacks at the same time. That means, first, for us to seek relief for him from the burden of his expense account and, second, to try to restore the purchasing power of his dollar by getting for him higher prices for the products of the soil.

Now, those two great purposes are, quite frankly, the basis of my farm policy, and I have definitely connected both of them with the broadest aspects of a new national economy, something that I like to label in simpler words, "A New Deal," covering every part of the Nation, and covering industry and business as well as farming, because I recognize, first of all, that from the soil itself springs our ability to restore our trade with the other Nations of the world.

First of all, I want to discuss with you one of the angles of the mounting expenses of agriculture in practically every community and in every State—the problem of taxes which we have to pay.

Let us examine the proportion of our expenditures that goes to the various divisions of Government. Half of what you and I pay for the support of the Government—in other words, on the average in this country fifty cents out of every dollar—goes to local government, that is, cities, townships, counties and lots of other small units; and the other half, the other fifty cents, goes to the State and Nation.

This fifty cents that goes to local government, therefore, points to the necessity for attention to local government. As a broad proposition you and I know we are not using our present agencies of local government with real economy and efficiency. That means we must require our public servants to give a fuller measure of service for what they are paid. It means we must eliminate useless office holders. It means every public official, every employee of local government must determine that he owes it to the country to cooperate in the great purpose of saving the taxpayers' money.

But it means more than that, my friends. I am going to speak very frankly to you. There are offices in most States that are provided for in the Constitution and laws of some of the States, offices that have an honorable history but are no longer necessary for the conduct of Government. We have too many tax layers, and it seems to me relief can come only through resolute, courageous cutting.

Some of you will ask why I, a candidate for the office of president of the United States, am talking to you about changes in local government. Now, it is perfectly clear that the president has no legal or constitutional control over the local government under which you people live. The President has, nevertheless, my friends, the right and even the duty of taking a moral leadership in this national task because it is a national problem, because in its scope it covers every State, and any problem that is national in this broader sense creates a national moral responsibility in the President of the United States himself.

And I propose to use this position of high responsibility to discuss up and down the country, in all seasons and at all times, the duty of reducing taxes, or increasing the efficiency of Government, of cutting out the underbrush around out governmental structure, of getting the most public service for every dollar paid in taxation. That I pledge you, and nothing I have said in the campaign transcends in importance this covenant with the taxpayers of the United States.

Now, of the other half dollar of your taxes, it is true that part goes to the support of State Governments. I am not going to discuss that end. In this field also I believe that substantial reductions can be made. While the President rightly has no authority over State budgets, he has the same moral responsibility of national leadership for generally lowered expenses, and therefore for generally lowered taxes.

It is in the field of the Federal Government that the office of President can, of course, make itself most directly and definitely felt. Over 30 percent of your tax dollar goes to Washington, and in their field also, items such as the interest can be accomplished. There are, of course, items such as the interest on the public debt which must be paid each year, and which can be reduced only through a reduction of the debt itself, by the creation of a surplus in the place of the present deficit in the national treasury, and it is perhaps worth while that I should tell you that I spent nearly eight years in Washington during the Administration of Woodrow Wilson, and that during those eight years I had a fair understanding of the problem of the national expenses, and that I knew first hand many of the details of actual administration of the different departments. Later in this campaign, I proposed to analyze the enormous increase in the growth of what you and I call bureaucracy. We are not getting an adequate return for the money we are spending in Washington, or to put it another way, we are spending altogether too much money for Government services that are neither practical nor necessary. And then, in addition to that, we are attempting too many functions. We need to simplify what the Federal Government is giving to the people.

I accuse the present Administration of being the greatest spending Administration in peace times in all our history. It is an Administration that has piled bureau on bureau, commission on commission, and has failed to anticipate the dire needs and the reduced earning power of the people. Bureaus and bureaucrats, commissions and commissioners have been retained at the expense of the taxpayer.

Now, I read in the past few days in the newspapers that the President is at work on a plan to consolidate and simplify the Federal bureaucracy. My friends, four long years ago, in the campaign of 1928, he, as a candidate, proposed to do this same thing. And today, once more a candidate, he is still proposing, and I leave you to draw your own inferences.

And on my part I ask you very simply to assign to me the task of reducing the annual operating expenses of your national Government.

Now I come to the other half of the farmer's problem, the increase of the purchasing power of the farm dollar. I have already gone at length into the emergency proposals relating to our major crops, and now I want to discuss in more detail a very important factor, a thing known as the tariff, and our economic relationship to the rest of this big round world. [Page 607]

From the beginning of our Government, one of the most difficult questions in our economic life has been the tariff. But it is a fact that it is now so interwoven with our whole economic structure, and that structure is such an intricate and delicate pattern of causes and effects, that tariff revision must be undertaken, with scrupulous care and only on the basis of established facts.

I have to go back in history a little way. In the course of his 1928 campaign, the present Republican candidate for President with great boldness laid down the propositions that high tariffs interfere only slightly, if at all, with our export or our import trade, that they are necessary to the success of agriculture and afford essential farm relief; that they do not interfere with the payments of debts by other Nations to us, and that they are absolutely necessary to the economic formula which he proposed at that time as the road to the abolition of poverty. And I must pause here for a moment to observe that the experience of the past four years has unhappily demonstrated the error, the gross, fundamental, basic error of every single one of those propositions—but four years ago!—that every one of them has been one of the effective causes of the present depression; and finally that no substantial progress toward recovery from this depression, either here or abroad, can be had without a forthright recognition of those errors.

And so I am asking effective action to reverse the disastrous policies which were based on them. As I have elsewhere remarked, the 1928 Republican leadership prosperity promise was based on the assertion that although our agriculture was producing a surplus far in excess of our power to consume, and that, due to the mass and automatic machine production of today, our industrial production had also passed far beyond the point of domestic consumption, nevertheless, we should press forward to increase industrial production as the only means of maintaining prosperity and employment. And the candidate of that year insisted that, although we could not consume all those things at home, there was some kind of unlimited market for our rapidly increasing surplus in export trade, and he boldly asserted that on this theory we were on the verge of the greatest commercial expansion in history. I do not have to tell you the later history of that.

And then, in the spring of 1929, ostensibly for the purpose of enacting legislation for the relief of agriculture, a special session of Congress was called, and the disastrous fruit of that session was the notorious and indefensible Grundy-Smoot-Hawley tariff.

As to the much-heralded purpose of that special session for the relief of agriculture, the result, my friends, was a ghastly jest. The principal cash crops of our farms are produced much in excess of our domestic requirements. And we know that no tariff on a surplus crop, no matter how high the wall—1,000 percent, if you like— has the slightest effect on raising the domestic price of that crop. Why, the producers of all those crops are so effectively thrust outside the protection of our tariff walls as if there were no tariff at all. But we still know that the tariff does protect the price of industrial products and raises them above world prices, as the farmer with increasing bitterness has come to realize. He sells on a free trade basis; he buys in a protected market. The higher industrial tariffs go, my friends, the greater is the burden of the farmer.

Now, the first effect of the Grundy tariff was to increase or sustain the cost of all that agriculture buys, but the harm to our whole farm production did not stop there.

The destructive effect of the Grundy tariff on export markets has not been confined to agriculture. It has ruined our export trade in industrial products as well. Industry, with its foreign trade cut off, naturally began to look to the home market—a market supplied for the greater part by the purchasing power of farm families—but for reasons that you and I know, it found that the Grundy tariff had reduced the buying power of the farmer.

So what happened? Deprived of any American market, the other industrial Nations in order to support their own industries, and take care of their own employment problem, had to find new outlets. In that quest they took to trade agreements with other countries than ourselves and also to the preservation of their own domestic markets against importations by trade restrictions of all kinds. An almost frantic movement toward self-contained nationalism began among other Nations of the world, and of course the direct result was a series of retaliatory and defensive measures on their part, in the shape of tariffs and embargoes and import quotas and international arrangements. Almost immediately international commerce began to languish. The export markets for our industrial and agricultural surplus began to disappear altogether.

In the year 1929, a year before the enactment of the Grundy tariff, we exported 54.8 percent of all the cotton produced in the United States—more than one-half. That means, Mr. Cotton Grower, that in 1929 every other row of your cotton was sold abroad. And you, the growers of wheat, exported 17 percent of your wheat, but your great foreign market had been largely sacrificed; and so, with the grower of rye, who was able to dispose of 20 percent of his crop to foreign markets. The grower of leaf-tobacco had a stake of 41 percent of his income overseas, and one-third of the lard production, 33 percent, was exported in the year 1929. Where does that come in? Well, it concerns the corn grower because some of us, even from the East, know that corn is exported in the shape of lard.

How were your interests taken care of? Oh, they gave you a tariff on corn—chicken feed—literally and figuratively, but those figures show how vitally you are interested in the preservation, perhaps I had better say the return, of our export trade.

Now, the ink on the Hawley-Smoot-Grundy tariff bill was hardly dry before foreign Nations commenced their program of retaliation. Brick for brick they built their walls against us. They learned the lesson from us. The villainy we taught them they practiced on us.

And the Administration in Washington had reason to know that would happen. It was warned. While the bill was before Congress, our State Department received 160 protests from 33 other nations, many of whom after the passage of the bill erected their own tariff walls to the detriment or destruction of much of our export trade. [Page 608]

Well, what is the result? In two years, from 1930 to May, 1932, to escape the penalty on the introduction of American-made goods, American manufacturers have established in foreign countries 258 separate factories; 48 of them in Europe; 12 in Latin American; 28 in the Far East, and 71 across the border in Canada. The Prime Minister of Canada said in a recent speech that a factory is moving every day of the year from the United States into Canada, and he assured those at the recent conferences at Ottawa that the arrangements made there with Great Britain and other colonies would take

$250,000,000 of Canadian trade that would otherwise go to the United States. So you see, my friends, what that tariff bill did there was to put more men on the street here, and to put more people to work outside our borders.

Now, there was a secondary and perhaps even more disastrous effect of Grundyism. Billions of dollars of debts are due to this country from abroad. If the debtor Nations cannot export goods, they must try to pay in gold. But we started such a drain on the gold reserves of the other Nations as to force practically all of them off the gold standard. What happened? The value of the money of each of these countries relative to the value of our dollar declined alarmingly and steadily. It took more Argentine pesos to buy an American plow. It took more English shillings to buy an American bushel of wheat, or an American bale of cotton.

Why, they just could not buy goods with their money. These goods then were thrown back upon our markets and prices fell still more.

And so, summing up, this Grundy tariff has largely extinguished the export markets for our industrial and our farm surplus; it has prevented the payment of public and private debts to us and the interest thereon, increasing taxation to meet the expense of our Government, and finally it has driven our factories abroad.

The process still goes on, my friends. Indeed, it may be only in its beginning. The Grundy tariff still retains its grip on the throat of international commerce.

There is no relief in sight, and certainly there can be no relief if the men in Washington responsible for this disaster continue in power. And I say to you, in all earnestness and sincerity, that unless and until this process is reversed throughout the world, there is no hope for full economic recovery, or for true prosperity in this beloved country of ours.

The essential trouble is that the Republican leaders thought they had a good patent on the doctrine of unscaleable tariff walls and that no other Nation could use the same idea. Well, either that patent has expired or else never was any good anyway; or else, one other alternative, all the other Nations have infringed on our patent and there is no court to which we can take our case. It was a stupid, blundering idea, and we know it today and we know it has brought disaster.

Do not expect our adroit Republican friends to admit this. They do not. On the contrary, they have adopted the boldest alibi in the history of politics. Having brought this trouble on the world, they now seek to avoid all responsibility by blaming the foreign victims for their own economic blundering. They say that all of our troubles come from abroad and that the Administration is not in the least to be held to answer. This excuse is a classic of impertinence. If ever a condition was more clearly traceable to two specific American-made causes, it is the depression of this country and the world. Those two causes are interrelated. The second one, in point of time, is the Grundy tariff. The first one is the fact that by improvident loans to "backward and crippled countries," the policy of which was specifically recommended by the President, we financed practically our entire export trade and the payment of interest and principal to us by our debtors, and even in part, the payment of German reparations.

When we began to diminish that financing in 1929 the economic structure of the world began to totter.

If it be fair to ask, What does the Democratic Party propose to do in the premises?

The platform declares in favor of a competitive tariff which means one which will put the American producers on a market equality with their foreign competitors, one that equalizes the difference in the cost of production, not a prohibitory tariff back of which domestic producers may combine to practice extortion of the American public.

I appreciate that the doctrine thus announced is not widely different from that preached by Republican statesmen and politicians, but I do know this, that the theory professed by them is that the tariff should equalize the difference in the cost of production as between this country and competitive countries, and I know that in practice that theory is utterly disregarded. The rates that are imposed are far in excess of any such difference, looking to total exclusion of imports—in other words, prohibitory rates.

Of course the outrageously excessive rates in that bill as it became law, must come down. But we should not lower them beyond a reasonable point, a point indicated by common sense and facts. Such revision of the tariff will injure no legitimate interest. Labor need have no apprehensions concerning such a course, for labor knows by long and bitter experience that the highly protected industries pay not one penny higher wages than the non-protected industries, such as the automobile industry, for example.

But, my friends, how is reduction to be accomplished? In view of present world conditions, international negotiation is the first, the most practical, the most common-sense, and the most desirable method. We must consent to the reduction to some extent of some of our duties in order to secure a lowering of foreign tariff walls over which a larger measure of our surplus may be sent.

I have not the fear that possesses some timorous minds that we should get the worst of it in such reciprocal arrangements. I ask if you have no faith in our Yankee tradition of good old-fashioned trading? Do you believe that our early instincts for successful barter have degenerated or atrophied? I do not think so. I have confidence that the spirit of the stalwart traders still permeates our people, that the red blood of the men who sailed our Yankee clipper ships around the Horn and Cape of Good Hope in the China trade still courses in our veins. I cannot picture Uncle Sam as a supine, white-livered, flabby-muscled old man, cooling his heels in the [Page 609] shade of our tariff walls. We may not have the astuteness in some forms of international diplomacy that our more experienced European friends have, but when it comes to good old-fashioned barter and trade—whether it be goods or tariff—my money is on the American. My friends, there cannot and shall not be any foreign dictation of our tariff policies, but I am willing and ready to sit down around the table with them.

And next, my friends, the Democrats propose to accomplish the necessary reduction through the agency of the Tariff Commission.

I need not say to you that one of the most deplorable features of tariff legislation is the log-rolling process by which it has been effected in Republican and Democratic Congresses. Indefensible rates are introduced through an understanding, usually implied rather than expressed among members, each of whom is interested in one or more individual items. Yet, it is a case of you scratch my back and I will scratch yours. Now, to avoid that as well as other evils in tariff making, a Democratic Congress in 1916 passed, and a Democratic President approved, a bill creating a bipartisan Tariff Commission, charged with the duty of supplying the Congress with accurate and full information upon which to base tariff rates. That Commission functioned as a scientific body until 1922, when by the incorporation of the so-called flexible provisions of the Act it was transformed into a political body. Under those flexible provisions—re-enacted in the Grundy tariff of 1930—the Commission reports not to a Congress but to the President, who is then empowered on its recommendation to raise or lower the tariff rates by as much as 50 percent. At the last session of Congress—this brings us down to date—by the practically unanimous action of the Democrats of both houses, aided by liberal-minded Republicans led by Senator Norris, of Nebraska, a bill was passed by the Congress, but vetoed by the President, which, for the purpose of preventing log-rolling provided that if a report were made by the Tariff Commission on a particular item, with a recommendation as to the rates of duty, a bill to make effective that rate would not be subject to amendment in the Congress so as to include any other items not directly affected by the change proposed in the bill. And in that way each particular tariff rate proposed would be judged on its merits alone. If that bill had been signed by the President of the United States, log-rolling would have come to an end.

I am confident in the belief that under such a system rates adopted would generally be so reasonable that there would be very little opportunity for criticism or even caviling as to them. I am sure that it is not that any duties are imposed that complaint is made, for despite the effort, repeated in every campaign, to stigmatize the Democratic Party as a free trade party, there never has been a tariff act passed since the Government came into existence, in which the duties were not levied with a view to giving the American producer an advantage over his foreign competitor. I think you will agree with me that the difference in our day between the two major parties in respect to their leadership on the subject of the tariff is that the Republican leaders, whatever may be their profession, would put the duties so high as to make them practically prohibitive and on the other hand that the Democratic leaders would put them as low as the preservation of the prosperity of American industry and American agriculture will permit.

Another feature of the bill to which reference has been made, a feature designed to obviate tariff log-rolling, contemplated the appointment of a public counsel who should be heard on all applications for changes in rates whether for increases sought by producers, sometimes greedy producers, or for decreases asked by importers, equally often actuated by purely selfish motives. And I hope some such change may speedily be enacted. It will have my cordial approval because, my friends, it means that the average citizen would have some representation.

Now, just a few words in closing. I want to speak to you of one other factor which enters into the dangerous emergency in which you farmers find yourselves at this moment. For more than a year I have spoken in my State and in other States of the actual calamity that impends on account of farm mortgages. Ever since my nomination on the first day of July, I have advocated immediate attention and immediate action looking to the preservation of the American home to the American farmer. But I recognize that I am not at the head of the National Administration nor shall I be until the March 4th next. Today I read in the papers that for the first time, so far as I know, the Administration of President Hoover has discovered the fact that there is such a thing as a farm mortgage or a home mortgage.

I do not have to tell you that, with the knowledge of conditions in my State which ranks fifth or sixth among the agricultural States of the Union and with the knowledge I have gleaned on this trip from coast to coast, I realize to the full the seriousness of the farm mortgage situation. And at least we can take a crumb of hope from his proposal for just another conference, a conference of some kind at least to discuss the situation. Seriously, my friends, all that I can tell you is that with you I deplore, I regret the inexcusable, the reprehensible delay of Washington, not for months alone, but for years. I have already been specific on this subject, upon mortgages, in my Topeka speech. All that I can promise you between now and the fourth of March is that I will continue to preach the plight of the farmer who is losing his home. All I can do is to promise you that when the authority of administration and recommendation to Congress is placed in my hands I will do everything in my power to bring the relief that is so long overdue. I shall not wait until the end of a campaign, I shall not wait until I have spent four years in the White House.

Herbert Hoover, Remarks to the Republican Joint National Planning Committee to Get Out the Negro Vote. October 1, 1932

Public Papers of the Presidents: Herbert Hoover (1929–33), National Archives and Records Administration.

I WISH to thank you for your coming and for the presentation to me of so touching a statement.

The platform of the Republican Party speaks with justifiable pride of the friendship of our party for the American Negro that has endured unchanged for 70 years. It pledges itself to the continued insistence upon his rights. That the friendship and consideration of the party for the American Negro has borne fruit is in the advancement of the race. That is evident in business, in the arts and sciences, in the professions, and recently we have seen a great achievement of two splendid youths, Tolan and Metcalfe, in world supremacy in the Olympiad.

It has been gratifying to me to have participated in many measures for advancement of education and welfare amongst the Negroes of our Nation. I have received the cooperation and counsel of a distinguished leadership of the Negroes themselves in these institutions and movements. No better example of this leadership than the contributions made by Negro representatives who participated in the recent White House Conference on Child Health and Protection and upon Home Building and Home Ownership. I recall also with great pleasure this cooperation and the evidence of fine leadership in the relief of the Mississippi floods, and more recently in relief of drought, and in the sound advice and assistance I have had in formulating relief from the present distress and unemployment.

You may be assured that our party will not abandon or depart from its traditional duty toward the American Negro. I shall sustain this pledge given in the first instance by the immortal Lincoln and transmitted by him to those who followed as a sacred trust. The right of liberty, justice, and equal opportunity is yours. The President of the United States is ever obligated to the maintenance of those sacred trusts to the full extent of his authority. I appreciate your presence here today as an evidence of your friendship.

Note: The President spoke at 12 noon in ceremonies welcoming 100 black Republicans to the White House. Prior to his remarks, the leaders of the delegation expressed their faith in him and asked for a message to the black community.

In his remarks, the President referred to Eddie Tolan, Olympic champion in the 100 and 200 meter dashes, and Ralph Metcalfe, runner-up in the 100 meter dash.

Herbert Hoover, Excerpt from Address at the Coliseum in Des Moines, Iowa. October 4, 1932

Public Papers of the Presidents: Herbert Hoover (1929–33), National Archives and Records Administration.

Now, an amazing statement was made a few days ago in this State that the passage of the Tariff Act of 1930 "started such a drain on the gold reserves of the principal commercial countries as to force practically all of them off the gold standard." The facts are that the Tariff Act was not passed until nearly a year after this depression began.

This earthquake started in Europe. The gold of Europe was not drained and never has been drained. It has increased in total every year since the passage of the Tariff Act and is right now $1,500 million greater than when the act was passed, and the tariff is still operating. It has been my daily task to analyze and to know the forces which brought these calamities. I have to look them in the face. They require far more penetration than such assertions as this would indicate.

The shocks which rocked these nations came from profound depths; their spread gave fearful blows to our own system, finally culminating October last in what, had they not been courageously met with unprecedented measures, would, because of our peculiar situation, have brought us to greater collapse than many of the countries of Europe.

The first effect of these shocks on us was from foreign dumping of American securities on our markets which demoralized prices upon our exchanges, depreciated the securities and investments held by our insurance companies and our trusts, foreign buying power stagnated because of their internal paralysis and this in turn stifled the markets for our farms and factories; it increased our unemployment and by piling up our surpluses demoralized our agricultural prices even further.

The frantic restrictive measures on exchanges which they took and the abandonment of gold standards made it impossible for American citizens to collect billions of the moneys due to us for goods which our citizens had sold abroad, or short-term loans they had made to facilitate commerce. At the same time citizens of those foreign countries demanded payment from our citizens of the moneys due for goods which they had sold to our merchants and for securities they had sold in our country.

Before the end foreign countries drained nearly a billion dollars of gold and a vast amount of other exchange from our coffers.

We had also to meet an attack upon our own flank from some of our own people who, becoming infected with world fear and panic, withdrew vast sums from our own banks and hoarded it from the use of our own people, to the amount of nearly $1,500 million. This brought its own train of failures and bankruptcies. Even worse, many of our less patriotic citizens started to export their money to foreign countries for fear we should be forced onto a paper money basis.

Now, all this cataclysm did not develop at once. It came blow by blow. Its effect upon us grew steadily, and our difficulties mounted higher day by day.

This is no time to trace its effect stage by stage. No statement of mine is needed to portray the effects which you have felt at your own door. No statement could portray the full measure of perils which threatened us as a nation.

Three of the great perils were invisible except to those who had the responsibility of dealing with the situation.

The first of these perils was the steady strangulation of credit through the removal of $3 billions of gold and currency by foreign drains and by the hoarding of our own citizens from the channels of our commerce and business. And let me remind you that credit is the lifeblood of business, the lifeblood of prices and of jobs.

Had the consequences of this action, of that drain been allowed to run their full extent, it would have resulted, under our system of currency and banking, in the deflation of credit anywhere from $20 to $25 billions, or the destruction of nearly one-half of the immediate working capital of the country. There would have been almost a universal call for the payment of debts which would have brought about inevitable universal bankruptcy because property could not be converted into cash, no matter what its value.

There were other forces equally dangerous. The tax income of the Federal Government is largely based upon profits and income. As these profits and income disappeared, the Federal resources fell by nearly one-half, and thus the very stability of the Federal Treasury was imperiled. The Government was compelled to borrow enormous sums to meet current expenses.

The third peril, which we escaped only by the most drastic action, was that of being forced off of the gold standard. I would like to make clear to you what that would have meant had we failed in that sector of the battle. Going off the gold standard in the United States would have been a most crushing blow to most of those with savings and those who owed money, and it was these we were fighting to protect.

Going off the gold standard is no academic matter. By going off that standard, gold goes to a premium, and the currency dollar becomes depreciated. In our country, largely as a result of fears generated by the experience after the Civil War and by the Democratic free-silver campaign in 1896, our people have long insisted upon writing a large part of their long-term debtor documents as payable in gold.

A considerable part of farm mortgages, most of our industrial and all of our Government, most of our State and municipal bonds, and most other long-term obligations are written as payable in gold.

This is not the case in foreign countries. They have no such practice. Their obligations are written in currency. When they abandon the gold standard and gold goes to a premium, the relation of their domestic debtors and creditors is unchanged because both he who pays and he who receives use the same medium. But if the United States had been forced off the gold standard, you in this city would have sold your produce for depreciated currency. You would be paid your bank deposits and your insurance policy in currency, but you would have to pay a premium on such of your debts as are written in gold. The Federal Government, many of the States, the municipalities, to meet their obligations, would either need to increase taxes which are payable in currency, or alternatively, to have repudiated their obligations.

Now, I believe I can also make it clear to you why we were in danger of being forced off the gold standard, even with our theoretically large stocks of gold. I have told you of the enormous sums of gold and exchange that were drained from us by foreigners. You will realize also that our citizens who hoard Federal Reserve and our other forms of currency are in effect hoarding gold because under the law we must maintain 40 percent gold reserve behind such currency. Owing to the lack in the Federal Reserve System of the kind of securities required by the law for the additional 60 percent of coverage of the currency, the Reserve System was forced to increase their gold reserve up to 75 percent. Thus with $1,500 million of hoarded currency, there was in effect over $1 billion of gold hoarded by our own citizens.

These drains had at one moment reduced the amount of gold we could spare for current payments to a point where the Secretary of the Treasury informed me that, unless we could put into effect a remedy, we could not hold to the gold standard in the United States for 2 weeks longer because of inability to meet the demands of foreigners and our own citizens for gold.

Being forced off the gold standard in the United States means chaos. Never was our Nation in greater peril, not alone in banks and financial systems, money and currency, but that forebode dangers—moral and social—with years of conflict and disarrangement.

In the midst of this hurricane the Republican administration kept a cool head, and it rejected every counsel of weakness and cowardice. Some of the reactionary economists urged that we should allow the liquidation to take its course until it had found its own bottom. Some people talked of vast issues of paper money. Some talked of suspending payments of Government issues. Some talked of setting up a Council of National Defense. Some talked foolishly of dictatorship—any one of which ideas would have produced panic in itself. Some assured me that no administration could propose increased taxes in the United States to balance the budget in the midst of a depression and survive an election.

However, we determined that we would not enter the morass of using the printing press for currency or bonds. All human experience has demonstrated that that path once taken cannot be stopped, and that the moral integrity of the Government would be sacrificed because ultimately both currency and bonds must become valueless.

We determined that we would not follow the advice of the bitter-end liquidationists and see the whole body of debtors of the United States brought to bankruptcy and the savings of our people brought to destruction.

We determined we would stand up like men and render the credit of the United States Government impregnable through the drastic reduction of Government expenditures and increased revenues until we balanced that budget. We determined that if necessary we should lend the full credit of the Government thus made impregnable to aid private institutions to protect the debtor and the savings of our people.

We decided, if necessary, upon changes in the Federal Reserve System which would make our gold active in commercial use, and that we would keep the American dollar ringing true in every city in America and every country in the world. We determined that we would expand credit to offset the contraction brought about by hoarding and foreign withdrawals; that we would strengthen the Federal land banks and all other mortgage institutions; that we would lend to the farmers for Production; that we would protect the insurance companies, the building and loan associations, the savings banks, the country banks, and every other point of weakness in this Nation.

We determined to place the shield of the Federal Government in front of those local communities in protection of those in distress, and that we would increase employment through profitable construction work with the aid of Government credit.

On the 3d of October last year, I called to Washington the leading bankers of the country and secured from them an agreement to combine the resources of the banks to stem the tide. They pledged themselves to $500 million for this purpose. On October 6, I called in the leaders of both political parties. I placed before them the situation at home and abroad. I asked for unity of national action. That unity was gladly given. We published a united determination to the country to meet the situation. Our people drew a breath of relief. The ship swung to a more even keel.

But by the 1st of December the storm had grown in further intensity abroad, and the menace became more serious than ever before. With the opening of Congress in December, I laid before it a program of unprecedented dimensions to meet our unprecedented situation.

Now, the battalions and regiments and armies which we thus mobilized for this great battle turned the tide toward victory by July. The foreigners drew out most of the money that they could get, but finding that the American dollar rang honest, they gained in confidence, and they are now sending it back. Since June, $275 million of gold has flowed back to us from abroad. Hoarders in our own country, finding our institutions safeguarded and safe, have returned $250 million to the useful channels of business. The securities held by our insurance companies, our savings banks, and our benevolent trusts have recovered in value.

The rills of credit are expanding. The pressure on the debtor to sacrifice his all in order to pay his debts is steadily relaxing. Men are daily being reemployed. If we calculate the values of this year's agricultural products compared with the low points, the farmers as a whole, despite the heartbreaking distress which still exists, are a billion dollars better off. Prices have a long way to go before the farmer has an adequate return, but at least the turn is toward recovery.

Now, I have been talking of gold and of currency, of credit and of banks and bonds and insurance policies and of loans. Do not think these things have no human interpretation. The happiness of 120 million people was at stake in the measure to enable the Government to meet its debts and obligations, to save the gold standard, in enabling 5,500 banks, insurance companies, building and loan associations, and a multitude of other institutions to pay their obligations and ease their pressure upon their debtors.

Primary Sources | 683

These institutions have been rendered safe and with them several million depositors, policyholders, and borrowers.

More than half of all of them were in the Midwest—500 in your own State of Iowa. Had they gone down, the shock of their failure would have carried down with them every man and institution who owed money and the whole employment and marketing fabric of the United States into chaos.

I wish I could translate what these perils, had they not been overcome, would have meant to each person in the United States. The financial system is not alone intrusted with your savings. Its failure means that the manufacturer cannot pay his worker, the worker cannot pay his grocer, the merchant cannot buy his stock of goods, the farmer cannot sell his products. The great clock of economic life stops. Had we failed, disaster would have translated itself into despair in every home, every village, and every farm.

Now, we won this great battle to protect our people at home. We held the Gibraltar of world stability. The world today has a chance. It is growing in strength. Let that man who complains that things could not be worse thank God for this victory and make reverent acknowledgement to the courage and stamina of a great democracy.

Let him also be thankful for the presence in Washington of a Republican administration. I say this with full consideration of its portent, for I wish to call your attention to the part which the dominating leadership, the majority of the Democratic Party has played in this crisis. I wish to bring before you the real doctrines and programs of the men who then and now and in the future will dominate that party.

You will recollect that the congressional election 2 years ago gave the control of the lower House of Congress to our opponents. They were also in position to control the policies of the Senate. After that election their leaders announced to the world that their party would present a program to restore prosperity. One year later, when the new Congress assembled last December in the midst of this crisis, they presented no program.

The administration did present a program which has saved the country from disaster. That program was patriotically supported by many members of the Democratic Party who joined in enactment of these measures. To these men, who placed patriotism above party, I pay tribute, but later in that session of Congress the opposition majority of the House of Representatives could not restrain the real purposes and doctrines of their party. It is of importance to the country to realize what that program was, for the American people are asked to intrust the future of the United States into the hands of these same men and to these policies.

At a time when the most vital need was for the reduction of expenditures and the balancing of the budget to preserve the stability of the Federal Government as the keystone of all stability, they produced a program of pork-barrel legislation in the sum of $1,200 million for nonproductive and unnecessary works at the expense of the American taxpayer. They produced the cash bonus bill. They passed that through the House of Representatives by their leadership. I opposed it. It failed in the Senate. Under that bill it was proposed to expend $2,300 million. Worse still, the bill that they passed provided the bonus should be paid through the creation of sheer fiat money. They would have made our currency a football to every speculator and every vicious element in the financial world at the very time when we were fighting for the honesty of the American dollar.

I can do no better than to quote Daniel Webster, who, 100 years ago, made one of the most prophetic statements ever made when he said:

"He who tampers with the currency robs labor of its bread. He panders, indeed, to greedy capital, which is keen-sighted and may shift for itself, but he beggars labor, which is unsuspecting and too busy with the pursuit: of the present to calculate for the future. The prosperity of the workpeople lives, moves and has its being in established credit and steady medium of payment."

The experience of scores of governments in the world since that day has confirmed Webster's statement, and yet the dominant leadership of the Democratic Party—and I am not accusing the Democratic minority who stood out against these things—but that dominant leadership passed that measure to issue paper money through the Democratic House of Representatives.

And, further, the administration proposed economy measures to bring about reduction in specialized governmental expenditures by $250 to $300 million. When those recommendations had passed through the filter of the Democratic majority of the House, only $50 million of savings were left, and yet we hear a multitude of speeches from them on the subject of governmental economy.

They passed a bill to destroy the effectiveness of the Tariff Commission. I vetoed that bill. They passed a price-fixing bill creating what might be colloquially called the "rubber dollar." I opposed that also. They passed a provision for loans to corporations and everybody else, whether they were affected and guarded by public interest or not. It would have made the Government the most gigantic pawnbroker of history. I vetoed that. They passed other measures with this same reckless disregard for the safety of the Nation.

All this undermined public confidence and delayed all the efforts of the administration and the powerful instrumentalities which we had placed in action to save the country. Those of you who will recollect will realize that last March there was a period of upward trend, and after that we descended again into the abyss through these destructive actions. These measures represented the dominant Democratic control, and they brought discouragement and delay to recovery.

That recovery began the moment when it was certain that these destructive measures of this Democratically-controlled House of Representatives had been stopped. Had that program passed, it would have been the end of recovery, and if it ever passes, it will end hope of recovery. These measures were not simply gestures for vote-catching. These ideas and measures represented the true sentiments and doctrines of the majority of the men who control the Democratic Party. A small minority of Democratic Members of the House and the Senate disapproved of these measures. These men obviously no longer voice the control of that party. This program was passed through the Democratic House of Representatives under the leadership of the gentleman who has been nominated the Democratic candidate for Vice-President, and thus these measures and policies were approved by that party.

At no time in public discussion of the vital issues of this campaign has any Democratic candidate, high or low, disavowed these destructive acts which must again emerge if they come to power. I ask you to compare this actual Democratic program and these

Democratic actions with the constructive program produced by the administration to meet the emergency. And I ask: Do you propose to place these men in power and subject this country to that sort of measures and policies? It is by their acts.in Congress and their leadership that you shall know them.

Now, of vital concern to you and to all the Nation are the difficulties of agriculture. They have been of vital concern to me for the whole of these difficult years. I have been at the post to which the first news of every disaster is delivered and to which no detail of human suffering is ever spared. I have heard the cries of distress, and not only as a sympathetic listener but as one oppressed by a deep sense of responsibility to do all that human ingenuity could devise. I wish to speak directly to those of my hearers who are farmers of what is on my mind, of what is in my heart, to tell you the conclusions that I have reached from this bitter experience of the years in dealing with these problems which affect agriculture at home and their relations abroad.

That agriculture is prostrate needs no proof. You have saved and economized and worked to reduce costs, but with all this, yours is a story of suffering and distress.

What the farmer wants and needs is higher prices, and in the meantime to keep from being dispossessed from his farm, to have a fighting chance to save his home. The immediate and pressing question is how these two things are to be attained. Every decent citizen wants to see the farmer receive higher prices and wants to see him keep his home. Every citizen realizes that the general recovery of the country cannot be attained unless these things are secured to the farmer.

Every thinking citizen knows that most of these low price levels and most of this distress, except in one or two commodities where there is an unwieldy surplus, are due to the decreased demand for farm products by our millions of unemployed and by foreign countries. Every citizen knows that part of this unemployment is due in turn to the inability of the farmer to buy the products of the factory. Every thinking citizen knows that the farmer, the worker, and the businessman are in the same boat and must all come to shore together.

Every citizen who stretches his vision across the whole United States realizes that for the last 3 years we have been on this downward spiral owing to the destructive forces some of which I have already described. If he has this vision, he today takes courage and hope because he also knows that these destructive forces have been stopped; that the spiral is now moving upward; that more men are being employed and are able to consume more agricultural products.

The policies of the Republican Party and the unprecedented instrumentalities and measures which have been put in motion—many of which are designed directly for agriculture—are winning out. If we continue to fight along these lines we shall win.

There are 12 facets of this subject, 12 parts of the problem that I should like to discuss with you. The first is that the very basis of safety to American agriculture is the protective tariff.

The Republican Party originated and proposes to maintain the protective tariff on agricultural products. We will even widen that tariff further if it is necessary to protect agriculture. Ninety percent of the farmer's market is at home, and we propose to reserve that market to him.

Now, has the Democratic Party ever proposed or supported a protective tariff on farm products? Has it ever given one single evidence of protection of this home market to the American farmer from the products raised by peasant labor on cheap land abroad?

The Democratic Party, as you know, took the tariff off a large part of farm products in 1913, and put them on the free list. A Republican Congress passed the emergency farm tariff in 1921, and a Democratic President vetoed it. The Democratic minority in the next Congress in 1921 voted against the revived emergency farm tariff. The Republican majority passed it, and the Republican President signed it.

The Democratic minority voted against the increase of agricultural tariffs in the Republican tariff of 1922. Most of the Democratic Members of Congress voted against the increases in the tariff bill of 1930. Their platform enunciates the principle of "a competitive tariff for revenue." What that competition must mean is peasant labor and cheap lands. That is the kind of competition we don't want. Their candidate states that: "We sit on a high wall of a Hawley-Smoot tariff;.... sealed by the highest tariffs in the history of the world"—which incidentally isn't true—"a wicked and exorbitant tariff." He calls it: "a ghastly jest," and states that "our policy declares for lowered tariffs." This is surely a promise of reducing farm tariffs. They will reduce farm tariffs if they come to power.

When you return to your homes you can compare prices with foreign countries and count up this proposed destruction at your own firesides. There are at this minute 2 million cattle in the northern States of Mexico seeking a market. The price is about $2.50 per 100 pounds on the south bank of the Rio Grande. It is $4.50 on the north bank—and only the tariff wall in-between.

Bad as our prices are, if we take comparable prices of farm products today in the United States and abroad, I am informed by the Department of Agriculture that you will find that, except for the guardianship of the tariff, butter could be imported for 25 percent below your prices, pork products for 30 percent below your prices, lamb and beef products from 30 to 50 percent below, flaxseed for 35 percent below, beans for 40 percent below, and wool 30 percent below your prices, Both corn and wheat could be sold in New York from the Argentine at prices below yours at this moment were it not for the tariff. I suppose these are ghastly jests.

Now, the removal of or reduction of the tariff on farm products means a flood of them into the United States from every direction, and either you would be forced to further reduce your prices, or your products would rot in your barns.

The opposition party has endeavored to persuade our farmers that increased tariffs abroad are the result of reprisals against the United States. There are a half dozen suppressions of truth in that statement that are of profound interest especially to the farmer. The first is that many increases in tariffs abroad took place before, and not after, our farm tariffs were increased. The second is that the restrictions on imports in most cases are not directed at the United States. They are for the purpose of reducing all expenditure of their people during their financial crises. The third is that if we survey the growls of some nations when our tariffs were changed, we find the objections in overwhelming majority were directed at the increase in our agricultural tariffs. American farmers are entitled to know this. The very object of our increases was to protect them in our home market.

The main thing that those countries want is entrance for their surplus agricultural products into our markets. Many of those countries would decrease their tariffs against our industrial goods tomorrow in exchange for reduction on their farm products to us, but that is no help to our farmer.

Now, the Democratic Party proposes that they would enter into bargaining tariffs to secure special concessions from other countries for the entry of American goods. They represent this to be in the farmer's interest. But I may tell you here and now that the largest part of the whole world desires to make only one bargain with the United States. The bargain these countries wish to make is to lower our tariff on agricultural products in exchange for lowering their tariffs on our industrial goods. American industrial leaders, realizing the needs of the American farmer, do not want to be a part of such bargains.

Now, all tariff acts contain injustices and inequities. That is the case in the last tariff bill. I have never said that tariff bill was perfect. Some people get too much, and some people get too little. But those of you who have followed the accomplishments of this administration will recollect that I secured in the last tariff act, 25 years after it had originally been advocated by President Theodore Roosevelt, the adoption of effective flexible tariff provisions to be administered by a bipartisan body. That authority of a bipartisan Tariff Commission to revise the tariff is based upon a definite principle of protection to our people, and it is one of the most progressive acts which have been secured in the history of all American tariff legislation.

By maintaining that reform the country need no longer be faced with heartbreaking logrolling, selfishness, and greed which come to the surface on every occasion when Congress tries to revise the tariff.

This bipartisan Commission has now been engaged for over 18 months in an effective revision of the tariff. It has heard every complaint. It has found that many rates were just. It found some were too high and some too low. But if there are tariffs which are too high and result in damage to the American people, those tariffs can be readjusted by mere application to the Commission and the presentation of the evidence thereof. That tribunal is open to all the people.

Now, our opponents opposed this reform in tariff legislation. They passed a bill last session to destroy the independence of the Commission. They propose in their platform to destroy it. The reasons for this action are obvious. The bipartisan Tariff Commission has proved a serious political embarrassment to them. Either one of the Houses of Congress has the right to call upon the Tariff Commission for reconsideration of any schedule by a mere resolution. Notwithstanding their outcries against the 1930 tariff act, the Democratic-controlled House of Representatives, after being in session for 7 months, did not pass a single resolution requesting readjustment of a single commodity or a single schedule.

What the Democratic Party proposes is to reduce your farm tariffs. Aside from ruin to agriculture, such an undertaking in the midst of the depression will disturb every possibility of recovery.

Roosevelt, Eleanor. "What Ten Million Women Want," March 1932

Speech and Article File, Anna Eleanor Roosevelt Papers, National Archives and Records Administration, Franklin D. Roosevelt Presidential Library, Hyde Park, NY.

What Ten Million Women Want

What do ten million women want in public life? That question could be answered in ten million different ways. For every woman, like every man, has some aspirations or desires exclusively her own.

We women are callow fledglings as compared with the wise old birds who manipulate the political machinery, and we still hesitate to believe that a woman can fill certain positions in public life as competently and adequately as a man.

For instance, it is certain that women do not want a woman for President. Nor would they have the slightest confidence in her ability to fulfill the functions of that office.

Every woman who fails in a public position confirms this, but every woman who succeeds creates confidence.

Judge Florence Allen on the Supreme Court Bench in Ohio, Frances Perkins as Labor Commissioner in New York, have done much to make women feel that a really fine woman, well trained in her work, can give as good an account of her stewardship as any man, and eventually women, and perhaps even men, may come to feel that sex should not enter into the question of fitness for office.

When it comes to the matter of having a woman as a member of the President's Cabinet, there are I think, many women who feel that the time has come to recognize the fact that women have practically just as many votes as men and deserve at least a certain amount of recognition.

Take the Department of Labor for instance. Why should not the Secretary of Labor be a woman, and would not a woman's point of view be valuable in the President's Council? There are many other places to which women may aspire, and the time will come when there will be new departments, some of which will undoubtedly need women at their heads.

When we come to finances we realize that after all, all government, whether it is that of village, city, state or nation, is simply glorified housekeeping.

Little by little we are getting budget systems into our public housekeeping and budgets are something all women understand.

Every woman knows that dire results happen when she exceeds her own budget, and it is only a short step from this to understanding what happens in the city, the state or the nation when finances are not carefully administered and watched. Every woman demands that her government be economically managed, but she knows, far better perhaps than the average man, that there are two kinds of economy. There is such a thing as parsimonious spending which in the end costs more than a wise study of the needs of the future, and the spending which takes into account the social side of life.

For instance, it may be wise to spend fifty thousand dollars this year in buying space for parks, first because the land will increase in value, secondly because we are beginning to recognize that for the youth growing up in the cities, play space in the city and play space in the country beyond, is most important for healthful development. Perhaps we could save this sum today, but it would cost us far more in physical and spiritual value twenty years from now, as well as in actual cash.

Women are detail minded, they have had to be for generations, therefore, they are much more apt to watch in detail what is done by their public officials in the case of finances than does the average man.

Ten million women may not at the moment be quite awake to their opportunities along this line, still I think we can safely say that this is one of the wants that lies back in the mind of every woman.

Do women want to take an active part in framing our laws? I think the answer to that is decidedly yes. There are more and more women elected to Legislative Bodies every year. This session of Congress has six Congresswomen on its roll, three Democrats and three Republicans.

The names of Ruth Bryan Owen and Mrs. McCormick are far better known than those of many male Congressmen. We have in this new Congress for a time at least, the first active woman United States Senator in Mrs. Caraway. She was elected this January for the full term and she will be, from all indications, a real power in the Upper House, and very far from a rubber stamp.

Welfare legislation touches very closely the home life of every woman, and therefore demands her interest and careful criticism both in the provisions of the laws, and in the administration of those laws when they actually become effective. Because these laws are interpreted and enforced by our courts, I think women feel they are entitled to places on the bench.

Women judges are no longer a novelty, and in some classes of courts, particularly those dealing with juvenile offenders, the women have proven themselves decidedly superior to the men.

I do not think women would approve of having women heads of police departments. I do think they feel policewomen and matrons a necessity for the proper care of girl and women offenders. As for a national police commissioner, male or female, I think women are decidedly opposed to it.

It is our conviction that crime to be dealt with successfully, must be dealt with locally with a thorough understanding of local conditions. Every woman is, of course, deeply interested in the crime situation.

But I think because of her education and knowledge of the home, she realizes that it is through better education and better living conditions in our crowded cities that the prevention of crime, which is the ultimate aim of all criminology, must be achieved.

While I do not believe in a national police commissioner, or a national police commission, I think women approve the recommendation that there should be available at Washington a national department where data relating to criminals, and statistics relating to crime should be available for the use of all the state and local police departments of the country.

I think that those women who have given this question of crime most serious consideration are generally in agreement that the first and most practical step to its eradication would be in the wiping out of certain tenement house localities in our big cities and the raising of educational standards generally.

Women to whom, after all, the education of the child is largely entrusted by the men, understand far better than the average man the need of education and improvement in teaching.

Too often, the father's actual knowledge of how his child is being educated is gleaned from a hasty scanning of the report card once a month, but the mother knows all the virtues of the successful teacher and the faults of the poor one. She understands the defects of our system which produces, I am sorry to say, so many who have not the heaven-sent gift of instructing the young successfully.

There is much research work that a Department of Education might be doing. What actual education possibilities does each state offer? Are all children furnished with standard textbooks? Are libraries accessible for all children? Do we need, for a great majority of children more specialized and vocational training?

All these questions should be made the subject of research on a national scale, but there is a great division of opinion as to what authority should be vested in a national department of education.

The women who travel over this country realize that standards of education are woefully low in certain places, and there is no doubt it would be most useful for the public at large to know that the actual standards vary greatly in different parts of the United States. But this is a very different thing from placing absolute control over the various state departments of education in a "Department of National Education," such as has been proposed by some.

What do women want to do about prohibition? Women generally consider prohibition as social legislation, not from the economic standpoint as the men do as a rule, but when you ask "what do women want to do about prohibition?," the answer is the same as it would be if we asked "what do men want to do about prohibition?"

Not only are political parties split, but there is no uniform answer to this in the case of either sex. No one can say what the women want to do about prohibition.

We can say this, however, that few women are completely satisfied with the present-day conditions, and many are not satisfied with any of the remedies which have been as yet set forth. Only a few fortunate people feel they have found the answer to this problem and not enough people agree with them as yet to settle it.

The matter of proper laws dealing with marriage has been one much considered by all women in every state in the union interested in social conditions. Everyone feels it should be harder to get married and more solemnity and sense of permanence should accompany the ceremony. Uniform divorce laws might help to this end.

My fourth point is the woman's desire to see government lighten her burdens. The first of these burdens is the taxes. On the whole when women see that taxes which they pay bring direct returns in benefits to the community, I do not think that they are averse to paying them, but I do think that our ten million women want much more careful accounting for how their taxes are expended in the local, state or national government. They want to see the actual good which comes to them from these expenditures.

They feel very strongly that governments should not add to their burdens but should lighten them. They are gradually coming to grasp the relation of legislation to the lightening of these burdens, for instance, in such questions as the regulation of public utilities and the development of the water power of our nation. They realize now that cheaper electricity means less work in the home, more time to give to their children, more time for recreation and greater educational opportunities.

In Canada, across the border from Buffalo, where so much power is generated, there are proportionately many more electric washing machines and ironers and electric stoves and vacuum cleaners and hot water heaters in use because of the cheaper cost of electricity, than we have on this side of the line, although we have the same possibilities before us, and the women are beginning to ask why they are not within our grasp. Hence their interest is growing daily in the aspects of the whole public utilities question.

Then we come to the fifth point, which after all while it is entirely in the hands of the national government, still comes back to the home of every individual woman. She may wake up someday to find that her nation is at war and her boys and even her girls in one war or another, are drafted into service, a service from which they may not return, or they may return with mangled bodies, but if they do return to her with physical bodies unchanged, there may be some kind of mental and spiritual change which will alter their characters and their outlook on life.

It may do them good, but the reading of history does not lead us to hope for great benefits for the younger generation from any war. Therefore, every woman's interest in the amicable relations of her country is very great and she has come to realize that this is not merely a question of polite phrases between diplomats.

The only danger that women will not get what they want lies in the fact that there are still a goodly number who do not know how to use their influence and how to make known their ideas.

I heard a teacher not long ago discussing a referendum with hr class; she suggested that in New York State such a referendum had been taken in the last election when the people voted on certain amendments. One of the children looked up brightly and said, "Oh, yes, my mother knew nothing about any of those so she voted 'no' on all of them!" This is a dangerous attitude for any woman to allow herself if she hopes to get what she wants from her government.

If ten million women really want security, real representation, honesty, wise and just legislation, happier and more comfortable conditions of living, and a future with the horrors of war removed from the horizon, then these ten million women must bestir themselves.

They can be active factors in the life of their communities and shape the future, or they can drift along and hide behind the men. Today is a challenge to women. Tomorrow will see how they answer the challenge!

Franklin D. Roosevelt. Inaugural Address. March 4, 1933

Public Papers of the Presidents: Franklin D. Roosevelt (1933–45), National
Archives and Records Administration.

I am certain that my fellow Americans expect that on my induction into the Presidency
I will address them with a candor and a decision which the present situation of our Nation impels. This is preeminently the time to speak the truth, the whole truth, frankly
and boldly. Nor need we shrink from honestly facing conditions in our country today.
This great Nation will endure as it has endured, will revive and will prosper. So, first
of all, let me assert my firm belief that the only thing we have to fear is fear itself—
nameless, unreasoning, unjustified terror which paralyzes needed efforts to convert
retreat into advance. In every dark hour of our national life a leadership of frankness
and vigor has met with that understanding and support of the people themselves which
is essential to victory. I am convinced that you will again give that support to leadership in these critical days.

This Nation asks for action, and action now. Our greatest primary task is to put
people to work. This is no unsolvable problem if we face it wisely and courageously.
It can be accomplished in part by direct recruiting by the Government itself, treating
the task as we would treat the emergency of a war, but at the same time, through this
employment, accomplishing greatly needed projects to stimulate and reorganize the
use of our natural resources.

Hand in hand with this we must frankly recognize the overbalance of population in
our industrial centers and, by engaging on a national scale in a redistribution, endeavor
to provide a better use of the land for those best fitted for the land. The task can be
helped by definite efforts to raise the values of agricultural products and with this the
power to purchase the output of our cities. It can be helped by preventing realistically
the tragedy of the growing loss through foreclosure of our small homes and our farms.
It can be helped by insistence that the Federal, State, and local governments act forth-
with on the demand that their cost be drastically reduced.

Finally, in our progress toward a resumption of work we require two safe-guards
against a return of the evils of the old order: there must be a strict supervision of all banking and credits and investments, so that there will be an end to speculation with other
people's money; and there must be provision for an adequate but sound currency.

Through this program of action we address ourselves to putting our own national
house in order and making income balance outgo. Our international trade relations,
though vastly important, are in point of time and necessity secondary to the establishment of a sound national economy. I favor as a practical policy the putting of first
things first. I shall spare no effort to restore world trade by international economic
readjustment, but the emergency at home cannot wait on that accomplishment.

It is to be hoped that the normal balance of Executive and Legislative authority may
be wholly adequate to meet the unprecedented task before us. But it may be that an unprecedented demand and need for undelayed action may call for temporary departure
from that normal balance of public procedure.

I am prepared under my constitutional duty to recommend the measures that a stricken Nation in the midst of a stricken world may require. These measures, or such other measures as the Congress may build out of its experience and wisdom, I shall seek, within my constitutional authority, to bring to speedy adoption.

But in the event that the Congress shall fail to take one of these two courses, and in the event that the national emergency is still critical, I shall not evade the clear course of duty that will then confront me. I shall ask the Congress for the one remaining instrument to meet the crisis—broad Executive power to wage a war against the emergency, as great as the power that would be given to me if we were in fact invaded by a foreign foe. For the trust reposed in me I will return the courage and the devotion that befit the time. I can do no less.

We do not distrust the future of essential democracy. The people of the United States have not failed. In their need they have registered a mandate that they want direct, vigorous action. They have asked for discipline and direction under leadership. They have made me the present instrument of their wishes. In the spirit of the gift I take it.

In this dedication of a Nation we humbly ask the blessing of God. May He protect each and every one of us. May He guide me in the days to come.

Franklin D. Roosevelt. Fireside Chat. July 24, 1933

Public Papers of the Presidents: Franklin D. Roosevelt (1933–45), National Archives and Records Administration.

Now I come to the links which will build us a more lasting prosperity. I have said that we cannot attain that in a nation half boom and half broke.

For many years the two great barriers to a normal prosperity have been low farm prices and the creeping paralysis of unemployment. These factors have cut the purchasing power of the country in half. I promised action. First, the Farm Act: It is based on the fact that the purchasing power of nearly half our population depends on adequate prices for farm products. We have been producing more of some crops than we consume or can sell in a depressed world market. The cure is not to produce so much. Without our help the farmers cannot get together and cut production, and the Farm Bill gives them a method of bringing their production down to a reasonable level and of obtaining reasonable prices for their crops.

It is obvious that if we can greatly increase the purchasing power of the tens of millions of our people who make a living from farming and the distribution of farm crops, we shall greatly increase the consumption of those goods which are turned out by industry. That brings me to the final step—bringing back industry along sound lines.

We can make possible by democratic self-discipline in industry general increases in wages and shortening of hours sufficient to enable industry to pay its own workers enough to let those workers buy and use the things that their labor produces. This can be done only if we permit and encourage cooperative action in industry, because it is either follow suit or close up shop. We have seen the result of action of that kind in the continuing descent into the economic hell of the past four years.

There is a clear way to reverse that process: If all employers in each competitive group agree to pay their workers the same wages—reasonable obvious that without united action a few selfish men in each competitive group will pay starvation wages and insist on long hours of work. Others in that group must either follow suit or close up shop. We have seen the result of action of that kind in the continuing descent into the economic hell of the past four years.

There is a clear way to reverse that process: If all employers in each competitive group agree to pay their workers the same wages—reasonable wages—and require the same hours—reasonable hours—then higher wages and shorter hours will hurt no employer. Moreover, such action is better for the employer than unemployment and low wages, because it makes more buyers for his product. That is the simple idea which is the very heart of the Industrial Recovery Act.

On the basis of this simple principle of everybody doing things together, we are starting out on this nationwide attack on unemployment. It will succeed if our people understand it—in the big industries, in the little shops, in the great cities and in the small villages. There is nothing complicated about it and there is nothing particularly new in the principle. It goes back to the basic idea of society and of the Nation itself that people acting in a group can accomplish things which no individual acting alone could even hope to bring about.

Here is an example. In the Cotton Textile Code and in other agreements already signed, child labor has been abolished. That makes me personally happier than any other one thing with which I have been connected since I came to Washington. In the textile industry—an industry which came to me spontaneously and with a splendid cooperation as soon as the Recovery Act was signed—child labor was an old evil. But no employer acting alone was able to wipe it out. If one employer tried it, or if one State tried it, the costs of operation rose so high that it was impossible to compete with the employers or States which had failed to act. The moment the Recovery Act was passed, this monstrous thing which neither opinion nor law could reach through years of effort went out in a flash. As a British editorial put it, we did more under a Code in one day than they in England had been able to do under the common law in eighty-five years of effort. I use this incident, my friends, not to boast of what has already been done but to point the way to you for even greater cooperative efforts this summer and autumn.

We are not going through another winter like the last. I doubt if ever any people so bravely and cheerfully endured a season half so bitter. We cannot ask America to continue to face such needless hardships. It is time for courageous action, and the Recovery Bill gives us the means to conquer unemployment with exactly the same weapon that we have used to strike down child labor.

The proposition is simply this: if all employers will act together to shorten hours and raise wages we can put people back to work. No employer will suffer because the relative level of competitive cost will advance by the same amount for all. But if any considerable group should lag or shirk, this great opportunity will pass us by and we shall go into another desperate winter. This must not happen.

We have sent out to all employers an agreement which is the result of weeks of consultation. This agreement checks against the voluntary codes of nearly all the large industries which have already been submitted. This blanket agreement carries the unanimous approval of the three boards which I have appointed to advise in this, boards representing the great leaders in labor, in industry, and in social service. The agreement has already brought a flood of approval from every State, and from so wide a cross-section of the common calling of industry that I know it is fair for all. It is a plan—deliberate, reasonable and just—intended to put into effect at once the most important of the broad principles which are being established, industry by industry, through codes. Naturally, it takes a good deal of organizing and a great many hearings and many months, to get these codes perfected and signed, and we cannot wait for all of them to go through. The blanket agreements, however, which I am sending to every employer will start the wheels turning now, and not six months from now.

There are, of course, men, a few men, who might thwart this great common purpose by seeking selfish advantage. There are adequate penalties in the law, but I am now asking the cooperation that comes from opinion and from conscience. These are the only instruments we shall use in this great summer offensive against unemployment. But we shall use them to the limit to protect the willing from the laggard and to make the plan succeed.

In war, in the gloom of night attack, soldiers wear a bright badge on their shoulders to be sure that comrades do not fire on comrades. On that principle, those who cooperate in this program must know each other at a glance. This is why we have provided a badge of honor for this purpose, a simple design with a legend, "We do our part," and I ask that all those who join with me shall display that badge prominently. It is essential to our purpose. Already all the great, basic industries have come forward willingly with proposed codes, and in these codes they accept the principles leading to mass reemployment. But, important as is this heartening demonstration, the richest field for results is among the small employers, those whose contribution will be to give new work for from one to ten people. These smaller employers are indeed a vital part of the backbone of our country, and the success of our plan lies largely in their hands.

When Andrew Jackson, "Old Hickory," died, someone asked, "Will he go to Heaven?" and the answer was, "He will go if he wants to." The essence of the plan is a universal limitation of hours of work per week for any individual by common consent, and a universal payment of wages above a minimum, also by common consent. I cannot guarantee the success of this nationwide plan, but the people of this country can guarantee its success. I have no faith in "cure-alls" but I believe that we can greatly influence economic forces. I have no sympathy with the professional economists who insist that things must run their course and that human agencies can have no influence on economic ills. One reason is that I happen to know that professional economists have changed their definition of economic laws every five or ten years for a very long time, but I do have faith, and retain faith,... in the strength of unified action taken by the American people.

Keynes, John Maynard. "An Open Letter to President Roosevelt."

Felix Frankfurter Collection, National Archives and Records Administration, Franklin D. Roosevelt Presidential Library, Hyde Park, NY, 1933.

Dear Mr. President,

You have made yourself the Trustee for those in every country who seek to mend the evils of our condition by reasoned experiment within the framework of the existing social system. If you fail, rational change will be gravely prejudiced throughout the world, leaving orthodoxy and revolution to fight it out. But if you succeed, new and bolder methods will be tried everywhere, and we may date the first chapter of a new economic era from your accession to office. This is a sufficient reason why I should venture to lay my reflections before you, though under the disadvantages of distance and partial knowledge.

At the moment your sympathisers in England are nervous and sometimes despondent. We wonder whether the order of different urgencies is rightly understood, whether there is a confusion of aim, and whether some of the advice you get is not crack-brained and queer. If we are disconcerted when we defend you, this may be partly due to the influence of our environment in London. For almost everyone here has a wildly distorted view of what is happening in the United States. The average City man believes that you are engaged on a hare-brained expedition in face of competent advice, that the best hope lies in your ridding yourself of your present advisers to return to the old ways, and that otherwise the United States is heading for some ghastly breakdown. That is what they say they smell. There is a recrudescence of wise head-waging by those who believe that the nose is a nobler organ than the brain. London is convinced that we only have to sit back and wait, in order to see what we shall see. May I crave your attention, whilst I put my own view?

You are engaged on a double task, Recovery and Reform;—recovery from the slump and the passage of those business and social reforms which are long overdue. For the first, speed and quick results are essential. The second may be urgent too; but haste will be injurious, and wisdom of long-range purpose is more necessary than immediate achievement. It will be through raising high the prestige of your administration by success in short-range Recovery, that you will have the driving force to accomplish long-range Reform. On the other hand, even wise and necessary Reform may, in some respects, impede and complicate Recovery. For it will upset the confidence of the business world and weaken their existing motives to action, before you have had time to put other motives in their place. It may over-task your bureaucratic machine, which the traditional individualism of the United States and the old "spoils system" have left none too strong. And it will confuse the thought and aim of yourself and your administration by giving you too much to think about all at once.

Now I am not clear, looking back over the last nine months, that the order of urgency between measures of Recovery and measures of Reform has been duly observed, or that the latter has not sometimes been mistaken for the former. In particular, I cannot detect any material aid to recovery in N.I.R.A., though its social gains have been large. The driving force which has been put behind the vast administrative task set by this Act has seemed to represent a wrong choice in the order of urgencies. The Act is on the Statute Book; a considerable amount has been done towards implementing it; but it might be better for the present to allow experience to accumulate before trying to force through all its details. That is my first reflection—that N.I.R.A., which is essentially Reform and probably impedes Recovery, has been put across too hastily, in the false guise of being part of the technique of Recovery.

My second reflection relates to the technique of Recovery itself. The object of recovery is to increase the national output and put more men to work. In the economic system of the modern world, output is primarily produced for sale; and the volume of output depends on the amount of purchasing power, compared with the prime cost of production, which is expected to come n the market. Broadly speaking, therefore, and increase of output depends on the amount of purchasing power, compared with the prime cost of production, which is expected to come on the market. Broadly speaking, therefore, an increase of output cannot occur unless by the operation of one or other of three factors. Individuals must be induced to spend more out o their existing incomes; or the business world must be induced, either by increased confidence in the prospects or by a lower rate of interest, to create additional current incomes in the hands of their employees, which is what happens when either the working or the fixed capital of the country is being increased; or public authority must be called in aid to create additional current incomes through the expenditure of borrowed or printed money. In bad times the first factor cannot be expected to work on a sufficient scale. The second factor will come in as the second wave of attack on the slump after the tide has been turned by the expenditures of public authority. It is, therefore, only from the third factor that we can expect the initial major impulse.

Now there are indications that two technical fallacies may have affected the policy of your administration. The first relates to the part played in recovery by rising prices. Rising prices are to be welcomed because they are usually a symptom of rising output and employment. When more purchasing power is spent, one expects rising output at rising prices. Since there cannot be rising output without rising prices, it is essential to ensure that the recovery shall not be held back by the insufficiency of the supply of money to support the increased monetary turn-over. But there is much less to be said in favour of rising prices, if they are brought about at the expense of rising output. Some debtors may be helped, but the national recovery as a whole will be retarded. Thus rising prices caused by deliberately increasing prime costs or by restricting output have a vastly inferior value to rising prices which are the natural result of an increase in the nation's purchasing power.

I do not mean to impugn the social justice and social expediency of the redistribution of incomes aimed at by N.I.R.A. and by the various schemes for agricultural restriction. The latter, in particular, I should strongly support in principle. But too much emphasis on the remedial value of a higher price-level as an object in itself may lead to serious misapprehension as to the part which prices can play in the technique of recovery. The stimulation of output by increasing aggregate purchasing power is the right way to get prices up; and not the other way round.

Thus as the prime mover in the first stage of the technique of recovery I lay over-whelming emphasis on the increase of national purchasing power resulting from governmental expenditure which is financed by Loans and not by taxing present incomes. Nothing else counts in comparison with this. In a boom inflation can be caused by allowing unlimited credit to support the excited enthusiasm of business speculators. But in a slump governmental Loan expenditure is the only sure means of securing quickly a rising output at rising prices. That is why a war has always caused intense industrial activity. In the past orthodox finance has regarded a war as the only legitimate excuse for creating employment by governmental expenditure. You, Mr. President, having cast off such fetters, are free to engage in the interests of peace and prosperity the technique which hitherto has only been allowed to serve the purposes of war and destruction.

The set-back which American recovery experienced this autumn was the predictable consequence of the failure of your administration to organise any material increase in new Loan expenditure during your first six months of office. The position six months hence will entirely depend on whether you have been laying the foundations for larger expenditures in the near future.

I am not surprised that so little has been spent up-to-date. Our own experience has shown how difficult it is to improvise useful Loan-expenditures at short notice. There are many obstacle to be patiently overcome, if waste, inefficiency and corruption are to be avoided. There are many factors, which I need not stop to enumerate, which render especially difficult in the United States the rapid improvisation of a vast programme of public works. I do not blame Mr Ickes for being cautious and careful. But the risks of less speed must be weighed against those of more haste. He must get across the crevasses before it is dark.

The other set of fallacies, of which I fear the influence, arises out of a crude economic doctrine commonly known as the Quantity Theory of Money. Rising output and rising incomes will suffer a set-back sooner or later if the quantity of money is rigidly fixed. Some people seem to infer from this that output and income can be raised by increasing the quantity of money. But this is like trying to get fat by buying a larger belt. In the United States to-day your belt is plenty big enough for your belly. It is a most misleading thing to stress the quantity of money, which is only a limiting factor, rather than the volume of expenditure, which is the operative factor.

It is an even more foolish application of the same ideas to believe that there is a mathematical relation between the price of gold and the prices of other things. It is true that the value of the dollar in terms of foreign currencies will affect the prices of those goods which enter into international trade. In so far as an over-valuation of the dollar was impeding the freedom of domestic price-raising policies or disturbing the balance of payments with foreign countries, it was advisable to depreciate it. But exchange depreciation should follow the success of your domestic price-raising policy as its natural consequence, and should not be allowed to disturb the whole world by preceding its justification at an entirely arbitrary pace. This is another example of trying to put on flesh by letting out the belt.

These criticisms do not mean that I have weakened in my advocacy of a managed currency or in preferring stable prices to stable exchanges. The currency and exchange policy of a country should be entirely subservient to the aim of raising output and employment to the right level. But the recent gyrations of the dollar have looked to me more like a gold standard on the booze than the ideal managed currency of my dreams.

You may be feeling by now, Mr President, that my criticism is more obvious than my sympathy. Yet truly that is not so. You remain for me the ruler whose general outlook and attitude to the tasks of government are the most sympathetic in the world. You are the only one who sees the necessity of a profound change of methods and is attempting it without intolerance, tyranny or destruction. You are feeling your way by trial and error, and are felt to be, as you should be, entirely uncommitted in your own person to the details of a particular technique. In my country, as in your own, your position remains singularly untouched by criticism of this or the other detail. Our hope and our faith are based on broader considerations.

If you were to ask me what I would suggest in concrete terms for the immediate future, I would reply thus.

In the field of gold-devaluation and exchange policy the time has come when uncertainty should be ended. This game of blind man's buff with exchange speculators serves no useful purpose and is extremely undignified. It upsets confidence, hinders business decisions, occupies the public attention in a measure far exceeding its real importance, and is responsible both for the irritation and for a certain lack of respect which exists abroad. You have three alternatives. You can devalue the dollar in terms of gold, returning to the gold standard at a new fixed ratio. This would be inconsistent with your declarations in favour of a long-range policy of stable prices, and I hope you will reject it. You can seek some common policy of exchange stabilisation with Great Britain aimed at stable price levels. This would be the best ultimate solution; but it is not practical politics at the moment unless you are prepared to talk in terms of an initial value of sterling well below $5 pending the realisation of a marked rise in your domestic price-level. Lastly you can announce that you will definitely control the dollar exchange by buying and selling gold and foreign currencies so as to avoid wide or meaningless fluctuations, with a right to shift the parities at any time but with a declared intention only so to do either to correct a serious want of balance in America's international receipts and payments or to meet a shift in your domestic price level relatively to price-levels abroad. This appears to me to be your best policy during the transitional period. In other respects you would regain your liberty to make your exchange policy subservient to the needs of your domestic policy—free to let out your belt in proportion as you put on flesh.

In the field of domestic policy, I put in the forefront, for the reasons given above, a large volume of Loan-expenditures under Government auspices. It is beyond my province to choose particular objects of expenditure. But preference should be given to those which can be made to mature quickly on a large scale, as for example the rehabilitation of the physical condition of the railroads. The object is to start the ball rolling. The United States is ready to roll towards prosperity, if a good hard shove can be given in the next six months. Could not the energy and enthusiasm, which launched the N.I.R.A. in its early days, be put behind a campaign for accelerating capital expenditures, as wisely chosen as the pressure of circumstances permits? You can at least feel sure that the country will be better enriched by such projects than by the involuntary idleness of millions.

I put in the second place the maintenance of cheap and abundant credit and in particular the reduction of the long-term rates of interest. The turn of the tide in great Britain is largely attributable to the reduction in the long-term rate of interest which ensued on the success of the conversion of the War Loan. This was deliberately engineered by means of the open-market policy of the Bank of England. I see no reason why you should not reduce the rate of interest on your long-term Government Bonds to 2½ per cent or less with favourable repercussions on the whole bond market, if only the Federal Reserve System would replace its present holdings of short-dated Treasury issues by purchasing long-dated issues in exchange. Such a policy might become effective in the course of a few months, and I attach great importance to it.

With these adaptations or enlargements of your existing policies, I should expect a successful outcome with great confidence. How much that would mean, not only to the material prosperity of the United States and the whole World, but in comfort to men's minds through a restoration of their faith in the wisdom and the power of Government!

With great respect,

Your obedient servant
J M Keynes

Indians at Work

John Collier

Source: Survey Graphic, Vol. 23, No. 6 (June, 1934), p. 261

IS it too late for Indian tribes, wards of the government, to demonstrate statesmanship? Have the Indians still a race to run?

The twelve months behind, even the five years behind, have supplied, for the Indians as a whole, merely the beginnings of a possible answer. Whether (ignoring the question of their capacity) the Indians shall be allowed to try to run their race at all, is still an unanswered question. It is discussed below. But let us start at the point of clearest evidence and greatest hope.

That point is the Navajo tribe and the Navajo regional plan. Forty-five thousand Indians, pure bloods and mostly non-English-speaking; in their religion, pre-Columbian; a nomad desert tribe, occupying nearly twenty-five thousand square miles of desert land of wild, somber and splendid beauty. They have multiplied nearly fourfold in seventy years. Their flocks have multiplied faster. They overpopulate and congest their barren range, and their sheep and goats desperately overgraze it. Their material standard of living very low indeed, their psychical standard is high, their elan vital is irrepressible. They are esthetes, adventurers, gamblers, sportsmen and nature-mystics. They have not the peasant's submissiveness to work, nor the bourgeoise idolatry toward it.

And suddenly the Navajos have been faced with a crisis which in some aspects is nothing less than a head-on collision between immediate advantages, sentiments, beliefs, affections and previously accepted preachments, as one colliding mass, and physical and statistical facts as the other.

The crisis consists in the fact that the soil of the Navajo reservation is hurriedly being washed away into the Colorado river. The collision consists in the fact that the entire complex and momentum of Navajo life must be radically and swiftly changed to a new direction and in part must be totally reversed.

And the changes must be made—if made at all—through the choice of the Navajos themselves; a choice requiring to be renewed through months and years, with increasing sacrifices for necessarily remote and hypothetical returns, and with a hundred difficult technical applications.

Nor is the burden of sacrifice an equal one; indeed, those Navajos, individuals and families, who have the greatest power to prevent the collective sacrifice from being made are the ones whose uncompensated individual sacrifice must be greatest.

It is the Navajos' past which has made their virtues. Their past still is, psychologically, their present. These virtues, aggressive and yet attractive and appealing, must not die from the new order which has suddenly become a matter of life or death. Yet can they live on? For human qualities are institutional products. The question is intense with sociological as well as with human interest.

About ten months ago, a joint committee of the Departments of Agriculture and Interior described the crisis and charted the emergency program. Soil erosion, they found, due to extreme overgrazing, had totally destroyed several hundred thousand acres of the Navajo range. It had seriously damaged millions of acres more. It was advancing not in arithmetical but in geometrical progression, and in fifteen, perhaps twenty years the Navajo reservation would be changed to a divinely painted desert and the Navajos would be homeless on the earth.

Whereupon, last July, the Navajo tribal council and two thousand other Navajos were brought together at Fort Wingate, New Mexico. With technical detail, through interpreters and endless hours of discussion the facts were supplied them. And the condition precedent to an ultimate saving of the soil was stated with no sparing of words That condition was a sacrifice of hundreds of thousands of their sheep and goats. But in addition there must be a planning of economic use for the whole reservation; range control, with redistribution of range privileges; an intensive revival of subsistence farming, irrigated and dry; a recasting and diminution of the road-building program; the fencing of areas of the range for soil experimentation, with total removal of stock from these areas; and erosion engineering and re-vegetative operations, under time pressure, throughout the wide region.

Nor could government funds pay for all the needed innovations. The Navajos themselves must pay, in labor and money.

The Navajo reservation is being washed into the Boulder Dam reservoir. That reservoir's rate of silting has been computed upon a static erosion rate which is but a fraction of the present and speeding-up rate. Hence; Southern California, as well as New Mexico and Arizona, is involved with the Navajos in their crisis. Actually, two thirds of the silt being fed to Boulder Dam is washed from the Navajo lands.

Mandatory sheep and goat reduction, mandatory range control, federal dominance over the Navajos' present and future program, are already possible in law and might be justified from the standpoint of national necessity.

But the Navajos were expressly and formally told that compulsion would not be used. This problem was their own and they, not the government, must do the things necessary to its solution. profound recasting of the economic and social life of a people must be sought through knowing consent of the people and must be forced through their own will, or it must fail.

How did the Navajos respond? The tribal council adopt the program, with the proviso that it must go by referendum to the whole Navajo people through those local "chapters" which are the ultimate units of Navajo government. The tribe adopted the program at this referendum

Again, after four months, a more drastic and more fast-moving program went before the council, was by it submitted to the people and was adopted. The Navajos through this decision surrendered ninety thousand of their sheep.

And again, after four months, a yet more drastic program was submitted. It called for the immediate sacrifice of 50,000 Navajo goats, and for coordinate adjustments that will cut the total of Navajo flocks by much more than one third. The cost of this latest stock reduction will be $225,000; the government does not undertake to pay the bill and the Navajos themselves are proposing to pay it, dependent on a government loan to the tribe. This latest sacrifice was adopted by referendum and confirmed by the tribal council in early April.

Meantime, the positive tasks of erosion control are well under way. The technical direction is being supplied by the Soil Erosion Service of the Department of the Interior. The Navajos are themselves carrying out the projects. In February, at Washington, the Carnegie Institute presented a photographic display showing erosion as a menacing condition threatening many parts of the United States. The exhibit climaxed with photographs of model erosion-control operations. The pictures bore no local designations, but they were photographs of the engineering works not merely built with Navajo hands but planned, practically in their entirety, by the Navajos. Four hundred Navajos had worked at the projects, assisted by only two white men.

I do not believe that any white community in the United States would have met a complicated and profound, urgent challenge, entailing the upset of widely distributed but unequal vested property interests, with the spirit, the audacity and the resourcefulness which the Navajo tribe has shown. Be it remembered that the Navajos are illiterates, in the main, and speak only the Navajo language, in the main And that the women are in most cases the owners of the goats and sheep; and that goats and sheep are viewed by the Navajos emotionally, all but as human children.

Let me quickly sketch the social program, going beyond erosion and range control, now being put into effect by the Navajos and by the government as their partner. First comes the drastic decentralization of Indian Service administration. The new Navajo capital (called Nee Alneeng, which means Center of the Navajo World) will be the Indian Service office for the whole reservation. Into it, whatever Washington authority can be legally transplanted will be transplanted. Under the pending Wheeler-Howard bill, discussed below, that will be substantially the whole authority of the federal government.

Here, likewise, will be the capitol of the tribe—the headquarters of the tribal council.

BUT beyond this headquarters, decentralization will be carried to the more than twenty-five sub-agencies, each the center of the locally organized Navajos and the administrative office for the school work, health work, agricultural extension, erosion, law-enforcement and other services of the government. These sub-agencies will be people's houses, and into them the formal schooling of the Navajos will be merged; indeed, if hopes are fulfilled there will be no formal schooling of the cloistrated or standardized order. All educational work will start from, and end in, the community group. The Navajo language will be used coordinately with English; Navajos and the government's workers with the Navajos will be bilingual in the future. The employee at these sub-agencies, and at the capital, will increasingly be (again, subject to the enactment of the Wheeler-Howard bill) Navajo Indians.

I have begun with this happy and inspiriting example, and I will give one bright instance more because it testifies to what qualities there are in all Indians; and then I will pass to the gloomy side. For it will become evident that the Indians, now as before, are shrouded in gloom.

Last May, President Roosevelt decided that 14,000 Indians in all parts of the Indian country should be admitted to emergency conservation camps, to work on reforestation, on water development and erosion control. We were glad, but we were frightened. For the permission extended beyond the Pueblos, Pimas, Papagos and Navajos, famed for their sobriety and their industry. It reached to the Oklahoma, Dakota, Montana and Pacific Coast tribes—to those Indians reputedly not willing to work and reputedly demoralized. Would the camps become centers of drink, of debauchery? Would the Indians respond to their opportunity, and after they responded, would they work?

The sequel has been, I believe, the most impressive event in Indian affairs in these "lonesome latter years" of Indian life. The Indians thronged to the camps and projects. The camps became and have uniformly remained (there has not arisen even one exception) models of orderly, happy living. The work-projects, involving every kind of technical operation connected with forestry and with land conservation and use, have been pursued with better than mere industry—rather, with joyous ardor. Of all the technical and supervisory positions, more than 60 percent are now being efficiently filled by Indians, and the rank-and-file of the workers is 100 percent Indian. But the main significance is here: that the southwestern tribes have in no degree, in no particular, excelled those of the other regions.

These Indians of the allotted areas have been, at the camps, like creatures released from prisons and dungeons. Once more they have been allowed to live in groups, to work in groups and to work for a common good. They have furnished the solution of the so-called problem of the American Indian. Just in such a way, the Mexican peons of yesterday, now members of the recreated pueblos or ejidos of Old Mexico, have furnished the solution of the problem of the Indians south of the Rio Grande.

Because this article has space limits I shall now deal with only one other matter, the Wheeler-Howard Indian land and home-rule bill and, in conclusion, with the objection raised against this bill, namely that it tends toward an unfortunate segregation Of the Indians.

Though this article will be published too late to have persuasive weight with the out going Congress, a description of the Wheeler-Howard bill will serve to give a perspective of the Indian situation as a whole, and will tell what it is that the present administration seeks to do. President Roosevelt has thus summarized the intent of the bill:

In offering the Indian these natural rights of man, we will more nearly discharge the federal responsibility for his welfare than through compulsory guardianship that has destroyed initiative and the liberty to develop his own culture.

The bill primarily drives against two states of fact—an Indian landholding system fatal, sinister and dishonest, and a system of law which makes of the executive an unreviewable czar over Indian life.

THE present system of land tenure was ushered in fifty-seven years ago with the passage of the General Allotment Act. Previous to this time the soil of the various Indian reservations was owned in common, title resting in the tribe. Every member of a tribe had the right to occupy as much land as he could beneficially use; his house and other improvements passed on to his heirs, but he could not alienate and dispose of a square foot of tribal soil. Those reservations which escaped allotment have today as much and frequently more land than they contained sixty years ago.

Through the General Allotment Act the government proceeded to break up the reservations, to attach to each Indian then living a tract of land as his individual property and throw the part of the reservations not used in this individual land distribution open to white settlement. Thus the Indian was to become an individualized farmer and assume all the white man's burden after a comparatively short "trust" period during which the privilege of mortgaging and selling his land was denied him.

After allotment the individualized land began to slip out of the Indian owners' hands at high speed. When the trust period expired or the Indian was declared "competent," he disposed of his land in short order, spent the proceed and went to live with his relatives. And when an allotted Indian died, the usual impossibility to make an equitable partition of the land forced its sale not to Indians, but to those who had the money to buy, to the waiting white people. Thus allotment dissipated, continues to dissipate the Indian estate.

In 1887, the Indians were owners of 136,340,950 acres of the best land. In 1933 they were owners of 47,311,099 acres, of which a full 20,000,000 acres were desert or semi-desert. The surface value of the Indian-owned lands had shrunk 90 percent in these forty-six years. Of the residual lands, 7,032,237 acres (the most covetable of the remnant) were awaiting "knock-down sale" to whites—sale conducted by the government itself, usually without reference to Indian choice. And of the usable land still owned by the allotted Indians, a full three fourths was already possessed and used by whites under the allotment leasing system. Such land is tax-exempt, and the white lessees (cattlemen, sheep-men, farmers and grain corporations) reap the benefit of tax exemption. Since 1887, one hundred and fifty thousand Indians have been rendered totally landless; and existing law—the practices mandatory or administratively inescapable under it—insured the dispossession of the remaining allotted Indians within the present generation.

WHAT the Indians themselves have done or have left undone has been a negligible factor in the above-stated record. The allotment law and system intends and compels the transfer of Indian title to whites. Less swift than treaty-breaking with Indians or than outright rape of Indian lands, but surer and cheaper, bloodless and silent, the allotment law has fulfilled the "civilizing" intentions of the government of 1887.

The facts of 1933 are the facts of today. I give some other facts of the workings and consequences of Indian land allotment.

The Indian lives in an ever-narrowing prison-pen of allotment until his last acre is gone, and then he is summarily cast out from federal responsibility. But the Indian service, hardly less than the Indian, lives, and endeavors to work, in a prison-pen of land allotment. Governmental appropriations into the millions each year, sorely needed for health service to Indians, for education, for relief, and for the economic rehabilitation of Indians, are of necessity diverted to the real-estate operations connected with the still-shrinking allotted lands. Pari passu with the swindling of the lands, the costs of administration rise. And there is no escape from these results under existing law.

I refer, of course, to the allotted areas, but these are all of the Indian country of Oklahoma and nearly all of the Indian country of Wisconsin, Minnesota, the Dakotas, Montana, Nebraska and Kansas, Wyoming, Oregon, Washington and California.

The allotment system fights against all the human services attempted for Indians. Two Oklahoma cases will serve as examples, chosen because the bitterest of the embittered opposition to the Wheeler-Howard bill comes from whites.

At the Kiowa and Comanche agency, the total government expenditure, school costs aside, is $80,000 a year. Of this total, only $15,000 can be used for health, relief, reimbursable loans, agricultural extension and all the other human services. Sixty-five thousand is required for the real-estate operations of the allotted lands. Meantime the lands inexorably pass to whites by government sale. About sixty of every hundred Indians in this jurisdiction are totally landless, all but a few are in poverty, and their needs for service are extreme. At most allotted jurisdictions, the proportion of the landless Indians is greater than at this one.

On its work other than schools, the Five Civilized Tribes agency of Oklahoma spends $300,000 a year. All except $60,000 of this total is devoured by the real-estate operations of the allotted lands. Of the 100,000 Five Tribes Indians, 72,000 are totally landless; the remaining lands are swiftly being forced into white ownership; and the per capita income of the Five Tribes, omitting oil and mineral royalties paid to a few individuals, is forty-seven dollars a year. These Five Tribes possessed, twenty-five years ago, 15 million acres of the best Oklahoma land; they now possess 1 ½ million acres.

Subdivision of inherited allotments, on a hundred reservations, has proceeded to that point where an individual equity is fixed by subdividing, for example, the sum 5200 into the sum 114,307,200, and the government solemnly pays each heir the value of a postage stamp once a month. The heir possesses an equity in ten, thirty, or fifty separate allotments. Administration costs more than the total rental, even the total value of the lands. Not merely farming lands, but grazing properties and even forests have been fractionated to these vanishing dimensions, making impossible the working of their own assets by the allotees; and the fading Indian lands are dots within the sea of white ownership. Twenty-five years ago the areas were solidly Indian.

The Wheeler-Howard Bill centers in the land problem. The bill's forty-eight pages are their own explanation, but the principles can be stated in a few words. Under the bill, individual allotted titles may be exchanged for equitable rights in a community title. Use of the land, ownership of the improvements, ownership of the rental value of the land, and the right to use an equal area or value of land within the community estate, is safeguarded and made into an inheritable vested right. The physical allotments may be inherited so long as their subdivision does not reach the point of destroying their economic use.

Under the bill, reservation areas are to be marked out for ultimate consolidation into unbroken Indian holdings. The new land procedures will apply only inside these consolidated areas. To buy the white-owned tracts, and to purchase the Indian heirship lands for the communities, the bill authorizes $2 million a year. This grant will be used likewise for buying land on which homeless Indians will be colonized. In addition, submarginal lands, now being purchased by the government, will be furnished the Indian communities, and funds from the subsistence homestead appropriation will be used for experimental colonies.

Financial credits which is now practically denied the Indians, is essential to the Wheeler-Howard plan, and the bill establishes a revolving fund of $10 million, which will be a federal grant, allocated to the Indian communities to be used by them as a revolving loan fund, capitalizing the individual and group enterprises.

The bill forbids any and all allotment of lands hereafter, and forbids the sale of Indian lands to whites, and through many devices seeks to enable the Indians to repossess their lands now rented to whites and to become their own operators.

The so-called home-rule provisions of the Wheeler-Howard Bill are "geared" with the land provisions, but their application is more general than that of the land provisions. Under existing law the secretary of the interior and Indian commissioner practically are forced to stand as absolutists over the Indians. Usually their actions are exempt from court review. But they, in turn, are victims of the mandatory allotment system and of an appropriation and budgeting system which conceals facts and which freezes government moneys into out-moded and sometimes even fictitious uses, leaving Congress itself helpless to control the expenditures, while the Indian office is no less helpless and the Indian is kept in the dark.

The total effect of these above conditions has been to impose on the Indian service an extreme centralization at the Washington Office. The free movement of ideas, of experimentation and of local adjustment is impeded everywhere, and in the allotted areas is all but prohibited. There has been a wealth of bold effort and of truly creative initiative within the Indian Service during the last four or five years, and by "main strength and awkwardness," as it were, some of this innovation has been pushed through to the Indians' actual life in the two hundred reservations. But the autocratic and centralized system practically defies the human effort, and the best administration, whether from the headquarters or from the field, is as water poured into the labyrinthine sands of bureaucracy which is forbidden by law to reorganize itself.

The Wheeler-Howard Bill cuts through the tangle of legal compulsions and inhibitions and provides for a radical decentralization of the Indian Service. Indians may organize and become chartered for any of the tasks or interests of their own lives; their organization may be geographical or functional, according to their wishes or requirements. When organized, the chartered Indian communities become instrumentalities of the federal government. Doing less or more according to the facts of the innumerable variable cases, these communities in their fullest development may become wholly self-governing, subject only to Congress and the Constitution. Any function of Indian Service, with the appurtenant federal moneys, may be transferred to these communities. The communities in turn may enter into contract with states, counties and any other local institutions.

A special Indian civil service is created by the bill, and communities may appoint their qualified members for any position of local Indian service, and power of recall over local government employees is given to the communities.

The bill in its Title 2 broadens the authority for Indian educational work, and through a system of loans and scholarship grants opens the colleges and the professional and technical schools to Indian youth.

Title 4 of the bill sets up a Court of Indian Affairs, with functions ministerial as well as judicial, and brings the Indian Service and the Indian communities under the review of this court. Through this court the constitutional rights will be insured, including minority rights, religious rights and the due process of law in matters of life and property which are necessarily withheld from Indians under the present system.

I conclude with some necessary remarks directed to the only reasoned criticism which has been brought against the Wheeler-Howard Bill and the Roosevelt-Ickes Indian policy. The bill and policy, it is contended, make for racial segregation and would wall the Indians off from civilization and from modern opportunity. To meet the contention is to bring the Indian situation under a sociological searchlight.

Where the trend or drift of a race has gone in one direction—in the case of most of the Indians, downhill—for a hundred years more or less, there cannot be any sudden or easy reversal of the trend. Subtle and deep readjustments, sociological, psychological and even biological, take place within peoples; human beings make structural adaptations to the life-limiting environment. The prison psychosis would furnish an illustration.

Space limits forbid the pursuit of this analysis, but as a practical matter, the Indian Service task has to be visioned in relation to such facts as the following.

The extreme poverty of the Indians, which was recognized as a controlling factor by the Institute for Government Research in 1928, continues unrelieved. Indeed, with data greatly enriched, the fact of Indian poverty has become more impressive. The shrinkage of landholdings, due to allotment, actually is smaller than the shrinkage of capital funds. These have disappeared altogether, in the cases of scores of tribes.

Earned income and subsistence production have continued at an almost unbelievably low level. Only when the land system is examined do the facts become credible, especially in the light of the proved readiness of Indians to work, and their ability to work efficiently, as displayed in emergency activities during the past year.

The incomplete returns have now been tabulated from ten allotted areas in the six states of South Dakota, North Dakota, California, Kansas, Montana and Oklahoma. The studies were remade by competent investigators employed under a Civil Works grant. Case records were made for families containing 38,772 individuals. The per capita per year income was found to be $47.78, after excluding the oil and mineral royalties paid to a handful of individuals in these ten areas.

This per capita income—$47.78—represents the earned income and the lease money and the market value of goods produced or consumed. These Indians have consumed no more than $47.78 worth of goods in the year. The ascertained figure is higher, not lower, than it would be in an average year, because federal emergency expenditures, on works projects in the Indian country, were rising toward their peak during the time of the survey.

The poverty of the Indians contributes to their continuing morbidity and deathrates. The deathrate, taking the Indians as a whole, continues at twice the deathrate of the general population including the Negroes. Tuberculosis, with an Indian deathrate more than seven times the white, is not yet being controlled. Trachoma is uncontrolled although clinical treatment has been multiplied tenfold since 1925.

Less tangible, but no less important, are the registrations of economic inferiority in the mental and social reactions of the Indians. Between the elder and younger generations, suppressed or open conflict rages. Between the pure bloods and the mixed bloods, conflict rages. Between the allotted Indians and the government, conflict rages. Rarely, where these conflicts go on, are the causes understood by the Indians. The causes are objective and imminent, residing as they do in the allotment system, in the dictatorial and centralized Bureau management and in the segregation forced upon the Indians by their poverty and their under-equipment. But the conflicts, psychologically analyzed, are essentially neurotic conflicts—compensations, escapes, and rationalizations of misery. And in the allotted areas, it is largely out of the question to recapture and harness these neurotic energies for practical social tasks, because the tasks are forbidden by the law and the system.

The total effect of these and related conditions is to degrade the Indian social level, and the degradation goes steadily forward. The real "values" of the Indian are driven inward, insulated from world intact, and compelled to face toward remembered glory, remembered plenty and power. And assimilation, whether biological or social, becomes for Indians, with each passing year, an assimilation into still inferior levels of the white life.

The Indian Rights Association, in company with some of the Missionaries' fears the policies of Secretary Ickes' administration, and looks with doubt on the Wheeler-Howard Bill, on the ground, stated above, that the policies and the bill are working toward the segregation of Indians. I have stated the facts of Indian poverty because from any point of view they are controlling in the appraisal of the Indian situation, but also because they dispose, I believe, of the segregation argument. The Indians today are segregated by factors all-penetrating, infinitely more potent than mere geographical segregations could ever be. Their extreme poverty segregates them. Their inferiority status in law intensifies their segregation. Their infectious diseases segregate them. Their inferiority sentiment, elaborately planted at the center of their consciousness by deliberate governmental policy as well as by the unintended action of poverty, effectually segregates them.

Their ancient interests and loyalties, which are far from being extinct, are by these same conditions imprisoned, and denied the chance to partake in social action, to salvage themselves through development and change.

And the Indian, in his profounder psyche, is condemned to that which could be termed a social-psychic infantilism, a dream-escape to the social mother—that social mother who, to the Indian, is always his own tribe. Yet even this escape takes with it a conflict into the very heart of the Indian's life. Due to the rendering of the ancient values powerless by social segregation, insecurity and inferiority haunt even this inmost refuge or shrine.

The mechanisms and policies of the Wheeler-Howard Bill are, first and last, a prescription for bringing this Indian segregation to an end.

Huey Long, Share Our Wealth

Source: Congressional Record, 74th Congress, 1st Session (1935), 7585–86, 7589–94.

Mr. LONG. Mr. President, about 4 weeks ago...the Senator from Arkansas [Mr. Robinson] and the Senator from Kentucky [Mr. Barkley] made speeches over the radio in which they...rather sneeringly referred to the phrase "share-our-wealth."

I desire to give them to understand where the "share-our-wealth" phrase was first used. I want them to understand that that "share-our-wealth" phrase did not come from the senior Senator from Louisiana, but was the phrase and promise of the present President of the United States in his acceptance speech delivered at the Chicago...Democratic National Convention of 1932...I am quoting Mr. Roosevelt:

Throughout the Nation, men and women, forgotten in the political philosophy of the Government of the last years look to us here for guidance and for more equitable opportunity to share-

S-H-A-R-E-

In the distribution of national wealth. [Applause and Cheering]

My friend from Kentucky was the keynoter of that convention. He forgot all about it and went on the radio to denounce "share-our-wealth" the other night. He has become disloyal to the party. [Laughter.] "Share our wealth," "share our national wealth," "share in the distribution of wealth," were the phrases of Franklin D. Roosevelt when he accepted the nomination in Chicago. I want my friend from Kentucky [Mr. Barkley]...and my friend from Arkansas [Mr. Robinson]...to realize when I first adopted that phrase for our organization. It is a pretty big organization in this country, Mr. President. It is in every State in the Union. It has thousands of members in every State. It has probably millions in some States, not counting, of course, that they may not all be voters. There may be many below the voting age. But the "share our wealth" phrase was the promise—yes; I said the "promise"—the "share our wealth" phrase was the promise of Franklin D. Roosevelt in the Chicago convention when he accepted the nomination.

What did Roosevelt say?...He said we have got to give a purchasing power to the masses. Then is when Franklin Delano Roosevelt announced that he was in favor of the share-our-wealth platform. Then is when he got up in the Chicago convention, when a man was supposed to be a man, and stood on his hind legs and said that "the crying need of the country is for more and equitable opportunity to share in the distribution of wealth," and our report says "applause and cheers" when he made that statement on the floor of the convention.

What did we do through the leadership of the Senator from Arkansas...What did we do? Did we come into the United States Senate and provide that we would give the people more money so they could buy the things which the United States Government said they had to have in order to live? Did we come here and provide that they could buy more and provide that instead of the farmer continuing underproduction he might produce what was expected to be consumed by the people?

No...We allowed the rich to become richer and the poor to become poorer...We gave the masses less with which to buy.

Why, Gentlemen of the Senate, someone has said I am at war with the President. With which President am I at war? Am I at war with the President who took the nomination of the Democratic convention in Chicago in 1932? No. That man is my brother. Is he demised?...Is that man to whom we gave the nomination and who uttered those words at the Chicago convention in 1932 still alive? If he is alive, he is a boon companion of mine because I am standing where he stood in 1932. Yea, more, I am standing where I stood before he took that stand.

We have reduced the purchasing power of the masses in the last 3 years; and the figures here show it. We have 22,000,000 on the relief dole and 10,000,000 to 15,000,000 more people trying to get on it. The United States Relief Department says that $8 is enough for one family to eat on, and, therefore, with that starvation diet we have prescribed under the dole they have forgotten the diet the health authorities of the Department of Agriculture, in 1929, and up to now, said was necessary for the human family, and have decided to reduce the people to where it is a bread-line proposition of getting a cup of soup for supper and some little hand-out for breakfast in the morning.

It makes me think of a man who seized the 140-acre farm of a man for a debt he owed to the store. The old man went off, and a few years later he came back, and meanwhile the other man has discovered oil on the land. The old man went in and said, "Mr. So-and-so, you seized that 140 acres of land for a $100 debt, and you have got $1,000,000 of oil off it. Don't you think you ought to help me out and give me a little something?" The man said, "Why, certainly my friend. I think I owe you something." He called his clerk and he said, "Come here, Jim. Go back of that counter and get this man a bottle of Sloan's liniment. He may have rheumatism for all I know." [Laughter.]

Mr. President, the Senators from Arkansas and Kentucky want me to tell them how I would draw the legislation [to share the wealth].

First, I would guarantee that there would be no such thing in the United States as a man possessing more than somewhere around 100 to 200 times the average family wealth. What would that mean in the United States today? It would mean that there would be nobody in the United States who could own more than between a million and a half and three million dollars as a fortune. I might get it down a little below that...No person shall own or possess wealth or property in the United States of America beyond an amount in excess of 200 times the average family fortune. This means that we would limit fortunes tomorrow to somewhere around $3,000,000.

[Second, I would guarantee] a homestead to every family in the United States of America.

No one should have a homestead worth less than one-third the average family fortune. How much would that have been, according to the United States estimates, in the prosperous days, and if my plan were adopted you would not find a record of a time in the past when our people were as prosperous as they would then be.

There was national wealth amounting to around $421,000,000,000 at one time, according to the estimates. Take that $421,000,000,000 and divide it into 24,000,000 families in the United States, and you have an average wealth of $17,000 to the family.

Guarantee to every family a homestead of one-third that amount, somewhere between five and six thousand dollars, and that will mean that every family of an average of four and a half to five people, according to the figures—the number varies depending on whether times are good or bad—would have a shelter under which to live, and would have those things necessary to enable them to live in respectable comfort and happiness. They would be able to have a home in which to live, land to till if they were farmers, and the furniture and the accoutrements of a house up to the value of $5,000, free of debt, and there would be no trouble about it. Each family might have some kind of automobile and radio. All free of debt.

[Third], the income of every family of America shall not be less than from one-third to one-half the average family income of the particular year. The income of no one person shall be more than 100 times the income of the average family for that year.

Without the least trouble at all there can be at least an average family income of around $5,000 a year in America if wealth and income are reasonably distributed, so that people can purchase, and mechanical appliances can be used, rather than prohibited because of a lack of distribution of income and capital.

Therefore if it can be guaranteed that a family will never be below the poverty line of somewhere around $2,000 in annual income, it would still leave somewhere around one-half of the income of the head of such a family, if not more—perhaps two-thirds of it—to be used and to be garnered by the man with better intellect and by the financial masters who weave not, but who nevertheless are arrayed in such manner that not even Solomon in all his glory appears as one of them.

Mr. President, how are we going to get this money? We are going to take into the ownership of the United States of America every dollar, every bit of property that anybody owns above a few million dollars, and we are going to distribute that property, either by selling it and distributing it or otherwise, to those who have less than a homestead of around $5,000. That is how we are going to get it.

It is said that cannot be done. It has been done. The Bible says it has been done. . . . The Bible says that every man will rest under his own vine and under his own tree, and that they who have houses, goods, and things of which they have no need, will bring them in to those who rule, and those who rule will distribute them out to those who have need of them. That is what is said in the Bible. You do not have to go very far to find out how it is all going to be done, or how it must be done.

Now, Mr. President, I have no objection to the Senate recessing.

Mr. BARKLEY. Mr. President, I do not know of anything, which the Senate would rather do at this moment.

Aubrey Williams, the Problem of Unemployment, January 16, 1935

Aubrey Williams Papers. National Archives and Records Administration, Franklin D. Roosevelt Presidential Library, Hyde Park, NY.

I am pleased with the opportunity of speaking before the Buffalo Council Agencies, for yours is a group with which I feel at home. By your training and the character of your work, I feel that you are gifted with the clearest perception of any professional group in the country of the problems which face America's millions of unemployed. By virtue of that fact I can approach you this evening on a basis of common understanding, for we are all working with the same tools toward common goal.

You and I know that the problem of unemployment does not stem directly from industrial depression. Depression aggravates unemployment and in the present instance has brought it to a nearly unbearable intensity. We know instead that it was spawned in an era of giddy expansionism; that it is an inescapable concomitant of our type of civilization, and that its roots are now sunk in the very bedrock of our capitalist society.

I do not think you will accuse me of pessimism when I say that unemployment—or better, disemployment—is, like the airplane, the radio, the weather and taxes, here to stay. Millions of those now out of jobs will never find jobs again. Thousands of young men and women leaving our schools each year are destined never to become self-supporting and independent in the sense that your and my generation were led to believe was our due.

The supply of workers exceeds the demand. Man power is a drug on the market. The productive forces of this country, are glutted with brawn and brain which they cannot use. And what can't be utilized, is simply laid aside to moulder and decay. Look about you and you'll see what I mean, Look at the case histories in your files and see the splendid, capable, intelligent workers for whom there are no jobs. Thumb through the cards in the National Reemployment Service. Look into the haggard faces of those who haunt the factory gates and the employment offices.

Civilization has done a great job of marching ahead in the last fifty years but it has been to the harsh, metallic beat of engines. Man has been thrust aside to make way for the machines, and the human carnage has not been reckoned. The stretch-out, the speed-up, and the soul-destroying regimentation of the production line are the grim symbols of our progress, and as they have been applied, a toll in human values has been taken.

Equally distorted has been the distribution of our national income, giving to our country today that inhumane paradox of need in the midst of plenty.

Is proof of these phenomena lacking? Turn to the United States Department of Labor, the files of the A. F. of L., the research findings of the Brookings Institution, the National Industrial Conference, and scores of the most able economists and sociologists in the land. Cumulative, progressive unemployment has been in progress since before the World War. Production methods have been steadily in favor of the machines as against human labor in practically any field you can name. Production ratios have doubled, trebled, and quadrupled while employment indices have remained static.

Incomes and the national wealth, meanwhile, have funneled into the coffers of the few. While 70 percent of our people are obliged to live in poverty on incomes of less than $1,500 a year—a sum insufficient to maintain health and decency for a family of five—a mere one-sixth of one percent of our people are privileged to enjoy the luxuries and good things of life which can be bought with incomes of $7,500 a year or more. Even in 1929, that false-faced Nirvana toward which the Bourbons still yearn, the Brookings Institution has revealed not more than ten percent of all our people were financially able to enjoy a liberal diet.

Now, these distressing conditions were not built up over night. They have been accumulating for the last fifty years when our physical frontiers were reached and overrun. Unseen for the most part save by a few inspired prophets whose warnings we scorned, they hung like the sword of Damocles over our heads, until the slender thread snapped in the fall of 1929.

Similarly, the damage is not to be repaired off hand. We have a long job of reconstruction ahead and as we build anew we must build for permanence. We must recognize that our cherished American liberties are but a pretense so long as three-fourths of our people do not know the meaning of security; when ten millions of our workers are denied the right to earn a living; while thousands of parents sit with helpless, folded hands while their children waste away from hunger.

It is along the line of a permanent correction of these inequalities that the Roosevelt New Deal has moved. Our efforts were clumsy at first, as naturally would result from attempting so momentous a task with not a single precedent or pattern to go by. But at least the direction was clear: it was not to spend the government's millions in salvaging railroads, banks, and insurance companies alone, but to spend them as well for the salvaging of human beings. For the first time in any national administration, President Roosevelt has thrown the spotlight of emphasis on human rather than material values.

The wails of protest from Park Avenue and Wall Street have, as you know, been piteous. I am fascinated by the glib wizardry of those who would care for these dispossessed millions and at the same time balance the budget, reduce taxes, end the war in Ethiopia and produce prosperity like a long eared rabbit from an opera hat. Theirs is the wistful, wishful thinking of adolescence.

You will be interested in some of the details of the very comprehensive picture we have been able to draw concerning our relief population. The trend of unemployment, the natural precursor of relief status, leaped upward from approximately 3,000,000 in March 1929, to an all-time high of 15,000,000 in the same month of 1933, when the present administration came into power. Last March, the estimates had dropped to 12,000,000, and today most reliable sources place the number of jobless at 10,000,000.

Relief trends followed those of unemployment, increasing from somewhere in the neighborhood of 400,000 in March 1929—a figure which we will never know with exactness—to about 18,000,000 in March 1933. With the introduction of organized Federal aid in that year, and as family resources among the unemployed finally broke under the long strain of joblessness, the number continued to increase until in January 1935, we had our maximum relief burden of 20,654,000 men, women and children, As of last May, one in every six persons in the cities, and one in every eight persons in the rural areas, were dependent upon public funds for support. The greatest proportion of these were under 20 years of age, while the next largest age group was that from 20 to 40—the period of greatest employability. Twenty-seven percent of all persons on relief were at that age when vitality and earning capacity should have been at its very peak, yet they were broke and without jobs, facing a hopeless future.

We have learned a great many other things about our relief group—where and in what sort of houses they live; their former usual occupations; the extent of their training and education; their general health status; their present employability, and many other details of their lives, character and capacities. We are able to answer with a defiant and emphatic "No!" those scornful critics who would make out our relief people to be idlers, wasters, and malingerers. We know that there are triflers in the lot, but by and large they are the same honest, industrious workers who contributed to America's prosperity of the 1920's. There are bankers, lawyers, architects, and ministers in the group as well as carpenters, bricklayers, farmers and laborers. A cross section of the relief rolls today would reveal a hardly discernible difference from any other segment of American life save for the one factor of dependence.

It was a tremendous statistical job to develop this picture on a national scale, but it had to be done if we were to use intelligent, long-range planning. This planning has assumed two general forms—employment at security wages for those who have been on relief, and the program of economic assurance against unemployment, old age, and sickness as embodied in the Social Security Act. Let's consider them separately and see to what extent they meet the needs imposed by the inequalities of civilization today.

Four billion, eight hundred million dollars were made available at the last session of Congress to take 3,500,000 Americans off the relief rolls. The dole was to be obliterated and relief clients were to be given jobs on constructive public works at wages on which they could decently support themselves and their families. That appropriation was bitterly fought when it was proposed and has been bitterly fought ever since, particularly by those who persist in thinking in terms of their own pocketbooks instead of the lives and welfare of other people. They would have perpetuated the dole because it was cheaper and would have ignored the waste of human values, the degradation, the smouldering resentment in honest hearts which such a system cannot help but inspire.

Now, what has the WPA done with its money? How much of it has gone into "boondoggling" and other channels of waste, inefficiency, or graft?

It should be borne in mind that the WPA did not get the entire four billion dollar fund. Not by any means. Only about 37 percent, or $1,082,900,000, went to that agency. The balance was distributed between the CCC, which got over $500,000,000, and certain other regular Government departments. Among the latter, the Department of Agriculture received over $500,000,000, the Public Works Administration $444,000,000 the Department of the Interior $118,000,000, the War Department $142,000,000, and so on.

As for the WPA's share, it is a simple matter to see to what purpose it is being put. Forty-two and one-half per cent of the entire fund has been earmarked for highway, road, and street projects. There are 20,950 such projects with an aggregate cost of $45S,055,892 already in operation or soon to be begun. Parks and playgrounds account for another 11.8 per cent, public buildings for 9.2 per cent, water supply and sewer systems for 9.1 per cent, flood control and other conservation projects for 5.9 per cent, sewing rooms and other production projects for 6.1 per cent, and white collar projects for 5.8 per cent.

Well, that list accounts for 90 per cent of all the funds allotted to the WPA and we haven't even touched on the health and sanitation projects, the airports, and a number of other groups of equal importance. I don't think any fair observer could complain of public funds being, spent for such meritorious purposes as these.

Now think what these undertakings mean to the communities in which they are operating. In practically every case you will find that the work being done is some essential construction or service which the community has long wanted but been unable to accomplish out of its own budget. Take your own state of New York, exclusive of New York City, and let's see what the program is doing here. One hundred fifty-eight thousand of your people have been given employment at wages ranging from $44 to $103 per month. One hundred thirty-four thousand of them are working for the WPA 16,000 of them are in the CCC and approximately 8,000 of them are engaged on projects sponsored by regular Governmental departments.

Forty-seven million, one hundred thirty-eight thousand dollars have been set aside to carry on the WPA program here, again, remember, exclusive of New York City. Forty-three per cent of this money is going into the building of new roads and streets and the maintenance of those already built. Farm-to-market roads, feeders from the hinterlands to the main arteries of traffic which will be passable throughout the year, constitute a large part of this highway work. Fourteen and one-half per cent of the money is being spent in the development of parks, playgrounds, swimming pools, not only for the children of such cities as Buffalo but for those in smaller towns and rural districts as well. Public building projects, which means, predominantly, schools, account for nine per cent of the funds. Not only are new schools being built, but thousands of gallons of paint, miles of roofing, millions of feet of lumber, and tons of brick, cement and steel are being used to make repairs and alterations which your school boards have long desired, but been unable to have.

A little over six per cent of the funds to be spent in New York State are going into projects for professional and non manual workers—white-collar people. Old, worn out court records are being recopied to withstand hard use, tax maps remade and brought up to date, surveys and studies of a dozen different kinds being carried or which will add materially to the value of services rendered by your various public bodies.

In Buffalo alone, $137,000 is being spent to provide much needed additional personnel in your public libraries. Another $44,000 is being used to employ extra help at the City Hospital in order to expand the services of its out-patient department. Many of your unemployed writers, artists, and musicians have been placed on projects where their talents will add to the cultural value of life. Such a list as this hardly scratches the surface of the varied activities which are being carried on in this field, yet it has been called "boondoggling," and as such is the favorite target of the critics.

Turning to the national scene again, we see that the youth of the country has not been forgotten. Fifty million dollars of WPA funds were set aside last June for the creation of the National Youth Administration so that young people in this particularly difficult period might not come to their majority under the blight of joblessness and destitution.

Up to this time we are maintaining more than 300,000 young people between the ages of 16 and 25 in high schools and colleges throughout the nation. Four thousand of them are pursuing graduate work on benefits averaging $25 a month. One hundred thousand are undergraduate students in some 1,600 colleges and universities and are receiving average benefits of $15 a month. Another 200,000 are students in high schools and are receiving $6 a month each. These, as you know, are not honorariums, but represent wages earned for constructive work in or about the schools and communities.

A little more than half of our $50,000,000 is being thus expended. The remainder is being applied as wages on work projects for those young people for whom further schooling is impossible or inadvisable. Special projects designed for young people have been set up in every state. Many of these have training as the predominant element. In other cases, young people are being employed part-time on regular WPA projects at one-third of the regular security wage. Many offices of the United States Employment Service have added young people to their staffs to seek particularly those jobs which are generally recognized as belonging to youth, and we are co-operating in full with the Federal Committee on Apprentice Training to place unemployed young people in apprentice jobs.

General control of the WPA program is retained in Washington. This, you will agree, is essential where one and not 48 separate objectives are sought. But the administration of the program, the shaping and fitting of plans and policies to the needs of individual localities, has been left with the various state and district administrators. Contrary to a belief which seems to have become general, there is no autocratic control vested in Washington. The greatest flexibility has been allowed the states to fit the program to their own needs, and it is, essentially, a state program in each state.

Localities design the types of projects they want. They are built around community needs and the abilities of the young people on relief. The communities contribute what they can toward the cost, and the project application is forwarded through local WPA headquarters to Washington. There it is judged in the light of certain essential requirements as to social and economic desirability, employment value, and cost. If these specifications are met, it is turned over to the Comptroller General for financial inspection, and finally to the Treasury for the actual allocation of funds. All along the line, greatest care is exerted to see that each project not only provides the requisite number of jobs, but constitutes a work or service of definite public value.

The WPA set out to remove the curse of the dole from American life and to substitute in its place honest jobs at honest rates of pay in which the unemployed might not only achieve a decent standard of living but retain their self-respect as well. In this I believe we are succeeding and I do not believe that a one of you here will tell me that our philosophy is wrong.

As to social security, the other half of our long-range program, I shall not go into detail. Briefly, it embodies unemployment compensation, old-age security, security for dependent children, aid to the blind, extension of public health services and vocational rehabilitation. It is much in the public prints at this time and most of you are familiar with its general procedure. I do wish to point out, however, how it and the WPA program of providing jobs for the unemployed complement one another and work to the greater security of the average American citizen.

I think I can be as lusty in my praise of America and American form of government as any professional patriot who ever waved a flag or damned a Communist, but I cannot blind myself to the abuses which have arisen about us. I cannot condone the inequalities, the injustices or the mass social crimes which have been perpetuated under the guise of American freedom and liberty. I get small consolation in counting the digits of our national wealth or hearing described our celestial standard of living when I know that these blessings have clogged up at the top of the social structure.

But it is not our part to concern ourselves over-much with the forms and processes of government. Ours must be the objective point of view. We must take hunger, destitution, and the mal-adjustments of society as we find them, and mitigate their effects as best we can within the limitations of the existing scheme of things.

But there is no law or rule or ethical precept which says we cannot exult when we see government concern itself with the problems in which we deal. And we must give our counsel and support to any political regime which says, as President Roosevelt said last June in submitting the draft of the Social Security Act, "Among our objectives I place the security of the men and women and children of the Nation first."

That, all along, has been the objective of those of us who have viewed unemployment and need as a professional problem. Now it has the sanction of a strong government and a courageous President and I think we may well be encouraged over the promise of fulfillment which they give.

Franklin D. Roosevelt. Fireside Chat. April 28, 1935

Public Papers of the Presidents: Franklin D. Roosevelt (1933–45), National Archives and Records Administration.

Since my annual message to the Congress on January fourth, last, I have not addressed the general public over the air. In the many weeks since that time the Congress has devoted itself to the arduous task of formulating legislation necessary to the country's welfare. It has made and is making distinct progress.

Before I come to any of the specific measures, however, I want to leave in your minds one clear fact. The Administration and the Congress are not proceeding in any haphazard fashion in this task of government. Each of our steps has a definite relationship to every other step. The job of creating a program for the Nation's welfare is, in some respects, like the building of a ship. At different points on the coast where I often visit they build great seagoing ships, and when one of these ships is under construction and the steel frames have been set in the keel, it is difficult for a person who does not know ships to tell how it will finally look when it is sailing the high seas. It may seem confused to some, but out of the multitude of detailed parts that go into the making of the structure the creation of a useful instrument for man ultimately comes.

It is that way with the making of a national policy. The objective of the Nation has greatly changed in three years. Before that time individual self-interest and group self-ishness were paramount in public thinking. The general good was at a discount.

Three years of hard thinking have changed the picture. More and more people, because of clearer thinking and a better understanding, are considering the whole rather than a mere part relating to one section or to one crop, or to one industry, or to an individual private occupation. That is a tremendous gain for the principles of democracy. The overwhelming majority of people in this country know how to sift the wheat from the chaff in what they hear and what they read. They know that the process of the constructive rebuilding of America cannot be done in a day or a year, but that it is being done in spite of the few who seek to confuse them and to profit by their confusion. Americans as a whole are feeling a lot better—a lot more cheerful than for many, many years.

The most difficult place in the world to get a clear open perspective of the country as a whole is Washington. I am reminded sometimes of what President Wilson once said: "So many people come to Washington who know things that are not so, and so few people who know anything about what the people of the United States are thinking about." That is why I occasionally leave this scene of action for a few days to go fishing or back home to Hyde Park, so that I can have a chance to think quietly about the country as a whole. "To get away from the trees", as they say, "and to look at the whole forest." This duty of seeing the country in a long-range perspective is one which, in a very special manner, attaches to this office to which you have chosen me. Did you ever stop to think that there are, after all, only two positions in the Nation that are filled by the vote of all of the voters—the President and the Vice-President? That makes it particularly necessary for the Vice-President and for me to conceive of our duty toward the entire country. I speak, therefore, tonight, to and of the American people as a whole.

My most immediate concern is in carrying out the purposes of the great work program just enacted by the Congress. Its first objective is to put men and women now on the relief rolls to work and, incidentally, to assist materially in our already unmistakable march toward recovery. I shall not confuse my discussion by a multitude of figures. So many figures are quoted to prove so many things. Sometimes it depends upon what paper you read and what broadcast you hear. Therefore, let us keep our minds on two or three simple, essential facts in connection with this problem of unemployment. It is true that while business and industry are definitely better our relief rolls are still too large. However, for the first time in five years the relief rolls have declined instead of increased during the winter months. They are still declining. The simple fact is that many million more people have private work today than two years ago today or one year ago today, and every day that passes offers more chances to work for those who want to work. In spite of the fact that unemployment remains a serious problem here as in every other nation, we have come to recognize the possibility and the necessity of certain helpful remedial measures. These measures are of two kinds. The first is to make provisions intended to relieve, to minimize, and to prevent future unemployment;

the second is to establish the practical means to help those who are unemployed in this present emergency. Our social security legislation is an attempt to answer the first of these questions; our work relief program the second.

The program for social security now pending before the Congress is a necessary part of the future unemployment policy of the government. While our present and projected expenditures for work relief are wholly within the reasonable limits of our national credit resources, it is obvious that we cannot continue to create governmental deficits for that purpose year after year. We must begin now to make provision for the future. That is why our social security program is an important part of the complete picture. It proposes, by means of old age pensions, to help those who have reached the age of retirement to give up their jobs and thus give to the younger generation greater opportunities for work and to give to all a feeling of security as they look toward old age.

The unemployment insurance part of the legislation will not only help to guard the individual in future periods of lay-off against dependence upon relief, but it will, by sustaining purchasing power, cushion the shock of economic distress. Another helpful feature of unemployment insurance is the incentive it will give to employers to plan more carefully in order that unemployment may be prevented by the stabilizing of employment itself.

Provisions for social security, however, are protections for the future. Our responsibility for the immediate necessities of the unemployed has been met by the Congress through the most comprehensive work plan in the history of the Nation. Our problem is to put to work three and one-half million employable persons now on the relief rolls. It is a problem quite as much for private industry as for the government.

We are losing no time getting the government's vast work relief program underway, and we have every reason to believe that it should be in full swing by autumn. In directing it, I shall recognize six fundamental principles:

First, the projects should be useful.

Secondly, the projects should be of a nature that a considerable proportion of the money spent will go into wages for labor.

Third, projects which promise ultimate return to the Federal Treasury of a considerable proportion of the costs will be sought.

Fourth, funds allotted for each project should be actually and promptly spent and not held over until later years.

Fifth, in all cases projects must be of a character to give employment to those on the relief rolls.

And finally, projects will be allocated to localities or relief areas in relation to the number of workers on relief rolls in those areas.

Next, I think that it will interest you to know exactly how we shall direct the work as a federal government.

First I have set up a Division of Applications and Information to which all proposals for the expenditure of money must go for preliminary study and consideration.

Secondly, after this Division of Applications and Information has sifted those projects, they will be sent to an Allotment Division composed of representatives of the more important governmental agencies charged with carrying on work relief projects. The group will also include representatives of cities, and of labor, farming, banking and industry. This Allotment Division will consider all of the recommendations submitted to it and such projects as they approve will be next submitted to the President who under the Act is required to make final allocations.

The next step will be to notify the proper government agency in whose field the project falls, and also to notify another agency which I am creating—a Progress Division. This Division will have the duty of coordinating the purchases of materials and supplies and of making certain that people who are employed will be taken from the relief rolls. It will also have the responsibility of determining work payments in various localities, of making full use of existing employment services and to assist people engaged in relief work to move as rapidly as possible back into private employment when such employment is available. Moreover, this Division will be charged with keeping projects moving on schedule.

Finally, I have felt it to be essentially wise and prudent to avoid, so far as possible, the creation of new governmental machinery for supervising this work. The National Government now has at least sixty different agencies with the staff and the experience and the competence necessary to carry on the two hundred and fifty or three hundred kinds of work that will be undertaken. These agencies, therefore, will simply be doing on a somewhat enlarged scale the same sort of things that they have been doing. This will make certain that the largest possible portion of the funds allotted will be spent for actually creating new work and not for building up expensive overhead organizations here in Washington.

For many months preparations have been under way. The allotment of funds for desirable projects has already begun. The key men for the major responsibilities of this great task already have been selected. I well realize that the country is expecting before this year is out to see the "dirt fly", as they say, in carrying on the work, and I assure my fellow citizens that no energy will be spared in using these funds effectively to make a major attack upon the problem of unemployment.

Our responsibility is to all of the people in this country. This is a great national crusade to destroy enforced idleness which is an enemy of the human spirit generated by this depression. Our attack upon these enemies must be without stint and without discrimination. No sectional, no political distinctions can be permitted.

It must, however, be recognized that when an enterprise of this character is extended over more than three thousand counties throughout the Nation, there may be occasional instances of inefficiency, bad management, or misuse of funds. When cases of this kind occur, there will be those, of course, who will try to tell you that the exceptional failure is characteristic of the entire endeavor. It should be remembered that in every big job there are some imperfections. There are chiselers in every walk of life; there are those in every industry who are guilty of unfair practices, every profession has its black sheep, but long experience in government has taught me that the exceptional instances of wrong-doing in government are probably less numerous than in almost every other line of endeavor. The most effective means of preventing such evils in this work relief program will be the eternal vigilance of the American people themselves. I call upon my fellow citizens everywhere to cooperate with me in making this the most efficient and the cleanest example of public enterprise the world has ever seen.

It is time to provide a smashing answer for those cynical men who say that a democracy cannot be honest and efficient. If you will help, this can be done. I, therefore, hope you will watch the work in every corner of this Nation. Feel free to criticize. Tell me of instances where work can be done better, or where improper practices prevail. Neither you nor I want criticism conceived in a purely fault-finding or partisan spirit, but I am jealous of the right of every citizen to call to the attention of his or her government examples of how the public money can be more effectively spent for the benefit of the American people.

I now come, my friends, to a part of the remaining business before the Congress. It has under consideration many measures which provide for the rounding out of the program of economic and social reconstruction with which we have been concerned for two years. I can mention only a few of them tonight, but I do not want my mention of specific measures to be interpreted as lack of interest in or disapproval of many other important proposals that are pending.

The National Industrial Recovery Act expires on the sixteenth of June. After careful consideration, I have asked the Congress to extend the life of this useful agency of government. As we have proceeded with the administration of this Act, we have found from time to time more and more useful ways of promoting its purposes. No reasonable person wants to abandon our present gains—we must continue to protect children, to enforce minimum wages, to prevent excessive hours, to safeguard, define and enforce collective bargaining, and, while retaining fair competition, to eliminate so far as humanly possible, the kinds of unfair practices by selfish minorities which unfortunately did more than anything else to bring about the recent collapse of industries.

There is likewise pending before the Congress legislation to provide for the elimination of unnecessary holding companies in the public utility field.

I consider this legislation a positive recovery measure. Power production in this country is virtually back to the 1929 peak. The operating companies in the gas and electric utility field are by and large in good condition. But under holding company domination the utility industry has long been hopelessly at war within itself and with public sentiment. By far the greater part of the general decline in utility securities had occurred before I was inaugurated. The absentee management of unnecessary holding company control has lost touch with and has lost the sympathy of the communities it pretends to serve. Even more significantly, it has given the country as a whole an uneasy apprehension of overconcentrated economic power.

You and I know that a business that loses the confidence of its customers and the good will of the public cannot long continue to be a good risk for the investor. This legislation will serve the investor by ending the conditions which have caused that lack of confidence and good will. It will put the public utility operating industry on a sound basis for the future, both in its public relations and in its internal relations.

This legislation will not only in the long run result in providing lower electric and gas rates to the consumer, but it will protect the actual value and earning power of properties now owned by thousands of investors who have little protection under the old laws against what used to be called frenzied finance. It will not destroy values.

Not only business recovery, but the general economic recovery of the Nation will be greatly stimulated by the enactment of legislation designed to improve the status of our transportation agencies. There is need for legislation providing for the regulation of interstate transportation by buses and trucks, to regulate transportation by water, new provisions for strengthening our Merchant Marine and air transport, measures for the strengthening of the Interstate Commerce Commission to enable it to carry out a rounded conception of the national transportation system in which the benefits of private ownership are retained, while the public stake in these important services is protected by the public's government.

And finally, the reestablishment of public confidence in the banks of the Nation is one of the most hopeful results of our efforts as a Nation to reestablish public confidence in private banking. We all know that private banking actually exists by virtue of the permission of and regulation by the people as a whole, speaking through their government. Wise public policy, however, requires not only that banking be safe but that its resources be most fully utilized, in the economic life of the country. To this end it was decided more than twenty years ago that the government should assume the responsibility of providing a means by which the credit of the Nation might be controlled, not by a few private banking institutions, but by a body with public prestige and authority. The answer to this demand was the Federal Reserve System. Twenty years of experience with this system have justified the efforts made to create it, but these twenty years have shown by experience definite possibilities for improvement. Certain proposals made to amend the Federal Reserve Act deserve prompt and favorable action by the Congress. They are a minimum of wise readjustment of our Federal Reserve system in the light of past experience and present needs.

These measures I have mentioned are, in large part, the program which under my constitutional duty I have recommended to the Congress. They are essential factors in a rounded program for national recovery. They contemplate the enrichment of our national life by a sound and rational ordering of its various elements and wise provisions for the protection of the weak against the strong.

Never since my inauguration in March, 1933, have I felt so unmistakably the atmosphere of recovery. But it is more than the recovery of the material basis of our individual lives. It is the recovery of confidence in our democratic processes and institutions. We have survived all of the arduous burdens and the threatening dangers of a great economic calamity. We have in the darkest moments of our national trials retained our faith in our own ability to master our destiny. Fear is vanishing and confidence is growing on every side, renewed faith in the vast possibilities of human beings to improve their material and spiritual status through the instrumentality of the democratic form of government. That faith is receiving its just reward. For that we can be thankful to the God who watches over America.

Robert Fechner to Thomas L. Griffith, September 21, 1935

Source: "CCC Negro Selection" file, BOX 700, General Correspondence of the Director, Record Group 35, National Archives, College Park, Maryland.

September 21, 1935

Mr. Thomas L. Griffith, Jr.
President
National Association for the Advancement of Colored People
1105 E. Vernon Avenue
Los Angeles, California

Dear Mr. Griffith:

The President has called my attention to the letter you addressed to him on September 14, 1935, in which you ask for information relating to the policy of segregation in CCC camps.

The law enacted by Congress setting up Emergency Conservation Work specifically indicated that there should be no discrimination because of color. I have faithfully endeavored to obey the spirit and letter of this, as well as all other provisions of the law.

At the very beginning of this work, I consulted with many representative individuals and groups who were interested in the work, and the decision to segregate white enrollees, negro enrollees, and war veterans, was generally approved. I believe that the record of the past thirty months will sustain the wisdom of our decision.

While segregation has been the general policy, it has not been inflexible, and we have a number of companies containing a small number of negro enrollees. I am satisfied that the negro enrollees themselves prefer to be in companies composed exclusively of their own race.

This segregation is not discrimination and cannot be so construed. The negro companies are assigned to the same types of work, have identical equipment, are served the same food, and have the same quarters as white enrollees. I have personally visited many negro CCC companies and have talked with the enrollees and have never received one single complaint. I want to assure you that I am just as sincerely interested as anyone in making this work of the greatest possible value to all who have a part in it.

Sincerely yours,

(Sgn) ROBERT FECHNER

ROBERT FECHNER
Director
RF/bp

Davis, Hallie Flanagan. "Is This the Time and Place?"

Papers of Hallie Flanagan Davis, Director Federal Theatre Project, Works Progress Administration. National Archives and Records Administration, Franklin D. Roosevelt Presidential Library, Hyde Park, NY.

This place in which we meet, at first glance so strangely inappropriate, becomes upon reflection one key to the situation, an epitome of one element in our American life which caused the situation.

Here we meet to discuss the problem of thousands of artists, no longer able to live in America except on charity; we meet to form a plan whereby people will again become enough interested in the work of artists to make such work a salable commodity. Behind us, hidden by a discreet panel, there is a carved wood serving table, imported from Italy, which cost $25,000. At the end of the hall, again cautiously veiled from the vandal or the irreverent, a buffet which cost $32,000. The hideousness of the chandeliers in the great ballroom, the busts and statues in the court, the gold faucet on the gigantic bathtubs, are only equaled by their excessive cost. In short, the McLean mansion, like many similar edifices throughout America, is a monument to the period of American culture in which the value of a work of art was measured in terms of its cost and the distance from which it was imported.

Irrespective of the merit of its art treasure, the McLean Mansion represents the conception of art as a commodity to be purchased by the rich, possessed by the rich, and shared on occasional Wednesday evenings with the populace who, gaping in ecstasy, were allowed to file past the accumulated treasures.

During the first days in this house I was haunted by a sense of having gone through this experience before; gradually that memory became focussed upon the golden places of Soviet Russia now turned into offices and orphans' homes and theatres for the Russian proletariat. I remembered a theatre meeting in the great Hall of Mirrors in Leningrad where reflected from every side in those mirrors which once gave back the image of the Empress, and later the execution of her officers, I saw the faces of Stalin, Litvinov, Lunachaisky, Petrov and other leaders of political, educational and theatrical life. They met to discuss their mutual problem: how the theatre could serve in educating the people and in enriching their lives.

I do not at this time wish to press the parallel or to argue as to its prophetic implications. I merely wish to say that the present state of this house, with typewriters clicking where once musicians played in the long galleries, with out of work painters and sculptors carefully averting their eyes from various art atrocities while they ask Mr. Cahill for jobs, is characteristic of the decline of a certain period in American art and life. For it is not only bad collections which have had their day, but all collections. Holger Cahill, director of the federal art project, came to this job after several years spent in disposing of art collections of the Morgans, and the Rockefellers, for whom he had previously assembled such collections. Mr. Cahill also feels that with the passing of the private art collections one whole period of American culture ends. Personally I cannot work up any regret over the demise. That works of art in America today should belong in small collections to individuals who care about them and share them with their friends, or to the museums, which are doing an increasingly good job of making art intelligible and exciting to everybody, seems to me a very satisfactory state of affairs.

I only wish we had a method of play distribution as satisfactory: perhaps it is our job to find one.

Unfortunately the theatre, more than any of the arts, still clings to the skirts of the 19th century. A recent advertisement in The Stage, for example, read:

The first ten rows are the people, the alert, challenging people whose opinion makes or breaks a play. These are the people who possess the gowns, the jewels, the furs, the country estates, the town cars—in short all the appurtenances of fine living around which the smart world of the theatre revolves.

In the economic fallacy of such a statement lies one reason for the decline of the stage.

That the stage is in a decline is obvious. Mr. Lee Shubert said the other day, with a bewilderment which I found rather touching,

Once the stage was the dog, and the movies were the tail; now the movies are the dog, and we are the tail.

And who should know better than Lee Shubert?

That the decline of the stage is not entirely due to the economic depression is one of the basic facts which we must consider. For if we attempt to put people back to work in theatre enterprises which are defunct, we are engaged in temporarily reviving a corpse which will never be alive again.

All the plans for reviving the road seem to me to be born of this naïve faith in resuscitation. Of course a great actress like Katharine Cornell touring the country in Romeo and Juliet will always have an audience; but the population of Oskaloosa, Iowa, or Fort Worth, Texas, is not going to be enraptured as in days of yore by a 3rd rate touring company in a mediocre play, just because such a company comes from New York. Oskaloos and Fort Worth have been educated by the cinema and the radio. They know a hawk from a hand saw. They no longer measure art by the distance from which it was imported.

Our whole emphasis in the theatre enterprises which we are about to undertake should be on re-thinking rather than on remembering. The good old days may have been very good days indeed, but they are gone. New days are upon us and the plays that we do and the ways that we do them should be informed by our consciousness of the art and economies of 1935.

We live in a changing world: man is whispering through space, soaring to the stars in ships, flinging miles of steel and glass into the air. Shall the theatre continue to huddle in the confines of a painted box? The movies, in their kaleidoscopic speed and juxtaposition of external objects and internal emotions are seeking to find visible and audible expression for the tempo and the psychology of our time. The stage too must experiment—with ideas, with psychological relationship of men and women, with speech and rhythm forms, with dance and movement, with color and light—or it must—and should—become a museum product.

In an age of terrific implications as to wealth and poverty, as to the functions of government, as to peace and war, as to the relation of the artist to all these forces, the theatre must grow up. The theatre must become conscious of the implications of the changing social order, or the changing social order will ignore, and rightly, the implications of the theatre.

Strategically, we are in a very fortunate position. Our liabilities, as is so often the case in life and art, are our assets. For we cannot subsidize existing theatrical enterprises, however excellent. The more fools we, then, if we model our new enterprises in the image of those now appealing to us for help. We cannot afford vast expenditures for scenery and costumes; another advantage, for scenery and costumes as we very well know have become too often the dog wagging the tail. We have plenty of designers—137 on relief rolls in New York City—we have a good many spot lights, and we have 250,000 yards of plain ticking in the government's surplus commodities; the result ought to be something pretty good, without benefit of Bergdorf-Goodman.

We should not be fatuous enough however to think that it will all be beer and skittles. If we have 6,000 theatre people on relief we all know that probably 4,000 of them are not of the calibre to experiment. However, we must keep steadily in mind that we do not work with the 6,000 alone. We work also with the 600 whom we may choose to work with them; and with the 300 whom we choose to direct them; and with as many apprentices as we can absorb from the National Youth Administration, who are ready and willing to pay underprivileged youths from 16 to 25 for studying with the various art groups.

Let us not, therefore, over emphasize the weaknesses of the material with which we work. Mr. Hopkins, in his last talk with the directors of the various art projects before he left on the western trip with President Roosevelt, reemphasized his position: that it was quality rather than quantity which was to be the keynote of the art program. He reaffirmed that we were to turn back to the employment service people who had no chance of making a living through the theatre after this project ends. That we were to bend our energies toward creating theatre units which would be so vital to community needs that they would continue to function after our funds are withdrawn. Our best efforts must be spent in finding intelligent and imaginative theatre plans, excellent direction and adequate sponsorship for such plans.

Now how much has been accomplished so far? In order to answer that question, I should like to trace briefly the development of the project thus far.

Early this year, President Roosevelt asked Congress to appropriate $4,800,000,000 for a Works Program. It immediately became known that a certain amount was to be spent for the relief of artists.

Late in May I received a telephone message to come to Washington to give professional judgment on the plans submitted thus far for the relief of theatre people. I spent several days going over those plans, which were for the most part requests for the government to back certain theatre companies or theatre artists. There were many plans for reviving the road, a few for Shakespearean companies, national academies, or the like.

The best plan which read at that time was one submitted by Elmer Rice, many elements of which are incorporated in our present plan. At that time I discussed with Mr. Hopkins and Mrs. Roosevelt the plan of the development of regional theatres, around the nucleus of existing theatres such as those represented here; a plan, which as you all know, had been advocated for years by George Pierce Baker, by Edith Iscair, Professor Koch, Professor Mabie, and many others. We discussed decentralization, the emphasis on experimental productions of new plays by unknown writers, and the limited touring, out of regional centers, of theatre units. In all of these plans, both the President and Mr. Hopkins are keenly interested. Work should have started then, but the abrupt termination of the N.R.A. made the W.P.A. officials decide to postpone all plans. Consequently it was not until September 10 that the bill allotting the money was actually stamped by the Comptroller of the Treasury. In the meantime, the 4 appropriations for the individual arts, were passed together as one project (Project I, W.P.A.). The total appropriation (which has never been broken up) was $27,000,000. This amount was for 6 months, though we are assured that a second allotment will carry us on through June 30.

Though the allotment was stamped on September 10, it has only now, on October 5, Saturday, been passed to the various states. Thus, up until now, all work has necessarily been preliminary.

The following steps in the F.T.P. have been taken:

I. The writing of some 2000 letters stating exactly what we can do with federal funds; i.e.,

1. Pay labor costs of people from relief rolls at the prevailing security wag given at the local W.P.A. office.
2. Pay the security wage for one person not on relief rolls for every nine who are.
3. Pay small superintendence salaries of $1,000–$2,500 in the ratio of one administrator to 20 relief rolls.
4. Pay 10% of the labor costs (1 and 2 above) for production costs.
5. Allow admissions of 10 cents to $1.00 to accrue through the sponsor, to the theatre project.

II. The compilation of the general procedure of W.P.A. Project I, involving the exact method under which all federal art projects will operate.

III. The compilation of the theatre manual, involving the particular procedure of our own project, together with classification of workers, wage rates, royalties, admission, etc.

This compilation involved conferences with statisticians, legal counsel, etc.

Both of these bulletins will be explained in detail by Mr. Lang and Mr. Goldschmidt.

IV. Discussion of the F. T. Project with the following groups, in order to secure cooperation:

The National Stage Hands Union

Several meetings were held in this office, one of which was attended by representatives of Actors Equity, Musicians' Union, and representatives of the Stage Hands' Unions from New York, Chicago, Boston, Philadelphia, and one national representative. A representative from this group was put on the reclassification board in N. Y. The general attitude was friendly. The decision was that we cannot run a union shop, but that preference is given to union workers because of their professional qualifications.

1. Actors' Equity.

Many conferences, here and in New York, resulted in Equity offering not only advice and cooperation, but the sponsorship of one New York unity (repertory of plays important in American theatre history).

Three meetings, in New York City, resulted in this group moving from complete antagonism to the project to the utmost cooperation, with an offer to sponsor several New York units as tryout theatres.

2. The Dramatists' Guild.

Several meetings with representatives of this group in New York resulted in our mutual decision that royalties must be paid dramatists; and that this group would interest itself in one of our units, a playwrights' theatre.

3. Federation of Actors.

Two meetings with Mr. Ralph Whitehead, representing vaudeville, variety, and circuses in a discussion of special problems.

4. Samuel French and the American Play Company.

Mr. Clark and Mr. Rumsey, representing respectively the above companies, came to an informal understanding that nay amateur theatre taking over a group of our people, would retain for a period of our experiment, amateur rights; our companies to pay stock prices, sealed low.

5. Chorus Equity.

A conference with Miss Bryant, speaking for Chorus Equity, resulted in a plan for musical comedy for chorus groups.

6. Cinema Interests.

A meeting with Mr. Will Hays in the hope of securing dark houses, resulted in nothing.

7. C.C.C. Camps.

A meeting with Mr. Oxley, director of education for the CCC Camps, and another meeting with Mr. Dunn, educational advisor for the 2nd corps area resulted in ideas for resident theatre instructor, which will be discussed by Mr. Oxley tomorrow.

8. National Youth Administration.

Meeting with representatives of this organization resulted in the plan for youths between 16 and 25 financed by the NYA, to work as students and apprentices in the arts. (This also will be discussed further tomorrow).

9. Theatre Arts Monthly, The New Theatre, the Mayor's Committee in New York.

This discussion led to a decision to have one project on research and publication to be based on the National Theatre Conference and to be headed by Rosamund Gilder.

V. An Analysis of the present New York situation.

This analysis led to the present detailed New York plan which will be explained by Mr. Rice and Mr. Askling.

VI. The reclassification of theatre people now on relief in New York City.

As no funds were yet available, this reclassification was financed by TERA. We now have case histories of 2000 theatre people in New York together with a summary of such value that Mr. Askling will present it to you in the hope that similar studies can be made in each of your regions.

VII. A field survey of the Southern States, conducted by Mr. John McGee with results which he will give you.

IX. A field survey of California, conducted by Mr. Howard Miller, who has gone back to California to start a project on the foundation of the survey.

X. The appointment of the slate of regional directors, in whose hands now rests the fate of the federal theatre project.

This, then, is the situation: several million dollars are allocated and will be in your various state banks within a few days. The procedure under which we work is ready. The plans which you have discussed with me, individually, will be approved. We hope to have several thousand people on the payroll by October 15 and several thousand more on the payroll by November 1. By January 1, I should like to turn in a report to Mr. Hopkins saying that all employable theatre people from relief rolls are at work on projects; more important still, that they have been put to work on theatre projects as intelligent, as vital, and as varied as the imaginations around this table.

The focus of most of the discussion during today and tomorrow will center, rightly, on how the theatre project can help the unemployed. Underneath this, however, let us continue to think how that it can help the theatre.

In a play, My County Right or Left, written by college students and produced on a college stage, there was a scene in which an intellectual, walking alone, philosophizing about art, is confronted by a woman who emerges from a motionless crowd of workers in the background.

The worker woman says, "Is this the appointed hour? Is this the time and place where we should meet?"

The intellectual, removing his hat, remarks cautiously,

"I do not think that we have met before."

To which the worker woman replies,

"I've walked the world for six years. I've noticed you. I knew that someday you would notice me."

Is it too much to think that, for two great forces, mutually in need of each other, the federal theatre project of 1935 may be the appointed time and place?

Southern Farm Tenancy: The Way Out of Its Evils, Edwin R. Embree

Source: Survey Graphic, Vol 25, No. 3 (March 1936), p. 149.

BOOKER T. WASHINGTON used to say, "To keep a black man in the gutter a white man must stay in the gutter to hold him there." The cotton tenants have gone Booker T. Washington one better. Two white men are in the sharecrop mire for every one Negro. Two million families, about eight and a half million people, are living in desperate conditions bordering on peonage in the southern cotton fields. These cotton tenants and sharecroppers make up seven percent of the total population of the nation. Economically they are at a bare subsistence level; mentally and morally they are dependents, without control over their own destinies, with little chance for self-respect or the exercise of individual responsibility, with so little hope that a defeatist attitude spreads like a pall amidst their squalid huts and straggling fields.

The facts are now widely known. The play "Tobacco Road" and the sharecroppers' insurrection in Arkansas have dramatized the story. Careful studies by many southern scholars have presented both the bizarre details and the appalling totals.

The whole jigsaw picture has been brought together recently in a booklet, The Collapse of Cotton Tenancy,[*] in such clear and simple form that he who runs may read.

The question is what we are going to do about it? A decadent nation lets such evils grow and fester. If America still has vitality and courage and imagination, we will not sit idly by while a great group of the population deteriorates, while a whole section of the country goes to ruin. Reorganization will not be easy and will be opposed by natural lethargy and by the complaisance of conservatives. But the issue is so acute, the area and the population concerned are so huge that it is not an overstatement to say that for the rural South the alternatives are reform or ruin.

Brief recital of main points will bring the picture before us. A wide belt extending 300 miles north and south and stretching 1600 miles from the Carolinas to western Texas is devoted almost exclusively to the single commercial crop of cotton. Over 60 percent of those engaged in the production of cotton are in this class. Furthermore tenancy for decades has been steadily increasing. It is an evil that, far from tending to remedy itself, is spread like a dismal infection. The number of farms operated by tenants in the South was high enough in 1880 when 36 percent were run by tenants. By 1920 the percentage of tenancy in the South had reached 49 and by 1930 it wet above 55. These figures are for the South as a whole. In the cotton belt the percentage is still higher. Out of every hundred cotton farms over 60 are operated by tenants.

Southern tenancy is also becoming increasingly a white problem. Up to the Civil War, cotton laborers were Negro slaves. After Emancipation, however, white people began to compete with Negroes for the new kind of slavery involved in tenancy. The white tenants have increased steadily and rapidly, filling the new openings in the expanding industry and taking places left vacant by Negroes who migrated from the plantations to northern or southern cities. In the decade from 1920 to 1930, white tenants in the cotton states increased by 200,000 families—approximately one million persons. During the same decade Negro tenants decreased by 2000 families as the result of mass movements to cities. Today the total number of individuals in cotton tenancy runs to approximately five and a half million whites and slightly over three million Negroes.

Southern sharecropping must not be confused with the condition of farm tenants elsewhere in the country. In many places in the North and West, where farming has a different tradition, tenants are an honorable and independent group. The evil is not in renting land; it is in he traditions and usages which have grown up about the share tenant group in the old South. The kingdom of cotton was reared first upon the backs of black slaves and, while today white workers in the cotton fields outnumber blacks almost two to one, the old pattern of "boss and black" persists. The system is shot through with the master and slave relationship. Practices which were set up "to keep the Negro in his place" have been transferred in large part to the whole group of dependent tenants, whether colored or white. Every kind of abuse and exploitation is permitted because of the old caste prejudice. Because of their insistence on degrading three million Negro tenants, five and a half million white workers continue to keep themselves in bondage.

TENANCY, as the term is commonly used in the South, does not include renters who hire land for a fixed price in money or commodities. It applies to those who use the land in return for a share of the crop which they raise. A difference is often made between share tenants and sharecroppers. The former furnish some of their own tools and work stock and in return pledge only a quarter or a third of their crop. The latter usually have nothing to offer but their labor and in return pledge half of the crop to the owner. In addition, both the share tenant and the sharecropper must pay out of their portion of the crop the cost of everything which the owner or commission merchant has furnished him—seed, fertilizer and often the supplies which the tenant and his family have consumed during the year. The difference in returns and in dependency is simply one of degree. As a matter of fact, over one third of all tenants in the South and over half of the Negro tenants are in the lowest category of poverty and dependence.

As a part of the age-old custom in the South, the landlord keeps the books and handles the sales of all products. The owner returns to the tenant only what is left over of his share of the profits after deduction of all items which the landlord has furnished to him during the year, plus interest on all indebtedness, plus a theoretical "cost of supervision." The landlord often supplies the food—"pantry supplies" or "furnish"—and other current necessities through his own store or commissary. Fancy prices at the commissary, exorbitant interest, and careless or manipulated accounts make it easy for the owner to keep his tenants constantly in debt.

The plight of the tenant at annual settlement time is so common that a whole folk-lore about it has grown up in the South.

A tenant offering five bales of cotton was told, after some owl-eyed figuring, that this cotton exactly balanced his debt. Delighted at the prospect of a profit this year, the tenant reported that he had one more bale which he hadn't yet brought in. "Shucks," shouted the boss, "why didn't you tell me before? Now I'll have to figure the account all over again to make it come out even."

Of course every story of this kind, and such stories are innumerable, can be matched by tales of unreliability and shiftlessness on the part of the tenant. The case against the system cannot be rested on any personal indictment of landlords any more than it can be vindicated by stories of the improvidence of tenants. The fact is that landlords generally act as they find it necessary to act under the system; tenants do likewise. The development of bad economic and social habits of whatever kind on the part of both landlords and tenants is direct evidence of a faulty system.

The cultural landscape of the cotton belt is a miserable panorama of unpainted shacks, rain-gullied fields, straggling fences, dirt, poverty, disease, drudgery, monotony. Submerged beneath the system which he supports, the cotton tenant's standard of living approaches the level of bare animal existence. The traditional standards of the slave required only subsistence. The cotton slave—white or colored—has inherited a role in which comfort, education, and self-development have no place. For the type of labor he performs, all that is actually required is a stomach indifferently filled, a shack to sleep in, some old jeans to cover his nakedness.

Although living on abundant land in the southern part of the temperate zone, tenant families have probably the most meager and ill-balanced diet of any large group in America. Devotion to the single cash crop makes it virtually impossible under the system to raise vegetables or to maintain cows, chickens, and other means of nourishing diet. Because the growing of his own produce does not fit into the economy of a cash crop, it is not encouraged by landlords whose prerogative it is to determine the crops grown. As a result the diet is limited largely to imported foods made available usually through the commissaries and local stores. This diet can be and commonly is strained down to the notorious three M's—meat (fat salt pork), meal and molasses. Evidence of the slow ravages of this diet are to be found in the widespread incidence of pellagra and in the general lack of robustness and energy throughout the tenant population.

The housing is as bad as the diet. A Children's Bureau study in the cotton-growing areas of Texas showed 64 percent of the white and 77 percent of the Negro families living under conditions of housing congestion—in spite of the common belief that overcrowding is a phenomenon of the city. The general condition of tenant houses is not exaggerated by the statement made by a tenant in Alabama: "My house is so rotten you can jest take up the boards in your hands and cromple 'em up. Everything done swunk about it."

The Landlord Suffers with the Tenant

FARM system might not be regarded as an unmitigated evil if only the laborers suffered. But in the case of cotton culture the owners are almost as much at the mercy of the system as the tenants. Even under slavery the chief capital supporting cotton cultivation was not available in the South, a situation which kept the whole area in a secondary slavery to the capital of the North. Throughout the whole history of cotton there has been a lack of short term credit to finance annual operations either of production or consumption.

Loans on cotton crops are speculative and this risk increases the cost. The hierarchy of these loans, with risk and service charges, brings an insuperable accumulation of credit costs for the groups lowest down. The credit merchant becomes an inescapable part of the credit structure. He is a response to the erratic nature of farm income under the exclusive one crop economy. These credit costs on the basis of studies made by the Department of Agriculture have been shown to drain off 25 to 30 percent from the operating capital of the small dependent farmers. The recent introduction of federal credit agencies has relieved the situation, but the old customs are so persistent in the South that the old habits, including the credit merchant, hang on. Since the owner is almost as dependent upon outside credit as the tenant, the landlord, as well as the workers, is in slavery to the system.

Louis Fourteenth of France observed with a grim irony that "Credit supports agriculture as the cord supports the hanged." Throughout its existence, cotton culture has been strangling under an almost impossible system of finance. Only a very favorable world market for this staple has permitted survival of the system and of the complex of social institutions bound up with it. Now, with increasing problems of production and consumption, cotton culture faces finally and perhaps fatally the consequences of unsound credit and an inhuman system.

King Cotton Doomed

MANY factors lead one to believe that King Cotton is doomed. Not only is the tenancy system intolerable on grounds of humanity but the dominance of cotton as a great commercial crop is threatened. The following are among the factors which threaten the wealth and prestige of the kingdom of cotton:

Loss of soil fertility: One of the major indictments of the one crop system is that it encourages waste and improvidence on the part of both landlord and tenant. Huge areas of the Old South have been literally worn out by the constant iteration of cotton crops. The tendency has been not to preserve existing acreage but to move ever westward until today cotton is produced chiefly and most successfully in Texas and the adjoining states rather than in the Old South. The fertility of the new land in the Southwest, together with its freedom from boll weevil and its adaptability to mechanical efficiencies, gives it an advantage which probably dooms the prestige of cotton in the Old South.

Loss of world markets: When the glut of overproduction or underconsumption brought world depression, cotton was at once recognized as a commodity in which production must be immediately and drastically curtailed if the collapsed prices were to be restored. The irony of half-clothed field workers destroying cotton because people were not able to buy it is now an old, if unpleasant, memory. But unless we are to move out of a money economy into a realm of production for communal needs, it is evident that cotton will never again be grown profitably in America in anything like its former quantity. Huge areas elsewhere in the world have proved their capacity to grow this commodity much more cheaply than we. India, Egypt, Brazil, large parts of Africa and of the Far East have increased their production enormously; Russia has proved able to supply her own needs and may later be ready to add a surplus to the world market. In 1921, for example, Russian cotton production was a bare 43,000 bales. In 1932–33 it jumped to 1,800,000 bales.

Competing fabrics: With the rise of other fabrics, the old position of cotton is menaced by factors other than barren soil and new areas. Rayon, made from wood pulp, is the most formidable of these new competitors. This industry, which was first confined chiefly to Europe, has recently made important strides even in the United States. In 1920 the world production of rayon was 50 million pounds. By 1932 this had been multiplied ten fold to 516 million pounds. The production of rayon in the United States has increased more than one hundred fold in two decades, from just over one million pounds in 1912 to 131 million pounds in 1932. In addition to rayon, other synthetic fabrics which can be cheaply manufactured are preferred to cotton for many types of wearing apparel and are gaining ground with menacing rapidity.

Just one word about the AAA. While this may have been a wise emergency measure to rescue the farmers from a collapsed market, it was never of any substantial benefit to the southern tenant. In many cases the farm owner, in reducing his acreage, simply turned off surplus tenants, who thus exchanged a previous miserable subsistence for future starvation or government relief. Where the tenants were supposed to receive a part of the government compensation, the "boss and slave" tradition again came into play. The recompense to the tenant was often simply "credited to his account" by the landlord who pocketed the cash. Harrison County, Texas, perfected a system, widely used throughout the South, whereby tenants endorsed their checks over to the company store by blindly signing the blank backs of the checks under instructions from the landlord or storekeeper that "the government wants you all to sign these here crop reduction contracts."

Significantly enough, as benefit payments for crop reduction increased, the relief load also increased in the same counties—clear evidence that the sharecroppers were losing rather than gaining by the program. Bolivar County, Mississippi, for example, up to August 1, 1934 received $380,394, the largest benefit payments in the state; yet from May 1933 to May 1934, the amount spent monthly on relief in the county increased from $1338 to $48,311. Sunflower County, with benefit payments of '1;275,875 to August 1, 1934, increased its relief expenditures between May 1933 and May 1934, from $5668 to $32,325. For the same periods, Dunklin County, Texas, received $164,524 in benefits, and increased its relief expenditures from $2584 to $10,909.

Neither the AAA nor its reversal by the Supreme Court has had much effect upon the tenant, except that each patching up of the existing order seems to be used to depress a little further this dependent group. The tenants' plight requires much more drastic and constructive treatment than is involved in merely tampering with the present system.

The Way Out

THE only question that confronts American statesmen is what are we going to do to correct the evils of cotton tenancy? As to the evils themselves, there is no question.

The system of cotton culture has been degrading and demoralizing to the workers, both white and colored, and has been neither satisfactory nor profitable to the owners. Furthermore, what profit there was in American cotton is likely to diminish rather than increase in the generation ahead.

The ideal, of course, is to transform the present tenants and sharecroppers into independent land owners. "A sturdy peasantry" is a phrase full of meaning where small farms are independently owned by the majority of the population. Yet it is clear that mere ownership will not transform overnight the habits and the competence of the great mass of farm workers who for generations have grown up in the dependence and shiftlessness inherent in the share tenant system. Provision must be made for supervision and guidance of these farm workers, even if they come into ownership of their own land. Furthermore some means of financing not only the purchase of the land but the necessary machinery, seed, and fertilizer must also be provided. And some form of farmers' cooperatives is needed both for efficient production and successful marketing.

The Way Out

Below in brief outline are the suggestions advanced almost unanimously by students of farm problems, southern statesmen and government officials

1. That the federal government (through some special agency set up for that purpose) buy up huge acreages of farm lands now in the hands of insurance companies, land banks and others, and distribute this land in small plots of minimum size required to support farm families, probably twenty to forty acres in the cotton area. The land may be allocated to the new owners either on long leases or through contracts of sale on long-time payment under easy forms. The aim is to give the new farmers a sense of ownership or stability and to prevent them from selling or mortgaging the holdings or otherwise alienating their new birthright.

2. That service agencies be set up by regions and local areas to supervise, guide and aid the new homesteaders. These service agencies should not only give expert counsel, but also provide seed, fertilizer and even certain of the current supplies which were heretofore furnished by the plantation owner. In certain instances the service agencies will have to finance buildings and farm animals, but these capital investments should be held to the very minimum so that the homesteaders will not start with too burdensome a debt. It is believed that the project can succeed on a large scale only if the capital investment (including land and whatever buildings, repairs and animals are required) does not exceed one thousand dollars to fifteen hundred dollars per family.

3. That along with this general wide-scale distribution of lands, experiments be conducted in unified and carefully directed types of communities, such

as (a) cooperative farm colonies, (b) communities with highly developed services in schools and health and recreational facilities, also with community incubators, breeding stock and marketing facilities, and (c) communities of the European type with homes and public services concentrated into villages with farm lands on the outskirts.

It is evident that only government funds and government direction can supply the needed reorganization. The pressing needs of the millions of tenants whose lives have always been barren and precarious and who now are in danger of being dispossessed from even the poor living they formerly had can be met only by some new distribution of farm ownership. On page 153 [above] are outlined the suggestions which have been advanced almost unanimously by students of farm problems, southern statesmen and government officials.

THE Re-Homesteading Project is intended to establish in farm ownership a huge number of families heretofore excluded from ownership and now being cut off even from tenancy or crop-sharing arrangements. To this end the provisions and stipulations must be few and simple.

The benefits are almost self-evident. First, hundreds of thousands of families will have a little land of their own. The effect of land ownership is striking and immediate in creating self-respect and stability. Second, the chief interest of a small farm owner is to raise food and supplies for his own use. A well-rounded diet and resulting improvements in health will come quickly if farm families are raising meat and vegetables and producing milk and eggs for their own tables.

Furthermore, many new cash crops can be developed: grapes, fruits, truck and dairy produce for nearby cities, livestock, and other new crops. A great variety of salable farm produce, needed in the South and throughout the country, can supplement cotton as a means of income.

Fortunately, these proposals are not entirely in the state of mere pious hopes. Through the federal and state relief administrations farm distribution, in general accord with the plans outlined above, has already proceeded to some extent in several of the cotton states. Through the large appropriation for public works voted by Congress in the spring of 1935, additional sums are made available for rural rehabilitation and resettlement. This makes possible expansion of the project for small farm ownership, and provides through work relief for the building and repair of homes and barns of schools and other community centers. Congress has before it a bill which has already passed the Senate which authorizes an issue of bonds to finance individual farm purchases on a wide scale. It looks very much as though, by these and other means, broad and effective measures may be taken to mitigate the tenancy evil and to rehabilitate area numbers of the population as self-supporting and self-respecting farmers.

It is of course not to be supposed that this scheme of land distribution, even if carried out wisely and on a wide scale, will solve all the problems of the rural South. There remain such severe ills as large stretches of worn-out soil; the long tradition of concentration on the single cash crop, cotton which the new farmers will find it hard to break away from; the vicious and enervating prejudice between the races which beclouds issues and makes almost impossible any concerted program of recovery and progress; and the traditions of dependence and the general shiftlessness and incompetence of the workers, both white and colored, who make up the large marginal farm population. But organization of the farm system is basic to reform in other matters. A group of independent farmers working together under competent leadership can begin to plan decent lives as well as a self-sustaining economy.

Robert Fechner to Robert J. Buckley, June 4, 1936

"CCC Negro Selection" file, Box 700, General Correspondence of the Director, Record Group 35, National Archives, College Park, MD.

EMERGENCY CONSERVATION WORK
OFFICE OF THE DIRECTOR
WASHINGTON, D.C.

June 4, 1936

Honorable Robert J. Buckley
Senate Office Building
Washington, D. C.

Honorable Vic Donahey
Senate Office Building
Washington, D. C.

My dear Senators:

I have letters from each of you under date of June 1, to which were attached identical letters addressed to you by Mr. Nimrod B. Allen, Secretary of the Columbus Urban League, Columbus, Ohio. I have carefully read this letter and I regret that apparently Mr. Allen is badly misinformed about our general policy of enrollments in the Civilian Conservation Corps, and particularly about the situation in Ohio.

You of course know that the original legislation setting up Emergency Conservation Work specifically provided that there should be no discrimination in enrollments because of race or color. We have faithfully observed both the spirit and letter of the law. The whole Civilian Conservation Corps organization was set up on a population percentage basis. That applied also to the proportionate enrollment of Whites and Negroes. From the vary start of this work we enrolled the full percentage of Negroes that the race had to the total population. At the present time this percentage of Negro enrollees is actually higher than the percents of the race to our total population.

I want to state definitely that the President has not prescribed any regulations relative to where enrollees in Civilian Conservation Corps companies should be sent. That is purely an administrative responsibility of this office. It is true that a number of White enrollees from Ohio have been sent into other States, and during the first year of this work this also applied to Negro enrollees.

Whether we like it or not, we cannot close our eyes to the feet that there are communities and States that do not want and will not accept a Negro Civilian Conservation Corps company. This is particularly true in localities that have a negligible Negro population. There were so many vigorous complaints and protests that I felt it was necessary to direct Corps Area Commanders to find a location within their State of origin for all Negro Civilian Conservation Corps companies. This applies to the entire company. Even this did not solve the situation because there was great difficulty in finding a community that was willing to accept a Negro company of its own citizens. In your own State we had a good example. In the Fourth Period of Emergency Conservation Work, a Civilian Conservation Corps camp had been assigned to a work project near one of your smaller cities. We went ahead and built and equipped the camp. When a company was selected to occupy the camp it was found that the only company available was one composed of Ohio Negro enrollees. When the citizens of the community learned that a Negro company was to be sent to the camp, they absolutely refused to permit the company to occupy the camp and we were forced to completely abandon the project. I therefore adopted the policy of having our representatives consult with the Governor of the State before attempting to assign a Negro Company to any locality.

We do not attempt to compel any community to accept a Negro company in a Civilian Conservation Corps camp against its will, but occasionally their refusal has meant that the Camp would not be established.

You know, of course, that beginning last October we started a reduction in the number of Civilian Conservation Corps camps and consequently in the number of Civilian Conservation Corps enrollees. This reduction has been effected by not filling vacancies. No enrollee, either white or colored, has been refused the privilege of continuing his enrollment it he conducted himself in accordance with established regulations. This policy meant that at each enrollment period we simply filled such vacancies as were necessary to maintain the companies at their authorized strength. This meant that selecting agencies only certified a definite number of both white and colored applicants for enrollment. There has been no discrimination against Negro enrollees but to the contrary, as stated above, the total percentage of Negro enrollees at the present time is larger than at any time singe this work started.

I return the letters.

Sincerely yours,

(Sgd) Robert Fechner

ROBERT FECHNER
Director
enclosures

Migratory Farm Labor in the United States

Taylor, Paul S. "Migratory Farm Labor in the United States," Monthly Labor Review (March 1937), Bureau of Labor Statistics, United States Department of Labor, Serial No. R. 530.

For thousands of years nomadism has been a way of life for whole peoples. Our cultural heritage has been enriched by its traditions, for there is something deeper than glamour in the simple life of roving peoples. Even today tribes of Asia Minor and Mongolia rhythmically follow grass like their ancestors. Folding their tents and driving their flocks and herds, they move en masse, keeping close to the basis of sustenance as it shifts periodically through the seasons.

Nomads have ever remained aloof from tillers of the soil, maintaining their own culture, and resisting settlement. But migratory farm labor shares little of the tradition of the nomads. Restless movement and a simple life it has, and its own ways of living, different from those of the settled folk among whom it moves. But migratory labor is a proletarian class, not a people with a developed culture. It is forced to till the soil for others. It lives in material poverty. To a large extent indispensable, nevertheless it is commonly exploited and substandard. It slips through stable and often rich communities, of which it is never an accepted part. It offers a breeding ground of social unrest. It migrates reluctantly, seeking a foothold on the land, which it seldom gains. It lends itself readily to the development of a form of agriculture which is not a way of life, but an industry. Thus it becomes an unwitting instrument in the breakdown of the traditional American ideal of the family farm.

Migratory labor is not peculiar to the United States. Irish laborers in the eighteenth and nineteenth centuries migrated to hop yards and other harvest fields of England. Since the 1870's Polish laborers have migrated seasonally to the sugar-beet fields of Saxony. By 1900 this annual migration had attained a magnitude of 200,000 people; by 1914 it reached 400,000, the majority of them women and young persons. With the depression, Polish migrants declined to 77,000 in 1930 and to 31,000 in 1932. In the years before the war, farm laborers migrating seasonally from Italy and Spain to the Argentine numbered as many as 60,000 annually. These are but illustrations.

In the United States, peak labor requirements of intensive crops have often drawn seasonal laborers from beyond the immediate vicinity. Fruit, truck, and berry crops in particular have induced heavy migration. Curiously, it was a field crop—wheat—which caused one of the largest and best known of American periodic rural migrations.

Wheat Belt Migration

From the early 1900's to the middle of the post-war decade, the wheat fields of the Middle West and Great Plains were scenes of great movement. A small amount of labor sufficed to sow the crop with machinery, but intensive labor was needed for the harvest, to shock and thresh the grain. To do this work as many as 250,000 men were annually on the move from field to field, following the ripening crop.

The harvest began about June 1 in Texas, and moved steadily northward, reaching North Dakota by the middle of August, and passing on into Canada. Some of the migrants moved all the way from Oklahoma and Texas to the Dakotas and Canada. But, as Lescohier has pointed out, there were several more restricted routes of migration, which were followed by a majority of the harvesters. The major portion of the harvest in each State was performed by men who migrated only within the State. The migration of another large group of men took place within the limits of the winter Wheat Belt, from Texas to Nebraska, and still another large group moved only through the spring Wheat Belt of the Dakotas, Minnesota, and Canada.

The harvest hands were men, traveling by train. Years before the war one could see the freights in July moving slowly through Sioux City into the Dakotas, the roofs and doorways of boxcars literally black with men en route to the wheat fields. In the second decade of the twentieth century, American radicalism in the form of the 1. W. W. spread rapidly among these men. It became unsafe to ride the freights unless one carried a "red card." Farmers learned the meaning of strikes for better wages and living conditions, and responded with vigilante mobs, driving agitators and workers from towns at the point of guns. Class warfare broke out in the most "American" sections of rural America.

With entry of the United States into the World War, the authorities stepped into the situation, suppressing the I. W. W. by criminal prosecutions of its leaders, on the one hand, and on the other by drafting a new and less radical type of young migrant from more remote rural districts. These rural youths were recruited in order to replace the "hobos" and "gandydancers" from the cities who were habitually exposed, and more susceptible, to "wobbly" agitation. These tactics had immediate effect. How effective they would have proved in the long run is another question, which was never answered. For the great migration began to collapse about the middle of the 1920's, and today it exists as but a fraction of its former size.

The death knell of the Wheat Belt migration was sounded by mechanization of the harvest. The combine harvester, enabling 5 men to do the work of 320, cut and threshed the grain in a single operation. Hand shocking is rendered unnecessary and wheat production is now mechanized from planting to harvest. It is metamorphosed from an intensive to an extensive crop. The Oklahoma Commissioner of Labor reports that laborers furnished by State employment offices to wheat farmers dropped from 11,296 in 1921 to 165 in 1932, and he states that the combine harvester has "completely reversed our harvest labor problems of finding and distributing an adequate supply of labor to that of preventing a surplus from coming into the State during the harvest season, as an oversupply of labor in any locality is almost as disastrous as a shortage and more so as far as the community in general is concerned."

As the use of the combine spread, migratory labor declined, and with it labor radicalism and the social problems caused by a great male migration disappeared from the harvest fields. When radicalism came again to the Middle West it was the farmers who agitated and organized, not the laborers.

Western Cotton Migration

The plight of the sharecropper in cotton has been well studied and effectively dramatized to the country. The existence and problems of the migratory cotton pickers of the

Southwest and the Pacific coast are not so well known. But it is important to note that American cotton production is sharply divided by the manner in which it is organized to meet its peak hand-labor requirements. For advancing mechanization, which has so thoroughly transformed planting and ginning, has not yet eliminated two sharp peak labor seasons-chopping in the early summer and picking in the fall.

The cotton-producing sections of the country meet these seasonal requirements in two ways. In the Old South and as far west as the Brazos bottoms of Texas, the old system of placing a large family upon each 15 to 20 acres, insures that large numbers of hands, young and old, will be available when needed. Thus the old Cotton Belt has been filled with under-employed labor sufficient to supply locally all normal peak needs. From central and south Texas westward, however, and including Arizona and California, a variant of the old plantation system has been developed upon the base of migratory labor. This has taken place mainly since 1910. Cotton farms are large, with only sufficient resident labor to supply minimum needs for planting the crop. Although California and Arizona, which depend upon migratory labor, produce only 3 percent of the Nation's cotton, they have within their borders approximately 47 percent of the large-scale cotton farms of the entire country. The sharecrop system, which binds the laborers to the soil throughout the year, is practically unknown. Wage labor from far and near chops and picks cotton on piece rates. The labor market is hundreds of miles in extent. Cotton harvesters for Arizona and California are drawn seasonally from as far east as Oklahoma, Arkansas, and Missouri. Until 1929, when immigration barriers were raised, they used to come also from the central plateau of Mexico. In Texas and Oklahoma there are probably more than 50,000 mobile cotton pickers—whites, Negroes, and Mexicans. They follow the opening bolls from Corpus Christi on the Gulf north and westward to the Texas Panhandle and Oklahoma, 600 to 900 miles distant.

This dependence of western cotton areas upon migratory laborers sharply distinguishes its social problems from those of the plantation and tenant system of the Old South. It is not necessary here to compare the distresses of migratory laborers and sharecroppers. But it is pertinent to observe that the western system, when employed in conjunction with other crops offering employment to migrants, represents more efficient utilization of labor than does the sharecrop system. And it is well to point out that if the Rust Brothers, or any other mechanical cotton picker proves successful, its effects on the social and economic structure built on cotton will be different in the area from central and south Texas to the Pacific coast than in the older cotton areas. In both areas the mechanization of the cotton harvest will displace labor. And the displacement will be facilitated by the less spectacular but important mechanization of chopping, through the cross-cultivation or check-row planting which has already begun. In the Old South, mechanization of cotton production may prove devastating in its displacement of labor population. In the Southwest and California, mechanization will end migration of labor in cotton, as the combine harvester is ending it in wheat. Loss of employment will go hard with the migrants, but the very fact that they constitute a mobile regional labor reserve means that fewer human beings will be displaced than under the system in which each plantation carries its own peak labor supply. The existence of other intensive crops in the same valleys will further cushion the shock. Rapid mechanization of cotton production is likely to burden labor severely in both areas, but its coming portends disturbances which will be much less severe in southwestern and Pacific coast cotton areas than in the Old South.

Berry Crop Migration

In many parts of the United States berry crops, which require large numbers of band pickers, have long been a cause of seasonal migration. Usually the distance covered by the migrants is not great. Thus, Italian berry pickers come from Philadelphia and Camden to harvest the crop of south Jersey, as they have done for 50 years; and now they are joined by Negroes from Delaware. Poles and Indians have for many years supplied the outside labor for the cranberry bogs of Wisconsin. In years of good crops a thin stream of migrant families works its way northward with the berry crops from the Gulf to Lake Michigan, a few following the whole way from the strawberry harvest of northern Florida in the spring to Tangipahoa Parish in Louisiana, next to Judsonia in central Arkansas, thence to Paducah, Ky., Vermillion or Farina, Ill., and Benton Harbor, Mich. After the berry harvest they pick grapes and peaches in northern Michigan.

Annual fluctuations in the volume of this migration are extreme, depending upon crop conditions and upon the degree to which general depression or prosperity have increased or decreased local labor reserves. Thus, it was estimated in 1934 that 20,000 people, most of them from outside the community, worked during the brief strawberry harvest in Arkansas. But in 1937 the crop is expected to be so small as to induce practically no migration. In 1938 and subsequent years, however, plantings may fluctuate upward, and when they do there will again be heavy migrations.

The routes of migrants are curiously varied and irregular. For example, in 1934 these migrant strawberry pickers of Arkansas were drawn from four principal groups:

Families from Arkansas, Oklahoma, and Texas, who return to their homes at the conclusion of the Arkansas harvest.

Families from north- and south-central States east of the Mississippi, who follow the strawberry harvest from Florida or Louisiana into Arkansas, Missouri, Illinois, Indiana, Ohio, and end their season picking the winter peach crop in the Michigan Peninsula and the islands of Lake Erie.

Pickers from various central States who follow the berry harvest in Arkansas and Missouri, then swing westward to follow the wheat harvest through Kansas, Nebraska, and the Dakotas into Canada.

Pickers from north central States who follow the berry harvest in Arkansas and Missouri, then turn southwestward into Texas for cotton picking, and return north for the winter.

Migration in the Southeast

In Florida many seasonal workers are employed in the winter and spring harvests of citrus, berry, fruit, and truck crops. White laborers predominate in the packing sheds, Negroes in the vegetable fields. Tens of thousands of these seasonal workers, both white and Negro, are migratory. Most of them are young males or couples; perhaps one-third move in family groups. The white packers are much more skilled and better paid than the field hands. They generally travel in their own cars and trailers, while the field laborers often travel in gangs in trucks.

Most of the migrants from outside Florida come from Alabama and Georgia, where many are sharecroppers. Others are from as far as Mississippi and even Arkansas. Many migrated to Florida for the first time in 1936. This migration pattern resembles the recently swelling migration from Oklahoma, Arkansas, and Texas to the harvest fields of Arizona and California. Depression or drought have dislodged them, and they have dropped into the ranks of migratory laborers completely, or they follow the crops seasonally in order to supplement a meager income at home. Some go southeast, others go west.

In the spring, those field and shed workers who do not return home, move northward from Florida. Some go to the peach orchards of Georgia, but more go to the strawberry, potato, and vegetable areas sprinkled along the Carolina coasts and as far as Norfolk, Va. From there, they follow the potato, vegetable, and berry harvests as they move steadily up the coasts along the Eastern Shore of Virginia, Maryland, and Delaware, and into New Jersey, whence they return to Florida in the fall. The vicinity of Norfolk in Virginia and the adjacent portion of North Carolina supplies a few thousand Negroes who participate in the northern portion of this seasonal swing.

Some of the white migrants who pack fruit and vegetables in Florida go to the vegetable harvests of Crystal Springs and Hazelhurst in southern Mississippi, then to the tomato harvest of Humboldt, Tenn. From there a few go to the apple harvest of the Shenandoah Valley of Virginia, or the fruit and vegetable harvests of northwestern New York. Yet other packers disperse in all directions, moving to the lower Rio Grande Valley of Texas, the Arkansas Valley of Colorado, and on to Oregon and Washington. These routes across the West are not well defined, nor followed by any "stream" of migrants, but the fruit and vegetable areas of the entire country from Florida to the State of Washington are known to the "fruit tramps", and are irregularly visited by them during a series of years.

No reliable estimate of the numbers which move up the eastern seaboard to serve in field, packing shed, and cannery is available. The range is, perhaps from 10,000 to 20,000. Fluctuations from year to year are great. Depression, for varied reasons has greatly reduced this migration during the past 6 years, and in some areas has stopped it.

Sugar Beet Migration

Migration of labor to the sugar-beet fields has been important since the early 1900's when, under stimulus of the tariff, acreage began rapidly to expand. Unlike much of the migratory labor, beet workers move only twice a year. They move in the spring to the farm where the crop is to be blocked, thinned, hoed, and topped on contract, and they move again to winter quarters or to seasonal work elsewhere when the harvest is over in the fall.

Sugar-beet production is an industrialized form of agriculture, with the influence of the sugar factories dominant throughout the process, from finance to seed and labor. Its labor history illustrates clearly, if in heightened degree, a number of characteristics common to the migratory-labor problem in other crops and areas. Beet growers, through the factories, have taken the initiative in recruitment of labor from afar. Agents recruit laborers for Montana, for example, in California, Colorado, New Mexico, and Texas. Until 1929 the labor market extended even into Central Mexico, and growers of beets, like the big cotton growers of Arizona and farmers of California, used all the influence they could muster to obtain congressional approval for seasonal importation of workers from Mexico. Many races have been mingled in the beet fields. In the Mountain States, German-Russians, Mexicans, Spanish-Americans from New Mexico, and even Japanese were brought in. For the Middle West, Belgians, Poles, and Mexicans were recruited. In 1930 even Filipinos were recruited in Seattle for shipment to Minnesota.

The necessity for migratory labor increases not only with expanding total acreage (which has characterized the main trend of beet production since the beginning), but also with the scale upon which the crop is produced by individual growers. In northeastern Colorado, where many seasonal workers have been imported, the fields are large. In Utah they are small-10 acres or less; and the farmer and his family do their own work, rendering migratory labor unnecessary. Indeed, the Mormon farmer boys of beet-growing central Utah even migrate to Idaho to work in the beet harvest there, where fields are larger.

The volume of migratory labor needed depends upon the acreage planted and upon the size of the resident labor supply. Since importations constitute only the margin of the labor supply, an increase of, say, 10 percent in acreage, may increase importations of migrants by 50 percent; or a decline of 10 percent may produce an equally disproportionate effect in the opposite direction. The annual importations of laborers by the Great Western Sugar Co. between 1915 and 1936 fluctuated irregularly between 150 to 14,500.

The beet industry has made great endeavors to build up the supply of field laborers permanently resident in its territory, in order to reduce the necessity of annual importations. In order to induce laborers to remain in the beet areas during the 6 slack months, assistance in obtaining housing in labor colonies, and opportunities for casual winter employment have been added to other forms of inducement. An illustration of the effectiveness of these efforts, and of the general tendency of seasonal laborers in most crops to settle wherever they can obtain a sufficient modicum of work in the "dead" season to enable them to avoid migration, is found in Great Western territory. Between 1921 and 1927, while the acreage of beets increased from 128,000 to 184,000, or 44 percent, the number of families of Mexican resident beet tenders rose from 537 to 2,084, or 269 percent.

In course of years, many who came originally as migrants have ascended the agricultural ladder to become farm operators. In northeastern Colorado, for example, the German-Russians, who were the earliest migrants, did this to a surprising extent. Between 1909 and 1927, German-Russian beet growers increased from 665 to 2,590, and from 17 to 35 percent of all beet growers. In California, Italians, Japanese, Hindustanis, Mexicans, and southwestern native whites have all shown strong tendencies to give up their migratory life at the least opportunity, and settle either as resident laborers or as farm managers and operators.

No reliable estimate of the annual number of migratory sugar-beet workers throughout the country is at hand. It may easily have reached 30,000 or more workers in peak years, but usually it is probably much less, especially since depression increased local labor supplies. It is probable that mechanization of the beet harvest will end migration as the combined harvester is ending it in wheat. Already mechanical blocking is advancing through the practice of cross cultivation, and mechanical beet toppers are being perfected. When success is achieved, there will be no peak needs for hand workers in beet production. Not only will migratory labor in the beet fields disappear, but a problem will arise, as with the unneeded sharecroppers of a mechanized cotton belt, or the stranded onion workers of Hardin County, Ohio, who struck in 1934-how will the colonies of resident beet tenders be able to maintain themselves?

Migration on the Pacific Coast

Since 1870, when completion of the transcontinental railroad opened eastern markets for fruits and vegetables and stimulated irrigation in California, large numbers of migrants have followed the western harvests. Today the greatest seasonal migrations of farm labor in the United States take place on the Pacific coast. The main whirlpool of migratory labor is in California, but the high mobility of the workers makes all the western areas parts of a common labor market. Seeking to dovetail brief seasons of employment, they move from Imperial Valley on the Mexican border to the Hood River Valley of Oregon and the Willamette and Yakima Valleys of Washington. Some go also to the lettuce, melon, or cotton harvests of the Salt River Valley of Arizona, the melon harvests of Colorado, the pea fields of Idaho, and the beet fields of Montana.

Since the beginning they have moved by train, by horse and wagon, or afoot with bundles over the shoulder. Today they travel about in old automobiles or light trucks, sometimes with home-made trailers attached. They pile their worldly possessions on car and trailer and cover them with old canvas or ragged bedding. Bedsprings, if any, go on top, the iron cook stove on the running board, and lantern and washtub behind. Grandmothers, children, and the dog fill the car to capacity.

The early migrants of the West, made known so well by Carleton Parker, were mostly single white men. The Chinese, Japanese, and Hindustanis, too, moved in gangs of males, as do the Filipinos today. But with the influx of Mexicans into California and Arizona during the war, western migratory labor became mainly family labor. Recently the number of migrant white families has been vastly increased by drought refugees from the Great Plains, notably from Oklahoma.

The routes of migratory farm laborers in California, where they are numerically the most important, follow patterns which are fairly well known. The best-traveled route within the State is between the Imperial and San Joaquin and Sacramento valleys, from 360 to 550 miles distant by line, and longer by road. The migrants move in great surges with the seasons, and ceaselessly shift from ranch to ranch to finish each crop.

No estimates of numbers of migrants in California are very reliable. Few measures are taken and fluctuations from year to year are great. The California E. R. A. estimated in 1935 that 198,000 laborers were needed at the harvest peak in 33 agricultural counties, and that 50,000 of these were nonresidents of the county where the crop grows. The number which actually migrates, of course, is very much larger than the number needed to perform the work, because labor distribution is far from perfect. Carleton Parker estimated 150,000 migratory workers on the coast in 1915, mostly farm workers. The California Board of Education reported 37,000 migratory children alone in 1927. The number of persons—men, women, and children—who follow the California crops away from home at some time during the year, may well have reached 150,000 in recent years, as some estimate.

Extent of Migration

It is impossible to estimate satisfactorily the number of persons who migrate with the crops in the United States. Even the definition of "migrant" is not entirely clear, for there are many who move short distances within the county or to an adjoining county for a brief season, or who move singly, or in such small groups or so irregularly that they are not regarded as migrants by those among whom they move. And the line blurs between those who live on a farm for a few weeks, returning to the city 40 miles away, who are not generally regarded nor included as migrants, and those who, like the sugar-beet workers, move 100 or several hundred miles for a long season, before returning, who are regarded as migrants and who should be included, So, defining migrants roughly as those field workers and their families, and packing-shed workers and their families, who follow crops in periodic movement, in groups or as part of a well-defined movement commonly recognized as a movement of migrants, so that for a few months, if not the full year, migratory labor becomes a way of life, shall we hazard a preliminary estimate that agricultural migrants in the United States number from 200,000 to 350,000?

Social Effects of Migratory Labor

Migratory agricultural labor is attended by characteristic social problems. First, earnings are low, with all that fact entails. During the late twenties some skilled packers made good earnings, but the field workers have always earned little. A recent study by the California Relief Administration of applicants for relief in 1935 reports average annual earnings of 775 migrant families, most of which received between $300 and $400 in 1930, and between $100 and $200 in 1935. By way of comparison, the cash income of 2,000 tenant families in the South was $105 in 1933, according to Will Alexander and his collaborators. In California living costs are higher, and migration imposes important expenditures for transportation not required of tenants.

Second, housing of migrants (with of course the usual exceptions) is universally a serious problem, whether today in the Imperial Valley of California, the Yakima Valley of Washington, the Salt River Valley of Arizona, the berry fields of Arkansas, Louisiana, and New Jersey, the tobacco fields of the Connecticut Valley, and the sugar-beet fields of the Middle West, or whether a century ago among the Irish harvest migrants in England. In California the ragged camps of migrants squatting in filth by the roadside, in open fields, along ditch banks, or on garbage dumps fairly beggar description. Large growers frequently provide good housing, but smaller growers with short peak seasons are often unable to do this. The Resettlement Administration has pointed a way for intelligent Government assistance by establishing the first two of a chain of camps for migrants. These have successfully demonstrated both their value to public health, decency, and morale, and (in the only camp where it has been tried) the feasibility of responsible, democratic management by the migrants themselves.

Third, migrants, like other farm workers, are left relatively unprotected by social-security legislation.

All the evils of migrant-labor life are aggravated when children must submit to its hardships. I shall mention only that migration cripples the education of the young. In California the school authorities have shown that serious efforts to enforce school attendance can be fairly successful, but at best the children suffer from continual shifting from school to school. In Colorado it has been customary to make little effort to enroll the beet tenders' children until after beet harvest, although the A. A. A. made a serious attempt to end child labor in the beet fields. And in Texas practically no attempt at all has been made to enroll the children of migrants. Indeed, I know of school districts where Mexicans predominate, where in fact their nonattendance at school was preferred, so that the State aid given because of their presence in the district might be spent on the local white American children.

In other respects, as well as in matters of education, the nomadic workers carry the stigma of outlanders. The white migrants of California complain that they are ostracized as "pea pickers." When race difference is added to nomadism, social ostracism becomes more strident. In community after community seasonal Filipino workers were subjected to violent attacks by mobs using guns and dynamite during the depression when competition for jobs was bitterest.

Settlement laws, which restrict the granting of relief to residents, work particular hardship on migratory labor. Harsh measures are sometimes employed, such as the "bum blockades" by Los Angeles police at the California border, by the militia in Colorado, by State authorities in Florida, and New Jersey where they turned back Negro migrants coming to the potato harvest. States as well as counties are unwilling that migrant laborers should remain long enough within their borders to become relief charges. At the conclusion of the pea harvest in 1934 the supervisors of San Luis Obispo County, Calif., voted $2,500 to supply the pea pickers with enough gasoline and food to get them into the next county. The authorities there sent back word that if the performance was repeated the migrants would be met at the county line with guns.

Finally, labor unrest is spreading among migratory agricultural workers. In 1931 there were half a hundred strikes among such workers in California, and they continue to occur. Underneath this of course lies the fact that agriculture is industrialized in many places where migrants are employed. In Imperial Valley, to cite an extreme example of the coincidence of industrialization, migration, and labor conflict, the amount spent on wage labor, per farm reporting such payments, was $3,498, as compared with a national average of only $363. Frequently large growers operate in several areas as employers of the same migrants, and conflict spreads quickly from one area to another. On December 21, 1936, a Federal injunction was issued on charges that growers and shippers in the Salinas and Imperial Valleys of California and the Salt River Valley of Arizona, who were willing to hire lettuce packers blacklisted because of activity in the

Salinas strike last September, were prevented from doing so by threats of having their supplies and bank credit cut off.

To sum it up, migratory farm labor is a focus of poverty, bad health, and evil housing conditions. Its availability in large numbers at low wages aids large-scale agriculture in its competition with the family farm. Migratory laborers are victims of all the prejudices of settled folk against outlanders and nomads, without the advantages of an organized group life of their own. They are discriminated against by arbitrary and illegal blockades. They cannot participate in democracy. The education of their children is seriously impaired if not completely neglected. Race prejudices are heightened and labor conflicts intensified. Migrants and public welfare suffer alike.

Migrants as Distinguished from Transients and Drought Refugees

The use of the word "transient" has been avoided, for "transients" should not be confused with "migrants." Transients, according to current usage, are applicants for relief, whose residence is in another State or county. This is an administrative classification into which, to be sure, migrants sometimes fall. But migrants are persons who seek a living by work, regularly following the crops. It is not sufficient to observe that the migrants move about like "transients" and need decent temporary quarters where they can eat, rest, and clean up. They are an integral part of the agriculture structure, for they meet its peak labor needs. Any adequate program must recognize this essential role of migrants, and must enable them to carry it out more efficiently, and under conditions more favorable to them and to the communities through which they move.

Neither should drought refugees from the Great Plains who have been pouring by scores of thousands to every part of the west coast, be confused with "transients," although they, too, sometimes become nonresident applicants for relief. These people are leaving areas where depopulation is desirable for the national economy, and are not drifting but are seeking resettlement. Whether these people, guided in their flight more by the hope of seasonal jobs in the fields than by accurate knowledge of available land, should be settled on the coast where they arrive, or elsewhere, is not the present question. In any case arbitrary restriction of movement is as uneconomic as encouragement of excessive movement.

Remedial Proposals

We can sympathize with localities which receive numbers of persons in need of relief and rehabilitation, whether drought refugees or migrants following seasonal agricultural work. Their burdens are heavy. The remedy, however, is not more "bum blockades" and settlement laws. It is a sharing by State and Nation of the financial burdens imposed on county and State by relief, rehabilitation, or resettlement of nonresidents. This is the most efficient, equitable, and economical way.

What can we do? I shall suggest only a few alternatives. Mechanization will end seasonal migration in crops like sugar beets and cotton, and some vegetable crops, as it is ending it in wheat. But for a long time to come, peach, apricot, prune, cherry, berry, grape, and many vegetable crops will require large numbers of seasonal workers. Revision of crop plantings to provide steady employment has long been urged, and to some extent practiced. It is desirable, but not much result should be expected. To drench the local labor market by building up excessive resident supplies is to apply a remedy worse than the disease, as witness the condition of the southeastern Cotton Belt However, stabilization on the soil of limited numbers of migrants in various localities represents a promising move. With this as an objective the Resettlement Administration is now initiating experiments with cooperative part-time farms, in Arizona and California.

The necessity for seasonal labor in agriculture will long remain. Indeed, a mobile labor reserve is efficient and desirable. For those whose migration is needed, conditions should be made as tolerable as possible. Facilities for efficient labor distribution will deflate their numbers to the minimum really required. Better machinery for mediation and arbitration will facilitate adjustment of labor relations. Decent camps and housing must be provided by private and public agencies. Migration by families should be replaced as far as possible by migration of unattached men or, better, by men and their older sons operating short distances from their home stakes on the soil. Decent camps and homesteads as started by the Resettlement Administration could well be included within the scope of a national tenancy act to relieve in a coordinated program all the submerged laborers of agriculture, whether they work for wages or for a share of the crop.

Radio Speech in the House of Representatives

Lamneck, Arthur, "Radio Speech in the House of Representatives," March 4, 1937, Congressional Record, 75th Congress, 1st Session (1937).

Mr. Chairman. The Supreme Court controversy is the most important issue that as confronted the country since the Civil War. Efforts are being made to becloud the issue by injecting politics. I want it clearly understood that I am a Democrat; that I loyally supported Mr. Roosevelt in both of his campaigns for the Presidency that I will continue to support him when I think he is right; but that I will oppose any effort to rob the people of the liberties and rights that have been so dearly gained. The question is not whether we shall or shall not support the President, but whether we shall do it within the framework of the Constitution. Since the almost total surrender by Congress of its power to the Executive, the Supreme Court remains the last bulwark of the people's rights.

Let us look back in history and note the struggles of the people to gain these rights. In ancient Rome the common people once left the city and refused to come back unless they were given written laws to protect their liberties. The freemen of England defeated the forces of King John and forced him to sign the Magna Carta—the bill of rights upon which Anglo-Saxon law is based. The Puritans, sailed the then unknown Atlantic to find a place where they could enjoy the right to worship God as they saw fit. The history of the Colonies is a history of the struggle of people for the right to govern themselves. Franklin, Jefferson, and the other signers of the Declaration of Independence pledged their lives, fortunes, and sacred honor in support of the Declaration, but it took seven long years of bloodshed and suffering to make independence a fact.

The people who have emigrated to America have come here seeking the free exercise of rights denied them in their own countries. The French Huguenots came here seeking the right to worship as they pleased—and found that right. The Irish fled their homeland because they could enjoy here the right of self-government. The subject people of Austria and Russia found in America that freedom denied them in their own lands. Many people came to this country from Germany shortly after the failure of the revolution of 1848, in which the German people rose against the ruling class and demanded their rights. After putting down the revolution, the rulers of Germany became increasingly oppressive and hundreds of thousands of the common people emigrated to other lands, the greater number to America.

Up to the present time the American people have continuously fought for, and succeeded in adding to, their rights Will it be said that in 1937 the tide turned and they commenced to lose them? Will the tide of freedom-seeking emigrants turn the other way? Will Americans have to leave their own country to seek their rights? I trust not.

To find the reason why the framers of our Constitution deliberately divided the powers of the Government into three branches we must first know the conditions as they existed prior to its adoption. The colonists had suffered from unchecked power in the hands of one man, George III. This British King controlled the Parliament and appointed and controlled the judges. The wise fathers of our country decided that they would not allow such a thing to happen in America. They gave the power of making laws to Congress, the power of interpreting the laws to the Courts, and the power of executing the laws to the President. They did this deliberately, so that no one man or group could centralize the power.

Let us see what former Presidents have said on this aggrandizement of power in the hands of one man. Washington, in his Farewell Address, said: "The spirit of encroachments tends to consolidate the powers of all the departments in one, and thus create, whatever the form of government, a real despotism."

Washington said further: "If in the opinion of the people the distribution of constitutional power be in any particular wrong, let it be corrected by an amendment, but let there be no change by usurpation."

Our fourth President, James Madison, wrote: "The accumulation of all powers—legislative executive, and judicial—in the same hands, whether of one, a few, or many, and whether hereditary, self-appointed, or elective, may justly be pronounced the very definition of tyranny."

Supporters of the President's proposal speak of a "mandate" given the President because of his overwhelming majority. Throughout his entire campaign the President spoke not a word about this proposed change. The Democratic national platform states:

"If problems cannot be effectively solved by legislation within the Constitution, we shall seek such clarifying amendments as will assure...power to enact these laws which...we...shall find necessary. Thus we propose to maintain the letter and spirit of the Constitution."

Every Congressman, every President, must take a solemn path to "preserve, protect, and defend" the Constitution undermining the Supreme Court in order to shove unconstitutional legislation down the throats of the people is as much a violation of this oath as it would be to tear the to shreds.

We have recently had a case of an executive undermining the judiciary in Michigan. Some automobile workers went on a strike and seized the factory of their employers. They comprised a very small minority of the total number of workers, but because of their key position they threw ten times their number out of work. The factory owner sought and received an injunction—the court ordering the men out of the factory. The men refused to go; and when the sheriff reported to the Governor that he did not have sufficient men to evict the strikers, but that the non-striking workers were about to evict them, the Governor had the National Guard surround the factory to protect the strikers in their illegal act.

This Governor, who is said to have White House ambitions, also took an oath to preserve, protect, and defend the constitution and faithfully execute the laws of the State of Michigan.

The right to enjoy one's property is a part of the Bill of Rights; and if the workers seize other people's property, how long can they be sure that their own property will be safe from seizure? I believe it was Lincoln who said, in effect, "Do not destroy your neighbor's house, lest your own house be destroyed."

Do not mistake me—I am a friend of labor. I believe the worker has the right to bargain collectively or individually as he chooses, to work if he chooses, quit when he chooses, and go on strike when he chooses.

Would-be dictators always incite the worker, recount the sufferings of the people, and then explain that in order to correct these conditions they must give up rights and powers. Once in possession of this power the dictator is no longer a would-be, but a reality. The people find that the silken threads have turned to chains, and that the long struggle to regain their lost rights has again begun.

Take Italy for example: Mussolini has placed Italy back on its feet, but at the cost of the people's rights. You are either in favor of the Fascist Government, or you are in jail. Germany is another example; Hitler has improved things. in a material way, but at the cost of free speech and free press. In Russia, anyone who has a different opinion from the ruling clique is soon liable to find him before a firing squad.

Let us see what happens to groups in dictator-controlled nations. In Russia, there is no such thing as freedom of religion. In Germany, the Nazis are in constant warfare with both the Catholic Church and the Protestants. In Mexico, a young girl suffers death for attending a religious ceremony in defiance of the law. In Italy the Masonic order is suppressed. In Germany the Jews are oppressed and have suffered the loss of their rights. Labor has suffered the loss of its rights in both Italy and Germany.

The people of these countries once had the rights we now enjoy, but were careless of them. They do not have them now. They cannot worship God as they please, or speak according to their conscience, or participate in the affairs of their government. These people can give Americans the answer to the question of what can happen to a nation that grows indifferent toward liberty. They lose it. And once lost, the reclaiming of liberty may be vastly more difficult, more bloody, and more tragic than the original winning of it.

These rights have been regarded by our ancestors as so precious that they have suffered untold hardships, and have even given up their lives to gain and preserve them. Are we to sit supinely by and see them taken away? Shall the sufferings, sacrifices, and struggles of our patriots have been in vain? Just as the fathers of our country dedicated their lives and fortunes to making America free, it is for us, the living, to dedicate our lives to keeping it free. "Eternal vigilance is the price of liberty."

In a world given over to one-man governments, the President has stood out as the defender of democracy—has made numerous speeches advocating that we Americans should prove to the world that "democracy will work." Can this be the same man who, controlling the legislative branch of the government, now seeks to gain control of the judiciary? Do we want a one-man government; no matter how benevolent?

I do not believe that Franklin Roosevelt has dictatorial ambitions; but we must remember that the term of Presidents is limited and that some other man in the White House might use the combined executive, legislative and judicial power to the detriment of the people and not to their advantage. I do not believe that the President now has any intention of taking away the liberties of our people; but I would like to make it clear to you that the Supreme Court is the last guardian of your rights. If you allow the Court to be packed today, you are liable to find that your liberties have vanished tomorrow.

An appeal is being made to the farmers to support the President in his demand. They are being told that the only way to give them the legislative aid they desire is this judiciary change. They are not told that this is the beginning of the probable loss of their rights—the right to plant what they want, when they please, and to sell their produce where they please—the right actually to hold property, the right of free speech. Are the farmers willing to risk losing their rights and independence for a small yearly soil-erosion or crop-curtailment check? Are they willing to sell their birthright for a mess of pottage?

The graveyard of the Democratic Party is strewn with the remains of Congressmen who, following the dictates of their conscience and the interests of their constituents, dared to vote against some of the administration's proposals. The Democratic Party will probably find itself in the graveyard as if it allows itself to be known as the party that surrendered are the hard-won rights of the American people.

The United States has done well under our present form of constitutional government. We have grown from thirteen sparsely settled States with a population of 3,000,000 to a great Nation, spanning the continent, with a population of 130,000,000 and a standard of living the highest the world en has ever known. The authors of the Declaration of Independence said:

"Prudence indeed will dictate that governments long established should not be changed for light and transient causes."

If we feel the need of a change in our form of government, we should remember that the Constitution provides for such a change by amendment. Opponents of the proposal to submit the issue to the people claim that it would take too long. This argument lacks force by reason of the fact that the prohibition repeal amendment was adopted a few short months after the people had been given the opportunity to vote on it. You can trust the American people. They have uncommonly good common sense. If we are to have a government of the people, by the people, and for the people, then we must let the people have final say on important of changes in the structure of the Government.

In conclusion, my fellow citizens, I again warn you that eternal vigilance is the price of liberty; and I appeal to you to make your wishes on this most important issue known to your servants in Congress. Let us keep our liberties intact, place patriotism above politics, and fritter not away for a momentary good the hard-won values of centuries of endeavor.

Address at Timberline Lodge

Address at Timberline Lodge, Franklin D. Roosevelt, President's Personal File Speeches, National Archives and Records Administration, Franklin D. Roosevelt Presidential Library, Hyde Park, NY, 1937.

Governor Martin, Ladies and Gentlemen:

HERE I am on the slopes of Mount Hood where I have always wanted to come.

I am here to dedicate the Timberline Lodge and I do so in the words of the bronze tablet directly in front of me on the coping of this wonderful building:

"Timberline Lodge, Mount Hood National Forest dedicated September 28, 1937, by the President of the United States as a monument to the skill and faithful performance of workers on the rolls of the Works Progress Administration."

In the past few days I have inspected many great governmental activities—parks and soil protection sponsored by the Works Progress Administration; buildings erected with the assistance of the Public Works Administration; our oldest and best-known National Park, the Yellowstone, under the jurisdiction of the National Park Service; great irrigation areas fathered by the Reclamation Service; and a few hours ago a huge navigation and power dam built by the Army engineers.

Now I find myself in one of our many national forests, here on the slopes of Mount Hood.

The people of the United States are singularly fortunate in having such great areas of the outdoors in the permanent possession of the people themselves—permanently available for many different forms of use.

In the total of this acreage the national forests already play an important part in our economy, and as the years go by, their usefulness is bound to expand.

A good many of us probably think of our forests as having the primary function of saving our timber resources, but they do far more than that; much of the timber in them is cut and sold under scientific methods, and replaced on the system of rotation by new stands of many types of useful trees. The National Forests, in addition, provide forage for livestock and game, they husband our water at the source; they mitigate our floods and prevent the erosion of our soil. Last but not least, our National Forests will provide constantly increasing opportunity for recreational use. This Timberline Lodge marks a venture that was made possible by W.P.A., emergency relief work, in order that we may test the workability of recreational facilities installed by the Government itself and operated under its complete control.

Here, to Mount Hood, will come thousands and thousands of visitors in the coming years. Looking east toward eastern Oregon with its great livestock raising areas, these visitors are going to visualize the relationship between the cattle ranches and the summer ranges in the forests. Looking westward and northward toward Portland and the Columbia River, with their great lumber and other wood using industries, they will understand the part which National Forest timber will play in the support of this important element of northwestern prosperity.

Those who will follow us to Timberline Lodge on their holidays and vacations will represent the enjoyment of new opportunities for play in every season of the year. I mention specially every season of the year because we, as a nation, I think, are coming to realize that the summer is not the only time for play. I look forward to the day when many, many people from this region of the Nation are going to come here for skiing and tobogganing and various other forms of winter sports. Among them, all of those visitors, in winter and summer, spring and autumn, there will be many from the outermost parts of our Nation, travelers from the Middle West, the South and the East, Americans who are fulfilling a very desirable objective of citizenship—getting to know their country better.

I am very keen about travel, not only personally—you know that—but also about travel for as many Americans as can possibly afford it, because those Americans will be getting to know their own country better; and the more they see of it, the more they will realize the privileges which God and nature have given to the American people.

So, I take very great pleasure in dedicating this Lodge, not only as a new adjunct of our National Forests, but also as a place to play for generations of Americans in the days to come.

Keepers of Democracy

Roosevelt, Eleanor. "Keepers of Democracy," Speech and Article File, Anna Eleanor Roosevelt Papers, National Archives and Records Administration, Franklin D. Roosevelt Presidential Library, Hyde Park, NY, 1939.

Recently a radio broadcast was given, based on a story written by H. G. Wells some years ago, called "War of the Worlds." For the purpose of dramatization it was placed in the United States with the names of regions and people who would naturally be involved if such a thing were to happen today. The basic idea was not changed; these invaders were supernatural beings from another planet who straddled the skyway and dealt in death rays, but it was dramatically done with many realistic touches.

I do not wish to enter into a discussion here as to whether the broadcasting company should do dramatizations of this type, nor do I wish to cast aspersions on people who may not have read the original book. But the results of this broadcast were the best illustration of the state of mind in which we as a nation find ourselves today. A sane people, living in an atmosphere of fearlessness, does not suddenly become hysterical at the threat of invasion, even from more credible sources, let alone by the Martians from another planet, but we have allowed ourselves to be fed on propaganda which has created a fear complex. For the past few years, nearly all of our organizations and many individuals have said something about the necessity for fighting dangerous and subversive elements in our midst.

If you are in the South someone tells you solemnly that all the members of the Committee of Industrial Organization are Communists, or that the Negroes are all Communists. This last statement derives from the fact that, being for the most part unskilled labor, Negroes are more apt to be organized by the Committee for Industrial Organization. In another part of the country someone tells you solemnly that the schools of the country are menaced because they are all under the influence of Jewish teachers and that the Jews, forsooth, are all Communists. And so it goes, until finally you realize that people have reached a point where anything which will save them from Communism is a godsend; and if Fascism or Nazism promises more security than our own democracy we may even turn to them.

It is all as bewildering as our growing hysterical over the invasion of the Martians! Somehow or other I have a feeling that our forefathers, who left their women and children in the wildernesses while they traveled weary miles to buy supplies, and who knew they were leaving them to meet Indians if need be, and to defend themselves as best they could, would expect us to meet present-day dangers with more courage than we seem to have. It is not only physical courage which we need, the kind of physical courage which in the face of danger can at least control the outward evidences of fear. It is moral courage as well, the courage which can make up its mind whether it thinks something is right or wrong, make a material or personal sacrifice if necessary, and take the consequences which may come.

I shall always remember someone, it may have been Theodore Roosevelt, saying in my hearing when I was young that when you were afraid to do a thing, that was the time to go and do it. Every time we shirk making up our minds or standing up for a cause in which we believe, we weaken our character and our ability to be fearless. There is a growing wave in this country of fear, and of intolerance which springs from fear. Sometimes it is a religious intolerance, sometimes it is a racial intolerance, but all intolerance grows from the same roots. I can best illustrate this fear by telling you that a short time ago someone told me in all seriousness that the American Youth Congress was a Communist organization and that the World Youth Congress was Communist controlled. This person really believed that the young people who were members of these organizations were attempting to overthrow by force the governments of the countries in which they belonged.

Undoubtedly, in the World Youth Congress there were young Communists, just as there are a group of young Communists and a group of young Socialists in the American Youth Congress, but this does not mean that either of these bodies is Communist controlled. It simply means that they conform to the pattern of society, which at all times has groups thinking over a wide range, from what we call extreme left to extreme right. The general movement of civilization, however, goes on in accordance with the thinking of the majority of the people, and that was exactly what happened in both the American Youth Congress and the World Youth Congress.

The resolutions finally passed by both bodies were rather sane and calm, perhaps a trifle idealistic and certainly very optimistic. There were amendments offered for discussion, and voted down, which many people might have considered radical; but since there is radical thinking among both young and old, it seems to me wiser to discuss and vote down an idea than to ignore it. By so doing we know in which direction the real trend of thought is growing. If we take the attitude that youth, even youth when it belongs to the Communist party, cannot be met on the basis of equal consideration and a willingness to listen, then we are again beginning to allow our fears of this particular group to overwhelm us and we are losing the opportunity to make our experience available and useful to the next generation.

I do not believe that oppression anywhere or injustice which is tolerated by the people of any country toward any group in that country is a healthy influence. I feel that unless we learn to live together as individuals and as groups, and to find ways of settling our difficulties without showing fear of each other and resorting to force, we cannot hope to see our democracy successful. It is an indisputable fact that democracy cannot survive where force and not law is the ultimate court of appeal. Every time we permit force to enter into a situation between employer and employee we have weakened the power of democracy and the confidence which a democratic people must have in their ability to make laws to meet the conditions under which they live, and, when necessary, to change those laws with due political process according to the will of the majority of the people.

When we permit religious prejudice to gain headway in our midst, when we allow one group of people to look down upon another, then we may for a short time bring hardship on some particular group of people, but the real hardship and the real wrong is done to democracy and to our nation as a whole. We are then breeding people who cannot live under a democratic form of government but must be controlled by force. We have but to look out into the world to see how easy it is to become stultified, to accept without protest wrongs done to others, and to shift the burden of decision and of responsibility for any action onto some vague thing called a government or some individual called a leader.

It is true today that democracies are in danger because there are forces opposed to their way of thinking abroad in the world; but more than democracies are at stake. When force becomes so necessary that practically all nations decide that they must engage in a race which will make them able to back up what they have to say with arms and will thus oblige the rest of the world to listen to them, then we face an ultimate Armageddon, unless at the same time an effort to find some other solution is never abandoned.

We in this country may look at it more calmly than the rest of the world, for we can pay for force over a longer period of time; and for a while at least our people will not suffer as much as some of the other nations of the world, but the building up of physical forces is an interminable race. Do you see where it will end unless some strong movement for an ultimate change is afoot?

Someone may say: "But we need only to go on until the men who at present have power in the world and who believe in force are gone." But when in the past has there been a time when such men did not exist? If our civilization is to survive and democracies are to live, then the people of the world as a whole must be stronger than such leaders. That is the way of democracy, that is the only way to a rule of law and order as opposed to a rule of force.

We can read the history of civilization, its ups and its down as they have occurred under the rule of force. Underlying that history is the story of each individual's fears. It seems to me a challenge to women in this period of our civilization to foster democracy and to refuse to fall a prey to fear. Only our young people still seem to have some strength and hope, and apparently we are afraid to give them a helping hand.

Someone said to me the other day that, acknowledging all the weaknesses of human nature, one must still believe in the basic good of humanity or fall into cynicism and the philosophy of old Omar Khayyam. I do still believe that there is within most of us a basic desire to live uprightly and kindly with our neighbors, but I also feel that we are at present in the grip of a wave of fear which threatens to overcome us. I think we need a rude awakening, to make us exert all the strength we have to face facts as they are in our country and in the world, and to make us willing to sacrifice all that we have from the material standpoint in order that freedom and democracy may not perish from this earth.

The Rising Tide of Anti-Semitism, Alvin Johnson

Source: Survey Graphic, Vol. 28, No. 2 (February 1939), p. 113.

Anti-Semitism is on the increase in America. This is to be sure just an opinion, for there are no reliable quantitative estimates available to the public. Private polls may even been held; there are not uncertain rumors afloat of such polls, and they are alleged to exhibit a marked increase in antagonism to the Jews. But polls of public opinion record only the view of an instant, and offer a very inadequate basis for conclusions on lasting realities. The Gallup poll of early December indicated that 94 per cent disapproved of Hitler's treatment of the Jews. But we cannot draw too heavily upon this particular fact. One may be anti-Semitic without approving of the pillage and murder of Jews.

What no one doubts may commonly be taken for pragmatically true, and no one, Gentile or Jew, doubts that there is more active anti-Semitism in present day America than there was, say, in 1930. No one believes that anti-Semitism has passed its peak, although there is much fragmentary evidence that it suffered a setback after the recent German pogrom. A considerable number of conservative Americans, who had viewed with complacency the sting of Jews from public offices, universities and the practice of law, have been deeply shocked by the brutal stacks on Jewish property. Property is property, and if it not sacred, what security is there in the world? But not too much dependence may be placed upon property owners' solidarity. The strength of the feudal aristocracy lay in the fact that the whole class was disposed to stand any members who fell into hard luck. The same thing true, within limits, of the modern proletariat. But the strength of the propertied middle class lies in the promptness with which it turns a cold shoulder on the dispropertied. A prince of the blood remained a prince even if he could not command the price of a breakfast. A prince of industry or finance becomes nothing at all promptly upon his bankruptcy. The sympathy of the propertied classes of the democracies for the Jews who have been expropriated likely to prove more touching than lasting. To be sure, Julius

Streicher's newly inaugurated campaign against the "white Jews," wicked Aryans who are making profits such as every American business man hopes to make, may do much to emphasize interracial propertied solidarity. The point is one that may be reserved, for the present.

Anti-Semitism is a social disease that, like syphilis, we have always had with us. Like syphilis it spares no section, no class. The gilded youth and the feebleminded are equally exposed to the infection. Not even the grandfathers are immune. Our racial body manages, however, to get on fairly well in spite of endemic syphilis, but it is always in danger of an epidemic that may prove fatal. Our social-political body is tolerant of a limited amount of anti-Semitism. But there is no one whose opinions are worth listening to, who does not know that a grave epidemic of anti-Semitism is capable of destroying the democratic liberal state. We have before us the example of Germany. Hitler could have talked himself black in the face on parliamentary shortcomings and the iniquity of the Treaty of Versailles. He had the genius to blow up into a flame the endemically smoldering embers of anti-Semitism. Every vulgar and designing scoundrel in America who schemes to substitute dictatorship for democracy casts a greedy eye upon the potentialities of an anti-Semitic campaign. We who love liberal democracy, who have faith in its unlimited possibilities for humanity and civilization, are dunces if we refuse to face the menace of anti-Semitism, and weaklings if we fail to apply our resources to combating it.

What Anti-Semitism Is Made Of

Let us try to break down the general phenomenon of anti-Semitism into its main constituent elements.

1. There is instinctive anti-alienism, which has always set us against unassimilated and partly assimilated members of our society. Four fifths of the Jews have been with us only since Kishineff; too many of them are only partly assimilated to the commanding externals of American life, language, dress and manners.

2. There is the age-old antipathy on the part of the farmer and manual worker to the "middleman," and the Jews still group themselves heavily in that class.

3. There is the fundamentalist hatred of the Jews on the basis of the over simplified view that the Jews crucified the Christ, never amplified to a recognition that Jesus, the Christ, was a Jew.

4. The business and professional hatred of the Jew as a redoubtable competitor.

5. What one may call parlor anti-Semitism, boldly paraded by well groomed young men of social status, who need to appear strong men to their women folk and know the passionate virtue of blood curdling sentiments.

6. The unhappy denizens of overtame environments, who were happy in spy hunting during the war and desire nothing so much as conspiracies to track down now, "Great Jewish conspiracies."

Who Promotes Anti-Semitism?

That, in brief, is the endemiology of American Anti-Semitism. These are the embers the present day propaganda is blowing upon, in the hope of consuming, not the Jew in particular, but democracy and liberalism also. It is an extensive propaganda. There are about 800 organizations in the United States carrying on a definite anti-Semitic propaganda. Some are nation-wide in their operations, some regional; but most of them are one man shows, with a few dues paying members and small sales of anti-Semitic literature, meagerly maintaining a bony, neurotic "president," mixed dunce and knave. The most important organizations are:

The Silver Shirts

The Defenders of the Christian Faith

The Industrial Defense Association

The American Nationalist Confederation

The James True Associates

The Knights of the White Camellia

Also, there is the notorious "Bund," a monstrous and impudent intrusion into our American life, far more worthy of expulsion than the half-witted bevies of "spies," but which blunders so egregiously that it ought to be subsidized by the Jews.

To this list we should add the most reckless one man show of the entire unsavory lot, Father Coughlin.

It is a motley array that has been waiting for years for a Hitler to come and organize them into a unified power.

Collectively they claim six million followers, and allege that they reach one third of the population of the United States by literature of personal agitation. There is no possibility of checking their claims; we may prudently assume that they do not understate them. Cut the claims in two: we still have to do with a stupendous anti-democratic activity. It is an activity that could not be carried on without considerable financial resources. It is not credible that these resources could be made up from the modest and occasional dues of the members and from sales of horrendous slanders at 3 or 4 cents a copy. Perhaps some part of Goebbels' $20 million for foreign propaganda reaches us here. This is, however, not a necessary conclusion. We have our fair share of rich men who would be glad to help us to a safe and sane dictatorship, and who have never stopped to consider that their privileges rest on the Bill of Rights.

The Appeal to Native Bigotry

The methods of the propaganda may be simply Classified. For the average timid soul, identification of the Jews with the Reds. For the romantic moron, the grand conspiracy of the Elders of Zion. For the blasé society lady, the fake letter of Franklin. For the anti-New Dealer, a catalogue of government posts held by Jews under the New Deal and "proof" that obnoxious New Deal measures were devised by Felix Frankfurter,

Mordecai Ezekiel or Jerome Frank. For the small business man, assertions that the great corporations destroying him are controlled by Jews. For the Fundamentalist, blood ritual whisperings. For the southern gentlemen, identification of the Jew with Negro domination. Nothing for the parlor anti-Semite, who hates the Jew on his own, to the admiration of his women folk.

One leaf the American anti-Semitic campaigners have taken out of Hitler's "Mein Kampf," a book otherwise too deep for them. That is the technology of the lie. A lie will nearly always travel faster than the pursuing truth. If the truth appears to be gaining on the lie, a covering bevy of lies can be launched. The truth has never really run down the Elders of Zion lie, nor the bogus statement of Franklin. It has never scotched the lie of the prevailing Jewish character of the Bolshevik party in Russia. It has not scotched the lie that Bernard Baruch ruled the United States for his own profit during the World War. In fact, the truth is ill adapted for the function of pursuit. The truth is a statue.

This is far from a reassuring picture. But wait: how large a proportion of the population of the United States is made up of the furious anti-New Dealers, the Fundamentalists, the oppressed small business men, the romantic morons and the parlor anti-Semites? Stretch your imagination as far as you please, it will not make a majority, or anywhere near it.

Organized labor is not anti-Semitic. Whether AF of L or CIO, it is perfectly aware that the Jew is only a stalking horse in the hunt aimed at organized labor. The farmers are not anti-Semitic. You may of course picture some of them in the long winter evenings, thrilling themselves with the Elders of Zion, just as they thrill themselves with "The Quadroon's Revenge" or "The True Story of Dillinger." But something tells the farmer that literature is always made up of lies. The women, save for the time-expired parlor heroines and the fluffy suburbanites who hear that a Jewish family might move into their environment and disturb their knitting raptures, are not anti-Semitic. They have an instinctive sense of bunk. Scarcely any of the unemployed has failed to receive a leaflet. "You haven't got a job. Who's got it? A Jew. How do you like it?" Momentarily at least this argument gets under the skin, although, strange as it may seem to the comfortable, the unemployed stand out for their common humanity. But the next leaflet may damn the "Jewish" New Deal policy of relief. That was intended for another group, but literature gets mixed in a society like ours.

Facing the Lies with American Facts

WE HAVE TOO MUCH anti-Semitism for the good of our democratic liberal state. We have not so much as to compel us to go about crying, "It can happen here, and it will." True, anti-Semitism enabled Hitler to overthrow the German democracy. But it was a weak democracy, forced upon a defeated people who had never had the opportunity to develop democrats, and without real democrats democracy is a mere book definition. It was a democracy sore with defeat, repeatedly humiliated and mistreated by the victors. German democracy was gradually struggling to its feet, and might have done so if it had not been afflicted with endemic anti-Semitism, which Hitler could fan into a flame. Given a similar situation of defeat and humiliation, of indemnities, inflation, the destruction of every hope of modest security, we could turn Nazi, too, and undoubtedly our designing Hitler would seize upon endemic anti-Semitism as a chief source of strength.

There is no need, however, to contemplate the ultimate extreme of a Nazi dictatorship. Our American democracy is far from a finished job. We are far from having attained satisfactory formulae covering the relations of employer and employee, of city and country, of state and individual. We have real issues before us, issues on which honest and intelligent men will differ. We know well that if we can fight out our political campaigns on these real issues, we can make whatever adjustments are necessary to the evolving requirements of the time. We can move toward a better state without revolutionary shock and disorder.

The interjection of a purely fantastic and corrupt issue like anti-Semitism menaces this orderly evolution of our national life. A wise political observer has predicted that the outcome of the next presidential election will be determined by the Jewish question. Is that not a shocking idea? That we should turn aside from the great questions of national defense, of reconstructing our agriculture, of employment, of collective bargaining and minimum wages, of the distribution of taxation, of public health, of education, to split on the question whether certain persons may adhere to a religion that antedates Christianity and after all, contributed the ethics without which Christianity would have been a dreary superstition.

If there are forces making for the increase in anti-Semitism, so also are there forces making for its abatement. Nazi Germany, identified with anti-Semitism, is not gaining in popularity in this country. I have mentioned the Gallup poll, with its evidence of almost universal condemnation of the treatment of the Jews in Germany. Nazi Germany will be still less popular with us when she really goes out to get the "white Jews," the business men who are making money, the Henry Fords and such. She has to go after them sooner or later, if only to meet her fiscal requirements. The identification of Nazism with American conservative capitalism will retire into the limbo whence it came, and therewith the sinews of propagandist anti-Semitism will be much slackened.

And on another side the conditions that give color to anti-Semitism are abating. The vast immigrant groups from Eastern Europe are now passing on into the third generation on American soil; Yiddish speech and Yiddish clannishness are giving way. The concentration of Jews in merchandising and the white-collar trades is gradually but surely breaking up. We have a fair beginning of a movement of Jews to the soil. The number of Jewish farmers is still undetermined, but there are certainly 16,000, on the whole succeeding well, and there are many stirrings to indicate an increasing movement to the land. A quarter of the union carpenters of New York City are Jews; a fifth of the electrical workers; nearly half the painters and paper hangers; half the plasterers; nearly half the plumbers and steam fitters; more than half the sheet metal workers. These are the union figures. The proportion of Jews among the non-union workers is greater—another story, however, that is not relevant here. The point is that the unhealthy concentration in commercial pursuits forced upon the Jew by the Old World anti-Semitism, itself operating to intensify anti-Semitism, is gradually breaking up here. People still say, to be sure, "You never see a Jewish artisan or farmer." Parrots will go on saying it.

The stars in their courses were fighting against Sisera, but that would not have helped much if the forces of the Lord had not fought too, and manfully. The stars in their courses are fighting against anti-Semitism in America, and that is the very reason why we who love our land, and who believe in our people, and have faith in our future as the richest, the most humane, the most orderly civilization ever created by man should fight the evil intelligently and manfully.

We cannot confront the anti-Semitic propagandist face to face, because he only flees, scattering lies behind him. We waste our time trying to confute the parlor anti Semite, because his anti-Semitism is a personal necessity. Besides, he is fickle in the objects of his manful hatred Not many years ago it was the Catholics; not many years hence it will be the Nazis, as it was the "Prussians" during the World War. We cannot do anything directly about Fundamentalist anti-Semitism, but with the advance in the standard of living and the extension of education this type of anti-Semitism loses in importance. We cannot do much about the romantic hunger for tales of conspiracy like the Protocols. A good ship can make headway though moderately barnacled, and if our ship of state is well handled, these anti-Semitic barnacles will slow us very little.

It Behooves Us to Do More than Wring Our Hands

FAR MORE IMPORTANT IS THE GENERAL DISPOSITION TO VIEW alienism and a permanent minority position with distrust. Toleration in the form in which it has been taught for the last two hundred years is essentially a liberal doctrine. It derived its force from antagonism to the absolute monarchy. Our present conflict is between democracy and dictatorship, and while democracy generates its own type of tolerance in contrast to dictatorial intolerance, the type is not necessarily the same as that of liberalism. The democracy has always exhibited certain reservations about persistent minority groupings. One may recall the universal response, at the time of the World War, to Theodore Roosevelt's attacks on the "hyphenated-Americans."

Is there any reason why democracy should not accept the Jew as unqualifiedly sound material for a democratic polity? Fundamentally, none. Most Jews of old American stock are so accepted. Differences in religion have never counted importantly with the democracy. Nevertheless, there is at present a disposition to impute permanent minority characteristics to the mass of the Jews. And this is a danger for the future. We shall see the current anti-Semitic wave subsiding, no doubt. But who shall say that in a future decade we may not be overwhelmed by a greater economic depression than the last, with a government less energetic in combating the general distress? In such event any weakness in our system may be disastrous, and latent anti-Semitism is one of the most dangerous.

It behooves us, as good American citizens, to set about building a bridge of under-standing between the two groups, Jewish and Christian. By good modern practice, a bridge is always begun from both sides of the river simultaneously. Most of the build-ing must be done from the side of the Christians, who have the most to lose from anti-Semitism, being the more numerous group. But the Jews have to do some build-ing, too. There was never a persecuted race that did not develop some characteris-tics that seemed to give color of justification to persecution. Abolish persecution and such characteristics disappear. In time, but in how much time? And does fate give us sufficient time?

It is wise not to presume on fate, at least so long as there is something we can do ourselves. It is still open to us to form an engineering organization representing both groups, to discuss frankly, without reservations or taboos, ways and means for softening the edges of inter-group conflict, of clearing away inter-group misunderstanding. At least we owe it to our democratic civilization to do something more than denounce and wring our hands. We can try.

Whither the American Indian? Alden Stevens

Source: *Survey Graphic,* Vol. 29, No. 3 (March 1, 1940), p. 168.

SIX YEARS AGO A TRIBE OF 700 INDIANS IN SOUTHERN New Mexico camped around the government agency, living in dilapidated tents, brush tepees, board shacks. Like hungry sparrows hoping for a crust of bread, these once proud people depended on their harassed agent to keep them somehow from starvation. What resources the tribe once owned had been dissipated in per capita payments, ill-advised loans which could never be repaid, care and training of the children which served only to male the younger generation as helpless and hopeless as the older.

Living on a reservation rich in natural resources and potentialities, they had never been taught or allowed to manage their own affairs. Instead, the Indian Bureau had handled—and mishandled—everything for them. Inevitably this tribe, lacking education, lacking any opportunities to become self-sufficient, bereft of all responsibility and not permitted to work out any small part of their own destiny, had become shiftless hangers-on at the agency, diseased, discouraged, broken in spirit.

Today many of the same people live in clean, comfortable homes; the children live with the parents and attend schools on the reservation, which prepare them for the problems they will face as adults. Their herds are sleek and fat—in 1937 the cattle income of the tribe was $101,000; the feed produced was worth more than $40,000. No longer are they discouraged and spiritless. NOW the tribe cares for its own old and indigent; the able-bodied care for themselves better than they have been able to do in many decades. This tribe, the Mescalero Apache, has come back. And there is no reason why the new order should not be permanent. They were fortunate in the natural resources available and in having an able superintendent to aid and advise them. But the reconstruction is their own doing, and other tribes less well equipped have also taken advantage of the same new devices with impressive results.

A Century and a Half of Dishonor

SINCE THE BEGINNING OF WHITE OCCUPATION OF THE North American continent the Indian has been trampled upon and exploited. Treaties have been made and violated; tribes deprived of their land, their living, their customs and religion. In 1838 the Cherokees were mercilessly driven westward from their homes in North Carolina and Georgia clear across the Mississippi. A few hid out in the mountains, but only a few. It was winter, and the soldiers who drove them cared little whether they lived or died. The best thing was to get rid of them anyway. One third of the tribe was buried or left to rot along the way.

At about the same time. on the western plain, the fur trading posts systematically debauched the Indians with cheap liquor, cheated them of their furs and sometimes of their land. Did a tribe rebel? Soldiers came quickly and taught them their place. Usually their place was underground.

Every effort was made, over a long period of time, to get rid of the Indian; to kill him off, starve him and discourage him into race suicide, in an effort to solve the Indian problem by eliminating the Indian. It didn't work, and today the Indian is actually gaining in numbers at a rate faster than that of the white population of the United States.

When Helen Hunt Jackson wrote "A Century of Dishonor" in 1881, the fashion of making treaties with tribes, and then conveniently breaking them by writing new ones, had just been abandoned. The book tells a long story of broken promises, systematic destruction and de. moralization, exploitation by traders, railroad companies and politicians. How much the book had to do with it is hard to say, but shortly after it was published a new Indian policy came into effect, based on the land needs of the tribes. This was urged by Carl Schurz and approved by Helen Hunt Jackson and other good friends of the Indian. It was recognized that ruthless destruction must stop. Instead, the Indian should be assimilated, gradually losing his identity until he became indistinguishable from a white man. This done successfully, the Indian problem would disappear, for certainly the Indian was dying out at that time—or being killed off; and Indian culture could not possibly last more than a few years, anyway. As a matter of fact little was said about Indian culture, the general feeling being that there wasn't any.

The General Allotment Act was passed in 1887, and many people regarded it as the final solution of the Indian problem. Each Indian was to be given 40 to 160 acres of land, with the stipulation that it must not be sold for twenty-five years except with the consent of the government. Agents were supposed to give instruction in farming methods and help along a little during the first few years.

It is doubtful whether anyone suspected that this act would work out even one tenth as badly as it did. In the first place the Indians were expected to adapt themselves almost immediately to a completely new way of life. The very concept of land ownership by individuals was foreign. Few of the tribes had done any farming or were interested in doing any. The facilities for educating them to the new ways were pitifully inadequate.

When all the Indians on a reservation had received their allotments, the remainder of the land was thrown open for white settlement. Nobody thought this mattered very much, since the Indians were a dying race, anyway, and would never need the land, especially now that each had a nice farm of his own. The tribes lost 20 percent of all their land within two years. By 1933 they had lost 90 million of the 138 million acres they had when the act was passed—nearly two thirds. "Checkerboarding" of reservations, leaving blocks of Indian land completely surrounded by white holdings, led to the gradual break-up of tribal life without the substitution of any other kind of community life. Whites more often than not regarded the Indians as inferior, and almost never would the two cultures mix.

But probably the worst feature of the allotment act was its inheritance provision. On the death of the original allottee, the land was to be divided among his heirs. Why no one thought of the way this would work out is hard to say; maybe some legislators did think of it, but they didn't do anything. Indians sometimes live a long time, and when Charley Yellowtail dies at the age of ninety-nine, the number of heirs may be something little less than astronomical. Forty acres of land divided among, say, 120 heirs, gives each just about enough to pitch a teepee.

The Indian Bureau attempted to solve difficulty by renting and in some cases selling the entire parcel, and dividing the proceeds among the heirs. More often than not a white man was on the other end of the deal. The Indians were left landless, and the rental checks sometimes amounted to as little as two or three cents a year. Some Indians might have these microscopic shares in a dozen or more estates. The bookkeeping was about all the Indian Bureau had time to handle.

It was an impossible situation, of course, and quite insoluble under the allotment act. Fortunately for them, the act was never applied to some groups, such as the Pueblos in New Mexico, who retained their land as tribes and lost nothing through allotment.

A Decade of Progress

THE GROUNDWORK FOR A CHANGE WAS LAID in 1928, when Lewis Meriam and his associates published their Institute of Government Research report. "The Problems of Indian Administration." In this comprehensive and fundamental study, the failure of the assimilation policy was boldly drawn, and practical, specific recommendations were made. Under President Hoover, Charles Rhoads and Henry Scattergood administered the Indian Office and began making the government a helpful friend instead of a despotic manager. A good spirit of cooperation between the government and the Indians came about. New emphasis on day schools marked the beginning of a better educational policy. Tribal skepticism and the novelty of the approach slowed the work, but a new day had definitely begun.

John Collier became Commissioner of Indian Affairs in 1933. For a number of years he had headed the militant Indian Defense Association, had saved the Pueblo lands from seizure by associates of Albert B. Fall by forcing the defeat of the anti-Indian Bursum bill, and had demonstrated his devotion to the Indian cause in many other ways.

Collier's plan was to make a clean sweep of the old ways and make it possible for Indians to live as Indians until a more natural and less destructive assimilation could come about. no matter how long this might cake. His first step was to get through a none-too-willing Congress the Wheeler-Howard bill, largely his own work, assisted by Nathan Margold and Felix Cohen, two Interior Department attorneys. In the end this emerged almost intact as the Indian Reorganization Act, and is the legal basis for Collier's program.

The act does not apply to any tribe which rejects it in an election, and though it does not appear that a tribe has anything to lose by accepting it, a considerable number have voted it down, including the Navajo. The administration frankly urges its adoption, sometimes with a fairly high pressure campaign, but there is no evidence of discrimination against those who reject it and nothing to cast suspicion on any of the elections. No tribe in the country has had a more comprehensive program of conservation work and general economic rehabilitation than the Navajo-but space is lacking for adequate discussion of this unique and particularly difficult situation.

Reorganization

THE ALLOTMENT POLICY IS ENDED, AND WHILE PRESENT HOLDINGS of individuals are not affected, no more allotments will be made. Indian owners of reservation land may now sell it, but only to the tribe, a provision which prevents further alienation of Indian land. Ceded lands which have neither been allotted nor settled by whites are returned to the tribe, and provision is made for small additions to Indian holdings where necessary. Management is by an elected tribal council, which (except where there is a shortage) assigns each member as much land as he can actually use. Thus one of the worst administrative headaches is on the way to a cure. and the shrinkage of Indian holdings is halted except for some of those tribes which have rejected the Reorganization Act. It is true that the problems of the checker-boarded reservations are not solved, and most of the old difficulties of rental and division of proceeds among heirs of allottees remain. But the new policy does turn land management back to the Indian; it goes far toward stabilization of the situation. and it seems to be working out well in most places.

No less important than the land provisions are the sections of the Reorganization Act enabling Indians to organize, adopt a constitution, and to incorporate. These give a measure of self-government greater than ever enjoyed before, though approval of the Secretary of the Interior is still required on many important matters. The constitutions are supposed to originate with the tribes, but government lawyers have usually helped frame them, and each must be approved by the Secretary before the tribe votes acceptance or rejection.

It is the Secretary of the Interior, too who issues a charter of incorporation when petitioned to do so. This also is subject to a vote on the reservation. Indians have never before had an opportunity to do much voting on what they wanted or didn't want. and not all tribes have taken kindly or intelligently to the democratic process thrust suddenly upon them under the New Deal. On some reservations, such as the Hopi, the idea of an all-tribal elected council is so foreign that many Indians simply do not recognize its authority and pay little attention to its activities. Poorly educated people commonly miss the full implications of an election and ignore it. After it is over, they may resent the powers acquired by the council members and regard them simply as government stooges.

Congress is authorized to appropriate $10 million as a revolving fund from which loans may be made to these chartered corporations for the purpose of promoting the economic development of the tribes. Repayments are credited to the revolving fund and are available for new loans. It was this fund which made possible the fresh start of the Mescalero Apache tribe. The record of collections on these loans has been very good.

About seventy-five of the tribal corporations are now functioning, with varying degrees of success, and the number continues to grow. The Jicarillas have bought their trading post and are running it; the Chippewas as run a tourist camp; the Northern Cheyennes have a very successful livestock cooperative: the Swinomish of Washington have a tribal fishing business. There are plenty of others to prove these corporations can be made to work

So far, however. it has shown up best where a small, close-knit group is involved, but less satisfactorily on such large reservations as those of the Sioux, where distances are great and there is a certain amount of mutual distrust and jealousy between communities. Smaller cooperatives, at least for the present, may be indicated. In the case of the Blackfeet, the tribal council, when elected, proved to be predominantly Indians of mixed blood, and the full bloods of the reservation, amounting to about 22 percent of the population, complained that their interests were being subordinated and neglected wherever they conflicted with those of the mixed bloods.

The election system was adjusted later to insure fair representation of the minority group. The difficulty about the system is that so many Indians on large reservations— and some on small—do not have a sense of common interest. The nine Hopi villages in Arizona have a long tradition of independent action as city states, with very little cooperation or friendly feeling between them. In other cases the desperately poor circumstances prevailing and the lack of resources to start with have caught tribes simply too run down and discouraged to put their shoulders to the wheel.

But all this new machinery gives Indians for the first time an opportunity to run their own affairs, to a limited extent it is true, but previously everything was handled by the government, and the Indians had to take it or leave it. Now a tribe, as a corporation, may purchase, operate and dispose of property, may hire counsel, engage in business enterprises of nearly any sort, and generally enjoy the legal privileges of a corporation. Management by the elected council is not always good, but at least it is management by Indians through democratic processes, and a nod of adjustment to the new way must be expected to produce mistakes and failures as well as successes. It has all been thrust upon the tribes very suddenly as such things go—too suddenly, say critics of the administration, and they may be right.

Indian families are definitely in the lower third of the American population, so far as income is concerned. The average for a family of four during 1937 was $600 or its equivalent in subsistence. Work relief and direct relief made up much too large a proportion of this. Only some of the families getting oil royalties and a very few others are in the tenth of the United States population with family incomes of more than $2500.

Indians at Work

About 40 PERCENT OF ALL INDIANS OVER TEN YEARS OLD ARE engaged for at least a part of the year in pursuits which bring in cash. Half of these are unskilled laborers, the other half do various types of semi-skilled and skilled work. Fishing brings in sizable amounts to some tribes in the Pacific Northwest. Lumbering is carried on in Oregon, Montana, Arizona, Wisconsin and other states. The sustained yield management of timber reserves now almost universally applied should insure an income indefinitely for the relatively small number of Indians with commercial forests. Nearly all Indians are farmers or stockbreeders, and as such raise at least a part of their own food supply. The cooperatives which are springing up all over the Indian country help with marketing and do much to improve farming methods and increase production of saleable crops.

A growing source of income has been the sale of arts and crafts. This has long brought in sizable sums to the southwest tribes, and everyone is familiar with Navajo blankets and jewelry and with Pueblo pottery. In fact, the popularity of these products has brought out a flood of inferior factory-made imitations which has hurt the sale of authentic items.

The Indian Arts and Crafts Board was set up by Congress in 1936 to give aid in marketing, and to keep up quality by setting standards for each type of object. Rene d'Harnoncourt, manager of the board, was responsible for the magnificent show of Indian products and Indian culture at the Golden Gate International Exposition in 1939, which was one of the really outstanding features of Treasure Island. New uses for Indian material in interior decoration were suggested to show the many attractive home furnishings, so thoroughly American, which Indians produce. The board is a promotional and advisory organization, working on a small budget. It has met opposition from traders and commercial firms—some of these are more friendly now—so that its influence is not yet widely felt. The publicity value of the exhibits at San Francisco, at Gallup, N.M., and elsewhere, together with marketing cooperatives the board has helped Indians establish on a number of reservations, has undoubtedly had a stimulating effect. Arts and crafts will never be one of the most important income sources except locally, but an increasing number of Indians are finding that there is money in it.

Homes and Health

HOUSING HAS BEEN FOR YEARS AS SERIOUS A PROBLEM ON THE Indian reservations as in city slums. Best housed are the Pueblos of New Mexico and Arizona, who escaped the destructive effects of the allotment act and early white penetration of their traditional homeland. Since they live in a mild climate, and have plenty of building materials—stone and adobe—they have managed well, and still do. On the plains it has been a different story. Nearly land: less, penniless, with no way to make a living, and no satisfactory natural building materials at hand, such tribes as the Sioux, Winnebago, Cheyenne and Arapaho have lived through the cold winters in dirt hovels, tarpaper shacks, ancient tents and other makeshift dwellings for many years.

The Mescalero and some of the plains tribes have accomplished a limited amount of rehousing with the aid of loans from the revolving fund set up under the Reorganization Act. Some Farm Security Administration money has been made available for housing planned by the Indian Office, most of the work being done by the Indians themselves. The general improvement in Indian income is reflected in repairs on old houses and in the building of some new ones by the Indians themselves. But it is still true, and will be for a long time, that these efforts merely scratch the surface. Indian housing remains woefully inadequate.

Health, so closely related to housing, is also still far from satisfactory, though probably better today than it has ever been before. Somewhat better food and shelter have made a difference, particularly in the greatest Indian scourge, tuberculosis. There is some indication that Indian resistance to disease is increasing, and certainly Indian resistance to white medicine is decreasing. When the new Navajo-Hopi health center was opened last year at Fort Defiance some of the prominent Navajo medicine men participated in the ceremonies with chants, speeches and offers of cooperation—evidence of an entirely new attitude toward the Indian Service, and one which has been brought about by the new attitude of the service itself toward the Indian.

Trachoma, a serious and persistent Indian disease, has been tackled with new vigor. Cooperative research with Columbia University at the Trachoma School on the Fort Apache Reservation in Arizona has definitely established the cause of trachoma as a filterable virus, and experiments with sulfanilamide give promise of an effective new treatment.

Educational About-Face

THE PROBLEM OF EDUCATION, SO VITAL TO THE SUCCESS OF any government program, has been a sore spot for more than a century, and the present administration has characteristically applied to it a fresh viewpoint; at the same time building on the work done by the previous administration under Commissioner Rhoads, who was one of the first to recognize the hopeless inadequacy of traditional policies.

The original colonies showed little concern for Indian education, although several colleges, including Dartmouth and Harvard, made provision for tuition-free admission of Indians, and the Continental Congress in 1775 employed a schoolmaster for the Delaware and made motions toward doing something for other tribes. The Revolution interrupted, and until 1819 Indian education was left entirely to a few missionary societies. From that year to 1873, $10,000 was appropriated annually for the work, and most of this was turned over to the missions. From 1873 on, the appropriations increased fairly regularly, until 1932, when $11,224,000 was set aside. The next few years saw slight reductions; the budget for 1939–1940 allow $10,523,745. (However, most post-1933 building was done with emerge funds not included in the departmental budget.) Until 1929, Indian education was pretty much a hodgepodge. More Indians attended public schools than other kind—this is still true. Large number were in mission schools. Many attended boarding schools both on and off the reservation These were established late in the last century when the accepted theory of Indian education called for remove the children from their parents and home life as much as possible so that they might be "civilized." Often the children were taken by force from their homes and subjected in the schools to a rigid discipline and a standardized, outmoded course of study. Half their time was devoted to school work, the other half to doing routine institutional tasks such as laundering, cleaning, wood-chopping and food preparation. Often this work was too hard and too many hours per day were devoted to it, so that it had a serious effect on health. Insufficient opera funds made the school and living standards dangerously low.

Forbidden to speak their own language in school, out of touch with family and tribal life, denied the normal experience and education needed to prepare them for life as Indians, the children would return home from school dissatisfied misfits, unable to readapt themselves to reservation life and equally unable to find a place in a white community. They had learned to read and write, but they were unfamiliar with the customs and language of own people, and found their schooling of little use in making a living.

The problem was a hard one, and perhaps the earlier officials should not be too harshly criticized for their failure to solve it. Indians are very diverse; they represent hundreds of cultures vastly different one from another. More than two hundred mutually unintelligible languages are spoken in the United States. The school program must be carefully fitted to each group since the needs vary so much. And undoubtedly the success of the present program rests partly on a study of previous failures.

The "about-face" in Indian education is designed to mesh with the "about-face" in general policy. Recognizing attempts to drag children from their families and "civilize" them as a total failure, the aim now is to give a basic education in the three R's without detaching them from their families, to teach hygiene and such mechanical skills as will be useful to each group. This is accomplished to an increasing extent in day schools, which are being established on as many reservations as possible. The children live at home and walk or ride to school. Native tongues are not forbidden, and an increasing number of Indians are on the teaching staffs. In the past ten years the Indian day school population (in all-Indian schools distinct from public schools) has risen from 4532 to 14,087. There are still over 10,000 in boarding schools on and off the reservations, and about 7000 in schools run by signs, states and private agencies.

The fact that facilities for education were so limited has made it impossible to abandon entirely the boarding schools, but the emphasis in these has been changed radically, and they are now used principally as vocational and trade schools. The boarding school at Flandreau, S.D., specializes in dairying; Haskell Institute (a high school) at Lawrence, Kan., gives business and commercial courses and shop work; that at Santa Fe, N.M., is for rents who wish to learn arts and crafts. Sherman Institute, at Riverside, Calif., teaches agriculture and industrial work. Thus it is possible for those who show aptitude and want training in trades to get it.

Some of these schools are accredited by higher institutions, and an educational loan fund of $250,000 enables young Indians to attend advanced trade and vocational schools as well as colleges. About 220 Indians are now receiving higher education, most of them in state universities.

Indian education is still much less complete than it should be. At least 10,000 children of school age are not oiled in any school. But never has an educational prom been so well adapted to the Indian's problem, and never have there been as many school-age children in school as there are today. The importance of education reflected in the fact that more than half the total staff the Office of Indian Affairs is engaged in this work.

Of 86,747 Indians between six and eighteen, 33,645 attend public schools not operated by the Office of Indian Affairs These are mostly in such states as California,

Minnesota, and Oklahoma, where a certain fount of assimilation is actually taking place. The arrangement does not work badly; and some educators feel that Indian children who attend public schools are better adapted to meet their problems as adults for the contacts made there. Since Indian land is exempt from taxation, the government pays a small tuition to the school district for each Indian pupil.

For the first time adult Indians are taking a real interest the education of their children d in the possibilities of the fool as a community center. the Rosebud reservation (Sioux, S.D.) a vegetable canning project by the women with some help from the school teacher was so successful that for the first time in many years a winter was passed without relief rations being sent into the area. There is an awakening of interest which has resulted in some rather astonishing initiative on the part of the Indians. In the Kallihoma district of Oklahoma some twenty-five children were without school facilities, but their parents got together, bought an abandoned hotel, remodeled it themselves, set up an Indian and his wife as teachers, and started a day school and community center which has been a most successful enterprise.

The Indian Administration

NO DISCUSSION OF COLLIER S POLICIES WOULD BE COMPLETE without mention of an important trend within the Office of Indian Affairs. The Reorganization Act is designed to set up mechanisms within the tribe which will perform the social services now provided by the government bureau. The result should be a gradual withering of the bureau as the new tribal machinery takes over the load. This withering process cannot be said to have begun as yet, but perhaps that would be expecting too much. Complete elimination of the bureau cannot be accomplished for many years, if ever, and meanwhile Indians are being trained and encouraged to seek government positions in it. About half the employee today are Indians, and the proportion is increasing. Nearly a hundred are in the Washington office—there were eleven there in 1933—and not a few are in highly responsible positions. The rest are scattered over the country; many are teaching in the new schools. These men and women are getting valuable experience in public administration, and as the office decreases in size many of them will be prepared to step into tribal government and perform there the greatest possible service to their people.

Indian civil liberties are in better shape than ever, though still rather restricted. Indians are citizens, but in some states. for a variety of reasons. they do not vote. Early in 1934 Congress repealed twelve old laws limiting Indian freedom of meeting, organization and communication, authorizing the Indian office to remove "undesirable persons", from reservations, permitting rather arbitrary action by the superintendents and approving repressive military measures. It is true that most of these laws had not been in use for many years, but it is good that they have been repealed. Bans on the use of Indian languages by children in school and restrictions on native religious ceremonies have been lifted.

An improved system of administration of justice to Indians was deleted from the Wheeler-Howard bill before passage. However, the judicial power of the reservation superintendents, once almost unlimited, has been sharply reduced, and the government has much less control over individual lives and activities than it formerly had.

The administration has come in for its share of criticism, much of it aimed at the Navajo service. The Navajo range was in extremely bad condition even before 1933, and by that year it was obvious that strong action was necessary if there was going to be any range left. It is a complicated story with, no doubt, much to be said on both sides, but the net result has been that in drastically reducing the Indian stock and instituting controls aimed at saving the range from destruction by erosion, a great deal of opposition was stirred up. There were claims of injustice, arbitrary seizure and more or less dictatorial methods. The Navajos expressed their displeasure by rejecting the Indian Reorganization Act, though by a fairly close margin. Last fall, when drought swept the West and crops everywhere were bad, critics pointed out thee if the administration hadn't been in such a rush to cut down the number of horses and get rid of the goats, the Navajos could now be eating them. On the other hand, feed for the remaining animals had to be brought onto the reservation because of the lack of grass, and had even more been destroyed this would not have been necessary.

Many sober observers have charged that Collier's program has been jammed through much too fast, and that this speed has brought about more trouble and resentment than it was worth. The Indian Rights Association, which has worked tirelessly for Indians since 1882, points to the good work of the previous administration as proof that it is not necessary to go so fast, and that order progress following careful experiment may result in more permanent reform with less upsetting opposition. There is evidence that the pace has now slowed down.

The administration has been publicized masterfully—perhaps too much so. One might gather from reading Indian Office releases that the Indian had never had a friend before, and that now every problem of the red man has been solved, or is on its way to a quick solution. Nothing has stirred up as much antagonism in the Indian country as the driving passion for immediate and complete reform, the impatience with criticism and the too enthusiastic press notices which have been characteristic since Collier took over.

Other critics have called Collier visionary, and his policies communistic. Some say Indians do not want to and are not competent to govern themselves. Occasionally, on the other hand, we hear that Collier is a sentimentalist, trying to hold the Indian back for the benefit of tourists and anthropologists, to keep him out of the main stream of American life. These groups, however, apparently have nothing to suggest but a return to the old assimilation policy which gave no promise of success and every evidence of complete and tragic failure during the long years of its history. Then there are many individual complaints against superintendents, physicians and other officials. There always have been these, and there always will be. "Too much education and not enough practical experience," says one New Mexico observer about local Indian office employee.

THE TWO MOST IMPORTANT INDEPENDENT ORGANIZATIONS working for the good of the Indian are the Indian Rights Association and the American Association on Indian Affairs. Both are friendly to the administration, the latter perhaps more so than the former. Each makes reports and suggestions, publicizes Indian needs, investigates complaints, and points out individual cases of bad administration. Although the Indian Rights Association is in sympathy with most of Collier's broad aims, it has taken some pretty energetic pot-shots in the past, and still takes every opportunity to point out that while good work is being done, there is still plenty left to do.

It has been a terrific problem. Hopelessly tangled in obsolete laws, nearly landless, poverty stricken, uneducated, prey to white interests everywhere, unable to defend themselves, and finally saddled with an administrative policy which regarded them as a dying people more in need of race euthanasia than anything else, the Indians could hardly have been worse off. As far back as 1862 Abraham Lincoln said, "If we get through this war, and I live, this Indian system shall be reformed." But it is only now that this is really taking place.

The truth is that the New Deal Indian administration is neither as successful as its publicity says it is, nor as black and vicious a failure as the severest critics would have us believe. Many Indian problems remain unsolved, but every one has been attacked. If eddies have been stirred up, there is still a powerful current in Indian affairs, and it seems to be in a direction which gives this splendid race an opportunity to shape its own destiny.

What the Civilian Conservation Corps (CCC) Is Doing for Colored Youth

Civilian Conservation Corps. "What the Civilian Conservation Corps (CCC) Is Doing for Colored Youth." Washington, D.C.: United States Government Printing Offices, 1941.

Approximately:

250,000 colored youth have served in the corps since President Roosevelt and the Congress initiated the Civilian Conservation Corps in 1933. Regular habits of work, training, discipline, fresh air and three well prepared and ample meals a day have combined to improve the health and morale of all enrollees. The gain in weight has ranged from seven to fifteen pounds for each boy.

30,000 young colored men and war veterans, one tenth of the total CCC enrollment, are actively participating in the Civilian Conservation Corps. They are engaged on work projects throughout the country, and the Virgin Islands.

$700,000 a month for the past year has been allotted by colored CCC boys to their parents and dependents back home.

90,000 books have been supplied through the War Department and the Office of Education for colored camp libraries. Current magazines, daily and weekly newspapers are made available in camp recreation halls.

12,000 colored CCC enrollees in the past five years have completed courses in first-aid through cooperation of the Civilian Conservation Corps and the National Red Cross.

2,000 colored project assistants' leaders and assistant leaders are on duty at CCC Camps.

600 colored cooks are steadily employed in CCC Mess Halls.

900 classes in Negro history were conducted in the camps during the past five years. National Negro Health exhibits have been shown for five consecutive years in cooperation with the U. S. Health Service.

800 colored boys have gained business training in the capacity of store clerks and mangers of the Post-Exchanges in CCC camps.

400 colored typists are assigned to CCC headquarters of commanding officers, camp superintendents and educational advisors.

147 colored college graduates are serving CCC camps as educational advisers.

1,200 part-time, experienced teachers are actively engaged in instruction of these colored enrollees at CCC camps.

25 colored medical reserve officers and chaplains of the U. S. Reserve Corps are on active duty in the nations CCC Camps.

106 colored CCC camps are located in forests, parks, recreational areas, fish and game reservations, and on drainage and mosquito control projects.

48 colored CCC companies are engaged on soil Conservation projects.

2 colored commending officers with the rank of Captain and Lieutenant, in the U.S. Reserve Corps are on active duty with the CCC; one at Gettysburg National Park, Pennsylvania, and the other at Fishers landing, New York. Four other line officers are on active duty at these two Camps.

4 colored engineers and six colored technical foremen have served Pennsylvania camps for more than two years, At Gettysburg, the camp superintendent is a Negro.

1 colored historian who received his Ph.D. degree from Columbia University is included in the camp personnel at Gettysburg.

1 colored CCC company is at work at Zanesville, Ohio on one of the largest tree nurseries in the U.S.

3 colored companies have made possible during the past five years the restoration of the battlefields at Yorktown, Virginia in the Colonial National Park.

1 colored company in Ohio, near the Taylorville Dam carriers on in the re-nowned Miami Conservation District, a flood control project started after the 1913 Dayton flood.

1 colored company has been engaged on the unique historic project at Williamsburg and Jamestown, Virginia.

1 colored company is located on the TVA site in Tennessee.

11,000 colored enrollees have been taught to read and write. More than 90 per cent of the colored CCC enrollees regularly attend classes from elementary to college level which are conducted in each camp's education building which is well equipped and especially constructed for vocational instruction. Howard University, Wilberforce University, Tuskegee Institute, Hampton Institute, Florida A. & M. College at Tallahassee, Tennessee A. & I. State College and a number of other Negro collages have granted scholarships and fellowships to CCC enrollees.

Industry Aided

The textile and food industries and the railroads have received orders for more than $33,000,000 worth of supplies needed to run colored CCC camps.

$15,000,000 has been obligated for clothing worn by colored enrollees, including shirts, underwear, trousers, socks, denim jumpers, shoes, caps, raincoats and overcoats.

$19,000,000 has been expended for food served colored boys and men at camp during the past 6 ½ years.

$1,500,000 has been received by railroads for transportation of colored CCC enrollees to camp and back home again.

Colored Men and Boy's Participation in the CCC

The Civilian Conservation Corps was established by President Roosevelt and the Congress on April 5, 1933. On the same day the late Robert Fechner was named Director. James J. McEntee, now Acting Director of the CCC, has been Assistant Director since its inception.

The purpose of Civilian Conservation Corps work is to relieve acute conditions of distress and unemployment in the United States and to provide for the restoration of the countries natural resources along with the advancement of an orderly program of useful public Works.

Civilian Conservation Corps enrollees are selected on a state-quota basis by the Labor Department from unemployed and needy young men. Veterans are selected by the Veterans' Bureau, and make up ten per cent of the total enrollment.

From the beginning of the Civilian Conservation Corps, colored youths have shared in the program. At the peak strength of the CCC, reached in August 1935, there were 506,000 young men and war veterans enrolled. Of this number, approximately 50,000 were colored.

Mindful of the health of these young men, medical officers from the U. S. Army Reserve Corps hare been assigned to look after their physical well being. Fourteen colored medical officers are now on active duty at CCC camps throughout the country. Each company is provided with a first-aid building, company, hospital, or dispensary with a medical officer in charge. Orderlies are appointed from among the enrollees.

The Office of Education has acted in an advisory capacity to the War Department in working out an educational and recreational program. Each company has an educational adviser, who develops a program suited to the individual needs of each camp. College graduates are appointed to fill these positions. Eleven thousand colored on rollees who were illiterate have been taught to read and write in classes offered by the CCC camps. There are today 147 colored men serving the CCC camps as education advisers. Most of the educational work is carried on at camp. Arrangements are often made, however, for enrollees to take additional school work in public school evening classes in nearby cities. The camp educational programs offer instruction in carpentry, shorthand, tying, forestry, auto mechanics, landscaping and numerous other vocational subjects. While attendance at classes is voluntary, approximately ninety per cent of the colored enrollees attend. Classes in first-aid, safety, morale, guidance, leadership and hygiene have been well attended. While at work, CCC enrollees are given practical instruction on the job by the project superintendent and the technical staff.

Baseball and soft ball diamonds, tennis courts and basket ball courts have been laid out to provide recreational facilities at the camps. Some of the camps have produced championship teams in baseball and other sports. Current movies, health education films, lectures on geography, conservation, history and other topics, and plays are included in the camp educational and entertainment program. Trips to nearby museums and other points of interest are frequently scheduled.

Six colored chaplains of the U.S. Army Reserve Corps direct the religious activities in a number of the colored camps. They are aided by ministers from nearby communities.

Through the experience and training received in the CCC, boys learn how to live together and work together amicably. Experience and training afforded by the CCC has helped many boys to secure employment. The specialized knowledge gained by filling such positions as mess sergeant, company clerk, assistant educational adviser, leaders, project assistants, store clerk manger, foreman and first-aid men has proved valuable to these enrollees in the Civilian Conservation Corps.

Food, Farmers, and Fundamentals, Henry A. Wallace

Source: Survey Graphic, Vol. 30, No. 7 (July 1941), p. 390.

Thanks to the ever-normal granary and the efficiency of modern farm production, we can approach the problem of nutrition more constructively than during the last war. There seems little likelihood that we shall have meatless days, or days without sugar. The problem today is to use our soil, our farmers, our processors, our distributors, and our knowledge to produce the maximum of abounding health and spirits—a broad foundation on which we can build all the rest of our hemispheric defense.

As goal number one we can wipe out deaths caused by dietary deficiency. No longer need we have pellagra.

As goal number two we can reduce those diseases such as tuberculosis toward which insufficient food predisposes.

To speed this task we must shift our agriculture more and more toward producing those foods which are rich in vitamins, minerals, and the right kind of proteins. We have started producing more of these foods, such as milk, eggs, tomatoes, dried beans, pork, etc., so that we may have an abundance, not only for ourselves but for Britain, to meet every possible kind of contingency. We are using the cow, the hen, and the pig to extract from our huge supplies of corn stored in the ever-normal granary the Vitamin B, the Vitamin A, the good minerals, and the proteins which will furnish the nervous energy to drive us through to victory. Some people may say, "Why haven't the farmers produced more of these fine protective foods before?"

The reason is simple. Protective foods demand more hard work from the farmer than the simple energy foods. A pound of dry matter in poultry, dairy, or meat products costs five or ten times as much human energy to produce as a pound of dry matter in wheat. The bottleneck has been the lack of consuming purchasing power. Today our factory payrolls are at least a third higher than they were a year ago, and the payrolls per employed person about 14 percent higher, but the cost of living of factory workers has gone up only about 3 percent. This means that millions of people can now spend more on protective foods.

At the same time, we must recognize that there are many millions who get paid very little and who are getting no more than they did a year ago. We are trying to take care of these people through the Surplus Marketing Administration, the free school lunches, low cost milk, and the Food Stamp Plan. The federal action programs have taken care of a large proportion of the ten million people in this country who are most needy. The increased payrolls are helping perhaps an additional ten or twenty million. But there still are perhaps twenty million people whose diet is woefully inadequate.

Many people of unusual intelligence in the high income brackets eat improperly. We must get nutrition information into every household, rich and poor, in the United States, so that the new knowledge of food may express itself in more vigor of living. Already we have made a start. We have state nutrition committees, schools, clinics, hospitals, public health nurses, as well as the Food Stamp Plan, the school lunch program, and various other federal programs for the distribution of food. Now we must focus the agencies available to our hands so that adequate nutrition standards can be put into life, so that there will be no more hidden hunger gnawing at our vital organs, so that our nerves will be strong and resolute.

Our program is just as good for peace as it is for war. It will never end until the soil and the farmers of the United States are fully geared to the job of bringing the maximum of health to every individual. At the moment we are taking an especial interest in seeing that the people of Britain, as well as our own, have an adequate supply of protective foods. And I am hopeful that the day will come when we shall cooperate with the governments of Latin America to help solve the unusual problems which exist there in agriculture, population, and nutrition.

What We Are Fighting for, Eleanor Roosevelt

Source: The American Magazine 134 (July 1942): 16–17, 60–62.

A young officer said to me the other day, "If I asked my men why they are fighting, the answer probably would be, 'Because those are our orders.'"

A great many people think in much the same terms—in fact, the great mass of people in our country, if asked why they are fighting, would answer, "Because we have to."

No great conviction seems to have come as yet to the people of the nation to make them feel that they fight for something so precious that any price is worth paying.

To me, it seems we fight for two things. First, for freedom. Under that we list:

Freedom to live under the government of our choice.

Freedom from economic want.

Freedom from racial and religious discrimination.

Second, for a permanent basis for peace in the world. Under this we list:

A world economy guaranteeing to all people free trade and access to raw materials.

A recognition of the rights and the dignity of the individual.

Machinery through which international difficulties may be settled without recourse to war. This necessitates international machinery as well as an international police force.

Gradually our people have accepted the fact that we are fighting for freedom, but I am constantly told that they are not really conscious of what freedom has been lost or endangered. They still feel safe. War is still remote, save for the families who have men in the Armed Forces. The individual civilian's place in this war is still not well defined.

Groups of people, especially young people, talk a great deal about post-war aims. They say the war is worth fighting only if, by fighting it, we are going to create a brave new world. But what kind of a new world?

We'd better be fairly sure of the kind of new world we want. When we look over the past few years, we discover that the war, as we know it now, is only a phase of something which has been going on ever since the last war—a kind of world revolution. It is a worldwide uprising by the people which manifested itself first in those countries where the pressure was greatest. It is a determination to accept whatever offered the promise of giving them and their families, their parents and their children, a better way of life.

Russia, Germany, and Italy had felt the pinch of material hardship. In addition, Germany felt spiritual humiliation because of the conditions laid down in the Versailles Treaty. This alone might not have been enough to galvanize the German people into action, but a strong personality appeared who offered them the type of organization they could understand. He promised them a life that provided them with the necessities of daily living in return for hard work. At the same time, he offered them an ideal which proclaimed them the super race of the world. He assured the German people they would dominate the world. This dream of power restored a lost self-respect and gave them a hope of eventually removing all the material difficulties under which they labored.

In Russia, in addition to material desires, the revolution was furthered by the ideal of a people's government. These revolutionary movements, of course, could have developed in one of two ways—the democratic way or the totalitarian way. They began in the totalitarian way but came at a time when the same type of revolution was brewing in many other countries—democratic countries. I think the Russian results have sometimes been very different from those originally envisioned. Russia hoped for a world revolution. Hitler, on the other hand, thought of revolution perhaps for his own people, but he did not realize that this was a world revolution. Nor did he see that in this world upheaval there would be only one point at issue—whether it would be carried out his way or the democratic way represented by the United States of America.

Once we recognize this basic issue between the two opposed types of revolutions, all the other things going on in the world are easier to understand. We know the conquered countries have never been really conquered. Czechoslovakia, Norway, Greece, the Balkan countries, the Free French, all are still fighting the totalitarian way of revolution in spite of persecution, hunger, and hardship. No one of them is resigned to accept the revolution on the basis of Hitler's totalitarianism.

Some people have questioned the wisdom of this. They ask, "What is the use of fighting against Germany? We might better accept the philosophy of Fascism."

We fight Germany simply because there are two methods of winning the revolution, and Hitler's way is not our way. His is a method by which you obtain certain material things, but by which you do not obtain the spiritual things. You accept bondage even though your masters may give you material things, such as better housing, a little more to eat and drink. The State will be paramount—the individual a controlled cog in the wheel. Our way permits the freedom of the individual.

Today we in the United States find ourselves a nation involved in this revolution, and the war is only its outward and visible sign. We are a part, our people are a part, of a worldwide desire for something better than has been had heretofore.

The same seeds have been germinating here that germinated and burst through the ground in Russia, Germany, Italy, Spain, and France. That they were still only germinating in Great Britain and in the United States when the war began is because we have been a little better off and have had people among us with sufficient wisdom to recognize some of the aspirations of human beings and to try to meet them. However, neither in Great Britain nor in the United States were they really being fully met.

Time and again I have heard the claim: "But what we have had has been good. Oh, to be sure, during the depression some of our people were hungry, some of our people went without shelter and clothing, but look at what we did for them! Our government began to feed them. We provided them with work which, though not very remunerative, kept them alive. Then they always had the hope that things would be better. We might get back to those good old days of the 20s, when all but some five million people actually had jobs, and some people really had more material things than they knew what to do with." But we were not getting back to "those good old days" as quickly as some people hoped. The five million had been added to, and there was a question in a great many people's minds whether the good old days were good enough for the vast majority of people.

I think most of us will agree that we cannot and do not want to go back to the economy of chance—the inequalities of the 20s. At the end of that period we entered an era of social and economic readjustment. The change in our society came about through the needs and the will of society. Democracy, in its truest sense, began to be fulfilled. We are fighting today to continue this democratic process. Before the war came, all the peoples of the world were striving for the same thing, in one way or another. Only if we recognize this general rising of the peoples of the world can we understand the real reason why we are in the war into which we were precipitated by the Japanese attack. Only if we realize that we in the United States are part of the world struggle of ordinary people for a better way of life can we understand the basic errors in the thinking of the America First people.

A few short months ago the America First people were saying that they would defend their own country, but that there was no menace to this country in the war going on in Europe and Asia. Why could we not stay within our own borders and leave the rest of the world to fight out its difficulties and reap the benefit ourselves of being strong from the material standpoint when others were exhausted? We would make money out of other nations. We would lose nothing, we would only gain materially, and we would be safe. Why stick our necks out? This sounded like an attractive picture to many people, but unfortunately it wasn't a true one.

One phase of the world revolt from which we could not escape concerns something which people do not like to talk about very much—namely, our attitude toward other races of the world. Perhaps one of the things we cannot have any longer is what Kipling called "The White Man's Burden." The other races of the world may be becoming conscious of the fact that they wish to carry their own burdens. The job which the white race may have had to carry alone in the past, may become a cooperative job.

One of the major results of this revolution may be a general acceptance of the fact that all people, regardless of race, creed, or color, rate as individual human beings. They have a right to develop, to carry the burdens which they are capable of carrying, and to enjoy such economic, spiritual, and mental growth as they can achieve.

In this connection, a problem which we Americans face now at home is the activity of the Japanese and Germans in sowing seeds of dissension among the ten percent of our population comprising the Negro race. The Negroes have been loyal Americans ever since they were brought here as slaves. They have worked here and they have fought for our country, and our county fought a bloody war to make them citizens and to insist that we remain a united nation.

They have really had equality only in name, however. Therefore, they are fertile ground for the seeds of dissension. They want a better life, an equality of opportunity, a chance to be treated like the rest of us before the law. They want a chance to hold jobs according to their ability, and not to be paid less because their skins are black. They want an equal break with the men and women whose skins happen to be white.

They must have a sense of economic equality, because without it their children cannot profit by equal education. Moreover, how can they have equal education if they haven't enough to eat, or if their home surroundings are such that they automatically sink to the level of the beasts? They must have, too, a sense that in living in a Democracy, they have the same opportunity to express themselves through their government and the same opportunity as other citizens for representation. They aspire to the same things as the yellow and brown races of the world. They want recognition of themselves as human beings, equal to the other human beings of the world.

Of course, they are a part of this revolution—a very active part because they have so much to gain and so little to lose. Their aspirations, like those of other races seeking recognition and rights as human beings, are among the things we are fighting for. This revolution will, I think, establish that the human beings of the world, regardless of race or creed or color, are to be looked upon with respect and treated as equals. We may prefer our white brothers, but we will not look down on yellow, black, or brown people.

Another of our aims undoubtedly is to assure that among our natural resources manpower is recognized as our real wealth. No future economic system will be satisfactory which does not give every man and woman who desires to work, an opportunity to work. Our people want to be able to earn, according to their abilities, not only what this generation considers the decencies of life, but whatever else they can gain by their labors. Standards of living may vary with the years, but we must see to it that all our men and women have the opportunity to meet them. The world we live in will not be the same after this war is over, but no one who travels through the length and breadth of the country will believe we need accept a low standard of living. We are still an un-developed country. We still have untold natural resources. All we have to do is to face the fact that real wealth lies in the resources of a country and in the ability of its people to work. You may lose everything you have put away in the safe-deposit box, but if you can work and produce with your hands or with your head, you will have wealth. For the wealth of a people lies in the land and in its people and not in the gold buried somewhere in vaults!

The economists can work out the details of our adjustments, but, in a broad way, this war will establish certain economic procedures. We will no longer cling to any type of economic system which leaves any human beings who are willing to work, without food and shelter and an opportunity for development. The people themselves are going to run their own affairs; they are not going to delegate them to a few people and become slaves to those few. Having established that, we will still be carrying out the revolution, the revolution of people all over the world.

Lastly, we are fighting, along with many other people, in other countries, for a method of world cooperation which will not force us to kill each other whenever we face new situations. From time to time we may have other world revolutions, but it is stupid that they should bring about wars in which our populations will increasingly be destroyed. If we destroy human beings fast enough, we destroy civilization. For many years after the war we will be finding ways to accomplish things which the people want to accomplish without destroying human beings in baffle. We must set up some ma-chinery, a police force, even an international court, but there must be a way by which nations can work out their difficulties peacefully.

The totalitarian way of revolution being abhorrent to us, we, in the United States, are dedicating all we have to the revolution which will make it possible for us to go forward in the ways of freedom. We cannot stand still for the pleasure of a few of our citizens who may grow weary of the forward march. We accept the will of the majority of our citizens. We fight this war in about the same spirit in which our first Revolution was carried on. We will have to part with many things we enjoy, but if we determine to preserve real values, the essentials of decent living for the people as a whole, and give up trying to keep them in the hands of a few, we will win the war in the democratic way. The ways of Fascism and Nazism will be defeated and the way of democracy will triumph.

Most of our present-day ideals were present in the last war twenty-five years ago. President Wilson's Fourteen Points really dealt with these same questions. The men who fought the war to end war—the war to establish democracy—were not as realistic as we are today, however. They had not been tried as we have been tried in the past few years. They had never been obliged to define the specific things for which they fought. Most of us today who have a clear picture of what we think is happening in the world are sure of the objectives for which we are going to sacrifice, but we are not willing to sacrifice for anything less than the attainment of these objectives.

Once the people as a whole understand that these are the objectives of the leaders of the United Nations, there will be sorrow at the young lives that are being sacrificed, but not bitterness. All will be willing to accept civilian hardships and sacrifice, for there will be full understanding that failure to win the revolution in the way of democracy would bring only unbearable disaster.

The war is but a step in the revolution. After the war we must come to the realization of the things for which we have fought—the dream of a new world.

Chronology

1920   Warren Harding is elected president in the November elections.

1921   American farmers overproduce, which causes crop prices to fall dramatically. The Warren Harding administration implements an emergency tariff on imported farm products.

President Warren Harding signs the Emergency Immigration Act on May 19 to restrict immigration to the United States from Europe. The act caps annual immigration at 350,000.

Lawlessness, whippings, brandings, tarrings, and destruction of the property of blacks and Catholics follow the reemergence of the Ku Klux Klan on August 21.

On July 14, radicals Nicola Sacco and Bartolomeo Vanzetti are convicted of robbery and murder on scant evidence and eventually sentenced to death. A public campaign is begun in their defense by supporters who believe that anticommunist panic in the United States precluded a fair trial.

1922   In New York City, the Harlem Renaissance, a flourishing of African American art and literature, begins.

Demonstrating their support for the Anti-Lynching Bill, African Americans from every state march in Washington, D.C., on June 14.

1923   The Department of Commerce estimates that by 1930, corporate profits will increase 62 percent, dividends 65 percent, and workers' income 11 percent.

In Adkins v. Children's Hospital (1923), the U.S. Supreme Court declares that the Washington, D.C., minimum wage law for women and children is unconstitutional on April 9.

In August, the United States Steel Corporation reduces its standard 12-hour day to 8 hours in response to labor activism. That change requires the hiring of 7,000 additional workers.

On August 2, President Warren Harding dies, and Vice President Calvin Coolidge is elevated to the presidency.

1924   On February 8, Congress passes a joint resolution calling for investigation into the illegal oil leases that were brought to light in the Teapot Dome scandal. The most egregious corruption that characterized the Warren Harding administration had occurred when Secretary of the Interior Albert B. Fall had secretly assigned oil drilling rights to private companies throughout the early 1920s in exchange for illegal payments and gifts.

On April 15, the Senate votes unanimously to bar immigration from Japan except for ministers, educators, and their families. Later, Congress passes the Nation Origins Act, which lowers the number of immigrants from southern and eastern European countries and forbids all immigration from East Asia.

The Dawes Plan, aimed at stabilizing the German economy in order to facilitate the payment of World War I reparations, is announced on April 16.

Calvin Coolidge is reelected president in the November elections.

1925   *The Great Gatsby* by F. Scott Fitzgerald is published. The novel includes his descriptions and criticisms of wanton 1920s lifestyles.

The Treasury Department uses U.S. Coast Guard vessels to wage an all-out campaign against rumrunners who have increased their activities along the Atlantic Seaboard.

Retail business grows as Sears, Roebuck & Company distributes 15 million catalogues and J. C. Penney opens its 500th store.

The Scopes trial begins in Dayton, Tennessee. On July 21, John Scopes is fined $100 for teaching evolutionary theory. In October, the Texas State Text Book Board bans the discussion of evolutionary theory in any of its school textbooks.

Over 40,000 Ku Klux Klan members from across the country march in Washington, D.C., on August 8 in an effort to broaden support for their organizations.

1926   The publishing of important American writing continues, including such works as Ernest Hemingway's *The Sun Also Rises,* which communicates his disillusionment after World War I, and Langston Hughes's influential essay "The Negro Artist and the Racial Mountain."

Due to Prohibition, the illegal liquor trade has become a $3.5 billion industry.

The Atlanta, Georgia Board of Education prohibits the teaching of evolutionary theory in its public schools on February 9.

1927   Al Capone's gang nets $60 million in the bootleg liquor trade.

The Jack Dempsey–Gene Tunney heavyweight championship boxing match is broadcast over radio.

Duke Ellington's orchestra begins performing at the Cotton Club in Harlem on December 4.

1928   President Calvin Coolidge vetoes a farm subsidy plan; he claims it is a "price fixing scheme."

Walter Chrysler announces plans for a 77-floor building in Manhattan. The Chrysler Building, designed by architect William Van Alen, becomes a landmark of Art Deco style.

Republican Herbert Hoover is elected president with some 21.4 million popular votes over the Democratic opponent, Alfred E. Smith, who gains only about 15 million.

1929   On February 14, Al Capone's gunmen execute seven members of a rival gang, and the murders become known as the St. Valentine's Day Massacre.

On September 3, the stock market reaches its all-time high of 381 points.

In what becomes known as Black Thursday, on October 24, the New York Stock Exchange crashes as the result of devaluations and massive sell-offs of stocks. In one day, the exchange loses $4 billion. On October 29, Black Tuesday, the market collapses. The Dow Jones Industrial Average plummets 30.57 points, and $30 billion is lost. The market hits bottom on November 13.

1930   For the first time, unemployment and poor economic conditions cause emigration from the United States to exceed immigration.

The Smoot-Hawley Tariff, the highest tariff in U.S. history, becomes law on June 17.

On August 7, unemployment reaches 4.5 million, and President Herbert Hoover appoints a Committee for Unemployment Relief.

The Bank of the United States in New York closes on December 11 and leaves over 400,000 depositors without their savings.

Also on December 11, filmmaker and comedian Charlie Chaplin releases the acclaimed film *City Lights*.

At President Herbert Hoover's request, on December 20, Congress appropriates $116 million for public works projects and $45 million for drought relief.

1931   In Los Angeles, California, in February, 6,024 Mexican Americans are "repatriated" and voluntarily or forcibly deported to Mexico under a program initiated by the Department of Labor.

In Alabama on March 25, the "Scottsboro Boys," nine young black men, are arrested and charged with the rape of two white women.

Between September and October, both the hoarding of gold and the number of bank failures increase. Depositors lose most of their savings.

1932 Four demonstrators are killed and over 100 are wounded outside the Ford Motor Plant in Dearborn, Michigan, when police fire into the crowd on March 7.

On March 23, Congress passes the Norris-La Guardia Act (1932), which states that no employer may use a contract to prohibit his employees from joining a union or to use injunctions against strikes.

Some 1,000 World War I veterans calling themselves the "Bonus Army" arrive in Washington, D.C., to urge Congress to allow early payment of the bonus money promised them in 1924. Within weeks, more than 20,000 veterans and their families are camped out in shanty towns around the city awaiting Congress' decision.

On July 28, after being ordered to disperse, the remainder of the Bonus Army is forced from its camp by U.S. Army troops commanded by Gen. Douglas MacArthur. President Herbert Hoover's popularity plummets when millions of movie-going Americans view newsreels of U.S. troops burning shacks and firing teargas at World War I veterans and their families.

In the entire month of October, General Motors sells a total of 5, 810 cars, the same number it sold per week in 1929.

Urging supporters to "Stay at Home! Buy Nothing! Sell Nothing!" the Iowa Farmers' Union stages a 30-day strike in November in the hope of forcing the federal government to institute a farm program to stabilize prices and provide mortgage relief.

On November 7, the Supreme Court rules in Powell v. Alabama (1932) that the Scottsboro Boys did not receive proper representation and are entitled to a new trial.

Democrat Franklin D. Roosevelt wins the presidential election by a landslide on November 8.

1933 The Twenty-first Amendment is adopted. It ends the prohibition of alcohol as enacted by the Eighteenth Amendment in 1919.

President Franklin D. Roosevelt in March appoints Frances Perkins as secretary of labor. She becomes the first female Cabinet member.

On March 9, Congress convenes to address the banking crisis. Thus begins the First Hundred Days, during which numerous bills aimed at economic recovery and relief for the poor and unemployed are passed.

On March 12, President Franklin D. Roosevelt delivers his first "fireside chat" radio broadcast, which explains the Emergency Banking Relief Act and significantly improves public confidence in the banking system.

Beginning its drive against segregation in American education, the National Association for the Advancement of Colored People unsuccessfully sues the University of North Carolina on March 15.

In May, the Tennessee Valley Authority (TVA) is created to help farmers and create jobs in one of the country's least developed regions. The TVA will provide cheap electric power, flood control, and recreational opportunities to the entire Tennessee River Valley.

To ensure labor's right to bargain collectively, on August 5, the Franklin D. Roosevelt administration creates the National Labor Board.

In response to increasing Nazi antiunion rhetoric in Germany, on October 20, the American Federation of Labor begins boycotting German-made goods.

In November, the drought-stricken Midwest suffers a huge dust storm that deposits Dakota soil as far as the Atlantic Ocean.

1934   Huey Long, liberal critic of the New Deal, receives the most mail of anyone in the United States in 1934.

In the Senate, the Nye Committee begins on April 12, 1934, to investigate profiteering by American businesses during World War I.

More dust storms rip through the plains states in May and blow 300 million tons of topsoil as far as the Atlantic Ocean.

On June 18, Congress approves the Indian Reorganization Act, also known as the Indian New Deal, aimed at improving the living conditions of American Indians in the United States.

A five-year moratorium on farm mortgage foreclosures is established by the Frazier-Lemke Farm Bankruptcy Act. Congress also passes the Taylor Grazing Act to control grazing and soil erosion in the West.

On September 3, George Gallup founds the American Institute of Public Opinion, which will use statistics and polling of small but representative segments of the population to ascertain the public's opinion. In 1936, the Gallup poll will predict the electoral returns more accurately than any other statistical group.

1935   President Franklin D. Roosevelt creates the Works Progress Administration (WPA) on May 6. He appoints Harry Hopkins to head the WPA, which will eventually hire over 8 million people to build parks, airports, and highways.

The Supreme Court declares the National Industrial Recovery Act of 1933 and the Frazier-Lemke Farm Bankruptcy Act of 1934 unconstitutional on May 27.

In July, union membership mushrooms due to the National Labor Relations Act, also known as the Wagner Act, which ensures the rights of workers to organize and bargain with employers for "fair labor practices."

Creating a nationwide system of old-age pensions and unemployment benefits, President Franklin D. Roosevelt signs the Social Security Act into law on August 14.

Huey Long is assassinated on September 8.

The Committee for Industrial Organization (later called the Congress of Industrial Organizations, or CIO) is created when members of the American Federation of Labor break with the union. John L. Lewis, president of the United Mine Workers, is the first CIO chairman.

In December, the Supreme Court in *Murray v. Maryland* (1935) orders the University of Maryland Law School either to admit the African American student Donald Murray or to create a segregated law school just for him.

1936   The Supreme Court on January 6 deems the Agricultural Adjustment Act of 1933 unconstitutional.

President Franklin D. Roosevelt appoints Mary McLeod Bethune head of the Division of Negro Affairs in the National Youth Administration in June.

In a landslide victory over Republican Alf Landon on November 3, Franklin D. Roosevelt is reelected for a second term. Only 89 Republicans remain in the House of Representatives and 16 in the Senate.

In Gibbs v. Board of Education (1936), brought forward by the National Association for the Advancement of Colored People, the Supreme Court rules that black schoolteachers deserve the same salaries as white schoolteachers.

1937   Hoping to aid the republican government against Francisco Franco's fascist forces in the Spanish Civil War, thousands of American men join the Abraham Lincoln Brigade. Authors John Dos Passos, Ernest Hemingway, Malcolm Cowley, and Upton Sinclair are among their ranks.

On February 5, President Franklin D. Roosevelt proposes legislation to Congress to enlarge the Supreme Court to 15 justices. Both his opponents and his supporters protest his Court-packing plan.

A sit-down strike in Flint, Michigan, ends on February 11, when General Motors recognizes the United Automobile Workers (UAW) as the sole bargaining agent for its employees. On May 26, Ford Motor Company police beat four UAW organizers at a union rally at Ford's River Rouge, Michigan, plant.

Following labor disputes, Chicago police attack a picnic of Republic Steel unionized workers on May 30, kill 10, and injure 84 in the Memorial Day Massacre.

Exercising the new rights guaranteed to them under the Wagner Act, workers hold 4,740 work stoppages, working strikes, and lockouts in factories nationwide during the course of the year.

On December 21, the first feature-length animated motion picture, Walt Disney's *Snow White,* is released.

1938   The House of Representatives forms the House Un-American Activities Committee on May 26, under the chairmanship of Texan Martin Dies, to investigate potentially "un-American" activities of communists, fascists, Nazis, and other suspect groups.

The Fair Labor Standards Act is passed on June 25 and affects 12.5 million American workers. Federal guidelines limit the work week to 44 hours, after which workers must be paid overtime. A minimum wage of 25 cents is also established and employment of children restricted.

On October 31, Orson Welles broadcasts "Invasion from Mars," a dramatization of H. G. Wells's *The War of the Worlds,* on his Mercury Theatre on the Air radio show. Many panicked listeners think Martians have landed in New Jersey.

In the case *Missouri ex rel. Gaines v. Canada* (1938), sponsored by the National Association for the Advancement of Colored People, the Supreme Court rules that states must provide equal, even if separate, educational facilities for blacks.

1939   The U.S. Department of Agriculture on May 16 implements the use of food stamps, which allows needy people to redeem them for surplus agricultural goods.

In July, New Deal programs are slashed when Congress cuts their budgets. Some 775,000 Works Progress Administration workers are laid off.

At the recommendation of fellow physicist Leo Szilard, Albert Einstein writes President Franklin D. Roosevelt on August 2 to suggest the development of an atomic bomb.

Responding to the outbreak of war in Europe, on September 8, President Franklin D. Roosevelt declares a limited state of emergency, which grants him additional presidential power to act in the international arena if necessary.

1940   Members of the America First Committee, including Henry Ford, encourage President Franklin D. Roosevelt to avoid U.S. involvement in World War II.

The U.S. War Department agrees to sell millions of dollars of outdated munitions and aircraft to Great Britain on June 3. The Naval Supply Act and the Military Supply Act are passed later in June and authorize $3.3 billion for defense projects.

Congress passes the Alien Registration Act (also known as the Smith Act) on June 28. The act states that it is against the law for any individual to call for the overthrow by force of any government in the United States, and unlawful to join or found any group that teaches such a doctrine.

On September 16, President Franklin D. Roosevelt signs the Selective Training and Service Act, which requires men ages 21 to 35 to register for military service.

On September 26, President Franklin D. Roosevelt declares an embargo on the exportation of scrap iron and steel except to Britain and the Western Hemisphere. The embargo will take effect on October 16 and cut off Japan from vital raw materials.

President Franklin D. Roosevelt on December 29 pledges that America will become the chief munitions supplier of the Allies in his "Arsenal of Democracy" speech.

1941   President Franklin D. Roosevelt asks Congress to support the lend-lease program on January 6 and explains that the Allies are fighting for "four essential freedoms": freedom of speech, freedom of worship, freedom from want, and freedom from fear.

On June 9, President Franklin D. Roosevelt orders troops to seize the North American Aviation Company after striking workers interfere with defense production.

By executive order on June 28, the Office of Scientific Research and Development is established with Dr. Vannevar Bush as chairman. It will coordinate the development of radar, sonar, and the first stages of the atomic bomb.

The U.S. destroyer *Reuben James* sinks off the coast of Iceland after being torpedoed by German U-boats on October 30. Though 100 U.S. sailors are killed in the attack, most Americans are still unwilling to go to war.

One day after the Japanese attack on Pearl Harbor, President Franklin D. Roosevelt asks Congress for a declaration of war on Japan and calls December 7 "a date that will live in infamy." This action officially ends U.S. neutrality and begins the nation's three-and-a-half-year involvement in World War II. War mobilization in the United States is also pivotal in bringing the United States out of the Great Depression.

A new draft act, requiring all males aged 18 to 65 to register for military service and all males 20 to 44 to be prepared to enter active duty, is signed by President Franklin D. Roosevelt on December 20.

1942   U.S. manufacturers strive to meet the challenge President Franklin D. Roosevelt has set: 60,000 planes, 45,000 tanks, and 800 million tons of ships to be built by the end of 1942.

On February 19, President Franklin D. Roosevelt issues Executive Order 9066, authorizing the relocation of Japanese Americans in California, Arizona, Oregon, and Washington from their homes to internment camps. By March 29, over 110,000 will have been uprooted and interned in the relocation camps.

The American Federation of Labor and the Congress of Industrial Organizations announce a no-strike agreement in order to ensure uninterrupted wartime production.

On November 29, President Franklin D. Roosevelt approves $400 million for the Manhattan Project. Two days later, physicist Enrico Fermi achieves the first controlled release of nuclear energy in a chain reaction.

1943   Labor shortages in defense plants result in new practices that improve conditions for workers. Awards, fringe benefits, piped-in music, coffee breaks, and suggestion boxes are all introduced in the workplace.

Beginning on January 1, meat is rationed at 28 ounces per person per week and butter at 4 ounces per week, the sale of sliced bread is banned, and flour and canned goods are also rationed. Shoes are rationed to three pairs a year; new sneakers are unavailable due to rubber shortages.

On April 26, American Jews begin a six-week period of "mourning and intercession" on behalf of European Jews "exterminated by Hitler."

Congress passes the Labor Disputes Act (Smith-Connally Anti-Strike Act) on June 25; it broadens the president's power to seize industrial plants where labor disturbances threaten to hinder war production.

1944   In February, Office of Price Administration director Chester Bowles announces that consumers are spending an estimated $1.2 billion on the black market.

After it defies an order from the National Labor Relations Board to extend a contract with its union employees, on April 26, the U.S. Army seizes Montgomery Ward.

On June 22, President Franklin D. Roosevelt signs the Serviceman's Readjustment Act (GI Bill of Rights), providing low-interest loans for postwar housing and funds for education. The bill alters the demographics of the United States by fostering suburbanization and opening up higher education to many working-class Americans.

1945   Statistics show that 18,610,000 women are employed outside the home. The Women's Bureau reports that 80 percent of them want to continue working after the war. Female autoworkers, laid off when their jobs are given to returning veterans, march in protests with posters stating, "Stop Discrimination Because of Sex."

Jazz musicians Charlie Parker and Dizzy Gillespie popularize bebop jazz.

In February, President Franklin D. Roosevelt, Soviet premier Joseph Stalin, and British Prime Minister Winston Churchill meet at Yalta in the Soviet Union to discuss the final phases of World War II and the postwar settlement.

President Franklin D. Roosevelt dies of a cerebral hemorrhage at Warm Springs, Georgia, on April 12. Harry Truman becomes president and the new commander in chief.

In May, Germany surrenders, bringing an end to World War II in Europe.

On July 16, the first atomic bomb is successfully detonated at Alamagordo, New Mexico.

Between July 17 and August 2, President Harry Truman, Soviet premier Joseph Stalin, and British Prime Minister Winston Churchill meet in Potsdam, Germany, to discuss the Allied occupation of Germany. Churchill is replaced by Clement Attlee after Attlee wins an election as prime minister on July 26. Having wrested Korea from the Japanese, the leaders decide to divide Korea along the 38th parallel. The Soviet Union will maintain control in northern Korea, and the United States will have sole influence in southern Korea.

The U.S. Senate votes overwhelmingly to approve the United Nations Charter on July 28.

The United States drops atomic bombs on Hiroshima, Japan, on August 6 and on Nagasaki on August 9. The Japanese surrender on August 14, ending World War II in Asia.

President Harry Truman orders the full restoration of civilian consumer production, collective bargaining, and the return of free markets on August 18.

1946   The end of the war brings great changes to U.S. society: a frenzy of consumer spending lifts the cost of living 33 percent higher than it was in 1941; 200,000 couples file for divorce in 1946; the birthrate shoots up 20 percent from 1945 as 74 percent of couples have their first child during their first year of marriage.

Index